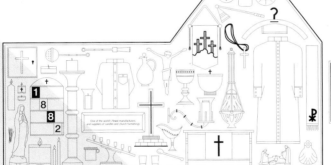

Christian Aid Scotland

Florence Muthiani at the Mikuyuni earth dam.

Stand together with Christian Aid to fight the climate crisis.

Find out more about Christian Aid prayers, bible readings and weekly worship at **christianaid.org.uk/Scotland**

Augustine United Church
41 George IV Bridge, Edinburgh, EH1 1EL, United Kingdom. Tel: 0131 220 1254

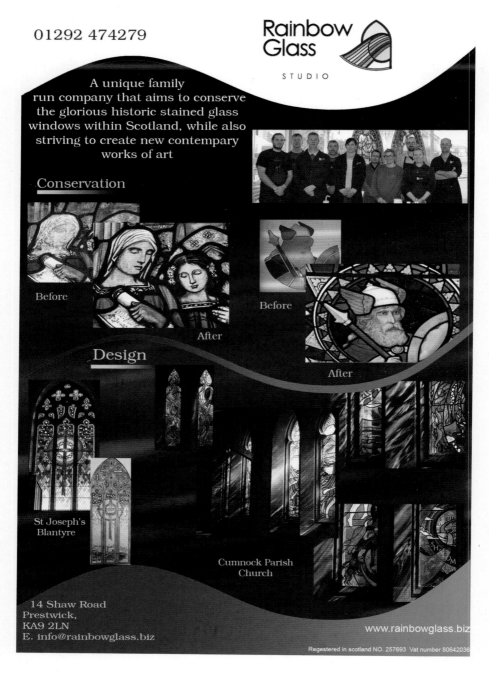

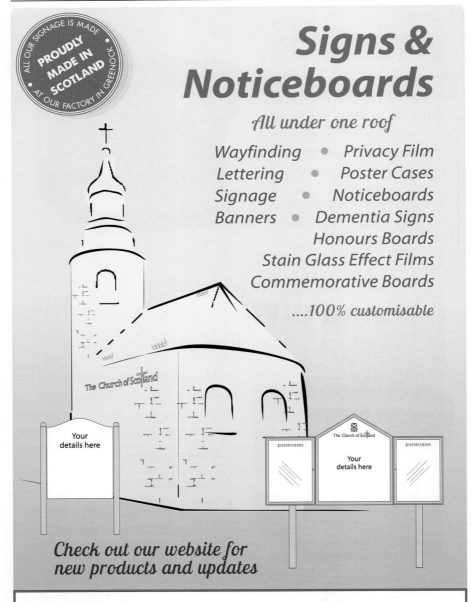

We'd love you to book our Scotland Speakers team

Let our speakers transport you to the ends of the earth as they tell MAF's exciting story. We cater for all types and sizes of meetings, completely free of charge.

In addition to hearing about the incredible ministry of MAF, we also offer the following: preaching, teaching, Bible studies and Mission-focused seminars. Please do get in touch to arrange a speaker or for any of the other services we offer to the National Church.

Email **scottishoffice@maf-uk.org** or phone **0141 332 5222** to find out more

Could you be their Chaplain?

As an RAF chaplain you'll be involved in the lives of our personnel, regardless of their rank or religious background. Your personal sacrifice may be considerable as you'll serve with our people wherever they go, providing vital spiritual, pastoral and ethical support in places of conflict, including on the front-line. Your home-based duties will be equally important, in support of personnel and their families.

A whole new congregation awaits you.

Contact the Branch Recruiting Officer now:
Christopher.Hodder101@mod.gov.uk

The Royal Air Force values every individual's unique contribution, irrespective of race, ethnic origin, religion, gender, sexual orientation or social background.

UK Ministry of Defence © Crown Copyright 2022

Designed with small groups in mind, and as a focus for churches thinking about resourcing and enabling their congregation to share their own faith naturally and authentically.

www.churcharmy.org/faithpictures

FAITH *Shared*

Designed to help churches to reflect on, pray about, and build a sustainable approach to mission and evangelism to their local communities over a course of six sessions.

www.churcharmy.org/faithshared

90kg Rice Challenge

THE ISSUE

Only 1 in 3 children can afford to go to secondary school in Malawi so many have no choice but to go work in the fields. Education is one of the most effective ways to escape poverty.

WHAT CAN YOU DO?

A bag of rice can change a life. 90kgs is the amount of rice a farmer has to sell to get a sustainable income to reinvest in their farms, feed and clothe their families and enable a child to attend secondary school for a year.

Can your church sell 90 bags of rice and change a life?

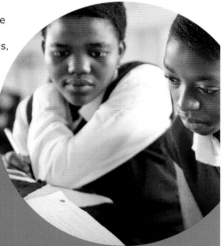

The 90kg challenge supports learning for all ages within these key Global Citizenship themes:

- Fair Trade
- Climate Justice
- Harvest Celebration

When you purchase the 90kg Rice Challenge, you receive a Challenge Pack which contains all the sermon outlines, prayers, case studies, and activities you need

THE 90KG RICE CHALLENGE COUNTS TOWARDS FAIR TRADE CHURCH STATUS

WWW.JTS.CO.UK/90KGRICECHALLENGE
EMAIL: NICOLA@JTS.CO.UK
PHONE: 0141 255 0901

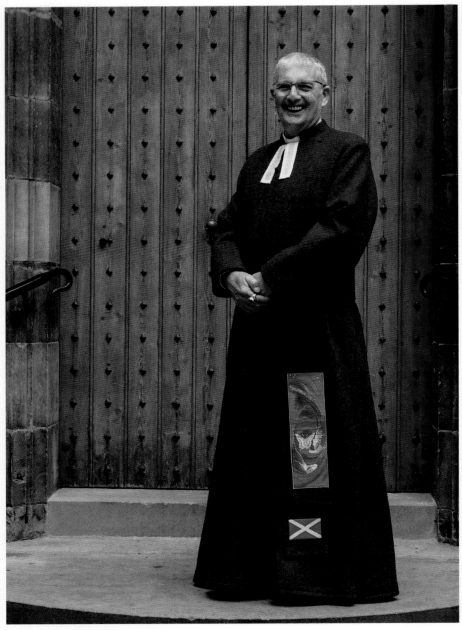

The Right Reverend Dr Iain M. Greenshields
MODERATOR

The Church of Scotland
YEAR BOOK
2022–2023

137th year of issue

Editor
David A. Stewart

Published on behalf of
THE CHURCH OF SCOTLAND
by SAINT ANDREW PRESS
121 George Street, Edinburgh EH2 4YN

THE OFFICES OF THE CHURCH

121 George Street, Edinburgh, EH2 4YN
0131 225 5722
Fax: 0131 220 3113
www.churchofscotland.org.uk

Office Hours: Monday–Friday 9:00am–5:00pm

CrossReach operates from Charis House, 47 Milton Road East, Edinburgh, EH15 2SR
0131 657 2000
Fax: 0131 657 5000
info@crossreach.org.uk
www.crossreach.org.uk

Scottish Charity Numbers

The Church of Scotland: unincorporated Councils and Committees	SC011353
The Church of Scotland General Trustees	SC014574
The Church of Scotland Investors Trust	SC022884
The Church of Scotland Trust	SC020269

For the Scottish Charity Numbers of presbyteries and congregations, see Section 7

Corrections and alterations to the Year Book
Contact the Editor, David A. Stewart:
yearbookeditor@churchofscotland.org.uk
0131 441 3362

The General Assembly of 2023 will convene on
Saturday 20 May

First published in 2022 by SAINT ANDREW PRESS, 121 George Street, Edinburgh EH2 4YN on behalf of THE CHURCH of SCOTLAND

Copyright © THE CHURCH of SCOTLAND, 2021

ISBN 978 1 80083 026 4

It is the Publisher's policy only to use papers that are natural and recyclable and that have been manufactured from timber grown in renewable, properly managed forests. All of the manufacturing processes of the papers are expected to conform to the environmental regulations of the country of origin.

Acceptance of advertisements for inclusion in *The Church of Scotland Year Book* does not imply endorsement of the goods or services or of any views expressed within the advertisements.

British Library Cataloguing in Publication Data
A catalogue record for this book is available from the British Library.

Printed and bound by Bell and Bain Ltd, Glasgow

CONTENTS

FROM THE MODERATOR

I have always considered the Year Book as an essential companion over these 38 years of ministry – a bit like the "Wee Red Book" produced yearly by the Evening Times in Glasgow, that kept me up to date with football; this bigger "red book" keeps me up to date with so much that is happening around and about the church.

It is an essential companion because I am kept abreast of the movements of people and their positions – people who perhaps I would not be in regular touch with but in whose life I have an interest. "The Big Red Book" is an essential guide to what help there is available to individual ministers and churches and down through the years I have found Section 2 in particular of value at a personal level and when seeking advice or potential funding for whatever church I was privileged to serve.

I am a statistics buff, and the congregational statistics fascinate me year on year. It helps me keep up to date with previous charges or churches with whom I have had an association. I find it interesting to note the changes and trends in the life of the church in that section.

This book is simply a valuable tool as a directory that gives immediate access to the phone numbers or email addresses of people throughout the church as well as offering good general information and contact details with respect to the officers and offices of the church.

Great that it is red because it stands out and is something that is of use to me on a weekly basis – an essential and invaluable tool.

Iain M. Greenshields

BHON MHODARÀTAIR

Tha mi riamh air a bhith a' meas an Leabhar Bliadhnail mar chompanach riatanach thairis air mo 38 bliadhna sa mhinistrealachd – beagan coltach ris an 'Leabhar Beag Dearg' a bhiodh an Evening Times ann an Glaschu a' foillseachadh gach bliadhna is a bhiodh a' toirt fios dhomh mu bhall-coise; tha an 'leabhar dearg' nas motha seo a' cumail fios rium mu na tha tachairt mu chuairt is mu dheidhinn na h-eaglaise.

'S e companach riatanach a th' ann seach gu bheil e ag innse dhomh mu ghluasadan dhaoine agus an suidhichidhean – daoine leis nach bithinn 's dòcha ann an todha gu cunbhalach ach anns am biodh ùidh agam nam beatha.

Tha 'An Leabhar Mòr Bliadhnail' na iùl riatanach don taic a tha ri fhaotainn do mhinistearan is eaglaisean fa leth agus, sìos tro na bliadhnaichean, tha Earrann 2 air a bhith gu h-àraidh feumail dhomh aig ìre phearsanta agus ann a bhith sireadh comhairle no ionmhais airson ge brith dè an eaglais san robh mi fortanach a bhith ri seirbheis.

Tha fìor ùidh agam ann an staitistearachd agus tha na h-àireamhan mu choitheanalan gam bheò-ghlacadh gach bliadhna. Tha iad a' leigeil leam cumail suas ri coitheanalan san robh mi cheana no ri eaglaisean leis an robh ceangal agam. Tha e inntinneach dhomh na h-atharrachaidhean agus na gluasadan ann am beatha na h-eaglaise fhaicinn san earrann sin.

Tha an leabhar seo dìreach na innleachd luachmhor mar iùl-lann a tha toirt slighe steach gu sgiobalta gu àireamhan fòn no seòlaidhean post-d dhaoine air feadh na h-eaglaise a bharrachd air a bhith a' tairgsinn fios math coitcheann agus seòlaidhean conaltraidh co-cheangailte ri oifigearan is oifisean na h-eaglaise.

Is math gu bheil e dearg oir tha e seasamh a-mach agus tha e na nì a tha feumail dhomh gach seachdain – innleachd riatanach agus ro luachmhor.

Iain M. Greenshields
Translation by Professor Boyd Robertson

EDITORIAL

The key changes in this edition, beside the usual extensive updating across virtually every page, are:

- In the Presbytery listings in Section 5:

  the Presbyteries of Edinburgh (1) and West Lothian (2) have been united as the Presbytery of Edinburgh and West Lothian (1);

  the Presbyteries of Annandale and Eskdale (7), Dumfries and Kirkcudbright (8), Wigtown and Stranraer (9), Ayr (10), Irvine and Kilmarnock (11) and Ardrossan (12) have been united as the Presbytery of the South West (7); and

  the Presbyteries of Lanark (13), Hamilton (17) and Falkirk (22) have been united as the Presbytery of Forth Valley and Clydesdale (17).

  As many more presbytery unions will follow next year, it is still not appropriate to renumber all the presbyteries.

- The list of ministers ordained sixty years and upwards has been restored to the printed book (List 6-O).

I am grateful to those readers who sent corrections and updates. Many people contribute to the Year Book. My thanks to the Presbytery Clerks and their secretaries, the staff in the Church offices (in particular my correspondents in Faith Nurture – especially Sheila MacRae), and those who compile some sections or subsections: Boyd Robertson and Duncan Sneddon (Gaelic), Sheena Orr (Prison Chaplains), Roy Pinkerton (church grid references, parish and congregational changes, index of parishes and places, and editorial advice), Madelaine Sproule (legal names and Scottish charity numbers) and Fiona Tweedie, Karen Bass and Sandy Gemmill (statistics). Thanks also to Claire Ruben of FairCopy for once again tackling the copy editing assiduously and to our contacts at Hymns Ancient and Modern who publish the book via the St Andrew Press.

Corrections, amendments and suggestions are always welcome.

David Stewart
yearbookeditor@churchofscotland.org.uk

SECTION 1

Assembly Trustees, Agencies, Committees and Departments

The symbol > used in website information indicates the headings to be selected as they appear

1. OFFICE OF THE GENERAL ASSEMBLY

The Office supports the General Assembly, Presbyteries and Kirk Sessions, the Moderator and the process of Presbytery reform. In addition, the staff service the following: Assembly Business Committee, Legal Questions Committee, Judicial Commission, Judicial Panel, Appeals Committee of the Commission of Assembly, Ministries Appeal Panel, Mission Plan Review Group, the Committee to Nominate the Moderator, the Chalmers Lectureship Trust, the Committee on Overtures and Cases, the Delegation of Assembly, the Committee on Classifying Returns to Overtures, the Ecumenical Relations Committee and the Theological Forum. The Clerks of Assembly are responsible for consultation on matters of Church Law, Practice and Procedure.

Secretaries:

Principal Clerk of the General Assembly:	Rev. Fiona E. Smith LLB BD
Depute Clerk:	Ms Christine Paterson LLB DipLP
Executive Assistant to the Principal Clerk:	Mrs Nicola Nicholls, 0131 240 2240

Senior Administration Officer
  (Assembly Arrangements
  and Moderatorial Support):
	Miss Catherine McIntosh MA, 0131 376 1594

Secretary, Ecumenical Relations Committee:	Rev. Dr John L. McPake
Secretary, Theological Forum:	Ms Nathalie A. Mareš MacCallum MA MTh

Personnel in this department are also listed with the bodies and Committees that they serve.
Contact: pcoffice@churchofscotland.org.uk   0131 240 2240   Fax: 0131 240 2239

2. OFFICE OF THE ASSEMBLY TRUSTEES

The Trustees have responsibility for governance, finance and stewardship, budgeting and general oversight of the agencies of the Church. They assist the General Assembly to determine the strategy and priorities of the Church, and seek to ensure the implementation of the policies, priorities and strategic objectives of the General Assembly through working with the agencies of the Church to achieve a collaborative approach to the nurturing of the people of the Church in their witness, worship and service. They are the Charity Trustees of the Church of Scotland (the Unincorporated Entities) Scottish Charity No. SC011353.

Assembly Trustees:

Convener:	Rev. David S. Cameron
Vice-Convener:	David Harrison
Administrative Trustee:	Ann Nelson
Other Trustees:	Jean Couper CBE
	Ian Forrester
	Rev. Barry J. Hughes
	Jennifer MacDonald

Rev. Donald G.B. McCorkindale
Rev. Dr Peter McEnhill
Geoff Miller
Rev. Gillian Paterson
Rev. Norman A. Smith
Rev. Prof. Philip G. Ziegler
and Chair of the General Trustees

Chief Officer:	Dave Kendall
Head of Analysis and Programme Development:	Catherine Skinner
Head of Faith Action Programme:	Rev. Dr Scott J.S. Shackleton
(see 3. and 4. below)	
Head of Estates and Procurement:	Liam Fennell 0131 376 1131
(see 12. below)	
Audit and Compliance Officer:	Debra Livingstone
Executive Officer:	Catherine Forsyth
Executive PA to the Chief Officer:	Carron Lunt
Senior Administration Officer:	Lynn Hall
Statistician:	Rev. Dr Fiona J. Tweedie
Research Officer:	Karen Bass
Grants Manager:	David Williams 0131 376 5846
	grants@churchofscotland.org.uk
Health and Safety Manager:	Jacqueline Collins

Contact: OATadmin@churchofscotland.org.uk   0131 240 2229

Further information:
www.churchofscotland.org.uk > About us > Our structure > The Assembly Trustees

3. FAITH IMPACT FORUM

The Forum's role is to enable the Church of Scotland to participate effectively in the Mission of God in the world, following the example and priorities of Jesus Christ and always seeking the guidance of the Holy Spirit. It works both nationally and internationally on behalf of the Church and with congregations and presbyteries, their members and adherents, to engage in global and national political and social issues. The Forum engages with leaders in civic society, public bodies and other networks; and nurtures and sustains relationships with the Church's international partners and others. The Forum seeks to enable the church locally to develop connections both internationally and locally, and to engage with national and global issues. This includes relationship building, promoting a just and green future, climate justice, engaging on issues of gender, inclusion and diversity, migration, refugees and asylum seekers. The Forum is also the principal link with Christian Aid. The Five Marks of Mission and the Faith Action Plan guide the work of the Forum. These emphasise that Christians are followers of Jesus Christ, here to live out God's mission as an expression of God's gracious love. The five marks are holistic and indivisible. The Good News is about being called into the church which will teach and nurture people in a discipleship which covers personal, societal and ecological witness, ethics and holiness; being called to love the whole world, to work for justice and peace, and to care for creation.

Acting Convener:	Rev. Karen E. Hendry BSc BD
Vice-Convener:	Rev. Karen E. Hendry BSc BD
Head of Faith Action Programme:	Rev. Dr Scott J.S. Shackleton
Global Justice:	Rev. Ian W. Alexander
Public Witness & Parliamentary Officer:	Mr David Bradwell
Congregational Engagement:	Ms Carol Finlay
Society, Religion and Technology:	Dr Murdo Macdonald
Interfaith, Equalities & Gender Justice:	Ms Mirella Yandoli
International Relationships:	Ms Jennie Chinembiri,
	Mr Sandy Sneddon,
	Mr Kenny Roger
Scottish Faiths Action for Refugees:	Ms Sabine Chalmers

Contact: faithimpact@churchofscotland.org.uk 0131 225 5722

Further information:
www.churchofscotland.org.uk > About us > Forums, committees and departments > Forums > Faith Impact Forum
www.churchofscotland.org.uk > Connect > Campaigns
www.churchofscotland.org.uk > Connect > Global Partnerships
www.churchofscotland.org.uk > Connect > Scottish Faiths Action for Refugees

---

4. FAITH NURTURE FORUM

The Forum seeks to support and resource congregations and presbyteries in sharing the good news of the Gospel, growing the church as part of the mission of God, nurturing faith and encouraging discipleship. It seeks to develop individual gifts and talents across all ages, and resource young people in their faith formation and participation in decision-making within the Church, building strong and accessible communities of worship and service, and learning from the successes in congregations. The Forum works on recruiting, training and supporting the recognised ministries of the Church, enabling Presbyteries to plan and resource congregations and mission, as congregations seek to give special priority to those living in poverty and at the margins.

Convener:	Rev. Rosemary Frew MA BD
Vice-Convener:	Rev. Dr Alan J. Hamilton
Head of Faith Action Programme:	Rev. Dr Scott J.S. Shackleton
Partnership Development:	Rev. Angus R. Mathieson MA BD
Mission Development:	Mrs Lesley Hamilton-Messer MA
Education and Learning:	Ms Kay Cathcart MA PGCE
Ministries Development:	Mr Daran Golby BA CIPD
*Priority Areas:	Ms Shirley Grieve BA PGCE (0141 248 2905)
Recruitment and Support:	Rev. Dr Lezley J. Stewart
Resourcing Worship:	Mr Phill Mellstrom BA
Sanctuary First:	Very Rev. Albert O. Bogle BD MTh

Contact: faithnurture@churchofscotland.org.uk 0131 240 2205

*The Priority Areas Team operates from 759 Argyle Street, Glasgow G3 8DS; 0141 248 2905

Further information:
www.churchofscotland.org.uk > About us > Forums, committees and departments > Forums > Faith Nurture Forum
www.churchofscotland.org.uk > Connect > Going for Growth
www.churchofscotland.org.uk > Connect > Priority Areas
www.churchofscotland.org.uk > Resources > Presbytery Planning
www.churchofscotland.org.uk > Serve > Faith Nurture Forum
www.churchofscotland.org.uk > Serve > Vocations
www.ascend.churchofscotland.org.uk
www.resourcingmission.org.uk

5. CROSSREACH

Charis House, 47 Milton Road East, Edinburgh EH15 2SR
0131 657 2000   Fax: 0131 657 5000
info@crossreach.org.uk   www.crossreach.org.uk

CrossReach, overseen by the CrossReach Board (formally recognised as the Social Care Council), provides social-care services as part of the Christian mission and ministry of the Church to the people of Scotland, and engages with other bodies in responding to emerging areas of need. CrossReach operates 73 services across the country.

Convener:	Rev. Thomas S. Riddell
Vice-Convener:	Sarah Wood
Chief Executive Officer:	Viv Dickenson (viv.dickenson@crossreach.org.uk)
Director of Services to Older People:	Allan Logan (allan.logan@crossreach.org.uk)
Director of Adult Care Services:	Vic Walker (vic.walker@crossreach.org.uk)
Director of Children and Families:	Sheila Gordon (sheila.gordon@crossreach.org.uk)
Director of Finance and Resources:	Eoin McDunphy (eoin.mcdunphy@crossreach.org.uk)
Director of Human Resources and Organisational Development:	Claire Hay (claire.hay@crossreach.org.uk)

Further information: www.crossreach.org.uk

For sharing local experience and initiatives: www.socialcareforum.scot

6. ASSEMBLY BUSINESS COMMITTEE

Convener:	Rev. Donald G.B. McCorkindale BD DipMin
Vice-Convener:	Rev. Michael J. Mair BD
Secretary:	Principal Clerk
	cmcintosh@churchofscotland.org.uk 0131 240 2240

Further information:
www.churchofscotland.org.uk > About us > General Assembly
www.churchofscotland.org.uk > About us > Forums, committees and departments > Committees
> Assembly Business

7. AUDIT COMMITTEE

Remit: to oversee the financial and other relevant reporting processes implemented by management; to work with the Assembly Trustees in setting appropriate standards of financial management and in overseeing compliance; and to keep under review the effectiveness of the systems for internal financial control, financial reporting and risk management, including compliance with the legal and regulatory environment.

Convener: Kenneth Baldwin

Contact: OATadmin@churchofscotland.org.uk 0131 240 2229

Further information:
www.churchofscotland.org.uk > About us > Forums, committees and departments > Committees
> Audit

8. CHURCH OF SCOTLAND TRUST

Chairman: Mr Leon M. Marshall CA
Vice-Chairman: Mrs Morag Angus MA DipLS FRICS
Treasurer: Mrs Anne F. Macintosh BA CA
Secretary and Clerk: Mrs Madelaine Sproule LLB MSc DipLP NP
                       msproule@churchofscotland.org.uk   0131 240 2215

Further information:
www.churchofscotland.org.uk > About us > Stewardship, finance and trusts > Church of Scotland Trust

9. COMMITTEE TO NOMINATE THE MODERATOR

Convener: The immediate past Moderator
Secretary: Principal Clerk
Contact: pcoffice@churchofscotland.org.uk 0131 240 2240

10. COMMUNICATIONS DEPARTMENT

Head of Communications:	Ruth MacLeod 0131 240 2243
Communications Manager:	Helen Silvis 0131 240 2268
Senior Communications Officer:	Cameron Brooks 0131 240 2204
Communications Officer:	Jane Bristow 0131 240 2204
Communications Officer:	Laura Crawford 0131 240 2268
Web Editor:	Brianne Moore
Web Developer:	Alan Murray
Design Team Leader:	Chris Flexen
Senior Designer:	Steve Walker

Contact the Media Team after hours: 07854 783539
Contact department: 0131 240 2268
Further information:
www.churchofscotland.org.uk > About us > Forums, committees and departments >
Departments > Communications

11. ECUMENICAL RELATIONS COMMITTEE

The Committee is composed of Convener, Vice Convener and eight members appointed by the General Assembly, plus representatives of other denominations in Scotland and Church of Scotland members elected to British and international ecumenical bodies.

Convener:	Rev. I. Ross Blackman BSc MBA BD CertTh
Vice-Convener:	Rev. Eileen A. Miller BD
Secretary and Ecumenical Officer:	Rev. Dr John L. McPake

Contact: ecumenical@churchofscotland.org.uk   0131 240 2208

Further information:
www.churchofscotland.org.uk > About us > Forums, committees and departments > Committees > Ecumenical Relations Committee
www.churchofscotland.org.uk > Connect > Ecumenical relations
World Council of Churches: www.oikumene.org
Churches Together in Britain and Ireland: www.ctbi.org.uk
Action of Churches Together in Scotland: www.acts-scotland.org
For other international ecumenical bodies see Committee's web pages as above
See also 'Other Churches in the United Kingdom' at Section 2.2.

12. ESTATES AND PROCUREMENT DEPARTMENT

Remit: to provide property, facilities, and procurement services to the Agencies and Departments of the central administration of the Church, and to manage the church offices.

Head of Estates and Procurement: Liam Fennell
Property Officer: Eunice Smith
Facilities Manager, Church Offices: Carole Tait
                                      ctait@churchofscotland.org.uk   0131 240 2214
Contact: cpd@churchofscotland.org.uk   0131 240 2254

Further information:
www.churchofscotland.org.uk > About us > Forums, committees and departments > Departments > Estates and Procurement

13. FORCES CHAPLAINS COMMITTEE

Convener: Rev. Scott J. Brown CBE
Vice-Convener: Group Captain Andrew G. Tait CEng FRAeS RAF(Ret'd)
Secretary: Daran Golby, Faith Nurture
                DGolby@churchofscotland.org.uk   0131 225 5722

Further information:
www.churchofscotland.org.uk > About us > Forums, committees and departments > Forces Chaplains Committee
A list of Chaplains is found at Section 6 G

14. GENERAL TRUSTEES

Chair: Vacant
Vice-Chair: Vacant
Chief Executive: Mr Barri S. Millar BSc MSc ICIOB MAPM
                                   MIoD FSAScot
PA to Chief Executive &
   Head of Administration: Mrs Eva Elder
Head of Building Safety,
   Risk & Compliance: Mr Brian Auld BSc PGDip ChEHO MREHIS MCIEH
                                   CEnvH MIISRM GradIOSH
Head of Land & Estates: Mrs Morag J. Menneer BSc MRICS
                                Ms Claire L. Cowell LLB
Head of Policy & Legislation: Mr Brian D. Waller LLB
Head of Projects & Development: Mr Neil Page BSc MCIOB

Sanctuary Development Officer:	Judith Roebuck BA PGDip
Health and Safety Advisor:	Mo D'Souli NEBOSH GradIOSH DipNCRQ REHIS
Fire Safety Officer:	Mr Robert Speedie BEng (Fire) GradIFireE
Project Surveyor:	Mr Robert Lee BSc MCIOB
Buildings Officer, North East:	Rev. B. Ian Murray BD
Buildings Officer, Fife:	Mr David Gillan BSc MRICS
Buildings Officer, Clyde:	Mr Jamie McNamara MA IHBC
Buildings Officer, Edinburgh and West Lothian:	Ms Katie Dunbar BSc MRICS
Energy Conservation:	Mr Robert Lindores FInstPa
Finance Manager:	Mr Simon Bree MA ACCA

Buildings insurance, all enquiries to	Church of Scotland Insurance Services Ltd. 121 George Street, Edinburgh EH2 4YN enquiries@cosic.co.uk 0131 220 4119
Chief Executive (COSIS):	Mr Barry Clarkson

Contact: gentrustees@churchofscotland.org.uk   0131 225 5722
Further information:
www.churchofscotland.org.uk > About us > Forums, committees and departments > Departments > General Trustees
www.churchofscotland.org.uk > About us > Forums, committees and departments > Committees > Church Art and Architecture
www.churchofscotland.org.uk > Resources > Subjects > Art and Architecture resources

15. THE GUILD

The Church of Scotland Guild is a movement within the Church of Scotland whose aim is 'to invite and encourage both women and men to commit their lives to Jesus Christ and to enable them to express their faith in worship, prayer, action and fellowship'.

Convener:	Helen Eckford, Inverclyde Guilds Together
Vice-Conveners:	Flora Buthlay, Gordon Guilds Together
	Morag Duncan, Lewis Guilds Together
	Rae Lind, Irvine and Kilmarnock Guilds Together
	Christina Patterson, Stirling and Clackmannshire Guilds Together
General Secretary:	Karen Gillon
Administrator:	Mandy Moir

Contact: guild@churchofscotland.org.uk   0131 240 2217

Further information:
www.cos-guild.org.uk
www.churchofscotland.org.uk > Serve > The Guild

16. HOUSING AND LOAN FUND

Chair: Rev. Dorothy U. Anderson LLB DipLP BD
Deputy Chair: Rev. Bruce H. Sinclair BA BD
Secretary: Hazel Bett
                      HBett@churchofscotland.org.uk   0131 225 5722 ext. 2310;
                        07929 418762
Property Manager: Hilary J. Hardy
Property Assistant: Selena MacArthur

Further information:
www.churchofscotland.org.uk > About us > Forums, committees and departments > Departments > Housing and Loan Fund

17. HUMAN RESOURCES DEPARTMENT

Head of Human Resources: Elaine McCloghry
Human Resources Managers: Karen Smith
                            Angela Ocak
Human Resources Advisers: Sarah-Jayne McVeigh
                            Stephanie Thomson

Contact: hr@churchofscotland.org.uk   0131 240 2270

Further information:
www.churchofscotland.org.uk > About us > Forums, committees and departments > Departments > Human Resources

18. INFORMATION TECHNOLOGY DEPARTMENT

Head of IT: Richard MacLennan
               0131 240 2247

Contact: itdept@churchofscotland.org.uk   0131 376 1597

Further information:
www.churchofscotland.org.uk > About us > Forums, committees and departments > Departments > IT

19. INVESTORS TRUST

Chairman:	Mr Robert D. Burgon
Vice-Chairman:	Ms Elaine Crichton
Treasurer:	Mrs Anne F. Macintosh BA CA
Executive Officer:	Mrs June Lee
	investorstrust@churchofscotland.org.uk 0131 376 3678

Further information:
www.churchofscotland.org.uk > About us > Stewardship, finance and trusts > Departments > Investors Trust

20. LAW DEPARTMENT

Solicitor of the Church and of the General Trustees:	Miss Mary Macleod LLB DipLP NP
Depute Solicitor:	Mrs Elspeth Annan LLB DipLP NP
Solicitors:	Miss Susan Killean LLB DipLP NP
	Mrs Anne Steele LLB DipLP NP
	Mrs Jennifer Campbell LLB LLM DipLP NP
	Gregor Buick LLB DipLP WS NP
	Mrs Madelaine Sproule LLB MSc DipLP NP
	Gordon Barclay LLB DipLP BSc MSc MPhil PhD FRSA
	David di Paola LLB DipLP NP
	John Wilson LLB DipLP NP
Data Protection Officer:	Alice Wilson BA PCDP

Contact: lawdept@churchofscotland.org.uk   0131 225 5722 ext. 2230; Fax: 0131 240 2246.

Further information:
www.churchofscotland.org.uk > About us > Forums, committees and departments > Departments > Law

21. LEGAL QUESTIONS COMMITTEE

Remit: to advise on legal questions of Church and civil law, assist in formulating responses to consultations by the Scottish and UK governments, provide the legislative drafting service for Agencies of the General Assembly, advise on reform to Church law in terms of practice and procedure, report on proposed amendments to Standing Orders, and inspect annually the records of Agencies and Presbyteries.

Convener:	Rev. S. Grant Barclay LLB DipLP BD MSc PhD
Vice-Convener:	Rev. Victoria J. Linford LLB BD
Secretary:	Principal Clerk
Depute Clerk:	Ms Christine Paterson LLB DipLP

Contact: NNicholls@churchofscotland.org.uk   0131 240 2240

Further information:
www.churchofscotland.org.uk > About us > Forums, committees and departments > Committees
> Legal Questions

22. LIFE AND WORK
the Church of Scotland's monthly magazine

The magazine's purpose is to keep the Church informed about events in church life at home and abroad and to provide a forum for Christian opinion and debate on a variety of topics. It has an independent editorial policy. Contributions which are relevant to any aspect of the Christian faith are welcome. The website, www.lifeandwork.org, includes up-to-date news, extracts from the magazine and additional features. To subscribe to the magazine through your church, speak to your Life and Work co-ordinator. To receive by post, call the number below or visit the website. A digital download, for reading on PC, tablet and smartphone, is also available.

Editor: Lynne McNeil   magazine@lifeandwork.org   0131 225 5722

Further information:
www.lifeandwork.org
www.churchofscotland.org.uk > News and Events > Life and Work

23. NOMINATION COMMITTEE

Remit: to bring before the General Assembly names of persons to serve on the Standing Committees of the General Assembly; to work with the Standing Committees to ensure an open, fair and robust process for identifying suitable persons to serve as Conveners; and to comment on recommendations for the appointment of Assembly Trustees.

Convener:	Rev. Julie M. Rennick BTh
Vice-Convener:	Rev. Dr Andrew Gardner

Contact: Nominations@churchofscotland.org.uk   0131 225 5722

Further information:
www.churchofscotland.org.uk > About us > Forums, committees and departments > Committees
> Nomination Committee

24. PENSION TRUSTEES

Chair:	Mr Graeme R. Caughey BSc FFIA
Vice-Chair:	Miss Lin J. Macmillan MA
Scheme Secretary and	
Pensions Manager:	Miss Jane McLeod BSc FPMI
Senior Pensions Administrator:	Mrs Fiona McCulloch-Stevenson
Pensions Administrators:	Ms Birgit Mosemann
	Mrs Lesley Elder
	Mrs Ruth Farquharson

Contact: pensions@churchofscotland.org.uk   0131 240 2255

Further information:
www.churchofscotland.org.uk > About us > Stewardship, finance and trusts > Pension Trustees

25. REGISTRATION OF MINISTRIES COMMITTEE

The Committee considers applications from ministers who wish to have the status of Category O, which entitles them to be inducted to a charge.

Convener:	Dr Hazel Hastie
Vice-Convener:	Rev. Hilary N. McDougall MA PGCE BD
Registrar:	Rev. Angus R. Mathieson MA BD

Contact: RegistrationofMinistries@churchofscotland.org.uk 0131 240 2205

Further information:
www.churchofscotland.org.uk > Forums, committees and departments > Committees > Registration of Ministries Committee

26. SAFEGUARDING SERVICE

The service ensures that the Church has robust structures and policies in place for the prevention of harm and abuse of children and adults at risk; and to ensure a timely and appropriate response when harm or abuse is witnessed, suspected or reported.

Convener:	Rev. Adam J. Dillon BD ThM
Vice-Convener:	Rev. Fiona J. Reynolds LLB BD FdSc
Service Manager:	Ms Julie Main BA DipSW

Contact: safeguarding@churchofscotland.org.uk   0131 240 2256

Further information:
www.churchofscotland.org.uk > About us > Forums, committees and departments > Departments > Safeguarding Service

27. SAINT ANDREW PRESS

Saint Andrew Press is managed on behalf of the Church of Scotland by Hymns Ancient and Modern Ltd and publishes a broad range of titles, focussing principally on resources for the mission and ministry of the contemporary church but also including backlist favourites such as William Barclay's much-loved *Daily Study Bible* commentaries. The full list of publications can be viewed on the Saint Andrew Press website (see below).

Contact: Christine Smith, Publishing Director christine@hymnsam.co.uk   0207 776 7546

Further information: www.standrewpress.com

28. SCOTTISH CHURCHES PARLIAMENTARY OFFICE
121 George Street, Edinburgh EH2 4YN

The purpose of the Scottish Churches Parliamentary Office is to build good relations between Scottish Churches, the Scottish and UK Parliaments and the Scottish and UK Governments. It aims to do this by: creating space for ecumenical fellowship and encounter on parliamentary and political affairs in Scotland; facilitating and enabling Scottish Churches to speak on legislation and political developments; and sharing news of parliamentary and political developments timeously and to the right people in the Churches.

Scottish Churches Parliamentary Officer: David Bradwell

Contact: DBradwell@churchofscotland.org.uk   0131 376 9104

Further information: www.scpo.scot

29. SCOTTISH STORYTELLING CENTRE (THE NETHERBOW)
43–45 High Street, Edinburgh EH1 1SR

The integrated facilities of the **Netherbow Theatre** and the **John Knox House**, together with the outstanding conference and reception areas, form an important cultural venue on the Royal Mile in Edinburgh. The Centre captures both the historical roots of storytelling and the forward-looking mission to preserve it: providing an extensive year-round cultural and literary programme. Faith Nurture Forum is pleased to partner with TRACS (Traditional Arts and Culture Scotland), a grant-funded body which provides advice and assistance nationally in the use of traditional arts in a diversity of settings.

Contact: reception@scottishstorytellingcentre.com   0131 556 9579

Further information: www.scottishstorytellingcentre.com

30. STEWARDSHIP AND FINANCE DEPARTMENT

General Treasurer: Anne F. Macintosh BA CA
Deputy Treasurer (Unincorporated Entities): Gillian E. Coghlan MA CA
Deputy Treasurer (Wider Church and Statutory Corporations): Leanne Thompson BSc CA
Finance Managers: Lisa Erskine BA FCCA
Elaine Macadie BA CA
Simon Bree MA ACCA
Jennifer Law BSc CA
Stewardship Team Leader: Pauline Wilson MA

Contact: sfadmin@churchofscotland.org.uk
Further information and details of consultants:
www.churchofscotland.org.uk > About us > Forums, committees and departments > Stewardship and Finance
www.churchofscotland.org.uk > Resources > Finance resources
www.churchofscotland.org.uk > Resources > Stewardship
www.churchofscotland.org.uk > About us > Stewardship Finance and Trusts

31. THEOLOGICAL FORUM

The purpose of the Forum is to continue to develop and bring to expression doctrinal understanding of the Church with reference to Scripture and to the confessional standards of the Church of Scotland, and the implications of this for worship and witness in and beyond contemporary Scotland. It responds to requests to undertake enquiries as they arise, draws the Church's attention to particular matters requiring theological work, and promotes theological reflection throughout the Church.

Convener: Rev. Liam J. Fraser LLB BD MTh PhD
Vice-Convener: Professor Paul T. Nimmo MA DipIA BD MTh PhD FHEA
Secretary: Nathalie A. Mareš MacCallum MA MTh

Contact: NMaresMacCallum@churchofscotland.org.uk
Further information:
www.churchofscotland.org.uk > About us > Forums, committees and departments > Committees > Theological Forum

SECTION 2

General Information

1. GAELIC DEVELOPMENT IN THE CHURCH OF SCOTLAND

Leasachadh na Gàidhlig ann an Eaglais na h-Alba
Tha comataidh na Gàidhlig air a bhith a' coinneachadh air loidhne am bliadhna.

A-nis agus eaglaisean a' cumail seirbheisean anns na toglaichean aca a-rithist, le cuinge-alachan Covid-19 air an togail, chan eil seirbheisean air a chraoladh air YouTube tro Eaglais Air-loidhne cho tric tuilleadh, ged a tha seirbheisean air a chraodhladh ann an Glaschu agus ann an Tairbeart na Hearadh (mar a bha iad mus tàinig Covid-19).

Tha coitheanal Eaglais Ghàidhlig Chaluim Chille ann an Glaschu (stèidhichte an-dràsta ann am Blawarthill Parish Church) ag obair air dòighean ùra gus coimhearsnachd na Gàidhlig ann an Glaschu a' ruigsinn. Aig an ìre-sa tha iad ag amas air cearcall còmhraidh a chur air dòigh.

Tha am fear a bha roimhe na Oifigear Gàidhlig aig an Eaglais a-nis fhathast a' ruith dà bhuidheann leughaidh air loidhne, gu saor-thoileach. Tha iad a' dol tron eadar-theangachadh ùr dhen Tiomnaidh Nuaidh.

A bharrachd air a sin, tha e air a bhith a' toirt comhairle agus taic do Chomann Bhìobaill na h-Alba, agus iad ag obair air Am Bìoball Gàidhlig (1992) fhoillseachadh ann an clò a-rithist, rud a tha air a bhith mach à chlò fad greis a-nis. Tha iad ag obair cuideachd còmhla ri *Faith Comes By Hearing*, buidhean anns na Stàitean Aonaichte, gus leabhar-fuaim a dhèanamh dhen eadar-theangachadh ùr dhen Tiomnaidh Nuaidh.

Tha adhartas air a bhith ann a thaobh tionndadh Gàidhlig a dhèanamh air goireasan *The God Question*. Chaidh an sgriobt eadar-theangachadh agus tha sinn a-nis a' sireadh maoineachaidh airson an ath cheum sa pròiseact seo.

Chaidh goireasan a bharrachd a chuir ris an làrach-lìn, An Sgeul Mòr (ansgeulmor.co.uk), le cuideam sònraichte air goireasan chloinne.

Tha *Na Duilleagan Gàidhlig* fhathast air fhoillseachadh gach ràith.

An t-Oll. Donnchadh Sneddon

Gaelic Development in the Church of Scotland
The Gaelic Committee has continued to meet online over the past year.

With services largely having resumed in person as Covid-19 restrictions have eased, the weekly services on the YouTube channel Eaglais Air-loidhne has largely wound down, though in-person services in Glasgow are being filmed and uploaded, and Tarbert Church of Scotland continues to make their Gaelic services available online as they have been doing since before the pandemic.

The congregation of St Columba Gaelic Church in Glasgow (currently based in Blawarthill Parish Church) are exploring new ways of reaching out to the Gaelic community of the city, and are planning to establish a Gaelic conversation group to that end.

The former Gaelic Language Officer, in a voluntary capacity, continues to run two weekly Gaelic reading groups online for learners, working through the new translation of the New Testament.

He has also been giving practical help and advice to the Scottish Bible Society as they work to republish the 1992 Revised Gaelic Bible (which has been out of print for some time) and to produce an audio version of the new translation of the New Testament with the US-based group *Faith Comes By Hearing*.

Progress has also been made on the production of the Gaelic version of *The God Question* materials. The script has been translated into Gaelic and funding is now being sought for the next steps in the project.

Materials have continued to be added to the website An Sgeul Mòr (ansgeulmor.co.uk), with a focus on resources for children.

Na Duilleagan Gàidhlig, the Gaelic supplement to *Life and Work*, continues to be produced on a quarterly basis.

Dr Duncan Sneddon

2. OTHER CHURCHES IN THE UNITED KINGDOM

ASSOCIATED PRESBYTERIAN CHURCHES: Clerk of Scottish Presbytery: Rev. J.R. Ross Macaskill (01470 582264; jrrm@gmail.com; www.apchurches.org).

BAPTIST UNION OF SCOTLAND: General Director: Rev. Martin Hodson, 48 Speirs Wharf, Glasgow G4 9TH (0141 433 4555; martin@scottishbaptist.org.uk; www.scottishbaptist.com).

CHURCH OF ENGLAND: Secretary General of General Synod: Mr William Nye, Church House, Great Smith Street, London SW1P 3AZ (020 7898 1000; enquiry@churchofengland. org).

CONGREGATIONAL FEDERATION IN SCOTLAND: Secretary: Miss Margaret McGuiness, Coatdyke Congregational Church, Kippen Street, Airdrie ML6 9AX (www. congregational.org.uk).

FREE CHURCH OF SCOTLAND: Principal Clerk: Rev. Callum Macleod, 15 North Bank Street, The Mound, Edinburgh EH1 2LS (0131 226 5286; offices@freechurch.org; www. freechurch.org).

FREE CHURCH OF SCOTLAND (CONTINUING): Principal Clerk: Rev. Graham Craig, Free Church Manse, 46A Craigie Road, Ayr KA8 0HA (01292 737447; principalclerk@ fccontinuing.org; www.freechurchcontinuing.org).

FREE PRESBYTERIAN CHURCH OF SCOTLAND: Clerk of Synod: Rev. Keith M. Watkins, Free Presbyterian Manse, Ferry Road, Leverburgh, Isle of Harris HS5 3UA (kmwatkins@fpchurch.org.uk; www.fpchurch.org.uk).

METHODIST CHURCH IN SCOTLAND: District Administrator: Sue Marshall-Jennings, Methodist Church District Office, Old Churches House, 1 Kirk Street, Dunblane FK15 0AL (07787 380823; DistrictAdmin@methodistchurchinscotland.net; methodistchurchinscotland.net).

PRESBYTERIAN CHURCH IN IRELAND: Clerk of the General Assembly and General Secretary: Rev. Trevor D. Gribben, Assembly Buildings, 2–10 Fisherwick Place, Belfast BT1 6DW (028 9041 7208; clerk@presbyterianireland.org; www.presbyterianireland.org).

PRESBYTERIAN CHURCH OF WALES: General Secretary: Rev. Meirion Morris, Tabernacle Chapel, 81 Merthyr Road, Whitchurch, Cardiff CF14 1DD (02920 627465; swyddfa. office@ebcpcw.org.uk; www.ebcpcw.cymru).

REFORMED PRESBYTERIAN CHURCH OF SCOTLAND: Clerk of Presbytery: Rev. Peter Loughridge, 7 West Pilton Road, Edinburgh EH4 4GX (07791 369626; peterloughridge@ hotmail.com; www.rpcscotland.org).

RELIGIOUS SOCIETY OF FRIENDS (QUAKERS): Clerk to the General Meeting for Scotland: Elizabeth Allen (scotfriends@gmail.com; www.quakerscotland.org).

ROMAN CATHOLIC CHURCH: Fr. Gerard Maguiness, General Secretary, Bishops' Conference of Scotland, 64 Aitken Street, Airdrie ML6 6LT (01236 764061; gensec@bcos. org.uk; www.bcos.org.uk).

SALVATION ARMY: Lt-Col. Carol Bailey, Secretary for Scotland, Scotland Office, 12A Dryden Road, Loanhead EH20 9LZ (0131 440 9109; carol.bailey@salvationarmy.org.uk; www.salvationarmy.org.uk).

SCOTTISH EPISCOPAL CHURCH: Secretary General: Mr John F. Stuart, 21 Grosvenor Crescent, Edinburgh EH12 5EE (0131 225 6357; secgen@scotland.anglican.org; www. scotland.anglican.org).

UNITED FREE CHURCH OF SCOTLAND: Principal Clerks: Rev. Martin C. Keane and Rev. Colin C. Brown, United Free Church Offices, 11 Newton Place, Glasgow G3 7PR (0141 332 3435; office@ufcos.org.uk; www.ufcos.org.uk).

UNITED REFORMED CHURCH: General Secretary: Rev. Dr John Bradbury, Church House, 86 Tavistock Place, London WC1H 9RT (020 7916 2020; john.bradbury@urc.org.uk; www.urc.org.uk).

UNITED REFORMED CHURCH SYNOD OF SCOTLAND: Synod Clerk: Rev. Jan Adamson, United Reformed Church, 3/2 Atlantic Chambers, 45 Hope Street, Glasgow G2 6AE (0141 248 5382; clerk@urcscotland.org.uk; www.urcscotland.org.uk).

---

3. OVERSEAS CHURCHES

See www.churchofscotland.org.uk > Connect > Global Partnerships > Partner Churches

---

4. HER MAJESTY'S HOUSEHOLD IN SCOTLAND
ECCLESIASTICAL

Dean of the Order of the Thistle and Dean of the Chapel Royal:	Very Rev. Prof. David A.S. Fergusson OBE MA BD DPhil DD FRSE FBA
Domestic Chaplains:	Rev. Kenneth I. Mackenzie DL BD CPS Rev. Neil N. Gardner OStJ MA BD
Chaplains in Ordinary:	Very Rev. Angus Morrison MA BD PhD DD Very Rev. E. Lorna Hood OBE MA BD DD Very Rev. Susan M. Brown BD DipMin DUniv Rev. Elizabeth M. Henderson OBE MA BD MTh Rev. George J. Whyte BSc BD DMin Rev. Marjory A. MacLean LLB BD PhD

Rev. S. Grant Barclay LLB DipLP BD MSc PhD
Rev. Prof. John Swinton BD PhD RMN RNMD FRSE
Rev. Moira McDonald MA BD

Extra Chaplains: Rev. John MacLeod MA
Very Rev. James A. Simpson BSc BD STM DD
Very Rev. James Harkness KCVO CB OBE MA DD
Rev. John L. Paterson MA BD STM
Rev. Charles Robertson LVO MA
Very Rev. John B. Cairns KCVO LTh LLB LLD DD
Very Rev. Gilleasbuig I. Macmillan
          KCVO MA BD Drhc DD FRSE HRSA FRCSEd
Very Rev. Finlay A.J. Macdonald MA BD PhD DD
Rev. Alastair H. Symington MA BD
Rev. James M. Gibson TD LTh LRAM
Very Rev. Prof. Iain R. Torrance KCVO Kt DD FRSE
Rev. Norman W. Drummond CBE MA BD DUniv FRSE
Rev. Alistair G. Bennett BSc BD
Very Rev. John P. Chalmers BD CPS DD

5. LORD HIGH COMMISSIONERS
TO THE GENERAL ASSEMBLY

* deceased

1969	Her Majesty the Queen attended in person
1980/81	The Earl of Elgin and Kincardine KT DL JP
1982/83	*Colonel Sir John Edward Gilmour Bt DSO TD
1984/85	*Charles Hector Fitzroy Maclean, Baron Maclean of Duart and Morvern KT GCVO KBE
1986/87	*John Campbell Arbuthnott, Viscount of Arbuthnott KT CBE DSC FRSE FRSA
1988/89	*Sir Iain Mark Tennant KT FRSA
1990/91	The Rt Hon. Donald MacArthur Ross FRSE
1992/93	The Rt Hon. Lord Macfarlane of Bearsden KT FRSE
1994/95	*Lady Marion Fraser KT
1996	Her Royal Highness the Princess Royal LT LG GCVO
1997	The Rt Hon. Lord Macfarlane of Bearsden KT FRSE
1998/99	*The Rt Hon. Lord Hogg of Cumbernauld CBE DL JP
2000	His Royal Highness the Prince Charles, Duke of Rothesay KG KT GCB OM
2001/02	*The Rt Hon. Viscount Younger of Leckie KT KCVO TD PC
	Her Majesty the Queen attended the opening of the General Assembly of 2002
2003/04	The Rt Hon. Lord Steel of Aikwood KT KBE
2005/06	The Rt Hon. Lord Mackay of Clashfern KT
2007	His Royal Highness the Prince Andrew, Duke of York KG KCVO
2008/09	The Rt Hon. George Reid PC MA
2010/11	Lord Wilson of Tillyorn KT GCMG PRSE

2012/13	The Rt Hon. Lord Selkirk of Douglas QC MA LLB
2014	His Royal Highness the Prince Edward, Earl of Wessex KG GCVO
2015/16	The Rt Hon. Lord Hope of Craighead KT PC FRSE
2017	Her Royal Highness the Princess Royal KG KT GCVO QSO
2018/19	The Duke of Buccleuch and Queensberry KT KBE DL FSA FRSE
2020	*The General Assembly in May was cancelled due to the pandemic*
2021	His Royal Highness the Prince William, Earl of Strathearn KG KT MA
2022	The Rt Hon. Lord Hodge PC QC MA LLB

6. MODERATORS
OF THE GENERAL ASSEMBLY

* deceased

1992	Hugh R. Wyllie MA DD FCIBS, Hamilton: Old
1993	*James L. Weatherhead CBE MA LLB DD, Principal Clerk of Assembly
1994	James A. Simpson BSc BD STM DD, Dornoch Cathedral
1995	James Harkness KCVO CB OBE MA DD, Chaplain General (Emeritus)
1996	*John H. McIndoe MA BD STM DD, London: St Columba's linked with Newcastle: St Andrew's
1997	*Alexander McDonald BA DUniv CMIWSc, General Secretary, Department of Ministry
1998	Alan Main TD MA BD STM PhD DD, University of Aberdeen
1999	John B. Cairns KCVO LTh LLB LLD DD, Dumbarton: Riverside
2000	Andrew R.C. McLellan CBE MA BD STM DD, Edinburgh: St Andrew's and St George's
2001	John D. Miller BA BD STM DD, Glasgow: Castlemilk East
2002	Finlay A.J. Macdonald MA BD PhD DD, Principal Clerk of Assembly
2003	Iain R. Torrance KCVO Kt DD FRSE, University of Aberdeen
2004	Alison Elliot CBE MA MSc PhD LLD DD FRSE, Associate Director, Centre for Theology and Public Issues, University of Edinburgh
2005	David W. Lacy DL BA BD DLitt, Kilmarnock: Henderson
2006	Alan D. McDonald LLB BD MTh DLitt DD, Cameron linked with St Andrews: St Leonard's
2007	Sheilagh M. Kesting BA BD DD DSG, Secretary of Ecumenical Relations Committee
2008	David W. Lunan MA BD DLitt DD, Clerk to the Presbytery of Glasgow
2009	William C. Hewitt BD DipPS, Greenock: Westburn
2010	John C. Christie BSc BD CBiol MRSB, Interim Minister
2011	A. David K. Arnott MA BD, St Andrews: Hope Park linked with Strathkinness
2012	Albert O. Bogle BD MTh, Bo'ness: St Andrew's
2013	E. Lorna Hood OBE MA BD DD, Renfrew: North
2014	John P. Chalmers BD CPS DD, Principal Clerk of Assembly
2015	Angus Morrison MA BD PhD DD, Orwell and Portmoak
2016	G. Russell Barr BA BD MTh DMin, Edinburgh: Cramond
2017	Derek Browning MA BD DMin, Edinburgh: Morningside
2018	Susan M. Brown BD DipMin DUniv, Dornoch Cathedral

2019	Colin A.M. Sinclair BA BD, Edinburgh: Palmerston Place
2020	W. Martin Fair BA BD DMin, Arbroath: St Andrew's
2021	James R. Wallace, The Rt Hon. Lord Wallace of Tankerness PC QC FRSE MA LLB DUniv
2022	Iain M. Greenshields BD CertMin DipRS ACMA MSc MTh DD, Dunfermline: St Margaret's

MATTER OF PRECEDENCE

The Lord High Commissioner (while the Assembly is sitting) ranks next to the Sovereign and before the rest of the Royal Family. The Moderator ranks next to the Lord Chancellor of Great Britain and before the Keeper of the Great Seal of Scotland (the First Minister) and the Dukes.

---

7. SCOTTISH DIVINITY FACULTIES

* denotes a Minister of the Church of Scotland

ABERDEEN
School of Divinity, History and Philosophy
50–52 College Bounds, Old Aberdeen AB24 3DS
01224 272366; divinity@abdn.ac.uk

Master of Christ's College:	Rev. Professor John Swinton* BD PhD RMN RNMD FRSE christs-college@abdn.ac.uk
Head of School:	Dr Paula Sweeney MA PhD
Head of Divinity:	Professor Paul T. Nimmo MA DipIA BD MTh PhD FHEA
Co-ordinator,	
Centre for Ministry Studies	Rev. Kenneth S. Jeffrey* BA BD PhD DMin ksjeffrey@abdn.ac.uk

For other teaching staff and further information see www.abdn.ac.uk/sdhp/

ST ANDREWS
University College of St Mary
The School of Divinity, South Street, St Andrews, Fife KY16 9JU
01334 462850; divinity@st-andrews.ac.uk

Principal and Head of School:	Professor Oliver Crisp BD MTh LLM PhD DLitt
Professor of World Christianity:	Professor Sabine Hyland BA MPhil PhD

For other teaching staff and further information see www.st-andrews.ac.uk/divinity/people

EDINBURGH
School of Divinity and New College
New College, Mound Place, Edinburgh EH1 2LX
0131 650 8959; divinity@ed.ac.uk

Head of School: Professor Helen K. Bond MTheol PhD
Principal of New College: Rev. Alison M. Jack* MA BD PhD SFHEA
Vice Principal of   Rev. Professor Susan Hardman Moore* MA MAR PhD FRHistS
New College:

For other teaching staff and further information see www.ed.ac.uk/schools-departments/divinity/

GLASGOW
School of Critical Studies
Theology and Religious Studies
4 Professors' Square, University of Glasgow, Glasgow G12 8QQ
0141 330 6526; trinitycollegeglasgow@gmail.com

Head of Subject: Dr Mia Spiro
Professor of Theology   Professor Heather Walton
and Creative Practice:
Principal of Trinity College: Rev. Doug C. Gay* MA BD PhD
Clerk of Trinity College and
Tutor in Pastoral Studies: Rev. Mark G. Johnston* BSc BD DMin

For other teaching staff and further information see www.gla.ac.uk/subjects/theology and www.
   trinitycollegeglasgow.co.uk

HIGHLAND THEOLOGICAL COLLEGE UHI
High Street, Dingwall IV15 9HA
01349 780000; htc@uhi.ac.uk

Principal of HTC: Rev. Hector Morrison* BSc BD MTh Cert ITL
Vice-Principal (Academic):   Jamie Grant LLB MA PhD
Vice Principal (Finance
and Operations):   Blair Gardner BSc PGDip
Programme Leader, Access
to Christian Theology
Programme: Rev. Jonathan Fraser* MA(Div) MTh ThM
Lecturer in Evangelism: Rev. Thomas MacNeil* MA BD
Lecturer in Understanding
Worship: Rev. Warren R. Beattie* BSc BD MSc PhD

For other teaching staff and further information see www.htc.uhi.ac.uk

8. SOCIETIES AND ASSOCIATIONS

* Church of Scotland Societies

ACTION OF CHURCHES TOGETHER IN SCOTLAND (ACTS) – Eaglaisean Còmhla an Gnìomh an Alba – was formed in 1990 as Scotland's national ecumenical instrument. It brings together nine denominations in Scotland who share a desire for greater oneness between churches, a growth of understanding and common life between churches, and unified action in proclaiming and responding to the gospel in the whole of life. The Member Churches of ACTS are in the process of transitioning the organisation into the Scottish Christian Forum, which would take forward the charitable purposes of ACTS. Address: Jubilee House, Forthside Way, Stirling, FK8 1QZ (www.acts-scotland.org).

* ASSEMBLY AND PRESBYTERY CLERKS FORUM: Secretary: Rev. Bryan Kerr, Greyfriars Parish Church, Bloomgate, Lanark ML11 9ET (01555 437050; 01555 663363; clerksforum@churchofscotland.org.uk).

BOYS' BRIGADE: A volunteer-led Christian youth organisation which was founded in Scotland in 1883 and now operates in many different countries around the world. Our vision is that children and young people experience life to the full (John 10:10). We provide opportunities for young people to learn, grow and discover in a safe, caring and fun environment. Contact: John Sharp, Carronvale House, Carronvale Road, Larbert FK5 3LH (01324 562008; support@boys-brigade.org.uk; www.boys-brigade.org.uk). Scottish Chaplain: Rev Derek Gunn (scottishchaplain@boys-brigade.org.uk).

BROKEN RITES: Support group for divorced and separated clergy spouses. (01896 759254; eshirleydouglas@hotmail.co.uk; www.brokenrites.org).

CHRISTIAN AID SCOTLAND: Sally Foster-Fulton, Head of Christian Aid Scotland, 41 George IV Bridge, Edinburgh EH1 1EL (0131 220 1254; edinburgh@christian-aid.org; www. christianaid.org.uk/get-involved-locally/scotland).

CHRISTIAN ENDEAVOUR IN SCOTLAND: Challenging and encouraging children and young people in the service of Christ and the Church, especially through the CE Award Scheme: 16 Queen Street, Alloa FK10 2AR (01259 215101; admin@cescotland.org; www.cescotland.org).

* CHURCH OF SCOTLAND ABSTAINERS' ASSOCIATION: Recognising that alcohol is a major – indeed a growing – problem within Scotland, the aim of the Church of Scotland Abstainers' Association, with its motto 'Abstinence makes sense', is to encourage more people to choose a healthy alcohol-free lifestyle. Further details are available from 'Blochairn', 17A Culduthel Road, Inverness IV24 4AG (jamwall@talktalk.net; www.kirkabstainers.org.uk).

* CHURCH OF SCOTLAND MILITARY CHAPLAINS' ASSOCIATION: The Association consists of serving and retired chaplains to HM Forces. It holds an annual meeting and lunch on Shrove Tuesday, and organises the annual Service of Remembrance in St Giles' Cathedral. Hon. Secretary: Rev. Stephen A. Blakey BSc BD OStJ, Balduff House, Kilry, Blairgowrie PH11 8HS (01575 560226; SBlakey@churchofscotland.org.uk).

* CHURCH OF SCOTLAND RETIRED MINISTERS' ASSOCIATION: The Association meets in St. Andrew's and St. George's West Church, George St., Edinburgh, normally on the first

Monday of the month, from October to April. The group is becoming increasingly ecumenical. Meetings include a talk, which can be on a wide variety of topics, which is followed by afternoon tea. Details of the programme from Hon. Secretary: Rev. Douglas A.O. Nicol, 1/2 North Werber Park, Edinburgh EH4 1SY (07811 437075; Douglas.Nicol@churchofscotland.org.uk).

* **CHURCH SERVICE SOCIETY:** Founded in 1865 to study the development of Christian worship through the ages and in the Reformed tradition, and to work towards renewal in contemporary worship. It has published since 1928, and continues to publish, a liturgical journal, archived on its website. Secretary: Rev. Dr Scott McKenna (01292 226075; SMcKenna@churchofscotland.org.uk; www.churchservicesociety.org).

* **COVENANT FELLOWSHIP SCOTLAND (formerly FORWARD TOGETHER):** An organisation for evangelicals within the Church of Scotland. Contact the Chairman, Rev. Louis Kinsey (07787 145918; LKinsey@churchofscotland.org.uk; http://covenantfellowshipscotland.com; https://www.facebook.com/covenantfellowshipscotland).

DAY ONE CHRISTIAN MINISTRIES: Day One has produced Christian literature for over 40 years. A variety of books are published for both adults and young people, as well as cards, bookmarks and stationery items. Ryelands Road, Leominster, Herefordshire HR6 8NZ. Contact Mark Roberts for further information (01568 613740; mark@dayone.co.uk; www.dayone.co.uk).

ECO-CONGREGATION SCOTLAND: An ecumenical environmental charity supporting the largest movement of community-based environment groups across Scotland to care and act for God's creation. Eco-Congregation Scotland offers a programme to help local congregations reduce their impact on climate change and live sustainably. 121 George Street, Edinburgh EH2 4YN (0131 240 2274; manager@ecocongregationscotland.org; www.ecocongregationscotland.org).

FELLOWSHIP OF ST ANDREW: The fellowship promotes dialogue between Churches of the east and the west in Scotland. Further information available from the Secretary, Rev. Dr Robert Pickles, The Manse, Thomas Telford Road, Langholm DG13 0BL (01387 380252; RPickles@churchofscotland.org.uk).

* **FRIENDS OF TABEETHA SCHOOL, JAFFA:** The Friends seek to support the only school run by the Church of Scotland in the world. Based in Jaffa, Israel, it seeks to promote tolerance and understanding amongst pupils and staff alike. President: Irene Anderson. Hon. Secretary: Rev. David J. Smith, 1 Cawdor Drive, Glenrothes KY6 2HN (01592 611963; David.Smith@churchofscotland.org.uk).

FRONTIER YOUTH TRUST: A movement journeying with young people on the margins of church and society. We host a community of practice for those working with young people in the community. We are resourcing the church to take pioneering risks in their work with young people. And we are calling others to join the pioneer movement to reach young people on the margins. Contact us for training and coaching, or find practical resources on our website at www.fyt.org.uk. Contact us at info@fyt.org.uk, 0121 771 2328 or find us on social media.

GIRLGUIDING SCOTLAND: 16 Coates Crescent, Edinburgh EH3 7AH (Tel: 0131 226 4511; administrator@girlguiding-scot.org.uk; www.girlguidingscotland.org.uk).

GIRLS' BRIGADE SCOTLAND: 11A Woodside Crescent, Glasgow G3 7UL (0141 332 1765; caroline.goodfellow@girls-brigade-scotland.org.uk; www.girls-brigade-scotland.org.uk).

INTERSERVE GREAT BRITIAN AND IRELAND: An international, evangelical and interdenominational organisation with 160 years of Christian service. The purpose of Interserve is 'to make Jesus Christ known through *wholistic* ministry in partnership with the global church, among the neediest peoples of Asia and the Arab world', and our vision is 'Lives and communities transformed through encounter with Jesus Christ'. Interserve supports over 800 people in cross-cultural ministry in a wide range of work including children and youth, the environment, evangelism, Bible training, engineering, agriculture, business development and health. We look to support churches and individuals as they seek to serve the Lord cross-culturally both locally and throughout Asia and the Arab world. (03333 601600; enquiries@interserve.org.uk; www.interserve.org.uk).

IONA COMMUNITY: We are an ecumenical Christian community with a dispersed worldwide membership, and an international network of supporters and volunteers. Inspired by our faith, we pursue justice and peace in and through community. Our Glasgow centre is the base for Wild Goose Publications and the Wild Goose Resource Group. The Iona Community welcomes thousands of visitors each year to its daily worship in Iona Abbey, and to its Welcome Centre and Community shop. It also welcomes guests to share in the common life on Iona and at Camas outdoor centre on Mull, which mainly hosts youth groups. Leader: Rev. Ruth Harvey, Suite 9, Fairfield, 1048 Govan Road, Glasgow, G51 4XS (0141 429 7281, admin@iona.org.uk; www.iona.org.uk; Facebook: Iona Community; Twitter: @ionacommunity). Iona Warden: Catriona Robertson, Iona Abbey, Isle of Iona, Argyll, PA76 6SN (01681 700404; enquiries@iona.org.uk).

* IRISH GATHERING: An informal annual meeting with a guest speaker; all those having a connection with or an interest in the Presbyterian Church in Ireland are very welcome. Treasurer: Rev. Richard Baxter, 31 Hughenden Gardens, Glasgow G12 9YH (07958 541418; RBaxter@churchofscotland.org.uk).

LEPROSY MISSION SCOTLAND: Working in over 30 countries, The Leprosy Mission is a global fellowship united by our Christian faith and commitment to finishing what Jesus started and making leprosy a thing of the past. The Leprosy Mission Scotland, Suite 2, Earlsgate Lodge, Livilands Lane, Stirling FK8 2BG (01786 449266; contactus@leprosymission.scot; www.leprosymission.scot).

PLACE FOR HOPE: exists to accompany and equip people and faith communities so that all may reach their potential as peacemakers, able to navigate change and conflict well. For over 10 years, Place for Hope has provided high quality mediation and training services in faith-based peace and reconciliation, supporting faith communities to notice brokenness and division, nurture relationships and community, navigate conflict with graciousness and nourish wholeness in themselves and their communities. In times of change and challenge, we know that practical support can help. We offer to congregations:
– support for groups and individuals experiencing conflict
– facilitation of sensitive or difficult group conversations, such as preparing for change or transition
– individual or team coaching
– community dialogues on difficult, potentially divisive issues
– training, workshops and resources for understanding and working with conflict and change.

Please get in touch for information, or a confidential conversation: 07884 580359; info@ placeforhope.org.uk; www.placeforhope.org.uk.

RELATIONSHIPS SCOTLAND: Scotland's largest provider of relationship counselling, family mediation and child contact centre services. Chief Executive: Mr Stuart Valentine, 18 York Place, Edinburgh EH1 3EP (Tel: 0345 119 2020; Fax: 0845 119 6089; enquiries@relationships-scotland.org.uk; www.relationships-scotland.org.uk).

ST COLM'S FELLOWSHIP: An association for all from any denomination who have trained, studied or been resident at St Colm's, either when it was a college or later as International House. There is an annual retreat and a meeting for Commemoration; and some local groups meet on a regular basis. Hon. Secretary: Rev. Margaret Nutter, 'Kilmorich', 14 Balloch Road, Balloch G83 8SR (01389 754505; maenutter@gmail.com).

SCOTTISH BIBLE SOCIETY: Chief Executive: Elaine Duncan, 7 Hampton Terrace, Edinburgh EH12 5XU (0131 337 9701; info@scottishbiblesociety.org; https://scottishbiblesociety.org).

SCOTTISH CHURCH HISTORY SOCIETY: Promoting interest in the history of Christianity in Scotland. Journal: *Scottish Church History*. Secretary: Dr Tristram Clarke (schssec@outlook. com; www.schs.org.uk).

* SCOTTISH CHURCH SOCIETY: Founded in 1892 to 'defend and advance Catholic doctrine as set forth in the Ancient Creeds and embodied in the Standards of the Church of Scotland', the Society meets for worship and discussion at All Saints' Tide, holds a Lenten Quiet Day, an AGM, and other meetings by arrangement; all are open to non-members. The Society is also now working closely with the Church Service Society and is arranging meetings which are of joint interest. Secretary: Rev. W. Gerald Jones MA BD MTh, The Manse, Patna Road, Kirkmichael, Maybole KA19 7PJ (01655 750286; WJones@churchofscotland.org.uk).

* SCOTTISH CHURCH THEOLOGY SOCIETY: The Society encourages theological exploration and discussion of the main issues confronting the Church in the twenty-first century. Rev. Alec Shuttleworth, 62 Toll Road, Kincardine, Alloa FK10 4QZ (01259 731002; AShuttleworth@churchofscotland.org.uk).

SCOTTISH CHURCHES ORGANIST TRAINING SCHEME (SCOTS): Established in 1995, SCOTS is run by the Royal College of Organists in partnership with the Scottish Federation of Organists, the Royal School of Church Music and the Scottish Churches. It is a self-propelled ecumenical scheme by which organists and those called upon to play the organ in churches follow a three-stage syllabus, receiving a certificate at each stage. Participants each have an Adviser whom they meet occasionally for help and assessment, and also take part in one of the Local Organ Workshops which are held in different parts of Scotland each year. Syllabus information at www.rco.org.uk/scots; information from Andrew Macintosh (01382 521210); andrew.macintosh@rco.org.uk.

SCOTTISH EVANGELICAL THEOLOGY SOCIETY: Seeks to promote theology which serves the church, is faithful to Scripture, grounded in scholarship, informed by worship, sharpened in debate, catholic in scope, with a care for Scotland and its people. Secretary: Rev. M.G. Smith, 0/2, 2008 Maryhill Road, Glasgow G20 0AB (0141 570 8680; sets.secretary@ gmail.com; www.s-e-t-s.org.uk).

SCOTTISH REFORMATION SOCIETY: Exists to defend and promote the work of the Protestant Reformation in Scotland by organising meetings, publishing literature and running an essay competition. Chairman: Rev. John Keddie. Vice-Chairman: Mr Allan McCulloch. Secretary: Rev. Dr Douglas Somerset. Treasurer: Mr Hugh Morrison. The Magdalen Chapel, 41 Cowgate, Edinburgh EH1 1JR (0131 220 1450; info@scottishreformationsociety.org; www.scottishreformationsociety.org).

SCOUTS SCOTLAND: Scottish Headquarters, Fordell Firs, Hillend, Dunfermline KY11 7HQ (01383 419073; hello@scouts.scot; www.scouts.scot).

SCRIPTURE UNION SCOTLAND: Scripture Union Scotland's vision is to see every child and young person in Scotland exploring the Bible and responding to the significance of Jesus. SU Scotland works in schools running SU groups and supporting Curriculum for Excellence. Its three activity centres, Lendrick Muir, Alltnacriche and Gowanbank, accommodate school groups and weekends away during term-time. During the school holidays it runs an extensive programme of events for school-age children – including residential holidays (some focused on disadvantaged children and young people), missions and church-based holiday clubs. In addition, it runs discipleship and training programmes for young people and is committed to promoting prayer for, and by, the young people of Scotland through a range of national prayer events and the *Pray for Schools Scotland* initiative. Scripture Union Scotland, 70 Milton Street, Glasgow G4 0HR (0141 332 1162; info@suscotland.org.uk; www.suscotland.org.uk).

* SOCIETY OF FRIENDS OF ST ANDREW'S JERUSALEM: In co-operation with the Faith Impact Forum, the Society seeks to provide support for the work of the Congregation of St Andrew's Scots Memorial Church, Jerusalem, and St Andrew's Guesthouse. Hon. Secretary and Membership Secretary: Walter T. Dunlop, c/o Faith Impact Forum, 121 George Street, Edinburgh, EH2 4YN.

STUDENT CHRISTIAN MOVEMENT: SCM is a student-led movement inspired by Jesus to act for justice and show God's love in the world. As a community we come together to pray, worship and explore faith in an open and non-judgemental environment. The movement is made up of a network of groups and individual members across Britain, as well as link churches and chaplaincies. As a national movement we come together at regional and national events to learn more about our faith and spend time as a community, and we take action on issues of social justice chosen by our members. SCM provides resources and training to student groups, churches and chaplaincies on student outreach and engagement, leadership and social action. Chief Executive: Rev. Naomi Nixon, SCM, Grays Court, 3 Nursery Road, Edgbaston, Birmingham B15 3JX (0121 426 4918; scm@movement.org.uk; www.movement.org.uk).

TEARFUND: Working alongside local partners and churches, in more than 50 countries, to tackle complex poverty through community development, humanitarian response and advocacy on a local, national and global level. 100 Church Road, Teddington TW11 8QE (020 3906 3906). Head of Tearfund Scotland: Graeme McMeekin, Baltic Chambers, Suite 529, 50 Wellington Street, Glasgow G2 6HJ (0141 332 3621; scotland@tearfund.org; www.tearfund.org).

WALDENSIAN MISSIONS AID SOCIETY FOR WORK IN ITALY: Supporting the outreach of the Waldensian Churches, including important work with immigrant communities in the *Mediterranean Hope* project. Scottish Charity No. SC001346. David A. Lamb SSC, 36 Liberton Drive, Edinburgh EH16 6NN (0131 664 3059; david@dlamb.co.uk; www.scottishwaldensian.org.uk).

WEST OF SCOTLAND BIBLE SOCIETY: Secretary: Rev. Robert Craig (01501 519085; secretary@westofscotlandbiblesociety.com; www.westofscotlandbiblesociety.com).

WORLD DAY OF PRAYER: SCOTTISH COMMITTEE: Convener: Mrs Margaret Broster, Bryn a Glyn, 27b Braehead, Beith KA15 1EF (01505 503300; margaretbroster@hotmail.co.uk). Secretary: Marjorie Paton, Muldoanich, Stirling Street, Blackford, Auchterarder PH4 1QG (01764 682234; marjoriepaton.wdp@btinternet.com; www.wdpscotland.org.uk).

YMCA SCOTLAND: Offers support, training and guidance to churches seeking to reach out to love and serve young people's needs. Chief Executive – National General Secretary: Mrs Kerry Reilly, YMCA Scotland, 1 Chesser Avenue, Edinburgh EH14 1TB (0131 228 1464; kerry@ymca.scot; www.ymca.scot).

YWCA SCOTLAND: Our vision is a world where every woman can shape her own life journey and fulfil her potential, where the voices of women are heard, respected and celebrated. We help to bring this about by creating empowering spaces for girls and young women to meet together in groups and clubs, activities and conversations. Chief Executive Officer: Dr Patrycja Kupiec, Wellpark/Kirkhaven Enterprise Centre, 120 Sydney Street, Glasgow G31 1JF (0141 465 4627; hello@ywcascotland.org; www.ywcascotland.org).

YOUTH FOR CHRIST: Youth for Christ is a national Christian charity committed to taking the Good News of Jesus Christ relevantly to every young person in Great Britain. In Scotland there are 5 locally governed, staffed and financed centres, communicating and demonstrating the Christian faith. Local Ministries Development Manager for Scotland: Sandra Blair (0121 502 9620; sandra.blair@yfc.co.uk; www.yfc.co.uk/local-centres/scotland).

YOUTH SCOTLAND: Balfour House, 19 Bonnington Grove, Edinburgh EH6 4BL (0131 554 2561; office@youthscotland.org.uk; www.youthscotland.org.uk).

9. TRUSTS AND FUNDS

ABERNETHY ADVENTURE CENTRES: Full board residential accommodation and adventure activities available for all Church groups, plus a range of Christian summer camps, gap year programmes and adventure leadership training courses at our two centres in Scotland. 01479 821279; info@abernethy.org.uk; www.abernethy.org.uk).

BAIRD TRUST: Assists in the building and repair of churches and halls, and generally assists the work of the Church of Scotland. Apply to Iain A.T. Mowat CA, 182 Bath Street, Glasgow G2 4HG (0141 332 0476; info@bairdtrust.org.uk; www.bairdtrust.org.uk).

Rev. Alexander BARCLAY BEQUEST: Assists a family member of a deceased minister of the Church of Scotland who at the time of his/her death was acting as his/her housekeeper and who is in needy circumstances, and in certain circumstances assists Ministers, Deacons, Ministries Development Staff and their spouses facing financial hardship. Applications can only be submitted to the trustees by the Faith Nurture Support Team, 121 George Street, Edinburgh EH2 4YN (pastoralsupport@churchofscotland.org.uk).

BELLAHOUSTON BEQUEST FUND: Gives grants to Protestant denominations in the City of Glasgow and certain areas within five miles of the city boundary for building and repairing churches and halls and the promotion of religion. Apply to Mrs Laura Schiavone, Mitchells Roberton, 36 North Hanover Street, Glasgow G1 2AD (0141 552 3422; info@mitchells-roberton.co.uk).

BEQUEST FUND FOR MINISTERS OF CHURCH OF SCOTLAND: Provides financial assistance to ministers towards the cost of manse furnishings, pastoral efficiency aids, and personal and family medical or educational costs. Apply to A. Linda Parkhill CA, 60 Wellington Street, Glasgow G2 6HJ (0141 226 4994; mail@parkhillmackie.co.uk).

CARNEGIE TRUST FOR THE UNIVERSITIES OF SCOTLAND: The Carnegie Trust invites applications by students who have had at least two years education at a secondary school in Scotland (or can demonstrate evidence of a substantial link to Scotland), for Tuition Fee Grants towards tuition fee costs for a first undergraduate degree at a Scottish university. For more information and a link to the online application form visit the Trust's website (https://www.carnegie-trust.org/award-schemes/undergraduate-tuition-fee-grants/) or contact the Carnegie Trust for the Universities of Scotland, Andrew Carnegie House, Pittencrieff Street, Dunfermline KY12 8AW (01383 724990; admin@carnegie-trust.org; www.carnegie-trust.org).

CHURCH HYMNARY TRUST: The trust is 'formed for the advancement of the Christian Faith through the promotion and development of hymnody in Scotland with particular reference to the Church of Scotland by assisting in the development, promotion, provision and understanding of hymns, psalms and paraphrases suitable for use in public worship, and in the distribution and making available of the same in books, discs, electronically and in other media for use by the Church of Scotland ....' The trust wishes to encourage applications for projects or schemes which are consistent with its purposes. These can include training courses, provision of music and guides to music, but the trust is not limited to those activities. The trust usually meets annually in early February, though applications may be considered out of committee. Applications should be made to the secretary and treasurer Hugh Angus, 56-66 Frederick Street, Edinburgh EH2 1LS, hugh.angus@balfour-manson.co.uk.

CHURCH OF SCOTLAND INSURANCE SERVICES LTD: Insurance intermediary, authorised and regulated by the Financial Conduct Authority, which arranges and manages the facility providing insurance protection for Church of Scotland congregations, including their activities and assets. Cover can also be arranged for other religious groups, charities, and non-profitmaking organisations. All profits are distributed to the General Trustees of the Church of Scotland through Gift Aid. Contact 121 George Street, Edinburgh EH2 4YN (Tel: 0131 220 4119; Fax: 0131 220 3113; b.clarkson@cosic.co.uk; www.cosic.co.uk).

CHURCH OF SCOTLAND MINISTRIES BENEVOLENT FUND: Makes grants to the following beneficiaries who are in need:
(a) any retired person who has been ordained or commissioned for the Ministry of the Church of Scotland;
(b) Minsters inducted or introduced to a charge or Ordained National Ministers appointed to posts under approval of Presbytery;
(c) Ministries Development Staff appointed to a Presbytery planned post (including Deacons);
(d) Ordained Local Minsters, Auxiliary Ministers or Deacons serving under the appointment of Presbytery;

(e) Readers set apart by Presbytery to carry out the work of the Church;
(f) any widow, widower and/or orphan of any person categorised in (a) to (e) above;
(g) any spouse or former spouse and/or child (natural or otherwise) of any person categorised by (a) to (e) above.
Contact pastoralsupport@churchofscotland.org.uk for an application form. Enquiries to Faith Nurture, Support Team, 121 George Street, Edinburgh EH2 4YN (0131 225 5722).

CINTRA BEQUEST: See 'Tod Endowment Trust ...' entry below.

CLAREMONT TRUST: aims to assist small, innovative projects of Christian witness, renewal and social action in their very early stages of development. Typically grants are of £500–£600 and not more than £1000. Completed application forms must be received by the last working day of April for consideration in May. Application forms available on www.claremonttrust.org.uk or the Secretary, Sylvia Marchant (01592 890986; smarchant1944@gmail.com)

CLARK BURSARY: Awarded to accepted candidate(s) for the ministry of the Church of Scotland whose studies for the ministry are pursued at the University of Aberdeen. Applications or recommendations for the Bursary to the Clerk to the Presbytery of Aberdeen and Shetland, Aberdeen North Church (Mastrick Building), Greenfern Road, Aberdeen AB16 6TR.

CRAIGCROOK MORTIFICATION: The Trust has power to award grants or pensions (1) to men and women of 60 years of age or over born in Scotland or who have resided in Scotland for not less than 10 years who appear to be in poor circumstances, and (2) to children of deceased persons who met those conditions at the time of death and who appear to require assistance. The Trust has made single payments but normally awards pensions of £1,030 payable biannually. Ministers are invited to notify the Clerk and Factor, Kirsty Ashworth, Exchange Place 3, Semple Street, Edinburgh EH3 8BL (0131 473 3500; SM-Charity@azets.co.uk) of deserving persons and should be prepared to act as a referee on the application form.

DRUMMOND TRUST: Makes grants towards the cost of publication of books of 'sound Christian doctrine and outreach'. The Trustees are also willing to receive grant requests towards the cost of audio-visual programme material, but not equipment, software but not hardware. Requests for application forms should be made to the Secretaries, Hill and Robb Limited, 3 Pitt Terrace, Stirling FK8 2EY (01786 450985; catherineberrill@hillandrobb.co.uk). Manuscripts should *not* be sent.

DUNCAN McCLEMENTS TRUST FOR ECUMENICAL TRAINING: Makes grants towards the cost of attendance at ecumenical assemblies and conferences; gatherings of young people; short courses or conferences promoting ecumenical understanding. Also to enable schools to organise one-off events to promote better understanding among differing communities and cultures with different religious backgrounds. The Trust also helps towards the cost of resources and study materials. Enquiries to: Committee on Ecumenical Relations, Church of Scotland, 121 George Street, Edinburgh EH2 4YN (ecumenicalofficer@churchofscotland.org.uk).

David DUNCAN TRUST: Makes grants annually (December) to students for the ministry and students in training to become deacons in the Church of Scotland in the Faculties of Arts and Divinity. All applications are considered with slight preference given to those born or educated within the bounds of the former Presbytery of Arbroath. Applications to be received no later than 27 October to Thorntons Law LLP, Brothockbank House, Arbroath DD11 1NE (reference: Glyn Roberts (Trust Manager); 01382 346299; groberts@thorntons-law.co.uk).

ERSKINE CUNNINGHAM HILL TRUST: Donates its annual income to charities and to CrossReach. Individual donations are in the region of £1,000. Priority is given to charities administered by voluntary or honorary officials, in particular charities registered and operating in Scotland and relating to the elderly, young people, ex-service personnel or seafarers. Application forms from the Secretary, Alan Ritchie, 121 George Street, Edinburgh EH2 4YN (0131 240 2260; aritchie@churchofscotland.org.uk).

ESDAILE TRUST: Assists the education and advancement of daughters of ministers, missionaries and widowed deaconesses of the Church of Scotland between 12 and 25 years of age. Applications are to be lodged by 31 May in each year with the Clerk and Treasurer, Kirsty Ashworth, Exchange Place 3, Semple Street, Edinburgh EH3 8BL (0131 473 3500; SM-Charity@azets.co.uk).

FERGUSON BEQUEST FUND: Assists with the building and repair of churches and halls and, more generally, with the work of the Church of Scotland. Priority is given to the Counties of Ayr, Kirkcudbright, Wigtown, Lanark, Dunbarton and Renfrew, and to Greenock, Glasgow, Falkirk and Ardrossan; applications are, however, accepted from across Scotland. Apply to Iain A.T. Mowat CA, 182 Bath Street, Glasgow G2 4HG (0141 332 0476; info@fergusonbequestfund. org.uk; www.fergusonbequestfund.org.uk).

James GILLAN'S BURSARY FUND: Bursaries are available for male or female Candidates for the Ministry in the Church of Scotland who are currently resident in, or were born and had their home for not less than three years continually in the Parishes of Dyke, Edinkillie, Forres St Leonard's and Rafford. In certain circumstances the Trustees may be able to make a grant to Church Candidates resident in the old counties of Moray or Nairn, but only while resident. Apply in writing to The Minister, St Leonard's Manse, Nelson Road, Forres IV36 IDR (01309 672380).

GLASGOW SOCIETY OF THE SONS AND DAUGHTERS OF MINISTERS OF THE CHURCH OF SCOTLAND: The Society's primary purpose is to grant financial assistance to children (no matter what age) of deceased ministers of the Church of Scotland. Applications for first grants can be lodged at any time. Thereafter annual applications must be lodged by 31 December for consideration by Council in February. To the extent that funds are available, grants are also given for the children of ministers or retired ministers, although such grants are normally restricted to university and college students. These latter grants are considered in conjunction with the Edinburgh-based Societies. Limited funds are also available for individual application for special needs or projects. Applications are to be submitted by 31 May in each year. Emergency applications can be dealt with at any time when need arises. More information can be found at www.mansebairnsnetwork.org. Application forms may be obtained from the Secretary and Treasurer, Kirsty Ashworth, Exchange Place 3, Semple Street, Edinburgh EH3 8BL (0131 473 3500; SM-Charity@azets.co.uk).

HAMILTON BURSARY: Awarded, subject to the intention on graduation to serve overseas under the Church of Scotland Faith Impact Forum or to serve with some other Overseas Mission Agency approved by the Forum, to a student at the University of Aberdeen (failing whom to Accepted Candidate(s) for the Ministry of the Church of Scotland whose studies for the Ministry are pursued at Aberdeen University). Applications or recommendations for the Bursary to the Clerk to the Presbytery of Aberdeen and Shetland, Aberdeen North Church (Mastrick Building), Greenfern Road, Aberdeen AB16 6TR.

Martin HARCUS BEQUEST: Makes annual grants to candidates for the ministry resident within the Presbytery of Edinburgh and West Lothian and currently under the jurisdiction of the Presbytery. Applications to the Principal's Secretary, New College, Mound Place, Edinburgh EH1 2LX (NewCollege@ed.ac.uk) by 15 October.

HOPE TRUST: In terms of its new constitution, gives support to organisations that (1) advance the cause of temperance through the promotion of temperance work and the combatting of all forms of substance abuse and (2) promote Reformed theology and Reformed church life especially in Scotland and the social mission of charities with historical or contemporary links to the Reformed tradition, and includes a scholarship programme, the appointment of a part-time post-doctoral fellowship and support for students in full time training. Apply to the Secretary, Lyn Sutherland, Glenorchy House, 20 Union Street, Edinburgh, EH1 3LR (Tel: 0131 226 5151; Fax: 0131 556 5354 or Email: hopetrust@drummondmiller.co.uk).

KEAY THOM TRUST: The purposes of the Trust are:
1. To benefit impoverished widows, widowers, surviving civil partners or relatives of deceased ministers, or of spouses or civil partners who have been deserted by ministers or have grounds for divorce or separation, who have been wholly dependent upon and assisted the minister in the fulfilment of his or her duties and who, by reason of death, divorce or separation, have been required to leave the manse. The Trust can assist in the purchase of a house or by providing financial or material assistance.
2. To assist financially in the education or training of the above relatives or children of deceased ministers.
Further information and application forms are available from Miller Hendry, Solicitors, 10 Blackfriars Street, Perth PH1 5NS (01738 637311; johnthom@millerhendry.co.uk).

LADIES' GAELIC SCHOOLS AND HIGHLAND BURSARY ASSOCIATION: Distributes small grants to students, preferably with a Highland/Gaelic background, who are training to be ministers in the Church of Scotland. Apply by 15 October in each year to the Secretary, Mrs Marion McGill, 61 Ladysmith Road, Edinburgh EH9 3EY (0131 667 4243; marionmcgill61@gmail.com).

LYALL BEQUEST: Offers grants to ministers:
1. Grants to individual ministers, couples and families, for a holiday for a minimum of seven nights. No reapplication within a three-year period; and thereafter a 50 per cent grant to those reapplying.
2. Grants towards sickness and convalescence costs so far as not covered by the National Health Service. Applications should be made to the Secretary and Clerk, The Church of Scotland Trust, 121 George Street, Edinburgh EH2 4YN (0131 376 1307; msproule@ churchofscotland.org.uk).

Gillian MACLAINE BURSARY FUND: Open to candidates for the ministry of the Church of Scotland of Scottish or Canadian nationality. Preference is given to Gaelic-speakers. Application forms available from Mr W Stewart Shaw DL BSc, Clerk to the Presbytery of Argyll, 59 Barone Road, Rothesay, Isle of Bute PA20 0DZ (07775 926541; argyll@churchofscotland.org.uk). Closing date for receipt of applications is 31 October.

Alexander J. MacLEOD GAELIC FUND: This historic bequeathed fund is able to support Ministers who wish to study Gaelic for preaching purposes or to enable Gaelic learning projects within a parish. Church of Scotland Ministers of full-time word and sacrament can apply for funding. The fund is administered by Faith Nurture. Applications must be received by the end of the second week in January to be considered for the annual allocation of grants. Decisions will be made in late January and grants will be paid upon the submission of receipts. A 300 word report on the impact of the work should be submitted along with receipts. Contact via ascend@ churchofscotland.org.uk

E. McLAREN FUND: The persons intended to be benefited are widows and unmarried ladies, preference being given to ladies above 40 years of age in the following order:
(a) Widows and daughters of Officers in the Highland Regiment, and
(b) Widows and daughters of Scotsmen.
Further details from the Secretary, The E. McLaren Fund, Messrs Wright, Johnston & Mackenzie LLP, Solicitors, St Vincent Plaza, 319 St Vincent Street, Glasgow G2 5RZ (Tel: 0141 248 3434; Fax: 0141 221 1226; rmd@wjm.co.uk).

MEIKLE AND PATON TRUST: Grants are available to Ministers and Missionaries for rest and recuperation at the following hotels: Crieff Hydro; Murraypark Hotel, Crieff; Peebles Hydro; Park Hotel, Peebles; Ballachulish Hotel and Isle of Glencoe Hotel. Grants are in addition to any discount offered by the hotels and give a subsidy for overnight residence, such subsidy being decreed by the Trustees at any given time, subject to a limit of seven nights in any one calendar year. Booking should be made online, via the respective hotel's website, quoting the promotion code MEIKLE22 and should be made no more than six months in advance in order to obtain Meikle Paton benefit. Chairman: Rev. Iain F. Paton (iain.f.paton@btinternet.com).

MORGAN BURSARY FUND: Makes grants to candidates for the Church of Scotland ministry studying at the University of Glasgow. Apply to the Clerk to the Presbytery of Glasgow, 260 Bath Street, Glasgow G2 4JP (0141 332 6606; glasgow@churchofscotland.org.uk). Closing date October 31.

NEW MINISTERS' FURNISHING LOAN FUND: Makes loans (of £1,000) to ministers in their first charge to assist with furnishing the manse. Apply to ministriesfinance@churchofscotland. org.uk. Enquiries to Faith Nurture Finance Team, 121 George Street, Edinburgh EH2 4YN (0131 225 5722).

NOVUM TRUST: Provides small short-term grants – typically between £300 and £2,500 – to initiate projects in Christian action and research which cannot readily be financed from other sources. Trustees welcome applications from projects that are essentially Scottish, are distinctively new, and are focused on the welfare of young people, on the training of lay people or on new ways of communicating the Christian faith. The Trust cannot support large building projects, staff salaries or individuals applying for maintenance during courses or training. Application forms and guidance notes from novumt@cofscotland.org.uk or Mrs Susan Masterton, Blair Cadell WS, The Bond House, 5 Breadalbane Street, Edinburgh EH6 5JH (0131 555 5800; www.novum.org.uk).

PARK MEMORIAL BURSARY FUND: Provides grants for the benefit of candidates for the ministry of the Church of Scotland from the Presbytery of Glasgow under full-time training. Apply to the Clerk to the Presbytery of Glasgow, 260 Bath Street, Glasgow G2 4JP (0141 332 6606; glasgow@churchofscotland.org.uk). Closing date November 15.

PRESBYTERY OF ARGYLL BURSARY FUND: Open to students who have been accepted as candidates for the ministry and the readership of the Church of Scotland. Preference is given to applicants who are natives of the bounds of the Presbytery, or are resident within the bounds of the Presbytery, or who have a strong connection with the bounds of the Presbytery. Application forms available from Mr W Stewart Shaw DL BSc, Clerk to the Presbytery of Argyll, 59 Barone Road, Rothesay, Isle of Bute PA20 0DZ (07775 926541; argyll@churchofscotland.org.uk). Closing date for receipt of applications is 31 October.

Margaret and John ROSS TRAVELLING FUND: Offers grants to ministers and their spouses for travelling and other expenses for trips to the Holy Land where the purpose is recuperation or relaxation. Applications should be made to the Secretary and Clerk, The Church of Scotland Trust, 121 George Street, Edinburgh EH2 4YN (0131 376 1307; msproule@churchofscotland. org.uk).

SCOTLAND'S CHURCHES TRUST: Seeks to preserve, promote and protect Scotland's rich ecclesiastical built heritage. Post-Covid, the Trust will focus its efforts on further improving the long-term sustainability of Scotland's places of worship, the recording of church buildings facing closure, growing its membership and developing new and its existing initiatives that strengthen the ties between the country's ecclesiastical built heritage, the communities that surround these buildings and the wider tourist economy. Our grants programmes are temporarily paused until a review process is completed. Scotland's Churches Trust, 15 North Bank Street, Edinburgh EH1 2LP (info@scotlandschurchestrust.org.uk; www.scotlandschurchestrust.org.uk).

SMIETON FUND: To assist ministers who would benefit from a holiday because of a recent pastoral need. Contact pastoralsupport@churchofscotland.org.uk for an application form. Enquiries to Faith Nurture, Support Team, 121 George Street, Edinburgh EH2 4YN (0131 225 5722).

Mary Davidson SMITH CLERICAL AND EDUCATIONAL FUND FOR ABERDEENSHIRE: Assists ministers who have been ordained for five years or over and are in full charge of a congregation in Aberdeen, Aberdeenshire and the north, to purchase books, or to travel for educational purposes, and assists their children with scholarships for further education or vocational training. Apply to Messrs Peterkins, 100 Union Street, Aberdeen AB10 1QR (01224 428000; maildesk@peterkins.com).

SOCIETY FOR THE BENEFIT OF THE SONS AND DAUGHTERS OF THE CLERGY OF THE CHURCH OF SCOTLAND: Annual grants are made to assist in the education of the children (normally between the ages of 12 and 25 years) of ministers of the Church of Scotland. The Society also gives grants to aged and infirm daughters of ministers and ministers' unmarried daughters and sisters who are in need. Applications are to be lodged by 31 May in each year with the Secretary and Treasurer, Kirsty Ashworth, Exchange Place 3, Semple Street, Edinburgh EH3 8BL (0131 473 3500; SM-Charity@azets.co.uk).

SOCIETY IN SCOTLAND FOR PROPAGATING CHRISTIAN KNOWLEDGE: The SSPCK gives grants to: 1. Resourcing mission within Scotland; 2. The training and education of Christians in Commonwealth countries overseas, aimed to equip them for service in the mission and outreach of the Church; 3.The training of British young people volunteering for periods of service in Christian mission and education overseas; 4. The resourcing of new initiatives in worldwide Christian mission. Chairman: Rev. Michael W. Frew; Secretary: Rev. Ian W.

Alexander, SSPCK, c/o 121 George Street, Edinburgh EH2 4YN (0131 225 5722; SSPCK@ churchofscotland.org.uk; www.sspck.co.uk).

Nan STEVENSON CHARITABLE TRUST FOR RETIRED MINISTERS: Provides loans and grants at or after retirement to ministers and others in a recognised ministry for the purchase, maintenance, repair or alteration of a property, primarily for those with a North Ayrshire connection. Secretary and Treasurer: Mrs Christine Thomas, 18 Brisbane Street, Largs KA30 8QN (01475 338564; 07891 838778; cathomas54@gmail.com).

Miss M.E. SWINTON PATERSON'S CHARITABLE TRUST: The Trust can give modest grants to support smaller congregations in urban or rural areas who require to fund essential maintenance or improvement works at their buildings providing that such works have been approved by the General Trustees of the Church of Scotland. Applications for grants should be made via the Trust's online application form available at www.swintonpatersontrust.org.uk.

SYNOD OF GRAMPIAN CHILDREN OF THE CLERGY FUND: Makes annual grants to children of deceased ministers. Apply to Rev. Iain U. Thomson, Clerk and Treasurer, 4 Keirhill Gardens, Westhill AB32 6AZ (01224 746743; iainuthomson@googlemail.com).

SYNOD OF GRAMPIAN WIDOWS' FUND: Makes annual grants (currently £450 p.a.) to widows or widowers of deceased ministers who have served in a charge in the former Synod. Apply to Rev. Iain U. Thomson, Clerk and Treasurer, 4 Keirhill Gardens, Westhill AB32 6AZ (01224 746743; iainuthomson@googlemail.com).

TOD ENDOWMENT TRUST; CINTRA BEQUEST; TOD ENDOWMENT SCOTLAND HOLIDAY FUND: The Trustees of the Cintra Bequest and of the Tod Endowment Scotland Holiday Fund can consider an application for a grant from the Tod Endowment funds from any ordained or commissioned minister or deacon in Scotland of at least two years' standing before the date of application, to assist with the cost of the beneficiary and his or her spouse or partner and dependants obtaining rest and recuperation in Scotland. The Trustees of the Tod Endowment Scotland Holiday Fund can also consider an application from an ordained or commissioned minister or deacon who has retired. Application forms are available from Madelaine Sproule, Law Department at msproule@churchofscotland.org.uk (for the Cintra Bequest), and from Faith Nurture Support Team at pastoralsupport@churchofscotland.org.uk (for the Tod Endowment Scotland Holiday Fund). The address in both cases is 121 George Street, Edinburgh EH2 4YN (0131 225 5722).

Stephen WILLIAMSON & ALEX BALFOUR FUND: Offers grants to Ministers in Scotland, with first priority being given to Ministers in the Presbyteries of Angus and Dundee, followed by the Presbytery of Fife, to assist with the cost of educational school/ college/university trips for sons and daughters of the Manse who are under 25 years and in full time education. Application for trips in any year will be considered by the Trustees in the January of that year, when the income of the previous financial year will be awarded in grants. The applications for trips in that calendar year must be submitted by 31 December of the preceding year. For applications from outwith the 3 priority Presbyteries the total cost of the trip must be in excess of £500, with the maximum grant which can be awarded being £200. The trustees will always give priority to new applicants. If funds still remain for distribution after the allocation of grants in January further applications for that year will be considered. Applications from the Presbyteries of Angus, Dundee and Fife will be considered at any time of year as the Trustees have retained income for these grants. Applications should be made to the Secretary and Clerk, The Church of Scotland Trust, 121 George Street, Edinburgh EH2 4YN (0131 376 1307; msproule@churchofscotland. org.uk).

10. LONG SERVICE CERTIFICATES

Long Service Certificates, signed by the Moderator, are available for presentation to elders and voluntary office bearers in respect of not less than thirty years of service. At the General Assembly of 2015, it was agreed that further certificates could be issued at intervals of ten years thereafter. It should be noted that the period is years of *service*, not (for example) years of ordination in the case of an elder. In the case of those volunteers engaged in children's and youth work, the qualifying period is twenty-one years of service. Certificates are not issued posthumously, nor is it possible to make exceptions to the rules, for example by recognising quality of service in order to reduce the qualifying period, or by reducing the qualifying period on compassionate grounds, such as serious illness. Applications for Long Service Certificates should be made in writing to the Principal Clerk at 121 George Street, Edinburgh EH2 4YN by the parish minister, or by the session clerk on behalf of the Kirk Session. Certificates are not issued from this office to the individual recipients, nor should individuals make application themselves. If a note of the award of the Certificate is to be inserted in *Life and Work* contact should be made with that publication direct.

11. RECORDS OF THE CHURCH OF SCOTLAND

Church records more than fifty years old, unless still in use, should be sent or delivered to the Principal Clerk for onward transmission to the National Records of Scotland. Where ministers or session clerks are approached by a local repository seeking a transfer of their records, they should inform the Principal Clerk, who will take the matter up with the National Records of Scotland.

12. FASTI ECCLESIAE SCOTICANAE

The *Fasti Ecclesiae Scoticanae* ('The Register of Officials of the Church of Scotland') is an ongoing series of volumes which documents the succession of the ordained ministry in the Church of Scotland. The initial volumes, published in the second half of the nineteenth century, offered a comprehensive account of the ministers of the church throughout the previous three hundred years. Since then there have been several updates, and the whole series now presents a complete record from the Reformation in the mid-sixteenth century to the present day of those who have served in parishes, as chaplains, as missionaries, and in academic, administrative and other appointments, including auxiliary and ordained local ministers. Since the bulk of the work is arranged by parishes, the *Fasti* also forms the only permanent record of unions, linkages and other forms of parish readjustment within the church.

The latest volume, volume XII, edited by Roy M. Pinkerton, covering the period from 1 October 1999 to 30 September 2020, was published in June 2021, and gives information about all those who have served as ordained ministers during the past twenty years. The cost of this volume is £30 plus p&p: to obtain a copy, please e-mail fasti@churchofscotland.org.uk confirming that you wish to purchase a copy and giving your full postal address. The book will be despatched along with an invoice asking you to make a bank transfer.

SECTION 3

Church Procedure

A. THE MINISTER AND BAPTISM

See www.churchofscotland.org.uk > Resources > Yearbook > Section 3A

B. THE MINISTER AND MARRIAGE

See www.churchofscotland.org.uk > Resources > Yearbook > Section 3B

C. CONDUCT OF MARRIAGE SERVICES (CODE OF GOOD PRACTICE)

See www.churchofscotland.org.uk > Resources > Yearbook > Section 3C

D. MARRIAGE AND CIVIL PARTNERSHIP (SCOTLAND) ACT 2014

See www.churchofscotland.org.uk > About us > Our views > Same-sex-marriage
Following the decision of the 2022 Assembly on same-sex marriage, the Legal Questions Committee is preparing a guidance document, which will be issued to Presbytery Clerks and placed on the website.

E. CONDUCT OF FUNERAL SERVICES: FEES

See www.churchofscotland.org.uk > Resources > Yearbook > Section 3E

F. PULPIT SUPPLY FEES AND EXPENSES

See www.churchofscotland.org.uk > Resources > Yearbook > Section 3F

G. PROCEDURE IN A VACANCY

See www.churchofscotland.org.uk > Serve > Faith Nurture Forum > Ministries handbooks, forms and guidance notes:
Vacancy Guidelines for Kirk Sessions and Interim Moderators (also covers appointing locums)
Guidelines for Nominating Committees
Guidelines for Advisory Committees
Guidance Notes on compiling Parish Profiles

SECTION 4

General Assembly 2022

The General Assembly of 2022 was held from 21-26 May with the majority of commissioners in the Assembly Hall, but some participating online via Zoom.

OFFICE-BEARERS OF THE GENERAL ASSEMBLY

The Lord High Commissioner:	The Rt Hon. Lord Hodge PC QC
Moderator:	Rev. Dr Iain M. Greenshields
Chaplains to the Moderator:	Rev. Monika R.W. Redman
	Rev. Allan P. Morton
Principal Clerk:	Rev. Dr George J. Whyte
Associate Principal Clerk:	Rev. Fiona E. Smith
Depute Clerk:	Ms Christine Paterson
Procurator:	Ms Laura Dunlop QC
Law Agent:	Miss Mary Macleod
Convener, Procedure Committee:	Rev. Donald G.B. McCorkindale
Vice-Convener, Procedure Committee:	Mrs Susan Pym
Precentor:	Rev. Colin C. Renwick
Chief Steward:	Mr Alexander F. Gemmill
Depute Steward:	Mr Neil Proven
Assembly Officer:	Mr William Mearns
Depute Assembly Officer:	Mrs Karen McKay

THE MODERATOR

The Right Reverend Iain MacLeod Greenshields
BD CertMin DipRS ACMA MSc MTh DD

We can perhaps all remember the first time we encountered someone who went on to be a significant influence in our lives. The elegant hand with which Iain wrote 30 years ago (e-mails and texts obscure so much, don't they), might have steered the reader towards an assumption of a brilliant mind (and that would be correct), but it also obscured so much about Iain that it is important to know. There is the enormous sense of fun, the commitment to spur-of-the-moment pranks, and the slavish loyalty to Partick Thistle that indicates, perhaps, a determination to counter a fiercely competitive streak by supporting the eternal underdog? (Fitter friends and colleagues will have encountered Iain's competitive streak on the badminton court, while the less fit have simply had their hands taken off in Snap!)

If – like many ministers – Iain gets caught up in an almost lyrical theological exposition that threatens to be disconnected from an everyday outworking of faith, then he is blessed with his wife Linda's very 'earthed' faith, and how it needs to be worked out in the relationships of their 6 children (usually expressed with an exasperated 'Haud yer wheesht!'). The whirl of the Greenie household is a miraculous delight to be caught up within, drawing influences from the airy highlands and islands of Iain's youthful holidays, the rich experience of the Glasgow schemes and the cultural heritage of China. And all of these things continue to be part of the plaid most recently woven with the people of Touch in Dunfermline.

Some back-story – Iain's background is in accounting, having worked for Weirs from when he left school at 17. A major road traffic accident required months in hospital and recuperation, and it was at this time that his life was transformed when he came to faith through the work of those at Gardner Street Church in Glasgow. There quickly followed a call to ministry and he began his studies at Trinity College in 1979. As a student, apart from the usual attachments, Iain also did placements at Barlinnie Prison and Gartnavel Royal Psychiatric Hospital – both of which have had an enduring impact on the course of his ministry.

In fact, ordination took Iain to the shadow of Barlinnie's walls, where Cranhill's manse was located, and also gave him opportunities to serve as chaplain in a number of psychiatric settings. His years in Greater Easterhouse have been formative in Iain's ministry, as both the congregation and community helped mould him. From Cranhill, Iain went to St Machan's in Larkhall, spearheading significant ecumenical work in a community determined to change. He also took the opportunity to add an MSc in Palliative Care to his MTh, continuing to extend his interest in chaplaincy both within care settings and the prison service.

In 2002 the family moved to Skye – a place that felt like home, being the place where his father was born and also near to his beloved Island of Lewis. Having always been very self-reflective and analytical of his ministry, Iain took the opportunity of his time on Skye to pull together all he had learned in pastoral ministry around bereavement into a Doctoral thesis – a process he found enriching. Always active within his local Presbytery, Iain also served on the Ministries Council for a decade, and as a national Assessor.

Iain comes to the call of Moderator from the parish of St Margaret's in Dunfermline, where he has served since 2007, both in the parish, and as Presbytery Clerk (2013 until the advent of Fife Presbytery). While not being as mysterious or spiritually satisfying as the Trinity, wrestling the 3-in-1 nature of Fife Presbytery has proved an enriching experience for Iain – involving as it did the interplay of relationships, structure and vision. Throughout ministry, Iain has always prioritised preaching and teaching…except when he has prioritised pastoral care and compassion…except when he has prioritised community mission and loving outreach… and then, of course, there are the times when he has prioritised the nurturing of the next generation of ministers…of whom we are two!

Allan Morton and Monika Redman
Moderator's Chaplains

REPORT FROM THE GENERAL ASSEMBLY 2022

The General Assembly gave final approval, by 274 votes to 136, to the legislation that will allow ministers to register to become celebrants of same sex marriages if they wish. In response to a question if a minister was taken to court over refusing to officiate a same sex marriage, the Procurator, Laura Dunlop QC, considered the protections built into the scheme, under which ministers are legally banned from officiating same sex marriages unless they 'opt in', to be sufficient.

The legislation had been approved in 2021 and subsequently by a majority of presbyteries under the Barrier Act. As regards the concern about the removal of the words 'husband and wife' in the Marriage Services Act, the Procurator said that the inclusive language in the Act, which meets the legal requirements for the solemnisation of marriage, did not preclude the use of additional wording.

The Assembly voted to introduce a scheme to support parish ministers facing hardship due to rising energy prices and later in the week the General Trustees accepted new measures aimed at making sure manses are energy efficient.

The Assembly heard several reminders of the need to keep up the pace of reforms in order to build a Church of Scotland which is relevant and fit for purpose, including further reform of the central structures, under which the work of the Faith Nurture and Faith Impact Forums will be brought together under a single Active Faith Leadership Team with four Programme Groups: Mission, People & Training, Public Life & Global Justice, and Resources & Presence; and an acknowledgement of the pain over the past year as the Church grappled with presbytery restructuring and Presbytery Mission Planning.

The process of merging presbyteries continued as the General Assembly approved the creation of four new presbyteries: Lothian and Borders (merging Duns, Jedburgh, Lothian, and Melrose & Peebles), Forth Valley & Clydesdale (Falkirk joining the existing presbytery of that name), Perth (merging Angus, Dundee, Dunkeld & Meigle, Perth, and Stirling); and the North East and Northern Isles (merging Aberdeen & Shetland, Buchan, Gordon, Kincardine & Deeside, Moray and Orkney).

Proposed arrangements for a Pioneer Mission Fund and the Seeds for Growth Fund, which will support the establishment of new worshipping communities and work with the under 40s, were also passed.

The General Assembly overwhelmingly approved a Declaration of Friendship with the Roman Catholic Church in Scotland, to be named the Saint Margaret Declaration, in which the two Churches 'recognise each other as brothers and sisters in Christ, and wish to express our friendship and respect for one another as fellow Christians, citizens and partners in announcing the kingdom of God in our land'.

The Assembly agreed to the creation of a new Book of Confessions, retaining the Westminster Confession of Faith as a subordinate standard of the church, but adding other confessions that 'express the range and depth of reformed thought', and to the preparation of teaching material on the confessional position of the church and the vows of office holders.

As is customary on 'Chaplains' Day' the Assembly was addressed by a senior member of the British military, Lieutenant General Nick Borton, Colonel of the Royal Regiment of Scotland, who said the Chaplains Department have 'a long and glorious history of providing pastoral care, spiritual support and moral guidance'.

The General Assembly condemned the Russian invasion of Ukraine, calling for an immediate ceasefire and a 'just and peaceful solution'.

The Faith Impact Forum introduced work on a Jewish-Christian glossary intended to aid understanding between the two faiths, as a way that the two communities can express opinions without offending each other.

The Chair of Christian Aid, Archbishop John Sentamu, challenged the Church not to resist change, and to continue its work in challenging poverty.

The outgoing Principal Clerk, the Rev. Dr George Whyte, urged the Church to show humility and listen to others… 'to God who might have new plans, or to the neighbour who might have new needs, new questions or… new insights'. The Rev. Fiona Smith was sworn in as Dr Whyte's successor, becoming the first woman to hold the role permanently.

Professor Jason Leitch, the Scottish Government's National Clinical Director, thanked the Church for everything it had done during the pandemic: 'Whether you run the tiniest church in Scotland or one of the largest fellowships, the work you've done for those you serve has been absolutely without precedent'.

The Convener of CrossReach, Rev. Thom Riddell, said that 'thousands of lives have continued to be transformed over the past year' by CrossReach services, and urges commissioners to make their voices heard as the Scottish Government presents legislation for a National Care Service in coming weeks.

During the report of the Iona Community Board, there was applause for the musician and worship leader Rev. Dr John Bell, who retires later this year.

The General Trustees encouraged commissioners to write to their MSPs to protest against new rules which will require church office bearers to be named on the Land Register.

Members of the Church were urged to put themselves forward to serve on the national committees: 'it's not just a privilege, it's often enjoyable too'.

The National Convener of the Church of Scotland Guild, Margaret Muir, said the last two years had proved the movement is not afraid of challenge or change.

The Lord High Commissioner, Lord Hodge, said that the week had given him 'a strong sense of the energy and vibrancy of initiatives being taken at a local level' across Scotland.

The Moderator, the Rt. Rev. Iain Greenshields, praised the Assembly's willingness to work together to find a way forward through difficult debates: 'If the Church is to do anything it has to work together on mission… and to bring Christ to the people and the people to Christ, and surely that is our greatest privilege'.

This is a summary of a report of proceedings which appeared in the July 2022 issue of Life and Work and online at www.lifeandwork.org

SECTION 5

Presbytery Lists

In each Presbytery list, the parishes/congregations ('charges') are listed in alphabetical order. In a linked charge, the names appear under the first-named. Under the name of the charge will be found the name of the minister and, where applicable, that of an associate minister, ordained local minister, auxiliary minister and member of the Diaconate. The years indicated after a name in the congregational section of each Presbytery list are the year of ordination (column 1) and the year of current appointment (column 2). Where only one date is given, it is both the year of ordination and the year of appointment. Where no other name is listed, the name of the session clerk(s) or interim moderator is given. (Some parishes have more than one church – see Section 8. For presbytery and parish boundaries, see the online map at http://arcg.is/11rSXH.)

In the second part of each Presbytery list, **B** comprises those ministers and deacons in other appointments (if any), while **C** comprises those members of Presbytery mainly registered as Category R (Retaining) and authorised to perform the functions of ministry outwith an appointment covered by Category O (a charge) or Category E (an employed appointment), though some of those listed who have ceased to hold an appointment may have chosen to retain Category O registration for a period of up to 3 years. The first date is the year of ordination, and the following date is the year of appointment or retirement. If the person concerned is retired, then the appointment last held will be shown in brackets.

F	A charge with a Facebook page.
GD	A charge where it is desirable that the minister should have a knowledge of Gaelic.
GE	A charge where public worship must be regularly conducted in Gaelic.
H	A hearing aid loop system has been installed.
L	A chair lift or lift has been installed.
T	A charge with a Twitter account.
W	A charge with a website.

PRESBYTERY NUMBERS (following unions 2, 8 to 13, 15, 18, 20 to 22, 25, 26 and 46 are no longer used)

1	Edinburgh and West Lothian	27	Dunkeld and Meigle	39	Ross
3	Lothian	28	Perth	40	Sutherland
4	Melrose and Peebles	29	Dundee	41	Caithness
5	Duns	30	Angus	42	Lochcarron-Skye
6	Jedburgh	31	Aberdeen and Shetland	43	Uist
7	South West	32	Kincardine and Deeside	44	Lewis
14	Clyde	33	Gordon	45	Orkney
16	Glasgow	34	Buchan	47	England
17	Forth Valley and Clydesdale	35	Moray	48	International Charges
19	Argyll	36	Abernethy	49	Jerusalem
23	Stirling	37	Inverness		
24	Fife	38	Lochaber		

(1) EDINBURGH AND WEST LOTHIAN (F W)

New presbytery formed by the union of the Presbytery of Edinburgh and the Presbytery of West Lothian on 1 January 2022.
Meets by Zoom on Tuesday 15 November 2022. In 2023 meets on 7 February, 20 June, 12 September and 7 November and, if required, on 28 March and 25 April.

Clerk:	REV. MARJORY McPHERSON LLB BD MTh	Postal Address: Morningside Parish Church, 2 Cluny Gardens, Edinburgh EH10 6BQ edinburghwestlothian@churchofscotland.org.uk	0131 225 9137
Depute Clerk:	HAZEL HASTIE MA CQSW PhD AIWS	Postal address as above HHastie@churchofscotland.org.uk	07827 314374

1 Abercorn (F H W) linked with Pardovan, Kingscavil (H) and Winchburgh (F H W)

Vacant				
Derek R. Henderson MA DipTCP DipCS	2017		The Manse, West End, Winchburgh, Broxburn EH52 6TT	01506 890919
(Ordained Local Minister)			45 Priory Road, Linlithgow EH49 6BP	01506 844787
			DHenderson@churchofscotland.org.uk	07968 491441

2 Armadale (H W)

Julia C. Wiley (Ms) MA(CE) MDiv	1998	2010	70 Mount Pleasant, Armadale, Bathgate EH48 3HB JWiley@churchofscotland.org.uk	01501 730358
Margaret Corrie (Miss) DCS	1989	2013	44 Sunnyside Street, Camelon, Falkirk FK1 4BH MCorrie@churchofscotland.org.uk	07955 633969

3 Avonbridge (H) linked with Torphichen (F H W)

Vacant			
Interim Moderator: W. Richard Houston	Manse Road, Torphichen, Bathgate EH48 4LT WHouston@churchofscotland.org.uk	01506 635957 01506 202246

4 Bathgate: Boghall (F H W)

Vacant			
Interim Moderator: Hanneke I. Janse van Vuren	1 Manse Place, Ash Grove, Bathgate EH48 1NJ HJansevanVuren@churchofscotland.org.uk	01506 652715

5 Bathgate: High (F H W)

Vacant			
Interim Moderator: Nelu I. Balaj	**info@bathgatehigh.com** NBalaj@churchofscotland.org.uk	**01506 650217** 01506 411888

6 Bathgate: St John's (H W)

Vacant			
Interim Moderator: Ian D. Maxwell	St John's Manse, Mid Street, Bathgate EH48 1QD IMaxwell@churchofscotland.org.uk	01506 653146 01506 239840

7	**Blackburn and Seafield (F H W)** Sandra Boyd (Mrs) BEd BD	2007	2019	The Manse, 5 MacDonald Gardens, Blackburn, Bathgate EH47 7RE SBoyd@churchofscotland.org.uk	07919 676242
8	**Blackridge (H) linked with Harthill: St Andrew's (F H)** Vacant Session Clerk, Blackridge: Jean Mowitt (Mrs) Session Clerk, Harthill: Alexander Kennedy			East Main Street, Harthill, Shotts ML7 5QW jean.mowitt@yahoo.com alex.kend@gmail.com	01501 751239 01501 750401 07590 901933 01501 752594
9	**Breich Valley (F H)** Robert Craig BA BD DipRS PGCertHC	2008	2020	49 Main Street, Stoneyburn, Bathgate EH47 8AU RCraig@churchofscotland.org.uk	01501 519085
10	**Broxburn (F H W)** Vacant Session Clerk: Anne Gunn (Mrs)			2 Church Street, Broxburn EH52 5EL anne.gunn42@gmail.com	01506 337560 07833 701274
11	**Edinburgh: Albany Deaf Church of Edinburgh (F H)** Albany Deaf Church is a Mission Initiative of Edinburgh: St Andrew's and St George's West			info@stagw.org.uk	**0131 444 2054**
12	**Edinburgh: Balerno (F H W)** Andre J. Groenewald BA BD MDiv DD CertPS DipPSRP	1995	2016	**bpc-admin@balernochurch.org.uk** 3 Johnsburn Road, Balerno EH14 7DN AGroenewald@churchofscotland.org.uk	**0131 449 7245** 0131 449 3830
13	**Edinburgh: Barclay Viewforth (F W)** David Clarkson BSc BA MTh	2010	2020	**admin@barclaychurch.org.uk** 113 Meadowspot, Edinburgh EH10 5UY DClarkson@churchofscotland.org.uk	**0131 229 6810** 0131 478 2376
14	**Edinburgh: Blackhall St Columba's (F T W)** Fergus M. Cook BD		2020	**secretary@blackhallstcolumba.org.uk** 5 Blinkbonny Crescent, Edinburgh EH4 3NB FCook@churchofscotland.org.uk	**0131 332 4431** 0131 466 7503
15	**Edinburgh: Bristo Memorial Craigmillar (F W)** Vacant Interim Moderator: Donald H. Scott			Donald.Scott@churchofscotland.org.uk	0131 468 1254

16 **Edinburgh: Broughton St Mary's (F H L W)** 1987
Laurene M. Lafontaine BA MDiv
2021
mail@bstmchurch.org.uk
78 March Road, Edinburgh EH4 3SY
LLafontaine@churchofscotland.org.uk
0131 556 4252
0131 312 7440

17 **Edinburgh: Canongate (F H T W)**
Neil N. Gardner OStJ MA BD
1991
2006
canongatekirk@btinternet.com
The Manse of Canongate, Edinburgh   EH8 8BR
NGardner@churchofscotland.org.uk
0131 556 3515
0131 556 3515

18 **Edinburgh: Carrick Knowe (H W)**
Fiona M. Mathieson (Mrs)
BEd BD PGCommEd MTh
1988
2001
ckchurch@talktalk.net
21 Traquair Park West, Edinburgh   EH12 7AN
FMathieson@churchofscotland.org.uk
0131 334 1505
0131 334 9774

19 **Edinburgh: Colinton (F H W)**
Rolf H. Billes BD
1996
2009
church.office@colinton-parish.com
The Manse, Dell Road, Colinton, Edinburgh   EH13 0JR
RBilles@churchofscotland.org.uk
0131 441 2232
0131 466 8384

20 **Edinburgh: Corstorphine Craigsbank (F H T W)**
Alan Childs BA BD MBA
2000
2019
admin@craigsbankchurch.org.uk
17 Craigs Bank, Edinburgh EH12 8HD
AChilds@churchofscotland.org.uk
0131 334 6365
0131 466 5196

21 **Edinburgh: Corstorphine Old (F H W)**
Moira McDonald MA BD
1997
2005
corold@aol.com
23 Manse Road, Edinburgh EH12 7SW
MMcDonald@churchofscotland.org.uk
0131 334 7864
0131 476 5893

22 **Edinburgh: Corstorphine St Anne's (F H L T W)**
James J. Griggs BD MTh ALCM PGCE
2011
2013
office@stannes.corstorphine.org.uk
1/5 Morham Gait, Edinburgh EH10 5GH
JGriggs@churchofscotland.org.uk
0131 316 4740
0131 447 7063

23 **Edinburgh: Corstorphine St Ninian's (F H W)**
James D. Aitken BD
2002
2017
office@st-ninians.co.uk
17 Templeland Road, Edinburgh EH12 8RZ
JAitken@churchofscotland.org.uk
0131 539 6204
0131 334 2978

24 **Edinburgh: Craiglockhart (F H T W)**
Gordon Kennedy BSc BD MTh
1993
2012
office@craiglockhartchurch.org
20 Craiglockhart Quadrant, Edinburgh   EH14 1HD
GKennedy@churchofscotland.org.uk
0131 455 8229
0131 444 1615

25 **Edinburgh: Craigmillar Park (F H W)**
linked with Edinburgh: Reid Memorial (F H W)
Alexander T. McAspurren BD MTh
CPS CertSMM
2002
2019
cpkirk@btinternet.com
reid.memorial@btinternet.com
14 Hallhead Road, Edinburgh EH16 5QJ
AMcAspurren@churchofscotland.org.uk
0131 667 5862
0131 662 1203
0131 667 1623

26 Edinburgh: Cramond (F H T W)
Vacant
Interim Moderator: Moira McDonald
cramond.kirk@blueyonder.co.uk
Manse of Cramond, Cramond Glebe Road, Edinburgh   EH4 6NS
MMcDonald@churchofscotland.org.uk
0131 336 2036
0131 336 2036
0131 476 5893

27 Edinburgh: Currie (F H W)
V. Easter Smart BA MDiv DMin   1996   2015
currie_kirk@btconnect.com
43 Lanark Road West, Currie   EH14 5JX
ESmart@churchofscotland.org.uk
0131 451 5141
0131 449 4719

28 Edinburgh: Dalmeny (F W) linked with Edinburgh: Queensferry (F H W)   office@qpcweb.org
David C. Cameron BD CertMin   1993   2009
1 Station Road, South Queensferry   EH30 9HY
DavidCCameron@churchofscotland.org.uk
0131 331 1100
0131 331 1100

29 Edinburgh: Davidson's Mains (F H W)
Daniel Robertson BA BD   2009   2016
life@dmainschurch.plus.com
1 Hillpark Terrace, Edinburgh   EH4 7SX
Daniel.Robertson@churchofscotland.org.uk
0131 312 6282
0131 336 3078
07909 840654

30 Edinburgh: Drylaw (F W)
Vacant
Interim Moderator: John S. (Iain) May
drylawparishchurch@btinternet.com
15 House o' Hill Gardens, Edinburgh   EH4 2AR
JMay@churchofscotland.org.uk
0131 332 6863
0131 332 0896
0131 555 0392

31 Edinburgh: Duddingston (F H W)
James A.P. Jack
BSc BArch BD DMin RIBA ARIAS   1989   2001
dodinskirk@aol.com
Manse of Duddingston, Old Church Lane, Edinburgh   EH15 3PX
JJack@churchofscotland.org.uk
0131 661 4240
0131 661 4240

32 Edinburgh: Fairmilehead (F H W)
Cheryl S. McKellar-Young (Mrs)
BA BD MSc PGCertHC   2013   2018
office@fhpc.org.uk
14 Margaret Rose Drive, Edinburgh   EH10 7ER
CMcKellarYoung@churchofscotland.org.uk
0131 445 2374
07590 230121

33 Edinburgh: Gorgie Dalry Stenhouse (F H T W)
Vacant
Interim Moderator: Gordon Kennedy
contactus@gdschurch.org.uk
90 Myreside Road, Edinburgh   EH10 5BZ
GKennedy@churchofscotland.org.uk
0131 337 7936
0131 337 2284
0131 444 1615

34 Edinburgh: Gracemount (F W) linked with Edinburgh: Liberton (F H T W)   churchsecretary@libertonkirk.net
John N. Young MA BD PhD   1996
7 Kirk Park, Edinburgh   EH16 6HZ
JYoung@churchofscotland.org.uk
Kay O. N. Haggarty BEd   2021
(Ordained Local Minister)
KHaggarty@churchofscotland.org.uk
0131 664 8264
0131 664 3067

No	Name		Contact	Phone
35	**Edinburgh: Granton (F H T W)** Norman A. Smith MA BD	1997 2005	**info@granton.org.uk** 8 Wardie Crescent, Edinburgh EH5 1AG NSmith@churchofscotland.org.uk	**0131 552 3033** 0131 551 2159
36	**Edinburgh: Greenbank (F H W)** Vacant Interim Moderator: Alistair P. Donald		**greenbankchurch@btconnect.com** 112 Greenbank Crescent, Edinburgh EH10 5SZ alistairpdonald@gmail.com	**0131 447 9969** 0131 447 4032
37	**Edinburgh: Greenside (H W)** Guardianship of the Presbytery Interim Moderator: Suzie M. Stark		**office@greenside.org.uk** 1B Royal Terrace, Edinburgh EH7 5AB sstark1962@btinternet.com	**0131 557 2124** 0131 551 1633
38	**Edinburgh: Greyfriars Kirk (F GE H T W)** Richard E. Frazer BA BD DMin	1986 2003	**enquiries@greyfriarskirk.com** 12 Tantallon Place, Edinburgh EH9 1NZ RFrazer@churchofscotland.org.uk	**0131 225 1900** 0131 667 6610
	Ruth D. Halley BEd BD PGCert (Associate Minister)	2012 2021	24 Connie Avenue, Dunbar EH42 1ZN RHalley@churchofscotland.org.uk	07530 307413
39	**Edinburgh: High (St Giles') (F T W)** Calum I. MacLeod BA BD	1996 2014	**alison.wylie@stgilescathedral.org.uk** St Giles' Cathedral, High Street, Edinburgh EH1 1RE Calum.MacLeod@churchofscotland.org.uk St Giles' Cathedral, High Street, Edinburgh EH1 1RE SMarten@churchofscotland.org.uk	**0131 225 4363** 0131 225 4363
	Sigrid Marten (Associate Minister)	1997 2021		0131 225 4363
40	**Edinburgh: Holy Trinity (F H W)** Ian A. MacDonald BD MTh	2005 2017	**admin@holytrinitywesterhailes.org.uk** 5 Baberton Mains Terrace, Edinburgh EH14 3DG Ian.Angus.MacDonald@churchofscotland.org.uk	**0131 442 3304** 0131 281 6153
	Rita M. Welsh BA PhD (Ordained Local Minister)	2017	19 Muir Wood Road, Currie EH14 5JW RWelsh@churchofscotland.org.uk	0131 451 5943
41	**Edinburgh: Inverleith St Serf's (F H W)** Vacant Interim Moderator: Ian W. Alexander		IAlexander@churchofscotland.org.uk	**0131 467 7185** 0131 225 5722
42	**Edinburgh: Juniper Green (F H W)** James S. Dewar MA BD	1983 2000	**jgpc@supanet.com** 476 Lanark Road, Juniper Green, Edinburgh EH14 5BQ JDewar@churchofscotland.org.uk	**0131 458 5147** 0131 453 3494
43	**Edinburgh: Kirkliston (F W)** G.F. (Erick) du Toit BTh	2016 2020	**kpc.officeangels@gmail.com** 43 Main Street, Kirkliston EH29 9AF EduToit@churchofscotland.org.uk	0131 333 3298

44 Edinburgh: Leith North (F H W)
Vacant
Interim Moderator: Karen W.F. McKay
nlpc-office@btinternet.com — 0131 553 7378
KarenMcKay_131241@churchofscotland.org.uk — 07921 317516

45 Edinburgh: Leith St Andrew's (F H W)
A. Robert A. Mackenzie LLB BD   1993
leithstandrews@yahoo.co.uk — 0131 553 8839
30 Lochend Road, Edinburgh EH6 8BS — 0131 553 2122
AMacKenzie@churchofscotlandorg.uk

46 Edinburgh: Leith South (H W)
John S. (Iain) May BSc MBA BD   2012
slpcoffice@gmail.com — 0131 554 2578
37 Claremont Road, Edinburgh EH6 7NN — 0131 555 0392
JMay@churchofscotland.org.uk

47 Edinburgh: Liberton See Edinburgh: Gracemount

48 Edinburgh: Liberton Northfield (F H W)
Vacant
Interim Moderator: Andre J. Groenewald
9 Claverhouse Drive, Edinburgh EH16 6BR — 0131 551 3847
AGroenewald@churchofscotland.org.uk — 0131 664 5490 / 0131 449 3830

49 Edinburgh: Marchmont St Giles' (F H T W)
Karen K. Campbell BD MTh DMin   1997
office@marchmontstgiles.org.uk — 0131 447 4359
2 Trotter Haugh, Edinburgh EH9 2GZ — 0131 447 2834
KKCampbell@churchofscotland.org.uk

50 Edinburgh: Mayfield Salisbury (F W)
Alexander C. Forsyth   2009
  LLB DipLP BD MTh PhD   2021
Kay McIntosh (Mrs) DCS   1990 / 2018
churchmanager@googlemail.com — 0131 667 1522
26 Seton Place, Edinburgh EH9 2JT — 0131 667 1286
AForsyth@churchofscotland.org.uk — 07739 639037
4 Jacklin Green, Livingston EH54 8PZ — 01506 440543
kay@backedge.co.uk

51 Edinburgh: Meadowbank (F T W)
Vacant
Interim Moderator: William M. Wishart
meadowbank@meadowbankchurch.com — 0131 237 5834
BWishart@churchofscotland.org.uk

52 Edinburgh: Morningside (F H W)
Derek Browning MA BD DMin   1987 / 2001
office@morningsideparishchurch.org.uk — 0131 447 6745
20 Braidburn Crescent, Edinburgh EH10 6EN — 0131 447 1617
Derek.Browning@churchofscotland.org.uk

53 Edinburgh: Morningside United (F H W)
Vacant
Interim Moderator:
churchoffice.muc@gmail.com — 0131 447 3152
1 Midmar Avenue, Edinburgh EH10 6BS — 0131 447 7943

Morningside United is a Local Ecumenical Partnership with the United Reformed Church

No.	Charge / Minister			Address / Email	Telephone
54	**Edinburgh: Murrayfield (F H W)** Keith Edwin Graham MA PGDipADS BD MTh	2008	2014	**mpchurch@btconnect.com** 45 Murrayfield Gardens, Edinburgh EH12 6DH KEGraham@churchofscotland.org.uk	**0131 337 1091** 0131 337 1364
55	**Edinburgh: Newhaven (F H W)** Peter B. Bluett BTh	1996	2007	158 Granton Road, Edinburgh EH5 3RF PBluett@churchofscotland.org.uk	0131 476 5212
56	**Edinburgh: Old Kirk and Muirhouse (F H T W)** Vacant Interim Moderator: Douglas A.O. Nicol			35 Silverknowes Road, Edinburgh EH4 5LL Douglas.Nicol@churchofscotland.org.uk	0131 476 2580 07811 437075
57	**Edinburgh: Palmerston Place (F H T W)** Vacant Interim Moderator: William R. Taylor			**admin@palmerstonplacechurch.com** 30B Cluny Gardens, Edinburgh EH10 6BJ wlretl@outlook.com	**0131 220 1690** 0131 447 9598 0131 443 5590 07447 258525
58	**Edinburgh: Pilrig St Paul's (F W)** Mark M. Foster BSc BD CertCS CertTM	1998	2013	**mail@pilrigstpauls.org.uk** Pilrig St Paul's, 1B Pilrig Street, Edinburgh EH6 5AS MFoster@churchofscotland.org.uk	**0131 553 1876** 0131 332 5736
59	**Edinburgh: Polwarth (F H W)** Jack Holt BSc BD MTh	1985	2011	**office@polwarth.org.uk** 88 Craiglockhart Road, Edinburgh EH14 1EP JHolt@churchofscotland.org.uk	**0131 346 2711** 0131 441 6105
60	**Edinburgh: Portobello and Joppa (F H W)** Stewart G. Weaver BA BD PhD	2003	2014	**office@portyjoppachurch.org** 6 St Mary's Place, Edinburgh EH15 2QF SWeaver@churchofscotland.org.uk	**0131 657 3401** 0131 669 2410
	Lourens de Jager PgDip MDiv BTh (Associate Minister)	2013	2015	1 Brunstane Road North, Edinburgh EH15 2DL LDeJager@churchofscotland.org.uk	07521 426644
61	**Edinburgh: Priestfield (F H W)** Donald H. Scott BA BD	1983	2018	13 Lady Road, Edinburgh EH16 5PA Donald.Scott@churchofscotland.org.uk	**0131 468 3302** 0131 468 1254 07720 040081
62	**Edinburgh: Queensferry** See Edinburgh: Dalmeny				
63	**Edinburgh: Ratho (F W)** Ian J. Wells BD	1999		2 Freelands Road, Ratho, Newbridge EH28 8NP IWells@churchofscotland.org.uk	0131 333 1346

64   Edinburgh: Reid Memorial See Edinburgh: Craigmillar Park

65   Edinburgh: Richmond Craigmillar (F H W)   1985   1997
Elizabeth M. Henderson
OBE MA BD MTh
Manse of Duddingston, Old Church Lane, Edinburgh EH15 3PX
EHenderson@churchofscotland.org.uk
0131 661 6561
0131 661 4240

66   Edinburgh: St Andrew's and St George's West (F H L W)   2009   2019
Rosemary E. Magee
BSc MSc MDiv DMin
info@stagw.org.uk
25 Comely Bank, Edinburgh EH4 1AJ
RMagee@churchofscotland.org.uk
0131 225 3847
0131 332 5848

67   Edinburgh: St Andrew's Clermiston (F W)
Vacant
Interim Moderator: Andrea E. Price
87 Drum Brae South, Edinburgh EH12 8TD
APrice@churchofscotland.org.uk
0131 339 4149
0131 443 4355

68   Edinburgh: St Catherine's Argyle (F H W)
Vacant
Interim Moderator: David Clarkson
5 Palmerston Road, Edinburgh EH9 1TL
DClarkson@churchofscotland.org.uk
0131 667 7220
0131 667 9344
0131 478 2376

69   Edinburgh: St Cuthbert's (F H L T W)   2017
Peter R.B. Sutton BA(AKC) BD MTh
PGCertCouns
office@st-cuthberts.net
St Cuthbert's Church, 5 Lothian Road, Edinburgh EH1 2EP
PSutton@churchofscotland.org.uk
0131 229 1142
07718 311319

70   Edinburgh: St David's Broomhouse (F H W)   2014
Michael J. Mair BD
33 Traquair Park West, Edinburgh EH12 7AN
MMair@churchofscotland.org.uk
0131 443 9851
0131 334 1730

71   Edinburgh: St John's Colinton Mains (F W)   2015
Peter Nelson BSc BD
2 Caiystane Terrace, Edinburgh EH10 6SR
PNelson@churchofscotland.org.uk
07500 057889

72   Edinburgh: St Margaret's (F H W)   1991   2020
John R. Wells BD PGCE DipMin
stmpc@btconnect.com
43 Moira Terrace, Edinburgh EH7 6TD
JWells@churchofscotland.org.uk
0131 554 7400
0131 322 9272

73   Edinburgh: St Martin's (F W)   2017
William M. Wishart BD
68 Milton Road West, Edinburgh EH15 1QY
BWishart@churchofscotland.org.uk
0131 237 5834

74 Edinburgh: St Michael's (H W)
Andrea E. Price (Mrs) — 1997 — 2018
office@stmichaels-kirk.co.uk
13 Dovecot Park, Edinburgh EH14 2LN
APrice@churchofscotland.org.uk
0131 478 9675
0131 443 4355

75 Edinburgh: St Nicholas' Sighthill (F T W)
Thomas M. Kisitu BD MTh PhD — 1993 — 2015
122 Sighthill Loan, Edinburgh EH11 4NT
TMKisitu@churchofscotland.org.uk
Nikki J. Kirkland BSc — 2021
(Ordained Local Minister)
St Nicholas' Sighthill Church, 124 Sighthill Loan EH11 4NT
NKirkland@churchofscotland.org.uk
07306 100111
0131 442 3978
07789 790483

76 Edinburgh: St Stephen's Comely Bank (F W)
George Vidits BD MTh — 2000 — 2015
office@comelybankchurch.com
8 Blinkbonny Crescent, Edinburgh EH4 3NB
GVidits@churchofscotland.org.uk
0131 315 4616
0131 332 3364

77 Edinburgh: Slateford Longstone (F W)
Samuel A.R. Torrens BSc BD — 1995 — 2019
50 Kingsknowe Road South, Edinburgh EH14 2JW
STorrens@churchofscotland.org.uk
0131 466 5308

78 Edinburgh: Stockbridge (F H T W)
Vacant
Interim Moderator: Peter B. Bluett
stockbridgechurch@btconnect.com
19 Eildon Street, Edinburgh EH3 5JU
PBluett@churchofscotland.org.uk
0131 332 0122
0131 557 6052
0131 476 5212

79 Edinburgh: Tron Kirk (Gilmerton and Moredun) (F W)
Cameron Mackenzie BSc BD — 1997 — 2010
Cammy.Mackenzie@churchofscotland.org.uk
80C Colinton Road, Edinburgh EH14 1DD
JMcKenzie@churchofscotland.org.uk
0131 664 7538
0131 444 2054
07980 884653

Janet R. McKenzie (Mrs) BA DipHS Cert CS — 2016
(Ordained Local Minister)
Liz Crocker DipComEd DCS — 1985 — 2015
77c Craigcrook Road, Edinburgh EH4 3PH
ECrocker@churchofscotland.org.uk
0131 332 0227

80 Edinburgh: Wardie (F H T W)
Dolly Purnell BD — 2003 — 2021
churchoffice@wardie.org.uk
35 Lomond Road, Edinburgh EH5 3JN
DPurnell@churchofscotland.org.uk
0131 551 3847
0131 552 0190

81 Edinburgh: Willowbrae (F H W)
Vacant
Interim Moderator: John N. Young
willowbrae@btinternet.com
19 Abercorn Road, Edinburgh EH8 7DP
JYoung@churchofscotland.org.uk
0131 661 8259
0131 652 2938
0131 664 3067

82 Fauldhouse: St Andrew's (H)
Scott Raby LTh CertMin — 1991 — 2018
7 Glebe Court, Fauldhouse, Bathgate EH47 9DX
SRaby@churchofscotland.org.uk
01501 771190

83 Harthill: St Andrew's See Blackridge

84 Kirknewton (H) and East Calder (F H W)
Alistair J. Cowper BSc BD 2011 8 Manse Court, East Calder, Livingston EH53 0HF 01506 357083
ACowper@churchofscotland.org.uk 07791 524504

85 Kirk of Calder (F H W)
Vacant
Interim Moderator: Jonanda Groenewald 19 Maryfield Park, Mid Calder, Livingston EH53 0SB 01506 882495
JGroenewald@churchofscotland.org.uk 0131 261 7977

86 Linlithgow: St Michael's (F H W)
Liam J. Fraser LLB BD MTh PhD 2017 2019 **info@stmichaels-parish.org.uk** **01506 842188**
St Michael's Manse, Kirkgate, Linlithgow EH49 7AL 01506 842195
LFraser@churchofscotland.org.uk
Thomas S. Riddell BSc CEng FIChemE 1993 1994 4 The Maltings, Linlithgow EH49 6DS 01506 843251
(Auxiliary Minister) TRiddell@churchofscotland.org.uk

87 Linlithgow: St Ninian's Craigmailen (H W)
W. Richard Houston BSc BD MTh 1998 2004 29 Philip Avenue, Linlithgow EH49 7BH 01506 202246
WHouston@churchofscotland.org.uk

88 Livingston: Old (F H W)
Nelu I. Balaj BD MA ThD 2010 2017 The Manse, Charlesfield Lane, Livingston EH54 7AJ 01506 411888
NBalaj@churchofscotland.org.uk

89 Livingston United (F W)
Marc B. Kenton BTh MTh 1997 2019 2 Eastcroft Court, Livingston EH54 7ET 01506 467426
MKenton@churchofscotland.org.uk
Livingston United is a Local Ecumenical Partnership with the Scottish Episcopal, Methodist and United Reformed Churches

90 Pardovan, Kingscavil and Winchburgh See Abercorn

91 Polbeth Harwood (F W) linked with West Kirk of Calder (F H W)
Jonanda Groenewald BA BD MTh DD 2000 2014 3 Johnsburn Road, Balerno EH14 7DN 0131 261 7977
JGroenewald@churchofscotland.org.uk
Alison I. Quilter DipCS 2018 27 Northfield Meadows, Longridge, Bathgate EH47 8SA 07741 985597
(Ordained Local Minister) AQuilter@churchofscotland.org.uk

92 **Strathbrock (F H T W)**
Hanneke I. Janse van Vuren (Ms) 2012 2020
BTh MDiv LTh MTh
1 Manse Park, Uphall, Broxburn EH52 6NX
HJansevanVuren@churchofscotland.org.uk
01506 856433
01506 206045

93 **Torphichen** See Avonbridge

94 **Uphall: South (F H W)**
Ian D. Maxwell MA BD PhD 1977 2013
8 Fernlea, Uphall, Broxburn EH52 6DF
IMaxwell@churchofscotland.org.uk
01506 239840

95 **West Kirk of Calder (H)** See Polbeth Harwood

96 **Whitburn: Brucefield (F H W)**
Vacant
Interim Moderator: Sandra Boyd
contact@brucefieldchurch.org.uk
48 Gleneagles Court, Whitburn, Bathgate EH47 8PG
SBoyd@churchofscotland.org.uk
01501 748666
01501 229354
07919 676242

97 **Whitburn: South (H W)**
Vacant
Interim Moderator: Robert Craig
admin@whitburnsouthparishchurch.org.uk
5 Mansewood Crescent, Whitburn, Bathgate EH47 8HA
RCraig@churchofscotland.org.uk
01501 740333
01501 519085

B. In other appointments

Alexander, Ian W. BA BD STM 1990 2020
Faith Impact Forum: Global Justice
121 George Street, Edinburgh EH2 4YN
IAlexander@churchofscotland.org.uk
0131 225 5722

Ashley-Emery, Stephen BD DPS RN 2006 2019
Royal Naval Chaplain, Portsmouth
Holmhill, East Main Street, Chirnside, Duns TD11 3XR
(Home) 07882 885684

Barclay, Iain C. MBE TD MA BD MTh MPhil PhD FRSA 1976 2020
Chaplain: The Robin Chapel
The Thistle Foundation, Edinburgh EH16 4EA
chaplain@robinchapel.org.uk
(Office) 07393 232736

Donald, Alistair P. MA PhD BD 1999 2009
Chaplain: Heriot-Watt University
The Chaplaincy, Heriot-Watt University, Edinburgh EH14 4AS
a.p.donald@hw.ac.uk
0131 451 4508

Evans, Mark BSc MSc DCS 1988 2006
Head of Spiritual Care NHS Fife
13 Easter Drylaw Drive, Edinburgh EH4 2QA
mark.evans59@nhs.scot
(Home) 0131 343 3089
(Office) 01383 674136

Fergusson, David A.S. (Prof.) OBE MA BD DPhil DD FRSE FBA 1984 2021
Regius Professor of Divinity, University of Cambridge
23 Riselaw Crescent, Edinburgh EH10 6HN
daf52@cam.ac.uk
0131 447 4022

Foster, Joanne G. (Mrs) DipTMus BD AdvDipCouns MBACP(Acc) 1996 2021
Chaplain, Royal Infirmary of Edinburgh
Royal Infirmary of Edinburgh, 51 Little France Crescent EH16 4SA
joanne.foster2@nhslothian.scot.nhs.uk
0131 242 1991

Galbraith, Christopher G. BA LLB BD 2012 2022
Team Leader, Faith Service Team, HM Prison Addiewell
HM Prison Addiewell, Station Road, Addiewell, West Calder EH55 8QA
chris.galbraith@sodexogov.co.uk
01506 874500

Glienecke, Urzula PhD 2022
Associate Chaplain, University of Edinburgh
Chaplaincy Centre, 1 Bristo Square, Edinburgh EH8 9AL
urzula.glienecke@ed.ac.uk
0131 650 2595

Hardman-Moore, Susan (Prof.) MA MAR PhD 2013 2022
Vice Principal, New College, University of Edinburgh (Ordained Local Minister)
New College, Mound Place, Edinburgh EH1 2LX
SHardman-Moore@churchofscotland.org.uk
0131 650 8908
07811 345699

Name	Position			Address / Contact	Phone
Howitt, Jane M. MA BD	Chaplain, Heriot-Watt University	1996	2020	The Chaplaincy, Heriot-Watt University, Edinburgh EH14 4AS j.m.howitt@hw.ac.uk	0131 451 4508
MacMurchie, F. Lynne LLB BD	Healthcare Chaplain	1998	2003	Royal Edinburgh Hospital, Community Mental Health, Astley Ainslie Hospital lynne.macmurchie@nhslothian.scot.nhs.uk	0131 537 6775
Mathieson, Angus R. MA BD	Faith Nurture Forum: Partnership Development	1988	2020	21 Traquair Park West, Edinburgh EH12 7AN AMathieson@churchofscotland.org.uk	0131 334 9774
McIntosh, Kay (Mrs) DCS	Deacon, Edinburgh: Mayfield Salisbury	1990	2018	4 Jacklin Green, Livingston EH54 8PZ kay@backedge.co.uk	01506 440543
McPheat, Elspeth DCS	Deacon: CrossReach	1985	2001	53 Wood Street, Grangemouth FK3 8LS elspeth176@sky.com	01324 282406
McPherson, Marjory (Mrs) LLB BD MTh	Presbytery Clerk: Edinburgh and West Lothian	1990	2017	Presbytery, c/o Morningside Parish Church, 2 Cluny Gardens, Edinburgh EH10 6BQ MMcPherson@churchofscotland.org.uk	0131 225 9137
McPherson, William BD DipEd	Chief Executive, The Vine Trust	1994	2003	83 Laburnam Road, Port Seton, Prestonpans EH32 0UD	01875 812252
Orr, Sheena BA MSc MBA BD DPT	Chaplaincy Adviser, Scottish Prison Service	2011	2018	Calton House, 5 Redheughs Rigg, South Gyle, Edinburgh EH12 9HW sheena.orr@prisons.gov.scot	0131 330 3575 07922 649160
Pennykid, Gordon J. BD DCS	Chaplain, HM Prison Edinburgh	2015	2018	8 Glenfield, Livingston EH54 7BG GPennykid@churchofscotland.org.uk	07747 652652
Robertson, Pauline (Mrs) DCS BA CertTheol	Port Chaplain, Sailors' Society: Leith and Forth Estuary	2003	2016	6 Ashville Terrace, Edinburgh EH6 8DD probertson@sailors-society.org	0131 554 6564 07759 436303
Stewart, Lezley J. BD ThM MTh DMin	Faith Nurture Forum: Recruitment and Support	2000	2017	121 George Street, Edinburgh EH2 4YN LStewart@churchofscotland.org.uk	0131 225 5722
Swan, David BVMS BD DipTh CDRS	Chaplain, HM Prison Edinburgh	2005	2018	159 Redhall Drive, Edinburgh EH13 2LR davidswan97@gmail.com	07944 598988
Tweedie, Fiona J. BSc PhD	Ordained Local Minister: Statistician, Office of Assembly Trustees	2011	2014	121 George Street, Edinburgh EH2 4YN FTweedie@churchofscotland.org.uk	0131 225 5722
Wishart, Erica M. (Mrs) MA BD	Hospice Chaplain	2014	2020	St Columba's Hospice, 15 Boswall Road, Edinburgh EH5 3RW EWishart@churchofscotland.org.uk	0131 551 1381 07503 170173

C. Retaining

Name	Position			Address / Contact	Phone
Aitchison, James W. BD	(Aberdalgie and Forteviot with Aberuthven and Dunning)	1993	2021	JAitchison@churchofscotland.org.uk	0131 346 0685
Alexander, Helen J.R. BD DipSW CQSW	(Assistant, Edinburgh: High (St Giles'))	1981	2019	7 Polwarth Place, Edinburgh EH11 1LG HAlexander@churchofscotland.org.uk	0131 226 4242
Anderson, Dorothy U. LLB DipLP BD	(Associate, Dunblane Cathedral)	2006	2021	4GF Glencairn Crescent, Edinburgh EH12 5BS DAnderson@churchofscotland.org.uk	07926 090489
Armitage, William L. BSc BD	(Edinburgh: London Road)	1976	2006	Flat 7, 4 Papermill Wynd, Edinburgh EH7 4GJ bill@billarm-plus.com	0131 558 8534
Baird, Kenneth S. MSc PhD BD MIMarEST	(Edinburgh: Leith North)	1998	2009	3 Maule Terrace, Gullane EH31 2DB	01620 843447

Name	Years	Role	Address	Contact
Barber, Peter I. MA BD	1984 2021	(Edinburgh: Gorgie Dalry Stenhouse)	39 Roseburn Drive, Edinburgh EH12 5NR	0131 552 8781
Bicket, Matthew S. BD	1989 2017	(Carnoustie: Panbride)	9/2 Connaught Place, Edinburgh EH6 4RQ / matthew.bicket1952@gmail.com	
Booth, Jennifer (Mrs) LTh BD	1996 2005	(Associate: Edinburgh: Leith South)	39 Lilyhill Terrace, Edinburgh EH7 7DR	0131 661 3813
Borthwick, Kenneth S. MA BD	1983 2016	(Edinburgh: Holy Trinity)	34 Rodger Crescent, Armadale EH48 3GR / kennysamuel@aol.com	07735 749594
Boyd, Kenneth M. (Prof.) MA BD PhD FRCPE	1970 2011	(University of Edinburgh: Medical Ethics)	1 Doune Terrace, Edinburgh EH3 6DY / k.boyd@ed.ac.uk	0131 225 6485
Brady, Ian D. BSc ARCST BD	1967 2001	(Edinburgh: Corstorphine Old)	28 Frankfield Crescent, Dalgety Bay, Dunfermline KY11 9LW / brady500@gmail.com	01383 825104
Brown, William D. BD CQSW	1987 2013	(Edinburgh: Murrayfield)	79 Carnbee Park, Edinburgh EH16 6GG / wdb@talktalk.net	0131 261 7297
Clark, Christine M. BA BD MTh DMin	2006 2019	(Chaplain, Royal Hospital for Sick Children, Edinburgh)	40 Pentland Avenue, Edinburgh EH13 0HY / CClark@churchofscotland.org.uk	07444 819237
Clinkenbeard, William W. BSc BD STM	1966 2000	(Edinburgh: Carrick Knowe)	3/17 Western Harbour Breakwater, Edinburgh EH6 6PA / bjclinks@compuserve.com	0131 629 0519
Cowie, John A. BSc BD DMin	1983 2021	(Edinburgh: Stockbridge)	1 Liberton Place, Edinburgh EH16 6NA / JCowie@churchofscotland.org.uk	0131 672 1766
Crawford, Morag (Miss) MSc DCS	1977 2021	(Deacon, Rosyth)	118 Wester Drylaw Place, Edinburgh EH4 2TG / MCrawford@churchofscotland.org.uk	0131 332 2253 / 07970 982563
Crossan, William	2014 2022	(Ordained Local Minister, Campbeltown: Lorne and Lowland)	57 Caldercruix Crescent, Eilburn, Livingston EH54 7FS / w.crossan@btinternet.com	07833 152345
Cuthell, Tom C. MA BD	1965 2007	(Edinburgh: St Cuthbert's)	Flat 10, 2 Kingsburgh Crescent, Waterfront, Edinburgh EH5 1JS	0131 476 3864
Darroch, Richard J.G. BD MTh MA(CMS)	1993 2010	(Whitburn: Brucefield)	23 Barnes Green, Livingston EH54 8PP / richdarr@aol.com	01506 436648
Davidson, D. Hugh MA	1965 2009	(Edinburgh: Inverleith)	Flat 1/2, 22 Summerside Place, Edinburgh EH6 4NZ / hdavidson35@btinternet.com	0131 554 8420
Donald, Alistair P. MA PhD BD	1999 2022	(Chaplain: Heriot-Watt University)	3 Coldstream Crescent, Leven KY8 5TD / alistairpdonald@gmail.com	
Douglas, Alexander B. BD	1979 2014	(Edinburgh: Blackhall St Columba's)	15 Inchview Gardens, Dalgety Bay, Dunfermline KY11 9SA / alexandjill@douglas.net	01383 791080
Dunleavy, Suzanne BD DipEd	1990 2016	(Bridge of Weir: St Machar's Ranfurly)	44 Tantallon Gardens, Bellsquarry, Livingston EH54 9AT / suzanne.dunleavy@btinternet.com	
Dunn, W. Iain C. DA LTh	1983 1998	(Edinburgh: Pilrig and Dalmeny Street)	10 Fox Covert Avenue, Edinburgh EH12 6UQ	0131 334 1665
Dunphy, Rhona B. (Mrs) BD DPTheol DrPhil	2005 2020	(Pastoral Support, Faith Nurture Forum)	92 The Vennel, Linlithgow EH49 7ET / RDunphy@churchofscotland.org.uk	07791 007158
Embleton, Brian M. BD CPS	1976 2015	(Edinburgh: Reid Memorial)	54 Edinburgh Road, Peebles EH45 8EB / bmembleton@gmail.com	01721 602157
Embleton, Sara R. (Mrs) BA BD MTh	1988 2010	(Edinburgh: Leith St Serf's)	54 Edinburgh Road, Peebles EH45 8EB / srembleton@gmail.com	01721 602157
Farquharson, Gordon MA BD DipEd	1998 2007	(Stonehaven: Dunnottar)	26 Learmonth Court, Edinburgh EH4 1PB / gfarqu@talktalk.net	0131 343 1047
Forrester, Margaret R. (Mrs) MA BD DD	1974 2003	(Edinburgh: St Michael's)	25 Kingsburgh Road, Edinburgh EH12 6DZ / margaret@rosskeen.org.uk	0131 337 5646

Name			Position	Address	Email	Phone
Fraser, Shirley A. (Miss) MA BD DipASS	1992	2008	(Scottish Field Director: Friends International)	6/50 Roseburn Drive, Edinburgh EH12 5NS		0131 347 1400
Frew, Michael W. BSc BD	1978	2017	(Edinburgh: Slateford Longstone)	37 Swanston Terrace, Edinburgh EH10 7DN		07712 162375
Gardner, John V.	1997	2003	(Glamis, Inverarity and Kinnettles)	75/1 Lockharton Avenue, Edinburgh EH14 1BD	jvgardner66@googlemail.com	0131 443 7126
Gilmour, Ian Y. BD CertMin	1985	2018	(Edinburgh: St Andrew's and St George's West)	1 Groathill Loan, Drylaw, Edinburgh EH4 2WL	ianyg2@gmail.com	07794 149852
Gordon, Margaret (Mrs) DCS	1998	2012	(Deacon)	92 Lanark Road West, Currie EH14 5LA		0131 449 2554
Graham, W. Peter MA BD	1967	2008	(Presbytery Clerk: Edinburgh)	23/6 East Comiston, Edinburgh EH10 6RZ		0131 445 5763
Greig, Ronald G. MA BD	1987	2018	(Livingston United)	47 Mallace Avenue, Armadale EH48 2QD rgglep@gmail.com		01501 731969 / 07787 887427
Harkness, James KVCO CB OBE QHC MA DD	1961	1995	(Chaplain General: Army)	Lang Glen, Durisdeer, nr Thornhill DG3 5BJ		01848 500225
Harley, Elspeth S. BA MTh	1991	2020	(Caddonfoot with Galashiels: Trinity)		eharley@hotmail.co.uk	07950 076528
Hay, Jared W. BA MTh DipMin DMin	1987	2017	(Edinburgh: Priestfield)	39 Netherbank, Edinburgh EH16 6YR jaredhay3110@gmail.com		07906 662515
Inglis, Ann (Mrs) LLB BD	1986	2015	(Langton and Lammermuir Kirk)	34 Echline View, South Queensferry EH30 9XL revainglis@gmail.com		0131 629 0233
Irving, William D. LTh	1985	2005	(Golspie)	122 Swanston Muir, Edinburgh EH10 7HY		0131 441 3384
Jamieson, Gordon D. MA BD	1974	2012	(Head of Stewardship)	41 Goldpark Place, Livingston EH54 6LW gordonjamieson182@gmail.com		01506 412020
Keil, Alistair H. BD DipMin	1989	2021	(Edinburgh: St Andrew's Clermiston)	14 Comiston Terrace, Edinburgh EH10 6AH AKeil@churchofscotland.org.uk		07758 009250
Kerr, Angus BD CertMin ThM DMin	1983	2019	(Whitburn: South)	27 Pelham Court, Jackton, East Kilbride G74 5PZ		01355 570962
Lawson, Kenneth C. MA BD	1963	1999	(Adviser in Adult Education)	56 Easter Drylaw View, Edinburgh EH4 2QP		0131 539 3311
Logan, Anne T. (Mrs) MA BD MTh DMin PhD	1981	2012	(Edinburgh: Stockbridge)	Sunnyside Cottage, 18 Upper Broomieknowe, Lasswade EH18 1LP annetlogan@sky.com		0131 663 9550
Lough, Adrian J. BD AFSERT MIERE DipSW	2012	2020	(Auchtergaven and Moneydie with Redgorton and Stanley)	12 Dundreman Cottages, Edinburgh EH16 5RG revlough@btinternet.com		
Mackay, Kenneth J. MA BD	1971	2007	(Edinburgh: St Nicholas' Sighthill)	46 Chuckethall Road, Livingston EH54 8FB knnth_mackay@yahoo.co.uk		01506 410884
Mackenzie, James G. BA BD	1980	2005	(Jersey: St Columba's)	26 Drylaw Crescent, Edinburgh EH4 2AU jgmackenzie@jerseymail.co.uk		0131 332 3720
Maclean, Ailsa G. (Mrs) BD DipCE	1979	2017	(Chaplain: George Heriot's School)	28 Swan Spring Avenue, Edinburgh EH10 6NJ		
Macmillan, Gilleasbuig I. KCVO MA BD Dthc DD FRSE HRSA FRCSEd	1969	2013	(Edinburgh: High (St Giles'))	207 Dalkeith Road, Edinburgh EH16 5DS gmacmillan1@btinternet.com		0131 667 5732
Marshall, A. Scott DipComm BD	1984	2021	(Abercorn with Pardovan, Kingscavil and Winchburgh)	13 Leyland Road, Bathgate EH48 2SG		07415 028678
McGregor, T. Stewart MBE MA BD	1957	1998	(Chaplain: Edinburgh Royal Infirmary)	19 Lonsdale Terrace, Edinburgh EH3 9HL cetsm@uwclub.net		0131 229 5332
McLaren, Glenda M. (Ms) DCS	1990	2020	(Deacon)	17 Heatherwood, Seafield, Bathgate EH47 7BX gmmclaren1330@gmail.com		01506 651401

Name			Role	Address / Email	Phone
McLarty, R. Russell MA BD DipArch	1985	2022	(Transition Minister, Edinburgh: Meadowbank)	9 Sanderson's Wynd, Tranent EH33 1DA / RussellMcLarty@churchofscotland.org.uk	01875 614496 / 07751 755986
McPake, John M. LTh	2000	2013	(Edinburgh: Liberton Northfield)	3 Kilburn Wood Drive, Roslin EH25 9AA / john_mcpake9@yahoo.co.uk	0131 285 8386
Moir, Ian A. MA BD	1962	2000	(Adviser for Urban Priority Areas)	28/6 Comely Bank Avenue, Edinburgh EH4 1EL	0131 332 2748
Morrison, Angus MA BD PhD DD	1979	2021	(Orwell and Portmoak)	170 The Murrays, Edinburgh EH17 8UP / AMorrison@churchofscotland.org.uk	
Mulligan, Anne MA DCS	1974	2013	(Deacon: Hospital Chaplain)	27A Craigour Avenue, Edinburgh EH17 1NH / mulliganne@aol.com	0131 664 3426
Munro, John R. BD	1976	2017	(Edinburgh: Fairmilehead)	23 Braid Farm Road, Edinburgh EH10 6LE / revjohnmunro@hotmail.com	0131 446 9363
Nelson, Georgina MA BD PhD DipEd	1990	2022	(Hospital Chaplain, NHS Lothian)	63 Hawthorn Bank, Seafield, Bathgate EH47 7EB	
Nicol, Douglas A.O. MA BD	1974	2018	(Hobkirk and Southdean with Ruberslaw)	1/2 North Werber Park, Edinburgh EH4 1SY / Douglas.Nicol@churchofscotland.org.uk	07811 437075
Paterson, Douglas S. MA BD DipTP	1976	2010	(Edinburgh: St Colm's)	4 Ards Place, High Street, Aberlady EH32 0DB	01875 870192
Povey, John M. DL BD PhD	1981	2021	(Kirk of Calder)	5 Ainslie Road, East Calder, Livingston EH53 0PU / RevJPovey@aol.com	07549 525498
Ramsay, A. Malcolm BA LLB DipMin	1986	2022	(Transition Minister, Edinburgh: Willowbrae)	Ford Cottage, Ford, Pathhead EH37 5RE / amalcolmramsay@gmail.com	
Rennie, Agnes M. (Miss) DCS	1974	2012	(Deacon)	3/1 Craigmillar Court, Edinburgh EH16 4AD	0131 661 8475
Ridland, Alistair K. MStJ MA BD DipDS MRAeS MInstLM RAFAC	1982	2022	(Chaplain: Western General Hospital)	13 Stewart Place, Kirkliston EH29 0BQ / a.ridland@btinternet.com	0131 333 2711
Robertson, Charles LVO MA	1965	2005	(Edinburgh: Canongate)	3 Ross Gardens, Edinburgh EH9 3BS / canongate1@aol.com	0131 662 9025
Roger, Alexander M. BD PhD	1982	2020	(Whitburn: Brucefield)	4 Lugton Circle, South Gilmerton Brae, Edinburgh EH17 8GT / amroger1951@outlook.com	0131 664 8109
Scott, Martin C. DipMusEd RSAM BD PhD	1986	2019	(Secretary, Council of Assembly)	52 Ravenscroft Gardens, Edinburgh EH17 8RP / martin.scott14@sky.com	0131 431 4195 / 07856 165820
Shaw, Duncan BD MTh	1975	2020	(Bathgate: St John's)	30 Meadowpark Crescent, Bathgate EH48 2SX / duncan.shaw11@btinternet.com	01506 654563
Smith, Angus MA LTh	1965	2006	(Chaplain to the Oil Industry)	3/7 West Powburn, West Savile Gait, Edinburgh EH9 3EW	0131 667 1761
Smith, Graham W. BA BD FSAScot	1995	2016	(Livingston: Old)	76 Bankton Park East, Livingston EH54 9BN / smithgraham824@gmail.com	01506 442917
Stark, Suzie M. BD CertMin	2013	2021	(Chaplain, St Columba's Hospice, Edinburgh)	The Lodge, 40 Warriston Gardens, Edinburgh EH3 5NE / sstark1962@btinternet.com	0131 551 1633
Stevenson, John MA BD PhD HonFEIS	1963	2001	(Department of Education)	12 Swanston Gardens, Edinburgh EH10 7DL	0131 445 3960
Tait, John M. BSc BD	1985	2012	(Edinburgh: Pilrig St Paul's)	82 Greenend Gardens, Edinburgh EH17 7QH / johmtait@me.com	0131 258 9105
Taylor, William R. MA BD MTh	1983	2018	(Chaplaincy Adviser, Scottish Prison Service)	33 Kingsknowe Drive EH14 2JY / wlretl@outlook.com	0131 443 5590
Teague, Yvonne (Mrs) DCS	1965	2002	(Board of Ministry)	46 Craigcrook Avenue, Edinburgh EH4 3PX / y.teague.1@blueyonder.co.uk	07447 258525 / 0131 336 3113

Watson, Nigel G. MA	1998 2012	(Associate: East Kilbride: Old/Stewartfield/West)	7 St Catherine's Place, Edinburgh EH9 1NU nigel.g.watson@gmail.com 0131 662 4191
Whyte, George J. BSc BD DMin	1981 2022	(Principal Clerk)	4 Baberton Mains Lea, Edinburgh EH14 3HB george.whyte@blueyonder.co.uk 07902 645109
Williams, Jenny M. BSc BD MTh CQSW	1996 2022	(Transition Minister, Edinburgh: Drylaw)	15 House o' Hill Gardens, Edinburgh EH4 2AR 0131 332 0896
Wynne, Alistair T.E. BA BD	1982 2009	(Nicosia Community Church, Cyprus)	Flat 6, 14 Burnbrae Drive, Edinburgh EH12 8AS awynne2@googlemail.com 0131 339 6462

EDINBURGH ADDRESSES

Albany	at St Andrew's and St George's West	Gorgie Dalry Stenhouse	Gorgie Road
Balerno	Johnsburn Road, Balerno	Gracemount	Gracemount Primary School
Barclay Viewforth	Barclay Place	Granton	Boswall Parkway
Blackhall St Columba's	Queensferry Road	Greenbank	Braidburn Terrace
Bristo Memorial Craigmillar	Peffermill Road, Craigmillar	Greenside	Royal Terrace
Broughton St Mary's	Bellevue Crescent	Greyfriars Kirk	Greyfriars Place
Canongate	Canongate	High (St Giles')	High Street
Carrick Knowe	North Saughton Road	Holy Trinity	Hailesland Place, Wester Hailes
Colinton	Dell Road	Inverleith St Serf's	Ferry Road
Corstorphine		Juniper Green	Lanark Road, Juniper Green
Craigsbank	Craigs Crescent	Kirkliston	The Square, Kirkliston
Old	Kirk Loan	Leith	
St Anne's	Kaimes Road	North	Madeira Street off Ferry Road
St Ninian's	St John's Road	St Andrew's	Easter Road
Craiglockhart	Craiglockhart Avenue	South	Kirkgate, Leith
Craigmillar Park	Craigmillar Park	Northfield	Kirkgate, Liberton
Cramond	Cramond Glebe Road	Liberton	Gilmerton Road, Liberton
Currie	Kirkgate, Currie	Marchmont St Giles'	Kilgraston Road
Dalmeny	Main Street, Dalmeny	Mayfield Salisbury	Mayfield Road x West Mayfield
Davidson's Mains	Quality Street	Meadowbank	Dalziel Road x London Road
Drylaw	Groathill Road North	Morningside	Cluny Gardens
Duddingston	Old Church Lane, Duddingston	Morningside United	Brunsfield Place x Chamberlain Rd
Fairmilehead	Frogston Road West, Fairmilehead	Murrayfield	Abinger Gardens
		Newhaven	Craighall Road
		Old Kirk and Muirhouse	Pennywell Gardens
		Palmerston Place	Palmerston Place

Pilrig St Paul's	Pilrig Street
Polwarth	Polwarth Terrace x Harrison Road
Portobello and Joppa	Abercorn Terrace
Priestfield	Dalkeith Road x Marchhall Place
Queensferry	The Loan, South Queensferry
Ratho	Baird Road, Ratho
Reid Memorial	West Savile Terrace
Richmond Craigmillar	Niddrie Mains Road
St Andrew's and St George's West	George Street
St Andrew's Clermiston	Clermiston View
St Catherine's Argyle	Grange Road x Chalmers Crescent
St Cuthbert's	Lothian Road
St David's Broomhouse	Broomhouse Crescent
St John's Colinton Mains	Oxgangs Road North
St Margaret's	Restalrig Road South
St Martin's	Magdalene Drive
St Michael's	Slateford Road
St Nicholas' Sighthill	Calder Road
St Stephen's Comely Bank	Comely Bank
Slateford Longstone	Kingsknowe Road North
Stockbridge	Saxe Coburg Street
Tron Kirk (Gilmerton and Moredun)	Craigour Gardens and Ravenscroft Street
Wardie	Primrosebank Road
Willowbrae	Willowbrae Road

(3) LOTHIAN (W)

Meets at Musselburgh: St Andrew's High Parish Church at 7pm on the last Thursday in November 2022. On 1 January 2023 it will unite with the Presbyteries of Melrose and Peebles, Duns, and Jedburgh to form the Presbytery of Lothian and Borders. That new Presbytery will meet on 21 January 2023 at a venue to be determined and thereafter as decided.

Clerk:	MR JOHN D. McCULLOCH DL	20 Tipperwell Way, Howgate, Penicuik EH26 8QP	01968 676300
		lothian@churchofscotland.org.uk	
Depute Clerk:	REV MICHAEL D. WATSON CertCS	2/1 Stanton Marches, Haddington EH41 3FB	01620 614009
		MWatson@churchofscotland.org.uk	

Aberlady (F H W) linked with Gullane (F H W)
Vacant   01875 870777
Interim Moderator: Jock Stein   jstein@handselpress.org.uk   01620 824896

Belhaven (F H T W) linked with Spott (F W)
Vacant   The Manse, Belhaven Road, Dunbar EH42 1NH   01368 860672
Interim Moderator: Brian C. Hilsley   BHilsley@churchofscotland.org.uk   07791 557350

Bilston linked with Roslin (H)
Vacant   31A Manse Road, Roslin EH25 9LG   0131 440 2012
June E. Johnston BSc MEd BD   2013   2020   21 Caberston Road, Walkerburn EH43 6AT   01896 870754
   (Ordained Local Minister)   June.Johnston@churchofscotland.org.uk   07754 448889
Interim Moderator: John Mitchell   JMitchell@churchofscotland.org.uk   0131 448 2676

Bonnyrigg (F H W)
Louise I. Purden BD   2020   9 Viewbank View, Bonnyrigg EH19 2HU   0131 258 6219
                                                                         LPurden@churchofscotland.org.uk

Cockenzie and Port Seton: Chalmers Memorial (F H W)   contact@chalmerschurch.co.uk
Robin N. Allison BD DipMin   1994   2018   2 Links Road, Port Seton, Prestonpans EH32 0HA   01875 812225
                                                                         RAllison@churchofscotland.org.uk

Cockenzie and Port Seton: Old (F H W)
Guardianship of the Presbytery
Session Clerk: Elizabeth W. Malcolm (Miss)   malcolm771@btinternet.com   01875 813659

Cockpen and Carrington (F H W) linked with Lasswade (H) and Rosewell (H W)
Lorna M. Souter MA BD MSc   2016   11 Pendreich Terrace, Bonnyrigg EH19 2DT   0131 663 6392
LSouter@churchofscotland.org.uk   07889 566418

Dalkeith: St John's and King's Park (F H W)
Keith L. Mack BD MTh DPS   2002   **sjkpdalkeith@gmail.com**   **0131 660 5871**
13 Weir Crescent, Dalkeith EH22 3JN   0131 454 0206
KMack@churchofscotland.org.uk

Dalkeith: St Nicholas Buccleuch (F H T W)
Alexander G. Horsburgh MA BD   1995   2004   1 Nungate Gardens, Haddington EH41 4EE   01620 824728
AHorsburgh@churchofscotland.org.uk

Dirleton (F H) linked with North Berwick: Abbey (F H W)
David J. Graham BSc BD PhD   1982   1998   **abbeychurch@abbeychurch.co.uk**   **01620 892800**
Sydserff, Old Abbey Road, North Berwick EH39 4BP   01620 890800
DGraham@churchofscotland.org.uk

Dunbar (H W)
Gordon Stevenson BSc BD   2010   The Manse, 10 Bayswell Road, Dunbar EH42 1AB   01368 865482
revgstev@gmail.com

Dunglass (W)
Suzanne G. Fletcher BA MDiv MA DMin   2001   2011   The Manse, Cockburnspath TD13 5XZ   01368 830713
SFletcher@churchofscotland.org.uk   07973 960544

Garvald and Morham (W) linked with Haddington: West (H W)
John D. Vischer   1993   2011   **hwcofs@hotmail.com**   01620 822213
15 West Road, Haddington EH41 3RD
JVischer@churchofscotland.org.uk

Gladsmuir linked with Longniddry (F H W)
Robin E. Hill LLB BD PhD   2004   The Manse, 8a Elcho Road, Longniddry EH32 0LB   01875 853195
RHill@churchofscotland.org.uk

Gorebridge (F H W)
Mark S. Nicholas MA BD   1999   **office@gorepc.com**   **01875 820387**
100 Hunterfield Road, Gorebridge EH23 4TT   01875 820387
MNicholas@churchofscotland.org.uk   07816 047493

Gullane See Aberlady

Haddington: St Mary's (F H T W)
Alison P. McDonald MA BD — 1991 — 2019 — 1 Nungate Gardens, Haddington EH41 4EE
Alison.McDonald@churchofscotland.org.uk — **01620 829354** / 01620 823109

Haddington: West See Garvald and Morham

Humbie (F W) linked with Yester, Bolton and Saltoun (F W)
Anikó Schütz Bradwell BA MA BD — 2015 — The Manse, Tweeddale Avenue, Gifford, Haddington EH41 4QN
ASchuetzBradwell@churchofscotland.org.uk — 01620 811193

Lasswade and Rosewell See Cockpen and Carrington

Loanhead (F T W)
Graham L. Duffin BSc BD DipEd — 1989 — 2001 — 120 The Loan, Loanhead EH20 9AJ
GDuffin@churchofscotland.org.uk — 0131 448 2459

Longniddry See Gladsmuir

Musselburgh: Northesk (F H W)
Hayley L. Cohen BA MDiv — 2020 — 34 Battlefield Drive, Musselburgh EH21 7DF
HCohen@churchofscotland.org.uk — 0131 665 8688

Musselburgh: St Andrew's High (H W)
A. Leslie Milton MA BD PhD — 1996 — 2019 — 8 Ferguson Drive, Musselburgh EH21 6XA
AMilton@churchofscotland.org.uk — **0131 665 7239** / 0131 665 1124

Musselburgh: St Clement's and St Ninian's
Guardianship of the Presbytery
Session Clerk: Ivor A. Highley — 110 Inveresk Road, Musselburgh EH21 7AY — 0131 665 5674

Musselburgh: St Michael's Inveresk (F W)
Malcolm M. Lyon BD — 2007 — 2017 — 5 Crookston Ct., Crookston Rd., Inveresk, Musselburgh EH21 7TR
MLyon@churchofscotland.org.uk — 0131 653 2411

Newbattle (F H W)
Gayle J.A. Taylor MA BD PGDipCouns — 1999 — 2019 — Parish Office, Mayfield and Easthouses Church, Bogwood Court,
(Transition Minister) — Easthouses EH22 5DG
GTaylor@churchofscotland.org.uk — **0131 663 3245** / 0131 663 3245

Newton
Guardianship of the Presbytery
Andrew Don MBA   2006   2013   5 Eskvale Court, Penicuik EH26 8HT   0131 663 3845
(Ordained Local Minister)   ADon@churchofscotland.org.uk   01968 675766

North Berwick: Abbey See Dirleton

North Berwick: St Andrew Blackadder (F H W)
Neil J. Dougall BD DipMin DMin   1991   2003   **admin@standrewblackadder.org.uk**   01620 892132
                7 Marine Parade, North Berwick EH39 4LD
                NDougall@churchofscotland.org.uk

Ormiston (W) linked with Pencaitland (F W)
David J. Torrance BD DipMin   1993   2009   The Manse, Pencaitland, Tranent EH34 5DL   01875 340963
                DTorrance@churchofscotland.org.uk

Pencaitland See Ormiston

Penicuik: North (F H W)
Graham D. Astles BD MSc   2007   2019   35 Esk Bridge, Penicuik EH26 8QR   07906 290568
                GAstles@churchofscotland.org.uk

Penicuik: Trinity (F H W)
John C.C. Urquhart MA MA BD   2010   2017   10 Fletcher Grove, Penicuik EH26 0JT   01968 382116
                JCUrquhart@churchofscotland.org.uk   07821 402901
New charge formed by the union of Penicuik: St Mungo's and Penicuik: South and Howgate

Prestonpans: Prestongrange (F W)
Kenneth W. Donald BA BD   1982   2014   The Manse, East Loan, Prestonpans EH32 9ED   01875 813643
                KDonald@churchofscotland.org.uk   07392 069957

Roslin See Bilston

Spott See Belhaven

Tranent (F W)
Katherine A. Taylor LLB MDiv   2021   1 Toll House Gardens, Tranent EH33 2QQ   01875 880011
                KTaylor@churchofscotland.org.uk

Traprain (W)

Name			Address	Tel
Douglas Hamilton LLB MSc MDiv	2022		dhamilton@churchofscotland.org.uk	
Michael D. Watson CertCS (Ordained Local Minister)	2013	2019	2/1 Stanton Marches, Haddington EH41 3FB MWatson@churchofscotland.org.uk	01620 614009

Tyne Valley (F H W)

Name			Address	Tel
Dale K. London BTh FSAScot	2011	2018	Cranstoun Cottage, Ford, Pathhead EH37 5RE DLondon@churchofscotland.org.uk	01875 321329

Yester, Bolton and Saltoun See Humbie

B. In other appointments

Name			Appointment	Address	Tel
Berry, Geoff T. BSc BD	2009	2011	Army Chaplain	3 SCOTS, Fort George, Ardersier, Inverness IV2 7TE revgeoffberry@gmail.com	
Cobain, Alan R. BD	2000	2017	Army Chaplain	Infantry Training Centre, Vimy Barracks, Catterick Garrison DL9 3PS	
Frail, Nicola R. BLE MBA MDiv	2000	2012	Army Chaplain	HQ 1 Army Infantry Brigade, Delhi Barracks, Tidworth SP9 7DX nrfscot@hotmail.com	
Harrison, Frederick CertCT		2013	Ordained Local Minister	50 Dundas Gardens, Gorebridge EH23 4BB FHarrison@churchofscotland.org.uk	07703 527240
Kellock, Chris N. MA BD	1998	2012	Army Chaplain	Defence Academy, Shrivenham, Swindon SN6 8LA nicandchris@hotmail.co.uk	
Wood, Peter J. MA BD	1993	2018	Pioneer New Housing Co-ordinator, Presbytery	49 Oxgangs Farm Drive, Edinburgh EH13 9PT PWood@churchofscotland.org.uk	07776 119901

C. Retaining

Name			Congregation	Address	Tel
Allison, Ann BSc PhD BD	2000	2017	(Crail with Kingsbarns)	99 Coalgate Avenue, Tranent EH33 1JW revann@sky.com	01875 571778 / 07857 525439 / 01875 819858
Atkins, Yvonne E.S. (Mrs) BD	1997	2018	(Musselburgh: St Andrew's High)	6 Robert de Quincy Place, Prestonpans EH32 9NS yveatkins@yahoo.com	
Burt, Thomas W. BD	1982	2013	(Carlops with Kirkurd and Newlands with West Linton: St Andrew's)	7 Arkwright Court, North Berwick EH39 4RT tomburt@westlinton.com	01620 895494
Campbell, Thomas R.	1986	1993	(Paisley: St James)	The White House, Nairns Mains, Haddington EH41 4HF tom@trcampbell.co.uk	07778 183830
Coltart, Ian O. CA BD	1988	2010	(Arbirlot with Carmyllie)	25 Bothwell Gardens, Dunbar EH42 1PZ	01368 860064
Dick, Andrew B. BD DipMin	1986	2015	(Musselburgh: St Michael's Inveresk)	4 Kirkhill Court, Gorebridge EH23 4TW dixbit@aol.com	07540 099480
Duncan, Maureen M. (Mrs) BD	1996	2018	(Lochend and New Abbey)	2 Chalybeate, Haddington EH41 4NX revmo43@gmail.com	01620 248559 / 07443 501738
Fraser, John W. MA BD	1974	2011	(Penicuik: North)	66 Camus Avenue, Edinburgh EH10 6QX jjjjj2005@hotmail.co.uk	0131 623 0647
Glover, Robert L. BMus BD MTh ARCO	1971	2010	(Cockenzie and Port Seton: Chalmers Memorial)	12 Seton Wynd, Port Seton, Prestonpans EH32 0TY rlglover@btinternet.com	01875 818759

Name	Ordained	Admitted	Charge/Role	Address / Email	Telephone
Gordon, Thomas J. MA BD	1974	2009	(Chaplain, Marie Curie Hospice, Edinburgh)	22 Gosford Road, Port Seton, Prestonpans EH32 0HF tom.swallowsnest@gmail.com	01875 812262
Hilsley, Brian C. LLB BD	1990	2020	(Aberlady with Gullane)	15 Letham Place, Dunbar EH42 1AJ BHilsley@churchofscotland.org.uk	07791 557350
Jones, Anne M. (Mrs) BD	1998	2011	(Hospital Chaplain)	7 North Elphinstone Farm, Tranent EH33 2ND revamjones@aol.com	01875 614442
Macaulay, Glendon D. BD ALCM	1999	2012	(Falkirk: Erskine)	43 Gavin's Lee, Tranent EH33 2AP gd.macaulay@btinternet.com	01875 615851
McNab, Douglas G. BA BD	1999	2021	(New Machar)	17 Wester Kippielaw Park, Dalkeith EH22 2GE dougie.mcnab@btinternet.com	0131 563 8034 07766 042033
Mitchell, John LTh CertMin	1991	2018	(Bonnyrigg)	28 Shiel Hall Crescent, Rosewell EH24 9DD JMitchell@churchofscotland.org.uk	0131 448 2676
Pirie, Donald LTh	1975	2006	(Bolton and Saltoun with Humbie with Yester)	46 Caiystane Avenue, Edinburgh EH10 6SH	0131 445 2654
Scott, Ian G. BSc BD STM	1965	2006	(Edinburgh: Greenbank)	50 Forthview Walk, Tranent EH33 1FE igscott50@btinternet.com	01875 612907
Simpson, Robert R. BA BD	1994	2014	(Callander)	19 Cadwell Walk, Gorebridge EH23 4LF robert@pansmanse.co.uk	01875 823180
Spence, Elisabeth G.B. BD DipEd	1995	2021	(Pioneer Minister, Hopefield Connections)	18 Castell Maynes Avenue, Bonnyrigg EH19 3RW revspence121@gmail.com	07772 548121
Steele, Marilynn J. (Mrs) BD DCS	1999	2012	(Deacon)	2 Northfield Gardens, Prestonpans EH32 9LQ marilynnsteele@aol.com	01875 811497
Stein, Jock MA BD PhD	1973	2008	(Tulliallan and Kincardine)	35 Dunbar Road, Haddington EH41 3PJ jstein@handselpress.org.uk	01620 824896
Stein, Margaret E. (Mrs) DA BD DipRE	1984	2008	(Tulliallan and Kincardine)	35 Dunbar Road, Haddington EH41 3PJ margaretestein@hotmail.com	01620 824896
Steven, Gordon R. BD DCS	1997	2012	(Deacon)	51 Nantwich Drive, Edinburgh EH7 6RB grsteven@btinternet.com	0131 669 2054 07904 385256
Thornthwaite, Anthony P. MTh	1995	2019	(Dundee: Coldside)	19 Dovecote Way, Haddington EH41 4HY tony.thornthwaite@sky.com	07706 761841
Watson, James B. BSc	1969	2009	(Coldstream with Eccles)	20 Randolph Crescent, Dunbar EH42 1GL jimwatson007@hotmail.com	01368 865045 07419 759451

(4) MELROSE AND PEEBLES (W)

Meets at Innerleithen on the first Tuesday of October, November and December 2022. On 1 January 2023 it will unite with the Presbyteries of Lothian, Duns, and Jedburgh to form the Presbytery of Lothian and Borders. That new Presbytery will meet on 21 January 2023 at a venue to be determined and thereafter as decided.

Clerk:	REV. VICTORIA J. LINFORD LLB BD	20 Wedale View, Stow, Galashiels TD1 2SJ melrosepeebles@churchofscotland.org.uk	01578 730237
Assistant Clerk:	MR PETER SANDISON MA CertEd DipLib	Lynhurst, Abbotsview Drive, Galashiels TD1 3SL petersandison@me.com	01896 758634 07805 637709

Ashkirk (W) linked with Ettrick and Yarrow (F W) linked with Selkirk (F H W)

office@selkirkparish.church — 01750 22078

Vacant

Interim Moderator: George C. Shand — 1 Loanside, Selkirk TD7 4DJ — 01750 23308 / 07765 987163

George.Shand@churchofscotland.org.uk

Bowden (H) and Melrose (F H W) — bowden.melrosepc@btinternet.com — 01896 823339

Rosemary Frew (Mrs) MA BD — 1988 2017 — The Manse, Tweedmount Road, Melrose TD6 9ST — 01896 822217

RFrew@churchofscotland.org.uk

Broughton, Glenholm and Kilbucho (F H W) linked with Carlops (W) linked with Kirkurd and Newlands (F H) linked with Skirling (F W)
 linked with Tweedsmuir (F H W) linked with West Linton: St Andrew's (F H W) (The West Tweeddale Parishes)

T.A. (Tony) Foley PhD — 1992 2021 — Old Joiners Croft, Skirling, Biggar ML12 6HD — 07793 294000

TFoley@churchofscotland.org.uk

Caddonfoot (H W) linked with Stow: St Mary of Wedale and Heriot (W)

Victoria J. Linford (Mrs) LLB BD — 2010 — 20 Wedale View, Stow, Galashiels TD1 2SJ — 01578 730237

VLinford@churchofscotland.org.uk

Carlops See Broughton, Glenholm and Kilbucho

Channelkirk and Lauder (F W) — The Manse, Brownsmuir Park, Lauder TD2 6QD — 01578 718996

Vacant — 01578 722848

Session Clerk: William Anderson — wdanderson0709@hotmail.com

Dryburgh District Churches (F W) Sheila W. Moir (Ms) MTheol	2008		**web4churches@gmail.com** 7 Strae Brigs, St Boswells, Melrose TD6 0DH SMoir@churchofscotland.org.uk	01835 822255
Earlston (F W) Vacant Session Clerk: Robert Turnbull			rgtapoth@btinternet.com	01896 848515
Eddleston (F H) linked with Peebles: Old (F H W) linked with Stobo and Drumelzier (F W) Aftab Gohar MA MDiv PgDip	1996	2021	**admin@topcop.org.uk** 7 Clement Gunn Square, Peebles EH45 8LW AGohar@churchofscotland.org.uk	**01721 723986** 07528 143784
Ettrick and Yarrow See Ashkirk				
Galashiels (H W) Graeme M. Glover MA MBA MSc	2017	2022	**office@galashielschurchofscotland.org.uk** Woodlea, Abbotsview Drive, Galashiels TD1 3SL GGlover@churchofscotland.org.uk	**01896 752967** 01896 209455
Innerleithen (H), Traquair and Walkerburn (W) Fraser Edwards BSc BA	2021		The Manse, 1 Millwell Park, Innerleithen, Peebles EH44 6JF FEdwards@churchofscotland.org.uk	01896 490742
Kirkurd and Newlands See Broughton, Glenholm and Kilbucho				
Lyne and Manor (W) linked with Peebles: St Andrew's Leckie (F H W) Malcolm S. Jefferson	2012		**office@standrewsleckie.co.uk** Mansefield, Innerleithen Road, Peebles EH45 8BE MJefferson@churchofscotland.org.uk	**01721 723121** 01721 725148

Peebles: Old See Eddleston
Peebles: St Andrew's Leckie See Lyne and Manor
Selkirk See Ashkirk
Skirling See Broughton, Glenholm and Kilbucho
Stobo and Drumelzier See Eddleston
Stow: St Mary of Wedale and Heriot See Caddonfoot
Tweedsmuir See Broughton, Glenholm and Kilbucho
West Linton: St Andrew's See Broughton, Glenholm and Kilbucho

B. In appointments

Name	2015	Ordained Local Minister	Address	Phone
Strachan, Pamela D. (Lady)	2015		Glenhighton, Broughton, Biggar ML12 6JF / PStrachan@churchofscotland.org.uk	01899 830423 / 07837 873688

C. Retaining

Name	Years	Ordained Local Minister	Address	Phone
Arnott, A. David K. MA BD	1971 2010	(St Andrews: Hope Park with Strathkinness)	53 Whitehaugh Park, Peebles EH45 9DB / adka53@btinternet.com	01721 725979 / 07759 709205
Dobie, Rachel J.W. (Mrs) LTh	1991 2008	(Broughton, Glenholm and Kilbucho with Skirling with Stobo and Drumelzier with Tweedsmuir)	20 Moss Side Crescent, Biggar ML12 6GE / revracheldobie@gmail.com	01899 229244
Dodd, Marion E. (Miss) MA BD LRAM	1988 2010	(Kelso: Old and Sprouston)	Esdaile, Tweedmount Road, Melrose TD6 9ST / mariondodd@btinternet.com	01896 822446
Donaldson, David MA BD DMin	1969 2018	(Manish-Scarista)	13 Rose Park, Peebles EH45 8HP / davidandjeandonaldson@gmail.com	07817 479866
Guy, Scott C. BD	1989 2020	(Aberdeen: Northfield)	41 Jenny Moore's Road, St Boswells TD6 0AN / scguy55@gmail.com	01835 274455
Hogg, Thomas M. BD	1986 2007	(Tranent)	22 Douglas Place, Galashiels TD1 3BT	01896 759381
Kellet, John M. MA	1962 1995	(Edinburgh: Leith South)	1 Dyers Close, Innerleithen EH44 6QF	01896 830201
Levison, Chris L. MA BD	1972 2010	(Health Care Chaplaincy Training and Development Officer)	Gardenfield, Nine Mile Burn, Penicuik EH26 9LT / chrislevison@hotmail.com	01968 674566
Macdonald, Finlay A.J. MA BD PhD DD	1971 2010	(Principal Clerk)	8 St Ronan's Way, Innerleithen EH44 6RG / finlay_macdonald@btinternet.com	01896 831631
Macdougall, Malcolm M. BD MTh DipCE	1981 2019	(Eddleston with Peebles: Old)	2 Woodilee, Broughton, Biggar ML12 6GB / calum.macdougall@btopenworld.com	01899 830615
Milloy, A. Miller DipPE LTh DipTrMan LHD	1979 2011	(General Secretary: United Bible Societies)	18 Kittlegairy Crescent, Peebles EH45 9NJ / ammilloy@aol.com	01721 723380
Moore, W. Haisley MA	1966 1996	(Secretary: The Boys' Brigade)	37 Wilkie Gardens, White Rose Place, Galashiels TD1 2FF / haisley37@outlook.com	01896 829809
Munson, Winnie (Ms) BD DipTh	1996 2006	(Delting with Northmavine)	6 St Cuthbert's Drive, St Boswells, Melrose TD6 0DF / wabsmith@btinternet.com	01835 823375
Norman, Nancy M. (Miss) BA MDiv MTh	1988 2012	(Lyne and Manor)	25 March Street, Peebles EH45 8EP / nancy.norman1@googlemail.com	01721 721699
Rennie, John D. MA	1962 1996	(Broughton, Glenholm and Kilbucho with Skirling with Stobo and Drumelzier with Tweedsmuir)	29/1 Rosetta Road, Peebles EH45 8HJ / tworennies@btinternet.com	01721 720963
Riddell, John A. MA BD	1967 2006	(Jedburgh: Trinity)	Orchid Cottage, Gingham Row, Earlston TD4 6ET	01896 848784
Shand, George C. MA BD	1981 2021	(Cairngryffe with Libberton and Quothquan with Symington)	15 Kittlegairy Place, Peebles EH45 9LW / George.Shand@churchofscotland.org.uk	07765 987163
Sinclair, Colin A.M. BA BD	1981 2022	(Edinburgh: Palmerston Place)	18 Dukehaugh, Peebles EH45 9DN / camsinclair90@gmail.com	07752 538954
Steele, Leslie M. MA BD	1973 2013	(Galashiels: Old Parish and St Paul's)	23 Mayburn Avenue, Loanhead EH20 9EY / lmslms@hotmail.com	
Steele, Margaret D.J. (Miss) BSc BD	2000 2022	(Ashkirk with Ettrick and Yarrow with Selkirk)	33 Anderson Drive, Perth PH1 1JX / MSteele@churchofscotland.org.uk	07801 365068
Wallace, James H. MA BD	1973 2011	(Peebles: St Andrew's Leckie)	52 Waverley Mills, Innerleithen EH44 6RH / jimwallace121@btinternet.com	01896 831637

(5) DUNS (F W)

Meets at 7pm on the first Tuesday of September and December 2022 in venues to be agreed. On 1 January 2023 it will unite with the Presbyteries of Lothian, Melrose and Peebles, and Jedburgh to form the Presbytery of Lothian and Borders. That new Presbytery will meet on 21 January 2023 at a venue to be determined and thereafter as decided.

Clerk:　　REV. H. DANE SHERRARD BD DMin　　Mount Pleasant Granary, Mount Pleasant Farm, Duns TD1 3HU　　01361 882254
duns@churchofscotland.org.uk　　07582 468468

Ayton (H) and District Churches (F)
Vacant
Session Clerk: Susan Patterson　　The Manse, Beanburn, Ayton, Eyemouth TD14 5QY　　01890 781333
aspatterson1960@gmail.com　　01289 386394

Berwick-upon-Tweed: St Andrew's Wallace Green (H) and Lowick (F W)
Adam J.J. Hood MA BD DPhil　　1989　2012　　3 Meadow Grange, Berwick-upon-Tweed TD15 1NW　　01289 332787
AHood@churchofscotland.org.uk

Chirnside (F) linked with Hutton and Fishwick and Paxton
Michael A. Taylor DipTh MPhil　　2006　2018　　The New Manse, The Glebe, Chirnside, Duns TD11 3XE　　01890 819947
MTaylor@churchofscotland.org.uk　　07479 985075

Coldingham and St Abbs (F W) linked with Eyemouth (F W)
Andrew N. Haddow BEng BD　　2012　　The Manse, Victoria Road, Eyemouth TD14 5JD　　01890 750327
AHaddow@churchofscotland.org.uk

Coldstream and District Parishes (H W) linked with Eccles and Leitholm
David J. Taverner MCIBS ACIS BD　　1996　2011　　36 Bennecourt Drive, Coldstream TD12 4BY　　01890 883887
DTaverner@churchofscotland.org.uk

Duns and District Parishes (F W)
Andrew J. Robertson BD　　2008　2019　　The Manse, Castle Street, Duns TD11 3DG　　01361 884502
ARobertson@churchofscotland.org.uk　　01361 883496

Eccles and Leitholm　See Coldstream
Eyemouth　See Coldingham and St Abbs

Fogo (F W)
H. Dane Sherrard BD DMin　　1971　2019　　Mount Pleasant Granary, Mount Pleasant Farm, Duns TD11 3HU　　01361 882254
(Non-Stipendiary)　　dane@mountpleasantgranary.net　　07582 468468

Gordon: St Michael's (F)
Guardianship of the Presbytery
Interim Moderator: Veronica Walker
walkerkenneth49@gmail.com — 01890 817102

Greenlaw (H)
Susan M. Brown (Mrs) BD DipMin DUniv   1985   2021   The Manse, Todholes, Greenlaw, Duns TD10 6XD   Susan.Brown@churchofscotland.org.uk — 07747 825755

Hutton and Fishwick and Paxton See Chirnside

Legerwood
Guardianship of the Presbytery
Interim Moderator: Kenneth D.F. Walker
walkerkenneth49@gmail.com — 01890 817102

C. Retaining

Name			Position	Address / Email	Phone
Brown, Derek G. BD DipMin DMin	1989	2021	(Lead Chaplain: NHS Highland)	The Manse, Todholes, Greenlaw, Duns TD10 6XD kerednodrog@outlook.com	01361 810316
Cartwright, Alan C.D. BSc BD	1976	2016	(Fogo and Swinton with Ladykirk and Whitsome with Leitholm)	Drumgray, Edrom, Duns TD11 3PX alan@cartwright-family.org.uk	01890 819191
Duncan, Rosslyn P. BD MTh	2007	2018	(Stonehaven: Dunnottar with Stonehaven: South)	Four Oaks, Broomdykes, Duns TD1 3LZ rosslynpduncan@gmail.com	07899 878427
Gaddes, Donald R.	1961	1994	(Kelso: North and Ednam)	2 Teindhill Green, Duns TD11 3DX drgaddes@btinternet.com	01361 883172
Hope, Geraldine H. (Mrs) MA BD	1986	2007	(Foulden and Mordington with Hutton and Fishwick and Paxton)	4 Well Court, Chirnside, Duns TD11 3UD geraldine.hope@virgin.net	01890 818134
Landale, William S.	2005	2016	(Auxiliary Minister)	Green Hope Guest House, Ellemford, Duns TD11 3SG WLandale@churchofscotland.org.uk	01361 890242
Neill, Bruce F. MA BD	1966	2007	(Maxton and Mertoun with Newtown with St Boswells)	18 Brierydean, St Abbs, Eyemouth TD14 5PQ bneill@phonecoop.coop	01890 771569
Paterson, William BD	1977	2001	(Bonkyl and Preston with Chirnside with Edrom Allanton)	Benachie, Gavinton, Duns TD11 3QT billdm.paterson@btinternet.com	01361 882727
Shields, John M. MBE LTh	1972	2007	(Channelkirk and Lauder)	12 Eden Park, Ednam, Kelso TD5 7RG john.shields118@btinternet.com	01573 229015
Walker, Kenneth D.F. MA BD PhD	1976	2008	(Athelstaneford with Whitekirk and Tyninghame)	Allanbank Kothi, Allanton, Duns TD11 3PY walkerkenneth49@gmail.com	01890 817102
Walker, Veronica (Mrs) BSc BD			(Licentiate)	Allanbank Kothi, Allanton, Duns TD11 3PY walkerkenneth49@gmail.com	01890 817102
Whyte, Norman R. BD MTh DipMin	1982	2022	(Ayton and District Churches)	34 Hollywood, Largs, KA30 8SP burraman@msn.co	07387 229806

(6) JEDBURGH

Meets at Denholm Church on the first Wednesday of October, November and December 2022. On 1 January 2023 it will unite with the Presbyteries of Lothian, Melrose and Peebles, and Duns to form the Presbytery of Lothian and Borders. That new Presbytery will meet on 21 January 2023 at a venue to be determined and thereafter as decided.

Clerk	REV. LISA-JANE RANKIN BD CPS	4 Wilton Hill Terrace, Hawick TD9 8BE 01450 370744
		jedburgh@churchofscotland.org.uk

Ale and Teviot United (F H W)
Vacant
Session Clerk: John Rogerson

22 The Glebe, Ancrum, Jedburgh TD8 6UX   01835 830318
B166ESS@yahoo.co.uk   07813 367533

Cavers and Kirkton (W) linked with Hawick: Trinity (H W)
Vacant
Session Clerk, Cavers and Kirkton: Jane Cox (Mrs)
Session Clerk, Hawick: Trinity: Muriel S. Bowie (Mrs)

trinityhawick@outlook.com   01450 378248
Trinity Manse, Howdenburn, Hawick TD9 8PH   01450 379171
jane.cox2401@btinternet.com   01450 372195
murielbowie80@outlook.com   07790 689997

Cheviot Churches (H W)
Colin D. Johnston MA BD   1986   2019

Cheviot Manse, Main Street, Morebattle, Kelso TD5 8QG   01573 440539
CDJohnston@churchofscotland.org.uk

Hawick: Burnfoot (F T W)
Vacant
Session Clerk: Scott Elliot

29 Wilton Hill, Hawick TD9 8BA   01450 373181
scott194elliot@btinternet.com   01450 375046

Hawick: St Mary's and Old (F H W) linked with Hawick: Teviot (H) and Roberton (F W)   info@smop-tero.org
Alistair W. Cook BSc CA BD   2008   2017   4 Heronhill Close, Hawick TD9 9RA   01450 378175
ACook@churchofscotland.org.uk   07802 616352

Hawick: Teviot and Roberton See Hawick: St Mary's and Old
Hawick: Trinity See Cavers and Kirkton

Hawick: Wilton linked with Teviothead
Lisa-Jane Rankin BD CPS — 2003 — 4 Wilton Hill Terrace, Hawick TD9 8BE / LRankin@churchofscotland.org.uk — 01450 370744

Hobkirk and Southdean (F W) linked with Ruberslaw (F W)
Rachel Wilson BA MTh — 2018 — The Manse, Leydens Road, Denholm, Hawick TD9 8NB / RWilson@churchofscotland.org.uk — 01450 870874

Jedburgh: Old and Trinity (F W)
Stewart M. McPherson BD CertMin (Interim Minister) — 1991 2020 — The Manse, Honeyfield Drive, Jedburgh TD8 6LQ / SMcPherson@churchofscotland.org.uk — 01835 863417 / 07814 901429

Kelso Country Churches (W)
Stephen Manners MA BD — 1989 2019 — 1 The Meadow, Stichill TD5 7TG / SManners@churchofscotland.org.uk — 01573 470663

Kelso: North (H) and Ednam (F H W)
Anna S. Rodwell BD DipMin — 1998 2016 — **office@kelsonorthandednam.org.uk** / The Manse, 20 Forestfield, Kelso TD5 7BX / ARodwell@churchofscotland.org.uk — **01573 224154** / 01573 224248 / 07508 810237

Kelso: Old and Sprouston (F)
Vacant
Session Clerk: Frances Gordon — The Manse, Glebe Lane, Kelso TD5 7AU / francesgordon38@btinternet.com — 01573 348749 / 07966 435484

Oxnam
Guardianship of the Presbytery
Session Clerk: Morag McKeand (Mrs) — mh.mckeand@gmail.com — 01835 840284

Ruberslaw See Hobkirk and Southdean
Teviothead See Hawick: Wilton

C. Retaining
Combe, Neil R. BSc MSc BD — 1984 2015 — (Hawick: St Mary's and Old with Hawick: Teviot and Roberton) — 2 Abbotsview Gardens, Galashiels TD1 3ER / neil.combe@btinternet.com — 01896 755869

Stewart, Una B. (Ms) BD DipEd — 1995 2014 — (Law) — 10 Inch Park, Kelso TD5 7BQ / rev.ubs@virgin.net — 01573 219231

HAWICK ADDRESSES

Burnfoot	Fraser Avenue
St Mary's and Old	Kirk Wynd
Teviot	St George's Lane
Trinity	Central Square
Wilton	Princes Street

(7) SOUTH WEST (W)

New presbytery formed by the union of the Presbyteries of Annandale and Eskdale, Ardrossan, Ayr, Dumfries and Kirkcudbright, Irvine and Kilmarnock, and Wigtown and Stranraer on 30 September 2022. It will meet on dates and at venues to be determined.

Clerk: Vacant   southwest@churchofscotland.org.uk

1 Alloway (F H W)
Neil A. McNaught BD MA   1987   1999
secretary.allowaypc@gmail.com   **01292 442083**
1A Parkview, Alloway, Ayr KA7 4QG   01292 441252
NMcNaught@churchofscotland.org.uk

David Hume MSc PhD CertHE   2020
(Ordained Local Minister)
8 Finlaggan Place, Kilmarnock KA3 1UY   07858 966367
DHume@churchofscotland.org.uk

2 Annan: Old (F H W) linked with Dornock (F)
David Whiteman BD   1998   2018
12 Plumdon Park Avenue, Annan DG12 6EY   01461 392048
DWhiteman@churchofscotland.org.uk

3 Annan: St Andrew's (H W) linked with Brydekirk (W)
John G. Pickles BD MTh MSc   2011
1 Annerley Road, Annan DG12 6HE   01461 202626
JPickles@churchofscotland.org.uk

4 Annbank (H W) linked with Tarbolton (F W)
Mandy R. H. Ralph RGN CertCS BTh   2013   2019
The Manse, Tarbolton, Mauchline KA5 5QJ   01292 541452
MRalph@churchofscotland.org.uk

5 Applegarth, Sibbaldbie (H) and Johnstone (F) linked with Lochmaben (H W)
Vacant
Interim Moderator: David Whiteman
The Manse, Barrashead, Lochmaben, Lockerbie DG11 1QF   01387 810640
DWhiteman@churchofscotland.org.uk   01461 392048

6 Ardrossan: Park (W)
Vacant
Session Clerk: Moira Crocker (Mrs)   **01294 463711**
35 Ardneil Court, Ardrossan KA22 7NQ   01294 468683
moirafcrocker@yahoo.co.uk

7 Ardrossan and Saltcoats: Kirkgate (F H W)
T. Nigel Chikanya BTh BA MTh   2014   2020
10 Seafield Drive, Ardrossan KA22 8NU   **01294 472001**
NChikanya@churchofscotland.org.uk   07566 278132

#	Charge / Minister	Ordained	Inducted	Address / Email	Telephone
8	**Arnsheen Barrhill and Colmonell: St Colmon (W) linked with Ballantrae (H W)**			The Manse, 1 The Vennel, Ballantrae, Girvan KA26 0NH	01465 831252
	Theodore L. Corney BA MTh GDipTh	2006	2019	TCorney@churchofscotland.org.uk	
9	**Auchinleck (F H) linked with Catrine (F)**			28 Mauchline Road, Auchinleck KA18 2BN	01290 424776
	Stephen F. Clipston MA BD	1982	2006	SClipston@churchofscotland.org.uk	
10	**Ayr: Auld Kirk of Ayr (St John the Baptist) (H L W)**			**auldkirkayr@hotmail.co.uk**	**01292 262938**
	David R. Gemmell MA BD	1991	1999	20 Seafield Drive, Ayr KA7 4BQ	01292 864140
				DGemmell@churchofscotland.org.uk	
11	**Ayr: Castlehill (F H W)**			**castlehillchurch44@gmail.com**	**01292 267520**
	Paul R. Russell MA BD	1984	2019	3 Old Hillfoot Road, Ayr KA7 3LW	01292 261464
				PRussell@churchofscotland.org.uk	
12	**Ayr: Newton Wallacetown (F H W)**			9 Nursery Grove, Ayr KA7 3PH	**01292 611371**
	Vacant			revronyoung@hotmail.com	01292 264251
	Interim Moderator: Rona M. Young				01292 471982
13	**Ayr: St Andrew's (F H W)**			**ayrstandrews@gmail.com**	01292 268164
	Stanley Okeke BA BD MSc	2012	2020	17 Whiteford View, Ayr KA7 3LL	
				SOkeke@churchofscotland.org.uk	
14	**Ayr: St Columba (F H W)**			**irene@ayrstcolumba.co.uk**	**01292 265794**
	Scott S. McKenna BA BD MTh MPhil PhD	1994	2019	3 Upper Crofts, Alloway, Ayr KA7 4QX	01292 226075
				SMcKenna@churchofscotland.org.uk	
15	**Ayr: St James' (F H W)**			**admin@stjamesayr.plus.com**	**01292 266993**
	Barbara V. Suchanek-Seitz CertMin DTh	2016		1 Prestwick Road, Ayr KA8 8LD	01292 262420
				BSuchanek-Seitz@churchofscotland.org.uk	
16	**Ayr: St Leonard's (F H W) linked with Dalrymple (F)**			**st_leonards@btinternet.com**	**01292 611117**
	Brian R. Hendrie BD CertMin	1992	2015	35 Roman Road, Ayr KA7 3SZ	01292 283825
				BHendrie@churchofscotland.org.uk	

17 Ayr: St Quivox (F H W)
John McCutcheon BA BD(Min)   2014   2019   11 Springfield Avenue, Prestwick KA9 2HA
JMcCutcheon@churchofscotland.org.uk   01292 861641

18 Ayrshire Mission to the Deaf
Richard C. Durno DipSW CQSW   1989   2013   31 Springfield Road, Bishopbriggs,
Glasgow G64 1PJ   (Voice/Text/Fax) 0141 772 1052
richard.durno@btinternet.com   (Voice/Text/Voicemail) 07748 607721

19 Ballantrae See Arnsheen Barrhill and Colmonell: St Colmon

20 Balmaclellan, Kells (H) and Dalry (H) linked with Carsphairn (H)
Vacant   The Manse, Dalry, Castle Douglas DG7 3PJ   01644 430380

21 Barr (F) linked with Dailly (F W) linked with Girvan: South (F)
Vacant   30 Henrietta Street, Girvan KA26 9AL   01465 713370
Interim Moderator: Theodore L. Corney   TCorney@churchofscotland.org.uk   01465 831252

22 Beith (F H W)   beithchurch@btinternet.com   **01505 502686**
Roderick I.T. MacDonald BD CertMin   1992   2005   2 Glebe Court, Beith KA15 1ET   01505 503858
RMacDonald@churchofscotland.org.uk
Fiona Blair DCS   1994   2015   9 Powgree Crescent, Beith KA15 1ES   07368 696550
FBlair@churchofscotland.org.uk

23 Bengairn Parishes (W) linked with Castle Douglas (H W)
Alison H. Burnside (Mrs) MA BD   1990   2018   1 Castle View, Castle Douglas DG7 1BG   01556 505983
ABurnside@churchofscotland.org.uk

24 Border Kirk (F W)   Chapel Street, Carlisle CA1 1JA   **01228 591757**
Wesley C. Brandon BA MDiv   2003   2022   95 Pinecroft, Carlisle CA3 0DB   01228 599572
WBrandon@churchofscotland.org.uk

25 Brodick (W) linked with Corrie linked with Lochranza and Pirnmill (W) linked with Shiskine (F H W)
brodickchurch@gmail.com;
info@lochranzachurch.org.uk; stmolios@gmail.com
Vacant   4 Manse Crescent, Brodick, Isle of Arran KA27 8AS   01770 860498
Session Clerk, Brodick: Shona Hume (Mrs)   shonah14@yahoo.co.uk
Session Clerk, Corrie: Anne Pringle (Mrs)   anne.m.pringle@btinternet.com
Session Clerk, Lochranza and Pirnmill: Bill Scott   bill.ormsay@btinternet.com
Session Clerk, Shiskine: John Kerr   kerrjh@btinternet.com

26 Brydekirk See Annan: St Andrew's

27 Caerlaverock (F) linked with Dumfries: St Mary's-Greyfriars' (F H W)
Vacant
Session Clerk, Caerlaverock: Sheila Wilson
Interim Moderator: Fiona A. Wilson
4 Georgetown Crescent, Dumfries DG1 4EQ
wilson.glencaple@btopenworld.com
FWilson@churchofscotland.org.uk
01387 270128
01387 770327
01556 610708

28 Caldwell (F W) linked with Dunlop (W)
Alison J.S. McBrier MA BD   2011   2017
4 Dampark, Dunlop, Kilmarnock KA3 4BZ
AMcBrier@churchofscotland.org.uk
01560 673686

29 Canonbie United (F H W) linked with Liddesdale (F H W)
Morag Crossan BA   2016   2020
churchoffice@liddesdalechurch.org.uk
23 Langholm Street, Newcastleton TD9 0QX
MCrossan@churchofscotland.org.uk
Liddesdale: 01387 375488
01387 375603
07861 736071

Canonbie United is a Local Ecumenical Partnership with the United Free Church

30 Carsphairn See Balmaclellan, Kells and Dalry
31 Castle Douglas See Bengairn Parishes
32 Catrine See Auchinleck

33 Closeburn linked with Kirkmahoe
Vacant
Session Clerk, Closeburn: Jack Tait
Session Clerk, Kirkmahoe: Bob McBride
The Manse, Kirkmahoe, Dumfries DG1 1ST
jacktait1941@gmail.com
rjmcbride91@hotmail.com
01387 710572
01848 331700
07717 247092

34 Colvend, Southwick and Kirkbean (W)
John A.H. Murdoch BA BD DPSS   1979   2022
The Manse, Colvend, Dalbeattie DG5 4QN
JMurdoch@churchofscotland.org.uk
01556 630255
07578 558978

35 Corrie See Brodick

36 Corsock and Kirkpatrick Durham (W) linked with Crossmichael, Parton and Balmaghie (W)
Vacant
Session Clerk, Corsock and Kirkpatrick Durham: Mary Burney
Session Clerk, Crossmichael, Parton and Balmaghie: Anne Carstairs
Knockdrocket, Clarebrand, Castle Douglas DG7 3AH
maryburney1@btinternet.com
annecarstairs@gmail.com
01556 503645
01556 650503
01556 670279

37 Coylton (F W) linked with Drongan: The Schaw Kirk (W)
Alwyn Landman BTh MDiv MTh DMin   2005   2019
4 Hamilton Place, Coylton, Ayr KA6 6JQ
ALandman@churchofscotland.org.uk
01292 571287

38 Craigie Symington (W) linked with Prestwick South (H W)
Kenneth C. Elliott BD BA Cert Min   1989
office.pwksouth@gmail.com
68 St Quivox Road, Prestwick KA9 1JF
KElliott@churchofscotland.org.uk
01292 678556
01292 478788

Tom McLeod   2014   2015
(Ordained Local Minister)
3 Martnaham Drive, Coylton KA6 6JE
TMcleod@churchofscotland.org.uk
01292 570100

39 Crosshill (H) linked with Maybole (F W)
Vacant
Interim Moderator: Paul R. Russell
74A Culzean Road, Maybole KA19 8AH
PRussell@churchofscotland.org.uk
01655 889454
01292 261464

40 Crosshouse (F H W)
Vacant
Interim Moderator: John A. Urquhart
John.Urquhart@churchofscotland.org.uk
01563 538289

41 Crossmichael, Parton and Balmaghie See Corsock and Kirkpatrick Durham

42 Cumbrae (F W) linked with Largs: St John's (F H W)
Vacant
Session Clerk, Cumbrae: Eleanor Browne (Mrs)
Session Clerk, Largs: St John's: Jim Welch
1 Newhaven Grove, Largs KA30 8NS
langeron@btinternet.com
jimwelch@ssky.com
Cumbrae: **01475 674468**
01475 329933
Cumbrae: **01475 531198** St John's: **01475 531198**

43 Cummertrees, Mouswald and Ruthwell (h W)
Vacant
Interim Moderator: Alison H. Burnside
The Manse, Ruthwell, Dumfries DG1 4NP
ABurnside@churchofscotland.org.uk
01387 870217
01556 505983

44 Dailly See Barr

45 Dalbeattie and Kirkgunzeon (F H W) linked with Urr (H W)
Fiona A. Wilson (Mrs) BD   2008   2014
36 Mill Street, Dalbeattie DG5 4HE
FWilson@churchofscotland.org.uk
01556 610708

46 Dalmellington (F) linked with Patna Waterside (F)
Vacant
Interim Moderator: Allan S. Vint
4 Carsphairn Road, Dalmellington, Ayr KA6 7RE
AVint@churchofscotland.org.uk
01292 551503
01290 518528

No.	Charge / Minister			Address / Email	Tel
47	**Dalry: St Margaret's (F W)** David A. Albon BA MCS	1991	2019	**stmargaret@talktalk.net** 33 Templand Crescent, Dalry KA24 5EZ DAlbon@churchofscotland.org.uk	**01294 832264** 01294 832747
48	**Dalry: Trinity (F H W)** Martin Thomson BSc DipEd BD	1988	2004	Trinity Manse, West Kilbride Road, Dalry KA24 5DX MThomson@churchofscotland.org.uk	01294 832363
49	**Dalrymple** See Ayr: St Leonard's				
50	**Dalton and Hightae (F) linked with St Mungo (F)** Vacant Session Clerk, Dalton: Isobel Tinning (Mrs) Session Clerk, St Mungo: Annie Hutchon (Mrs)			The Manse, Hightae, Lockerbie DG11 1JL isobel.tinning@gmail.com anniehutchon45@gmail.com	01387 811499 01387 269133 01576 510280
51	**Darvel (F W)** Vacant Session Clerk: John Grier Interim Moderator: Margaret A. Hamilton (Mrs)			46 West Main Street, Darvel KA17 0AQ johngrier46@btinternet.com mahamilton1@outlook.com	**01560 322924** 01560 322924 01560 321355 01563 534431
52	**Dornock** See Annan: Old				
53	**Dreghorn and Springside (T W)** Jamie W. Milliken BD PGCertADS	2005	2020	7 Sycamore Wynd, Perceton, Irvine KA11 2FA JMilliken@churchofscotland.org.uk	01294 211893
54	**Drongan: The Schaw Kirk** See Coylton				
55	**Dumfries: Maxwelltown West (H W)** Johannes Wildner MTh	2006	2021	Maxwelltown West Manse, 11 Laurieknowe, Dumfries DG2 7AH JWildner@churchofscotland.org.uk	**01387 255900** 01387 257238
56	**Dumfries: Northwest (F T)** Vacant Session Clerk: Clara Jackson			c/o Church Office, Dumfries Northwest Church, Lochside Road, Dumfries DG2 0DZ sessionclerk.dumfriesnorthwest@gmail.com	01387 249964 01387 249964

57 Dumfries: St George's (F H W)
Donald Campbell BD   1997
office@saint-georges.org.uk
9 Nunholm Park, Dumfries DG1 1JP
DCampbell@churchofscotland.org.uk
01387 **267072**
01387 252965

58 Dumfries: St Mary's-Greyfriars' See Caerlaverock

59 Dumfries: St Michael's and South (W)
Vacant
Session Clerk: Esther Preston
39 Cardoness Street, Dumfries DG1 3AL
prestoncraigavon@supanet.com
01387 253849
01387 263402

60 Dumfries: Troqueer (F H W)
John R. Notman BSc BD   1990   2015
secretary@troqueerparishchurch.com
Troqueer Manse, Troqueer Road, Dumfries DG2 7DF
JNotman@churchofscotland.org.uk
01387 253043

61 Dundonald (H W)
Lynsey J. Brennan BScN MSc BA   2019
64 Main Street, Dundonald, Kilmarnock KA2 9HG
LBrennan@churchofscotland.org.uk
01563 850243

62 Dunlop See Caldwell

63 Dunscore (F W) linked with Glencairn and Moniaive (F W)
Mark R.S. Smith BSc CertMin   1990   2020
The Manse, Wallaceton, Auldgirth, Dumfries DG2 0TJ
Mark.Smith@churchofscotland.org.uk
01387 820245

64 Durisdeer linked with Penpont, Keir and Tynron linked with Thornhill (H)
Vacant
Interim Moderator: David Gibson (Mr)
The Manse, Manse Park, Thornhill DG3 5ER
gibson186@btinternet.com
01848 331191
01387 250318

65 Ervie Kirkcolm (H W) linked with Leswalt (W)
Guardianship of the Presbytery
Session Clerk, Ervie Kirkcolm:
  Jennifer Comery (Mrs)
Session Clerk, Leswalt: Fiona McColm (Mrs)
Skellies Knowe West, Leswalt, Stranraer DH9 0RY

sessionclerk@leswaltparishchurch.org.uk
01776 854277

01776 870555

66 Fairlie (F H W) linked with Largs: St Columba's (F W)
Graham McWilliams BSc BD DMin   2005   2019
secretary@largscolumba.org
14 Fairlieburne Gardens, Fairlie, Largs KA29 0ER
GMcWilliams@churchofscotland.org.uk
01475 **686212**
01475 568515

No.	Congregation / Name		Address / Email	Telephone
67	**Fenwick (F H W)** Vacant			
	Interim Moderator: Kim Watt		KWatt@churchofscotland.org.uk	07881 680982
68	**Fisherton (H) linked with Kirkoswald (H W)** Vacant			
	Session Clerk, Fisherton: Elspeth Carter (Mrs)		The Manse, Kirkoswald, Maybole KA19 8HZ elspeth@kinmount222.plus.com	01655 760532 01292 443954
	Session Clerk, Kirkoswald: Elizabeth Veitch (Mrs)		eveitch@btinternet.com	01465 714966
69	**Galston (F H W)** Kristina I. Hine BS MDiv	2011 2016	19 Manse Gardens, Galston KA4 8DJ KHine@churchofscotland.org.uk	**01563 820136** 01563 257172
70	**Gatehouse and Borgue linked with Tarff and Twynholm** Valerie J. Ott (Mrs) BA BD DipARSM	2002	The Manse, Planetree Park, Gatehouse of Fleet, Castle Douglas DG7 2EQ VOtt@churchofscotland.org.uk	01557 814233
71	**Girvan: North (F H W)** Vacant		**churchoffice12@btconnect.com** 38 The Avenue, Girvan KA26 9DS	**01465 712672** 01465 713203
	Interim Moderator: James Anderson (Dr)		jc.anderson2@talktalk.net	01465 710059
72	**Girvan: South** See Barr			
73	**Glasserton and Isle of Whithorn linked with Whithorn: St Ninian's Priory (F W)**			
	Alexander I. Currie BD CPS	1990	The Manse, St Ninian's Grove, Whithorn, Newton Stewart DG8 8PT 01988 500267 ACurrie@churchofscotland.org.uk	
74	**Glencairn and Moniaive** See Dunscore			
75	**Gretna: Old (H), Gretna: St Andrew's (H), Half Morton and Kirkpatrick Fleming (F)**			
	Eleanor J. McMahon BEd BD (Interim Minister)	1994 2020	81 Moorpark Square, Renfrew PA4 8DB EMcMahon@churchofscotland.org.uk	07974 116539
76	**Hoddom, Kirtle-Eaglesfield and Middlebie (F W)** Vacant			
	Session Clerk: John Bicket		The Manse, Main Road, Ecclefechan, Lockerbie DG11 3BU johnbicket44@gmail.com	01576 300108 07517 169847

77 Hurlford (F H W)
Vacant
Session Clerk: Elizabeth F.G. Lauchlan
Interim Moderator: Colin G.F. Brockie

12 Main Road, Crookedholm, Kilmarnock KA3 6JT
elizabeth.lauchlan@btinternet.com
revcolin@uwclub.net

01563 539739
01563 537381
01563 559960

78 Inch linked with Luce Valley (F W)
Stephen Ogston MPhys MSc BD   2009   2017

Ladyburn Manse, Main Street, Glenluce, Newton Stewart DG8 0PU
SOgston@churchofscotland.org.uk

01581 300316

79 Irongray, Lochrutton and Terregles
Gary J. Peacock MA BD MTh   2015

The Manse, Shawhead, Dumfries DG2 9SJ
GPeacock@churchofscotland.org.uk

01387 730759

80 Irvine: Fullarton (F H T W)
Neil Urquhart BD DipMin DipSC   1989

secretary@fullartonchurch.co.uk
48 Waterside, Irvine KA12 8QJ
NUrquhart@churchofscotland.org.uk

01294 273741
01294 279909

81 Irvine: Girdle Toll (F H) linked with Irvine: St Andrew's (F H)
Vacant
Interim Moderator: Barbara Urquhart (Mrs)

barbaraurquhart1@gmail.com

01294 276051

01563 538289

82 Irvine: Mure Relief (F H)
Vacant
Interim Moderator: Jamie W. Milliken

9 West Road, Irvine KA12 8RE
JMilliken@churchofscotland.org.uk

01294 279916
01294 211893

83 Irvine: Old (F H)
Vacant
Interim Moderator: Alexander C. Wark

22 Kirk Vennel, Irvine KA12 0DQ
alecwark@yahoo.co.uk

01294 273503
01294 279265
01563 559581

84 Irvine: St Andrew's See Irvine: Girdle Toll

85 Kilbirnie: Auld Kirk (F H W)
Vacant
Session Clerk: Archie Currie

49 Holmhead, Kilbirnie KA25 6BS
archiecurrie@yahoo.co.uk

01505 682342
01505 681474

86 Kilbirnie: St Columba's (H W)
Fiona C. Ross (Miss) BD DipMin   1996   2004

Manse of St Columba's, Dipple Road, Kilbirnie KA25 7JU
FRoss@churchofscotland.org.uk

01505 685239
01505 683342

87 Kilmarnock: Kay Park (F H W)
Fiona E. Maxwell BA BD   2004   2018
chrchdmnstr@outlook.com
1 Glebe Court, Kilmarnock KA1 3BD
FMaxwell@churchofscotland.org.uk
01563 574106
01563 521762

88 Kilmarnock: New Laigh Kirk (F H W)
David S. Cameron BD   2001
newlaighkirkchurch@hotmail.com
1 Holmes Farm Road, Kilmarnock KA1 1TP
David.Cameron@churchofscotland.org.uk
01563 573307
01563 525416

89 Kilmarnock: St John's Onthank (F H W)
Vacant
Interim Moderator: Fiona E. Maxwell
84 Wardneuk Drive, Kilmarnock KA3 2EX
FMaxwell@churchofscotland.org.uk
07716 162380
01563 521762

90 Kilmarnock: St Kentigern's (F W)
Vacant
Interim Moderator: George K. Lind
hub@stkentigern.org.uk
gklind@talktalk.net
01560 428732

91 Kilmarnock: St Marnock's (F W)
James McNaughtan BD DipMin   1983   1989
35 South Gargieston Drive, Kilmarnock KA1 1TB
JMcNaughtan@churchofscotland.org.uk
01563 521665

92 Kilmaurs: St Maur's Glencairn (H)
John A. Urquhart BD   1993
9 Standalane, Kilmaurs, Kilmarnock KA3 2NB
John.Urquhart@churchofscotland.org.uk
01563 538289

93 Kilmory (F W) linked with Lamlash (W)
Vacant
Session Clerk, Kilmory: Mairi Duff (Mrs)
Session Clerk, Lamlash: Lilias Nicholls (Mrs)
The Manse, Margnaheglish Road, Lamlash, Isle of Arran KA27 8LL
mairiduff@btinternet.com
lnicholls21@hotmail.com
01770 600074

94 Kilwinning: Abbey (F W)
Vacant
Isobel Beck BD DCS   2014   2016
Session Clerk: Fiona Silver (Mrs)
54 Dalry Road, Kilwinning KA13 7HE
16 Patrick Avenue, Stevenston KA20 4AW
lBeck@churchofscotland.org.uk
fionamfrew@aol.com
01294 552606
01294 552606
07919 193425
01294 556297

95 Kilwinning: Mansefield Trinity (F W)
Hilary J. Beresford BD PGCertCS   2000   2018
Mansefield Trinity Church, West Doura Way, Kilwinning KA13 6DY
HBeresford@churchofscotland.org.uk
01294 550746
01294 550746

96 Kirkconnel (H) linked with Sanquhar: St Bride's (F H W)
Vacant
Session Clerk, Kirkconnel: Fay Rafferty — fayrafferty1957@gmail.com — 01659 67650
Session Clerk, Sanquhar: Duncan Close — dunruth@btinternet.com — 01659 50596

97 Kirkcowan (H) linked with Wigtown (F H W)
Eric Boyle BA MTh   2006
Seaview Manse, Church Lane, Wigtown, Newton Stewart DG8 9HT — 01988 402314
EBoyle@churchofscotland.org.uk

98 Kirkcudbright (H W)
James F. Gatherer BD   1984   2020
church@kirkcudbrightparishchurch.org.uk — 01557 339108
6 Bourtree Avenue, Kirkcudbright DG6 4AU
JGatherer@churchofscotland.org.uk

99 Kirkinner linked with Mochrum linked with Sorbie (H)
Vacant
Session Clerk, Kirkinner: John W. MacDonald (Dr) — jwamacdonald1@gmail.com — 01988 402329
Session Clerk, Mochrum: Jenny Gray (Mrs) — j.saunders201@btinternet.com — 01988 700948
Session Clerk, Sorbie: Morag Donnan (Mrs) — morag.donnan1@btinternet.com — 01988 850288

100 Kirkmabreck (W) linked with Monigaff (H W)
Vacant
Session Clerk, Kirkmabreck: Robert McQuistan — mcquistan@mcquistan.plus.com — 01671 403361
— — 01671 820327
Session Clerk, Monigaff: Margaret McDowall (Mrs) — monigaffsessionclerk@gmail.com — 01671 403847
Monigaff Manse, Creebridge, Newton Stewart DG8 6NR

101 Kirkmahoe See Closeburn

102 Kirkmaiden (H)
Guardianship of the Presbytery
Session Clerk, Kirkmaiden: Maureen Graham (Mrs) — maureen.grahamm@btinternet.com — 01776 840209

103 Kirkmichael linked with Straiton: St Cuthbert's (W)
W. Gerald Jones MA BD ThM   1984   1985
The Manse, Patna Road, Kirkmichael, Maybole KA19 7PJ — 01655 750286
WJones@churchofscotland.org.uk

104 Kirkmichael, Tinwald and Torthorwald (W)
Vacant
Mhairi Wallace (Mrs)   2013   2017
(Ordained Local Minister)
Manse of Tinwald, 6 Sundew Lane, Dumfries DG1 3TW — 07701 375064
5 Dee Road, Kirkcudbright DG4 4HQ
MWallace@churchofscotland.org.uk

105 Kirkoswald See Fisherton

106 Kirkpatrick Juxta (F) linked with Moffat: St Andrew's (F H W) linked with Wamphray (F) standrewsmoffat@gmail.com
Elsie Macrae BA   2020
The Manse, 1 Meadow Bank, Moffat DG10 9LR
Elsie.Macrae@churchofscotland.org.uk   01683 225159

107 Lamlash See Kilmory

108 Langholm, Eskdalemuir, Ewes and Westerkirk (W) leewparishchurch@outlook.com
Robert G. D. W. Pickles BD MPhil PhD   1984   2019
The Manse, Thomas Telford Road, Langholm DG13 0BL
RPickles@churchofscotland.org.uk   01387 380252

109 Largs: Clark Memorial (H W)
T. David Watson BSc BD   1988   2014
31 Douglas Street, Largs KA30 8PT
DWatson@churchofscotland.org.uk   **01475 675186**
                                                          01475 672370

110 Largs: St Columba's See Fairlie
111 Largs: St John's See Cumbrae
112 Leswalt See Ervie Kirkcolm
113 Liddesdale See Canonbie United

114 Lochend and New Abbey
Vacant
New Abbey Manse, 32 Main Street, New Abbey, Dumfries DG2 8BY 01387 850490
Elizabeth A. Mack (Miss) DipPE   1994   2018
24 Roberts Crescent, Dumfries DG2 7RS   01387 264847
(Auxiliary Minster)
mackliz@btinternet.com

115 Lochmaben See Applegarth, Sibbaldbie and Johnstone
116 Lochranza and Pirnmill See Brodick

117 Lockerbie: Dryfesdale, Hutton and Corrie (F W)
Vacant
Dryfesdale Manse, 5 Carlisle Road, Lockerbie DG11 2DW   01576 204188
Interim Moderator: Wesley C. Brandon
WBrandon@churchofscotland.org.uk   01228 599572

118 Luce Valley See Inch

119 Lugar (W) linked with Old Cumnock: Old (H)
John W. Paterson BSc BD DipEd   1994
33 Barrhill Road, Cumnock KA18 1PJ
paterson-j6@sky.com   01290 420769

120 Mauchline (H W) linked with Sorn
Allan S. Vint BSc BD MTh PhD   1989   2021
mauchlineparish@yahoo.com
4 Westside Gardens, Mauchline KA5 5DJ   01290 518528
AVint@churchofscotland.org.uk   07795 483070

121 Maybole See Crosshill
122 Mochrum See Kirkinner
123 Moffat: St Andrew's See Kirkpatrick Juxta
124 Monigaff See Kirkmabreck

125 Monkton and Prestwick: North (F H T W)
Vacant   office@mpnchurch.org.uk   **01292 678810**
Interim Moderator: Brian R. Hendrie   40 Monkton Road, Prestwick KA9 1AR   01292 471379
    BHendrie@churchofscotland.org.uk   01292 283825

126 Muirkirk (H W) linked with Old Cumnock: Trinity (F W)
Vacant   46 Ayr Road, Cumnock KA18 1DW   01290 422145
Interim Moderator: Alwyn Landman   ALandman@churchofscotland.org.uk   01292 571287

127 New Cumnock (F H W)
Vacant   37 Castle, New Cumnock, Cumnock KA18 4AG   01290 338296
Interim Moderator: Kenneth B. Yorke   kenyorke@yahoo.com   01292 670476

128 Newmilns: Loudoun (F H T W)
Vacant   Loudoun Manse, 116A Loudoun Road, Newmilns KA16 9HH   01560 320174
Interim Moderator: Andrew R. Black   andrewblack@tiscali.co.uk   01294 673090

129 Ochiltree (W) linked with Stair (F W)
Vacant   10 Mauchline Road, Ochiltree KA18 2PZ   01290 700365
Interim Moderator: George R. Fiddes   grfiddes@outlook.com   01292 737512

130 Old Cumnock: Old See Lugar
131 Old Cumnock: Trinity See Muirkirk
132 Patna Waterside See Dalmellington

133 Penninghame (F H)
Edward D. Lyons BD MTh   2007
The Manse, 1A Corvisel Road, Newton Stewart DG8 6LW   01671 404425
ELyons@churchofscotland.org.uk

134 Penpont, Keir and Tynron See Durisdeer

135 Portpatrick linked with Stoneykirk
Vacant
Session Clerk, Portpatrick: D. Maxwell (Mr)
Session Clerk, Stoneykirk: Gillian Lynn (Mrs)

Church Road, Sandhead, Stranraer DG9 9JJ
maxwell@supanet.com
randglynn@btinternet.com

01776 830757
01776 704045
01776 860665

136 Prestwick: Kingcase (F H W)
Ian Wiseman BTh DipHSW   1993

office@kingcase.co.uk
15 Bellrock Avenue, Prestwick KA9 1SQ
IWiseman@churchofscotland.org.uk

01292 470755
01292 479571

137 Prestwick: St Nicholas' (H W)
Vacant
Interim Moderator: David R. Gemmell

office@stnicholasprestwick.org.uk
3 Bellevue Road, Prestwick KA9 1NW
DGemmell@churchofscotland.org.uk

01292 671547

01292 864140

138 Prestwick: South See Craigie Symington
139 St Mungo See Dalton and Hightae

140 Saltcoats: North (W)
Vacant
Session Clerk: Rosann McLean (Mrs)

25 Longfield Avenue, Saltcoats KA21 6DR

01294 464679
01294 604923
01294 467106

141 Saltcoats: St Cuthbert's (H W)
Sarah E.C. Nicol (Mrs) BSc BD MTh   1985   2018

10 Kennedy Road, Saltcoats KA21 5SF
SNicol@churchofscotland.org.uk

01294 605109

142 Sanquhar: St Bride's See Kirkconnel
143 Shiskine See Brodick
144 Sorbie See Kirkinner
145 Sorn See Mauchline
146 Stair See Ochiltree

147 Stevenston: Ardeer (F W) linked with Stevenston: Livingstone (F H W)
Vacant
Session Clerk, Livingstone: Alexander Hershaw

27 Cuninghame Drive, Stevenston KA20 4AB
gavsandor@aol.com

01294 608993
01294 466293

148 Stevenston: High (F H W)
M. Scott Cameron MA BD   2002

High Kirk Manse, Stevenston KA20 3DL
Scott.Cameron@churchofscotland.org.uk

01294 463356

149 Stevenston: Livingstone See Stevenston: Ardeer

150 Stewarton: John Knox (F T W)
Gavin A. Niven BSc MSc BD   2010
getconnected@johnknox.org.uk
27 Avenue Street, Stewarton, Kilmarnock KA3 5AP
GNiven@churchofscotland.org.uk
01560 **484560**
01560 482418

151 Stewarton: St Columba's (H W)
Vacant
Interim Moderator: T. Alan W. Garrity
1 Kirk Glebe, Stewarton, Kilmarnock KA3 5BJ
alangarrity@btinternet.com
01560 485113
01560 486879

152 Stoneykirk See Portpatrick
153 Straiton: St Cuthbert's See Kirkmichael

154 Stranraer (F H W)
Vacant
Session Clerks, Stranraer: Isobel Irving (Mrs)
  Louise McCandlish (Mrs)
Church Road, Sandhead, Stranraer DG9 9JJ
irvingisobel217@gmail.com
lmccandlish27@gmail.com
01776 830757
01776 820643
01776 704916

155 Tarbolton See Annbank
156 Tarff and Twynholm See Gatehouse and Borgue
157 Thornhill See Durisdeer

158 Troon: Old (F H W)
Vacant
Session Clerk: Andrew Fell (Mr)
office@troonold.org.uk
85 Bentinck Drive, Troon KA10 6HZ
sessionclerk@troonold.org.uk
01292 **313520**
01292 313644
01292 313520

159 Troon: Portland (F H W)
Vacant
Interim Moderator: Bill Duncan (Mr)
office@troonportlandchurch.org.uk
89 South Beach, Troon KA10 6EQ
bill.jan.duncan@gmail.com
01292 **317929**
01292 318929
01292 440560

160 Troon: St Meddan's (F H T W)
Vacant
Interim Moderator: James Hogg
stmeddanschurch@gmail.com
27 Bentinck Drive, Troon KA10 6HX
JHogg@churchofscotland.org.uk
01292 **317750**
07974 576295

161 Tundergarth
Guardianship of the Presbytery
Session Clerk: David Paterson
jilljoe@tiscali.co.uk
07982 037029

162 Urr See Dalbeattie and Kirkgunzeon

163 Wamphray See Kirkpatrick Juxta

164 West Kilbride (F H T W)
James J. McNay MA BD   2008   **office@westkilbrideparishchurch.org.uk**   **01294 829902**
The Manse, Goldenberry Avenue, West Kilbride KA23 9LJ   01294 823186
JMcNay@churchofscotland.org.uk

165 Whithorn: St Ninian's Priory See Glasserton and Isle of Whithorn

166 Whiting Bay and Kildonan
Vacant   The Manse, Whiting Bay, Brodick, Isle of Arran KA27 8RE   01770 700289
Session Clerk: Sharon MacLeod (Mrs)   macleodsharon@hotmail.com

167 Wigtown See Kirkcowan

B. In other appointments

Name		Appointment	Address	Tel
Bellis, Pamela A. BA DipTheol	2004	Ordained Local Minister	12 Woodlands Avenue, Kirkcudbright DG6 4BP PBellis@churchofscotland.org.uk	07751 379249
Blackshaw, Christopher J. BA(Theol) *Chris Blackshaw is a Methodist Minister*	2015 2017	Pioneer Minister, Farming Community	Ellwood Croft, Gamblesby, Penrith CA10 1HY CBlackshaw@churchofscotland.org.uk	07980 975062
Campbell, Neil G. BA BD	1988 2018	Chaplain, HM Prison Dumfries	12 Charles Street, Anman DG12 5AJ neil.campbell2@prisons.gov.scot	
Clancy, P. Jill (Mrs) BD DipMin	2000 2017	Chaplain, HM Prison Barlinnie	27 Cross Street, Galston KA4 8AA JClancy@churchofscotland.org.uk	07956 557087
Harvey, P. Ruth (Ms) MA BD	2007 2020	Leader, Iona Community	Croslands, Beacon Street, Penrith CA11 7TZ ruth@iona.org.uk	01768 840749 07403 638339
Hogg, James	2018	Ordained Local Minister	JHogg@churchofscotland.org.uk	07974 576295
Watt, Kim CertThS	2015	Ordained Local Minister, Presbytery	Reddans Park Gate, The Crescent, Stewarton, Kilmarnock KA3 5AY KWatt@churchofscotland.org.uk	01560 482267

C. Retaining

Name		Former charge	Address	Tel
Adamson, R. Angus BD	2006 2020	(Brodick with Corrie with Lochranza and Pirnmill with Shiskine)	Otterburn, Corriecravie, Isle of Arran KA27 8PD RAdamson@churchofscotland.org.uk	01770 870228
Aitken, Fraser R. GCSJ MA BD	1978 2019	(Ayr: St Columba)	Sandringham, 38 Coylebank, Prestwick KA9 2DH sandringham381@outlook.com	01292 225087
Anderson, Robert A. MA BD DPhil	1984 2017	(Blackburn and Seafield)	Aiona, 8 Old Auchans View, Dundonald KA2 9EX robertanderson307@btinternet.com	01563 850554 07484 206190

Name			Charge	Address	Tel.
Baker, Carolyn M. (Mrs) BD	1997	2008	(Ochiltree with Stair)	Clanary, 1 Maxwell Drive, Newton Stewart DG8 6EL; cncbaker@btinternet.com	01671 404292
Bartholomew, David S. BSc MSc PhD BD	1994	2022	(Balmaclellan, Kells and Dalry with Carsphairn)	Craigend Cottage, Broughton, Biggar ML12 6HH; dhbart99@gmail.com	
Becker, Allison E. BA MDiv	2015	2022	(Kilmarnock: St John's Onthank)	ABecker@churchofscotland.org.uk	0131 225 3393
Beveridge, S. Edwin P. BA	1959	2004	(Brydekirk with Hoddom)	19 Rothesay Terrace, Edinburgh EH3 7RY	
Birse, G. Stewart CA BD BSc	1980	2013	(Ayr: Newton Wallacetown)	9 Calvinston Road, Prestwick KA9 2EL; stewart.birse@gmail.com	01292 474556
Black, Andrew R. BD CertMin	1987	2018	(Irvine: Relief Bourtreehill)	4 Nursery Wynd, Kilwinning KA13 6ER; andrewblack@tiscali.co.uk	01294 673090
Bogle, Thomas C. BD CPS HDipRE	1983	2003	(Fisherton with Maybole: West)	38 McEwan Crescent, Mossblown, Ayr KA6 5DR	01292 521215
Bond, Maurice S. BA DipEd MTh PhD BSc(Eng) BD SOSc	1983	2019	(Dumfries: St Michael's and South)	15 Pleasance Avenue, Dumfries DG2 7JJ	
Brockie, Colin G.F.	1967	2007	(Kilmarnock: Grange)	36 Brachead Court, Kilmarnock KA3 7AB; colin@brockie.org.uk	01563 559960
Brown, H. Taylor BD CertMin FRAI	1997	2022	(Kilmarnock: St Marnock's)	HBrown@churchofscotland.org.uk	07596 111310
Brown, Jack M. BSc BD	1977	2012	(Applegarth, Sibbaldbie and Johnstone with Lochmaben)	69 Berelands Road, Prestwick KA9 1ER; jackmbrown47@gmail.com	01292 477151
Burgess, Paul C.J. MA	1970	2003	(World Mission Partner, Gujranwala Theological Seminary, Pakistan)	Springvale, Halket Road, Lugton, Kilmarnock KA4 3EE; paulandcathie@gmail.com	01505 850254
Burns, John H. BSc BD	1985	2019	(Inch with Portpatrick with Stranraer: Trinity)	The Cabin, Dundeugh, Dalry DG7 3SY	01644 460595
Cairns, Alexander B. MA	1957	2009	(Turin)	Beechwood, Main Street, Sandhead, Stranraer DG9 91G; dorothycairns@aol.com	01776 830389
Cant, Thomas M. MA BD	1964	2004	(Paisley: Laigh Kirk)	3 Meikle Cutstraw, Stewarton, Kilmarnock KA3 5HU; revtmcant@aol.com	01560 480566
Christie, Robert S. MA BD ThM	1964	2000	(Kilmarnock: West High)	24 Homeroyal House, 2 Chalmers Crescent, Edinburgh EH9 1TP	07549 988643
Crichton, James MA BD MTh	1969	2010	(Crosshill with Dalrymple)	60 Kyle Court, Ayr KA7 3AW; crichton.james@btinternet.com	
Cruickshank, Norman BA BD	1983	2006	(West Kilbride: Overton)	24D Faulds Wynd, Seamill, West Kilbride KA23 9FA	01294 822239
Cuthbert, Helen E. MA MSc BD	2009	2021	(New Cumnock)	63 Haining Avenue, Bellfield, Kilmarnock KA1 3QN; helenncuthbertk21@hotmail.co.uk	07941 027480
Davidson, Amelia (Mrs) BD	2004	2011	(Coatbridge: Calder)	11 St Mary's Place, Saltcoats KA21 5NY	
Dee, Oonagh	2014	2019	(Ordained Local Minister)	Kendoon, Merse Way, Kippford, Dalbeattie DG5 4LL; ODee@churchofscotland.org.uk	01556 620001
Dempster, Eric T. MBA	2016	2021	(Ordained Local Minister)	Annanside, Wamphray, Moffat DG10 9LZ	01576 470496
Dickie, Michael M. BSc	1955	1993	(Ayr: Castlehill)	8 Noltmire Road, Ayr KA8 9ES	01292 618512
Falconer, Alan D. MA BD DLitt DD	1972	2011	(Aberdeen: St Machar's Cathedral)	18 North Crescent Road, Ardrossan KA22 8NA; alanfalconer@gmx.com	07491 484800
Faris, Janice M. (Mrs) BSc BD	1991	2018	(Innerleithen, Traquair and Walkerburn)	Overdale Cottage, Grange Park Road, Orton Grange, Carlisle CA5 6LT; revjfaris@gmail.com	07427 371239
Fiddes, George R. BD	1979	2019	(Prestwick: St Nicholas')	4 St Cuthbert's Crescent, Prestwick KA9 2EG; grfiddes@outlook.com	01292 737512 / 07925 004062
Finch, Graham S. MA BD	1977	2015	(Cadder)	32a St Mary Street, Kirkcudbright DG6 4DN; gsf231@gmail.com	01557 620123

Name	Ord.	Ind.	(Charge/Designation)	Address / Email	Telephone
Finlay, William P. MA BD	1969	2000	(Glasgow: Townhead Blochairn)	High Corrie, Brodick, Isle of Arran KA27 8JB	01770 810689
Ford, Alan A. BD	1977	2013	(Glasgow: Springburn)	14 Corsankell Wynd, Saltcoats KA21 6HY alan.andy@btinternet.com	01294 465740
Garrity, T. Alan W. BSc BD MTh	1969	2008	(Bermuda: Christ Church, Warwick)	17 Solomon's View, Dunlop, Kilmarnock KA3 4ES alangarrity@btinternet.com	01560 486879
Geddes, Alexander J. MA BD	1960	1998	(Stewarton: St Columba's)	2 Gregory Street, Mauchline KA5 6BY sandy270736@gmail.com	01290 518597
Gibb, J. Daniel M. BA LTh	1994	2006	(Aberfoyle with Port of Menteith)	1 Beechfield, Newton Aycliffe DL5 7AX dannygibb@hotmail.co.uk	01560 483778
Gillon, C. Blair BD	1975	2007	(Glasgow: Ibrox)	East Muirshiel Farmhouse, Dunlop, Kilmarnock KA3 4EJ charlesgillon21@gmail.com	
Glencross, William M. LTh	1968	1999	(Bellshill: Macdonald Memorial)	1 Lochay Place, Troon KA10 7HH	01292 317097
Godfrey, Linda BSc BD	2012	2014	(Ayr: St Leonard's with Dalrymple)	9 Taybank Drive, Ayr KA7 4RL godfreykayak@aol.com	07825 663866
Guthrie, James A.	1969	2005	(Corsock and Kirkpatrick Durham with Crossmichael and Parton)	2 Barrhill Road, Pinwherry, Girvan KA26 0QE p.h.m.guthrie@btinternet.com	01465 841236
Hall, William M. BD	1972	2010	(Kilmarnock: Old High Kirk)	33 Cairns Terrace, Kilmarnock KA1 2JG revwillie@talktalk.net	01563 525080
Hammond, Richard J. BA BD	1993	2007	(Kirkmahoe)	3 Marchfield Mount, Marchfield, Dumfries DG1 1SE libby.hammond@virgin.net	07764 465783
Harper, David L. BSc BD	1972	2012	(Troon: St Meddan's)	19 Calder Avenue, Troon KA10 7JT d.l.harper@btinternet.com	01292 312626
Hewitt, William C. BD DipPS	1977	2017	(Presbytery Clerk: Glasgow)	60 Woodlands Grove, Kilmarnock KA3 1TZ WHewitt@churchofscotland.org.uk	01563 533312
Hogg, William T. MA BD	1979	2018	(Kirkconnel with Sanquhar: St Bride's)	30 Castle Street, Kirkcudbright DG6 4JD WHogg@churchofscotland.org.uk	07515 102776
Holland, William MA	1967	2009	(Lochend and New Abbey)	Ardshean, 55 Georgetown Road, Dumfries DG1 4DD billholland55@btinternet.com	01387 256131 07766 531732
Horsburgh, Gary E. BA	1977	2015	(Dreghorn and Springside)	1 Woodlands Grove, Kilmarnock KA3 1TY garyhorsburgh@hotmail.co.uk	01563 624508
Howie, Marion L.K. (Mrs) MA ARCS	1992	2019	(Auxiliary Minister)	51 High Road, Stevenston KA20 3DY MHowie@churchofscotland.org.uk	01294 466571
Huggett, Judith A. (Miss) BA BD	1990	2021	(Lead Chaplain, NHS Ayrshire and Arran)		
Hutcheson, Norman M. MA BD	1973	2013	(Dalbeattie with Urr)	66 Maxwell Park, Dalbeattie DG5 4LS norman.hutcheson@gmail.com	01556 610102
Irving, Douglas R. LLB BD WS	1984	2016	(Kirkcudbright)	17 Galla Crescent, Dalbeattie DG5 4JY douglas.irving@outlook.com	01556 610156
Jackson, Nancy M. CertThRS CertChS	2009	2015	(Auxiliary Minister)	35 Auchentrae Crescent, Ayr KA7 4BD nancyjaxon@btinternet.com	01292 262034
Jackson, William BD CertMin	1994	2020	(Airdrie: New Monkland with Greengairs)	15 Dalwhinnie Crescent, Kilmarnock KA3 1QS	
Keating, Glenda K. (Mrs) MTheol	1996	2015	(Craigie Symington)	8 Wardlaw Gardens, Irvine KA11 2EW kirkglen@btinternet.com	01294 218820

Name	Year	Year	Charge	Address / Email	Phone
Kelly, William W. BSc BD	1994	2014	(Dumfries: Troqueer)	8 Talia Drive, Stirling, WA 6021 Australia / wwkelly@yahoo.com	04 11 104890
Kyle, Caryl A.E. (Mrs) BD DipEd	2008	2021	(Holytown with New Stevenston: Wrangholm Kirk)	58 Kelvin Walk, Netherhall, Largs KA30 8SJ / caryl_kyle@hotmail.com	01475 310390
Lacy, David W. DL BA BD DLitt	1976	2017	(Kilmarnock: Kay Park)	4 Cairns Terrace, Kilmarnock KA1 2JG / DLacy@churchofscotland.org.uk	01563 624034 / 07974 760272
Lamarti, Samuel H. BD MTh PhD	1979	2006	(Stewarton: John Knox)	7 Dalwhinnie Crescent, Kilmarnock KA3 1QS / samlamar@pobroadband.co.uk	01563 529632
Lennox, Lawrie I. MA BD DipEd	1991	2006	(Cromar)	7 Carwinshoch View, Ayr KA7 4AY / lennox127@btinternet.com	01292 288658
Lind, George K. BD MCIBS	1998	2017	(Stewarton: St. Columba's)	Endrig, 98 Loudoun Road, Newmilns KA16 9HQ / gklind@talktalk.net	01560 428732
Lochrie, John S. BSc BD MTh PhD	1967	2008	(Arnsheen Barrhill and Colmonell: St Colmon)	Cosyglen, Kilkerran, Maybole KA19 8LS / revjslochrie@btinternet.com	01465 811262
Macintyre, Thomas MA BD	1972	2011	(Sandsting and Aithsting with Walls and Sandness)	the2macs.macintyre@btinternet.com	
Mackay, Marjory H. (Mrs) BD DipEd CCE	1998	2008	(Cumbrae)	4 Golf Road, Millport, Isle of Cumbrae KA28 0HB / marjory.mackay@gmail.com	01475 530388
MacKinnon, Ronald M. DCS	1996	2012	(Deacon)	32 Strathclyde House, Shore Road, Skelmorlie PA17 5AN / ronnie@ronniemac.plus.com	01475 521333 / 07594 427960
MacLeod, Ian LTh BA MTh PhD	1969	2006	(Brodick with Corrie)	Cromla Cottage, Corrie, Isle of Arran KA27 8JB / i.macleod829@btinternet.com	01770 810237
MacPherson, Gordon C. MA BD MTh	1963	1988	(Associate, Kilmarnock: Henderson)	6 Crosbie Place, Troon KA10 6EY / ggmacpherson@btinternet.com	01292 679146
Matthews, John C. OBE MA BD MTh	1992	2010	(Glasgow: Ruchill Kelvinside)	12 Arrol Drive, Ayr KA7 4AF / mejohnmatthews@gmail.com	01292 264382
Mayes, Robert BD CertMin	1982	2017	(Dundonald)	Garfield Cottage, Sorn Road, Mauchline KA5 6HQ / bobmayes3@gmail.com	01290 519869
McAllister, Anne C. BSc DipEd CCS	2013	2021	(Ordained Local Minister)	39 Bowes Rigg, Stewarton, Kilmarnock KA3 5EN / AMcAllister@churchofscotland.org.uk	01560 483191
McCallum, Alexander D. BD	1987	2005	(Saltcoats: New Trinity)	59 Woodcroft Avenue, Largs KA30 9EW / sandyandjose@madasafish.com	01475 670133
McCulloch, James D. BD MIOP MIP3 FSAScot	1996	2015	(Hurlford)	18 Edradour Place, Dunsmuir Park, Kilmarnock KA3 1US / mccullochmanse1@btinternet.com	01563 535833
McGurk, Andrew F. BD	1983	2011	(Largs: St. John's)	15 Fraser Avenue, Troon KA10 6XF / afmcg.largs@talk21.com	01292 676008
McKay, David M. MA BD	1979	2007	(Kirkpatrick Juxta with Moffat: St Andrew's with Wamphray)	20 Auld Brig View, Auldgirth, Dumfries DG2 0XE / davidmckay20@tiscali.co.uk	01387 740013
McKenzie, William M. DA	1958	1993	(Dumfries: Troqueer)	41 Kingholm Road, Dumfries DG1 4SR / mckenzie.dumfries@btinternet.com	01387 253688
McKinnon, Lily F. H. (Mrs) MA BD PGCE	1993	2021	(Kilmory with Lamlash)	Rowan Cottage, 6 Sheean Drive, Brodick, Isle of Arran KA27 8DH / lily.mackinnon@yahoo.co.uk	07917 548357
McLauchlan, Mary C. (Mrs) LTh	1997	2013	(Mochrum)	3 Ayr Street, Moniaive, Thornhill DG3 4HP / mary@revmother.co.uk	01848 200786

Name	Years	Charge	Address / Email	Phone
McLeod, David C. BSc MEng BD	1969 2001	(Dundee: Fairmuir)	76 Ayr Road, Prestwick KA9 1RR	01292 442554
McNidder, Roderick H. BD DipCE	1987 2007	(Chaplain: NHS Ayrshire and Arran Trust)	6 Hollow Park, Alloway, Ayr KA7 4SR / roddymcnidder@sky.com	
McPhail, Andrew M. BA	1968 2002	(Ayr: Wallacetown)	25 Maybole Road, Ayr KA7 2QA	01292 282108
Mitchell, D. Ross BA BD	1972 2007	(West Kilbride: St Andrew's)	11 Dunbar Gardens, Saltcoats KA21 6GJ / ross.mitchell@virgin.net	01294 474375
Moore, Douglas T.	2003 2019	(Auxiliary Minister)	9 Midton Avenue, Prestwick KA9 1PU / douglastmoore@hotmail.com	01292 671352
Morrison, Alistair H. BTh DipYCS	1985 2004	(Paisley: St Mark's Oldhall)	92 St Leonard's Road, Ayr KA7 2PU / alistairhmorrison@gmail.com	01292 266021
Ness, David T. LTh	1972 2008	(Ayr: St Quivox)	17 Winston Avenue, Prestwick KA9 2EZ / davidtness@gmail.com	01292 471625
Ogston, Edgar J. BSc BD	1976 2017	(North West Lochaber)	14 North Park Avenue, Girvan KA26 9DH / edgar.ogston@macfish.com	01465 713081
Owen, John J.C. LTh	1967 2001	(Applegarth and Sibbaldbie with Lochmaben)	5 Galla Avenue, Dalbeattie DG5 4JZ / jj.owen@onetel.net	01556 612125
Paterson, John H. BD	1977 2000	(Kirkintilloch: St David's Memorial Park)	Creag Bhan, Golf Course Road, Whiting Bay, Isle of Arran KA27 8QT	01770 700569
Paterson, John L. MA BD STM	1964 2003	(Linlithgow: St Michael's)	9 The Pines, Murdoch's Lane, Alloway, Ayr KA7 4WD / lip38rev@gmail.com	01292 443615
Rae, Scott M. MBE BD CPS	1976 2016	(Muirkirk with Old Cumnock: Trinity)	2 Primrose Place, Kilmarnock KA1 2RR / scottrae1@btopenworld.com	01563 532711
Roy, Iain M. MA BD	1960 1997	(Stevenston: Livingstone)	2 The Fieldings, Dunlop, Kilmarnock KA3 4AU	01560 483072
Sanderson, Alastair M. LTh BA	1971 2007	(Craigie with Symington)	26 Main Street, Monkton, Prestwick KA9 2QL / aesanderson2@gmail.com	01292 475819
Scott, Thomas T.	1968 1989	(Kilmarnock: St Marnock's)	4c Seamore Street, Largs KA30 9AP / tomtscott@btinternet.com	
Shaw, Catherine A.M. MA	1998 2005	(Auxiliary Minister)	40 Merrygreen Place, Stewarton, Kilmarnock KA3 5EP / catherine.shaw@tesco.net	01560 483352
Sheppard, Michael J. BD	1997 2016	(Ervie Kirkcolm with Leswalt)	4 Mill Street, Drummore, Stranraer DG9 9PS / michaelsheppard00@gmail.com	01776 840369
Simpson, Edward V. BSc BD	1972 2009	(Glasgow: Giffnock South)	7 Whitehill Grove, Newton Mearns, Glasgow G77 5DH / eddie.simpson3@talktalk.net	0141 237 4048 / 07896 013605
Sorensen, Alan K. DL BD MTh DipMin FSAScot	1983 2022	(Greenock: Wellpark Mid Kirk)	51A Castlepark Terrace, Fairlie KA29 0DG / ASorensen@churchofscotland.org.uk	01475 568314
Steele, Hugh D. LTh DipMin	1994 2020	(Kelty)	23 Mossgiel Avenue, Troon KA10 7DQ / hugdebra@btinternet.com	07449 974940
Stewart, David MA DipEd BD MTh	1977 2013	(Howwood)	72 Glen Avenue, Largs KA30 8QQ / revdavidst@aol.com	01475 675159
Stirling, Ian R. BSc BD MTh MSc DPT	1990 2021	(Fisherton with Kirkoswald)	lStirling@churchofscotland.org.uk	
Strachan, Alexander E. MA BD	1974 2012	(Chaplain, Dumfries Hospitals)		
Sutherland, Colin A. LTh	1995 2007	(Blantyre: Livingstone Memorial)	71 Caulstran Road, Dumfries DG2 9FJ / colin.csutherland@btinternet.com	01387 279954

Name	Years	Role / Congregation	Address	Phone
Taylor, Andrew S. BTh FPhS	1959 1992	(Greenock: The Union)	9 Raillies Avenue, Largs KA30 8QY andrew.taylor_123@btinternet.com	01475 674709
Telfer, Alan B. BA CQSW BD	1983 2021	(Strathaven: Avendale Old and Drumclog)	22 Crawford Avenue, Prestwick KA9 2BN ATelfer@churchofscotland.org.uk	01292 474041
Travers, Robert BA BD	1993 2015	(Irvine: Old)	74 Caledonian Road, Stevenston KA20 3LF roberttravers@live.co.uk	01294 279265
Urquhart, Barbara (Mrs) DCS	1986 2017	(Deacon)	9 Standalane, Kilmaurs, Kilmarnock KA3 2NB barbaraurquhart1@gmail.com	01563 538289
Ward, Alan H. MA BD	1978 2015	(Interim Minister)	47 Meadowfoot Road, West Kilbride KA23 9BU	01475 822244 07709 906130
Wark, Alexander C. MA BD STM	1982 2017	(Mid Deeside)	43 Mure Avenue, Kilmarnock KA 3 1TT alecwark@yahoo.co.uk	01563 559581
Watson, Elizabeth R.L. (Miss) BA BD	1981 2021	(Whiting Bay and Kildonan)	3 Fernside, Brisbane Street, Largs KA30 8QG revewatson@btinternet.com	01475 673548
Welsh, Alex M. MA BD	1979	(Hospital Chaplain, NHS Ayrshire and Arran)	8 Greenside Avenue, Prestwick KA9 2HB alexandevelyn@hotmail.com	01292 475341
Whitecross, Jeanette BD	2002 2019	(Kilwinning: Old)	4 Fir Bank, Ayr KA7 3SX jeanettewx@yahoo.com	07803 181150
Wilson, Muriel (Miss) MA BD DCS	1997 2011	(Deacon)	28 Bellevue Crescent, Ayr KA7 2DR me.wilson28@btinternet.com	01292 264039
Wotherspoon, Robert C. LTh	1976 1998	(Corsock and Kirkpatrick Durham with Crossmichael and Parton)	5 Goddards Green Cottages, Goddards Green, Beneden, Cranbrook TN17 4AW	01580 243091
Yorke, Kenneth B. BD DipEd	1982 2009	(Dalmellington with Patna Waterside)	13 Annfield Terrace, Prestwick KA9 1PS kenyorke@yahoo.com	01292 670476
Young, Rona M. (Mrs) BD DipEd	1991 2015	(Ayr: St Quivox)	16 Macintyre Road, Prestwick KA9 1BE revronyoung@hotmail.com	01292 471982

TOWN ADDRESSES

Ayr

Auld Kirk	Kirkport (116 High Street)
Castlehill	Castlehill Road x Hillfoot Road
Newton Wallacetown	Main Street
St Andrew's	Park Circus
St Columba	Midton Road x Carrick Park
St James'	Prestwick Road x Falkland Park Road
St Leonard's	St Leonard's Road x Monument Road

Dumfries

Maxwelltown West	Laurieknowe
Northwest	Lochside Road
St George's	George Street
St Mary's-Greyfriars	St Mary's Street
St Michael's and South	St Michael's Street
Troqueer	Troqueer Road

Girvan

North	Montgomerie Street
South	Stair Park

Irvine

Fullarton	Marress Road x Church Street
Girdle Toll	Bryce Knox Court
Mure Relief	West Road
Old	Kirkgate
St Andrew's	Caldon Road x Oaklands Ave

Kilmarnock

Ayrshire Mission to the Deaf	10 Clark Street
Kay Park	London Road
New Laigh Kirk	John Dickie Street
St John's Onthank	84 Wardneuk Street
St Marnock's	St Marnock Street
St Kentigern's	Dunbar Drive

Prestwick

Kingcase	Waterloo Road
Monkton and Prestwick North	Monkton Road
St Nicholas	Main Street
South	Main Street

Troon

Old	Ayr Street
Portland	St Meddan's Street
St Meddan's	St Meddan's Street

(14) CLYDE (W)

Meets on dates and venues to be decided.

Clerk: REV. PETER McENHILL BD PhD
The Presbytery Office (see below)
clyde@churchofscotland.org.uk
'Homelea', Faith Avenue, Quarrier's Village, Bridge of Weir
PA11 3SX
Tel 07837 729333
Fax 01505 615033
01505 615088

Presbytery Office:

No.	Congregation	Ind.	Adm.	Minister / Contact	Address / Email	Tel	Fax
1	**Arrochar (F W) linked with Luss (F W)**			Vacant Interim Moderator: Grace Rogerson (Dr)	ggrogerson@btinternet.com	0141 956 5165	
2	**Baldernock (H) linked with Milngavie: St Paul's (F H W)**			Vacant	stpauls@btconnect.com 8 Buchanan Street, Milngavie, Glasgow G62 8DD	0141 956 4405	0141 956 1043
3	**Barrhead: Bourock (F H W)**	2006	2014	Pamela Gordon BD	14 Maxton Avenue, Barrhead, Glasgow G78 1DY PGordon@churchofscotland.org.uk	0141 881 9813	0141 881 8736
4	**Barrhead: St Andrew's (F H W)**	2020		Timothy Mineard BA BD	10 Arthurlie Avenue, Barrhead, Glasgow G78 2BU TMineard@churchofscotland.org.uk	0141 881 8442	0141 587 7913
5	**Bearsden: Baljaffray (F H W)**	2008		Ian K. McEwan BSc PhD BD FRSE FRAE	5 Fintry Gardens, Bearsden, Glasgow G61 4RJ IMcEwan@churchofscotland.org.uk	0141 942 5304	0141 942 0366
6	**Bearsden: Cross (F H W)**	2006	2013	Graeme R. Wilson MCIBS BD ThM DMin	secretary@bearsdencross.org 61 Drymen Road, Bearsden, Glasgow G61 2SU GWilson@churchofscotland.org.uk	0141 942 0507	0141 942 0507
7	**Bearsden: Killermont (F H W)**	2003		Alan J. Hamilton LLB BD PhD	8 Clathic Avenue, Bearsden, Glasgow G61 2HF AHamilton@churchofscotland.org.uk	0141 942 0021	
8	**Bearsden: New Kilpatrick (F H W)**	1992	2011	Roderick G. Hamilton MA BD	mail@nkchurch.org.uk 51 Manse Road, Bearsden, Glasgow G61 3PN Roddy.Hamilton@churchofscotland.org.uk	0141 942 8827	0141 942 0035

9 Bearsden: Westerton Fairlie Memorial (H W)
Christine M. Goldie LLB BD MTh DMin   1984   2008
westertonchurch@talktalk.net
3 Canniesburn Road, Bearsden, Glasgow   G61 1PW
CGoldie@churchofscotland.org.uk
0141 942 6960
0141 942 2672

10 Bishopton (F H W)
Yvonne Smith BSc BD   2017
office@bishoptonkirk.org.uk
The Manse, Newton Road, Bishopton PA7 5IP
YSmith@churchofscotland.org.uk
01505 862583
01505 862161

11 Bonhill (F H W) linked with Renton: Trinity (F H)
Vacant
Interim Moderator: Graeme R. Wilson
bonhillchurchoffice@gmail.com
1 Glebe Gardens, Bonhill G83 9NZ
GWilson@churchofscotland.org.uk
Bonhill: 01389 756516
01389 609329
0141 942 0507

12 Bridge of Weir: Freeland (F H W)
Kenneth N. Gray BA BD   1988
15 Lawmarnock Crescent, Bridge of Weir PA11 3AS
aandkgray@btinternet.com
01505 612610
01505 690918

13 Bridge of Weir: St Machar's Ranfurly (F W)
Hanneke A.S. Marshall (Mrs) MTh MA   2017
PGCE CertMin
9 St Andrew's Drive, Bridge of Weir PA11 3HS
Hanneke.Marshall@churchofscotland.org.uk
01505 612975
01505 612975

14 Cardross (F H W)
Margaret McArthur BD DipMin   1995   2015
16 Bainfield Road, Cardross G82 5JQ
MMcArthur@churchofscotland.org.uk
01389 841322
01389 849329
07799 556367

15 Clydebank: Faifley (F W)
Gregor McIntyre BSc BD   1991
Kirklea, Cochno Road, Hardgate, Clydebank   G81 6PT
Gregor.McIntyre@churchofscotland.org.uk
01389 876836

16 Clydebank: Kilbowie St Andrew's (F) linked with Clydebank: Radnor Park (H)
Vacant
Session Clerk, Kilbowie St Andrew's: Derek W. Smith
11 Tiree Gardens, Old Kilpatrick, Glasgow G60 5AT
ann.smith@live.co.uk
01389 875599
0141 952 8425
07703 185423
Session Clerk, Radnor Park: Mabel Baillie (Mrs)
r.baillie1@ntlworld.com
0141 579 5957

17 Clydebank: Radnor Park See Clydebank: Kilbowie St Andrew's

18 Clydebank: Waterfront (F W) linked with Dalmuir: Barclay (F W)
Vacant
Interim Moderator: Gregor McIntyre
16 Parkhall Road, Dalmuir, Clydebank G81 3RJ
Gregor.McIntyre@churchofscotland.org.uk
Dalmuir Barclay: 0141 941 3988
0141 941 3317
01389 876836

19 Craigrownie (F W) linked with Garelochhead (F W) linked with Rosneath: St Modan's (F H W)   Garelochhead: **01436 810589**

Christine M. Murdoch BD   1999   2015   The Manse, Argyll Road, Kilcreggan, Helensburgh G84 0JW   01436 842274
CMurdoch@churchofscotland.org.uk   07973 331890

Ian J. Millar BA   2020   Lochfada House, Succoth, Arrochar G83 7AL   01301 702133
(Ordained Local Minister)   IMillar@churchofscotland.org.uk

20 Dalmuir: Barclay See Clydebank: Waterfront

21 Dumbarton: Riverside (F H W) linked with Dumbarton: St Andrew's (H W) linked with Dumbarton: West Kirk (F H W)   Riverside: **01389 742551**
office@dumbartonriverside.org.uk
administration@standrewsdumbarton.co.uk

Vacant   18 Castle Road, Dumbarton G82 1JF   01389 726685
Interim Moderator:

22 Dumbarton: St Andrew's See Dumbarton: Riverside
23 Dumbarton: West Kirk See Dumbarton: Riverside

24 Duntocher: Trinity (F H L T W)   info@duntochertrinitychurch.co.uk
Vacant   The Manse, Roman Road, Duntocher, Clydebank G81 6BT
Session Clerk: Colin G. Dow   colin.g.dow@ntlworld.com   01389 380038

25 Elderslie Kirk (F H W)
G. Gray Fletcher BSc BD   1989   2019   282 Main Road, Elderslie, Johnstone PA5 9EF   **01505 323348**
GFletcher@churchofscotland.org.uk   01505 321767

26 Erskine (F T W)
David Nicolson BA   2019   The Manse, 7 Leven Place, Linburn, Erskine PA8 6AS   **0141 812 4620**
DNicolson@churchofscotland.org.uk   0141 570 8103

27 Garelochhead See Craigrownie

28 Gourock: Old Gourock and Ashton (H W) linked wth Greenock: St Ninian's   secretary@ogachurch.org.uk
David W.G. Burt BD DipMin MTh   1989   2014   331 Eldon Street, Greenock PA16 7QN   01475 633914
DBurt@churchofscotland.org.uk

29 Gourock: St John's (F H T W)
Teri C. Peterson BMus MDiv   2006   2018
office@stjohns-gourock.org.uk
6 Barrhill Road, Gourock PA19 1JX
TPeterson@churchofscotland.org.uk
01475 632143

30 Greenock: East End (F) linked with Greenock: Mount Kirk (F W)
Francis E. Murphy BEng DipDSE BD   2006
info@themountkirk.org.uk
76 Finnart Street, Greenock PA16 8HJ
FMurphy@churchofscotland.org.uk
01475 722338

31 Greenock: Lyle Kirk (F T W)
Jonathan C. Fleming MA BD   2012   2021
office@lylekirk.org
39 Fox Street, Greenock PA16 8PD
JFleming@churchofscotland.org.uk
01475 727694
01475 717229

32 Greenock: Mount Kirk   See Greenock: East End

33 Greenock: St Margaret's (F W)
Guardianship of the Presbytery
Interim Moderator: Teri C. Peterson
TPeterson@churchofscotland.org.uk
01475 781953
01475 632143

34 Greenock: St Ninian's   See Gourock: Old Gourock and Ashton

35 Greenock: Wellpark Mid Kirk (F)
Vacant
Interim Moderator: William A. Boyle
101 Brisbane Street, Greenock PA16 8PA
WBoyle@churchofscotland.org.uk
01475 721741
01475 745407

36 Greenock: Westburn (F W)
Karen E. Harbison (Mrs) MA BD   1991   2014
50 Ardgowan Street, Greenock PA16 8EP
KHarbison@churchofscotland.org.uk
01475 720257
01475 721048

37 Helensburgh (F W) linked with Rhu and Shandon (F W)
Vacant
Interim Moderator: Roderick G. Hamilton
hello@helensburghcos.org
35 East Argyle Street, Helensburgh G84 7EL
Roddy.Hamilton@churchofscotland.org.uk
Helensburgh: 01436 676880
Rhu and Shandon: 01436 820605
01436 673365
0141 942 0035

38 Houston and Killellan (F H W)
Gary D. Noonan BA   2018
The Manse of Houston, Main Street, Houston, Johnstone PA6 7EL
GNoonan@churchofscotland.org.uk
01505 612569

39 Howwood (W) linked with Johnstone: St Paul's (F H W)
Alistair N. Shaw MA BD MTh PhD   1982   2003
9 Stanley Drive, Brookfield, Johnstone PA5 8UF
Alistair.Shaw@churchofscotland.org.uk
St Paul's: 01505 **321632**
01505   320060

40 Inchinnan (F H W)
Ann Knox BD Cert.Healthc.Chap   2017
51 Old Greenock Road, Inchinnan, Renfrew PA4 9PH
AKnox@churchofscotland.org.uk
0141 812 1263
0141 389 1724
07534 900065

41 Inverkip (H W) linked with Skelmorlie and Wemyss Bay (W)
Vacant
admin@inverkip.org.uk
3a Montgomerie Terrace, Skelmorlie PA17 5DT
01475   529320

42 Johnstone: High (F H W)
Ann C. McCool (Mrs) BD DSD IPA ALCM 1989   2001
76 North Road, Johnstone PA5 8NF
AMcCool@churchofscotland.org.uk
01505 **336303**
01505   320006

43 Johnstone: St Andrew's Trinity
Vacant
Interim Moderator: Stephen J. Smith
45 Woodlands Crescent, Johnstone PA5 0AZ
SSmith@churchofscotland.org.uk
01505 **337827**
01505   672908
01505   702621

44 Johnstone: St Paul's See Howwood

45 Kilbarchan (F T W)
Stephen J. Smith BSc BD   1993   2015
41 Shuttle Street, Kilbarchan PA10 2JR
SSmith@churchofscotland.org.uk
01505   702621

46 Kilmacolm: Old (F H W)
Vacant
Interim Moderator: Gary D. Noonan
The Old Kirk Manse, Glencairn Road, Kilmacolm PA13 4NJ
GNoonan@churchofscotland.org.uk
01505 **873911**
01505   873174
01505   612569

47 Kilmacolm: St Columba (F H)
Vacant
Interim Moderator: William R. Armstrong
6 Churchill Road, Kilmacolm PA13 4LH
w.armstrong@btinternet.com
01505   873271
01475   520891

48 Kilmaronock Gartocharn linked with Lomond (F W)
Vacant
Session Clerk, Kilmaronock Gartocharn: Mark Smith
kilgartoch@gmail.com
01389   830785
07796   938318

Session Clerks, Lomond: Linda Cust (Miss)
Robert M. Kinloch
lindaccust@btinternet.com
rkinloch@blueyonder.co.uk
01389   754502
07760   276505

No.	Name / Minister			Contact	Telephone
49	**Langbank (F T W)** Guardianship of the Presbytery Interim Moderator: Stuart C. Steell			info@langbankparishchurch.co.uk SSteell@churchofscotland.org.uk	0141 387 2464
50	**Linwood (F H)** Vacant Interim Moderator: Ann C. McCool			1 John Neilson Avenue, Paisley PA1 2SX AMcCool@churchofscotland.org.uk	0141 887 2801 01505 320006
51	**Lomond** See Kilmaronock Gartocharn				
52	**Luss** See Arrochar				
53	**Milngavie: Cairns (H W)** Andrew Frater BA BD MTh	1987	1994	**office@cairnschurch.org.uk** 4 Cairns Drive, Milngavie, Glasgow G62 8AJ AFrater@churchofscotland.org.uk	**0141 956 4868** 0141 956 1717
54	**Milngavie: St Luke's (W)** Ramsay B. Shields BA BD	1990	1997	70 Hunter Road, Milngavie, Glasgow G62 7BY RShields@churchofscotland.org.uk	**0141 956 4226** Tel 0141 577 9171 Fax 0141 577 9181
55	**Milngavie: St Paul's** See Baldernock				
56	**Neilston (F W)** Matthew D. Ritchie BA	2020		The Church Hall, 45 High Street, Neilston, Glasgow G78 3HJ Matthew.Ritchie@churchofscotland.org.uk	**0141 881 9445** 07548 342672
57	**Old Kilpatrick Bowling** Scott McCrum BD	2015	2018	The Manse, 175 Dumbarton Road, Old Kilpatrick, Glasgow G60 5JQ SMcCrum@churchofscotland.org.uk	08005 668242
58	**Paisley: Abbey (F H W)** Elspeth M. McKay LLB LLM PGCert BD	2014	2021	**info@paisleyabbey.org.uk** 1 Carriagehall Drive, Paisley PA2 6JG EMcKay@churchofscotland.org.uk	**0141 889 7654; Fax 0141 887 3929** 07789 993535
59	**Paisley: North (F W)** Vacant Stuart Davidson BD (Pioneer Minister)	2008	2017	**wallneuknorthchurch@gmail.com** 5 Glenvilla Crescent, Paisley PA2 8TL 25H Cross Road, Paisley PA2 9QJ SDavidson@churchofscotland.org.uk	**0141 889 9265** 0141 884 4429 07717 503059

60 Paisley: Oakshaw Trinity (F H W)
Gordon B. Armstrong BD FIAB BRC CertCS   1998   2012
The Manse, 52 Balgonie Drive, Paisley PA2 9LP   **0141 887 4647; Fax 0141 848 5139**
GArmstrong@churchofscotland.org.uk   0141 587 3124
Oakshaw Trinity is a Local Ecumenical Partnership with the United Reformed Church

61 Paisley: St George's (F W T)
Vacant
Mhairi M. Breingan BSc CertCS   2011   2019
(Ordained Local Minister)
6 Park Road, Inchinnan, Renfrew PA4 4QJ   0141 812 1425
mhairi.b@btinternet.com

62 Paisley: St Mark's Oldhall (F H L W)   2020
A. Sonia Blakesley MB ChB BD
office@stmarksoldhall.org.uk   **0141 882 2755**
36 Newtyle Road, Paisley PA1 3JX   0141 258 1161
SBlakesley@churchofscotland.org.uk

63 Paisley: Sherwood Greenlaw (F H W)   1988   2014
John Murning BD CPS
5 Greenlaw Drive, Paisley PA1 3RX   **0141 889 7060**
JMurning@churchofscotland.org.uk   0141 316 2678

64 Paisley: South (F H W)   1997   2020
David P. Hood BD CertMin IOB(Scot)
6 Southfield Avenue, Paisley PA2 8BY   **0141 561 7139**
DHood@churchofscotland.org.uk   0141 587 9374

65 Paisley: West
Vacant
Interim Moderator: G. Gray Fletcher
GFletcher@churchofscotland.org.uk   01505 321767

66 Port Glasgow: Hamilton Bardrainney (F)
Guardianship of the Presbytery
Interim Moderator: Francis E. Murphy
80 Bardrainney Avenue, Port Glasgow PA14 6HD   01475 701213
FMurphy@churchofscotland.org.uk   01475 722338

67 Port Glasgow: New (F H W)   2020
William A. Boyle BA
New Parish Church Manse, Barr's Brae Lane, Port Glasgow   01475 745407
PA14 5QA
WBoyle@churchofscotland.org.uk

68 Renfrew: North (F T W)   1998   2018
Philip D. Wallace BSc BTh DTS
contact@renfrewnorth.org.uk   **0141 530 1308**
1 Alexandra Drive, Renfrew PA4 8UB   0141 570 3502
PWallace@churchofscotland.org.uk

69 Renfrew: Trinity (F H W)
Stuart C. Steell BD CertMin   1992 2015   25 Paisley Road, Renfrew PA4 8JH   **0141 885 2129**
SSteell@churchofscotland.org.uk   0141 387 2464

70 Renton: Trinity See Bonhill
71 Rhu and Shandon See Helensburgh
72 Roseneath: St Modan's See Craigrownie
73 Skelmorlie and Wemyss Bay See Inverkip

B. In other appointments

Dalton, Mark BD DipMin RN	2002		Chaplain: Royal Navy	Royal Naval Air Station Culdrose, Helston, Cornwall TR12 7RH mark.dalton242@mod.gov.uk	
McEnhill, Peter BD PhD	1992	2021	Presbytery Clerk: Clyde	Flat 3/1, 112 Cloch Road, Gourock PA19 1FN PMcEnhill@churchofscotland.org.uk	07837 729333
Peel, Jeanette L. BA BD MTh	2020		Healthcare Chaplain	Royal Alexandria Hospital, Corsebar Road, Paisley PA2 9PN Jeanette.Peel@churchofscotland.org.uk	0141 314 9561 0141 314 7365
Stevenson, Stuart CertCE	2011		Ordained Local Minister	143 Springfield Park, Johnstone PA5 8JT SStevenson@churchofscotland.org.uk	0141 886 2131

C. Retaining

Armstrong, William R. BD	1979	2008	(Skelmorlie and Wemyss Bay)	25A The Lane, Skelmorlie PA17 5AR w.armstrong@btinternet.com	01475 520891
Bell, Ian W. LTh	1990	2011	(Erskine)	40 Brueacre Drive, Wemyss Bay PA18 6HA revianbell@gmail.com	01475 529312
Bell, May (Mrs) LTh	1998	2012	(Johnstone: St Andrew's Trinity)	40 Brueacre Drive, Wemyss Bay PA18 6HA revmaybell22@gmail.com	01475 529312
Buchanan, Fergus C. MA BD MTh	1982	2022	(Baldernock with Milngavie: St Paul's)	114 Moorpark Square, Renfrew PA4 8JF Fergus.Buchanan@churchofscotland.org.uk	07760 138960
Cameron, Ann J. (Mrs) CertCS	2005	2019	(Auxiliary Minister)	Water's Edge, Ferry Road, Rosneath, Helensburgh G84 0RS ACameron@churchofscotland.org.uk	01436 831800
Cameron, Charles M. BA BD PhD	1980	2021	(Johnstone: St Andrew's Trinity)	5 Weavers Road, Paisley PA2 9DP charlescameron@hotmail.co.uk	07469 198443
Campbell, Donald BD	1998	2016	(Houston and Killellan)	15 Garshake Road, Dumbarton G82 3LH	01389 739353
Clark, David W. MA BD	1975	2014	(Helensburgh: St Andrew's Kirk with Rhu and Shandon)	3 Ritchie Avenue, Cardross, Dumbarton G82 5LL clarkdw@talktalk.net	01389 849319
Coull, Morris C. BD	1974	2018	(Greenock St Margaret's)	14 Kelvin Gardens, Largs KA30 8SY	01475 338674
Cowie, Marian (Mrs) MA BD MTh	1990	2012	(Aberdeen: Midstocket)	2 Glenmore Avenue, Alexandria, Glasgow G83 0QA mcowieou@aol.com	07740 174969
Currie, Ian S. MBE BD	1975	2010	(The United Church of Bute)	26 Old Bridge of Weir, Houston PA6 7EB ianscurrie@tiscali.co.uk	07764 254300
Easton, Lilly C. (Mrs)	1999	2012	(Renfrew: Old)	Flat 0/2, 90 Beith Street, Glasgow G11 6DG revlillyeaston@hotmail.co.uk	0141 586 7628

Name	Parish/Role		Address	Tel
Geddes, Elizabeth (Mrs) DCS	(Ordained Local Minister)	2013 2021	9 Shillingworth Place, Bridge of Weir PA11 3DY geddes_liz@hotmail.com	01505 612639
Gray, Greta (Miss) DCS	(Deacon)	1992 2014	67 Crags Avenue, Paisley PA3 6SG greta.gray@ntlworld.com	0141 884 6178
Hamilton, David G. MA BD	(Braes of Rannoch with Foss and Rannoch)	1971 2004	79 Finlay Rise, Milngavie, Glasgow G62 6QL davidhamilton40@googlemail.com	0141 956 4202
Hood, E. Lorna OBE MA BD DD	(Renfrew: North)	1978 2016	4 Thornly Park Drive, Paisley PA2 7RR revlornahood@gmail.com	0141 384 9516
Houston, Elizabeth W. MA BD DipEd	(Alexandria)	1985 2018	Croftengea, 25 Honeysuckle Lane, Jamestown, Alexandria G83 8PL Cleric2@hotmail.com	01389 721165
Kay, David BA BD MTh	(Paisley: Sandyford: Thread Street)	1974 2008	36 Donaldswood Park, Paisley PA2 8RS david.kay500@o2.co.uk	0141 884 2080
Kemp, Tina MA	(Auxiliary Minister)	2005 2021	12 Oaktree Gardens, Dumbarton G82 1EU TKemp@churchofscotland.org.uk	01389 730477
Lees, Andrew P. BD	(Baldernock)	1984 2017	58 Lindores Drive, Stepps G33 6PD andrew.lees@yahoo.co.uk	0141 389 5840
Leitch, Maureen (Mrs) BA BD DipPhysEd	(Barrhead: Bourock)	1995 2011	Rockfield, 92 Paisley Road, Barrhead G78 1NW maureen.leitch@ntlworld.com	0141 580 2927
Macdonald, Alexander MA BD	(Neilston)	1966 2006	35 Lochore Avenue, Paisley PA3 4BY alexsmacdonald42@aol.com	0141 889 0066
Manson, Eileen (Mrs) DipCE	(Auxiliary Minister)	1994 2021	1 Cambridge Avenue, Gourock PA19 1XT EManson@churchofscotland.org.uk	01475 632401
Marshall, T. Edward BD CertMin	(Crosshouse)	1987 2020	20 Alloway Drive, Paisley PA2 7DS	
McFarlane, Robert G. BD	(Paisley St Mark's Oldhall)	2001 2018	990 Crookston Road, Glasgow G53 7DY	
Miller, Ian H. BD BA	(Bonhill)	1975 2012	Derand, Queen Street, Alexandria G83 0AS revianmiller@btinternet.com	01389 753039
Moore, Norma MA BD	(Jamestown)	1995 2017	25 Miller Street, Dumbarton G82 2JA norma-moore@sky.com	
Nutter, Margaret A.E. BA BD MFPh	(Ordained Local Minister)	2014 2021	Kilmorich, 14 Balloch Road, Balloch, Alexandria G83 8SR MNutter@churchofscotland.org.uk	01389 754505
O'Donnell, Barbara A. BD PGSE	(Bonhill with Renton: Trinity)	2007 2022	Ashbank, 258 Main Street, Alexandria G83 0NU revbarb1@gmail.com	01389 752356
Ramsden, Iain R. MStJ BTh	(Killearnan with Knockbain)	1999 2013	Flat 1/1, 15 Cardon Square, Renfrew PA4 8BY s4rev@sky.com	07795 972560
Read, Paul R. BSc DipEd MA(Th)	(Applegarth, Sibbaldbie and Johnstone with Lochmaben)	2000 2021	21 Brechanshaw, Erskine PA8 7EZ prr747@icloud.com	0141 560 0561 07791 724162
Robertson, Isbhel A. R. MA BD	(Ordained Local Minister)	2013 2018	Oakdene, 81 Bonhill Road, Dumbarton G82 2DU mawhyte@hotmail.com	01389 763436
Whyte, Margaret A. (Mrs) BA BD	(Glasgow: Pollokshaws)	1988 2011	4 Springhill Road, Barrhead G78 2AA mawhyte@hotmail.co.uk	0141 881 4942
Wilson, John BD CPS	(Glasgow: Temple Anniesland)	1985 2010	4 Carron Crescent, Bearsden, Glasgow G61 1HJ revjwilson@btinternet.com	0141 931 5609
Yule, Margaret J.B. BD DipDSc PGCE	(Clydebank: Kilbowie St Andrew's with Radnor Park)	1992 2019	4 Overtoun Road, Clydebank G81 3QY mjbyule@yahoo.co.uk	0141 390 3243

TOWN ADDRESSES

Bearsden
Baljaffray — Grampian Way
Cross — Drymen Road
Killermont — Rannoch Drive
New Kilpatrick — Manse Road
Westerton — Crarae Avenue

Clydebank
Faifley — Faifley Road
Kilbowie St Andrew's — Kilbowie Road
Radnor Park — Radnor Street
Waterfront — Town Centre

Dumbarton
Riverside — High Street
St Andrew's — Aitkenbar Circle
West Kirk — West Bridgend

Gourock
Old Gourock and Ashton — 41 Royal Street
St John's — Bath Street x St John's Road

Greenock
East End — 49–51 Belleville Street
Lyle Kirk — Newark Street x Bentinck Street
Mount Kirk — Dempster Street at Murdieston Park
St Margaret's — Finch Road x Kestrel Crescent
St Ninian's — Warwick Road, Larkfield
Wellpark Mid Kirk — Cathcart Square
Westburn — 9 Nelson Street

Helensburgh — Colquhoun Square

Milngavie
Cairns — Buchanan Street
St Luke's — Kirk Street

St Paul's — Strathblane Road

Paisley
Abbey — Cotton Street
North — off Renfrew Road
Oakshaw Trinity — Churchill
St George's — Causeyside Street, and Nethercraigs Drive
St Mark's Oldhall — Glasgow Road, Ralston
Sherwood Greenlaw — Glasgow Road
South — Rowan Street off Neilston Road
West — King Street

Port Glasgow
Hamilton Bardrainney — Bardrainney Avenue x Auchenbothie Road
New — Princes Street

(16) GLASGOW (F W)

Meets at 7pm on the second Tuesday of every month apart from June when it is the third Tuesday and July, August and January when it does not meet. Details of the venue are displayed on the Presbytery website.

Clerk: REV. S. GRANT BARCLAY LLB DipLP BD MSc PhD 260 Bath Street, Glasgow G2 4JP **0141 332 6606**
glasgow@churchofscotland.org.uk **07743 779929**

Depute Clerk: REV. HILARY N. McDOUGALL MA PGCE BD HMcDougall@churchofscotland.org.uk

Treasurer: MRS ALISON WHITELAW treasurer@presbyteryofglasgow.org.uk

1 **Bishopbriggs: Kenmure (F W)** 100 Kenmure Avenue, Bishopbriggs, Glasgow G64 2DB **0141 762 4242**
Vacant **0141 390 3598**
Session Clerk: Jim Wright jim@auchendavie.co.uk **07808 365845**

2 **Bishopbriggs: Springfield Cambridge (F W)** 1995 2006 springfieldcamb@btconnect.com **0141 772 1596**
64 Miller Drive, Bishopbriggs, Glasgow G64 1FB **0141 772 1540**
Ian Taylor BD ThM DipPSRP ITaylor@churchofscotland.org.uk

#	Name / Minister			Address / Contact	Tel / Fax
					Tel
					Fax
3	**Broom (F W)** James A.S. Boag BD CertMin	1992	2007	office@broomchurch.org.uk 3 Laigh Road, Newton Mearns, Glasgow G77 5EX JBoag@churchofscotland.org.uk	**0141 639 3528** 0141 639 2916 0141 639 3528
4	**Burnside Blairbeth (F W)** William T.S. Wilson BSc BD	1999	2006	theoffice@burnsideblairbeth.church 59 Blairbeth Road, Burnside, Glasgow G73 4JD WWilson@churchofscotland.org.uk	**0141 634 7383** 0141 583 6470
5	**Busby (F W)** Jeremy C. Eve BSc BD	1995	1998	17A Carmunnock Road, Busby, Glasgow G76 8SZ JEve@churchofscotland.org.uk	**0141 644 2073** 0141 644 3670
6	**Cadder (F W)** John B. MacGregor BD	1999	2017	231 Kirkintilloch Road, Bishopbriggs, Glasgow G64 2JB JMacGregor@churchofscotland.org.uk	**0141 772 7436** 0141 576 7127
7	**Cambuslang (F W)** Peter W. Nimmo BD ThM	1996	2020	office@churchofscotland.org.uk 74 Stewarton Drive, Cambuslang, Glasgow G72 8DG PNimmo@churchofscotland.org.uk	**0141 642 9271** 0141 641 2028
	Karen M. Hamilton (Mrs) DCS	1995	2014	6 Beckfield Gate, Glasgow G33 1SW KHamilton@churchofscotland.org.uk	0141 558 3195 07514 402612
8	**Cambuslang; Flemington Hallside (F W)** Ian A. Cathcart BSc BD	1994	2018	59 Hay Crescent, Cambuslang, Glasgow G72 6QA ICathcart@churchofscotland.org.uk	0141 641 1049 07588 441895
9	**Campsie (F W)** Jane M. Denniston MA BD MTh DPT DipPSRP	2002	2016	campsieparishchurch@gmail.com Campsie Parish Church, 130 Main Street, Lennoxtown, Glasgow G66 7DA Jane.Denniston@churchofscotland.org.uk	**01360 310939** 07738 123101
10	**Chryston (H T W)** Mark Malcolm MA BD	1999	2008	chrystonchurch@hotmail.com The Manse, 109 Main Street, Chryston, Glasgow G69 9LA MMalcolm@churchofscotland.org.uk	**0141 779 4188** 0141 779 1436 07731 737377
11	**Cumbernauld: Abronhill (H W)** Joyce A. Keyes (Mrs) BD	1996	2003	26 Ash Road, Cumbernauld, Glasgow G67 3ED JKeyes@churchofscotland.org.uk	01236 723833

12	**Cumbernauld: Condorrat (H W)**				
	Vacant			11 Rosehill Drive, Cumbernauld, Glasgow G67 4EQ	01236 452090
	Session Clerk: Gordon Ross			g8dross@gmail.com	07979 911647
13	**Cumbernauld: Kildrum (H W) linked with Cumbernauld St Mungo's (W)**				
	Vacant			18 Fergusson Road, Balloch, Cumbernauld, Glasgow G67 1LS	01236 721513
14	**Cumbernauld: Old (H W)**				
	Vacant			The Manse, 23 Baronhill, Cumbernauld, Glasgow G67 2SD	01236 728853
	Valerie S. Cuthbertson (Miss)	2003		2 Muirhill Court, Hamilton ML3 6DR	01698 429232
	DipTMus DCS			VCuthbertson@churchofscotland.org.uk	
15	**Cumbernauld: St Mungo's** See Cumbernauld: Kildrum				
16	**Eaglesham (F W)**			**office@eagleshamparishchurch.co.uk**	**01355 302087**
	Jade M. Ableitner BA	2021		2 West Glebe, Cheapside Street, Eaglesham, Glasgow G76 0NS	07470 046982
				Jade.Ableitner@churchofscotland.org.uk	
17	**Fernhill and Cathkin (F W)**				
	Aquila R. Singh BA PGCE BD	2017		20 Glenlyon Place, Rutherglen, Glasgow G73 5PL	0141 389 3599
				ASingh@churchofscotland.org.uk	
18	**Gartcosh (F H T W) linked with Glenboig (F T W)**				Gartcosh: **01236 872274**
	David G. Slater BSc BA DipThRS	2011		26 Inchnock Avenue, Gartcosh, Glasgow G69 8EA	07722 876616
				DSlater@churchofscotland.org.uk	
19	**Giffnock: Orchardhill (F W)**				
	Gillian Rooney BA	2021		23 Huntly Avenue, Giffnock, Glasgow G46 6LW	**0141 638 3604**
				GRooney@orchardhill.org.uk	0141 387 8254
20	**Giffnock: South (F W)**				
	Catherine J. Beattie (Mrs) BD	2008	2011	164 Ayr Road, Newton Mearns, Glasgow G77 6EE	**0141 638 2599**
				CBeattie@churchofscotland.org.uk	0141 258 7804
21	**Giffnock: The Park (F W)**			**contact@parkchurch.org.uk**	**0141 620 2204**
	Calum D. Macdonald BD CertMin	1993	2001	41 Rouken Glen Road, Thornliebank, Glasgow G46 7JD	0141 638 3023
				CMacdonald@churchofscotland.org.uk	

22	**Glenboig** See Gartcosh			
23	**Greenbank (F H W)** Jeanne N. Roddick BD	2003	greenbankoffice@tiscali.co.uk Greenbank Manse, 38 Eaglesham Road, Clarkston, Glasgow G76 7DJ JRoddick@churchofscotland.org.uk	**0141 644 1841** 0141 644 1395
24	**Kilsyth: Anderson (F T W)** Vacant Session Clerk: Christine Johnston		Anderson Manse, 1 Kingston Road, Kilsyth, Glasgow G65 0HR johnstonchristine@hotmail.co.uk	01236 822345 01236 821060
25	**Kilsyth: Burns and Old (F W)** Robert Johnston BD MSc FSAScot	2017	**boldchurch@hotmail.com** 23 Cavalry Park, Kilsyth, Glasgow G65 0AU RJohnston@churchofscotland.org.uk	07810 377582
26	**Kirkintilloch: St Columba's Hillhead (H W)** Philip A. Wright BSc MSc PhD BTh	2017	stcolumbassecretary@outlook.com 6 Glenwood Road, Lenzie, Glasgow G66 4DS PWright@churchofscotland.org.uk	**0141 578 0016** 07427 623393
	New charge formed by the union of Kirkintilloch: Hillhead and Kirkintilloch: St Columba's			
27	**Kirkintilloch: St David's Memorial Park (F H W)** Vacant Session Clerk: David S. Forsyth		sdmp2@outlook.com 2 Roman Road, Kirkintilloch, Glasgow G66 1EA forsyth12@btinternet.com	**0141 776 4989** 0141 588 3570 07715 971397
28	**Kirkintilloch: St Mary's (W)** Ruth H.B. Morrison MA BD PhD	2009 2021	**office.stmarys@btconnect.com** 23 Braes o' Yetts, Kirkintilloch, Glasgow G66 3FF RMorrison@churchofscotland.org.uk	**0141 775 1166** 07557 657079
29	**Lenzie: Old (H W)** Louise J.E. McClements BD	2008 2016	41 Kirkintilloch Road, Lenzie, Glasgow G66 4LB LMcClements@churchofscotland.org.uk	0141 573 5006
30	**Lenzie: Union (F H W)** Daniel J.M. Carmichael MA BD	1994 2003	**office@lenzieunion.org** 1 Larch Avenue, Lenzie, Glasgow G66 4HX DCarmichael@churchofscotland.org.uk	**0141 776 1046** 0141 776 3831

	Congregation / Minister			Contact	Tel/Fax
31	**Maxwell Mearns Castle (W)** Scott R.M. Kirkland BD MAR DMin	1996	2011	office@maxwellmearns.org.uk 122 Broomfield Avenue, Newton Mearns, Glasgow G77 5JR SKirkland@churchofscotland.org.uk	**0141 639 5169** 0141 560 5603
32	**Mearns (F H W)** Joseph A. Kavanagh BD DipP'Th MTh MTh	1992	1998	office@mearnskirk.church 11 Belford Grove, Newton Mearns, Glasgow G77 5FB JKavanagh@churchofscotland.org.uk	**0141 639 6555** 0141 384 2218
33	**Milton of Campsie (F H W)** Julie H.C. Moody BA BD PGCE	2006		16 Cannerton Park, Milton of Campsie, Glasgow G66 8HR JMoody@churchofscotland.org.uk	01360 310548
34	**Moodiesburn (F W)** Mark W.J. McKeown MEng MDiv DipMin	2013	2020	info@moodiesburn.church 6 Glenapp Place, Moodiesburn, Glasgow G69 0HS MMcKeown@churchofscotland.org.uk	**01236 870515** 01236 263406 07761 097633
35	**Netherlee and Stamperland (F H W)** Scott Blythe BSc BD MBA	1997	2017	nethandstamchurch@gmail.com 25 Ormonde Avenue, Netherlee, Glasgow G44 3QY SBlythe@churchofscotland.org.uk	**0141 637 2503** 0141 533 7147 07504 692046
36	**Newton Mearns (F H W)** Stuart J. Crawford BD MTh	2017		office@churchatthecross.org.uk 28 Waterside Avenue, Newton Mearns, Glasgow G77 6TJ SCrawford@churchofscotland.org.uk	**0141 639 7373** 07912 534280
37	**Rutherglen: Old (F H T W)** Jean J. de Villiers BATheol BTh HonPsych	2003	2021	31 Highburgh Drive, Rutherglen, Glasgow G73 3RR JdeVilliers@churchofscotland.org.uk	0141 534 7477
38	**Rutherglen: Stonelaw (F T W)** Neil H. Watson BD	2017	2021	info@stonelawchurch.org 12 Hawthorn Way, Cambuslang, Glasgow G72 7AF NWatson@churchofscotland.org.uk	**0141 647 5113** 07871 615840
39	**Rutherglen: West and Wardlawhill (F W)** Malcolm Cuthbertson BA BD	1984	2017	info@westandwardlawhill.org 12 Albert Drive, Rutherglen, Glasgow G73 3RT MCuthbertson@churchofscotland.org.uk	**0844 736 1470** 07864 820612
40	**Stepps (F H W)** Gordon MacRae BD MTh	1985	2014	112 Jackson Drive, Crowwood Grange, Stepps, Glasgow G33 6GF GMacRae@churchofscotland.org.uk	0141 779 5742

41   Thornliebank (F H W)
Mike R. Gargrave BD
2008   2014
12 Parkholm Quadrant, Thornliebank, Glasgow G53 7ZH
MGargrave@churchofscotland.org.uk
0141 880 5532

42   Torrance (F T W)
Stuart D. Irvin BD
2013   2021
1 Atholl Avenue, Torrance, Glasgow G64 4JA
SIrvin@churchofscotland.org.uk
01360 620970
07421 352 893

43   Williamwood (F W)
Janet S. Mathieson MA BD ALCM PGSE
2003   2015
125 Greenwood Road, Clarkston, Glasgow G76 7LL
JMathieson@churchofscotland.org.uk
0141 638 2091
0141 579 9997

44   Glasgow: Baillieston Mure Memorial (F W) linked with Glasgow: Baillieston St Andrew's (F W)
Sandra Black BSc BD
(Interim Minister)
1988   2019
36 Glencairn Drive, Glasgow G41 4PW
SBlack@churchofscotland.org.uk
Mure Memorial: 0141 773 1216
07703 827057

45   Glasgow: Baillieston St Andrew's See Glasgow: Baillieston Mure Memorial

46   Glasgow: Balshagray Victoria Park (W)
Vacant
Session Clerk: Ranald McTaggart
20 St Kilda Drive, Glasgow G14 9JN
ranaldbvp@btinternet.com
0141 954 9780
07969 567807

47   Glasgow: Barlanark Greyfriars (W)
Vacant
Session Clerk: Jemima Bell (Mrs)
enquiries@barlanark-greyfriars.co.uk
4 Rhindmuir Grove, Baillieston, Glasgow G69 6NE
jemima.bell@ntlworld.com
0141 771 6477
0141 771 7103
0141 771 3468

48   Glasgow: Blawarthill (F T W)
G. Melvyn Wood MA BD
1982   2009
46 Earlbank Avenue, Glasgow G14 9HL
GMelvynWood@churchofscotland.org.uk
0141 579 6521

49   Glasgow: Bridgeton St Francis in the East (F H L W)
Vacant
Session Clerk: Barbara Jennings (Mrs)
bridgetonsfrancis@gmail.com   **0141 556 2830 (Church House: 0141 554 8045)**
barbara.jennings1@ntlworld.com
07856 912267

50   Glasgow: Broomhill Hyndland (F W)
George C. Mackay
BD CertMin CertEd DipPC
1994   2014
info@broomhillhyndlandchurch.org
27 St Kilda Drive, Glasgow G14 9LN
GMackay@churchofscotland.org.uk
0141 334 2540
0141 959 8697
07711 569127

No.	Name / Details			Address	Contact
51	**Glasgow: Calton Parkhead**				
	Alison E.S. Davidge MA BD	1990	2008	98 Drumover Drive, Glasgow G31 5RP ADavidge@churchofscotland.org.uk	**0141 554 3866** 07843 625059
52	**Glasgow: Cardonald (F W)**				
	Gavin McFadyen BEng BD	2006	2018	133 Newtyle Road, Paisley PA1 3LB GMcFadyen@churchofscotland.org.uk	**0141 882 6264** 0141 576 6818 07960 212106
53	**Glasgow: Carmunnock (F)**				
	Vacant				**0141 644 0655**
	Session Clerk: George Dow			george.dow@macmic.co.uk	0141 644 0689 07801 613 127
54	**Glasgow: Carmyle (W) linked with Glasgow: Kenmuir Mount Vernon (F W)**				
	Murdo MacLean BD CertMin	1997	1999	3 Meryon Road, Glasgow G32 9NW Murdo.MacLean@churchofscotland.org.uk	**0141 778 4186** 0141 770 9247 0141 774 4250
	Roland Hunt BSc PhD CertEd (Ordained Local Minister)	2016		4 Flora Gardens, Bishopbriggs, Glasgow G64 1DS RHunt@churchofscotland.org.uk	0141 778 2625 0141 563 3257
55	**Glasgow: Carntyne**				
	Vacant				
	Session Clerk: May Fawns			163 Lethamhill Road, Glasgow G33 2SQ mayfawns@sky.com	
56	**Glasgow: Carnwadric (F L W)**				
	James Gemmell BD MTh	1999	2020	62 Loganswell Road, Thornliebank, Glasgow G46 8AX JGemmell@churchofscotland.org.uk	0141 638 5884
	Mary S. Gargrave (Mrs) DCS	1989	2007	12 Parkholm Quadrant, Thornliebank, Glasgow G53 7ZH Mary.Gargrave@churchofscotland.org.uk	0141 880 5532 07896 866618
57	**Glasgow: Castlemilk (F H W)**				
	Vacant				**0141 634 7113**
	John Paul Cathcart DCS	2000	2017	156 Old Castle Road, Glasgow G44 5TW 9 Glen More, East Kilbride, Glasgow G74 2AP John.Cathcart@churchofscotland.org.uk	0141 637 5451 01355 243970 07708 396074
58	**Glasgow: Cathcart Old (F)**				
	Neil W. Galbraith BD CertMin	1987	1996	21 Courthill Avenue, Cathcart, Glasgow G44 5AA NGalbraith@churchofscotland.org.uk	Tel/Fax **0141 637 4168** 0141 633 5248

59 Glasgow: Cathcart Trinity (F H W)
Alasdair R. MacMillan LLB BD — 2015
office@cathcarttrinity.org.uk
21 Muirhill Avenue, Glasgow G44 3HP
Alasdair.MacMillan@churchofscotland.org.uk
0141 637 6658
0141 391 9102

60 Glasgow: Cathedral (High or St Mungo's) (F W)
Mark E. Johnstone DL MA BD — 1993 2019
41 Springfield Road, Bishopbriggs, Glasgow G64 1PL
Mark.Johnstone@churchofscotland.org.uk
0141 552 8198
07515 285374

61 Glasgow: Causeway (Tollcross) (F)
Monica Michelin-Salomon BD — 1999 2007
228 Hamilton Road, Glasgow G32 9QU
MMichelin-Salomon@churchofscotland.org.uk
0141 778 2413

62 Glasgow: Clincarthill (F H W)
Stuart Love BA MTh — 2016
90 Mount Annan Drive, Glasgow G44 4RZ
SLove@churchofscotland.org.uk
0141 632 4206
0141 632 2985

63 Glasgow: Colston Milton
Christopher J. Rowe BA BD — 2008
118 Birsay Road, Milton, Glasgow G22 7QP
CRowe@churchofscotland.org.uk
0141 772 1922
0141 564 1138

64 Glasgow: Colston Wellpark (F H W)
Guardianship of the Presbytery
Leslie E.T. Grieve BSc BA — 2014
(Ordained Local Minister)
23 Hertford Avenue, Kelvindale, Glasgow G12 0LG
LGrieve@churchofscotland.org.uk
0141 772 8672
07813 255052

65 Glasgow: Cranhill (F H W)
Vacant
31 Lethamhill Crescent, Glasgow G33 2SH
0141 774 3344
0141 770 6873

66 Glasgow: Croftfoot (F H W)
Robert M. Silver BA BD — 1995
4 Inchmurrin Gardens, High Burnside, Rutherglen, Glasgow G73 5RU
RSilver@churchofscotland.org.uk
0141 637 3913
0141 258 7268

67 Glasgow: Dennistoun New (F H W)
Ian M.S. McInnes BD DipMin — 1995 2008
31 Pencaitland Drive, Glasgow G32 8RL
IMcInnes@churchofscotland.org.uk
0141 554 1350
0141 564 6498

No.	Charge / Minister			Address / Email	Telephone
68	**Glasgow: Drumchapel St Andrew's (F W)** Vacant			6 Firdon Crescent, Old Drumchapel, Glasgow G15 6QQ	**0141 944 3758** 0141 944 4566
69	**Glasgow: Drumchapel St Mark's (F)** Audrey J. Jamieson BD MTh	2004	2007	146 Garscadden Road, Glasgow G15 6PR AJamieson@churchofscotland.org.uk	0141 944 5440
70	**Glasgow: Easterhouse (F W)** Derek W. Hughes BSc BD DipEd	1990	2018	3 Barony Gardens, Springhill, Glasgow G69 6TS DHughes@churchofscotland.org.uk	07723 578573
71	**Glasgow: Eastwood (F W)** James R. Teasdale BA BD	2009	2016	54 Mansewood Road, Eastwood, Glasgow G43 1TL JTeasdale@churchofscotland.org.uk	0141 571 7648
72	**Glasgow: Gairbraid (F H W)** Donald Michael MacInnes BD	2002	2011	4 Blackhill Gardens, Summerston, Glasgow G23 5NE DMacInnes@churchofscotland.org.uk	0141 946 0604
73	**Glasgow: Gallowgate** Peter L. V. Davidge BD MTh	2003	2009	98 Drumover Drive, Glasgow G31 5RP	07765 096599
74	**Glasgow: Garthamlock and Craigend (F W)** I. Scott McCarthy BD	2010	2018	9 Craigievar Court, Garthamlock, Glasgow G33 5DJ ISMcCarthy@churchofscotland.org.uk	07725 037394
75	**Glasgow: Gorbals** Vacant Session Clerk: Douglas Ellis			6 Stirlingfauld Place, Gorbals, Glasgow G5 9QF dandvellis@btinternet.com	07786 678783
76	**Glasgow: Govan and Linthouse (F T W)** David T. Gray BArch BD	2010	2020	**glpcglasgow@googlemail.com** 44 Forfar Avenue, Glasgow G52 3JQ DGray@churchofscotland.org.uk	**0141 445 2010** 07789 718622
77	**Glasgow: Hillington Park (F H W)** David A. Sutherland BD	2001	2022	81 Raeswood Road, Glasgow G53 7HH DSutherland@churchofscotland.org.uk	0141 463 3203

78 **Glasgow: Ibrox (F H W)**
Tara P. Granados (Ms) BA MDiv   2018
ibroxparishchurch@gmail.com
Ibrox Parish Church, 67 Clifford Street, Glasgow G51 1QH
TGranados@churchofscotland.org.uk
07380 **830030**
07380 830030

79 **Glasgow: John Ross Memorial Church for Deaf People (W)**   1989 1998
Richard C. Durno DipSW CQSW
31 Springfield Road, Bishopbriggs, Glasgow G64 1PJ
RDurno@churchofscotland.org.uk
Voice/Text 0141 420 1391; Fax 0141 420 3778
Voice/Text/Fax 0141 772 1052
Voice/Text/Voicemail 07748 607721

80 **Glasgow: Jordanhill (F W)**   2009 2015
Bruce H. Sinclair BA BD
jordchurch@btconnect.com
12 Priorwood Gardens, Academy Park, Glasgow G13 1GD
BSinclair@churchofscotland.org.uk
0141 959 2496
0141 959 1310

81 **Glasgow: Kelvinbridge (F W)**   1987 2003
Gordon Kirkwood BSc BD MTh
MPhil PGCE
Flat 2/2, 94 Hyndland Road, Glasgow G12 9PZ
GKirkwood@churchofscotland.org.uk
0141 339 1750
0141 334 5352

82 **Glasgow: Kelvinside Hillhead (F W)**
Vacant
Roger D. Sturrock (Prof.) BD MD FCRP   2014
(Ordained Local Minister)
36 Thomson Drive, Bearsden, Glasgow G61 3PA
RSturrock@churchofscotland.org.uk
0141 334 2788
0141 942 7412

83 **Glasgow: Kenmuir Mount Vernon** See Glasgow: Carmyle

84 **Glasgow: King's Park (F H W)**
Vacant
Session Clerks: Ian and Eunice Black
office@kingspark.church.co.uk
1101 Aikenhead Road, Glasgow G44 5SL
office@kingsparkchurch.co.uk
0141 636 8688

85 **Glasgow: Kinning Park (W)**   1988 2000
Margaret H. Johnston BD DipPEd
168 Arbroath Avenue, Cardonald, Glasgow G52 3HH
MHJohnston@churchofscotland.org.uk
0141 810 3782

86 **Glasgow: Knightswood Anniesland Trinity (F H W)**   1997 2011
Fiona M.E. Gardner (Mrs) MA MLitt BD
info@tachurch.org.uk
76 Victoria Park Drive North, Glasgow G14 9PJ
FGardner@churchofscotland.org.uk
0141 530 9745
0141 959 5647

Ruth Forsythe (Mrs) DipRS MCS   2017 2018
(Ordained Local Minister)
28 Gardenside Avenue, Carmyle, Glasgow G32 8DY
RForsythe@churchofscotland.org.uk
07824 641212
New charge formed by the union of Glasgow: Knightswood St Margaret's and Glasgow: Temple Anniesland

87	**Glasgow: Langside (F T W)** Vacant		**langsidechurch@gmail.com** 36 Madison Avenue, Glasgow G44 5AQ	**0141 632 7520** 0141 637 0797
88	**Glasgow: Maryhill (F H W)** Stuart C. Matthews BD MA	2006	2010	251 Milngavie Road, Bearsden, Glasgow G61 3DQ SMatthews@churchofscotland.org.uk	**0141 946 3512** 0141 942 0804
	James Hamilton DCS	1997	2000	6 Beckfield Gate, Glasgow G33 1SW James.Hamilton@churchofscotland.org.uk	0141 558 3195 07584 137314
89	**Glasgow: Merrylea (F W)** Vacant Session Clerk: Ralph P. Boettcher			4 Pilmuir Avenue, Glasgow G44 3HX merryleasessionclerk@outlook.com	**0141 637 2009** 07806 453724
90	**Glasgow: Newlands South (H T W)** R. Stuart M. Fulton BA BD PGCE	1991	2017	**secretary@newlandschurch.org.uk** 24 Monreith Road, Glasgow G43 2NY SFulton@churchofscotland.org.uk	**0141 632 3055** 0141 632 2588
91	**Glasgow: Partick South (F H W)** James Andrew McIntyre BD	2010		3 Branklyn Crescent, Glasgow G13 1GJ Andy.McIntyre@churchofscotland.org.uk	**0141 339 8816** 0141 959 3732
92	**Glasgow: Partick Trinity (F H T W)** Timothy D. Sinclair MA MDiv	2018		**enquiry@particktrinity.org.uk** 99 Balshagray Avenue, Glasgow G11 7EQ TSinclair@churchofscotland.org.uk	0141 563 6424
93	**Glasgow: Pollokshaws (F)** Roy J.M. Henderson MA BD DipMin	1987	2013	33 Mannering Road, Glasgow G41 3SW RHenderson@churchofscotland.org.uk	**0141 649 1879** 0141 632 8768
94	**Glasgow: Pollokshields (F H T W)** David R. Black MA BD	1986	1997	36 Glencairn Drive, Glasgow G41 4PW DBlack@churchofscotland.org.uk	0141 423 4000
95	**Glasgow: Possilpark (F)** Vacant Session Clerk: Karen Ritchie (Miss)			1262 Balmuildy Road, Glasgow G23 5HE karen.ritchie7@ntlworld.com	**0141 336 8028** 07973 439938

96 Glasgow: Queen's Park Govanhill (F W)
Vacant
Session Clerk: Jonathan Gibb
officeQPG@btinternet.com — 0141 423 3654
jogibb60@gmail.com — 07522 997748

97 Glasgow: Robroyston (F W)
Jonathan A. Keefe BSc BD   2009
info@robroystonchurch.org.uk — 0141 558 8414
7 Beckfield Drive, Glasgow G33 1SR — 0141 558 2952
JKeefe@churchofscotland.org.uk

98 Glasgow: Ruchazie (F)
Guardianship of the Presbytery
Session Clerk: Margaret Dott
— 0141 774 2759
— 0141 572 0451

99 Glasgow: Ruchill Kelvinside (W)
Vacant
ruchill.kelvinside@gmail.com — 0141 533 2731
41 Mitre Road, Glasgow G14 9LE — 0141 959 6718

100 Glasgow: St Andrew and St Nicholas (F W)
Vacant
Session Clerk: Stewart Boyle
80 Tweedsmuir Road, Glasgow G52 2RX — 0141 882 3601
stewartmboyle@gmail.com — 0141 883 9873
— 0141 427 2666

101 Glasgow: St Andrew's East (F W)
Vacant
Session Clerk: Elizabeth McIvor
43 Broompark Drive, Glasgow G31 2JB — 0141 554 1485
emcivor@talktalk.net — 0141 556 4838

102 Glasgow: St Andrew's West (F W)   1998   2019
Kleber Machado BD MTh
BTh MSc PhD
Tel: 0141 332 4293; Fax: 0141 332 8482
info@rsschurch.org.uk — 0141 332 8482
101 Hill Street, Glasgow G3 6TY — 0141 353 6551
KMachado@churchofscotland.org.uk

103 Glasgow: St Christopher's Priesthill and Nitshill (W)
Vacant
Session Clerk: Douglas MacLaren
— 0141 881 6541
douglas_maclaren@hotmail.co.uk — 07948 193783

104 Glasgow: St Columba (F GE W)
Vacant
Session Clerk: Duncan Mitchell
dpm@addapt.org.uk — 0141 221 3305
— 0141 339 9679

No.	Charge / Minister	Years	Address	Contact
105	**Glasgow: St David's Knightswood (F)** Graham M. Thain LLB BD	1988 1999	60 Southbrae Drive, Glasgow G13 1QD GThain@churchofscotland.org.uk	**0141 954 1081** 0141 959 2904
106	**Glasgow: St Enoch's Hogganfield (F H W)** Vacant		church@st-enoch.org.uk	Tel 0141 770 5694; Fax 08702 840084
107	**Glasgow: St George's Tron (F W)** Alastair S. Duncan MA BD	1989 2013	info@sgt.church 29 Hertford Avenue, Glasgow G12 0LG ADuncan@churchofscotland.org.uk	**0141 229 5746** 07968 852083
108	**Glasgow: St James' (Pollok)** Vacant Session Clerk: David T. Arbuckle		davidtarbuckle@outlook.com	**0141 882 4984** 07469 878303
109	**Glasgow: St John's Renfield (F W)** Vacant Interim Moderator: Kleber Machado		office@sjrchurch.com 26 Leicester Avenue, Glasgow G12 0LU KMachado@churchofscotland.org.uk	**0141 334 0782** 0141 339 4637 0141 353 6551
110	**Glasgow: St Paul's (F T W)** Vacant Session Clerk: Scott Stewart		38 Lochview Drive, Glasgow G33 1QF scottstewart@live.co.uk	**0141 770 8559** 0141 770 1561 07999 007900
111	**Glasgow: St Rollox (F W)** Vacant		inbox@strollox.co.uk 42 Melville Gardens, Bishopbriggs, Glasgow G64 3DE	**0141 558 1809** 0141 581 0050
112	**Glasgow: Sandyford Henderson Memorial (F H L T W)** Benjamin Thorp BD	2021	enquiries@sandyfordhenderson.net 66 Woodend Drive, Glasgow G13 1TG BThorp@churchofscotland.org.uk	**0141 226 3696** 0141 954 9013
113	**Glasgow: Sandyhills (W)** Norman A. Afrin BA MRes	2018	60 Wester Road, Glasgow G32 9JJ NAfrin@churchofscotland.org.uk	**0141 778 3415** 0141 778 1213
114	**Glasgow: Scotstoun (W)** Richard Cameron BD DipMin	2000	15 Northland Drive, Glasgow G14 9BE RCameron@churchofscotland.org.uk	0141 959 4637

115 Glasgow: Shawlands Trinity (F W)
Vacant
Interim Moderator: Stuart J. Crawford

29 St Ronan's Drive, Glasgow G41 3SQ
SCrawford@churchofscotland.org.uk

0141 649 0266
0141 258 6782
07912 534280

116 Glasgow: Sherbrooke Mosspark (F H W) 2003   2021
Adam J. Dillon BD ThM

sherbrooke-init@btconnect.com
114 Springkell Avenue, Glasgow G41 4EW
ADillon@churchofscotland.org.uk

0141 427 1968
0141 737 7299

117 Glasgow: Shettleston New (F W) 2017
W. Louis T. Reddick MA BD

211 Sandyhills Road, Glasgow G32 9NB
LReddick@churchofscotland.org.uk

0141 778 4769
0141 230 7365
07843 083548

118 Glasgow: Springburn (F H T W) 2014
Brian M. Casey MA BD

springburnparishchurch@btconnect.com
c/o Springburn Parish Church, 180 Springburn Way,
Glasgow G21 1TU
BCasey@churchofscotland.org.uk

0141 557 2345
07703 166772

119 Glasgow: Toryglen (F H T W)
Guardianship of the Presbytery

toryglenparish@gmail.com

07587 207981

120 Glasgow: Trinity Possil and Henry Drummond (W) 1990   1995
Richard G. Buckley BD MTh DMin

tphdcofs@yahoo.com
50 Highfield Drive, Glasgow G12 0HL
RBuckley@churchofscotland.org.uk

0141 339 2870

121 Glasgow: Tron St Mary's (F) 2015
Rhona E. Graham BA BD

30 Louden Hill Road, Robroyston, Glasgow G33 1GA
RGraham@churchofscotland.org.uk

122 Glasgow: Wallacewell (New Charge Development) (F T W) 1984   2011
Daniel L. Frank BA MDiv DMin

info@wallacewell.org
8 Streamfield Gate, Glasgow G33 1SJ
DFrank@churchofscotland.org.uk

0141 558 4466
0141 585 0283

123 Glasgow: Wellington (F H T W)
Richard Baxter MA BD   1997   2022
(Transition Minister)
Roger D. Sturrock (Prof.) BD MD FCRP   2014
(Ordained Local Minister)

wellingtonchurch@btinternet.com
31 Hughenden Gardens, Glasgow G12 9YH
RBaxter@churchofscotland.org.uk
36 Thomson Drive, Bearsden, Glasgow G61 3PA
RSturrock@churchofscotland.org.uk

0141 339 0454
07958 541418

0141 942 7412

124 Glasgow: Whiteinch (F W)
Laura Digan
2021
65 Victoria Park Drive South, Glasgow G14 9NX
LDigan@churchofscotland.org.uk
0141 959 9317
0141 576 9020

125 Glasgow: Yoker (F T)
Karen E. Hendry BSc BD
2005
15 Coldingham Avenue, Glasgow G14 0PX
KHendry@churchofscotland.org.uk
0141 952 3620

B. In other appointments

Name	Years	Appointment	Address / Email	Phone
Barclay, S. Grant LLB DipLP BD MSc PhD	1995 2021	Presbytery Clerk: Glasgow	Presbytery Office, 260 Bath Street, Glasgow G2 4JP GBarclay@churchofscotland.org.uk	0141 332 6606
Bell, John L. MA BD FRSCM DUniv	1978 1988	Iona Community	148 West Princes Street, Glasgow G4 9DA	0141 387 7628
Christie, Helen F. (Mrs) BD	1998 2015	Chaplain: (part-time) Forth Valley Hospitals	4B Glencairn Road, Cumbernauld G67 2EN andychristie747@yahoo.com	01236 611583
Forrest, Martin R. BA MA BD	1988 2012	Chaplain: HM Prison Low Moss	4/1, 7 Blochairn Place, Glasgow G21 2EB martinrforrest@gmail.com	0141 552 1132
Foster-Fulton, Sally BA BD	1999 2016	Head of Christian Aid Scotland	24 Monreith Road, Glasgow G43 2NY sallyfulton01@gmail.com	07850 937226
Gardner, Peter M. MA BD	1988 2016	Pioneer Minister, Glasgow Arts Community	Flat 3/2, 10 Haggswood Avenue, Glasgow G41 4RE PGardner@churchofscotland.org.uk	07743 539654
Gay, Douglas C. MA BD PhD	1998 2005	University of Glasgow: Trinity College	4 Copland Place, Glasgow G51 2RS douggay@mac.com	0141 330 2073 / 07971 321452
Herbert, Claire DCS	2019	Chaplain, Lodging House Mission, Glasgow	35 East Campbell Street, Glasgow G51 5DT CHerbert@churchofscotland.org.uk	0141 552 0285
Johnston, Mark G. BSc BD DMin	1998 2020	Tutor in Pastoral Studies, Trinity College, University of Glasgow	4 Professors' Square, Glasgow G12 8QQ mark.johnston.2@glasgow.ac.uk	0141 330 6526
Kelly, Carolyn PhD	2015 2020	Chaplain, University of Glasgow	West Quadrangle, University Avenue, Glasgow G12 8QQ chaplaincy@glasgow.ac.uk	0141 331 4160
Kelly, Ewan R. BSc MB ChB BD PhD	1994 2020	Lecturer in Healthcare Chaplaincy, University of Glasgow	Flat 1/2, 17 Overdale Street, Glasgow G42 9PZ ewan.kelly@glasgow.ac.uk	0141 649 2714
Love, Joanna R. (Ms) BSc DCS	1992 2009	Iona Community: Wild Goose Resource Group	92 Everard Drive, Glasgow G21 1XQ jo@wildgoose.scot	(Office) 0141 429 7281
MacDonald, Anne (Miss) BA DCS	1980 2002	Healthcare Chaplain	Chaplaincy Office, Glasgow Royal Infirmary G4 0SF	0141 211 4661
Maxwell, David	2014	Ordained Local Minister	248 Old Castle Road, Glasgow G44 5EZ DMaxwell@churchofscotland.org.uk	0141 569 6379
McDougall, Hilary N. (Mrs) MA PGCE BD	2004 2013	Depute Clerk & Congregational Facilitator: Presbytery of Glasgow	Presbytery Office, 260 Bath Street, Glasgow G2 4JP HMcdougall@churchofscotland.org.uk	07561 427802 / 0141 332 6606
McPake, John L. BA BD PhD	1987 2017	Ecumenical Officer, Church of Scotland	121 George Street, Edinburgh EH2 4YN JMcPake@churchofscotland.org.uk	07539 321832 / 0131 240 2208
Peat, Derek A. BA BD MTh	2013 2021	Strategy Officer: Presbytery of Glasgow	Presbytery Office, 260 Bath Street, Glasgow G2 4JP DPeat@churchofscotland.org.uk	0141 332 6606

C. Retaining

Name	Charge		Years	Address	Phone
Alexander, Eric J. MA BD	(Glasgow: St George's Tron)		1958 1997	77 Norwood Park, Bearsden, Glasgow G61 2RZ	0141 942 4404
Beaton, Margaret S. (Miss) DCS	(Deacon)		1989 2015	64 Gardenside Grove, Carmyle, Glasgow G32 8EZ margaretbeaton.54@hotmail.com	0141 646 2297 07796 642382
Birch, James PgDip FRSA FIOC	(Auxiliary Minister)		2001 2007	1 Kirkhill Grove, Cambuslang, Glasgow G72 8EH	0141 583 1722
Black, Ian W. MA BD	(Grangemouth: Zetland)		1976 2013	Flat 1R, 2 Carrickvale Court, Carrickstone, Cumbernauld, Glasgow G68 0LA iwblack@hotmail.com	01236 453370
Black, William B. MA BD	(Stornoway: High)		1970 2011	33 Tankerland Road, Glasgow G44 4EN revwillieblack@gmail.com	0141 637 4717
Blount, A. Sheila (Mrs) BD BA	(Cupar: St John's and Dairsie United)		1978 2010	28 Alcaig Road, Mosspark, Glasgow G52 1NH asheilablount@gmail.com	0141 419 0746
Campbell, John LTh BA MA BSc	(Caldwell)		1973 2009	96 Boghead Road, Lenzie, Glasgow G66 4EN johncampbell.lenzie@gmail.com	0141 776 0874
Cartlidge, Graham R.G. MA BD STM	(Glasgow: Eastwood)		1977 2015	5 Briar Grove, Newlands, Glasgow G43 2TG	0141 637 3228
Clark, Douglas W. LTh	(Lenzie: Old)		1993 2015	2 Poplar Drive, Lenzie, Glasgow G66 4DN douglaswclark@hotmail.com	0141 776 1298
Cunningham, Alexander MA BD	(Presbytery Clerk: Glasgow)		1961 2002	18 Lady Jane Gate, Bothwell, Glasgow G71 8BW	01698 811051
Denniston, David W. BD DipMin	(Interim Minister, Glasgow: Queen's Park Govanhill)		1981 2022	c/o Campsie Parish Church, 130 Main Street, Lennoxtown, Glasgow G66 7DA DDenniston@churchofscotland.org.uk	07903 926727
Drummond, John W. MA BD	(Rutherglen: West and Wardlawhill)		1971 2011	25 Kingsburn Drive, Rutherglen, Glasgow G73 2AN	0141 571 6002
Duff, T. Malcolm F. MA BD MTh	(Glasgow: Queen's Park)		1985 2009	54 Hawkhead Road, Paisley PA1 3NB	0141 570 0614 07846 926584
Dutch, Morris M. BD BA Dip BTI	(Costa del Sol)		1998 2013	41 Baronald Drive, Glasgow G12 OHN mmdutch@yahoo.co.uk	0141 357 2286
Easton, David J.C. MA BD	(Burnside Blairbeth)		1965 2005	6 Peveril Court, Burnside, Glasgow G73 4RE deaston@btinternet.com	0141 634 9775
Farrington, Alexandra LTh	(Campsie)		2003 2015	'Glenburn', High Banton, Kilsyth G65 0RA revsfarrington@aol.co.uk	01236 824516
Ferguson, James B. LTh	(Lenzie: Union)		1972 2002	3 Bridgeway Place, Kirkintilloch, Glasgow G66 3HW	0141 588 5868
Finnie, Bill H. BA DipSW CertCRS	(Ordained Local Minister, Kirkintilloch: Hillhead)		2015 2022	27 Hallside Crescent, Cambuslang, Glasgow G72 7DY BFinnie@churchofscotland.org.uk	07518 357138
Fraser, Alexander M. BD DipMin	(Glasgow: Knightswood St Margaret's)		1985 2019	39 McConnell Road, Lochwinnoch PA12 4EB	07753 686603
Galloway, Ian F. BA BD	(Glasgow: Gorbals)		1977 2021	IGalloway@churchofscotland.org.uk	
Haley, Derek BD DPS	(Chaplain: Gartnavel Royal Hospital)		1960 1999	9 Kinnaird Crescent, Bearsden, Glasgow G61 2BN	0141 942 9281
Hope, Evelyn P. (Miss) BA BD	(Wishaw: Thornlie)		1990 1998	Flat 0/1, 48 Moss Side Road, Glasgow G41 3UA	0141 649 1522
Hudson, Howard R. MA BD	(Glasgow: Bridgeton St Francis in the East)		1982 2021	4 Larch Square, Cambuslang, Glasgow G72 7BQ	
Hughes, Helen (Miss) DCS	(Deacon)		1977 2008	2/2, 43 Burnbank Terrace, Glasgow G20 6UQ helhug35@gmail.com	0141 333 9459 07752 604817

Name	(Role)	Years	Address	Phone
Hunter, Alastair G. BSc MSc BD	(University of Glasgow)	1976 2009	6 Whittingehame Court, 1350 Great Western Road, Glasgow G12 0BG ian.ciw.johnson@btinternet.com	07484 256472
Johnson, C. Ian W. MA BD	(Dumbarton: Riverside with Dumbarton: St Andrew's with Dumbarton: West)	1997 2022	13 Kilmardinny Crescent, Bearsden, Glasgow G61 3NP	0141 931 5862
Johnston, Robert W.M. MA BD STM	(Glasgow: Temple Anniesland)	1964 1999	3/1, 952 Pollokshaws Road, Glasgow G41 2ET	0141 636 5819
Johnstone, H. Martin J. MA BD MTh PhD	(Secretary: Church and Society Council)	1989 2020	MJohnstone@churchofscotland.org.uk	
Lunan, David W. MA BD DLitt DD	(Presbytery Clerk: Glasgow)	1970 2009	30 Mill Road, Banton, Glasgow G65 0RD	01236 824110
Lyall, Ann DCS	(Deacon, Glasgow: Baillieston Mure Memorial with St Andrew's; Glasgow: Govan and Linthouse)	1980 2022	117 Barlia Drive, Glasgow G45 0AY ALyall@churchofscotland.org.uk	0141 631 3643
MacDonald, Kenneth D. MA BA	(Auxiliary Minister)	2001 2006	5 Henderland Road, Bearsden, Glasgow G61 1AH	0141 943 1103
MacFadyen, Anne M. (Mrs) BSc BD FSAScot	(Auxiliary Minister)	1995 2003	295 Mearns Road, Glasgow G77 5LT	0141 639 3605
Mackenzie, Gordon R. BScAgr BD	(Chapelhall)	1977 2014	16 Crowhill Road, Bishopbriggs, Glasgow G64 1QY rev.g.mackenzie@btopenworld.com	0141 772 6052
Mackinnon, Campbell BSc BD	(Glasgow: Balshagray Victoria Park)	1982 2019	campbellbvp@live.com	0141 772 3811
MacKinnon, Charles M. BD CertMin	(Kilsyth: Anderson)	1989 2009	36 Hilton Terrace, Bishopbriggs, Glasgow G64 3HB cm.ccmackinnon@gmail.com	
Macleod, Donald BD LRAM DRSAM	(Blairgowrie)	1987 2008	9 Millersneuk Avenue, Lenzie G66 5HJ donmac2@sky.com	0141 776 6235
MacQuarrie, Stuart D. JP BD BSc MBA MPhil	(Chaplain: University of Glasgow)	1984 2020		
MacRae, Elaine H. (Mrs) BD	(Glasgow: St Enoch's Hogganfield)	1985 2021	112 Jackson Drive, Crowwood Grange, Stepps, Glasgow G33 6GF EMacRae@churchofscotland.org.uk	0141 779 5742 07834 269487
Manastireanu, Daniel BA MTh AdvDipTCouns	(Glasgow: St Paul's)	2010 2020	61 Vancouver Walk, Glasgow G40 4TP DManastireanu@churchofscotland.org.uk	
McLachlan, David N. BD	(Glasgow: Langside)	1985 2021	16 Kinpurnie Road, Paisley PA1 3HH eric.janis@btinternet.com	0141 810 5789
McLachlan, Eric BD MTh CPS	(Glasgow: Cardonald)	1978 2005		
McLachlan, T. Alastair BSc	(Craignish with Kilbrandon and Kilchattan with Kilninver and Kilmelford)	1972 2009	9 Alder Road, Milton of Campsie, Glasgow G66 8HH talastair@btinternet.com	01360 319861
McLaren, D. Muir BA BD MTh PhD	(Glasgow: Mosspark)	1971 2001	House 44, 145 Shawhill Road, Glasgow G43 1SX muir44@yahoo.co.uk	07931 155779
McLellan, Margaret DCS	(Deacon)	1986 2018	18 Broom Road East, Newton Mearns, Glasgow G77 5SD margaretdmclellan@outlook.com	0141 639 6853
McWilliam, Alan BD MTh	(Glasgow: Whiteinch)	1993 2019	1 Springbank Gardens, Glasgow G31 4QD AMcWilliam@churchofscotland.org.uk	
Miller, Elsie M. (Miss) DCS	(Deacon)	1974 2001	30 Swinton Avenue, Rowanbank, Baillieston, Glasow G69 6JR	0141 771 0857
Miller, John D. BA BD STM DD	(Glasgow: Castlemilk East)	1971 2007	98 Kirkcaldy Road, Glasgow G41 4LD rev.john.miller@btinternet.com	0141 423 0221
Moffat, Thomas BSc BD	(Culross and Torryburn)	1976 2008	Flat 8/1, 8 Cranston Street, Glasgow G3 8GG tom@gallus.org.uk	0141 248 1886
Nelson, Thomas BSc BD	(Netherlee)	1992 2002	11a Crosshill Drive, Rutherglen, Glasgow G73 3QU	0141 534 7834

Name	Charge / position			Address / contact	Telephone
Nicholson, David DCS	(Deacon)	1994	2020	2D Doonside, Kildrum, Cumbernauld, Glasgow G67 2HX	01236 732260
Nicol, Douglas M. CA BD	(Glasgow: St Christopher's Priesthill and Nitshill)	1987	2021	19 Rockmount Avenue, Thornliebank, Glasgow G46 7BU DNicol@churchofscotland.org.uk	0141 569 7848
Ninian, Esther J. (Miss) MA BD DipLib	(Newton Mearns)	1993	2015	21 St Ronan's Drive, Burnside, Rutherglen G73 3SR estherninian5914@btinternet.com	0141 647 9720
Paciti, Stephen A. MA	(Black Mount with Culter with Libberton and Quothquan)	1963	2003	157 Nithsdale Road, Glasgow G41 5RD	0141 423 5792
Pearson, Wilma (Mrs) BD	(Associate, Glasgow: Cathcart Trinity)	2004	2018	90 Newlands Road, Glasgow G43 2JR WPearson@churchofscotland.org.uk	0141 632 2491
Pollock, Thomas L. BA BD MTh FSAScot JP	(Glasgow: Sherbrooke Mosspark)	1982	2021	27 Dorchester Court, Monmouth Avenue, Glasgow G12 0BT TPollock@churchofscotland.org.uk	
Purves, John S. LLB BD	(Glasgow: Drumchapel St Andrew's)	1983	2022	28 Cloberhill Road, Glasgow G13 2JL johnpurves278@btinternet.com	0141 286 0917
Raeburn, Alan C. MA BD	(Glasgow: Battlefield East)	1971	2010	3 Orchard Gardens, Strathaven ML10 6UN acraeburn@hotmail.com	01357 522924
Ramsay, W.G.	(Glasgow: Springburn)	1967	1999	53 Kelvinvale, Kirkintilloch, Glasgow G66 1RD billram@btopenworld.com	0141 776 2915
Reid, Iain M.A. BD CQSW DipSW	(Paisley Glenburn)	1990	2017	16 Walker Court, Glasgow G16 6QP ireid@churchofscotland.org.uk	0141 577 1200
Ross, Donald M. MA	(Industrial Mission Organiser)	1953	1993	14 Cartsbridge Road, Busby, Glasgow G76 8DH	0141 644 2220
Ross, Joan BSc BD PhD	(Glasgow: Carntyne)	1999	2022	4 Moncrieff Gardens, Lenzie G66 4NN	
Smith, G. Stewart MA BD STM	(Glasgow: King's Park)	1966	2006	33 Brent Road, Stewartfield, East Kilbride, Glasgow G74 4RA stewartandmary@googlemail.com	Tel/Fax 01355 226718
Spencer, John MA BD	(Dumfries: Lincluden with Holywood)	1962	2001	10 Kinkell Gardens, Kirkintilloch, Glasgow G66 2HJ	0141 777 8935
Stewart, Diane E. BD CertMin	(Milton of Campsie)	1988	2006	4 Miller Gardens, Bishopbriggs, Glasgow G64 1FG destewart@givemail.co.uk	0141 762 1358
Stewart, Norma D. (Miss) MA MEd BD MTh	(Glasgow: Strathbungo Queen's Park)	1977	2000	127 Nether Auldhouse Road, Glasgow G43 2YS	0141 637 6956
Thomson, Andrew BA	(Airdrie: Broomknoll)	1976	2007	3 Laurel Wynd, Drumsagard Village, Cambuslang, Glasgow G72 7BH AThomson@churchofscotland.org.uk	0141 641 2936 07772 502774
Tuton, Robert M. MA	(Glasgow: Shettleston Old)	1957	1995	6 Holmwood Gardens, Uddingston, Glasgow G71 7BH	01698 321108
White, C. Peter BVMS BD	(Glasgow: Sandyford Henderson Memorial)	1974	2011	2 Hawthorn Place, Torrance, Glasgow G64 4EA revcpw@gmail.com	01360 622680
White, David M. BA BD DMin	(Kirkintilloch: St Columba's)	1988	2016	9 Lapwing Avenue, Lenzie, Glasgow G66 3DJ drdavidmwhite@btinternet.com	0141 578 4357
Whyte, James BD	(Fairlie)	1981	2011	32 Torbum Avenue, Giffnock, Glasgow G46 7RB jameswhyte89@btinternet.com	0141 620 3043
Wilson, Phyllis M. (Mrs) DipCom DipRE CertMin	(Motherwell: South Dalziel)	1985	2006	Glasgow thomas.wilson38@btinternet.com	
Younger, Adah (Mrs) BD LLB	(Glasgow: Dennistoun Central)	1978	2004	Flat 2/3, 53 Barloch Street, Glasgow G22 5BX	07947 580924

ADDRESSES

Bishopbriggs	
Kenmure	Viewfield Road, Bishopbriggs
Springfield Cambridge	The Leys, off Springfield Road
Broom	Mearns Road, Newton Mearns
Burnside Blairbeth	Church Avenue, Burnside
	Kirkriggs Avenue, Blairbeth
Busby	Church Road, Busby
Cadder	Cadder Road, Bishopbriggs
Cambuslang	Arnott Way
Flemington Hallside	Hutchinson Place
Campsie	Main Street, Lennoxtown
Chryston	Main Street, Chryston
Cumbernauld	
Abronhill	Larch Road
Condorrat	Main Road
Kildrum	Clouden Road
Old	Baronhill
St Mungo's	St Mungo's Road
Eaglesham	Montgomery Street, Eaglesham
Fernhill and Cathkin	Neilvaig Drive
Gartcosh	113 Lochend Road, Gartcosh
Giffnock	
Orchardhill	Church Road
South	Eastwood Toll
The Park	Ravenscliffe Drive
Glenboig	Main Street, Glenboig
Greenbank	Eaglesham Road, Clarkston
Kilsyth	
Anderson	Kingston Road, Kilsyth
Burns and Old	Church Street, Kilsyth
Kirkintilloch	Newdyke Road and
St Columba's	Waterside Road nr Auld Aisle Road
Hillhead	Alexandra Street
St David's Mem Pk	Cowgate
St Mary's	
Lenzie	
Old	Kirkintilloch Road x Garngaber Ave
Union	65 Kirkintilloch Road

Maxwell	Waterfoot Road
Mearns Castle	
Mearns	Mearns Road, Newton Mearns
Milton of Campsie	Locheil Drive, Milton of Campsie
Moodiesburn	20 Blackwoods Crescent, Moodiesburn
Netherlee	Ormonde Drive x Ormonde Avenue
and Stamperland	
Newton Mearns	Ayr Road, Newton Mearns
Rutherglen	
Old	Main Street at Queen Street
Stonelaw	Stonelaw Road x Dryburgh Avenue
West and Wardlawhill	3 Western Avenue
Stepps	Whitehill Avenue
Thornliebank	61 Spiersbridge Road
Torrance	School Road, Torrance
Williamwood	4 Vardar Avenue, Clarkston
Glasgow	
Baillieston	
Mure Memorial	Maxwell Drive, Garrowhill
St Andrew's	Bredisholm Road
Balshagray Victoria Pk	218–230 Broomhill Drive
Barlanark Greyfriars	Edinburgh Rd x Hallhill Rd (365)
Blawarthill	Millbrix Avenue
Bridgeton St Francis in the East	26 Queen Mary Street
Broomhill Hyndland	64–66 Randolph Rd (x Marlborough Ave)
Calton Parkhead	122 Helenvale Street
Cardonald	2155 Paisley Road West
Carmunnock	Kirk Road, Carmunnock
Carmyle	155 Carmyle Avenue
Carntyne	358 Carntynehall Road
Carnwadric	556 Boydstone Road, Thornliebank
Castlemilk	1 Dougrie Road
Cathcart	
Old	119 Carmunnock Road
Trinity	90 Clarkston Road

Cathedral	Cathedral Square, 2 Castle Street
Causeway, Tollcross	1134 Tollcross Road
Clincarthill	1216 Cathcart Road
Colston Milton	Egilsay Crescent
Colston Wellpark	1378 Springburn Road
Cranhill	109 Bellrock St (at Bellrock Cr)
Croftfoot	Croftpark Ave x Crofthill Road
Dennistoun New	9 Armadale Street
Drumchapel	
St Andrew's	153 Garscadden Road
St Mark's	281 Kinfauns Drive
Easterhouse	Boyndie Street
Eastwood	Mansewood Road
Gairbraid	1517 Maryhill Road
Gallowgate	Calton Parkhead halls
	122 Helenvale Street
Garthamlock and Craigend	46 Porchester Street
Gorbals	1 Errol Gardens
Govan and Linthouse	Govan Cross
Hillington Park	24 Berryknowes Road
Ibrox	Carillon Road x Clifford Street
John Ross Memorial	at Queen's Park Govanhill Church
Jordanhill	28 Woodend Drive (x Munro Road)
Kelvinbridge	Belmont Street at Belmont Bridge
Kelvinside Hillhead	Observatory Road
Kenmuir Mount Vernon	2405 London Road, Mount Vernon
King's Park	242 Castlemilk Road
Kinning Park	Eaglesham Place
Knightswood	2000 Great Western Road
Anniesland Trinity	869 Crow Road
Langside	167–169 Ledard Road (x Lochleven Road)
Maryhill	1990 Maryhill Road
Merrylea	78 Merrylee Road
Newlands South	Riverside Road x Langside Drive

Church	Address
Partick South	259 Dumbarton Road
Partick Trinity	20 Lawrence Street x Elie Street
Pollokshaws	223 Shawbridge Street
Pollokshields	Albert Drive x Shields Road
Possilpark	124 Saracen Street
Queen's Park Govanhill	170 Queen's Drive
Robroyston	34 Saughs Road
Ruchazie	4 Elibank Street (x Milncroft Road)
Ruchill Kelvinside	Shakespeare Street nr Maryhill Rd
St Andrew and St Nicholas	224 Hartlaw Crescent
St Andrew's East	681 Alexandra Parade
St Andrew's West	260 Bath Street
St Christopher's Priesthill and Nitshill	100 Priesthill Rd (x Muirshiel Cr)
St Columba	300 St Vincent Street
St David's Knightswood	66 Boreland Drive (nr Lincoln Avenue)
St Enoch's Hogganfield	860 Cumbernauld Road
St George's Tron	163 Buchanan Street
St James' (Pollok)	Lyoncross Road x Byrebush Road
St John's Renfield	22 Beaconsfield Road
St Paul's	30 Langdale St (x Greenrig St)
St Rollox	70 Fountainwell Road
Sandyford Henderson Memorial	Kelvinhaugh Street at Argyle Street
Sandyhills	28 Baillieston Rd nr Sandyhills Rd
Scotstoun	Earlbank Ave x Ormiston Ave
Shawlands Cross	(1114 Pollokshaws Road)
Shawlands Trinity	Nithsdale Rd x Sherbrooke Avenue
Sherbrooke Mosspark	679 Old Shettleston Road
Shettleston New	180 Springburn Way
Springburn	Glenmore Ave nr Prospecthill Road
Torglen	2 Crowhill Street (x Broadholm Street)
Trinity Possil and Henry Drummond	128 Red Road
Tron St Mary's	57 Northgate Rd. Balornock
Wallacewell	University Ave x Southpark Ave
Wellington	1a Northinch Court
Whiteinch	10 Hawick Street
Yoker	

(17) FORTH VALLEY AND CLYDESDALE (F W)

New presbytery formed by the union of the Presbyteries of Hamilton and Lanark on 1 January 2022 and of Falkirk on 1 June 2022.
Meets in 2022 on 4 October and 26 November and in 2023 on the first Saturday of March, June and September and the last Saturday of November at GLO Centre, Motherwell and Motherwell: Dalziel St Andrew's Church.

Presbytery Office:		Rex House, 103 Bothwell Road, Hamilton ML3 0DW	01698 285672
		fvandc@churchofscotland.org.uk	
Clerk:	REV. JULIE M. RENNICK BTh	c/o The Presbytery Office; jrennick@churchofscotland.org.uk	
Depute Clerk:	REV. BRYAN KERR BA BD	c/o The Presbytery Office; bkerr@churchofscotland.org.uk	
Treasurer:	MR DAVID J. WATT BAcc CA CPFA	c/o The Presbytery Office; david.j.watt@btinternet.com	

1   Airdrie: Cairnlea (F H W) linked with Calderbank (F T)
Peter H. Donald MA PhD BD   1991   2018
31 Victoria Place, Airdrie ML6 9BU
PDonald@churchofscotland.org.uk
Cairnlea: 01236 762101
01236 753159

2   Airdrie: Clarkston (F W)
Hanna I. Rankine BA BD   2018
enquiries@airdrieclarkstonparishchurch.org.uk
66 Wellhall Road, Hamilton ML3 9BY
HRankine@churchofscotland.org.uk
01236 756862

3   Airdrie: High (W) linked with Caldercruix and Longriggend (H)
Ian R.W. McDonald BSc BD PhD   2007
17 Etive Drive, Airdrie ML6 9QL
IMcDonald@churchofscotland.org.uk
High: 01236 779620
01236 760023

4   Airdrie: Jackson (W)
Kay Gilchrist (Miss) BD CertMin DipPC   1996   2008
48 Dunrobin Road, Airdrie ML6 8LR
KGilchrist@churchofscotland.org.uk
01236 597649

5   Airdrie: New Monkland (F H W) linked with Greengairs (F W)
Vacant
Session Clerk, Airdrie: New Monkland: Helene Marshall
Session Clerk, Greengairs: Sheena Walker
3 Dykehead Crescent, Airdrie ML6 6PU
helenemarshall@blueyonder.co.uk
sheena.walker4@icloud.com
01236 761723
01236 751945
01236 830347

6   Airdrie: New Wellwynd (W)
Robert A. Hamilton BA BD   1995   2001
72 Inverlochy Road, Airdrie ML6 9DJ
RHamilton@churchofscotland.org.uk
01236 748646
01236 763022

7	**Airdrie: St Columba's (F)**				
	Margaret F. Currie BEd BD	1980	1987	52 Kennedy Drive, Airdrie ML6 9AW	01236 763173
				MCurrie@churchofscotland.org.uk	
8	**Airth (F H)**				
	James F. Todd BD CPS	1984	2012	The Manse, Airth, Falkirk FK2 8LS	01324 831120
				JTodd@churchofscotland.org.uk	
9	**Bellshill: Central (F T W)**				
	Kevin M. de Beer BTh	1995	2016	32 Adamson Street, Bellshill ML4 1DT	01698 841176
				KdeBeer@churchofscotland.org.uk	07555 265609
10	**Bellshill: West (F H W)**				
	Vacant			16 Croftpark Street, Bellshill ML4 1EY	**01698 747581**
	Session Clerk: Annabel Leitch			leitch.a@sky.com	01698 842877
					01698 810143
11	**Biggar (F H W) linked with Black Mount**			**biggarkirk09@gmail.com**	**01889 229291**
	Mike D. Fucella BD MTh	1997	2013	'Candlemas', 6C Leafield Road, Biggar ML12 6AY	01899 229291
				MFucella@churchofscotland.org.uk	
12	**Black Mount** See Biggar				
13	**Blackbraes and Shieldhill (W) linked with Muiravonside (F W)**				
	Vacant				
	Interim Moderator: Scott W. Burton			Scott.Burton@churchofscotland.org.uk	01324 712062
14	**Blantyre: Livingstone Memorial (F W) linked with Blantyre St Andrew's (F) info@livingstonechurch.org.uk**				
	Murdo C. Macdonald MA BD	2002	2017	332 Glasgow Road, Blantyre, Glasgow G72 9LQ	01698 769699
				Murdo.Macdonald@churchofscotland.org.uk	
15	**Blantyre: Old (F H T W)**				
	Vacant			The Manse, Craigmuir Road, High Blantyre, Glasgow G72 9UA	01698 769046
	Session Clerk: Mary Gallacher			mary.gallacherclerk@yahoo.com	01698 821958
16	**Blantyre: St Andrew's** See Blantyre: Livingstone Memorial				

17 Bo'ness: Old (F H T W)
Amanda J. MacQuarrie MA PGCE MTh   2014   2016
10 Dundas Street, Bo'ness EH51 0DG
A.MacQuarrie@churchofscotland.org.uk
01506 828504

18 Bo'ness: St Andrew's (F W)
Vacant
Interim Moderator: David Wandrum
St Andrew's Manse, 11 Erngath Road, Bo'ness EH51 9DP
DWandrum@churchofscotland.org.uk
01506 825803
01506 822195
01236 723288

19 Bonnybridge: St Helen's (F H W)
Vacant
Interim Moderator: Ronald Matandakufa
The Manse, 32 Reilly Gardens, High Bonnybridge FK4 2BB
RMatandakufa@churchofscotland.org.uk
01324 874807
01324 337885

20 Bothkennar and Carronshore (W)
Andrew J. Moore BSc BD   2007
11 Hunter Place, Greenmount Park, Carronshore, Falkirk FK2 8QS
AMoore@churchofscotland.org.uk
01324 570525

21 Bothwell (F H W)
Iain M.T. Majcher BD   2020
office@bothwellparishchurch.org.uk
Bothwell Parish Church, Main Street, Bothwell, Glasgow G71 8EX
IMajcher@churchofscotland.org.uk
01698 854903
01698 600933

22 Brightons (F H T W)
Scott W. Burton BA BA   2019
info@brightonschurch.org.uk
Brightons Manse, Maddiston Road, Brightons, Falkirk FK2 0JP
Scott.Burton@churchofscotland.org.uk
01324 713855
01324 715565

23 Cairngryffe (F W) linked with Libberton and Quothquan (F H W) linked with Symington (F W) (The Tinto Parishes)
contactus@symingtonkirk.com
Vacant
Session Clerk, Cairngryffe: Rosmairi J. Galloway (Dr)   16 Abington Road, Symington, Biggar ML12 6JX
Session Clerk, Libberton and Quothquan: Paul J. Dobie   pepperknowes@btinternet.com
paul.dobie@hebrides.net
Session Clerk, Symington: Robert Carson   robertdcarson@yahoo.com
01899 309400
07733 446567
01899 308248
07717 847446
01899 309061

24 Calderbank See Airdrie: Cairnlea
25 Caldercruix and Longriggend See Airdrie: High

26 Carluke: Kirkton (H W)
Iain D. Cunningham MA BD   1979   1987
kirktonchurch@btconnect.com
9 Station Road, Carluke ML8 5AA
ICunningham@churchofscotland.org.uk
01555 750778
01555 771262

27 Carluke: St Andrew's (H W)
Helen E. Jamieson (Mrs) BD DipEd — 1989
standrewscarluke@btinternet.com
120 Clyde Street, Carluke ML8 5BG
HJamieson@churchofscotland.org.uk
01555 771218

28 Carluke: St John's (F H W)
Elijah O. Obinna BA MTh PhD — 2002, 2016
18 Old Bridgend, Carluke ML8 4HN
EObinna@churchofscotland.org.uk
01555 751730
01555 752389

29 Carnwath (H) linked with Carstairs (W)
Sumit Harrison BA DipTh BTh — 2013, 2020
11 Range View, Cleghorn, Carstairs, Lanark ML11 8TF
SHarrison@churchofscotland.org.uk
01555 668868

30 Carriden (H W)
Vacant
David C. Wandrum — 1993, 2017
(Auxiliary Minister)
The Spires, Foredale Terrace, Carriden, Bo'ness EH51 9LW
5 Cawder View, Carrickstone Meadows, Cumbernauld, Glasgow G68 0BN
DWandrum@churchofscotland.org.uk
PHacking@churchofscotland.org.uk
01506 822141
01236 723288

Interim Moderator: Philip R. Hacking
01324 337936

31 Carstairs See Carnwath

32 Chapelhall (F H W) linked with Kirk o' Shotts (F H W)
Vacant
The Manse, Russell Street, Chapelhall, Airdrie ML6 8SG
bettymcl175@btinternet.com
rossdrumduff@gmail.com
01236 763439
01236 765249
07450 275307
Session Clerk, Chapelhall: Betty McLean
Session Clerk, Kirk o' Shotts: Eileen Ross

33 Cleland (F H) linked with Wishaw: St Mark's (F)
Vacant
3 Laburnum Crescent, Wishaw ML2 7EH
craig.mains@yahoo.co.uk
barbaracurtin47@gmail.com
01698 384596
01698 814875
07939 102784
Session Clerk, Cleland: Craig Mains
Session Clerk, Wishaw: St Mark's: Barbara Curtin

34 Coalburn and Lesmahagow (F H W)
Morag V. Garrett (Mrs) BD — 2011, 2021
candle.church2@gmail.com
9 Elmbank, Lesmahagow ML11 0EA
MGarrett@churchofscotland.org.uk
01555 892425
01555 890460

35 Coatbridge: Blairhill Dundyvan (H W) linked with Coatbridge: Middle (W)
Blairhill Dundyvan:
Vacant
1 Nelson Terrace, East Kilbride, Glasgow G74 2EY
myrafraser@hotmail.co.uk
01236 435198
01355 520093
01236 421728
Session Clerk, Blairhill Dundyvan: Myra Fraser

36 Coatbridge: Calder (F H W) linked with Coatbridge: Old Monkland (F W)
Vacant   26 Bute Street, Coatbridge ML5 4HF   01236 421516
Session Clerk, Old Monkland: Alison McGowan (Mrs)   alisonrobertsonmcgowan@gmail.com   07798 644253

37 Coatbridge: Middle See Coatbridge: Blairhill Dundyvan

38 Coatbridge: New St Andrew's (W)
Fiona M. Nicolson BA BD CQSW   1996   2005   77 Eglinton Street, Coatbridge ML5 3JF   01236 437271
                                              FNicolson@churchofscotland.org.uk

39 Coatbridge: Old Monkland See Coatbridge: Calder

40 Coatbridge: Townhead (F H)
Ecito Selemani LTh MTh   1993   2004   The Manse, Crinan Crescent, Coatbridge ML5 2LH   01236 702914
                                              ESelemani@churchofscotland.org.uk

41 Crossford (H) linked with Kirkfieldbank
Steven Reid BAcc CA BD   1989   1997   74 Lanark Road, Crossford, Carluke ML8 5RE   01555 860415
                                              SReid@churchofscotland.org.uk

42 Dalserf (F H)
Vacant   Manse Brae, Dalserf, Larkhall ML9 3BN   01698 882195
Session Clerk: Joan Pollok   joan.pollok@btinternet.com   07728 337212

43 Denny: Old (W) linked with Haggs (H W)
Raheel Arif MSc MEd BA   2019   **haggschurch1@yahoo.co.uk**   01324 819149
                                              57 Singers Place, Dennyloanhead FK4 1FD
                                              RArif@churchofscotland.org.uk

44 Denny: Westpark (F H W)
D. I. Kipchumba Too BTh MTh MSc 2017   13 Baxter Crescent, Denny FK6 5EZ   01324 882220
                                              KToo@churchofscotland.org.uk   07340 868067

45 Douglas Valley (F W)
Guardianship of the Presbytery   **office.tdvc@yahoo.co.uk**   **01555 850000**
Session Clerk: Andy Robinson   The Manse, Douglas, Lanark ML11 0RB   01555 851246
                                              gavdrewandjoe@aol.com

No.	Charge / Minister	Ord.	Ind.	Address / Contact	Phone
46	**Dunipace (F H W)** Jean W. Gallacher BD CertMin CertTheol DMin	1989		The Manse, 239 Stirling Street, Dunipace, Denny FK6 6QJ JGallacher@churchofscotland.org.uk	01324 824540
47	**East Kilbride: Claremont (F H W)** Vacant Session Clerk: Moraig Drumgold			**office@claremontparishchurch.co.uk** 17 Deveron Road, East Kilbride, Glasgow G74 2HR mogie.drumgold@btinternet.com	**01355 238088** 01355 248826 01355 231815
48	**East Kilbride: Greenhills** Vacant Interim Moderator: Mahboob Masih			21 Turnberry Place, East Kilbride, Glasgow G75 8TB MMasih@churchofscotland.org.uk	**01355 221746** 01355 242564 01355 224469
49	**East Kilbride: Moncrieff (F H W)** Sarah L. Ross BD MTh PGDipCS	2004	2020	**theoffice@moncrieffparishchurch.co.uk** 16 Almond Drive, East Kilbride, Glasgow G74 2HX SRoss@churchofscotland.org.uk	**01355 223328** 01355 715735
50	**East Kilbride: Mossneuk (F)** Vacant Session Clerk: Mhairi MacLeod			30 Eden Grove, Mossneuk, East Kilbride, Glasgow G75 8XU sessionclerk@mossneuk.church	**01355 260954** 01355 234196
51	**East Kilbride: Old (H W)** Anne S. Paton BA BD	2001		**ekopc.office@btconnect.com** 40 Maxwell Drive, East Kilbride, Glasgow G74 4HJ APaton@churchofscotland.org.uk	**01355 279004** 01355 220732
52	**East Kilbride: South (F H W)** Terry Ann Taylor BA MTh	2005	2017	7 Clamps Wood, St Leonard's, East Kilbride, Glasgow G74 2HB TTaylor@churchofscotland.org.uk	01355 902758
53	**East Kilbride: Stewartfield (F)** Vacant Interim Moderator: Colin Russell			russellc56@gmail.com	01555 759993
54	**East Kilbride: West (F H W)** Mahboob Masih BA MDiv MTh	1999	2008	4 East Milton Grove, East Kilbride, Glasgow G75 8SN MMasih@churchofscotland.org.uk	01355 224469

55 East Kilbride: Westwood (H W)
Kevin Mackenzie BD DipPS   1989 1996
16 Inglewood Crescent, East Kilbride, Glasgow G75 8QD
Kevin.Mackenzie@churchofscotland.org.uk
01355 245657
01355 223992

56 Falkirk: Bainsford (F H T W)
Vacant
Andrew Sarle BSc BD   2013
(Ordained Local Minister)
1 Valleyview Place, Newcarron Village, Falkirk FK2 7JB
114 High Station Road, Falkirk FK1 5LN
ASarle@churchofscotland.org.uk
07743 726013
Interim Moderator: Alastair M. Horne
AHorne@churchofscotland.org.uk
01324 623308

57 Falkirk: Camelon (F W)
Vacant
30 Cotland Drive, Falkirk FK2 7GE
Interim Moderator: Jean W. Gallacher
JGallacher@churchofscotland.org.uk
01324 870011
01324 623631
01324 824450

58 Falkirk: Grahamston United (F H T W)
Hilda M. Warwick (Methodist Minister)   2017 2022
13 Wallace Place, Falkirk FK2 7EN
warwickhilda@gmail.com
Anne W. White BA CQSW DipHE   2018
(Ordained Local Minister)
94 Craigleith Road, Grangemouth FK3 0BA
Anne.White@churchofscotland.org.uk
01324 880864
Grahamston United is a Local Ecumenical Partnership with the Methodist and United Reformed Churches

59 Falkirk: Laurieston (W) linked with Redding and Westquarter (W)
Vacant
11 Polmont Road, Laurieston, Falkirk FK2 9QQ
Interim Moderator: Deborah L. van Welie
DLVanWelie@churchofscotland.org.uk
01324 621196
01324 713427

60 Falkirk: St Andrew's West (H W)
Alastair M. Horne BSc BD   1989 1997
1 Maggiewood's Loan, Falkirk FK1 5SJ
AHorne@churchofscotland.org.uk
01324 622091
01324 623308

61 Falkirk: Trinity (F H T W)
Robert S.T. Allan LLB DipLP BD   1991 2003
office@falkirktrinity.org.uk
9 Major's Loan, Falkirk FK1 5QF
RAllan@churchofscotland.org.uk
01324 611017
01324 625124

62 Forth: St Paul's (F H W)
Vacant
22 Lea Rig, Forth, Lanark ML11 8EA
Session Clerk: Margaret Hunter
sclerkforthstpauls@outlook.com
01555 728837

63 **Grangemouth: Abbotsgrange (F T W)**
Vacant
Interim Moderator: Andrew Sarle
8 Naismith Court, Grangemouth FK3 9BQ
ASarle@churchofscotland.org.uk
01324 482109
07743 726013

64 **Grangemouth: Kirk of the Holy Rood (F W)**
Ronald Matandakufa BTh MA   2014   2019
The Manse, Bowhouse Road, Grangemouth FK3 0EX
RMatandakufa@churchofscotland.org.uk
01324 337885

65 **Grangemouth: Zetland (F H W)**
Alison A. Meikle (Mrs) BD   1999   2014
Ronaldshay Crescent, Grangemouth FK3 9JH
AMeikle@churchofscotland.org.uk
01324 336729

66 **Greengairs** See Airdrie: New Monkland
67 **Haggs** See Denny: Old

68 **Hamilton: Cadzow (F H W)**
W. John Carswell BS MDiv DPT   1996   2009
contact@cadzowchurch.org.uk
3 Carlisle Road, Hamilton ML3 7BZ
JCarswell@churchofscotland.org.uk
01698 428695
01698 426682

69 **Hamilton: Gilmour and Whitehill (H W) linked with Hamilton: West (H W)**
Vacant
Session Clerk, Gilmour: Ann Paul
Session Clerk, West: Ian Hindle
annepaul.gandw@gmail.com
ianmarilyn.hindle@googlemail.com
West: 01698 284670
01698 284670
01698 421697
01698 429080

70 **Hamilton: Hillhouse (F W)**
Christopher A. Rankine MA MTh PgDE   2016
66 Wellhall Road, Hamilton ML3 9BY
CRankine@churchofscotland.org.uk
01698 327579

71 **Hamilton: Old (F H W)**
I. Ross Blackman BSc MBA BD CertTh   2015
office@hamiltonold.co.uk
1 Chateau Grove, Hamilton ML3 7DS
RBlackman@churchofscotland.org.uk
01698 281905
01698 640185

72 **Hamilton: St John's (H W)**
Joanne C. Hood (Miss) MA BD   2003   2012
9 Shearer Avenue, Ferniegair, Hamilton ML3 7FX
JHood@churchofscotland.org.uk
01698 283492
01698 425002

73 Hamilton: South (F H) linked with Quarter (F)
Andrew (Drew) Gebbie BTh   2021
The Manse, Limekilnburn Road, Quarter, Hamilton ML3 7XA
DGebbie@churchofscotland.org.uk
South: 01698 281014
01698 424511
07498 947412

74 Hamilton: Trinity
Vacant
69 Buchan Street, Hamilton ML3 8JY
Session Clerk: Catherine Hamilton
cathiehamilton@hotmail.com
01698 284254
01698 284919

75 Hamilton: West See Hamilton: Gilmour and Whitehill

76 Holytown (W) linked with New Stevenston: Wrangholm Kirk (W)
Vacant
The Manse, 260 Edinburgh Road, Holytown, Motherwell ML1 5RU
Session Clerk, Holytown: Stewart McNeil   asmcneil@aol.com
Session Clerk, New Stevenston: Wrangholm Kirk: Netta Lithgow   n.lithgow@btinternet.com
01698 832622
01698 831269
01698 833743

77 Kirkfieldbank See Crossford

78 Kirkmuirhill (F H W)
Andrew D. Rooney BSc BD   2019
kirkmuirhillchurch@btinternet.com
The Manse, 82 Vere Road, Kirkmuirhill, Lanark ML11 9RP
ARooney@churchofscotland.org.uk
01555 895593
01555 892409

79 Kirk o' Shotts (H) See Chapelhall

80 Lanark: Greyfriars (F H T W)
Bryan Kerr BA BD   2002   2007
office@lanarkgreyfriars.com
Greyfriars Manse, 3 Bellefield Way, Lanark ML11 7NW
BKerr@churchofscotland.org.uk
01555 437050
01555 663363

81 Lanark: St Nicholas' (F H W)
Louise E. Mackay BSc BD   2017
lanarkstnicholas@outlook.com
2 Kairnhill Court, Lanark ML11 9HU
01555 666220
01555 661936

82 Lanark: East (F W)
Vacant
1 Cortachy Avenue, Carron, Falkirk FK2 8DH
Session Clerk: Margaret Tooth   margaret.tooth@larberteast.church
01324 562402

83 Larbert: Old (F H W)
Guardianship of the Presbytery
The Manse, 38 South Broomage Avenue, Larbert FK5 3ED
Session Clerk: Eric Appelbe   larbertoldcontact@gmail.com
01324 872760
01324 556551

84	**Larbert: West (F H W)** Vacant Session Clerk: Carol Sergeant			27 Drysdale Avenue, Kinnaird, Larbert FK2 8RE casergeant@btinternet.com	07368 198182
85	**Larkhall: New (F H W)** Alastair G. McKillop BD DipMin	1995	2004	2 Orchard Gate, Larkhall ML9 1HA AMcKillop@churchofscotland.org.uk	01698 321976
86	**Larkhall: Trinity** Vacant Session Clerk: Wilma Gilmour (Miss)			13 Machan Avenue, Larkhall ML9 2HE gilmourgilmour@btinternet.com	01698 881401 01698 883002
87	**Law (F W)** Paul G.R. Grant BD MTh	2003	2018	**info@lawparishchurch.org** 3 Shawgill Court, Law, Carluke ML8 5SJ PGrant@churchofscotland.org.uk	01698 373180
88	**Libberton and Quothquan** See Cairngryffe				
89	**Motherwell: Crosshill (F H W) linked with Motherwell: St Margaret's (F W)** info@crosshillparishchurch.org.uk Vacant Session Clerk, Motherwell: Crosshill: Willie Talbot			talbottally@aol.com	01698 269598
90	**Motherwell: Dalziel St Andrew's (F H T W)** Alistair S. May LLB BD PhD	2002	2020	4 Pollock Street, Motherwell ML1 1LP AMay@churchofscotland org.uk	**01698 264097** 01698 263414
91	**Motherwell: North (F W) linked with Wishaw: Craigneuk and Belhaven (H)** Derek H.N. Pope BD DipYCW	1987	1995	35 Birrens Road, Motherwell ML1 3NS DPope@churchofscotland.org.uk	01698 266716
92	**Motherwell: St Margaret's** See Motherwell: Crosshill				
93	**Motherwell: St Mary's (F H T W)** Bryce Calder MA BD	1995	2017	**office@stmarysmotherwell.org.uk** 19 Orchard Street, Motherwell ML1 3JE BCalder@churchofscotland.org.uk	**01698 268554** 07986 144834

94 Motherwell: South (H T W)
Alan W. Gibson BA BD   2001   2016
62 Manse Road, Motherwell ML1 2PT
Alan.Gibson@churchofscotland.org.uk
01698 239279

95 Muiravonside See Blackbraes and Shieldhill

96 Newarthill and Carfin (F H T W)
Elaine W. McKinnon MA BA BD   1988   2014
Church Street, Newarthill, Motherwell ML1 5HS
EMcKinnon@churchofscotland.org.uk
01698 296850

97 Newmains: Bonkle (F H W) linked with Newmains: Coltness Memorial (F H W)
Graham Raeburn MTh   2004
5 Kirkgate, Newmains, Wishaw ML2 9BT
GRaeburn@churchofscotland.org.uk
01698 344001
01698 383858

98 Newmains: Coltness Memorial See Newmains: Bonkle
99 New Stevenston: Wrangholm Kirk See Holytown

100 Overtown (F W)
Lorna I. MacDougall MA DipGC BD   2003   2017
The Manse, 146 Main Street, Overtown, Wishaw ML2 0QP
LMacDougall@churchofscotland.org.uk
01698 358727
01698 352090

101 Polmont: Old (F W)
Deborah L. van Welie (Ms) MTheol   2015
3 Orchard Grove, Polmont, Falkirk FK2 0XE
DLVanWelie@churchofscotland.org.uk
01324 715995
01324 713427

102 Quarter See Hamilton: South
103 Redding and Westquarter See Falkirk: Laurieston

104 Shotts: Calderhead Erskine
Vacant
Session Clerk: Liam T. Haggart SSC
The Manse, 9 Kirk Road, Shotts ML7 5ET
a2lth@hotmail.com
01501 823204
07896 557687

105 Slamannan
Vacant
Monica J. MacDonald (Mrs)   2014
(Ordained Local Minister)
60 Kennedy Way, Airth FK2 8GG
Monica.MacDonald@churchofscotland.org.uk
01324 832782

106 Stenhouse and Carron (F H)
William Thomson BD — 2001 — 2007
The Manse, 21 Tipperary Place, Stenhousemuir, Larbert FK5 4SX
WThomson@churchofscotland.org.uk
01324 416628

107 Stonehouse: St Ninian's (F H T W)
Stewart J. Cutler BA MSc DipHE — 2017
info@st-ninians-stonehouse.org.uk
4 Hamilton Way, Stonehouse, Larkhall ML9 3PU
revstewartcutler@gmail.com
01698 791508

Stonehouse: St Ninian's is a Local Ecumenical Partnership with the United Reformed Church

108 Strathaven: Avendale Old and Drumclog (F H W)
Calum M. Stark LLB BD — 2011 — 2021
info@avendale-drumclog.org.uk
4 Fortrose Gardens, Strathaven ML10 6FH
CStark@churchofscotland.org.uk
01357 671557
01357 523031

109 Strathaven: Trinity (F H W)
Shaw J. Paterson BSc BD MSc DPT — 1991
15 Lethame Road, Strathaven ML10 6AD
SPaterson@churchofscotland.org.uk

Fiona Anderson DipHE — 2020
(Ordained Local Minister)
52 Cooper Crescent, Ferniegair, Hamilton ML3 7FT
FAnderson@churchofscotland.org.uk

Tel 01357 520019
    01357 529316
Fax 07913 153608

110 Symington See Cairngryffe

111 Uddingston: Burnhead (F H W)
Les N. Brunger BD — 2010
90 Laburnum Road, Uddingston, Glasgow G71 5DB
LBrunger@churchofscotland.org.uk
01698 813716

112 Uddingston: Old (F H W)
Fiona L.J. McKibbin (Mrs) MA BD — 2011
1 Belmont Avenue, Uddingston, Glasgow G71 7AX
FMcKibbin@churchofscotland.org.uk
01698 814015
01698 814757

113 Uddingston: Viewpark (F H W)
Michael G. Lyall BD CertMin — 1993 — 2001
14 Holmbrae Road, Uddingston, Glasgow G71 6AP
MLyall@churchofscotland.org.uk
01698 810478
01698 813113

114 Upper Clyde (F W)
Nikki M. Macdonald BD MTh PhD — 2014
31 Carlisle Road, Crawford, Biggar ML12 6TP
NMacdonald@churchofscotland.org.uk
01864 502139

115 Wishaw: Cambusnethan North (F H W)
Vacant
Session Clerk: Tom McIvor   350 Kirk Road, Wishaw ML2 8LH   01698 381305
tommcivor13@yahoo.co.uk   01698 383815

116 Wishaw: Cambusnethan Old and Morningside
Vacant
Session Clerk: Graeme Vincent   22 Coronation Street, Wishaw ML2 8LF   01698 384235
gvincent@theiet.org   01555 752166

117 Wishaw: Craigneuk and Belhaven See Motherwell: North

118 Wishaw: Old (F H)
Vacant
Session Clerk: Thomas W. Donaldson   130 Glen Road, Wishaw ML2 7NP   **01698 376080**
tomdonaldson@talktalk.net   01698 375134
01698 357605

119 Wishaw: St Mark's See Cleland

120 Wishaw: South Wishaw (F H W)   **southwishaw@tiscali.co.uk**   **01698 375306**
Terence C. Moran BD CertMin   1995   2015   3 Walter Street, Wishaw ML2 8LQ   01698 767459
TMoran@churchofscotland.org.uk

B. In other appointments

Name			Appointment	Address	Phone
Bogle, Albert O. BD MTh	1981	2016	Pioneer Minister, Sanctuary First	49a Kenilworth Road, Bridge of Allan FK9 4RS AlbertBogle@churchofscotland.org.uk	07715 374557
Brydson, Angela (Mrs) DCS	2015	2021	Community Outreach Worker, Southern Ministry Cluster	52 Victoria Park, Lockerbie DG11 2AY ABrydson@churchofscotland.org.uk	07543 796820
Buck, Maxine SRN ONC CertMgtS	2007	2015	Auxiliary Minister, Presbytery	Brownlee House, Mauldslie Road, Carluke ML8 5HW MBuck@churchofscotland.org.uk	01555 759063
Fyfe, Lorna K. BD		2020	Ordained Local Minister	20 Kennoway Crescent, Hamilton ML3 7WQ LFyfe@churchofscotland.org.uk	01698 633304
Hacking, Philip R.	2021	2022	Head of Spiritual Care and Bereavement, NHS Lothian (Ordained Local Minister)	101 Craig's Crescent, Falkirk FK2 0ET PHacking@churchofscotland.org.uk	01324 337936
Macpherson, Duncan J. BSc BD	1993	2002	Deputy Assistant Chaplain General: Army	177 Station Road, Shotts ML7 4BA padredjm@btinternet.com	01501 821484
Murphy, Jim		2014	Ordained Local Minister	10 Hillview Crescent, Bellshill ML4 1NX JMurphy@churchofscotland.org.uk	01698 740189
Rennick, Julie M. (Mrs) BTh	2005	2022	Presbytery Clerk: Forth Valley and Clydesdale	Presbytery Office, Rex House, 103 Bothwell Road, Hamilton ML3 0DW JRennick@churchofscotland.org.uk	01698 285672
Stevenson, Beverley		2020	Ordained Local Minister	68 Dundrennan Drive, Chapelhall, Airdrie ML6 8GT BStevenson@churchofscotland.org.uk	01698 734791

C. Retaining

Name	(Charge)	Ord.	Ret.	Address	Tel
Barrie, Arthur P. LTh	(Hamilton: Cadzow)	1973	2007	30 Airbles Crescent, Motherwell ML1 3AR	01698 261147
Baxendale, Georgina M. DipEd BD DMin	(Motherwell: South)	1981	2014	32 Meadowhead Road, Plains, Airdrie ML6 7HG; georgiebaxendale@btinternet.com	01236 842752
Campbell, James W. BD	(Ceres, Kemback and Springfield)	1995	2020	145 Mungalhead Road, Falkirk FK2 7JH	01324 638686, 07975 976024
Colvin, Sharon E.F. (Mrs) BD LRAM LTCL	(Airdrie: Jackson)	1985	2008	25 Balblair Road, Airdrie ML6 6GQ; dibleycol@hotmail.com	01236 590796
Cook, J. Stanley BD DipPSS DipPC	(Hamilton: West)	1974	2001	Mansend, 137A Old Manse Road, Netherton, Wishaw ML2 0EW; stancook@blueyonder.co.uk	01698 299600
Cowan, James S.A. BD DipMin	(Barrhead: St Andrew's)	1986	2019	30 Redding Road, Falkirk FK2 9XJ; jim_cowan@ntlworld.com	07966 489609
Crosthwaite, Melville D. BD DipEd DipMin	(Larbert: East)	1984	2021	16 Southend Drive, Strathaven ML10 6QT; revcrosthwaite@gmail.com	
Doyle, David W. MA BD	(Motherwell: St Mary's)	1977	2015	76 Kethers Street, Motherwell ML1 3HN	01698 263472
Fuller, Agnes A. (Mrs) BD	(Bellshill: West)	1987	2014	14 Croftpark Street, Bellshill ML14 1EY; revamoore2@tiscali.co.uk	01698 748244
Gibson, James M. TD LTh LRAM	(Bothwell)	1978	2019	22 Kirklands Crescent, Bothwell, Glasgow G71 8HU; jamesmgibson@msn.com	01698 854907
Gilroy, Lorraine (Mrs) DCS	(Deacon)	1988	1994	68 Clement Drive, Airdrie ML16 7FB; lorraine.gilroy@sky.com	07923 540602
Gunn, F. Derek BD	(Airdrie: Clarkston)	1986	2017	6 Yardley Place, Falkirk FK2 7FH; RevDerekGunn@hotmail.com	01324 624938
Jones, Robert BSc BD	(Rosskeen)	1990	2017	3 Grantown Avenue, Airdrie ML6 8HH; rob2jones@btinternet.com	07761 782714
Kent, Robert M. MA BD	(Hamilton: St John's)	1973	2011	48 Fyne Crescent, Larkhall ML9 2UX; robertmkent@talktalk.net	01698 769244
Macdonald, Mhorag (Ms) MA BD	(Wishaw: Cambusnethan North)	1989	2021	Mhorag.Macdonald@churchofscotland.org.uk	01698 301230
MacKenzie, Ian C. MA BD	(Interim Minister, Carnwath)	1970	2011	21 Wilson Street, Motherwell ML1 1NP; iancmac@blueyonder.co.uk	
Mathers, Alexena (Sandra)	(Ordained Local Minister)	2015	2018	10 Ercall Road, Brightons, Falkirk FK2 0RS; SMathers@churchofscotland.org.uk	01324 872253
McKee, Norman B. BD	(Uddingston: Old)	1987	2010	148 Station Road, Blantyre, Glasgow G72 9BW; normanmckee946@btinternet.com	01698 827358
Murdoch, Iain C. MA LLB DipEd BD	(Wishaw: Cambusnethan Old and Morningside)	1995	2017	2 Pegasus Avenue, Carluke ML8 5TN; iaincmurdoch@btopenworld.com	01555 773891
Ogilvie, Colin BA DCS	(Deacon)	1998	2015	21 Neilsland Drive, Motherwell ML1 3DZ; colinogilvie2@gmail.com	01698 321836, 07837 287804
Palmer, Gordon R. MA BD STM	(East Kilbride: Claremont)	1986	2022	GPalmer@churchofscotland.org.uk	07804 817522
Ross, Eileen M. (Mrs) BD MTh	(Linwood)	2005	2022	2 Millburn Way, East Kilbride, Glasgow G75 8EB	
Ross, Keith W. MA BD MTh	(Congregational Development Officer)	1984	2015	Easter Bavelaw House, Pentland Hills Regional Park, Balerno EH14 7JS; keithwross@outlook.com	07855 163449

Name		Charge	Address	Phone
Salmond, James S. BA BD MTh ThD	1979 2003	(Holytown)	165 Torbothie Road, Shotts ML7 5NE	01698 817582
Stevenson, John LTh	1998 2006	(Cambuslang: St Andrew's)	20 Knowehead Gardens, Uddingston, Glasgow G71 7PY therev20@sky.com	
Stewart, William T. BD DipPS	1980 2018	(Glassford with Strathaven: East)	8 Cot Castle Grove, Stonehouse ML9 3RQ	01698 793979
Thomson, John M.A. TD JP BD ThM	1978 2014	(Hamilton: Old)	8 Skylands Place, Hamilton ML3 8SB jt@john1949.plus.com	01698 422511
Turnbull, S. Lindsay A. BSc BD	2014 2021	(Hamilton: Trinity)		
Waddell, Elizabeth A. (Mrs) BD	1999 2014	(Hamilton: West)	114 Branchalfield, Wishaw ML2 8QD elizabethwaddell@tiscali.co.uk	01698 382909
Wallace, Douglas W. MA BD	1981 2019	(East Kilbride: Stewartfield)	11 Cromalt Avenue, East Kilbride, Glasgow G75 GQ DWallace@churchofscotland.org.uk	01355 260879
Zambonini, James LIADip	1997 2015	(Auxiliary Minister)	100 Old Manse Road, Netherton, Wishaw ML2 0EP	01698 350889

TOWN ADDRESSES

Airdrie
Cairnlea — 89 Graham Street
Clarkston — Forrest Street
High — North Bridge Street
Jackson — Glen Road
New Monkland — Glenmavis
New Wellwynd — Wellwynd
St Columba's — Thrashbush Road

Bo'ness
Old — Panbrae Road
St Andrew's — Grahamsdyke Avenue
Carriden — Carriden Brae

Carluke
Kirkton — Station Road
St Andrew's — Mount Stewart Street
St John's — Hamilton Street

Coatbridge
Blairhill Dundyvan — Blairhill Street
Calder — Calder Street
Middle — Bank Street
New St Andrew's — Church Street
Old Monkland — Woodside Street
Townhead — Crinan Crescent

Denny
Old — Denny Cross
Westpark — Duke Street
Dunipace — Stirling Street

East Kilbride
Claremont — High Common Road, St Leonard's
Greenhills — Greenhills Centre
Moncrieff — Calderwood Road
Mossneuk — Eden Drive
Old — Montgomery Street
South — Baird Hill, Murray
Stewartfield — Stewartfield Community Centre
West — Kittoch Street
Westwood — Belmont Drive, Westwood

Falkirk
Bainsford — Hendry Street, Bainsford
Camelon — Dorrator Road
Grahamston United — Bute Street
Laurieston — Polmont Road
St Andrew's West — Newmarket Street
Trinity — Kirk Wynd

Grangemouth
Abbotsgrange — Abbot's Road
Kirk of the Holy Rood — Bowhouse Road
Zetland — Ronaldshay Crescent

Hamilton
Cadzow — Woodside Walk
Gilmour and Whitehill — Glasgow Road, Burnbank
Hillhouse — Clerkwell Road
Old — Leechlee Road
St John's — Duke Street
South — Strathaven Road
Trinity — Neilsland Square off Neilsland Road
West — Burnbank Road

Larbert
East — Kirk Avenue
Old — Denny Road x Stirling Road
West — Main Street

Motherwell
Crosshill — Windmillhill Street x Airbles Street
Dalziel St Andrew's — Merry Street x Muir Street
North — Chesters Crescent
St Margaret's — Shields Road
St Mary's — Avon Street
South — Gavin Street

Uddingston
Burnhead — Laburnum Road
Old — Old Glasgow Road
Viewpark — Old Edinburgh Road

Wishaw
Cambusnethan North — Kirk Road
Old — Kirk Road
Craigneuk and Belhaven — Craigneuk Street
Old — Main Street
St Mark's — Coltness Road
South Wishaw — East Academy Street

(19) ARGYLL (F W)

Meets in the Village Hall, Tarbert, Loch Fyne, Argyll on the first Tuesday or Wednesday of March, June, September and December. For details, contact the Presbytery Clerk.

| Clerk: | MR W. STEWART SHAW DL BSc | 59 Barone Road, Rothesay, Isle of Bute PA20 0DZ
argyll@churchofscotland.org.uk | 07775 926541 |
| Treasurer: | REV. DAVID CARRUTHERS BD | The Manse, Park Road, Ardrishaig, Lochgilphead PA30 8HE
DCarruthers@churchofscotland.org.uk | 01546 603269 |

Appin (F) linked with Lismore

| Dugald J. Cameron BD DipMin MTh | 1990 | 2021 | An Mansa, 11 Tyneribbie Place, Appin, Argyll PA38 4DS
Dugald.Cameron@churchofscotland.org.uk | Appin 01631 730280 |

Ardchattan (F H W) linked with Coll (F W) linked with Connel (F W)

| Willem J. Bezuidenhout BA BD MHEd MEd | 1977 | 2019 | St Oran's Manse, Connel, Oban PA37 1PJ
WBezuidenhout@churchofscotland.org.uk | 01631 710214
07484 333923
Coll 01879 230366 |

Ardrishaig (H) linked with South Knapdale

| David Carruthers BD | 1998 | | The Manse, Kilduskland Road, Ardrishaig, Lochgilphead PA30 8HE 01546 603269
DCarruthers@churchofscotland.org.uk | |

Barra (GD) linked with South Uist (GD W)

| Lindsay Schluter ThE CertMin PhD | 1995 | 2016 | The Manse, Cuithir, Isle of Barra HS9 5XU
LSchluter@churchofscotland.org.uk | 01871 810230
07835 913963 |

Bute, United Church of (F W)

| John Owain Jones MA BD FSAScot | 1981 | 2011 | 10 Bishop Terrace, Rothesay, Isle of Bute PA20 9HF
JJones@churchofscotland.org.uk | 01700 504502 |

Campbeltown: Highland (H W) linked with Saddell and Carradale (H W) linked with Southend (F H W)

| Vacant | | | St Blaan's Manse, Southend, Campbeltown PA28 6RQ | 01586 830504 |

Campbeltown: Lorne and Lowland (F H)

| Vacant
Interim Moderator: Alison Hay (Mrs) | | | Lorne and Lowland Manse, Castlehill, Campbeltown PA28 6AN
AHay@churchofscotland.org.uk | 01586 552468
01546 886213
07887 760086 |

Coll See Ardchattan

Colonsay and Oronsay (W)
Guardianship of the Presbytery
Session Clerk: Kevin Bryne

colonsaybryne@gmail.com   01950 200320

Connel See Ardchattan

Cowal Kirk (F H W)
Vacant

Alexander J. (Sandy) MacPherson MA BSc   2021
FRSA (Ordained Local Minister)
Interim Moderator: Alison Hay (Mrs)

The Manse, 13 Dhailling Park, Hunter Street,   01369 702256
  Kirn, Dunoon, PA23 8FB
8 Queens View, Marine Parade, Kirn, Dunoon   PA23 8LF 01369 707969
SMacPherson@churchofscotland.org.uk
AHay@churchofscotland.org.uk   01546 886213
                                                       07887 760086

Craignish
Vacant
Interim Moderator: David Carruthers

DCarruthers@churchofscotland.org.uk   01546 603269

Gigha and Cara (GD H W) linked with Kilcalmonell (W) linked with Killean and Kilchenzie (H W)
Vacant
Session Clerk, Gigha and Cara: Alasdair McNeill
Session Clerk, Kilcalmonell: Elizabeth M. Ball (Mrs)
Session Clerk, Killean and Kilchenzie: Anne Littleson (Miss)

The Manse, Muasdale, Tarbert, Argyll PA29 6XD   01583 421086
amacneill@gigha.org.uk   01583 505271
johnball56@btinternet.com   01880 740650
anne.littleson@btinternet.com   01583 421241

Glassary, Kilmartin and Ford linked with North Knapdale (W)
Vacant
Session Clerk, Glassary, Kilmartin and Ford: Linda Tighe
Session Clerk, North Knapdale: Catherine Paterson

The Manse, Kilmichael Glassary, Lochgilphead PA31 8QA 01546 606926
chalin@tiscali.co.uk   01546 600330
catherine@dochasfund.org.uk   01546 603772

Glenorchy and Innishael (W) linked with Strathfillan (W)
Vacant
Session Clerk, Strathfillan: Mary Anderson

m.anderson53@btinternet.com   01838 300253

Iona (W) linked with Kilfinichen and Kilvickeon and the Ross of Mull (W)
Jenny Earl MA BD   2007   2018

1 The Steadings, Achavaich, Isle of Iona PA76 6SW   07769 994680
JEarl@churchofscotland.org.uk

Jura (GD) linked with North and West Islay (GD) linked with South Islay (GD H W) (Islay and Jura)
Vacant — The Manse, Bowmore, Isle of Islay PA43 7LH — 01496 810271
Session Clerk, Jura: Heather Cameron — h.cameronjura@btinternet.com — 01496 820371
Session Clerk, North and West Islay: — marsalithomson@outlook.com — 01496 810236
Marsali Thomson
Session Clerk, South Islay: Sue Hind — eddieandsue2000@yahoo.co.uk — 01496 311494

Kilbrandon and Kilchattan linked with Kilninver and Kilmelford (Netherlorn F W)
Vacant — The Manse, Kilmelford, Oban PA34 4XA — 01852 200565
Session Clerk, Kilbrandon and Kilchattan: — jandjalex@gmail.com — 01852 314242
Jean Alexander
Session Clerk, Kilninver and Kilmelford: — sallyinglis12@gmail.com — 01852 316271
Sally Inglis

Kilcalmonell See Gigha and Cara

Kilchrenan and Dalavich (W) linked with Muckairn (W)
Thomas W. Telfer BA MDiv   1986   2018 — Muckairn Manse, Taynuilt PA35 1HW — 01866 822204
TTelfer@churchofscotland.org.uk

Kilfinan linked with Kilmodan and Colintraive linked with Kyles (H) (West Cowal)
David Mitchell BD DipPTheol MSc   1988   2006 — West Cowal Manse, Kames, Tighnabruaich PA21 2AD — 01700 811045
DMitchell@churchofscotland.org.uk

Kilfinichen and Kilvickeon and the Ross of Mull See Iona
Killean and Kilchenzie See Gigha and Cara
Kilmodan and Colintraive See Kilfinan

Kilmore and Oban (F GD W)
Vacant — obancofs@btinternet.com — **01631 562405**
Session Clerks: Sine MacVicar (Miss) — Kilmore and Oban Manse, Ganavan Road, Oban   PA34 5TU — 01631 566253
John MacLean — s.macvicar52@btinternet.com — 01631 710090
john.maclean56@btinternet.com — 01631 565519

Kilmun, Strone and Ardentinny: The Shore Kirk (H W)
Vacant — The Manse, Blairmore, Dunoon PA23 8TE — 01369 840601
Janet K. MacKellar BSc ProfCertMgmt   2019 — Laurel Bank, 23 George Street, Dunoon PA23 8TE — 01369 705549
FCMI (Ordained Local Minister) — JMackellar@churchofscotland.org.uk

Kilninver and Kilmelford See Kilbrandon and Kilchattan

Kyles See Kilfinan
Lismore See Appin

Lochgilphead (F W)
Vacant
Interim Moderator: Alison Hay (Mrs)   Parish Church Manse, Manse Brae, Lochgilphead PA31 8QZ   01546 602238 / 01546 886213 / 07887 760086
AHay@churchofscotland.org.uk

Lochgoilhead (H) and Kilmorich linked with Strachur and Strathlachlan (Upper Cowal)
Robert K. Mackenzie MA BD PhD   1976   1998   The Manse, Strachur, Cairndow PA27 8DG   01369 860246
RKMackenzie@churchofscotland.org.uk

Muckairn See Kilchrenan and Dalavich
North and West Islay See Jura
North Knapdale See Glassary, Kilmartin and Ford

North Mull (F GD H W)
Elizabeth A. Gibson (Mrs) MA MLitt BD   2003   2021   The New Manse, Gruline Road, Salen, Aros, Isle of Mull PA72 6JF   01680 300655
egibson@churchofscotland.org.uk

Rothesay: Trinity (H W)
Sibyl A. Tchaikovsky BA BD MLitt   2018   12 Crichton Road, Rothesay, Isle of Bute PA20 9JR   01700 504047
STchaikovsky@churchofscotland.org.uk

Saddell and Carradale See Campbeltown: Highland

Skipness (F) linked with Tarbert, Loch Fyne and Kilberry (F H W)
Lyn M. Peden (Mrs) BD   2010   2020   The Manse, Campbeltown Road, Tarbert, Argyll PA29 6SX   01880 820158
LPeden@churchofscotland.org.uk

Southend See Campbeltown: Highland
South Islay See Jura
South Knapdale See Ardrishaig
South Uist See Barra
Strachur and Strathlachlan See Lochgoilhead and Kilmorich
Strathfillan See Glenorchy and Innishael
Tarbert, Loch Fyne and Kilberry See Skipness

Tiree (F GD W)
Vacant
Interim Moderator: Douglas Allan
The Manse, Scarinish, Isle of Tiree PA77 6TN
douglas.allan423@gmail.com
01879 220377
01700 502331
07478 134946

West Lochfyneside: Cumlodden, Inveraray and Lochgair (F W)
Dorothy M. Wallace BA   2021
The Manse, Inveraray PA32 8XT
Dorothy.Wallace@churchofscotland.org.uk
01499 302459

B. In other appointments

Name	Years	Appointment	Address	Tel
Anderson, David P. BSc BD	2002 2007	Senior Army Chaplain	4 Infantry Brigade and HQ North East, Bourlon Barracks, Pluymer Road, Catterick Garrison DL9 3AD padre.anderson180@mod.gov.uk	
Ross, Kenneth R. OBE BA BD PhD	1982 2019	Theological Educator, Africa	Zomba Theological College, PO Box 130, Zomba, Malawi kross@thinkingmission.org	

C. Retaining

Name	Years	Charge	Address	Tel
Acklam, Clifford R. BD MTh	1997 2018	(Glassary, Kilmartin and Ford with North Knapdale)	4 Knoll View Terrace, Westtown, New York 10998, United States of America	
Barge, Nigel L. BSc BD	1991 2021	(Torrance)	2 Lephinmore Cottage, Strathlachlan, Cairndow PA27 8BU NBarge@churchofscotland.org.uk	
Campbell, Andrew B. BD DPS MTh	1979 2018	(Gargunnock with Kilmadock with Kincardine-in-Menteith)	Seahaven, Ganavan, Oban PA34 5TU beachcomber53@gmail.com	07523 420079
Campbell, Roderick D.M. TD MStJ BD DMin FSAScot	1975 2019	(Cumlodden, Lochfyneside and Lochgair with Glenaray and Inveraray)	Windy Ridge, Glen Loanan, Taynuilt PA35 1EY Roderick.Campbell@churchofscotland.org.uk	01866 822623
Cringles, George G. BD CertMin	1981 2017	(Coll with Connel)	The Moorings, Ganavan Road, Oban PA34 5TU george.cringles@gmail.com	01631 564215
Dunlop, Alistair J. MA	1965 2004	(Saddell and Carradale)	8 Pipers Road, Cairnbaan, Lochgilphead PA31 8UF dunrevn@btinternet.com	01546 600316
Fulcher, Christine P. BEd CertCS	2012 2022	(Ordained Local Minister, Team Minister, South Argyll)	Kilmelford CFulcher@churchofscotland.org.uk	
Fulcher, Stephen BA MA	1993 2022	(Campbeltown: Highland with Saddell and Carradale with Southend)	Kilmelford SFulcher@churchofscotland.org.uk	
Gray, William LTh	1971 2006	(Kilberry with Tarbert)	Lochnagar, Longsdale Road, Oban PA34 5DZ gray98@hotmail.com	01631 567471
Griffiths, Ruth I. (Mrs)	2004 2020	(Auxiliary Minister)	Kirkwood, Mathieson Lane, Innellan, Dunoon PA23 7TA	01369 830145
Henderson, Grahame McL. BD CPS	1974 2008	(Kirn)	6 Gerhallow, Bullwood Road, Dunoon PA23 7QB ghende5884@aol.com	01369 702433
Hood, H. Stanley C. MA BD	1966 2000	(London: Crown Court)	10 Dalriada Place, Kilmichael Glassary, Lochgilphead PA31 8QA	01546 606168

Name			(Charge)	Address	Phone
Lind, Michael J. LLB BD	1984	2012	(Campbeltown: Highland)	Maybank, Station Road, Conon Bridge, Dingwall IV7 8BJ mijylind@gmail.com	01349 865932
Macfarlane, James MTh PhD	1991	2011	(Lochgoilhead and Kilmorich)	'Lindores', 11 Bullwood Road, Dunoon PA23 7QJ mac.farlane@btinternet.com	01369 710626
Marshall, Freda (Mrs) BD FCII	1993	2005	(Colonsay and Oronsay with Kilbrandon and Kilchattan)	Allt Mhaluidh, Glenview, Dalmally PA33 1BE mail@freda.org.uk	01838 200693
McIvor, Anne (Miss) SRD BD	1996	2013	(Gigha and Cara)	20 Albyn Avenue, Campbeltown PA28 6LY annemcivor@btinternet.com	07901 964825
Mill, David GCSJ MA BD	1978	2018	(Kilmun, Strone and Ardentinny: The Shore Kirk)	The Hebrides, 107 Bullwood Road, Dunoon PA23 7QN revandevmill@aol.com	01369 707544
Millar, Margaret R.M. (Miss) DipChE BTh	1977	2008	(Kilchrenan and Dalavich with Muckairn)	Fearnoch Cottage, Fearnoch, Taynuilt PA35 1JB macoje@btinternet.com	01866 822416
Morrison, Angus W. MA BD	1959	1999	(Kildalton and Oa)	1 Livingstone Way, Port Ellen, Isle of Islay PA42 7EP	01496 300043
Park, Peter B. BD MCIBS	1997	2014	(Fraserburgh: Old)	Hillview, 24 McKelvie Road, Oban PA34 4GB peterpark9@btinternet.com	01631 565849
Ritchie, Walter M.	1973	1999	(Uphall: South)	Hazel Cottage, Barr Mor View, Kilmartin, Lochgilphead PA31 8UN	01546 510343
Scott, Randolph MA BD	1991	2013	(Jersey: St Columba's)	18 Lochan Avenue, Kirn, Dunoon PA23 8HT rev.rs@hotmail.com	01369 703175
Smith, Hilda C. (Miss) MA BD MSc	1992	2021	(Lochgilphead)	Ardmore, Kilmory Road, Lochgilphead PA31 8SZ hilda.smith2@btinternet.com	01546 603191
Stewart, Joseph LTh	1979	2011	(Dunoon: St John's with Sandbank)	7 Glenmorag Avenue, Dunoon PA23 7LG	01369 703438
Wilkinson, W. Brian MA BD	1968	2007	(Glenaray and Inveraray)	3 Achlonan, Taynuilt PA35 1JJ williambrian35@btinternet.com	01866 822036

(23) STIRLING (F W)

Meets at Bridge of Allan Parish Church on the first Thursday of November 2022, at the Moderator's church on the first Thursday of December 2022, and for conference on the first Thursday of October 2022. On 1 January 2023 it will unite with the Presbyteries of Dunkeld and Meigle, Perth, Dundee and Angus to form a new Presbytery of Perth. That Presbytery will meet on a date and in a venue to be determined and thereafter as decided.

Clerk:	REV. ALAN F. MILLER BA MA BD	7 Windsor Place, Stirling FK8 2HY AMiller@churchofscotland.org.uk	01786 465166 07535 949258
Depute Clerk:	MR EDWARD MORTON	22 Torry Drive, Alva FK12 5LN edmort@aol.com	01259 760861 07525 005028
Treasurer:	MR MARTIN DUNSMORE	60 Brookfield Place, Alva FK12 5AT m.dunsmore53@btinternet.com	01259 762262
Presbytery Office:		Park Church, Park Terrace, Stirling FK8 2NA stirling@churchofscotland.org.uk	01786 465166

Aberfoyle (H W) linked with Port of Menteith (H W)
Vacant
Interim Moderator: Dan Gunn   degunn@hotmail.co.uk   01786 823798

Alloa: Ludgate (F W)
Dawn A. Laing BEd PGCertPD BD   2020   28 Alloa Park Drive, Alloa FK10 1QY   01259 213134
                                                                                                                            DLaing@churchofscotland .org.uk

Alloa: St Mungo's (F H T W)
Sang Y. Cha BD MTh   2011   contact@alloastmungos.org   **01259 723004**
                                                                                37A Claremont, Alloa FK10 2DG   01259 213872
                                                                                SCha@churchofscotland.org.uk

Alva (F W)
James N.R. McNeil BSc BD   1990   1997   alvaparishchurch@gmail.com
                                                                                34 Ochil Road, Alva FK12 5JT   01259 760262
                                                                                JMcNeil@churchofscotland.org.uk
Anne F. Shearer BA DipEd CertCS   2010   2018   10 Colsnaur, Menstrie FK11 7HG   01259 769176
(Auxiliary Minister)   AShearer@churchofscotland.org.uk

Balfron (F W) linked with Fintry (F H W)
Vacant   admin@balfronchurch.org.uk
                                                                                7 Station Road, Balfron, Glasgow G63 0SX   01360 440285
Lesley A. Stanley MA PhD FBTS   2021   Lilac Cottage, Main Street, Gartmore, Stirling FK8 3RN   01506 671532
(Ordained Local Minister)   LStanley@churchofscotland.org.uk
Interim Moderator: Jeffrey A. McCormick   JMcCormick@churchofscotland.org.uk   01877 330474

Balquhidder linked with Killin and Ardeonaig (H W)
Russel Moffat BD CPS MTh PhD — 1986 — 2016 — The Manse, Killin FK21 8TN / Russel.Moffat@churchofscotland.org.uk — 01567 820247

Bannockburn: Allan (F H T W) linked with Cowie and Plean (H T)
hiya@allanchurch.org
Peter G. Gill MA BA — 2008 — 2021 — The Manse, Bogend Road, Bannockburn, Stirling FK7 8NP / PGill@churchofscotland.org.uk — 01786 814692

Bannockburn: Ladywell (F H W)
Elizabeth M.D. Robertson (Miss) BD CertMin — 1997 — 57 The Firs, Bannockburn FK7 0EG / ERobertson@churchofscotland.org.uk — 01786 812467

Bridge of Allan (F H W)
office@bridgeofallanparishchurch.org.uk
Daniel (Dan) J. Harper BSc BD — 2016 — 29 Keir Street, Bridge of Allan, Stirling FK9 4QJ / DHarper@churchofscotland.org.uk — 01786 834155 / 01786 832753

Buchanan linked with Drymen (F W)
Vacant
Interim Moderator: Murdo M. Campbell — Buchanan Manse, Drymen, Glasgow G63 0AQ / MCampbell@churchofscotland.org.uk — 01360 660370 / 01360 870212 / 01360 770226

Buchlyvie (H W) linked with Gartmore (H W)
buchlyviechurch@gmail.com   gartmorechurch@gmail.com
Scott J. Brown CBE BD — 1993 — 2019 — Buchlyvie Parish Church, Main Street, Buchlyvie, Stirling FK8 3LX / SJBrown@churchofscotland.org.uk — 07824 805888

Callander (F H W)
Jeffrey A. McCormick BD DipMin — 1984 — 2018 — 21 Glenartney Road, Callander FK17 8EB / JMcCormick@churchofscotland.org.uk — Tel/Fax: 01877 331409 / 01877 330474

Cambusbarron: The Bruce Memorial (F H W)
Graham P. Nash MA BD — 2006 — 2012 — 14 Woodside Court, Cambusbarron, Stirling FK7 9PH / GPNash@churchofscotland.org.uk — 01786 442068

Clackmannan (H W)
office@clackmannankirk.org.uk
Vacant
Interim Moderator: James N.R. McNeil — The Manse, Port Street, Clackmannan FK10 4JH / JMcNeil@churchofscotland.org.uk — 01259 214238 / 07824 505211 / 01259 760262

Cowie and Plean See Bannockburn: Allan

Dollar (F H W) linked with Glendevon linked with Muckhart (W) info@dollarparishchurch.org.uk   muckhartchurch@gmail.com
Vacant   2 Princes Crescent East, Dollar FK14 7BU
Interim Moderator: Ellen M. Larson Davidson   ELarsonDavidson@churchofscotland.org.uk   01259 740286
                                                                                                                          01786 871249

Drymen See Buchanan

Dunblane: Cathedral (F H T W)   **office@dunblanecathedral.org.uk**   **01786 825388**
Colin C. Renwick BMus BD   1989   2014   Cathedral Manse, The Cross, Dunblane   FK15 0AQ   01786 822205
                                                              CRenwick@churchofscotland.org.uk
Alastair Munro RN BSc   2022   AMunro@churchofscotland.org.uk
  (Ordained Local Minister)

Dunblane: St Blane's (F H W) linked with Lecropt (F H W)
Gary J. Caldwell BSc BD   2007   2015   46 Kellie Wynd, Dunblane FK15 0NR   01786 825324
                                                              GCaldwell@churchofscotland.org.uk

Fallin (F W)   **info@fallinchurch.com**
Alison J. Grainger BD CertEd   1995   2021   5 Fincastle Place, Cowie, Stirling FK7 7DS   01786 760512
                                                              AGrainger@churchofscotland.org.uk

Fintry See Balfron

Gargunnock (W) linked with Kilmadock (W) linked with Kincardine-in-Menteith (W)
Vacant
Interim Moderator: Val Rose   val.rose@btinternet.com   01259 722221

Gartmore See Buchlyvie
Glendevon See Dollar

Killearn (F H W)
Stuart W. Sharp MTheol DipPA   2001   2018   Killearn Kirk, Balfron Road, Killearn G63 9NL   01360 550101
                                                              SSharp@churchofscotland.org.uk

Killin and Ardeonaig See Balquhidder
Kilmadock See Gargunnock
Kincardine-in-Menteith See Gargunnock

Kippen (F H W) linked with Norrieston (F W)
Ellen M. Larson Davidson BA MDiv	2007	2015	The Manse, Main Street, Kippen, Stirling FK8 3DN ELarsonDavidson@churchofscotland.org.uk	01786 871249

Lecropt See Dunblane: St Blane's

Logie (F H W)
Jan J. Steyn BA BD DipTheol	1988	2022	21 Craiglea, Causewayhead, Stirling FK9 5EE JSteyn@churchofscotland.org.uk	01786 271809

Menstrie (F H T W)
Michael J. Goodison BSc BD	2013	2022	7 Long Row, Menstrie FK11 7BA MGoodison@churchofscotland.org.uk	

Muckhart See Dollar
Norrieston See Kippen
Port of Menteith See Aberfoyle

Sauchie and Coalsnaughton (F)
Vacant
Interim Moderator: Scott McInnes	SMcInnes@churchofscotland.org.uk	01786 463376

Stirling: Church of the Holy Rude (F H W) linked with Stirling: Viewfield Erskine (H)   holyrude@holyrude.org
Alan F. Miller BA MA BD	2000	2010	7 Windsor Place, Stirling FK8 2HY AMiller@churchofscotland.org.uk	01786 465166

Stirling: North (F H W)   info@stirlingnorth.org
Scott McInnes MEng BD	2016		13 Calton Crescent, Stirling FK7 0BB SMcInnes@churchofscotland.org.uk	01786 463376 01786 463376

Stirling: Park (F H T W)   parkchurchstirling@gmail.com
Attie van Wyk BTh LMus MDiv MTh	2005	2022	24 Laurelhill Gardens, Stirling FK8 2PT AvanWyk@churchofscotland.org.uk	01786 462400 01786 478269

Stirling: St Mark's (T W)   stmarksstirling1@gmail.com
Barry J. Hughes MA BA	2011	2018	St Mark's Parish Church, Drip Road, Stirling FK8 1RE BHughes@churchofscotland.org.uk	01786 470733 07597 386762

Stirling: St Ninians Old (F H W)
Gary J. McIntyre BD DipMin — 1993 1998 — 7 Randolph Road, Stirling FK8 2AJ / GMcIntyre@churchofscotland.org.uk — 01786 474421

Stirling: Viewfield Erskine See Stirling: Church of the Holy Rude

Strathblane (F H T W)
Murdo M. Campbell BD DipMin — 1997 2017 — strathblanekirk@gmail.com / 2 Campsie Road, Strathblane, Glasgow G63 9AB / MCampbell@churchofscotland.org.uk — 01360 770418 / 01360 770226

Tillicoultry (F H W)
Alison E.P. Britchfield (Mrs) MA BD — 1987 2013 — The Manse, 17 Dollar Road, Tillicoultry FK13 6PD / ABritchfield@churchofscotland.org.uk — 01259 750340 / 01259 750340

Tullibody: St Serf's (H W)
Drew Barrie BSc BD — 1984 2016 — 22, The Cedars, Tullibody, Alloa FK10 2PX / DBarrie@churchofscotland.org.uk — 01259 213326

B. In other appointments

Name		Appointment	Address	Phone
Allen, Valerie L. BMus MDiv DMin	1990 2015	Presbytery Chaplain	16 Pine Court, Doune FK16 6JE / VL2allen@btinternet.com	01786 842577 / 07801 291538
Begg, Richard J. MA BD	2008 2016	Army Chaplain	12 Whiteyetts Drive, Sauchie FK10 3GE / rbegg711@aol.com	07525 612914
Boyd, Ronald M.H. BD DipTheol	1993 2010	Queen Victoria School	6 Victoria Green, Queen Victoria School, Dunblane FK15 0JY / ron.boyd@qvs.org.uk	07766 004292
Jack, Alison M. MA BD PhD SFHEA	1998 2022	Principal and Senior Lecturer, New College, Edinburgh	5 Murdoch Terrace, Dunblane FK15 9JE / alisonjack809@btinternet.com	01786 826953

C. Retaining

Name			Address	Phone
Clark, Marion A. (Rae) MA BD	2014 2022	(Clackmannan)	11A Tulipan Crescent, Callander FK17 8AR / david.cloggie@hotmail.co.uk	01877 331021
Cloggie, June (Mrs)	1997 2006	(Auxiliary Minister)		
Cochrane, James P.N. LTh	1994 2012	(Tillicoultry)	12 Sandpiper Meadow, Alloa Park, Alloa FK10 1QU / jamescochrane@pobroadband.co.uk	01259 218883
Cook, Helen K.M. (Mrs) MA BD DipSW MComC	1974 2012	(Kingussie)	60 Pelstream Avenue, Stirling FK7 0BG / revhcook@btinternet.com	01786 464128

Name			Role	Address	Phone
Dunnett, Linda (Mrs) BA DCS	1976	2016	(Deacon)	9 Tulipan Crescent, Callander FK17 8AR / lindadunnett@sky.com	01877 339640 / 07838 041683
Gaston, A. Ray C. MA BD	1969	2002	(Leuchars: St Athernase)	'Hamewith', 13 Manse Road, Dollar FK14 7AL / gaston.arthur@yahoo.co.uk	01259 743202
Goring, Iain M. BSc BD	1976	2015	(Interim Minister)	4 Argyle Grove, Dunblane FK15 9DU / imgoring@gmail.com	01786 821688
Izett, William A.F.	1968	2000	(Law)	1 Duke Street, Clackmannan FK10 4EF / william.izett@talktalk.net	01259 724203
Mack, Lynne (Mrs)	2013	2019	(Ordained Local Minister)	36 Middleton, Menstrie FK11 7HD / LMack@churchofscotland.org.uk	01259 761465
Malloch, Philip R.M. LLB BD	1970	2009	(Killearn)	8 Michael McParland Drive, Torrance, Glasgow G64 4EE / pmalloch@mac.com	01360 620089
Mathew, J. Gordon MA BD	1973	2011	(Buckie: North)	45 Westhaugh Road, Stirling FK9 5GF / jg.mathew@btinternet.com	01786 445951
McKenzie, Alan BSc BD	1988	2013	(Bellshill: Macdonald Memorial with Bellshill: Orbiston)	89 Drip Road, Stirling FK8 1RN / rev.a.mckenzie@btopenworld.com	01786 430450
McNicol, Bruce BL BD	1967	2006	(Jedburgh: Old and Edgerston)	22 Beechwood Gardens, Stirling FK8 2AX / mcnicol942@gmail.com	01786 358308
Ogilvie, Catriona (Mrs) MA BD	1999	2015	(Cumbernauld: Old)	Seberham Flat, 1A Bridge Street, Dollar FK14 7DF / catriona.ogilvie1@btinternet.com	01259 742155
Ovens, Samuel B. BD	1982	1992	(Slamannan)	21 Bevan Drive, Alva FK12 5PD	01259 763456
Porter, Jean T. (Mrs) BD DCS	2006	2022	(Deacon, Stirling: St Mark's)	3 Cochrie Place, Tullibody FK10 2RR / JPorter@churchofscotland.org.uk	07729 316321
Rose, Dennis S. DipTh LTh	1996	2016	(Arbuthnott, Bervie and Kinneff)	69 Blackthorn Grove, Menstrie FK11 7DX / dennis2327@aol.com	01259 692451
Russell, Kenneth G. BD CertCE CertCounsS PGCertHC DipPRSP	1986	2020	(Prison Chaplain)	158 Bannockburn Road, Stirling FK7 0EW / kenrussell1000@hotmail.com	01786 812680
Sewell, Paul M.N. MA BD	1970	2010	(Berwick-upon-Tweed: St Andrew's Wallace Green and Lowick)	7 Bohun Court, Stirling FK7 7UT / paulmsewell@btinternet.com	01786 489969
Thomson, Raymond BD DipMin	1992	2013	(Slamannan)	8 Rhodders Grove, Alva FK12 5ER	01259 769083
Wilson, Hazel MA BD DipEd DipMS	1991	2015	(Dundee: Lochee)	2 Boe Court, Springfield Terrace, Dunblane FK15 9LU / hmwilson704@gmail.com	01786 825850

STIRLING ADDRESSES

Holy Rude	St John Street	
North	Springfield Road	
Park	Park Terrace	
St Mark's	Drip Road	
St Ninians Old	Kirk Wynd, St Ninians	
Viewfield Erskine	Barnton Street	

(24) FIFE (F W)

Meets in varying locations on the third Saturday in February, June, September and November.

| Clerk: | REV. DAVID G. COULTER CB OStJ QHC BA BD MDA PhD | Presbytery Office, Wellesley Centre, Wellesley Parish Church, Wellesley Road, Methil KY8 3PD
fife@churchofscotland.org.uk | 07340 461921 |
| Mission Director: | MR NEIL CAMPBELL MA | Neil.Campbell@churchofscotland.org.uk | 07999 349587 |

1 Aberdour: St Fillan's (H W)
Peter S. Gerbrandy-Baird MA BD MSc FRSA FRGS   2004
St Fillan's Manse, 36 Bellhouse Road, Aberdour, Fife KY3 0TL
PGerbrandy-Baird@churchofscotland.org.uk   01383 861522

2 Anstruther and Cellardyke: St Ayle (H W) linked with Crail (F)
John W. Murray LLB BA   2001 2020
16 Taeping Close, Cellardyke, Anstruther KY10 3YL
JMurray@churchofscotland.org.uk   01333 311630

3 Auchterderran Kinglassie (F W)
Donald R. Lawrie MA BD DipCouns   1991 2018
7 Woodend Road, Cardenden, Lochgelly KY5 0NE
DLawrie@churchofscotland.org.uk   01592 720508

4 Auchtertool (W) linked with Kirkcaldy: Linktown (F H W)
Vacant   **01592 641080**
Session Clerk, Auchtertool
Session Clerk, Kirkcaldy: Linktown: J. Stewart Milne
16 Raith Crescent, Kirkcaldy KY2 5NN   01592 265536
jstewartmilne@blueyonder.co.uk   01592 266018

5 Balmerino (H W) linked with Wormit (F H W)
Vacant
Session Clerk, Balmerino: Christopher Hill
5 Westwater Place, Newport-on-Tay DD6 8NS   01382 542626
christopherhill566@btinternet.com   01382 330459
Session Clerk, Wormit: Kimberley Falconer
kimberleywatt1960@gmail.com   01334 838827

6 Beath and Cowdenbeath: North (F H W)
Deborah J. Dobby (Mrs) BA BD PGCE RGN RSCN   2014 2018
42 Woodside Avenue, Rosyth KY11 2LA
DDobby@churchofscotland.org.uk   01383 325520

7 Boarhills and Dunino linked with St Andrews: Holy Trinity (F W) holytrinitystandrews@gmail.com — 01334 478317
Guardianship of the Presbytery
Session Clerk, Boarhills and Dunino: Kenneth S. Morris kensm48@gmail.com — 01334 474468
Session Clerk, Holy Trinity: Michael Stewart (Dr) htsessionclerk@gmail.com — 01334 461270

8 Buckhaven and Wemyss (F) — 01592 715577
Vacant
Jacqueline Thomson (Mrs) MTh DCS 2004 2008 16 Aitken Place, Coaltown of Wemyss, Kirkcaldy KY1 4PA — 07806 776560
Jacqueline.Thomson@churchofscotland.org.uk

9 Burntisland (F H)
Vacant
Session Clerk: William Sweenie 21 Ramsay Crescent, Burntisland KY3 9JL — 01592 873567
billsweenie01@gmail.com

10 Cairneyhill (F H W) linked with Limekilns (F H W) office@limekilnschurch.org Cairneyhill: 01383 882352 Limekilns: 01383 873337
Norman M. Grant BD DipMin 1990 The Manse, 10 Church Street, Limekilns, Dunfermline KY11 3HT — 01383 872341
NGrant@churchofscotland.org.uk

11 Cameron (F W) linked with St Andrews: St Leonard's (F H W) stlencam@btconnect.com — 01334 478702
Graeme W. Beebee BD 1993 2017 1 Cairnhill Gardens, St Andrews KY16 8QY — 01334 472793
GBeebee@churchofscotland.org.uk

12 Carnbee linked with Pittenweem
Vacant
Session Clerk, Carnbee: Henry Watson 29 Milton Road, Pittenweem, Anstruther KY10 2LN — 01333 312838
Session Clerk, Pittenweem: to be appointed — 01333 313796

13 Carnock and Oakley (F H W)
Charles M.D. Lines BA 2010 2017 The Manse, Main Street, Carnock, Dunfermline KY12 9JG — 01383 247209
CLines@churchofscotland.org.uk — 07909 762257

14 Ceres, Kemback and Springfield (W) info@ckschurch.org
Jane L. Barron (Mrs) BA DipEd BD 1999 2021 Denhead Old Farm, St Andrews KY16 8PA — 01334 850135
JBarron@churchofscotland.org.uk — 07545 904541

15 Cowdenbeath: Trinity (F H W)
Vacant
Session Clerk: John Bain 2 Glenfield Road, Cowdenbeath KY4 9EL — 01383 510696
johnbain1@btinternet.com — 01383 512779

16	Crail See Anstruther and Cellardyke: St Ayle		
17	**Creich, Flisk and Kilmany (W)** Guardianship of the Presbytery Session Clerk: Patricia Pearce	p.pearce@tiscali.co.uk	01334 655799
18	**Culross and Torryburn (H)** Vacant	Contact via Presbytery Office	
19	**Cupar: Old and St Michael of Tarvit (H W) linked with Monimail** Jeffrey A. Martin BA MDiv 1991 2016	76 Hogarth Drive, Cupar KY15 5YU JMartin@churchofscotland.org.uk	01334 656181
20	**Cupar: St John's and Dairsie United (F W)** Gavin W.G. Black BD 2006 2019	The Manse, 23 Hogarth Drive, Cupar KY15 5YH GBlack@churchofscotland.org.uk	01334 650751
21	**Dalgety (H W)** Christine M. Sime (Miss) BSc BD 1994 2012	office@dalgety-church.co.uk 9 St Colme Drive, Dalgety Bay, Dunfermline KY11 9LQ CSime@churchofscotland.org.uk	**01383 824092** 01383 822316
22	**Dunfermline: Abbey (F H T W)** MaryAnn R. Rennie (Mrs) BD MTh CPS 1998 2012	dunfermline.abbey.church@gmail.com 3 Perdieus Mount, Dunfermline KY12 7XE MARennie@churchofscotland.org.uk	**01383 724586** 01383 727311
23	**Dunfermline: East (F W)** Andrew A. Morrice MA BD 1999 2010	71 Swift Street, Dunfermline KY11 8SN AMorrice@churchofscotland.org.uk	01383 223144 07815 719301
24	**Dunfermline: Gillespie Memorial (F H W)** Michael A. Weaver BSc BD 2017	office@gillespiechurch.org 4 Killin Court, Dunfermline KY12 7XF MWeaver@churchofscotland.org.uk	**01383 621253** 01383 724347
25	**Dunfermline: North** Guardianship of the Presbytery Session Clerk: Graham Primrose	sessionclerk@dunfermlinenorthparishchurch.co.uk	07920 445669

26 Dunfermline: St Andrew's Erskine (F W) 2006
Muriel F. Willoughby (Mrs) MA BD   2013
staechurch@standrewserskine.org.uk
71A Townhill Road, Dunfermline KY12 0BN
MWilloughby@churchofscotland.org.uk
01383 **841660**
01383 738487

27 Dunfermline: St Leonard's (F W)
Vacant
Margaret B. Mateos   2018
(Ordained Local Minister)
office@slpc.org
12 Torvean Place, Dunfermline KY11 4YY
43 South Street, Lochgelly KY5 9LJ
MMateos@churchofscotland.org.uk
01383 **620106**
01383 300092
01592 780073

28 Dunfermline: St Margaret's (F W)   1985
Iain M. Greenshields   2007
BD CertMin DipRS ACMA MSc MTh DD
38 Garvock Hill, Dunfermline KY12 7UU
IGreenshields@churchofscotland.org.uk
01383 723955
07427 477575

29 Dunfermline: St Ninian's (F W)   2009
Carolann Birnie BD DipPSRP   2018
51 St John's Drive, Dunfermline KY12 7TL
CBirnie@churchofscotland.org.uk
01383 271548

30 Dunfermline: Townhill and Kingseat (F H W)
Vacant
Session Clerk: David Henderson
info@townhillandkingseatchurchofscotland.org
7 Lochwood Park, Kingseat, Dunfermline KY12 0UX
davidw-henderson@sky.com
01383 723691
01383 737679

31 Dysart: St Clair (F H W)
Vacant
Session Clerk: Raymond Domin
42 Craigfoot Walk, Kirkcaldy KY1 1GA
raymonddomin@blueyonder.co.uk
01592 561967
01592 203620

32 East Neuk Trinity (F H W) linked with St Monans (F H W)
Douglas R. Creighton BSc BTh   2020
eastneuktrinityoffice@btconnect.com
6 Reaper Lane, Anstruther KY10 3FR
DCreighton@churchofscotland.org.uk
01333 311045

33 Edenshead (F W)
Vacant
Session Clerk: Liz Slattery
The Manse, Kirk Wynd, Strathmiglo, Cupar KY14 7QS
halhill14@gmail.com
01337 860256
07719 724730

34 Falkland (F W) linked with Freuchie (H W)
Guardianship of the Presbytery
Session Clerk, Falkland: Marion Baldie
Session Clerk, Freuchie: Margaret Cuthbert
1 Newton Road, Falkland, Cupar KY15 7AQ
sessionclerk.falkland@gmail.com
cuthbertmargaret@yahoo.co.uk
01337 858557
07951 824488
01337 830940

35 Freuchie See Falkland

36 Glenrothes: Christ's Kirk (H W)
Vacant
Session Clerk: Ruth Anderson

christskirkglenrothes@yahoo.com — **01592 745938**
ruthp.anderson@yahoo.com — 07970 594033

37 Glenrothes: St Columba's (F W)
Alan W.D. Kimmitt BSc BD — 2013

info@st-columbas.com — **01592 752539**
40 Liberton Drive, Glenrothes KY6 3PB — 01592 742233
Alan.Kimmitt@churchofscotland.org.uk

38 Glenrothes: St Margaret's (F H W)
Vacant
Session Clerk: Catriona Redpath — 2014

office@stmargaretschurch.org.uk — **01592 328162**
8 Alburne Park, Glenrothes KY7 5RB — 01592 752241
catriona.redpath@outlook.com — 01592 753534

39 Glenrothes: St Ninian's (F H W)
David J. Smith BD DipMin — 1992 2017

office@stninians.co.uk — **01592 610560**
1 Cawdor Drive, Glenrothes KY6 2HN — 01592 611963
David.Smith@churchofscotland.org.uk

40 Howe of Fife (F W)
William F. Hunter MA BD — 1986 2011

The Manse, 83 Church Street, Ladybank, Cupar KY15 7ND — 01337 832717
WHunter@churchofscotland.org.uk

41 Inverkeithing (F W) linked with North Queensferry (W)
Colin M. Alston BMus BD BN RN — 1975 2012

32c Townhill Road, Dunfermline KY12 0QX — 01383 621050
CAlston@churchofscotland.org.uk

42 Kelty (W)
Vacant
Session Clerk: Veronica Forrest

info@keltychurch.co.uk — **01383 831219**
15 Arlick Road, Kelty KY4 0BH — 01383 831362
forveronica2@gmail.com — 01383 830130

43 Kennoway, Windygates and Balgonie: St Kenneth's (F W)
Allan P. Morton MA BD PGDip — 2018

stkennethsparish@gmail.com — **01333 351372**
2 Fernhill Gardens, Windygates, Leven KY8 5DZ — 01333 350240
AMorton@churchofscotland.org.uk

44 Kilrenny (W)
Guardianship of the Presbytery
Session Clerk: Corinne Peddie

corinne@peddies.com — 01333 311408

No.	Charge / Name			Address / Email	Tel
45	**Kinghorn (F W)** James Reid BD	1985	1997	17 Myre Crescent, Kinghorn, Burntisland KY3 9UB JReid@churchofscotland.org.uk	01592 890269
46	**Kingsbarns (F H)** Guardianship of the Presbytery Session Clerk: Elizabeth Spittal			elibby.121@btinternet.com	01334 880387
47	**Kirkcaldy: Abbotshall (F H T W)** Vacant Session Clerk: Morag Michael			83 Milton Road, Kirkcaldy KY1 1TP msmichael@icloud.com	01592 267915 01592 263087
48	**Kirkcaldy: Bennochy (F W)** Robin J. McAlpine BDS BD MTh	1988	2011	25 Bennochy Avenue, Kirkcaldy KY2 5QE RMcAlpine@churchofscotland.org.uk	**01592 201723** 01592 643518
49	**Kirkcaldy: Linktown** See Auchtertool				
50	**Kirkcaldy: Pathhead (F H W)** Andrew C. Donald BD DPS	1992	2005	**pathheadchurch@btconnect.com** 73 Loughborough Road, Kirkcaldy KY1 3DB ADonald@churchofscotland.org.uk	**01592 204635** 01592 652215
51	**Kirkcaldy: St Bryce Kirk (F H T W)** Vacant Session Clerk: Margaret Hunter			**office@stbrycekirk.org.uk** mannehunter@hotmail.com	**01592 640016** 01592 265927
52	**Kirkcaldy: Templehall and Torbain United (F W)** Vacant Brian W. Porteous BSc DipRM DipCS CertCounsS (Ordained Local Minister)	2018		Kildene, Westfield Road, Cupar KY15 5DS BPorteous@churchofscotland.org.uk	01334 653561
53	**Largo (F W)** Gavin R. Boswell BTheol	1993	2018	1 Castaway Lane, Lower Largo KY8 6FA GBoswell@churchofscotland.org.uk	01333 320850
54	**Largoward (H W)** Guardianship of the Presbytery Session Clerk: Robert Scott			bobandandge@gmail.com	

55 Leslie: Trinity
Guardianship of the Presbytery
Session Clerk: Alec Redpath — sessionclerk@leslietrinitychurch.co.uk — 01592 742636

56 Leuchars: St Athernase (F)
Vacant
Session Clerk: Richard Trewern — 7 David Wilson Park, Balmullo, St Andrews KY16 0NP — 01334 870038
rrit_lucklaw@btinternet.com

57 Leven (F)
Vacant — **levenparish@tiscali.co.uk** — **01333 423969**
Session Clerk: Linda Archer — lindaarcher847@ymail.com — 01333 329850

58 Limekilns See Cairneyhill

59 Lindores (F H)
Guardianship of Presbytery
Session Clerk: Elizabeth Lee — 2 Guthrie Court, Cupar Road, Newburgh, Cupar KY14 6HA — 01337 842228
elee1963.el@gmail.com — 07761 342131

60 Lochgelly and Benarty: St Serf's (F W)
Zoltán Sáfrány BD 2000 2020 — 82 Main Street, Lochgelly KY5 9AA — 01592 780435
ZSafrany@churchofscotland.org.uk — 07411 444743
Pamela Scott (Mrs) BD DCS 2017 — 177 Primrose Avenue, Rosyth KY11 2TZ — 01383 410530
PScott@churchofscotland.org.uk — 07548 819334

61 Markinch and Thornton (F W)
Conor Fegan MA MTh PhD 2022 — 7 Guthrie Crescent, Markinch, Glenrothes KY7 6AY — 01592 758264
CFegan@churchofscotland.org.uk

62 Methil: Wellesley (F H W)
Gillian Paterson (Mrs) BD 2010 — 10 Vettriano Vale, Leven KY8 4GD — 01333 423147
GPaterson@churchofscotland.org.uk

63 Methilhill and Denbeath (F)
Elisabeth F. Cranfield (Ms) MA BD 1988 — 9 Chemiss Road, Methilhill, Leven KY8 2BS — 01592 713142
ECranfield@churchofscotland.org.uk

64 Monimail See Cupar: Old and St Michael of Tarvit

65 Newport-on-Tay (F H W)
Amos B. Chewachong BTh MTh PhD   2005   2017   17 East Station Place, Newport-on-Tay DD6 8EG   01382 542893
AChewachong@churchofscotland.org.uk

66 North Queensferry See Inverkeithing
67 Pittenweem See Carnbee

68 Rosyth (F W)   rpc@cos82a.plus.com   **01383 412534**
D. Brian Dobby BA MA   1999   2018   42 Woodside Avenue, Rosyth KY11 2LA   01383 412776
BDobby@churchofscotland.org.uk

69 St Andrews: Holy Trinity See Boarhills and Dunino
70 St Andrews: St Leonard's See Cameron

71 St Andrews: St Mark's (F H W)   admin@hpmchurch.org.uk   **01334 478144**
Allan McCafferty BSc BD   1993   2011   20 Priory Gardens, St Andrews KY16 8XX   Tel/Fax 01334 478287
AMcCafferty@churchofscotland.org.uk
New charge formed by the union of St Andrews: Hope Park and Martyrs and Strathkinness

72 St Monans See East Neuk Trinity

73 Saline and Blairingone (F W) linked with Tulliallan and Kincardine (F W)   tulliallanandkincardine@gmail.com
Alexander J. Shuttleworth MA BD   2004   2013   62 Toll Road, Kincardine, Alloa FK10 4QZ   01259 731002
AShuttleworth@churchofscotland.org.uk

74 Tayport (F W)   bwd.hmd@btinternet.com   01382 553634
Guardianship of the Presbytery
Session Clerk: Heather Davidson

75 Tulliallan and Kincardine See Saline and Blairingone
76 Wormit See Balmerino

B. In other appointments
Coulter, David G. CB OStJ QHC   1989 2021   Presbytery Clerk: Fife   62B Buchanan Gardens, St Andrews KY16 9LX   01334 473836
BA BD MDA PhD   DCoulter@churchofscotland.org.uk
MacEwan, Donald G. MA BD PhD   2001 2011   Chaplain: University of St Andrews   Chaplaincy Centre, 3A St Mary's Place, St Andrews KY16 9UY   01334 462865
dgm21@st-andrews.ac.uk   07713 322036

Name			Role	Address / Email	Tel
Miller, Eileen A. BD DipComEd AdvDipCouns MBCAP(Snr Accred.)	2014	2022	Chaplain, Queen Margaret Hospital, Dunfermline	9 Car Craig View, Burntisland KY3 0DS / EMiller@churchofscotland.org.uk	07923 033933
Smith, Fiona E. (Mrs) LLB BD	2010	2022	Principal Clerk	11 Bridge Street, Saline, Dunfermline KY12 9TS / FSmith@churchofscotland.org.uk	07824 037271
Strang, Gordon I. BSc BD	2014	2021	Chaplain, NHS Fife	Department of Spiritual Care, Victoria Hospital, Kirkcaldy KY2 5AH / GStrang@churchofscotland.org.uk	01592 648158

C. Retaining

Name			Role	Address / Email	Tel
Adams, David G. BD	1991	2011	(Cowdenbeath: Trinity)	13 Fernhill Gardens, Windygates, Leven KY8 5DZ / adams.69@btinternet.com	01333 351214
Allardice, Michael MA MPhil DipTheol FHEA	2014	2020	(Ordained Local Minister)	2 Station Road, Kingskettle, Cupar KY15 7PR / MAllardice@churchofscotland.org.uk	01337 597073 / 07936 203465
Barr, G. Russell BA BD MTh DMin	1979	2020	(Edinburgh: Cramond)	4 Balone Steading, St Andrews KY16 8NS / GBarr@churchofscotland.org.uk	01334 781142
Boyle, Robert P. LTh CPS	1990	2010	(Saline and Blairingone)	23 Farnell Way, Dunfermline KY12 0SR / boab.boyle@btinternet.com	01383 729568
Bradley, Ian C. (Prof.) MA BD DPhil	1990	2018	(University of St Andrews)	4 Donaldson Gardens, St Andrews KY16 9DN / icb@st-andrews.ac.uk	01334 475389
Brewster, John MA BD DipEd	1988	2021	(East Kilbride: Greenhills)	82 Harcourt Road, Kirkcaldy KY2 5HF / johnbrewster@blueyonder.co.uk	07917 333812
Campbell, Reginald F. BSc BD DipChEd	1979	2015	(Daviot and Dunlichity with Moy, Dalarossie and Tomatin)	12 Alloway Drive, Kirkcaldy KY2 6DX / campbell1578@talktalk.net	
Chalmers, John P. BD CPS DD	1979	2017	(Principal Clerk)	10 Liggars Place, Dunfermline KY12 7XZ / JChalmers@churchofscotland.org.uk	01383 739130
Christie, Arthur A. BD	1997	2018	(Anstruther and Cellardyke: St Ayle with Kilrenny)	194 Foulford Road, Cowdenbeath KY4 9AX / revac@btinternet.com	01383 511326
Clark, David M. MA BD	1989	2013	(Dundee: The Steeple)	2b Rose Street, St Monans, Anstruther KY10 2BQ / dmclark72@gmail.com	01333 739034
Connolly, Daniel BD DipTh DipMin	1983	2015	(Army Chaplain)	2 Cairngreen, Cupar KY15 2SY / dannyconnolly@hotmail.co.uk	07951 078478
Deans, Graham D.S. MA BD MTh MLitt DMin	1978	2017	(Aberdeen: Queen Street)	38 Sir Thomas Elder Way, Kirkcaldy KY2 6ZS / graham.deans@btopenworld.com	01592 641429
Dick, John H.A. (Ian) MA MSc BD	1982	2012	(Aberdeen: Ferryhill)	18 Fairfield Road, Kelty KY4 0BY	01383 271147
Elston, Ian J. BD MTh	1999	2019	(Kirkcaldy: Torbain)	65 Longbrae Gardens, Kirkcaldy KY2 5YJ / IElston@churchofscotland.org.uk	01592 592393
Fairlie, George BD BVMS MRCVS	1971	2002	(Crail with Kingsbarns)	41 Warrack Street, St Andrews KY16 8DR	01334 475868
Farquhar, William E. BA BD	1987	2006	(Dunfermline: Townhill and Kingseat)	29 Queens Drive, Middlewich, Cheshire CW10 0DG	01606 835097
Fisk, Elizabeth A. BD	1996	2022	(Culross and Torryburn)	30 Masterton Road, Dunfermline KY11 8RB / EFisk@churchofscotland.org.uk	01383 730039
Foggie, Janet P. MA BD PhD	2003	2021	(Pioneer Minister, University of Stirling)	Old Schoolhouse, Dunbog, Newburgh KY14 6JF	07899 349246
Forrester, Ian L. MA	1964	1996	(Friockheim Kinnell with Inverkeilor and Lunan)	8 Bennochy Avenue, Kirkcaldy KY2 5QE	01592 260251

Name			Charge	Address / Email	Tel
Forsyth, Alexander R. TD BA MTh	1973	2014	(Markinch)	49 Scaraben Crescent, Formonthills, Glenrothes KY6 3HL / alex@arforsyth.com	01592 749049 / 07483 232581
Fraser, Ann G. BD CertMin	1990	2007	(Auchtermuchty)	24 Irvine Crescent, St Andrews KY16 8LG / anngilfraser@btinternet.com	01334 461329
Froude, J. Kenneth (Ken) MA BD	1979	2020	(Kirkcaldy: St Bryce Kirk)	44 Templars Crescent, Kinghorn KY3 9XS / JFroude@churchofscotland.org.uk	01592 892512
Galbraith, D. Douglas MA BD BMus MPhil ARSCM PhD	1965	2005	(Office for Worship, Doctrine and Artistic Matters)	34 Balbirnie Street, Markinch, Glenrothes KY7 6DA / dgalbraith@churchofscotland.org.uk	01592 752403
Gordon, Ian D. LTh	1972	2001	(Markinch)	2 Somerville Way, Glenrothes KY7 5GE	01592 742487
Hamilton, Ian W.F. BD LTh ALCM AVCM	1978	2012	(Nairn: Old)	Mossneuk, 5 Windsor Gardens, St Andrews KY16 8XL / reviwfh@btinternet.com	01334 477745
Harrison, Cameron BSc MEd	2006	2010	(Auxiliary Minister)	Woodfield House, Priormuir, St Andrews KY16 8LP / cameron@harrisonleimon.co.uk	01334 478067
Henderson, J. Mary MA BD DipEd PhD	1990	2020	(Falkirk: Laurieston with Redding and Westquarter)	8 Miller Terrace, St Monans KY10 2BB / jmary.henderson1@gmail.com	01333 730138
Jenkins, Gordon F.C. MA BD PhD	1968	2006	(Dunfermline: North)	2 Balrymonth Court, St Andrews KY16 8XT / jenkinsgordon1@sky.com	01335 477194
Johnston, Thomas N. LTh	1972	2008	(Edinburgh: Priestfield)	71 Main Street, Newmills, Dunfermline KY12 8ST / tomjohnston@blueyonder.co.uk	01383 889240
Kenny, Elizabeth S.S. BD RGN SCM	1989	2010	(Carnock and Oakley)	5 Cobden Court, Crossgates, Cowdenbeath KY4 8AU / esskenny@btinternet.com	07831 763494
Kesting, Sheilagh M. BA BD DD DSG	1980	2016	(Ecumenical Officer, Church of Scotland)	Restalrig, Chance Inn, Cupar KY15 5QJ / smkesting@btinternet.com	01334 829485
Laidlaw, Victor W.N. BD CertCE	1975	2008	(Edinburgh: St Catherine's Argyle)	9 Tern Road, Dunfermline KY11 8GA / v9wintern@hotmail.com	01383 620134
Lane, Margaret R. (Mrs) BA BD MTh	2009	2019	(Edinburgh: Kirkliston)	6 Overhaven, Limekilns KY11 3JH / margaretlane@btinternet.com	01383 873328
Leitch, D. Graham MA BD	1974	2012	(Tyne Valley)	9 St Margaret Wynd, Dunfermline KY12 0UT / dgrahamleitch@gmail.com	01383 249245
McCulloch, William B. BD	1997	2016	(Rome: St Andrew's)	81 Meldrum Court, Dunfermline KY11 4XR / revwbmculloch@hotmail.com	01383 730305
McDonald, Tom BD	1994	2015	(Kelso: North and Ednam)	12 Woodmill Grove, Dunfermline KY11 4JR / revtomparadise12@gmail.com	01383 695365
McKay, Violet C.C. BD	1988	2017	(Rosyth)	20B Blane Crescent, Dunfermline KY11 8ZF / violetcm@gmail.com	01383 727255
McKimmon, Eric G. BA BD MTh PhD	1983	2014	(Cargill Burrelton with Collace)	14 Marionfield Place, Cupar KY15 5JN / ericmckimmon@gmail.com	01334 659650
McLean, John P. BSc BPhil BD	1994	2013	(Glenrothes: St Margaret's)	72 Lawmill Gardens, St Andrews KY16 8QS / jpmclean72@gmail.com	01334 470803
McLellan, Andrew R.C. CBE MA BD STM DD	1970	2009	(HM Chief Inspector of Prisons for Scotland)	4 Liggars Place, Dunfermline KY12 7XZ / iamclellan4@gmail.com	01383 725959
McLeod, Alistair G.	1988	2005	(Glenrothes: St Columba's)	13 Greenmantle Way, Glenrothes KY6 3QG / alistairmcleod1936@gmail.com	01592 744558

Name	Ord	Ind	Charge	Address / Email	Telephone
McNaught, Samuel M. MA BD MTh	1968	2002	(Kirkcaldy: St John's)	6 Munro Court, Glenrothes KY7 5GD / sjmcnaught@btinternet.com	01592 742352
Meager, Peter MA BD CertMgmt(Open)	1970	1998	(Elie with Kilconquhar and Colinsburgh)	7 Lorraine Drive, Cupar KY15 5DY / meager52@btinternet.com	01334 656991
Melville, David D. BD	1989	2008	(Kirkconnel)	28 Porterfield, Comrie, Dunfermline KY12 9HJ / revddm@gmail.com	01383 850075
Munro, Andrew MA BD PhD	1972	2000	(Glencaple with Lowther)	7 Dunvegan Avenue, Kirkcaldy KY2 5SG / am.smm@blueyonder.co.uk	01592 566129
Neilson, Peter MA BD MTh	1975	2016	(Mission Consultant)	Linne Bheag, 2 School Green, Anstruther KY10 3HF / neilson.peter@btinternet.com	01333 310477 / 07818 418608
Nicol, George G. BD DPhil	1982	2013	(Falkland with Freuchie)	48 Fidra Avenue, Burntisland KY3 0AZ / ggnicol@totalise.co.uk	01592 873258
Nisbet, Gilbert C. CA BD	1993	2019	(Leven)	Upper Flat, 2 Temple Crescent, Crail KY10 3RS / gcn@insprint.co.uk	01333 450929
Paterson, Andrew E. JP	1994	2020	(Auxiliary Minister)	6 The Willows, Kelty KY4 0FQ	01383 830998
Paterson, Maureen (Mrs) BSc	1992	2010	(Auxiliary Minister)	91 Dalmahoy Crescent, Kirkcaldy KY2 6TA / m.e.paterson@blueyonder.co.uk	01592 262300
Paton, Marion J. (Miss) MA BMus BD	1991	2017	(Dundee: St David's High Kirk)	18 Winram Place, St Andrews KY16 8XH / mjpdht@gmail.com	01334 208743
Redmayne, David W. BSc BD	2001	2017	(Beath and Cowdenbeath: North)	10 Hawthorn Park, Dunfermline KY12 0DY	01383 738137
Reid, David MSc LTh FSAScot	1962	1992	(Largoward with St Monans)	North Lethans, Saline, Dunfermline KY12 9TE	01383 733144
Robb, Nigel J. FCP MA BD ThM MTh	1981	2014	(Associate Secretary, Mission and Discipleship Council)		07966 286958
Rose, Margaret E.S. BD	2007	2022	(Carnbee with Pittenweem)	10a Dunlop Street, Strathaven ML10 6LA / MRose@churchofscotland.org.uk	
Roy, Allistair D. BD DipSW PgDip	2007	2016	(Glenrothes: St Ninian's)	39 Ravenswood Drive, Glenrothes KY6 2PA / minister@revroy.co.uk	
Scott, David D. BSc BD	1981	2019	(Traprain)	259 Lamond Drive, St Andrews KY16 8RR / revddd.scott@gmail.com	01334 473460
Sharp, Alan BSc BD	1980	2019	(Burntisland)	29 Cromwell Road, Burntisland KY3 9EH / alansharp03@aol.com	
Sinclair, David I. BSc BD PhD DipSW CQSW	1990	2020	(Ecumenical and International Officer, Evangelical Church of the Czech Brethren)	42 South Road, Cupar KY15 5JF / davidsinclair@btinternet.com	01334 659171
Symington, Alastair H. MA BD	1972	2012	(Troon: Old)	70 The Walled Garden, Abbey Park Avenue, St Andrews KY16 9JW / revdahs@virginmedia.com	07703 176717
Templeton, James L. BSc BD	1975	2012	(Innerleven: East)	29 Coldstream Avenue, Leven KY8 5TN / jamietempleton@btinternet.com	01333 427102
Thom, Ian G. BSc PhD BD	1990	2020	(Dunfermline: North)	4 Calaiswood Crescent, Dunfermline KY11 8ZR / ianthom58@btinternet.com	01383 733471
Thomson, John D. BD	1985	2005	(Kirkcaldy: Pathhead)	3 Tottenham Court, Hill Street, Dysart, Kirkcaldy KY1 2XY / j.thomson10@sky.com	01592 655313 / 07885 414979
Tomlinson, Bryan L. TD	1969	2003	(Kirkcaldy: Abbotshall)	2 Duddingston Drive, Kirkcaldy KY2 6JP / abbkirk@blueyonder.co.uk	01592 564843

Name			Address	Tel
Torrance, Alan J. (Prof.) MA BD DrTheol ARCM	(University of St Andrews)	1984 2020	Kincaple House, Kincaple, St Andrews KY16 9SH	01334 850755
Unsworth, Ruth BA BD CertMHS PgDipCBP BABCP	(Glasgow Pollokshaws)	1984 1987	5 Lindsay Gardens, St Andrews KY16 8XB RUnsworth@churchofscotland.org.uk	07894 802119
Walker, James B. MA BD DPhil	(Chaplain: University of St Andrews)	1975 2011	5 Priestden Park, St Andrews KY16 8DL	01334 472839
Wallace, Hugh M. MA BD	(Newhills)	1980 2018	15 West End, St Monans KY10 2BX	
Watt, Robert J. BD	(Dumbarton: Riverside)	1994 2009	101 Birrell Drive, Dunfermline KY11 8FA robertwatt101@gmail.com	01383 735417 07753 683717
Wilson, Tilly (Miss) MTh	(Dysart)	1990 2012	6 Citron Glebe, Kirkcaldy KY1 2NF tillywilson1@sky.com	01592 263134
Wotherspoon, Ian G. BA LTh	(Coatbridge: St Andrew's)	1967 2004	12 Cherry Lane, Cupar KY15 5DA wotherspoonrig@aol.com	01334 650710
Wright, Lynda BEd DCS	(Community Chaplaincy Listening Co-ordinator, NHS Fife)	1979 2021	71a Broomhill Avenue, Burntisland KY3 0BP lyndawright20@gmail.com	07835 303395

TOWN ADDRESSES

Cupar
Old and St Michael of Tarvit — Kirkgate
St John's and Dairsie United — Bonnygate / Main Street, Dairsie

Dunfermline
Abbey — St Catherine's Wynd
East — Nightingale Place
Gillespie Memorial — Chapel Street
North — Golfdrum Street
St Andrew's Erskine — Robertson Road
St Leonard's — Brucefield Avenue
St Margaret's — Abel Place
St Ninian's — Allan Crescent
Townhill and Kingseat — Main Street, Townhill / Church Street, Kingseat

Glenrothes
Christ's Kirk — Pitcoudie Avenue
St Columba's — Church Street
St Margaret's — Woodside Road
St Ninian's — Durris Drive

Kirkcaldy
Abbotshall — Abbotshall Road
Bennochy — Elgin Street
Linktown — Nicol Street x High Street
Pathhead — Harriet Street x Church Street
St Bryce Kirk — St Brycedale Avenue x Kirk Wynd
Templehall and Torbain United — Beauly Place / Carron Place

St Andrews
Holy Trinity — South Street
St Leonard's — Donaldson Gardens
St Mark's — St Mary's Place

(27) DUNKELD AND MEIGLE

Meets at Pitlochry on the fourth Tuesday of October and the first Tuesday of December 2022. On 1 January 2023 it will unite with the Presbyteries of Stirling, Perth, Dundee and Angus to form a new Presbytery of Perth. That Presbytery will meet on a date and in a venue to be determined and thereafter as decided.

Clerk:	**REV. JOHN RUSSELL MA**		**Kilblaan, Gladstone Terrace, Birnam, Dunkeld PH8 0DP**	**01350 728896**
			dunkeldmeigle@churchofscotland.org.uk	
Depute Clerk:	**REV. R. FRASER PENNY BA BD**		**Cathedral Manse, Dunkeld PH8 0AW**	**01350 727249**
			RPenny@churchofscotland.org.uk	

Aberfeldy (F H W) linked with Dull and Weem (H W) linked with Grantully, Logierait and Strathtay (F W)

Neil M. Glover BSc BD	2005	2017	The Manse, Taybridge Terrace, Aberfeldy PH15 2BS	01887 820819
			NGlover@churchofscotland.org.uk	07779 280074

Alyth (F H W)

Michael J. Erskine MA BD	1985	2012	The Manse, Cambridge Street, Alyth, Blairgowrie PH11 8AW	01828 632238
			erskinemike@gmail.com	

Ardler, Kettins and Meigle (F W)

Vacant			The Manse, Dundee Road, Meigle, Blairgowrie PH12 8SB	01828 640074
Interim Moderator: Michael J. Erskine			erskinemike@gmail.com	01828 632238

Bendochy (W) linked with Coupar Angus: Abbey (W)

Andrew F. Graham BTh DPS	2001	2016	Caddam Road, Coupar Angus, Blairgowrie PH13 9EF	01828 627864
			Andrew.Graham@churchofscotland.org.uk	

Blair Atholl and Struan linked with Braes of Rannoch linked with Foss and Rannoch (H)

Vacant			The Manse, Blair Atholl, Pitlochry PH18 5SX	01796 481213
Interim Moderator: Grace M. F. Steele			GSteele@churchofscotland.org.uk	01887 820025

Blairgowrie (F W)   blairgowrieparishchurch@gmail.com

Benjamin J. A. Abeledo BTh DipTh PTh	1991	2019	The Manse, Upper David Street, Blairgowrie PH10 6HB	01250 870986
			BAbeledo@churchofscotland.org.uk	

Braes of Rannoch See Blair Atholl and Struan

Caputh and Clunie (H) linked with Kinclaven (H)

Vacant				
Interim Moderator: Richard S. Campbell			revrichards@yahoo.co.uk	01250 876386

Coupar Angus: Abbey See Bendochy
Dull and Weem See Aberfeldy

Dunkeld (H W)
R. Fraser Penny BA BD   1984   2001
The Manse, Cathedral Street, Dunkeld PH8 0AW   01350 727249
RPenny@churchofscotland.org.uk

Fortingall, Glenlyon, Kenmore (H) and Lawers (W)
Vacant
Interim Moderator: Robert D. Nicol
The Manse, Balnaskeag, Kenmore, Aberfeldy PH15 2HB   01887 830218
RNicol@churchofscotland.org.uk   01887 820242

Foss and Rannoch See Blair Atholl and Struan
Grantully, Logierait and Strathtay See Aberfeldy
Kinclaven See Caputh and Clunie

Kirkmichael, Straloch and Glenshee (W) linked with Rattray (H W)
Linda Stewart (Mrs) BD   1996   2012
The Manse, Alyth Road, Rattray, Blairgowrie PH10 7HF   01250 872462
Linda.Stewart@churchofscotland.org.uk

Pitlochry (H W)
Vacant
Interim Moderator: R. Fraser Penny
thetryst@btconnect.com   **01796 474010**
Manse Road, Moulin, Pitlochry PH16 5EP   01796 472774
RPenny@churchofscotland.org.uk   01350 727249

Rattray See Kirkmichael, Straloch and Glenshee

Tenandry
Guardianship of the Presbytery
Interim Moderator: Neil M. Glover
NGlover@churchofscotland.org.uk   01887 820819
07779 280074

B. In other appointments
Nicol, Robert D. MA   2013   2019   Ordained Local Minister: Presbytery-wide   Rappla Lodge, Camserney, Aberfeldy PH15 2JF   01887 820242
RNicol@churchofscotland.org.uk
Russell, John MA   1959   2000   Presbytery Clerk: Dunkeld and Meigle   Kilblaan, Gladstone Terrace, Birnam, Dunkeld PH8 0DP   01350 728896
Steele, Grace M.F. MA BTh   2014   Ordained Local Minister: Presbytery-wide   12a Farragon Drive, Aberfeldy PH15 2BQ   01887 820025
GSteele@churchofscotland.org.uk

C. Retaining

Name	Charge	Years	Address / Email	Phone
Campbell, Richard S. LTh	(Gargunnock with Kilmadock with Kincardine-in-Menteith)	1993 2010	3 David Farquharson Road, Blairgowrie PH10 6FD revrichards@yahoo.co.uk	01250 876386
Dingwall, Brian BTh CQSW	(Arbirlot with Carmyllie)	1999 2020	10 New Road, Rattray, Blairgowrie PH10 7RA brian.d12@btinternet.com	07906 656847
Ewart, William BSc BD	(Caputh and Clunie with Kinclaven)	1972 2010	22 Muirend Avenue, Perth PH1 1JL ewel@btinternet.com	
Ewart-Roberts, Peggy BA BD	(Caputh and Clunie with Kinclaven)	2003 2022	22 Muirend Avenue, Perth PH1 1JL PEwart-Roberts@churchofscotland.org.uk	07775 712686
Haddow, Mary M. (Mrs) BD	(Pitlochry)	2001 2022	16 Hobens Drive, North Berwick EH39 5GZ mary_haddow@btconnect.com	
Knox, John W. MTheol	(Lochgelly: Macainsh)	1992 1997	2 Darroch Gate, Blairgowrie PH10 6GT ian.knox5@btinternet.com	01250 872733
MacRae, Malcolm H. MA PhD	(Kirkmichael, Straloch and Glenshee with Rattray)	1971 2010	10B Victoria Place, Stirling FK8 2QU malcolm.macrae1@btopenworld.com	01786 465547
McLachlan, Ian K. MA BD	(Barr with Dailly with Girvan: South)	1999 2019	22 Beeches Road, Blairgowrie PH10 6PN iankmclachlanyetiville53@gmail.com	01250 369224
Mowbray, Harry BD CA	(Blairgowrie)	2003 2018	12 Isla Road, Blairgowrie PH10 6RR	01250 873479
Nelson, Robert C. BA BD	(Kilninian and Kilmore with Salen and Ulva with Tobermory with Torosay and Kinlochspelvie)	1980 2010	St Colme's, Perth Road, Birnam, Dunkeld PH8 0BH rcnelson49@btinternet.com	01350 727455
Notman, Alison BD	(Ardler, Kettins and Meigle)	2014 2020	6 Hall Street, Kettlebridge, Cupar KY15 7QF	
Ormiston, Hugh C. BSc BD MPhil PhD	(Kirkmichael, Straloch and Glenshee with Rattray)	1969 2004	Cedar Lea, Main Road, Woodside, Blairgowrie PH13 9NP	01828 670539
Robertson, Matthew LTh	(Cawdor with Croy and Dalcross)	1968 2002	Inver, Strathtay, Pitlochry PH9 0PG	01887 840780
Rodger, Matthew A. BD	(Ellon)	1978 1999	1 Bank House, Airlie Street, Alyth PH11 8AH	01828 634265
Wallace, Sheila D. (Mrs) BA BD DCS	(Deacon)	2009 2020	Little Orchard, Blair Atholl, Pitlochry PH18 5SH	01796 481647 07733 243046
Whyte, William B. DipArch ARIBA BD	(Nairn: St Ninian's)	1973 2004	The Old Inn, Park Hill Road, Rattray, Blairgowrie PH10 7DS	01250 874401
Wilson, John M. MA BD	(Altnaharra and Farr)	1967 2004	Berbice, The Terrace, Blair Atholl, Pitlochry PH18 5SZ	01796 481619

(28) PERTH (W)

Meets at 7pm on the second Tuesday of November. On 1 January 2023 it will unite with the Presbyteries of Stirling, Dunkeld and Meigle, Dundee and Angus to form a new Presbytery of Perth. That Presbytery will meet on date and in a venue to be determined and thereafter as decided.

Clerk:	**REV. J. COLIN CASKIE BA BD**		
Presbytery Office:		**209 High Street, Perth PH1 5PB** **perth@churchofscotland.org.uk**	**01738 451177**

Aberdalgie and Forteviot (F H W) linked with Aberuthven and Dunning (F H W)
Vacant
Interim Moderator: Allan J. Wilson
awilson@churchofscotland.org.uk   01738 812211

Abernethy and Dron and Arngask (F W)
Stanley Kennon BA BD CertEd   1992   2018
3 Manse Road, Abernethy, Perth PH2 9JP   01738 850194
SKennon@churchofscotland.org.uk

Aberuthven and Dunning See Aberdalgie and Forteviot

Almondbank Tibbermore (F W) linked with Methven and Logiealmond (F W)
Robert J. Malloch BD   1987   2019
The Manse, Dalcrue Road, Pitcairngreen, Perth PH1 3EA   01738 583727
RMalloch@churchofscotland.org.uk

Ardoch (H W) linked with Blackford (F H W)
Mairi Perkins BA BTh   2012   2016
info@ardochparishchurch.org
Manse of Ardoch, Feddal Road, Braco, Dunblane FK15 5RE   01786 880948
MPerkins@churchofscotland.org.uk

Auchterarder (F H T W)
Lynn M. McChlery BA BD MLitt PhD   2005   2019
22 Kirkfield Place, Auchterarder PH3 1FP   01764 662399
LMcChlery@churchofscotland.org.uk

Auchtergaven and Moneydie (F W) linked with Redgorton and Stanley (W)
Vacant
Interim Moderator: James C. Stewart
JStewart@churchofscotland.org.uk   **01738 788017**
01738 624167

Blackford See Ardoch

Cargill Burrelton (F) linked with Collace (F)
Steven Thomson BSc BD   2001   2016   The Manse, Manse Road, Woodside, Blairgowrie PH13 9NQ   01828 670384
SThomson@churchofscotland.org.uk

Cleish (H W) linked with Fossoway: St Serf's and Devonside (F W)
Elisabeth M. Stenhouse BD   2006   2014   Station House, Station Road, Crook of Devon, Kinross KY13 0PG   01577 842128
EStenhouse@churchofscotland.org.uk

Collace See Cargill Burrelton

Comrie (F H W) linked with Dundurn (F H)
Craig Dobney BA BD   2020   **strathearnkirks@btinternet.com**   **01764 679555**
The Manse, Strowan Road, Comrie, Crieff PH6 2ES   01764 679196
CDobney@churchofscotland.org.uk

Crieff (F H W)
Andrew J. Philip BSc BD   1996   2013   8 Strathearn Terrace, Crieff PH7 3AQ   01764 218976
APhilip@churchofscotland.org.uk

Dunbarney (H) and Forgandenny (F W)
Allan J. Wilson BSc MEd BD   2007   **dfpoffice@btconnect.com**   **01738 812463**
Dunbarney Manse, Manse Road, Bridge of Earn, Perth PH2 9DY   01738 812211
AWilson@churchofscotland.org.uk

Dundurn See Comrie

Errol (F H W) linked with Kilspindie and Rait
Vacant   South Bank, Errol, Perth PH2 7PZ   01821 642279
Interim Moderator: Graham W. Crawford   GCrawford@churchofscotland.org.uk   01738 626046

Fossoway: St Serf's and Devonside See Cleish
Kilspindie and Rait See Errol

Kinross (F H W)
Alan D. Reid MA BD   1989   2009   **office@kinrossparishchurch.org**   **01577 862570**
15 Green Wood, Kinross KY13 8FG   01577 862952
AReid@churchofscotland.org.uk

Methven and Logiealmond See Almondbank Tibbermore

Mid Strathearn (H W)
Vacant
Interim Moderator: Marjorie Clark (Miss)
Beechview, Abercairney, Crieff PH7 3NF
marjorie.clark@btinternet.com
01764 652116
01738 637017

Muthill (F H W) linked with Trinity Gask and Kinkell (F W)
Vacant
Interim Moderator: Mairi Perkins
The Manse, Station Road, Muthill, Crieff PH5 2AR
mperkins@churchofscotland.org.uk
01764 681205
01786 880948

Orwell and Portmoak (F H W)
Vacant
Interim Moderator: Alan D. Reid
orwellandportmoakchurch@gmail.com
41 Auld Mart Road, Milnathort, Kinross KY13 9FR
areid@churchofscotland.org.uk
01577 862100
01577 863461
01577 862952

Perth: Craigie and Moncreiffe (F W)
Vacant
Robert F. Wilkie CertCS   2011   2012
(Auxiliary Minister)
Interim Moderator: Robert J. Malloch
The Manse, 46 Abbot Street, Perth PH2 0EE
24 Huntingtower Road, Perth PH1 2JS
RWilkie@churchofscotland.org.uk
RMalloch@churchofscotland.org.uk
01738 623748
01738 628301
01738 583727

Perth: Kinnoull (F H W)
Graham W. Crawford BSc BD STM   1991   2016
1 Mount Tabor Avenue, Perth PH2 7BT
GCrawford@churchofscotland.org.uk
01738 626046
07817 504042

Perth: Letham St Mark's (F H W)
James C. Stewart BD DipMin   1997
office@lethamstmarks.org.uk
35 Rose Crescent, Perth PH1 1NT
JStewart@churchofscotland.org.uk
01738 446377
01738 624167

Perth: North (F W)
Kenneth D. Stott MA BD   1989   2017
info@perthnorthchurch.org.uk
2 Cragganmore Place, Perth PH1 3GJ
KStott@churchofscotland.org.uk
01738 622298
01738 625728

Perth: Riverside (F W)
David R. Rankin MA BD   2009   2014
perthriverside.bookings@gmail.com
44 Hay Street, Perth PH1 5HS
DRankin@churchofscotland.org.uk
01738 622341
07810 008754

Perth: St John's Kirk of Perth (F H W) linked with Perth: St Leonard's-in-the-Fields (H W)   St John's: 01738 633192   St Leonard's: 01738 632238
Vacant
Interim Moderator: Maudeen I. MacDougall
Ferntower, Kinfauns Holdings, Perth PH2 7JY
rev.maudeen@gmail.com
01738 628378
01738 551942

Perth: St Leonard's-in-the-Fields See Perth: St John's Kirk of Perth

Perth: St Matthew's (F T W)   office@stmatts.org.uk   Office: 01738 636757; Vestry: 01738 630725
Fiona C. Bullock (Mrs) MA LLB BD   2014   12 Craigieknowes Avenue, Perth PH2 0DL   01738 570241
                                                                 FBullock@churchofscotland.org.uk

Redgorton and Stanley See Auchtergaven and Moneydie

St Madoes and Kinfauns (F W)
Marc F. Bircham BD MTh   2000   The Manse, St Madoes, Glencarse, Perth PH2 7NF   01738 860837
                                                                 MBircham@churchofscotland.org.uk

Scone and St Martins (F W)   sconeandstmartinschurch@talktalk.net   01738 553900
Maudeen I. MacDougall BA BD MTh   1978   2019   The Manse, Burnside, Scone PH2 6LP   01738 551942
                                                                 rev.maudeen@gmail.com

Trinity Gask and Kinkell See Muthill

B. In other appointments
Michie, Margaret   2013   Ordained Local Minister: Loch Leven   3 Loch Leven Court, Wester Balgedie, Kinross KY13 9NE   01592 840602
                                                    Parish Grouping   margaretmichie@btinternet.com
Pandian, Ali R. BA BD PGCertHC   2017   2022 Chaplain, Rachel House Children's   95 Baron's Hill Avenue, Linlithgow EH49 7JQ   07966 368344
  DipPS   Hospice, Kinross   APandian@churchofscotland.org.uk
Shuttleworth, Margaret MA BD   2013   2020 Chaplain, HM Prison Perth   62 Toll Road, Kincardine, Alloa FK10 4QZ   01259 731002
                                                                                                 margaret.shuttleworth@prisons.gov.scot
Steenbergen, Pauline (Ms) MA BD   1996   2022 Chaplain, The Bield Retreat and   The Bield, Blackruthven House, Tibbermore, Perth PH1 1PY 01738 583238
                                                          Conference Centre   p.steenbergen1@gmail.com
Stewart, Anne E. BD CertMin   1998   2007 Chaplain: HM Prison Castle Huntly   35 Rose Crescent, Perth PH1 1NT   01738 624167
                                                                                                 anne.stewart2@prisons.gov.scot
Stott, Anne M.   2019   Ordained Local Minister: Presbytery   2 Cragganmore Place, Perth PH1 3GJ   01738 625728
                                                    Pioneer Worker, Bertha Park   AStott@churchofscotland.org.uk
Thorburn, Susan MTh   2014   Ordained Local Minister; Mission   3 Daleally Farm Cottages, St Madoes Road, Errol, Perth PH1 7TJ 01821 642681
                                                    Development Worker, Fife Presbytery   SThorburn@churchofscotland.org.uk
Wallace, Catherine PGDipC DCS   1987   2021 Clinical Manager, Harbour   21 Durley Dene Crescent, Bridge of Earn PH2 9RD   01738 621709
                                                          Counselling Service, Perth   secretary@churchofscotland.org.uk
Wylie, Jonathan BSc BD MTh   2000   2016 Chaplain: Strathallan School   Strathallan School, Forgandenny, Perth PH2 9EG   01738 815098
                                                                                                 chaplain@strathallan.co.uk

C. Retaining

Name			(Charge)	Address / Email	Telephone
Ballentine, Ann M. MA BD DipRE	1981	2007	(Kirknewton and East Calder)	17 Nellfield Road, Crieff PH7 3DU / annmballentine@gmail.com	01764 652567
Barr, T. Leslie LTh	1969	1997	(Kinross)	8 Fairfield Road, Kelty KY4 0BY / leslie_barr@yahoo.co.uk	07727 718076
Brennan, Anne J. BSc BD MTh	1999	2019	(Fortingall, Glenlyon, Kenmore and Lawers)	Dunmore House, Findo Gask, Auchterarder PH3 1HS / annebrennan@yahoo.co.uk	01738 730350
Brown, Elizabeth JP RGN	1996	2007	(Auxiliary Minister)	8 Viewlands Place, Perth PH1 1BS / liz.brown@blueyonder.co.uk	01738 552391
Brown, Marina D. MA BD MTh	2000	2012	(Hawick: St Mary's and Old)	Moneydie School Cottage, Luncarty, Perth PH1 3HZ / revmdb1711@btinternet.com	01738 582163
Cairns, Evelyn BD	1987	2012	(Chaplain: Rachel House)	15 Talla Park, Kinross KY13 8AB / revelyn@btinternet.com	01577 863990
Caskie, J. Colin BA BD	1977	2012	(Rhu and Shandon)	13 Anderson Drive, Perth PH1 1JZ / jcolincaskie@gmail.com	01738 445543
Coleman, Sidney H. BA BD MTh	1961	2001	(Glasgow: Merrylea)	15 Richmond Terrace, Dundee DD2 1BQ / sidney.h.coleman@gmail.com	01382 645824
Corbett, Richard T. BSc MSc PhD BD	1992	2019	(Kilmallie)	Flat 309, Knights Court, 1 North William Street, Perth PH1 5NB / richard.t.corbett@btinternet.com	01738 626315
Craig, Joan H. MTheol DipCE CPS	1986	2005	(Orkney: East Mainland)	7 Jedburgh Place, Perth PH1 1SJ / joanhcraig@btinternet.com	01738 580180
Gilchrist, Ewen J. BD DipMin DipComm	1982	2017	(Cults)	9 David Douglas Avenue, Scone PH2 6QQ / ewengilchrist@btconnect.com	07747 746418
Graham, Alasdair G. BD DipMin	1981	2019	(Arbroath: West Kirk)	5 Robb Place, Perth PH2 0GB / alasdairgraham704@btinternet.com	01738 626952
Graham, Sydney S. DipYL MPhil BD	1987	2009	(Iona with Kilfinichen and Kilvickeon and the Ross of Mull)	'Aspen', Milton Road, Luncarty, Perth PH1 3ES / syd@sydgraham.plus.com	01738 829350
Gregory, J.C. LTh	1968	1992	(Blantyre: St Andrew's)	2 Southlands Road, Auchterarder PH3 1BA	01764 664594
Gunn, Alexander M. MA BD	1967	2006	(Aberfeldy with Amulree and Strathbraan with Dull and Weem)	'Navarone', 12 Cornhill Road, Perth PH1 1LR / sandygunn@btinternet.com	01738 443216
Halliday, Archibald R. BD MTh	1964	1999	(Duffus, Spynie and Hopeman)	8 Turretbank Drive, Crieff PH7 4LW / roberthalliday343@btinternet.com	01764 656464
Kelly, T. Clifford	1973	1993	(Ferintosh)	20 Whinfield Drive, Kinross KY13 8UB	01577 864946
Lawson, James B. MA BD	1961	2002	(South Uist)	4 Cowden Way, Comrie, Crieff PH6 2NW / james.lawson7@btopenworld.com	01764 679180
MacDonald, James W. BD	1976	2012	(Crieff)	'Mingulay', 29 Hebridean Gardens, Crieff PH7 3BP / rev_up@btinternet.com	01764 654500
Macgregor, John BD	2001	2020	(Errol with Kilspindie and Rait)	1 Le Petit Vierzon, 16490 Hiesse, France / john_macg@hotmail.com	
MacMillan, Riada M. BD	1991	1998	(Perth: Craigend Moncreiffe with Rhynd)	73 Muirend Gardens, Perth PH1 1JR	01738 447259
Main, Douglas M. BD	1986	2014	(Errol with Kilspindie and Rait)	14 Madoch Road, St Madoes, Perth PH2 7TT / revdmain@sky.com	01738 860867

Name	Dates	Charge / Role	Address / Email	Telephone
Majcher, Philip L. BD	1982 2020	(London: Crown Court)	5 Strathallan Bank, Ardargie, Forgandenny, Perth PH2 9FE pmajcher@me.com	01738 710979
Malcolm, Alistair BD DPS	1976 2012	(Inverness: Inshes)	11 Kinclaven Gardens, Murthly, Perth PH1 4EX amalcolm067@btinternet.com	
McCarthy, David J. BSc BD	1985 2020	(Fresh Expressions Development Worker, Faith Nurture Forum)	Orchard House, Croft Avenue, Dunning PH2 0SG djmcclv@gmail.com	
McCormick, Alastair F.	1962 1998	(Creich with Rosehall)	14 Balmanno Park, Bridge of Earn, Perth PH2 9RJ	01738 813588
McCrum, Robert BSc BD CertMin	1982 2014	(Ayr: St James')	28 Rose Crescent, Perth PH1 1NT robert.mccrum@virgin.net	01738 447906
McFadzean, Iain MA BD CMgr FCMI MHGI	1989 2019	(Chief Executive: Work Place Chaplaincy Scotland)	2 Lowfield Crescent, Luncarty, Perth PH1 3FG iain.mcfadzean@wpcscotland.co.uk	01738 827338 07969 227696
McIntosh, Colin G. MA BD	1976 2013	(Dunblane: Cathedral)	Drumhead Cottage, Drum, Kinross KY13 0PR colinmcintosh4@btinternet.com	01577 840012
McNaughton, David J.H. BA CA	1976 1995	(Killin and Ardeonaig)	14 Rankine Court, Wormit, Newport-on-Tay DD6 8TA	
Millar, Alexander M. MA BD MBA	1980 2018	(Stirling: St Columba's)	17 Mapledene Road, Scone, Perth PH2 6NX alexmillar0406@gmail.com	01738 550270
Millar, Jennifer M. (Mrs) BD DipMin	1986 2021	(Teacher: Religious and Moral Education)	17 Mapledene Road, Scone, Perth PH2 6NX ajrmillar@blueyonder.co.uk	01738 550270
Milne, Robert B. BTh	1999 2017	(Broughton, Glenholm and Kilbucho with Skirling with Stobo and Drumelzier with Tweedsmuir)	3 Mid Square, Comrie PH6 2EG rbmilne@aol.com	07803 609387
Mitchell, Alexander B. BD	1981 2014	(Dunblane: St Blane's)	24 Hebridean Gardens, Crieff PH7 3BP alex.mitchell6@btopenworld.com	01764 652241
Munro, Gillian BSc BD	1989 2018	(Head of Spiritual Care, NHS Tayside)	The Old Town House, 53 Main Street, Abernethy, Perth PH2 9JH munrooth@aol.com	01738 850066
Munro, Patricia M. BSc DCS	1986 2016	(Deacon)	4 Hewat Place, Perth PH1 2UD patmunrodcs@gmail.com	01738 443088 07814 836314
Paton, Iain F. BD FCIS	1980 2006	(Elie with Kilconquhar and Colinsburgh)	Muldoanich, Stirling Street, Blackford, Auchterarder PH4 1QG iain.f.paton@btinternet.com	01764 682234
Philip, Elizabeth A. C. MA BA PGCSE DCS	2007 2018	(Deacon)	8 Strathearn Terrace, Crieff PH7 3AQ ephilipstitch@gmail.com	01764 218976 07970 767851
Quigley, Barbara D. (Mrs) MTheol ThM DPS	1979 2019	(Glasgow: St Andrew's East)	33 Castle Drive, Auchterarder PH3 1FU bdquigley@aol.com	07926 064235
Redpath, James G. BD DipPTh	1988 2016	(Auchtermuchty with Edenshead and Strathmiglo)	9 Beveridge Place, Kinross KY13 8QY JRedpath@churchofscotland.org.uk	07713 919442
Searle, David C. MA DipTh FSAScot	1965 2002	(Warden: Rutherford House)	Stonefall Lodge, 30 Abbey Lane, Grange, Errol PH2 7GB dcs@davidsearle.plus.com	01821 641004
Shewan, Michael R.R. MA BD CPS	1985 2022	(Aberdeen: North)	13 Hatton Road, Luncarty, Perth PH1 3UZ	
Simpson, James A. BSc BD STM DD	1960 1999	(Interim Minister, Brechin Cathedral)	'Dornoch', Perth Road, Bankfoot, Perth PH1 4ED ja@simpsondornoch.co.uk	01738 787710
Sloan, Robert P. MA BD	1968 2007	(Interim Minister, Armadale)	1 Broomhill Avenue, Perth PH1 1EN sloan12@virginmedia.com	01738 443904
Stenhouse, W. Duncan MA BD	1989 2006	(Dunbarney and Forgandenny)	32 Sandport Gait, Kinross KY13 8FB	01577 866992

Name	Years	Description	Address	Phone
Stewart, Alexander T. MA BD FSAScot	1975 2022	(Associate, Perth: St John's Kirk of Perth with St Leonard's-in-the-Fields	36 Viewlands Terrace, Perth PH1 1BZ alex.t.stewart@blueyonder.co.uk	01738 566675
Stewart, Robin J. MA BD STM	1959 1995	(Orwell with Portmoak)	'Oakbrae', Perth Road, Murthly, Perth PH1 4HF	01738 710220
Wallace, James K. MA BD STM	1988 2015	(Perth: St John's Kirk of Perth with St Leonard's-in-the-Fields)	21 Durley Dene Crescent, Bridge of Earn PH2 9RD jkwministry@hotmail.com	01738 621709

PERTH ADDRESSES

Church	Address
Craigie	Abbot Street
Kinnoull	Dundee Rd near Queen's Bridge
Letham St Mark's	Rannoch Road
Moncreiffe	Glenbruar Crescent
North	Mill Street near Kinnoull Street
Riverside	Bute Drive
St John's	St John's Street
St Leonard's-in-the-Fields	Marshall Place
St Matthew's	Tay Street

(29) DUNDEE (F W)

Meets at Dundee: The Steeple, Nethergate, on the fourth Wednesday of November 2022. On 1 January 2023 it will unite with the Presbyteries of Stirling, Dunkeld and Meigle, Perth and Angus to form a new Presbytery of Perth. That Presbytery will meet on a date and in a venue to be determined and thereafter as decided.

Clerk:	MR TIM PODGER	dundee@churchofscotland.org.uk tpodger@churchofscotland.org.uk	01382 350575
Depute Clerk:	MR DAVID INGLIS	davel146@btinternet.com	01382 533516
Presbytery Office:		Whitfield Parish Church, Haddington Crescent, Dundee DD4 0NA	01382 503012

Abernyte (W) linked with Inchture and Kinnaird (F W) linked with Longforgan (F H W)

Catriona M. Morrison MA BD	1995	2 Boniface Place, Invergowrie, Dundee DD2 5DR CMorrison@churchofscotland.org.uk	01382 561523
Marc A. Prowe	2000	2 Boniface Place, Invergowrie, Dundee DD2 5DR MProwe@churchofscotland.org.uk	01382 561523

Auchterhouse (F H W) linked with Monikie and Newbigging and Murroes and Tealing (F H W)   office@sidlawchurches.org.uk   01382 350182

Vacant			
Interim Moderator: Auchterhouse: Donna M. Hays		DHays@churchofscotland.org.uk	01382 580210
Interim Moderator: Monikie: Caroline Taylor		caro234@btinternet.com	01382 770198

Dundee: Balgay (F H W)

Nardia J. Sandison BAppSc BD MLitt	2019	150 City Road, Dundee DD2 2PW NSandison@churchofscotland.org.uk	01382 903446

Dundee: Barnhill St Margaret's (F H W)   church.office@btconnect.com   01382 737294

Andrew Gardner BSc BD PhD (Interim Minister)	1997	2 St Margaret's Lane, Barnhill, Dundee DD5 2PQ AGardner@churchofscotland.org.uk	01382 503012 07411 989344

Dundee: Broughty Ferry New Kirk (F H T W)   office@broughtyferrynewkirk.org.uk   01382 738264

Vacant		New Kirk Manse, 25 Ballinard Gardens, Broughty Ferry, Dundee DD5 1BZ	01382 778874
Interim Moderator: Roderick J. Grahame		RGrahame@churchofscotland.org.uk	01382 561873

Dundee: Broughty Ferry St James' (F H)

Guardianship of the Presbytery			
Session Clerks: Lyn Edwards (Mrs)		kathelyneedwards@gmail.com	01382 730552
David J.B. Murie		d.j.b.murie@gmail.com	01382 320493

Dundee: Broughty Ferry St Luke's and Queen Street (F W)
Vacant
Session Clerk: Kenneth Andrew   22 Albert Road, Broughty Ferry, Dundee DD5 1AZ   01382 732094 / 01382 779212 / 01382 776765
kga@scot-int.com

Dundee: Broughty Ferry St Stephen's and West (H W) linked with Dundee: Dundee (St Mary's) (H W)   office@dundeestmarys.co.uk
Keith F. Hall MA BD   1981   1994   33 Strathern Road, West Ferry, Dundee DD5 1PP   01382 226271 / 01382 778808
KHall@churchofscotland.org.uk

Dundee: Camperdown (H)
Guardianship of the Presbytery
Interim Moderator: Roderick J. Grahame   Camperdown Manse, Myrekirk Road, Dundee DD2 4SF   01382 561872
RGrahame@churchofscotland.org.uk

Dundee: Chalmers-Ardler (F H W)
Vacant
Interim Moderator: Andrew Gardner   40 St Martin Crescent, Dundee DD3 0SU   07411 989344
AGardner@churchofscotland.org.uk

Dundee: Coldside (F W)
Vacant
Session Clerk: Yvonne Grant (Miss)   9 Abercorn Street, Dundee DD4 7HY   01382 458314 / 01382 652705
ymgrant@sky.com

Dundee: Craigiebank (H W) linked with Dundee: Douglas and Mid Craigie (F W)
Vacant
Interim Moderator: Kenneth Andrew   kga@scot-int.com   01382 731173 / 01382 776765

Dundee: Douglas and Mid Craigie   See Dundee: Craigiebank

Dundee: Downfield Mains (F H W)   downfieldmainsoffice@gmail.com   07979 939092 / 07977 042166
Nathan S. McConnell BS MA ThM   2002   2016   9 Elgin Street, Dundee DD3 8NL
NMcConnell@churchofscotland.org.uk

Dundee: Dundee (St Mary's)   See Dundee: Broughty Ferry St Stephen's and West

Dundee: Fintry (F W)
Colin M. Brough BSc BD   1998   2002   4 Clive Street, Dundee DD4 7AW   01382 458629
CBrough@churchofscotland.org.uk
Catherine J. Brodie MA BA MPhil PGCE   2017   48h Cleghorn Street, Dundee DD2 2NJ   07432 513375
(Ordained Local Minister)   CBrodie@churchofscotland.org.uk

Dundee: Lochee (F H)
Roderick J. Grahame BD CPS DMin DipPSRP   1991   2018
32 Clayhills Drive, Dundee DD2 1SX
RGrahame@churchofscotland.org.uk
01382 561872

Dundee: Logie and St John's Cross (F H W)
Grant R. MacLaughlan BA BD   1998   2021
administrator@logies.org
7 Hyndford Street, Dundee DD2 1HQ
GMaclaughlan@churchofscotland.org.uk
01382 668514
07790 518041

Dundee: Meadowside St Paul's linked with Dundee: St Andrew's (F H T W)   **standrewsdundee@outlook.com**
Anita D.C. Kerr MA   2007   2020
27 Mayfield Grove, Dundee DD4 7GZ
Anita.Kerr@churchofscotland.org.uk
01382 224860
01382 456659

Dundee: Menzieshill (F W)
Robert Mallinson BD   2010
The Manse, Charleston Drive, Dundee DD2 4BD
RMallinson@churchofscotland.org.uk
01382 667446
07595 249089

Dundee: St Andrew's See Dundee: Meadowside St Paul's

Dundee: St David's High Kirk (H W)
Emma McDonald BD   2013   2018
St David's High Kirk, 119A Kinghorne Road, Dundee DD3 6PW
EMcDonald@churchofscotland.org.uk
01382 322746

Dundee: The Steeple (F H T W)
Vacant
Interim Moderator: Emma McDonald
office@thesteeplechurch.org.uk
EMcDonald@churchofscotland.org.uk
01382 200031
01382 322746

Dundee: Stobswell (F H W) linked with Dundee: Trinity (H W)   Stobswell: **secretary@trinitychurchdundee.org**
Jean A. Kirkwood BSc PhD BD   2015   2021
65 Clepington Road, Dundee DD4 7BQ
JKirkwood@churchofscotland.org.uk
Stobswell: **01382 461397**
01382 526071

Dundee: Strathmartine (F H W)
Stewart McMillan BD   1983   1990
19 Americanmuir Road, Dundee DD3 9AA
SMcMillan@churchofscotland.org.uk
01382 825817
01382 812423

Dundee: Trinity See Dundee: Stobswell

Dundee: West (F W)
James Connolly DipTh CertMin MA(Theol) DMin   1982   2020
enquiries@dundeewestchurch.org
22 Hyndford Street, Dundee DD2 1HX
JConnolly@churchofscotland.org.uk
07341 **255354**
07711 177655

Dundee: Whitfield (H)
Vacant
Interim Moderator: Kenneth Andrew
53 Old Craigie Road, Dundee DD4 7JD
kga@scot-int.com
01382 **503012**
01382 776765

Fowlis and Liff (F T W) linked with Lundie and Muirhead (F H T W)
Donna M. Hays (Mrs) MTheol DipEd DipTMHA   2004
enquiries@churches-flandlm.co.uk
149 Coupar Angus Road, Muirhead of Liff, Dundee DD2 5QN
DHays@churchofscotland.org.uk
01382 580210

Inchture and Kinnaird See Abernyte

Invergowrie (H W)
Catriona M. Morrison MA BD   1995   2020
hello@invergowrieparishchurch.org
2 Boniface Place, Invergowrie, Dundee DD2 5DR
CMorrison@churchofscotland.org.uk
01382 561523

Marc A. Prowe   2000   2020
2 Boniface Place, Invergowrie, Dundee DD2 5DR
MProwe@churchofscotland.org.uk
01382 561523

Longforgan See Abernyte
Lundie and Muirhead See Fowlis and Liff

Monifieth (F H W)
Fiona J. Reynolds LLB BD FdSc   2018
office@monifiethparishchurch.co.uk
8 Church Street, Monifieth, Dundee DD5 4JP
FReynolds@churchofscotland.org.uk
01382 699183

Monikie and Newbigging and Murroes and Tealing See Auchterhouse

B. In other appointments

Name	Years	Appointment	Address	Phone
Campbell, Gordon A. MA BD CDipAF DipHSM CMgr MCMI MIHM AssocCIPD AFRIN ARSGS FRGS FSAScot	2001 2004	Auxiliary Minister; an Honorary Chaplain: University of Dundee	2 Falkland Place, Kingoodie, Invergowrie, Dundee DD2 5DY g.a.campbell@dundee.ac.uk	01382 561383
Douglas, Fiona C. MBE MA BD PhD	1989 1997	Chaplain: University of Dundee	10 Springfield, Dundee DD1 4JE f.c.douglas@dundee.ac.uk	01382 384157
McDonald, Ian J.M. MA BD	1984 2020	Chaplain, Palliative Care, Roxburghe House, NHS Tayside	11 James Grove, Kirkcaldy KY1 1TN IanJMMcdonald@churchofscotland.org.uk	07421 775644
Strachan, Willie D. DipYCW MBA CertCS	2013 2020	Ordained Local Minister: Presbytery-wide	Ladywell House, Lucky Slap, Monikie, Dundee DD5 3QG WStrachan@churchofscotland.org.uk	07432 513375

C. Retaining

Name	Years	Former charge	Address	Phone
Allan, Jean (Mrs) DCS	1989 2011	(Deacon)	12C Hindmarsh Avenue, Dundee DD3 7LW jeannieallan45@googlemail.com	01382 827299 07709 959474
Barrett, Leslie M. BD FRICS	1991 2014	(Chaplain: University of Abertay, Dundee)	Dunelm Cottage, Logie, Cupar KY15 4SJ lesliembarrett@btinternet.com	01334 870396
Calvert, Robert A. BSc BD DMin PhD	1983 2021	(Dundee: The Steeple)	5 Cowiefaulds Cottages, Gateside, Cupar KY14 7ST robertacalvert@gmail.com	07532 029343
Collins, Catherine E.E. (Mrs) MA BD	1993 2021	(Dundee: Broughty Ferry New Kirk)	Eden Cottage, 16 Melville Road, Ladybank, Cupar KY15 7LU revdacollins@btinternet.com	01337 830707
Collins, David A. BSc BD	1993 2016	(Auchterhouse with Monikie and Newbigging and Murroes and Tealing)	Eden Cottage, 16 Melville Road, Ladybank, Cupar KY15 7LU revdacollins@btinternet.com	01337 830707
Dempster, Colin J. BD CertMin	1990 2016	(Mearns Coastal)	35 Margaret Lindsay Place, Monifieth DD6 4RD Coldcoast@btinternet.com	01382 532368
Duncan, John C. MBE BD MPhil	1987 2021	(Leuchars: St Athernase)	21 Ravenscraig Gardens, Broughty Ferry, Dundee DD5 1LT JDuncan@churchofscotland.org.uk	01382 480772
Fraser, Donald W. MA	1958 2010	(Monifieth)	1 Blake Avenue, Broughty Ferry, Dundee DD5 3LH fraserdonald37@yahoo.co.uk	01382 477491 07531 863316
Kay, Elizabeth (Miss) DipYCS	1993 2007	(Auxiliary Minister)	1 Kintail Walk, Inchture, Perth PH14 9RY ekay007@btinternet.com	01828 686029
Laing, David J.H. BD DPS	1976 2014	(Dundee: Trinity)	18 Kerrington Crescent, Barnhill, Dundee DD5 2TN david.laing@live.co.uk	01382 739586
Lillie, Fiona L. (Mrs) BA BD MLitt	1995 2017	(Glasgow: St John's Renfield)	4 McVicars Lane, Dundee DD1 4LH fionalillie@btinternet.com	01382 229082
Mair, Michael V.A. MA BD	1968 2007	(Dundee: Craigiebank with Douglas and Mid Craigie)	48 Panmure Street, Monifieth DD5 4EH mvamair@gmail.com	01382 530538
McMillan, Edith F. (Mrs) MA BD	1981 2018	(Dundee: Craigiebank with Douglas and Mid Craigie)	19 Americanmuir Road, Dundee DD3 9AA wee_rev_edimac@btinternet.com	01382 812423
Reid, R. Gordon BSc BD MIEE	1993 2010	(Carriden)	6 Bayview Place, Monifieth, Dundee DD5 4TN GordonReid@aol.com	01382 520519 07952 349884

Robertson, James H. BSc BD	1975	2014	(Culloden: The Barn)	'Far End', 35 Mains Terrace, Dundee DD4 7BZ jimrob838@gmail.com	01382 522773 07595 465838
Robson, George K. LTh DPS BA	1983	2011	(Dundee: Balgay)	11 Ceres Crescent, Broughty Ferry, Dundee DD5 3JN gkrobson@virginmedia.com	01382 901212
Rose, Lewis (Mr) DCS	1993	2010	(Deacon)	6 Gauldie Crescent, Dundee DD3 0RR lewis_rose48@yahoo.co.uk	01382 816580 07899 790466
Scott, James MA BD	1973	2010	(Drumoak-Durris)	3 Blake Place, Broughty Ferry, Dundee DD5 3LQ jimscott73@yahoo.co.uk	01382 739595
Taylor, Caroline (Mrs)	1995	2014	(Leuchars: St Athernase)	7 Sunart Street, Broughty Ferry, Dundee DD5 3HW caro234@btinternet.com	01382 770198
Taylor, C. Graham D. BSc BD FIAB	2001	2020	(Dundee: Broughty Ferry St Luke's and Queen Street)	The Smithy, Grange, Errol, Perth PH2 7TB cgdtaylor@btinternet.com	07804 527103
Wilson, James L. BD CPS	1986	2022	(Dundee: Whitfield)	Burnside Cottage, 97 Peebles Drive, Dundee DD4 0TF r3vjw@aol.com	07885 618659

DUNDEE ADDRESSES

Balgay	200 Lochee Road
Barnhill St Margaret's	10 Invermark Terrace
Broughty Ferry	
New Kirk	370 Queen Street
St James'	5 Fort Street
St Luke's and Queen Street	5 West Queen Street
St Stephen's and West	96 Dundee Road
Camperdown	22 Brownhill Road
Chalmers-Ardler	Turnberry Avenue
Coldside	Isla Street x Main Street
Craigiebank	Craigie Avenue at Greendykes Road
Douglas and Mid Craigie	Balbeggie Place
Downfield Mains	Haldane Street off Strathmartine Road
Dundee (St Mary's)	Nethergate
Fintry	Fintry Road x Fintry Drive
Lochee	191 High Street, Lochee
Logie and St John's Cross	Shaftesbury Rd x Blackness Ave
Meadowside St Paul's at St Andrew's	2 King Street
Menzieshill	Charleston Drive, Menzieshill
St Andrew's	2 King Street
St David's High Kirk	119A Kinghorne Road
Steeple	Nethergate
Stobswell	170 Albert Street
Strathmartine	507 Strathmartine Road
Trinity	73 Crescent Street
West	130 Perth Road
Whitfield	Haddington Crescent

(30) ANGUS (W)

Meets at Forfar in St Margaret's Church Hall on the first Tuesday of November and December 2022. On 1 January 2023 it will unite with the Presbyteries of Stirling, Dunkeld and Meigle, Perth and Dundee to form a new Presbytery of Perth. That Presbytery will meet on a date and in a venue to be determined and thereafter as decided.

Clerk:	REV. IAN A. McLEAN BSc BD DMin	angus@churchofscotland.org.uk	
Depute Clerk:	REV. MARGARET J. HUNT MA BD		
Presbytery Office:		St Margaret's Church, West High Street, Forfar DD8 1BJ	01307 464224

Aberlemno (H W) linked with Guthrie and Rescobie (W)
Vacant
Interim Moderator: Margaret J. Hunt

The Manse, Guthrie, Forfar DD8 2TP — 01241 828243
MHunt@churchofscotland.org.uk — 01307 462044

Arbirlot linked with Carmyllie
Vacant
Interim Moderator: Annette Gordon

The Manse, Arbirlot, Arbroath DD11 2NX — 01241 874613
AGordon@churchofscotland.org.uk — 01241 854478

Arbroath: Old and Abbey (F H W)
Vacant
Session Clerk: Carole J. Munro (Mrs)

church.office@old-and-abbey-church.org.uk — **01241 877068**
51 Cliffburn Road, Arbroath DD11 5BA — Tel/Fax 01241 872196
cj.munro@btinternet.com — 01241 874133

Arbroath: St Andrew's (F H W)
1992 W. Martin Fair BA BD DMin

office@arbroathstandrews.org.uk — **01241 431135**
92 Grampian Gardens, Arbroath DD11 4AQ — Tel/Fax 01241 873238
MFair@churchofscotland.org.uk

Arbroath: St Vigeans (F H W)
Guardianship of the Presbytery
Session Clerk: Margaret Pullar (Mrs)

office.stvigeans@gmail.com — **01241 879567**
The Manse, St Vigeans, Arbroath DD11 4RF — 01241 873206
margaret.pullar@btinternet.com — 01241 876667

Arbroath: West Kirk (F H W)
2020 Christine Hay LLB CA BD

arbroathwestkirk2019@gmail.com — **01241 434721**
1 Charles Avenue, Arbroath DD11 2EY — 01241 554189
Christine.Hay@churchofscotland.org.uk

Barry (W) linked with Carnoustie (F W)
1991 2003 Michael S. Goss BD DPS

44 Terrace Road, Carnoustie DD7 7AR — 01241 410194
MGoss@churchofscotland.org.uk — 07787 141567

Brechin (F H T W) linked with Farnell (W)
Vacant
Session Clerk, Brechin:
    Dorothy Black (Miss)

office@gardnermemorial.plus.com
15 Caldhame Gardens, Brechin DD9 7JJ
dorothy.black6@btinternet.com

Brechin: **01356 629191**
01356 622034
01356 622614

Carmyllie See Arbirlot
Carnoustie See Barry

Carnoustie: Panbride (F H W)
Annette M. Gordon BD   2017

8 Arbroath Road, Carnoustie DD7 6BL
AGordon@churchofscotland.org.uk

01241 854478

Colliston linked with Friockheim Kinnell linked with Inverkeilor and Lunan (H)
Peter A. Phillips BA   1995   2004

The Manse, Inverkeilor, Arbroath DD11 5SA
PPhillips@churchofscotland.org.uk

01241 830464

Dun and Hillside (F)
Vacant
Interim Moderator: Christine Hay

4 Manse Road, Hillside, Montrose DD10 9FB
Christine.Hay@churchofscotland.org.uk

01674 830288
01241 554189

Dunnichen, Letham and Kirkden (W)
Guardianship of the Presbytery
Session Clerk: Irene McGugan

irene.mcgugan@btinternet.com

01307 818436

Eassie, Nevay and Newtyle
Carleen J. Robertson (Miss) BD CertEd   1992

2 Kirkton Road, Newtyle, Blairgowrie PH12 8TS
CRobertson@churchofscotland.org.uk

01828 650461

Edzell Lethnot Glenesk (F H W) linked with Fern Careston Menmuir (F W) elgparish@btconnect.com
A.S. Wayne Pearce MA PhD   2002   2017   19 Lethnot Road, Edzell, Brechin DD9 7TG
                                                          ASWaynePearce@churchofscotland.org.uk

01356 647815
01356 648117

Farnell See Brechin
Fern Careston Menmuir See Edzell Lethnot Glenesk

Forfar: East and Old (F H W) eando_office@yahoo.co.uk
Barbara Ann Sweetin BD   2011   The Manse, Lour Road, Forfar DD8 2BB
                                                        BSweetin@churchofscotland.org.uk

01307 248228

Forfar: Lowson Memorial (F H W)
Karen M. Fenwick BSc BD MPhil PhD   2006
1 Jamieson Street, Forfar DD8 2HY
KFenwick@churchofscotland.org.uk
01307 **460576**
01307 468585

Forfar: St Margaret's (F H W)
Margaret J. Hunt (Mrs) MA BD   2014
stmargaretsforfar@gmail.com
St Margaret's Manse, 15 Potters Park Crescent, Forfar   DD8 1HH
MHunt@churchofscotland.org.uk
01307 **464224**
01307 462044

Friockheim Kinnell See Colliston

Glamis (H), Inverarity and Kinnettles (F W)
Guardianship of the Presbytery
Session Clerk: Mary Reid (Mrs)
mmreid@btinternet.com
01307 840999

Guthrie and Rescobie See Aberlemno
Inverkeilor and Lunan See Colliston

Montrose: Old and St Andrew's (F W)
Ian A. McLean BSc BD DMin   1981   2008
2 Rosehill Road, Montrose DD10 8ST
IMcLean@churchofscotland.org.uk
01674 672447

Ian Gray   2013   2017
(Ordained Local Minister)
The Mallards, 15 Rossie Island Road, Montrose   DD10 9NH
IGray@churchofscotland.org.uk
01674 677126

Montrose: South and Ferryden (F W)
Geoffrey Redmayne BSc BD MPhil   2000   2016
Inchbrayock Manse, Usan, Montrose DD10 9SD
GRedmayne@churchofscotland.org.uk
01674 675634

Oathlaw Tannadice (F W) linked with The Glens and Kirriemuir United (F W)
John K. Orr BD MTh   2012
26 Quarry Park, Kirriemuir DD8 4DR
JOrr@churchofscotland.org.uk
01575 **572819**
01575 572610

The Glens and Kirriemuir United See Oathlaw Tannadice

The Isla Parishes (F W)
Stephen A. Blakey BSc BD OStJ   1977   2018
Balduff House, Kilry, Blairgowrie PH11 8HS
SBlakey@churchofscotland.org.uk
01575 560226

B. In other appointments

Name	Dates	Appointment	Address	Phone
Gourlay, Heather	2021	Ordained Local Minister: supporting rural ministry in Angus	The Schoolhouse, Pitkennedy, Forfar DD8 2UJ HGourlay@churchofscotland.org.uk	01397 830372

C. Retaining

Name	Dates	Charge	Address	Phone
Buchan, Alexander MA BD PGCE	1975 1992	(North Ronaldsay with Sanday)	59 Cliffburn Road, Arbroath DD11 5BA revjcbuchan@bluebucket.org	01241 878862
Buchan, Isabel C. (Mrs) BSc BD RE(PgCE)	1975 2019	(Buckie: North with Rathven)	59 Cliffburn Road, Arbroath DD11 5BA revicbuchan@bluebucket.org	01241 878862
Buwert, Klaus O.F. LLB BD DMin	1984 2022	(Muthill with Trinity Gask and Kinkell)	55 Duncan Road, Letham, Forfar DD8 2PN	01241 852666
Edwards, Dougal BTh	2013 2017	(Ordained Local Minister)	25 Mackenzie Street, Carnoustie DD7 6HD	07891 838379
Gough, Ian G. MA BD MTh DMin	1974 2009	(Arbroath: Knox's with Arbroath: St Vigeans)	23 Keptie Road, Arbroath DD11 3ED iangough@btinternet.com	
Humphrey, Jonathan W. BSc BD PhD	2015 2021	(Dundee: Chalmers Ardler)	Burnside, Kilcaldrum, Forfar DD8 1TW JHumphrey@churchofscotland.org.uk	07587 186424
Nicoll, A. Norman BD	2003 2020	(Corby: St Andrew's)	14 Victoria Street, Forfar DD8 3BA	
Norrie, Graham MA BD	1967 2007	(Forfar: East and Old)	'Novar', 14A Wyllie Street, Forfar DD8 3DN grahamnorrie@hotmail.com	01307 468152
Oxburgh, Brian H. BSc BD	1980 2019	(Tayport)	50 Ravensbay Park Gardens, Carnoustie DD7 7NY	01241 828243
Ramsay, Brian BD DPS MLitt	1980 2022	(Aberlemno with Guthrie and Rescobie)	The Manse, Guthrie, Forfar DD8 2TP	01356 647322
Robertson, George R. LTh	1985 2004	(Udny and Pitmedden)	3 Slateford Gardens, Edzell, Brechin DD9 7SX geomag.robertson@btinternet.com	
Rooney, Malcolm I.G. DipPE BEd BD	1993 2017	(The Glens and Kirriemuir: Old)	23 Mart Lane, Northmuir, Kirriemuir DD8 4TL malc.rooney@gmail.com	01575 575334 07909 993233
Smith, Hamish G.	1965 1993	(Auchterless with Rothienorman)	11A Guthrie Street, Letham, Forfar DD8 2PS	01307 818973
Saunders, Grace I.M. BSc BTh	2007 2022	(Cumbernauld: Condorrat)	65 Slade Gardens Kirriemuir DD8 5AG	
Thomas, Martyn R.H. CEng MIStructE	1987 2002	(Fowlis and Liff with Lundie and Muirhead of Liff)	14 Kirkgait, Letham, Forfar DD8 2XQ martyn317thomas@btinternet.com	01307 818084
Watt, Alan G.N. MTh CQSW DipCommEd	1996 2009	(Edzell Lethnot Glenesk with Fern Careston Menmuir)	6 Pine Way, Friockheim, Arbroath DD11 4WF watt455@btinternet.com	01241 826018
Webster, Allan F. MA BD	1978 2013	(Workplace Chaplain)	42 McCulloch Drive, Forfar DD8 2EB allanfwebster@aol.com	01307 464252 07546 276725

TOWN ADDRESSES

Arbroath: Old and Abbey	West Abbey Street
St Andrew's	Hamilton Green
St Vigeans	St Vigeans Brae
West Kirk	Keptie Street
Brechin	South Esk Street
Carnoustie:	Dundee Street
Panbride	Arbroath Road
Forfar: East and Old	East High Street
Lowson Memorial	Jamieson Street
St Margaret's	West High Street
Kirriemuir: United	High Street
Montrose: Old and St Andrew's	High Street
Montrose: South and Ferryden	Church Road, Ferryden

(31) ABERDEEN AND SHETLAND (F W)

Meets at Aberdeen Queen's Cross in November 2022 and at other times as it may determine. On 1 January 2023 it will unite with the Presbyteries of Buchan, Gordon, Kincardine and Deeside, Moray and Orkney to form the Presbytery of the North East and the Northern Isles. That new Presbytery will meet on-line on 10 January 2023 and thereafter as decided.

Clerk:	REV. JOHN A. FERGUSON BD DipMin DMin
Depute Clerk:	MRS CHERYL L. BRANKIN BA
Treasurer:	MR WILLIAM D. ANDERSON CA
Presbytery Office:	Aberdeen North Church, Greenfern Road, Aberdeen AB16 6TR
	aberdeenshetland@churchofscotland.org.uk
	01224 662560

Aberdeen: Bridge of Don Oldmachar (F H W)
Vacant
Session Clerk: Judith Byers
secretary@oldmacharchurch.org
60 Newburgh Circle, Aberdeen AB22 8QZ
judithmbyers@gmail.com
01224 709299
01224 823283
01224 826480

Aberdeen: Craigiebuckler (F H W)
Kenneth L. Petrie MA BD   1984   1999
office@craigiebuckler.org.uk
185 Springfield Road, Aberdeen AB15 8AA
KP East Academy Street etrie@churchofscotland.org.uk
01224 315649
01224 315125

Aberdeen: Ferryhill (F H W)
J. Peter N. Johnston BSc BD   2001   2013
office@ferryhillparishchurch.org
54 Polmuir Road, Aberdeen AB11 7RT
PJohnston@churchofscotland.org.uk
01224 213093
01224 414747

Aberdeen: High Hilton (F H W)
G. Hutton B. Steel MA BD   1982   2013
1 Fairview Road, Bridge of Don, Aberdeen   AB22 8ZG
Hutton.Steel@churchofscotland.org.uk
01224 494717
07917 012024

Aberdeen: Holburn West (F H W)
Duncan C. Eddie MA BD   1992   1999
churchoffice@holburnwestchurch.org.uk
31 Cranford Road, Aberdeen AB10 7NJ
DEddie@churchofscotland.org.uk
01224 571120
01224 325873

Aberdeen: Mannofield (F H T W)
Keith T. Blackwood BD DipMin   1997   2007
office@mannofieldchurch.org.uk
21 Forest Avenue, Aberdeen AB15 4TU
KBlackwood@churchofscotland.org.uk
01224 310087
01224 315748

Aberdeen: Midstocket (H W)
Tanya J. Webster BCom DipAcc BD   2011   2019
secretary@midstocketchurch.org.uk
182 Midstocket Road, Aberdeen AB15 5HS
TWebster@churchofscotland.org.uk
01224 319519
01224 561358

Aberdeen: North (F H W)
Vacant
Session Clerk: Ian Ingram
office@aberdeennorthchurch.co.uk
ianingram890@gmail.com
01224 694121
07479 927052

Aberdeen: Queen's Cross (F H W)
Vacant
Session Clerk (Joint): Mike Leys
office@queenscrosschurch.org.uk
1 St Swithin Street, Aberdeen AB10 6XH
mikeleys41@gmail.com
01224 644742
01224 322549
07770 720721

Aberdeen: Rubislaw (F H W)
Robert L. Smith BS MTh PhD   2000   2013
rubislawchurch@btconnect.com
13 Oakhill Road, Aberdeen AB15 5ER
RSmith@churchofscotland.org.uk
01224 645477
01224 314773

Aberdeen: Ruthrieston West (F W)
Benjamin D.W. Byun BA MDiv MTh PhD   1992   2008
53 Springfield Avenue, Aberdeen   AB15 8JJ
BByun@churchofscotland.org.uk
01224 312706

Aberdeen: St Columba's Bridge of Don (F H W)
Louis Kinsey BD DipMin TD   1991
administrator@stcolumbaschurch.org.uk
151 Jesmond Avenue, Aberdeen   AB22 8UG
LKinsey@churchofscotland.org.uk
01224 825653
01224 705337

Aberdeen: St John's Church for Deaf People
P. Mary Whittaker BSc BD   2011   2018
11 Templand Road, Lhanbryde, Elgin IV30 8BR
MWhittaker@churchofscotland.org.uk
Text only 07501 454766
or contact Aberdeen: St Mark's

Aberdeen: St Machar's Cathedral (F H T W)
Sarah A. Brown (Ms)   2012   2021
MA BD ThM DipYW/Theol PDCCE DipPS
office@stmachar.com
39 Woodstock Road, Aberdeen AB15 5EX
Sarah.Brown@churchofscotland.org.uk
01224 485988
01224 539630

New charge formed by the union of Aberdeen: St George's Tillydrone and Aberdeen: St Machar's Cathedral

Aberdeen: St Mark's (F H W)
Vacant
Session Clerks: Helen Burr (Mrs)
Dianne Morrison (Miss)
office@stmarksaberdeen.org.uk
helen.burr@hotmail.co.uk
diannemorrison@talktalk.net
01224 640672
07751 851610
07767 140582

Aberdeen: St Mary's (F H W)
Elsie J. Fortune (Mrs) BSc BD — 2003
stmaryschurch924@btinternet.com
456 King Street, Aberdeen AB24 3DE
EFortune@churchofscotland.org.uk
01224 **487227**
01224 633778

Aberdeen: St Nicholas Kincorth, South of (W)
Edward C. McKenna BD DPS — 1989 2002
The Manse, Kincorth Circle, Aberdeen AB12 5NX
EMcKenna@churchofscotland.org.uk
01224 872820

Joseph K. Somevi BSc MSc PhD BTh
MRICS MRTPI MIEMA CertCRS
(Ordained Local Minister) — 2015 2021
97 Ashwood Road, Aberdeen AB22 8QX
JSomevi@churchofscotland.org.uk
01224 826362
07886 533259

Aberdeen: St Stephen's (F H W)
Maggie Whyte BD — 2010
6 Belvidere Street, Aberdeen AB25 2QS
Maggie.Whyte@churchofscotland.org.uk
01224 **624443**
01224 635694

Aberdeen: South Holburn (H W)
David J. Stewart BD MTh DipMin — 2000 2018
contact@southholburn.org
54 Woodstock Road, Aberdeen AB15 5JF
DStewart@churchofscotland.org.uk
07498 **781457**
01224 317975

Aberdeen: Stockethill (F W)
Ian M. Aitken MA BD — 1999
52 Ashgrove Road West, Aberdeen AB16 5EE
IAitken@churchofscotland.org.uk
01224 686929

Aberdeen: Torry St Fittick's (F H W)
Edmond Gatima BEng BD MSc MPhil PhD — 2013
st.fitticks@btconnect.com
11 Devanha Gardens East, Aberdeen AB11 7UH
EGatima@churchofscotland.org.uk
01224 **899183**
01224 588245

Joseph K. Somevi BSc MSc PhD BTh
MRICS MRTPI MIEMA CertCRS
(Ordained Local Minister) — 2015 2021
97 Ashwood Road, Aberdeen AB22 8QX
JSomevi@churchofscotland.org.uk
01224 826362
07886 533259

Aberdeen: Woodside (F H W)
Vacant
Interim Moderator: Manson C. Merchant
officewpc@talktalk.net
MMerchant@churchofscotland.org.uk
01224 **277249**
01224 722380

Brimmond (F H W)
Jonathan A. Clipston BSc MDiv — 2020
office@newhillschurch.org.uk
Newhills Manse, Bucksburn, Aberdeen AB21 9SS
JClipston@churchofscotland.org.uk
New charge formed by the union of Bucksburn Stoneywood and Newhills
01224 **716161**
01224 712594

Cults (F H T W)
Shuna M. Dicks BSc BD — 2010 — 2018
cultsparishchurch@btinternet.com
1 Cairnlee Terrace, Bieldside, Aberdeen AB15 9AE
SDicks@churchofscotland.org.uk
01224 **869028**
01224 861692

Dyce (F H T W)
Manson C. Merchant BD CPS — 1992 — 2008
dyceparishchurch@outlook.com
100 Burnside Road, Dyce, Aberdeen AB21 7HA
MMerchant@churchofscotland.org.uk
01224 **771295**
01224 722380

Joan I. Thorne BA TQFE CertCS — 2019
(Ordained Local Minister)
85 Mosside Drive, Portlethen, Aberdeen AB12 4QY
JThorne@churchofscotland.org.uk
07368 390832

Kingswells (F H W)
Vacant
Session Clerk: Lorna Graham
lorna.graham15@btinternet.com
07527 581941

Peterculter (F H W)
John A. Ferguson BD DipMin DMin — 1988 — 1999
secretary@culterkirk.co.uk
7 Howie Lane, Peterculter AB14 0LJ
JFerguson@churchofscotland.org.uk
01224 **735845**
01224 735041

Shetland (F)
ShetlandParish@churchofscotland.org.uk
Frances M. Henderson BA BD PhD — 2006 — 2018
(Transition Minister/ Minister)
The Manse, 25 Hogalee, East Voe, Scalloway, Shetland ZE1 0UU
FHenderson@churchofscotland.org.uk
01585 881184

Irene A. Charlton (Mrs) BTh CPS — 1994 — 1997
(Team Minister)
The Manse, Marrister, Symbister, Whalsay, Shetland ZE2 9AE
ICharlton@churchofscotland.org.uk
01806 566767

Lynn Brady BD DipMin — 1996 — 2020
(Interim Minister)
The North Isles Manse, Gutcher, Yell, Shetland ZE2 9DF
LBrady@churchofscotland.org.uk
07815 922889

B. In other appointments
Craig, Gordon T. QHC BD DipMin — 1988 — 2012
Chaplain to UK Oil and Gas Industry
Shell Exploration and Production, Tullos Complex,
1 Altens Farm Road, Aberdeen AB12 3FY
gordon.craig@ukoilandgaschaplaincy.com
01224 882600

Jeffrey, Kenneth S. BA BD PhD DMin — 2002 — 2014
University of Aberdeen
The North Steading, Dalgairn, Cupar KY15 4PH
ksjeffrey@btopenworld.com
01334 653196

Swinton, John (Prof.) BD PhD — 1999
RMN RNMD FRSE
University of Aberdeen
51 Newburgh Circle, Bridge of Don, Aberdeen AB22 8XA
j.swinton@abdn.ac.uk
01224 825637

C. Retaining

Name	Years	Role / (Previous charge)	Address	Phone
Lundie, Ann V. (Miss) DCS	1972 2007	(Deacon)	20 Langdykes Drive, Cove, Aberdeen AB12 3HW ann.lundie@btopenworld.com	01224 898416
Montgomerie, Jean B. (Miss) MA BD	1973 2006	(Forfar: St Margaret's)	12 St Ronan's Place, Peterculter, Aberdeen AB14 0QX revjeanb@tiscali.co.uk	01224 732350
Rodgers, D. Mark BA BD MTh	1987 2021	Head of Spiritual Care, NHS Grampian	63 Cordiner Place, Hilton, Aberdeen AB24 4SB dmrodgers16@gmail.com	01224 379135
Sheret, Brian S. MA BD DPhil	1982 2009	(Glasgow: Drumchapel Drumry St Mary's)	59 Airyhall Crescent, Aberdeen AB15 7QS	01224 323032
Sutherland, Susan J. (Mrs) BD	2009 2022	(Aberdeen: North)	53 Westhill Grange, Westhill AB32 6QJ SSutherland@churchofscotland.org.uk	
Weir, James J.C.M. BD CertMin	1991 2018	(Aberdeen: St George's Tillydrone)	114 Hilton Heights, Woodside, Aberdeen AB24 4QF	01224 901430
Youngson, Elizabeth J.B. BD	1996 2015	(Aberdeen: Mastrick)	47 Corse Drive, The Links, Dubford, Aberdeen AB23 8LN elizabeth.youngson@btinternet.com	07788 294745

ABERDEEN ADDRESSES

Parish	Address	Parish	Address	Parish	Address
Bridge of Don Oldmachar	Ashwood Park	Mannofield	Great Western Road x Craigton Road	St Machar's Cathedral	The Chanonry
Brimmond	west of Bucksburn	Midstocket	Mid Stocket Road	St Mark's	Rosemount Viaduct
Craigiebuckler	Springfield Road	North	Greenfern Road, Mastrick	St Mary's	King Street
Cults	Quarry Road, Cults	Peterculter	Craigton Crescent	St Nicholas Kincorth, South of	Kincorth Circle
Dyce	Victoria Street, Dyce	Queen's Cross	Albyn Place	St Stephen's	Powis Place
Ferryhill	Fonthill Road x Polmuir Road	Rubislaw	Queen's Gardens	South Holburn	Holburn Street
High Hilton	Hilton Drive	Ruthrieston West	Broomhill Road	Stockethill	Cairncry Community Centre
Holburn West	Great Western Road	St Columba's Bridge of Don	Braehead Way, Bridge of Don at St Mark's	Torry St Fittick's	Walker Road
Kingswells	Old Skene Road, Kingswells	St John's for the Deaf		Woodside	Church Street, Woodside

Worship in the Parish of Shetland held at:

Place	Address	Place	Address
Aith	11 Wirliegert, Aith, Bixter ZE2 9NW	Lunna St Margaret's	Methodist Chapel, Vidlin, Lunnasting ZE2 9QE
Baltasound St John's	Baltasound, Unst ZE2 9DX	Ollaberry	Ollaberry, Northmavine ZE2 9QW
Brae	Grindwell, Brae, Delting ZE2 9QW	Sandwick	Sandwick ZE2 9HW
Bridgend, Burra Isle	Freefield Road, Bridge End, Burra Isle ZE2 9LD	Scalloway	Main Street, Scalloway ZE1 0TR
Cullivoe	Cullivoe, Yell ZE2 9DD	Walls St Paul's	Pier Road, Walls ZE2 9PF
Lerwick St Columba's	Greenfield Place, Lerwick ZE1 0EQ	Whalsay	Church Hall, Symbister, Whalsay ZE2 9AD

(32) KINCARDINE AND DEESIDE (W)

Meets in various locations as arranged on the first Tuesday of October, November and December 2022 at 7pm. On 1 January 2023 it will unite with the Presbyteries of Aberdeen and Shetland, Buchan, Gordon, Moray and Orkney to form the Presbytery of the North East and the Northern Isles. That new Presbytery will meet on-line on 10 January 2023 and thereafter as decided.

Clerk:	REV. HUGH CONKEY BSc BD		39 St Ternans Road, Newtonhill, Stonehaven AB39 3PF kincardinedeeside@churchofscotland.org.uk	01569 739297
Aberluthnott (F W) linked with Laurencekirk (F H W)				
Rosalind (Linda) E. Pollock (Miss) BD ThM ThM	2001	2021	contact@parishchurchofaberluthnottandlaurencekirk.co.uk The Manse, Aberdeen Road, Laurencekirk AB30 1AJ RPollock@churchofscotland.org.uk	01561 377013
Aboyne-Dinnet (F H W) linked with Cromar (F W)				
Frank Ribbons MA BD DipEd	1985	2011	49 Charlton Crescent, Aboyne AB34 5GN FRibbons@churchofscotland.org.uk	01339 887267
Arbuthnott, Bervie and Kinneff (F T W)				
Andrew R. Morrison MA BA	2019		5 West Park Place, Inverbervie, Montrose DD10 0XA Andrew.Morrison@churchofscotland.org.uk	01561 362530
Banchory-Ternan: East (F H W)				
Alan J.S. Murray BSc BD PhD	2003	2013	info@banchoryeastchurch.com East Manse, Station Road, Banchory AB31 5YP AJSMurray@churchofscotland.org.uk	**01330 820380** 01330 822481
Banchory-Ternan: West (F H T W)				
Antony A. Stephen MA BD	2001	2011	office@banchorywestchurch.com The Manse, 2 Wilson Road, Banchory AB31 5UY TStephen@churchofscotland.org.uk	**01330 822006** 01330 822006 07866 704738
Birse and Feughside (W)				
Amy C. Pierce BA BD	2017	2019	The Manse, Finzean, Banchory AB31 6PB ACPierce@churchofscotland.org.uk	01330 850736 07814 194997
Braemar and Crathie (F W)				
Kenneth I. Mackenzie DL BD CPS	1990	2005	The Manse, Crathie, Ballater AB35 5UL KMacKenzie@churchofscotland.org.uk	01339 742208

Cromar See Aboyne-Dinnet

Drumoak-Durris (F H W)
Jean A. Boyd MSc BSc BA   2016
drumoakdurrischurch2020@gmail.com
26 Sunnyside Drive, Drumoak, Banchory AB31 3EW
JBoyd@churchofscotland.org.uk
01330 811031

Glenmuick (Ballater) (H W)
David L.C. Barr   2014
The Manse, Craigendarroch Walk, Ballater AB35 5ZB
DBarr@churchofscotland.org.uk
01339 756111

Laurencekirk See Aberluthnott

Maryculter Trinity (W)
Vacant
David Galbraith (Ordained Local Minister)   2021
marycultertrinitychurch@btinternet.com
The Manse, Kirkton of Maryculter, Aberdeen   AB12 5FS
Myreside Steading, Auchenblae, Laurencekirk   AB30 1TX
David.Galbraith@churchofscotland.org.uk
01224 **735983**
01224 730150
01561 320779

Interim Moderator: Antony A. Stephen
TStephen@churchofscotland.org.uk
01330 822811

Mearns Coastal (F W)
Guardianship of the Presbytery
Norman D. Lennox-Trewren CertCS   2018
(Ordained Local Minister)
32 Haulkerton Crescent, Laurencekirk AB30 1FB
NLennoxTrewren@churchofscotland.org.uk
01561 377359

Mid Deeside (F W)
Holly Smith BSIS MDiv MEd   2009   2019
Lochnagar, Beltie Road, Torphins, Banchory AB31 4U
Holly.smith@churchofscotland.org.uk
01339 **889160**
01339 882915

Newtonhill (F W)
Hugh Conkey BSc BD   1987   2001
39 St Ternans Road, Newtonhill, Stonehaven AB39 3PF
HConkey@churchofscotland.org.uk
01569 730143

Portlethen (F H W)
Rodolphe Blanchard-Kowal MTh MDiv   2013   2017
(Exchange Minister)
portlethenpc@btconnect.com
18 Rowanbank Road, Portlethen, Aberdeen AB12 4NX
RKowal@churchofscotland.org.uk
01224 **782883**
01224 780211

Stonehaven: Carronside (H W)
Sarah Smith BA MDiv MA   2017   2021
secretary.dunnottarchurch@outlook.com
Dunnottar Manse, Stonehaven AB39 3XL
Sarah.Smith@churchofscotland.org.uk
01569 **760930**
01569 762166

Stonehaven: Fetteresso (H W)				**office@fetteresso.org.uk**	**01569 767689**
Mark Lowey BD DipTh	2012	2021		11 South Lodge Drive, Stonehaven AB39 2PN	01569 549960
				MLowey@churchofscotland.org.uk	
West Mearns (F W)					
Brian D. Smith BD	1990	2016		The Manse, Fettercairn, Laurencekirk AB30 1UE	01561 340203
				BSmith@churchofscotland.org.uk	

C. Retaining

Birss, Alan D. DL OStJ MA BD	1979	2020	(Paisley: Abbey)	36 Marquis Drive, Aboyne AB34 5FD	01339 886231
				alan.birss@btinternet.com	07411 088786
Blair, Fyfe BA BD DMin	1989	2019	(Stonehaven: Fetteresso)	19 Crichie Place, Fettercairn, Laurencekirk AB30 1EZ	01561 340579
				Fyfe.Blair@churchofscotland.org.uk	
Broadley, Linda J. (Mrs) LTh DipEd	1996	2013	(Dun and Hillside)	Snaefell, Lochside Road, St Cyrus, Montrose DD10 0DB	01674 850141
				lindabroadley@btinternet.com	
Lamb, A. Douglas MA	1964	2002	(Dalry: St Margaret's)	9 Luther Drive, Laurencekirk AB30 1FE	01561 376816
				lamb.edzell@talk21.com	
Purves, John P. S. MBE BSc BD	1978	2013	(Colombo, Sri Lanka: St Andrew's Scots Kirk)	Lonville Cottage, 20 Viewfield Road, Ballater AB35 5RD	01339 754081
				john@thepurves.com	
Wallace, William F. BDS BD	1968	2008	(Wick: Pulteneytown and Thrumster)	Lachlan Cottage, 29 Station Road, Banchory AB31 5XX	01330 822259
				williamfwallace39@gmail.com	
Watson, John M. LTh	1989	2009	(Aberdeen: St Mark's)	20 Greystone Place, Newtonhill, Stonehaven AB39 3UL	01569 730604
				johnmutchwatson2065@btinternet.com	07733 334380

(33) GORDON (F W)

Meets at various locations on the first Tuesday of October, November and December 2022. On 1 January 2023 it will unite with the Presbyteries of Aberdeen and Shetland, Buchan, Kincardine and Deeside, Moray and Orkney to form the Presbytery of the North East and the Northern Isles. That new Presbytery will meet on-line on 10 January 2023 and thereafter as decided.

Clerk:	REV. G. EUAN D. GLEN BSc BD		The Manse, 26 St Ninians, Monymusk, Inverurie AB51 7HF gordon@churchofscotland.org.uk	01467 651470

Barthol Chapel (F) linked with Tarves (F W)
Alison I. Swindells (Mrs) LLB BD DMin   1998   2017   8 Murray Avenue, Tarves, Ellon AB41 7LZ   01651 851295
ASwindells@churchofscotland.org.uk

Belhelvie (F H W)
Paul McKeown BSc PhD BD   2000   2005   **belhelviecofs@btconnect.com**
Belhelvie Manse, Balmedie, Aberdeen AB23 8YR   01358 742227
PMcKeown@churchofscotland.org.uk

Blairdaff and Chapel of Garioch (F W)
Vacant
Interim Moderator: Neil W. Meyer   The Manse, Chapel of Garioch, Inverurie AB51 5HE   01467 681619
NMeyer@churchofscotland.org.uk   01467 632219

Cluny (F H W) linked with Monymusk (F H W)
G. Euan D. Glen BSc BD   1992   The Manse, 26 St Ninians, Monymusk, Inverurie AB51 7HF   01467 651470
GGlen@churchofscotland.org.uk

Culsalmond and Rayne (F W) linked with Daviot (F H W)
Mary M. Cranfield MA BD DMin   1989   The Manse, Daviot, Inverurie AB51 0HY   01467 671241
MCranfield@churchofscotland.org.uk

Cushnie and Tough (F H)
Vacant
Simon A. Crouch MCIPD CertCS   2019   The Manse, Muir of Fowlis, Alford AB33 8JU   01975 581239
 (Ordained Local Minister)   Delhandy, Corgarff, Strathdon AB36 8YB   01975 651779
Interim Moderator: John A. Cook   SCrouch@churchofscotland.org.uk   07713 101358
John.Cook@churchofscotland.org.uk   01975 562282

Daviot See Culsalmond and Rayne

Echt and Midmar (F H W) Sheila M. Mitchell BD MTh	1995	2018	The Manse, Echt, Westhill AB32 7AB SMitchell@churchofscotland.org.uk	01330 860004
Ellon (F T W) Alastair J. Bruce BD MTh PGCE	2015		**info@ellonparishchurch.co.uk** The Manse, 12 Union Street, Ellon AB41 9BA ABruce@churchofscotland.org.uk	**01358 725690** 01358 723787
Fintray Kinellar Keithhall (F W) Vacant Interim Moderator: Sheila A. Craggs			sacraggs@outlook.com	**01224 790439** 01358 723055
Foveran (W) Vacant Interim Moderator: Ibidun B. Daramola			The Manse, Foveran, Ellon AB41 6AP IDaramola@churchofscotland.org.uk	01358 789288 07395 006113
Howe Trinity (F W) John A. Cook MA BD DMin	1986	2000	**enquiries@howetrinity.org.uk** The Manse, 110 Main Street, Alford AB33 8AD John.Cook@churchofscotland.org.uk	**01975 562829** 01975 562282
Huntly Cairnie Glass (F) Thomas R. Calder LLB BD WS	1994		The Manse, Queen Street, Huntly AB54 8EB TCalder@churchofscotland.org.uk	01466 792630
Insch-Leslie-Premnay-Oyne (F H W) Kay F. Gauld BD STM PhD	1999	2015	66 Denwell Road, Insch AB52 6LH KGauld@churchofscotland.org.uk	01464 820404
Inverurie: St Andrew's (F W) Carl J. Irvine BSc MEd BA	2017	2020	**standrews@btinternet.com** 1 Ury Dale, Inverurie AB51 3XW CIrvine@churchofscotland.org.uk	**01467 628740** 01467 629163
Inverurie: West (F T W) Rhona P. Cathcart BA BSc BD	2017		**admin@inveruriewestchurch.org** West Manse, 1 Westburn Place, Inverurie AB51 5QS RCathcart@churchofscotland.org.uk	**01647 620285** 01467 620285

			Tel/Fax	**01467 643883** 01467 642219

Kennay (F T W)
Joshua M. Mikelson BA MDiv

2008   2015

office@kemnayparish.church
15 Kirkland, Kemnay, Inverurie AB51 5QD
JMikelson@churchofscotland.org.uk
01467 643883
01467 642219

Kintore (F H W)
Neil W. Meyer BD MTh

2000   2014

28 Oakhill Road, Kintore, Inverurie AB51 0FH
NMeyer@churchofscotland.org.uk
01467 632219

Meldrum and Bourtie (F W)
Alisa L. McDonald BA MDiv

2008   2020

info@meldrumandbourtiechurch.com
The Manse, Urquhart Road, Oldmeldrum, Inverurie AB51 0EX
Alisa.McDonald@churchofscotland.org.uk
01651 872059

Methlick (F W)
William A. Stalder BA MDiv MLitt PhD

2014

The Manse, Manse Road, Methlick, Ellon AB41 7DG
WStalder@churchofscotland.org.uk
01651 806264

Monymusk See Cluny

New Machar (F W)
Vacant
Interim Moderator: Carl J. Irvine

The New Manse, Newmachar, Aberdeen AB21 0RD
CIrvine@churchofscotland.org.uk
01651 862278
01467 629163

Noth
Regine U. Cheyne (Mrs) MA BSc BD

1988   2010

Manse of Noth, Kennethmont, Huntly AB54 4NP
RCheyne@churchofscotland.org.uk
01464 831690

Skene (F H W)
Stella Campbell MA (Oxon) BD

2012

Ibidun B. Daramola BA MA PhD
(Associate Minister)

2020

info.skeneparish@gmail.com
The Manse, Manse Road, Kirkton of Skene, Westhill AB32 6LX
SCampbell@churchofscotland.org.uk
Trinity Church Office, Westhill Drive, Westhill AB32 6FY
IDaramola@churchofscotland.org.uk
01224 742512
01224 745955

07395 006113

Strathbogie Drumblade (F W)
Vacant
Interim Moderator: Carol H.M. Ford

49 Deveron Park, Huntly AB54 8UZ
CFord@churchofscotland.org.uk
01466 792702
01464 820332

Tarves See Barthol Chapel

Udny and Pitmedden (F W)
Vacant
Interim Moderator: Sheila M. Mitchell
The Manse, Manse Road, Udny Green, Ellon AB41 7RS
SMitchell@churchofscotland.org.uk
01651 843794
01330 860004

Upper Donside (F H)
Vacant
upperdonsideparishchurch@btinternet.com

Simon A. Crouch MCIPD CertCS (Ordained Local Minister)	2019	Delhandy, Corgarff, Strathdon AB36 8YB SCrouch@churchofscotland.org.uk	01975 651779 07713 101358

Interim Moderator: Regine U. Cheyne
RCheyne@churchofscotland.org.uk
01464 831690

B. In other appointments

Mitchell, Valerie A. MA FSA	2019	2021	Ordained Local Minster: Presbytery-wide	Brownhill of Ardo, Methlick AB41 7HS VMitchell@churchofscotland.org.uk	01651 806005

C. Retaining

Name			Position	Address	Phone
Christie, Andrew C. LTh	1975	2000	(Banchory-Devenick and Maryculter/Cookney)	17 Broadstraik Close, Elrick, Aberdeen AB32 6JP	01224 746888
Craggs, Sheila A. (Mrs)	2001	2016	(Auxiliary Minister)	7 Morar Court, Ellon AB41 9GG sacraggs@outlook.com	01358 723055
Craig, Anthony J.D. BD	1987	2009	(Glasgow: Maryhill)	4 Hightown, Collieston, Ellon AB41 8RS aacraig@btinternet.com	01358 751247
Dryden, Ian MA DipEd	1988	2001	(New Machar)	16 Glenhome Gardens, Dyce, Aberdeen AB21 7FG ian@idryden.freeserve.co.uk	01224 722820
Falconer, James B. MBE BD CertMin	1982	2018	(Hospital Chaplain)	3 Brimmond Walk, Westhill AB32 6XH	01224 744621
Ford, Carolyn (Carol) H.M. DSD RSAMD BD	2003	2018	(Edinburgh: St Margaret's)	4 Mitchell Avenue, Huntly AB54 8DW CFord@churchofscotland.org.uk	01464 820332
Greig, Alan BSc BD	1977	2017	(Interim Minister)	1 Dunnydeer Place, Insch AB52 6HP greig@kincarr.free-online.co.uk	01464 820332
Hawthorn, Daniel MA BD DMin	1965	2004	(Belhelvie)	7 Crimond Drive, Ellon AB41 8BT danhawthorn@compuserve.com	01358 723981
Macalister, Eleanor E. DipCEd BD	1994	2006	(Ellon)	Quarryview, Ythan Bank, Ellon AB41 7TH macall.ster@aol.com	01358 761402
McLeish, Robert S. LTh	1970	2000	(Insch-Leslie-Premnay-Oyne)	19 Western Road, Insch AB52 6JR	01464 820749
Noble, Alexander B. MA BD ThM	1982	2020	(Saltcoats: North)	93 Snipe Street, Ellon AB41 9FW	01358 268705
Reid, Richard M.C. BSc BD MTh	1991	2021	(Foveran)	13 Morningside Crescent, Inverurie AB51 4FA reidricky322@gmail.com	07474 010915
Sanders, Martyn S. BA CertEd	2013	2020	(Blairdaff and Chapel of Garioch)	140 The Homend, Ledbury, Herefordshire HR8 1BZ	07814 164373
Telfer, Iain J.M. BD DPS	1978	2018	(Chaplain: Royal Infirmary of Edinburgh)	66 High Street, Inverurie AB51 3XS iain_telfer@yahoo.co.uk	07749 993070
Thomson, Iain U. MA BD	1970	2011	(Skene)	4 Keirhill Gardens, Westhill AB32 6AZ iainuthomson@googlemail.com	01224 746743

(34) BUCHAN (W)

Meets at St Kane's Centre, New Deer, Turriff on the first Tuesday of November 2022. On 1 January 2023 it will unite with the Presbyteries of Aberdeen and Shetland, Gordon, Kincardine and Deeside, Moray and Orkney to form the Presbytery of the North East and the Northern Isles. That new Presbytery will meet on-line on 10 January 2023 and thereafter as decided.

Clerk:	REV. SHEILA M. KIRK BA LLB BD		The Manse, Abbey Street, Old Deer, Peterhead AB42 5JB buchan@churchofscotland.org.uk	01771 623582
Aberdour linked (W) with Pitsligo (F W)				
Vacant			31 Blairmore Park, Rosehearty, Fraserburgh AB43 7NZ	01346 571823
Interim Moderator: Ruth Mackenzie (Miss)			ursular@tiscali.co.uk	01779 480680
Auchaber United (W) linked with Auchterless (W)				
Stephen J. Potts BA	2012		The Manse, Auchterless, Turriff AB53 8BA	01888 511058
			SPotts@churchofscotland.org.uk	
Auchterless See Auchaber United				
Banff (F W) linked with King Edward (F W)				
Vacant			info@banffparishchurchofscotland.org.uk	**01262 818211**
Interim Moderator: Colin A. Strong			7 Colleonard Road, Banff AB45 1DZ	01261 812107
			CStrong@churchofscotland.org.uk	01771 637365
Crimond (F W) linked with Lonmay (W)				
Vacant			The Manse, Crimond, Fraserburgh AB43 8QJ	01346 532431
Session Clerk, Crimond: Irene Fowlie (Mrs)			fowlie@hotmail.com	
Session Clerk, Lonmay: Roy Kinghorn			strathelliefarm@btinternet.com	01346 532436
Cruden (F H W)				
Sean Swindells BD DipMin MTh	1996	2019	8 Murray Avenue, Tarves, Ellon AB41 7LZ	01651 851295
			SSwindells@churchofscotland.org.uk	07791 755976
Deer (F H)				
Sheila M. Kirk BA LLB BD	2007	2010	The Manse, Abbey Street, Old Deer, Peterhead AB42 5JB	01771 623582
			SKirk@churchofscotland.org.uk	
Fraserburgh: Old (W)				
Vacant			fraserburghopc@btconnect.com	**01346 510139**
Interim Moderator: James Givan			4 Robbie's Road, Fraserburgh AB43 7AF	01346 515332
			jim.givan@btinternet.com	01261 833318

Fraserburgh: South (H) linked with Inverallochy and Rathen: East
Vacant
Session Clerk, Fraserburgh: South:

Fraserburgh: West (F H T W) linked with Rathen: West (T W)
Vacant
Session Clerk, Fraserburgh: West: Jill Smith (Mrs)
Session Clerk, Rathen: West: Ian J. Campbell
4 Kirkton Gardens, Fraserburgh   AB43 8TU
jill@fraserburgh-harbour.co.uk
cicfarmers@hotmail.co.uk
01346 513303
01346 517972
01346 532062

Fyvie linked (F W) with Rothienorman (F)
Alison Jaffrey (Mrs) MA BD FSAScot   1990   2019
The Manse, Peterwell Road, Fyvie, Turriff   AB53 8RD
AJaffrey@churchofscotland.org.uk
01651 891961

Inverallochy and Rathen: East See Fraserburgh: South
King Edward See Banff

Longside (W)
Robert A. Fowlie BD   2007
The Manse, Abbey Street, Old Deer, Peterhead   AB42 5JB
RFowlie@churchofscotland.org.uk
01771 622228

Lonmay See Crimond

Macduff (F T W)
Hugh O'Brien CSS MTheol   2001   2016
contactus@macduffparishchurch.org
10 Ross Street, Macduff AB44 1NS
HOBrien@churchofscotland.org.uk
01261 832316

Marnoch (F W)
Vacant
Marnoch Manse, 53 South Street, Aberchirder, Huntly AB54 7TS
01466 781143

Maud and Savoch (F W) linked with New Deer: St Kane's (F W)
Aileen M. McFie (Mrs) BD   2003   2018
The Manse, Fordyce Terrace, New Deer, Turriff   AB53 6TD
ARobson@churchofscotland.org.uk
01771 644097
01771 644631

Monquhitter and New Byth linked with Turriff: St Andrew's (F)
James M. Cook BSc MBA MDiv   1999   2002
info@standrewsturriff.co.uk
St Andrew's Manse, Balmellie Road, Turriff   AB53 4DP
JCook@churchofscotland.org.uk
01888 560304

New Deer: St Kane's See Maud and Savoch

New Pitsligo linked with Strichen and Tyrie (F W)
Colin A. Strong BSc BD   1989   Kingsville, Strichen, Fraserburgh AB43 6SQ   01771 637365
CStrong@churchofscotland.org.uk

Ordiquhill and Cornhill (H) linked with Whitehills
Vacant   6 Craigneen Place, Whitehills, Banff AB45 2NE   01261 861317
Session Clerk, Ordiquhill and Cornhill: Frances Webster (Mrs)   william.webster@btconnect.com   01466 751230
Session Clerk, Whitehills: Jenny Abel (Mrs)   jennyabel14@hotmail.co.uk   01261 861386

Peterhead: New (F)
Julia Pizzuto-Pomaco BA MA MDiv PhD   1999   2021   **contact@peterheadnew.org**   01779 471714
15 Inchmore Gardens, Boddam, Peterhead AB42 3BG
JPizzuto-Pomaco@churchofscotland.org.uk

Peterhead: St Andrew's (H W)
Guardianship of the Presbytery   eil.ian@btinternet.com   01779 470571
Session Clerk: John Leslie

Pitsligo See Aberdour

Portsoy (W)
John Gow BA   2021   **portsoychurch@gmail.com**   **01261 843125**
The Manse, 4 Seafield Terrace, Portsoy, Banff AB45 2QB   01261 842272
JGow@churchofscotland.org.uk

Rathen: West See Fraserburgh: West
Rothienorman See Fyvie

St Fergus (F)
Jeffrey Tippner BA MDiv MCS PhD   1991   2012   26 Newton Road, St Fergus, Peterhead AB42 3DD   01779 838287
JTippner@churchofscotland.org.uk

Sandhaven
Guardianship of the Presbytery   CStrong@churchofscotland.org.uk   01771 637365
Interim Moderator: Colin A. Strong

Strichen and Tyrie See New Pitsligo
Turriff: St Andrew's See Monquhitter and New Byth

Turriff: St Ninian's and Forglen (H L W) **01888 560282**
Kevin R. Gruer BSc BA   2011   01888 563850
info@stniniansandforglen.org.uk
4 Deveronside Drive, Turriff AB53 4SP
KGruer@churchofscotland

Whitehills See Ordiquhill and Cornhill

B. In other appointments

Stewart, William	2015	2016	Ordained Local Minister, Presbytery-wide	Denend, Strichen, Fraserburgh AB43 6RN 01771 637256
				billandjunes@live.co.uk
van Sittert, Paul BA BD	1997	2011	Chaplain: Army	32 Engineer Regiment, Marne Barracks, Catterick Garrison DL10 7NP
				padre.pvs@gmail.com

C. Retaining

Coutts, Fred MA BD	1973	2012	(Hospital Chaplain)	Ladebank, 1 Manse Place, Hatton, Peterhead AB42 0UQ 01779 841320
				fred.coutts@btinternet.com
Fawkes, G.M. Allan BSc BA JP	1979	2000	(Lonmay with Rathen: West)	3 Northfield Gardens, Hatton, Peterhead AB42 0SW 01779 841814
				afawkes@aol.com
Griffiths, Melvyn J. BTh DipTheol DMin	1978	2021	(Maryculter Trinity)	2 Chalmers Place, Fetterangus AB42 4ED 01771 624684
				thehayvn@btinternet.com
Macgregor, Alan BA BD PhD	1992	2022	(Marnoch)	Culag, 139 Main Street, Aberchirder, Huntly AB54 7TB 01261 815647
Macnee, Iain LTh BD MA PhD	1975	2011	(New Pitsligo with Strichen and Tyrie)	Wardend Cottage, Alvah, Banff AB45 3TR
				macneeiain4@googlemail.com
Murray, Alistair BD	1984	2018	(Inverness: Trinity)	7 Clunie Street, Banff AB45 1HY 01261 390154
				a.murray111@btinternet.com
Noble, George S. DipTh	1972	2000	(Carfin with Newarthill)	Craigowan, 3 Main Street, Inverallochy, Fraserburgh AB43 8XX 01346 582749
Ross, David S. BSc MSc PhD BD	1978	2013	(Chaplain: Scottish Prison Service)	3–5 Abbey Street, Old Deer, Peterhead AB42 5LN 01771 623994
				padsross@btinternet.com
Thorburn, Robert J. BD DipPS	1978	2017	(Fyvie with Rothienorman)	12 Slackadale Gardens, Turriff AB53 4UA 01888 562278
				rjthorburn@aol.com
Verster, W. Myburgh BA BTh LTh MTh	1981	2019	(Ordiquhill and Cornhill with Whitehills)	32 Newtown Drive, Macduff AB44 1SR
				myburghverster@gmail.com

(35) MORAY (F W)

Meets at St Andrew's-Lhanbryd and Urquhart on the first Tuesday of October, November and December 2022. On 1 January 2023 it will unite with the Presbyteries of Aberdeen and Shetland, Gordon, Kincardine and Deeside, Moray and Orkney to form the Presbytery of the North East and the Northern Isles. That new Presbytery will meet on-line on 10 January 2023 and thereafter as decided.

Clerk:	MRS JANET WHYTE		1 Lemanfield Crescent, Garmouth IV32 7LS moray@churchofscotland.org.uk	01343 870667
Aberlour (F H W) Andrew I. M. Kimmitt MA(Div)	2020		The Manse, Mary Avenue, Aberlour AB38 9QU AKimmitt@churchofscotland.org.uk	01340 871909 07752 306462
Bellie and Speymouth (F W) Seòras I. Orr MSc MTh	2018		11 The Square, Fochabers IV32 7DG SOrr@churchofscotland.org.uk	01343 820256
Birnie and Pluscarden (W) linked with Elgin: High (W) Vacant Session Clerk, Birnie and Pluscarden: Alistair Farquhar Session Clerk, Elgin: High: Hazel Dickson			The Manse, 7 Kirkton Place, Elgin IV30 6JR alistair.farquhar@btinternet.com hazelandjohn@mypostoffice.co.uk	01343 541328 01343 540949
Buckie: North (F H W) linked with Rathven (F) Jacobus Boonzaaier BA BCom(OR) BD MDiv PhD	1996	2021	20 Netherton Terrace, Findochty, Buckie AB56 4QD JBoonzaaier@churchofscotland.org.uk	01542 649644
Buckie: South and West (F H) linked with Enzie (F) Vacant Session Clerk, Buckie: South and West: Wilma Smith Session Clerk, Enzie: Gladys Murray (Mrs)			Craigendarroch, 14 Cliff Terrace, Buckie AB56 1LX parkgrove10@gmail.com	01542 833895 01542 832383
Cullen and Deskford (F T W) Douglas F. Stevenson BD DipMin DipHE MScR MCOSCA MBACP	1991	2010	14 Seafield Road, Cullen, Buckie AB56 4AF DStevenson@churchofscotland.org.uk	01542 841963
Duffus, Spynie and Hopeman (F H W) Jenny M. Adams BEng BD MTh	2013		The Manse, Duffus, Elgin IV30 5QP JAdams@churchofscotland.org.uk	01343 830276

Elgin: High See Birnie and Pluscarden

Elgin: St Giles' (H) and St Columba's South (F W)
Deon F. Oelofse BA MDiv LTh MTh   2002   2017
stgileselgin@gmail.com
18 Reidhaven Street, Elgin IV30 1QH
DOelofse@churchofscotland.org.uk
01343 551501
01343 208786

Sonia Palmer RGN   2017
(Ordained Local Minister)
94 Ashgrove Park, Elgin IV30 1UT
Sonia.Palmer@churchofscotland.org.uk
07748 700929

Enzie See Buckie: South and West

Findochty (F T W) linked with Portknockie (F T W)
Vacant
Interim Moderator: Louis C. Bezuidenhout
20 Netherton Terrace, Findochty, Buckie AB56 4QD
macbez@gmail.com
01542 649644
01542 839493

Keith: North, Newmill, Boharm and Rothiemay (F H W)
Amy C. Bender BA PhD DDiv   2022
knnbrchurch@btconnect.com
North Manse, Church Road, Keith AB55 5BR
ABender@churchofscotland.org.uk
01542 886390
01542 780486

Keith: St Rufus, Botriphnie and Grange (F H W)
J.P.L. (Wiekus) van Straaten BA BTh   1997   2020
St Rufus Manse, Church Road, Keith AB55 5BR
WvanStraaten@churchofscotland.org.uk
01542 882799

Knockando, Elchies and Archiestown (H W) linked with Rothes (W) info@moraykirk.co.uk
Vacant
Session Clerk, Knockando, Elchies and Archiestown: Patricia North
Session Clerk, Rothes: Dennis Malcolm
The Manse, Rothes, Aberlour AB38 7AF
patnorth82@gmail.com
dennis.malcolm46@icloud.com
01340 831497
01340 831381
01340 810687
01340 831319
07399 420695

Lossiemouth: St Gerardine's High (H W) linked with Lossiemouth: St James (F T W)
Geoffrey D. McKee BA BA DipPS   1997   2014
The Manse, St Gerardine's Road, Lossiemouth IV31 6RA
GMcKee@churchofscotland.org.uk
01343 208852

Lossiemouth: St James' See Lossiemouth: St Gerardine's High

Mortlach and Cabrach (F H)
Eduard Enslin BTh MDiv MTh LLB   2010   2020
Mortlach Manse, Ardean, Church Street, Dufftown, Keith
  AB55 4AR
EEnslin@churchofscotland.org.uk
01340 820380

Portknockie See Findochty
Rathven See Buckie: North
Rothes See Knockando, Elchies and Archiestown

St Andrew's-Lhanbryd and Urquhart (F H W)

C. Breda Ludik BA BTh DipTheol MTh PhD	1979	2020		39 St Andrews Road, Lhanbryde, Elgin IV30 8PU BLudik@churchofscotland.org.uk	01343 842017

B. In other appointments

Lancaster, Craig MA BD	2004	2011	RAF Senior Chaplain	St Aidan's Church, RAF Lossiemouth, Moray IV31 6DS craig.lancaster102@mod.gov.uk	01343 817193
Murray, B. Ian BD	2002	2021	Buildings Officer, Presbyteries of the North East and Northern Isles	Kilmorie House, 6 Institution Road, Elgin IV30 1RP IMurray@churchofscotland.org.uk	0131 376 3647
Young, David T. BA BD MTh	2007	2022	Chaplain: RAF	RAF Lossiemouth, Moray IV31 6DS david.young137@mod.gov.uk	01434 817193

C. Retaining

Anderson, Robert J.M. BD FInstLM	1993	2022	(Knockando, Elchies and Archiestown with Rothes)	20 Park Street, Burghead, Elgin IV30 5UG bobjmanderson@gmail.com	01343 835401
Attenburrow, A. Anne BSc MB ChB	2006	2018	(Auxiliary Minister)	4 Jock Inksons Brae, Elgin IV30 1QE AAttenburrow@churchofscotland.org.uk	01343 552330
Bain, Brian LTh	1980	2007	(Gask with Methven and Logiealmond)	Bayview, 13 Stewart Street, Portgordon, Buckie AB56 5QT bricoreen@gmail.com	01542 831215
Bezuidenhout, Louis C. BA MA BD DD	1978	2020	(Interim Minister)	76 East Church Street, Buckie AB56 1LQ macbez@gmail.com	01542 839493
Boyd, Barry J. LTh DPS	1993	2020	(Forres: St Laurence)		07778 73 1018
Duff, Stuart M. BA	1997	2019	(Birnie and Pluscarden with Elgin: High)	7 Kirkton Place, Elgin IV30 6JR stuart.duff@gmail.com	01343 200233
King, Margaret MA DCS	2002	2012	(Deacon)	56 Murrayfield, Fochabers IV32 7EZ margaretking889@gmail.com	01343 820937
Legge, Rosemary (Mrs) BSc BD MTh	1992	2017	(Cushnie and Tough)	57 High Street, Archiestown, Aberlour AB38 7QZ revr1192@aol.com	01340 810304
Morton, Alasdair J. MA BD DipEd FEIS	1960	2000	(Bowden with Newtown)	16 St Leonard's Road, Forres IV36 1DW alasgilmor@hotmail.co.uk	01309 671719
Rollo, George B. BD	1974	2010	(Elgin: St Giles' and St Columba's South)	'Struan', 13 Meadow View, Hopeman, Elgin IV30 5PL rollos@gmail.com	01343 835226
Ross, William B. LTh CPS	1988	2016	(Aberdour with Pitsligo)	5 Strathlene Court, Rathven AB55 3DD williamross278@btinternet.com	01542 834418

Smith, Morris BD CertCE	1988 2013	(Cromdale and Advie with Dulnain Bridge with Grantown-on-Spey)	1 Urquhart Grove, New Elgin IV30 8TB mosmith.themanse@btinternet.com	01343 545019
Whyte, David W. LTh	1993 2011	(Boat of Garten, Duthil and Kincardine)	1 Lemanfield Crescent, Garmouth, Fochabers IV32 7LS whytedj@btinternet.com	01343 870667

(36) ABERNETHY (W)

Meets at Boat of Garten on the first Tuesday of February, March, May, September, October, November and December, and on the last Tuesday of June.

Clerk:	REV JAMES A.I. MacEWAN MA BD	Rapness, Station Road, Nethy Bridge PH25 3DN abernethy@churchofscotland.org.uk	**01479 821116**

Abernethy (F H W) linked with Boat of Garten (H), Carrbridge (H) and Kincardine (F W)

Graham T. Atkinson MA BD MTh	2006 2019	The Manse, Deshar Road, Boat of Garten PH24 3BN GAtkinson@churchofscotland.org.uk	01479 831637

Alvie and Insh (H W) linked with Rothiemurchus and Aviemore (H W)

Charles J. Finnie LTh DPS	1991 2019	The Manse, 8 Dalfaber Park, Aviemore PH22 1QF CFinnie@churchofscotland.org.uk	01479 810280

Boat of Garten, Carrbridge and Kincardine See Abernethy

Cromdale (H) and Advie (F W) linked with Dulnain Bridge (H W) linked with Grantown-on-Spey (F H W)

Vacant		The Manse, Golf Course Road, Grantown-on-Spey PH26 3HY	01479 872084
Mary B. Duncanson (Ms) BTh (Ordained Local Minister)	2013 2017	3 Balmenach Road, Cromdale, Grantown-on-Spey PH26 3LJ MDuncanson@churchofscotland.org.uk	01479 872165
Session Clerk, Cromdale and Advie: Diane Brazier (Mrs)		dbrazier39@gmail.com	01479 872547
Session Clerk, Dulnain Bridge: Ruth Coker (Mrs)		ruth.coker@btopenworld.com	01479 851797
Session Clerk, Grantown-on-Spey: William Steele (Dr)		wmsteele33@aol.com	01479 870154

Dulnain Bridge See Cromdale and Advie
Grantown-on-Spey See Cromdale and Advie

Kingussie (F H W) linked with Laggan (H) and Newtonmore (H W)

Vacant		The Manse, Fort William Road, Newtonmore PH20 1DG	01540 673238
Session Clerk, Kingussie: Sandy Peebles (Mr)		sandy@ats.me.uk	01540 661965
Session Clerk, Laggan and Newtonmore: Alison Armstrong (Mrs)		alisonmabel@hotmail.com	07841 502991

Laggan and Newtonmore See Kingussie
Rothiemurchus and Aviemore See Alvie and Insh

Tomintoul (H), Glenlivet and Inveraven
Guardianship of the Presbytery
Session Clerk: Margo Stewart (Mrs)   margoandedward@hotmail.co.uk   01807 580239

B. In other appointments

Thomson, Mary Ellen (Mrs)	2014	Ordained Local Minister: Presbytery Chaplain to Care Homes	Kerrowside, 3 Hillside Avenue, Kingussie PH21 1PA Mary.Thomson@churchofscotland.org.uk	01540 661772

C. Retaining

MacEwan, James A.I. MA BD	1973	2012	(Abernethy with Cromdale and Advie)	Rapness, Station Road, Nethy Bridge PH25 3DN wurrus@hotmail.co.uk	01479 821116
Ritchie, Christine A.Y. (Mrs) BD DipMin	2002	2012	(Braes of Rannoch with Foss and Rannoch)	25 Beachen Court, Grantown-on-Spey PH26 3JD gandcritchie70@gmail.com	01479 873419
Walker, Donald K. BD	1979	2018	(Abernethy with Boat of Garten, Carrbridge and Kincardine)	Jabulani, Seafield Avenue, Grantown-on-Spey PH26 3JQ dwalkerjabulani@gmail.com	01479 870104

(37) INVERNESS (W)

Meets at Inverness, in Inverness: Inshes (2022) on the second Saturday of September, the third Tuesday of November, (2023) the second Saturday of March and the last Tuesday of June; Saturday meetings preceded by a presbytery conference.

| Clerk: | REV. TREVOR G. HUNT BA BD | 7 Woodville Court, Culduthel Avenue, Inverness IV2 6BX
inverness@churchofscotland.org.uk | 01463 250355
07753 423333 |

Alves and Burghead (F W) linked with Kinloss and Findhorn (W)

| Dewald Louw BTh MDiv | 2007 | 2021 | The Manse, 4 Manse Road, Kinloss, Forres IV36 3GH
DLouw@churchofscotland.org.uk | 01309 690474
07464 847803 |

Ardersier (H) linked with Petty (F)

Vacant
Interim Moderator: Fiona S. Morrison

The Manse, Ardersier, Inverness IV2 7SX
FMorrison@churchofscotland.org.uk

01667 462224
07710 331746

Cawdor (F H) linked with Croy and Dalcross (F H)

| Robert E. Brookes BD | 2009 | 2016 | Hillswick, Regoul, Geddes, Nairn IV12 5SB
RBrookes@churchofscotland.org.uk | 01667 404686 |

Croy and Dalcross See Cawdor

Culloden: The Barn (F H W)

Vacant
Interim Moderator: David Whillis

admin@barnchurch.org.uk
45 Oakdene Court, Culloden IV2 7XL
DWhillis@churchofscotland.org.uk

01463 798946
01463 795430
01463 232304

Dallas linked with Forres: St Leonard's (F H W) linked with Rafford (F)   stleonardsforres@gmail.com

| Donald K. Prentice BSc BD
DipPsych MSc MLitt | 1989 | 2010 | St Leonard's Manse, Nelson Road, Forres IV36 1DR
DPrentice@churchofscotland.org.uk | 01309 672380 |
| John A. Morrison BSc BA PGCE
(Ordained Local Minister) | | 2013 | 35 Kirkton Place, Elgin IV30 6JR
JMorrison@churchofscotland.org.uk | 01343 550199 |

Daviot and Dunlichity (W) linked with Moy, Dalarossie and Tomatin (W)

Vacant
Interim Moderator: Robert E. Brookes

RBrookes@churchofscotland.org.uk

01667 404686

Dores and Boleskine
Vacant
Interim Moderator: Scott A. McRoberts
SMcRoberts@churchofscotland.org.uk
01463 230308
07535 290092

Dyke and Edinkillie (F W)
Richard G. Moffat BD   1994
Dyke and Edinkillie Manse, Westview, Mundole, Forres IV36 2TA
RMoffat@churchofscotland.org.uk
01309 271321

Forres: St Laurence (F H W)
Vacant   2019
Interim Moderator: Sonia Palmer
office@stlaurencechurchforres.org.uk
12 Mackenzie Drive, Forres IV36 2JP
Sonia.Palmer@churchofscotland.org.uk
01309 672260
07748 700929

Forres: St Leonard's   See Dallas

Inverness: Crown (F H W)
Douglas R. Robertson BSc BD   1991
office@crown-church.co.uk
39 Southside Road, Inverness IV2 4XA
DRRobertson@churchofscotland.org.uk
01463 231140
01463 230537

Inverness: Dalneigh and Bona (GD H W)
Vacant   2020
Interim Moderator: Len Cazaly
9 St Mungo Road, Inverness IV3 5AS
len_cazaly@btinternet.com
01463 232339
01463 794469

Inverness: East (F GD H W)
Vacant
Interim Moderator: Hugh F. Watt
inverneesseastoffice@gmail.com
39 Appin Drive, Inverness IV2 7AL
HWatt@churchofscotland.org.uk
01463 236695
01456 450231

Inverness: Hilton (F W)
Duncan MacPherson LLB DipLP BD   1994
office@hiltonchurch.org.uk
66 Culduthel Mains Crescent, Inverness IV2 6RG
DMacPherson@churchofscotland.org.uk
01463 233310
01463 231417

Inverness: Inshes (H W)
David S. Scott MA BD   1987   2013
48 Redwood Crescent, Milton of Leys, Inverness IV2 6HB
David.Scott@churchofscotland.org.uk
01463 226727
01463 772402

Inverness: Kinmylies (F H W)
Scott Polworth LLB BD   2009   2018
2 Balnafettack Place, Inverness IV3 8TQ
SPolworth@churchofscotland.org.uk
01463 714035
01463 559137

Inverness: Ness Bank (F H T W)
Vacant
Interim Moderator: Ian A. Manson
nessbankchurch@gmail.com — **01463 221812**
15 Ballifeary Road, Inverness IV3 5PJ — 01463 234653
IManson@churchofscotland.org.uk — 01463 783824

Inverness: Old High St Stephen's (T W)
Vacant
Interim Moderator: Scott Polworth
invernesschurch@gmail.com — **07934 285924**
24 Damfield Road, Inverness IV2 3HU — 01463 250802
SPolworth@churchofscotland.org.uk — 01463 559137

Inverness: St Columba's (F H T W)
Scott A. McRoberts BD MTh — 2012
info@stcolumbainverness.org — 01463 832601
25 Moriston Road, Inverness IV2 6HN
SMcRoberts@churchofscotland.org.uk

Inverness: Trinity (F H W)
Vacant
Interim Moderator: Fraser K. Turner
invernesstrinitychurch@yahoo.co.uk — **01463 221490**
60 Kenneth Street, Inverness IV3 5PZ — 01463 234756
fraseratq@yahoo.co.uk — 01463 794004

Kilmorack and Erchless (F W)
Ian A. Manson BA BD — 1989   2016
'Roselynn', Croyard Road, Beauly IV4 7DJ — 01463 783824
IManson@churchofscotland.org.uk

Kiltarlity and Kirkhill (F W)
Andrew (Drew) P. Kuzma DipTheol BA — 2007   2021
Wardlaw Manse, Wardlaw Road, Kirkhill IV5 7NZ — 01463 831132
AKuzma@churchofscotland.org.uk

Kinloss and Findhorn See Alves and Burghead
Moy, Dalarossie and Tomatin See Daviot and Dunlichity

Nairn: Old (H W)
Alison C. Mehigan BD DPS — 2003   2015
secretary.nairnold@btconnect.com — **01667 452382**
15 Chattan Gardens, Nairn IV12 4QP — 01667 453777
AMehigan@churchofscotland.org.uk

Nairn: St Ninian's (H) and Auldearn and Dalmore (F W)
Thomas M. Bryson BD — 1997   2015
The Manse, Auldearn, Nairn IV12 5SX — 01667 451675
TBryson@churchofscotland.org.uk

Petty See Ardersier
Rafford See Dallas

Urquhart and Glenmoriston (F H W)

Name	Ord.	Ind.	Charge/Appointment	Address	Tel
Hugh F. Watt BD DPS DMin	1986	1996		Blairbeg, Drummadrochit, Inverness IV3 6UG HWatt@churchofscotland.org.uk	01456 450231

B. In other appointments

Name			Appointment	Address	Tel
Archer, Morven (Mrs)	2013	2020	Ordained Local Minister: Presbytery Assistant Minister	42 Firthview Drive, Inverness IV3 8QE MArcher@churchofscotland.org.uk	01463 237840
Fraser, Jonathan MA(Div) MTh ThM	2012	2019	Lecturer: Highland Theological College	9 Broom Drive, Inverness IV2 4EG Jonathan.Fraser@uhi.ac.uk	07749 539981
Morrison, Fiona S. BA	2019		Ordained Local Minister	8 Essich Gardens, Inverness IV2 6BW FMorrison@churchofscotland.org.uk	07710 331746
Morrison, Hector BSc BD MTh CertITL	1981	2009	Principal: Highland Theological College	24 Oak Avenue, Inverness IV2 4NX	01463 238561
Robertson, Michael A. BA	2014	2022	Chaplain, Raigmore Hospital, Inverness	Raigmore Hospital, Old Perth Road, Inverness IV2 3UJ Michael.Robertson@churchofscotland.org.uk	07740 984395
Whillis, David (Dr) DipHE	2020		Ordained Local Minister: Presbytery-wide minister to over 60s community	Helen's Lodge, Inshes, Inverness IV2 5BG DWhillis@churchofscotland.org.uk	01463 232304

C. Retaining

Name			Charge	Address	Tel
Andrews, J. Edward MA BD DipCG FSAScot	1985	2005	(Armadale)	Dunnichen, 1B Cameron Road, Nairn IV12 5NS edward.andrews@btinternet.com	01667 459466 07808 720708
Archer, Nicholas D.C. BA BD	1971	1992	(Dores and Boleskine)	3 Ferntower Place, Culloden, Inverness IV2 7TL na.overcome7@gmail.com	01463 793538
Buell, F. Bart BA MDiv	1980	1995	(Urquhart and Glenmoriston)	6 Towerhill Place, Cradlehall, Inverness IV2 5FN bartbuell@talktalk.net	01463 794634
Cleland, Robert	1997	2022	(Ardersier with Petty)	35 High Street, Ardersier, Inverness IV2 7QE	01808 521450
Forbes, Farquhar A.M. MA BD	2016	2022	(Associate, Inverness: Inshes)	The Heights, Inverarnie, Inverness IV2 6XA FForbes@churchofscotland.org.uk	01463 716051
Getliffe, Dot L.J. (Mrs) BA BD DipEd DCS	2006	2021	(Deacon)	136 Ardness Place, Lochardil, Inverness IV2 4QY DGetliffe@churchofscotland.org.uk	
Hunt, Trevor G. BA BD	1986	2011	(Evie with Firth with Rendall)	7 Woodville Court, Culduthel Avenue, Inverness IV2 6BX trevorghunt@gmail.com	01463 250355 07753 423333
MacGregor, Neil I.M. BD	1995	2019	(Strathbogie Drumblade)	1 Abban Place, Inverness IV3 8GZ NMacGregor@churchofscotland.org.uk	07989 902722
McRoberts, T. Douglas BD CPS FRSA	1975	2014	(Malta: St Andrew's Scots Church)	24 Redwood Avenue, Inverness IV2 6HA doug.mcroberts@btinternet.com	01463 772594
Mitchell, Joyce (Mrs) DCS	1994	2010	(Deacon)	Sunnybank, Farr, Inverness IV2 6XG stanleymitchell121@btinternet.com	01808 521285
Morton, Gillian M. (Mrs) MA BD PGCE	1983	1996	(Hospital Chaplain)	16 St Leonard's Road, Forres IV36 1DW gillianmorton@hotmail.co.uk	01309 671719

Ritchie, Bruce BSc BD PhD	1977	2013	(Dingwall: Castle Street)	16 Brinckman Terrace, Westhill, Inverness IV2 5BL brucezomba@hotmail.com	01463 791389
Robertson, Peter BSc BD	1988	1998	(Dallas with Forres: St Leonard's with Rafford)	17 Ferryhill Road, Forres IV36 2GY peterrobertsonforres@talktalk.net	01309 676769
Turner, Fraser K. LTh	1994	2007	(Kiltarlity with Kirkhill)	20 Caulfield Avenue, Inverness IV2 5GA fraseratq@yahoo.co.uk	01463 794004
Walker, Linda A.W. BA CertCS	2008	2022	(Auxiliary Minister, Presbytery of Glasgow)		
Younger, Alastair S. BScEcon ASCC	1969	2008	(Inverness: St Columba High)	33 Duke's View, Slackbuie, Inverness IV2 6BB younger873@btinternet.com	01463 242873

INVERNESS ADDRESSES

Inverness

Crown	Kingsmills Road x Midmills Road
Dalneigh and Bona	St Mary's Avenue
East	Academy Street x Margaret Street
Hilton	Druid Road x Tomatin Road
Inshes	Inshes Retail Park
Kinmylies	Kinmylies Way
Ness Bank	Ness Bank x Castle Road
Old High	Old Edinburgh Road x Southside Road
St Stephen's	Drummond School, Drummond Road
St Columba	
Trinity	Huntly Place x Upper Kessock Street

Nairn

Old	Academy Street x Seabank Road
St Ninian's	High Street x Queen Street

(38) LOCHABER (F W)

Meets at Caol, Fort William, in Kilmallie Church Hall at 6pm, on the first Tuesday of September and December, on the last Tuesday of October and on the fourth Tuesday of March. The June meeting is held at 6pm on the second Tuesday in the church of the incoming Moderator. The Presbytery Annual Conference is held in February.

Clerk: REV STEWART GOUDIE BSc BD — Church of Scotland Manse, Annie's Brae, Mallaig PH41 4RG
lochaber@churchofscotland.org.uk — **01687 462514 / 07957 237757**

Treasurer: MRS CONNIE ANDERSON — faoconnie@gmail.com

Acharacle (F H W) linked with Ardnamurchan (F W)
Vacant
Session Clerk, Acharacle: Ella Gill (Mrs) — ellagill768@gmail.com — 01967 431834
Session Clerk, Ardnamurchan: Bridget Cameron (Mrs) — branault@googlemail.com — 01972 510284

Ardgour and Kingairloch (F H T W) linked with Morvern (F H T W) linked with Strontian (F H T W)
Donald G.B. McCorkindale BD DipMin 1992 2011 The Manse, 2 The Meadows, Strontian, Acharacle PH36 4HZ 01967 402234
DMcCorkindale@churchofscotland.org.uk 07554 176580

Ardnamurchan See Acharacle

Duror (F H W) linked with Glencoe: St Munda's (F H W)
Vacant
Session Clerk, Duror: Janice Cameron (Miss)
Session Clerk, Glencoe: St Munda's: Ella Gill (Mrs)

9 Cameron Brae, Kentallen, Duror PA38 4BF
janiceann271@btinternet.com
ellagill768@gmail.com

01631 740285
01631 740271
01967 431834

Fort Augustus (W) linked with Glengarry (W)
Anthony M. Jones   1994   2018
BD DPS DipTheol CertMin FRSA

The Manse, Fort Augustus PH32 4BH
AJones@churchofscotland.org.uk

01320 366210

Fort William Kilmallie (F H W) linked with Kilmonivaig (F W)
Vacant
Rory N. MacLeod BA BD   1986   2021
(Team Minister)
Session Clerk, FWK: Mabel Wallace (Mrs)
Session Clerk, Kilmonivaig: Gordon Smith

The Manse, The Parade, Fort William PH33 6BA
Kilmallie Manse, Corpach, Fort William PH33 7JS
RNMacLeod@churchofscotland.org.uk
thewallace@talk21.com
gordonsmith934@btinternet.com

01397 702297
01397 772736

01397 703635
01397 712375

Glencoe: St Munda's See Duror
Glengarry See Fort Augustus
Kilmonivaig See Fort William Kilmallie

Kinlochleven (H W) linked with Nether Lochaber (H W)
Malcolm A. Kinnear MA BD PhD   2010

The Manse, Lochaber Road, Kinlochleven PH50 4QW
MKinnear@churchofscotland.org.uk

01855 831227

Morvern See Ardgour
Nether Lochaber See Kinlochleven

North West Lochaber (F H W)
Stewart Goudie BSc BD   2010   2018

Church of Scotland Manse, Annie's Brae, Mallaig PH41 4RG
SGoudie@churchofscotland.org.uk

01687 462514
07957 237757

Strontian See Ardgour

B. In other appointments

Kinnear, Marion (Mrs) BD	2009 2021	Auxiliary Minister : Southern Lochaber Group	The Manse, Lochaber Road, Kinlochleven PH50 4QW Marion.Kinnear@churchofscotland.org.uk	01855 831227 07519 635976

C. Retaining

Anderson, David M. MSc FCOptom	1984 2017	(Ordained Local Minister)	'Mirlos', 1 Dumfries Place, Fort William PH33 6UQ david@mirlos.co.uk	01397 702091
Muirhead, Morag Y. (Mrs)	2013 2022	(Ordained Local Minister)	6 Dumbarton Road, Fort William PH33 6UU MMuirhead@churchofscotland.org.uk	01397 703643
Stoddart, Alexander C. BD	2001 2022	(Duror with Glencoe: St Munda's)	sandystoddart1@outlook.com	
Varwell, Adrian P.J. BA BD PhD	1983 2011	(Fort Augustus with Glengarry)	19 Enrick Crescent, Kilmore, Drumnadrochit, Inverness IV63 6TP adrian.varwell@btinternet.com	01456 459352
Winning, A. Ann MA DipEd BD	1984 2006	(Morvern)	'Westering', 13C Carnoch, Glencoe, Ballachulish PH49 4HQ awinning009@btinternet.com	01855 811929

(39) ROSS (W)

Meets on the first Tuesday of September in the church of the incoming Moderator; and in Dingwall: Castle Street Church on the first Tuesday of October, November, December, February, March and May, and on the last Tuesday of June.

Clerk:	MRS CATH CHAMBERS	184 Kirkside, Alness IV17 0RH ross@churchofscotland.org.uk	01349 882026

Alness

Vacant				
Michael J. Macdonald (Auxiliary Minister)	2004	2014	27 Darroch Brae, Alness IV17 0SD 73 Firhill, Alness IV17 0RT Michael.Macdonald@churchofscotland.org.uk	01349 882238 01349 884268

Avoch (W) linked with Fortrose and Rosemarkie (W)

Warren R. Beattie BSc BD MSc PhD	1990	2019	5 Ness Way, Fortrose IV10 8SS WBeattie@churchofscotland.org.uk	01381 620111

Contin (H W) linked with Fodderty and Strathpeffer (H W)

Ronald Gall BSc BD	1985	2021	The Manse, Contin, Strathpeffer IV14 9ES RGall@churchofscotland.org.uk	01997 421028

Cromarty (W) linked with Resolis and Urquhart (W)
Terrance T. Burns BA MA — 2004 — 2017
The Manse, Culbokie, Dingwall IV7 8JN
TBurns@churchofscotland.org.uk
01349 877452

Dingwall: Castle Street (F H W)
Drausio P. Goncalves — 1993 — 2019
16 Achany Road, Dingwall IV15 9JB
DGoncalves@churchofscotland.org.uk
01349 866792

Dingwall: St Clement's (H W)
Bruce Dempsey BD — 1997 — 2014
8 Castlehill Road, Dingwall IV15 9PB
BDempsey@churchofscotland.org.uk
01349 292055

Fearn Abbey and Nigg (W) linked with Tarbat (W)
Vacant
Session Clerk, Fearn Abbey and Nigg: James Maxwell
Session Clerk, Tarbat: Douglas Gordon
jimmymaxwell62@gmail.com
d.gordon123@btinternet.com
01862 871883

Ferintosh (F W)
Stephen Macdonald BD MTh — 2008 — 2018
Ferintosh Manse, Leanaig Road, Conon Bridge,
Dingwall IV7 8BE
SMacdonald@churchofscotland.org.uk
01349 861275
07570 804193

Fodderty and Strathpeffer See Contin
Fortrose and Rosemarkie See Avoch

Invergordon (W)
Brian Macleod BA MDiv — 2021 — 2022
invergordonparishchurch@live.co.uk
The Manse, Cromlet Drive, Invergordon IV18 0BA
BMacleod@churchofscotland.org.uk

Killearnan (F H W) linked with Knockbain (F H W)
Susan Cord — 2016
14 First Field Avenue, North Kessock, Inverness IV1 3JB
SCord@churchofscotland.org.uk
01463 731930

Kilmuir and Logie Easter (F)
Alistair J. Drummond BSc BD ThM — 1986 — 2020
The Manse, Delny, Invergordon IV18 0NW
ADrummond@churchofscotland.org.uk
01862 842280

Kiltearn (H)

Donald A. MacSween BD	1991	1998	The Manse, Swordale Road, Evanton, Dingwall IV16 9UZ DMacSween@churchofscotland.org.uk	01349 830472

Knockbain See Killearnan

Lochbroom and Ullapool (F GD W)

Heidi J. Hercus BA		2018	**info@ullapoolkirk.co.uk** The Manse, 11 Royal Park, Mill Street, Ullapool IV26 2XT HHercus@churchofscotland.org.uk	**01854 612360** 01854 613146

Resolis and Urquhart See Cromarty

Rosskeen (F W)

Philip Gunn BSc BA		2020	Rosskeen Manse, 15 Perrins Road, Alness IV17 0SX PGunn@churchofscotland.org.uk	01349 884252
Carol Rattenbury BA (Ordained Local Minister)		2017	Balloan Farm House, Alcaig, Conon Bridge, Dingwall IV7 8HU CRattenbury@churchofscotland.org.uk	01349 877323

Tain (F W)

Andrew P. Fothergill BA	2012	2017	14 Kingsway Avenue, Tain IV19 1NJ AFothergill@churchofscotland.org.uk	01862 892296

Tarbat See Fearn Abbey and Nigg

Urray and Kilchrist (F W)

Monika R.W. Redman BA BD	2003	2021	**urraychurch@gmail.com** Woodville, Ord Road, Muir of Ord IV6 7XL MRedman@churchofscotland.org.uk	01463 871625

B. In other appointments

Bissett, James	2016	2021	Ordained Local Minister, on loan to Inverness: Old High Stephen's	JBissett@churchofscotland.org.uk	
McGowan, Andrew T. B. (Prof) BD STM PhD	1979	2019	Director, Rutherford Centre for Reformed Theology	18 Davis Drive, Alness IV17 0ZD AMcGowan@churchofscotland.org.uk	01340 880762
Munro, Irene BA		2019	Ordained Local Minister: Presbytery Chaplain to vulnerable groups in residential care	1 Wyvis Crescent, Conon Bridge, Dingwall IV7 8BZ IMunro@churchofscotland.org.uk	01349 865752

C. Retaining

Name	Ord.	Ind.	Charge	Address	Tel.
Bell, Graeme K. BA BD CertMS	1983	2017	(Glasgow: Carnwadric)	4 Munro Terrace, Rosemarkie, Fortrose IV10 8UR graemekbell@googlemail.com	07591 180101
Dupar, Kenneth W. BA BD PhD	1965	1993	(Christ's College, Aberdeen)	The Old Manse, The Causeway, Cromarty IV11 8XJ	01381 600428
Horne, Douglas A. BD	1977	2009	(Tain)	151 Holm Farm Road, Culduthel, Inverness IV2 6BF douglas.horne@talktalk.net	01463 712677
Lincoln, John BA BD MPhil	1986	2014	(Balquhidder with Killin and Ardeonaig)	59 Obsdale Park, Alness IV17 0TR johnlincoln@minister.com	01349 882791
MacLennan, Alasdair J. BD DipCE	1979	2001	(Resolis and Urquhart)	Airdale, Seaforth Road, Muir of Ord IV6 7TA	01463 870704
MacLeod, Kenneth Donald BD CPS	1989	2019	(Invergordon)	10 Scott Crescent, Greenfaulds, Cumbernauld, Glasgow G67 4LG kd-macleod@tiscali.co.uk	07808 416767
McDonald, Alan D. LLB BD MTh DLitt DD	1979	2016	(Cameron with St Andrews: St Leonard's)	7 Duke Street, Cromarty IV11 8YH alan.d.mcdonald@talk21.com	01381 600954
McLeod, John MA	1958	1993	(Resolis and Urquhart)	'Benview', 19 Balvaird, Muir of Ord IV6 7RQ sheilaandjohn@yahoo.co.uk	01463 871286
Munro, James A. BD DMS	1979	2013	(Port Glasgow: Hamilton Bardrainney)	1 Wyvis Crescent, Conon Bridge, Dingwall IV7 8BZ james781munro@btinternet.com	01349 865752
Scott, David V. BTh	1994	2014	(Fearn Abbey and Nigg with Tarbat)	29 Sunnyside, Culloden Moor, Inverness IV2 5ES	01463 795802
Smith, Russel BD	1994	2013	(Dingwall: St Clement's)	1 School Road, Conon Bridge, Dingwall IV7 8AE russanntwo@btinternet.com	01349 861011
Warwick, Ivan C. TD BD DipPS DipEcum	1980	2014	(Paisley: St James')	Ardcruidh Croft, Heights of Dochcarty, Dingwall IV15 9UF L70rev@btinternet.com	01349 861464 07787 535083

(40) SUTHERLAND (F)

Meets at Lairg on the first Tuesday of March, May, September, November and December, and on the first Tuesday of June at the Moderator's church.

Clerk:	REV. IAN W. McCREE BD	Tigh Ardachu, Mosshill, Brora KW9 6NG sutherland@churchofscotland.org.uk	01408 621185

Altnaharra and Farr (F W) linked with Melness and Tongue (F H)

Name	Ord.	Ind.	Address	Tel.
Beverly W. Cushman BA MDiv MA PhD	1977	2017	The Manse, Bettyhill, Thurso KW14 7SS BCushman@churchofscotland.org.uk	01641 521208

Assynt and Stoer (F W)

Name	Ord.	Ind.	Address	Tel.
Iain A. MacLeod BA	2012	2020	The Manse, Canisp Road, Lochinver, Lairg IV27 4LH IMacleod@churchofscotland.org.uk	01571 844342 07795 014889

Clyne (H W) linked with Kildonan and Loth Helmsdale (F H W)   info@brorachurchofscotland.org
Lorna H. Tunstall MA MDiv   2020   40 Golf Road, Brora KW9 6QS
    LTunstall@churchofscotland.org.uk   01408 536005

Creich (W) linked with Kincardine Croick and Edderton (W) linked with Rosehall (W)   info@kyleofsutherlandchurches.org
Vacant   The Manse, Ardgay IV24 3BG   01863 766285
Interim Moderator: John B. Sterrett   JSterrett@churchofscotland.org.uk   Tel/Fax 01408 633295

Dornoch Cathedral (F H W)
Vacant   1 Allan Gardens, Dornoch IV25 3PD   01862 810296
Interim Moderator: Lorna H. Tunstall   LTunstall@churchofscotland.org.uk   01408 536005

Durness and Kinlochbervie (F W)
Andrea M. Boyes (Mrs) RMN BA(Theol)   2013   2017   Manse Road, Kinlochbervie, Lairg IV27 4RG   01971 521287
    ABoyes@churchofscotland.org.uk

Eddrachillis
Vacant   Church of Scotland Manse, Scourie, Lairg IV27 4TQ   01971 502431
Interim Moderator: John B. Sterrett   JSterrett@churchofscotland.org.uk   01408 633295

Golspie (W)   pray@standrewgolspie.org
John B. Sterrett BA BD PhD   2007   The Manse, Fountain Road, Golspie KW10 6TH   Tel/Fax 01408 633295
    JSterrett@churchofscotland.org.uk

Kildonan and Loth Helmsdale See Clyne
Kincardine Croick and Edderton See Creich

Lairg (F H W) linked with Rogart (H W)
Vacant
Hilary M. Gardner (Miss)   2010   2018   Cayman Lodge, Kincardine Hill, Ardgay IV24 3DJ   01863 766107
   (Auxiliary Minister)   HGardner@churchofscotland.org.uk   01408 621569
Interim Moderator: Sydney L. Barnett   sydneylb43@gmail.com

Melness and Tongue See Altnaharra and Farr
Rogart See Lairg
Rosehall See Creich

B. In other appointments

Stobo, Mary J. (Mrs) BA	2013	Ordained Local Minister; Community Healthcare Chaplain	Druim-an-Sgairnich, Ardgay IV24 3BG MStobo@churchofscotland.org.uk	01863 766868

C. Retaining

Chambers, S. John OBE BSc	1972 2009	(Inverness: Ness Bank)	Bannlagan Lodge, 4 Earls Cross Gardens, Dornoch IV25 3NR chambersdornoch@btinternet.com	01862 811520
Goskirk, J. Leslie LTh	1968 2010	(Lairg with Rogart)	Rathvilly, Lairgmuir, Lairg IV27 4ED leslie_goskirk@sky.com	01549 402569
MacPherson, John BSc BD	1993 2021	(Eddrachillis)	23 Drumfield Road, Inverness IV2 4XH	01463 230038
McCree, Ian W. BD	1971 2011	(Clyne with Kildonan and Loth Helmsdale)	Tigh Ardachu, Mosshill, Brora KW9 6NG ianmccree@live.co.uk	01408 621185
McKay, Margaret M. (Mrs) MA BD MTh	1991 2003	(Auchaber United with Auchterless)	2 Mackenzie Gardens, Dornoch IV25 3RU megsie38@gmail.com	01862 811859

(41) CAITHNESS (W)

Meets alternately at Wick and Thurso on the first Tuesday of February, March, May, September, November and December, and the third Tuesday of June.

Clerk:	**REV. HEATHER STEWART**	**Burnthill, Thrumster, Wick KW1 5TR** **caithness@churchofscotland.org.uk**	**01955 651717**

Halkirk Westerdale linked with Watten

Vacant

Interim Moderator: Sheila Cormack (Mrs)		Wester Cottage, Dunnet, by Thurso KW14 8XP	01847 851274

Latheron (W)

Vacant — parish-of-latheron@btconnect.com

Heather Stewart (Mrs) (Ordained Local Minister)	2013	2017	Central Manse, Main Street, Lybster KW3 6BN Burnthill, Thrumster, Wick KW1 5TR Heather.Stewart@churchofscotland.org.uk	01593 721706 01955 651717

North Coast (F W)

David J.B. Macartney BA	2017	Church of Scotland Manse, Reay, Thurso KW14 7RE DMacartney@churchofscotland.org.uk	01847 811734

Pentland

Janet A. Easton-Berry BA BA	2016	2021	The Manse, Canisbay, Wick KW1 4YH JEaston-Berry@churchofscotland.org.uk	01847 895186

Thurso: St Peter's and St Andrew's (F H W)

David S.M. Malcolm BD	2011	2014	11 Castle Gardens, Barrock Street, Thurso KW14 7GZ David.Malcolm@churchofscotland.org.uk	01847 811734

Thurso: West (H W)

Vacant
Interim Moderator: David J.B. Macartney   DMacartney@churchofscotland.org.uk

Watten See Halkirk Westerdale

Wick: Pulteneytown (H) and Thrumster (F W)

Andrew A. Barrie BD	2013	2017	The Manse, Coronation Street, Wick KW1 5LS Andrew.Barrie@churchofscotland.org.uk	01955 606192 07791 663439

Wick: St Fergus (F W)

Vacant
Interim Moderator: David S.M. Malcolm   Mansefield, Miller Avenue, Wick KW1 4DF   01955 602167
David.Malcolm@churchofscotland.org.uk   01847 895186

C. Retaining

Duncan, Esme (Miss)	2013 2017	(Ordained Local Minister)	Avalon, Upper Warse, Canisbay, Wick KW1 4YD EDuncan@churchofscotland.org.uk	01955 611455
Nugent, John BD	1999 2020	(Wick: St Fergus)		07511 503946
Rennie, Lyall	2014 2019	(Ordained Local Minister)	Ruachmarra, Lower Warse, Canisbay, Wick KW1 4YB LRennie@churchofscotland.org.uk	01955 611756

CAITHNESS Communion Sundays

Halkirk Westerdale	Apr, Jul, Oct
Latheron	Apr, Jul, Sep, Nov
North Coast	Mar, Easter, Jun, Sep, Dec
Pentland:	
Canisbay	1st Jun, Nov
Dunnet	last May, Nov
Keiss	1st May, 3rd Nov
Olrig	last May, Nov
Thurso: St Peter's and St Andrew's	Mar, Jun, Sep, Dec
West	4th Mar, Jun, Nov
Watten	1st Jul, Dec
Wick: Pulteneytown and Thrumster	1st Mar, Jun, Sep, Dec
St Fergus	Apr, Oct

(42) LOCHCARRON – SKYE

Meets in conference annually and in Kyle as required and, where possible, online.

Clerk:	REV. RODERICK A.R. MacLEOD MA MBA BD DMin		The Manse, 6 Upper Breakish, Isle of Skye IV42 8PY lochcarronskye@churchofscotland.org.uk	01471 822416

Applecross, Lochcarron and Torridon (F GD)
Guardianship of the Presbytery
Interim Moderator: Stuart J. Smith

The Manse, Colonel's Road, Lochcarron, Strathcarron IV54 8YG
Stuart.Smith@churchofscotland.org.uk

01520 722783
01445 712645

Bracadale and Duirinish (GD)
Guardianship of the Presbytery
Interim Moderator: Alisdair T. MacLeod-Mair

AMacLeod-Mair@churchofscotland.org.uk

Gairloch and Dundonnell (F W)
Stuart J. Smith BEng BD MTh   1994   2016

Church of Scotland Manse, The Glebe, Gairloch IV21 2BT
Stuart.Smith@churchofscotland.org.uk

01445 712645

Glenelg, Kintail and Lochalsh (F W)
Frederick W. Vincent BA BD MPhil   1990   2021

The Manse, Glebe Road, Inverinate, Kyle of Lochalsh IV40 8HE
FVincent@churchofscotland.org.uk

07971 507952

Kilmuir and Stenscholl (F GD)
Vacant
Interim Moderator: John H. Lamont

1 Totescore, Kilmuir, Isle of Skye IV51 9YN
jhlamont@btinternet.com

01470 542297
01445 731888
07714 720753

Portree (GD W)
Sandor Fazakas BD MTh   1977   2007

Viewfield Road, Portree, Isle of Skye IV51 9ES
SFazakas@churchofscotland.org.uk

01478 611868

Snizort (GD H)
Vacant

The Manse, Kensaleyre, Snizort, Portree, Isle of Skye IV51 9XE

01470 532453

Strath and Sleat (F GD W)

Roderick A.R. MacLeod MA MBA BD DMin	1994	2015	The Manse, 6 Upper Breakish, Isle of Skye IV42 8PY RMacLeod@churchofscotland.org.uk	01471 822416

C. Retaining

MacLeod-Mair, Alisdair T. MEd DipTheol	2001	2022	(Snizort)	AMacLeod-Mair@churchofscotland.org.uk	
Martin, George M. MA BD	1987	2005	(Applecross, Lochcarron and Torridon)	8(1) Buckingham Terrace, Edinburgh EH4 3AA	0131 343 3937
Morrison, Derek	1995	2013	(Gairloch and Dundonnell)	2 Cliffton Place, Poolewe, Achnasheen IV22 2JU derekmorrison1@aol.com	01445 781333
Stutter, Anita Drs (MA)	2008	2020	(Applecross, Lochcarron and Torridon)	Aros, Slumbay, Lochcarron IV54 8YQ AStutter@churchofscotland.org.uk	01520 722139

(43) UIST

Meets on the first Tuesday of February, March, September and November in Lochmaddy; and on the third Tuesday of June in Leverburgh.

Clerk:	**REV. GAVIN J. ELLIOTT MA BD**	**5a Aird, Isle of Benbecula HS7 5LT** **uist@churchofscotland.org.uk**	**01870 602726**

Benbecula (F GD H) linked with Carinish (F GD H W) info@carinish-church.org.uk

Vacant				
Isabel Macdonald (Ordained Local Minister)	2011		'Cleat Afe Ora', 18 Carinish, Isle of North Uist HS6 5HN Ishie.Macdonald@churchofscotland.org.uk	01876 580367

Berneray and Lochmaddy (GD H) linked with Kilmuir and Paible (GD)

Alen J.R. McCulloch MA BD	1990	2017	Church of Scotland Manse, Paible, Isle of North Uist HS6 5HD AMcCulloch@churchofscotland.org.uk	01876 510310

Carinish See Benbecula
Kilmuir and Paible See Berneray and Lochmaddy

Manish-Scarista (GD H)

Vacant Session Clerk: Paul Alldred	Church of Scotland Manse, Scarista, Isle of Harris HS3 3HX paul.alldred@outlook.com	01859 550200 01859 520494

Tarbert (F GD H T W)

Ian Murdo M. MacDonald DPA BD	2001	2015	The Manse, Manse Road, Tarbert, Isle of Harris HS3 3DF Ian.MacDonald@churchofscotland.org.uk	01859 502231

C. Retaining

Elliott, Gavin J. MA BD	1976	2015	(Ministries Council)	5a Aird, Isle of Benbecula HS7 5LT gavkondwani@gmail.com	01870 602726
MacIver, Norman BD	1976	2011	(Tarbert)	57 Boswell Road, Wester Inshes, Inverness IV2 3EW norman@n-cmaciver.freeserve.co.uk	01463 236586
Morrison, Donald John	2001	2019	(Auxiliary Minister)	22 Kyles, Tarbert, Isle of Harris HS3 3BS DMorrison@churchofscotland.org.uk	01859 502341
Petrie, Jackie G.	1989	2011	(South Uist)	7B Malaclete, Isle of North Uist HS6 5BX jackiegpetrie@yahoo.com	01876 560804
Smith, John M.	1956	1992	(Lochmaddy)	Hamersay, Clachan, Locheport, Lochmaddy, Isle of North Uist HS6 5HD	01876 580332
Smith, Murdo MA BD	1988	2011	(Manish-Scarista)	Aisgeir, 15A Upper Shader, Isle of Lewis HS3 3MX	

UIST Communion Sundays

Benbecula	2nd Mar, Sep	Carinish	4th Mar, Aug
Bernera and Lochmaddy	4th Jun, last Oct	Kilmuir and Paible	1st Jun, 3rd Nov
		Manish-Scarista	3rd Apr, 1st Oct
		Tarbert	2nd Mar, 3rd Sep

(44) LEWIS

Meets at Stornoway, in St Columba's Church Hall, on the second Tuesday of March, June, September and November and at other times as required.

Clerk:	MR JOHN CUNNINGHAM	1 Raven's Lane, Stornoway, Isle of Lewis HS2 0EG **lewis@churchofscotland.org.uk**	**01851 709977** **07789 878840**

Barvas (F GD H W)

Dougie Wolf BA(Theol)	2017	Church of Scotland Manse, Lower Barvas, Isle of Lewis HS2 0QY DWolf@churchofscotland.org.uk	01851 840218

Carloway (F GD H)

Duncan M. Macaskill BA BD MPhil DMin	1992	2019	Church of Scotland Manse, Knock, Carloway, Isle of Lewis HS2 9AU DMacaskill@churchofscotland.org.uk	**01851 643211** 01851 643255

Cross Ness (F GD H T W)
John M. Nicolson BD DipMin — 1997   2019

crossnesschurch@gmail.com
Church of Scotland Manse, Cross Skigersta Road, Ness,
Isle of Lewis HS2 0TB
JNicolson@churchofscotland.org.uk
07899 235355

Kinloch (F GD H)
Iain M. Campbell BD — 2004   2008

Laxay, Lochs, Isle of Lewis HS2 9LA
ICampbell@churchofscotland.org.uk
01851 830218

Knock (GD H)
Guardianship of the Presbytery
Interim Moderator: Iain M. Campbell

ICampbell@churchofscotland.org.uk
01851 830218

Lochs-Crossbost (GD H)
Guardianship of the Presbytery
Interim Moderator: Donald Macleod

donaldmacleod25@btinternet.com
01851 704516

Lochs-in-Bernera (F GD H) linked with Uig (F GD H)
Hugh Maurice Stewart DPA BD — 2008

Church of Scotland Manse, Uigen, Miavaig, Isle of Lewis HS2 9HX
HStewart@churchofscotland.org.uk
01851 672388

Stornoway: High (F GD H W)
Gordon M. Macleod BA — 2017   2019

Woodside, Laxdale Lane, Stornoway, Isle of Lewis HS1 0DR
GMacleod@churchofscotland.org.uk
07717 065739

Stornoway: Martin's Memorial (F H W)
Thomas MacNeil MA BD — 2002   2006

enquiries@martinsmemorial.org.uk
Martin's Memorial Church, Matheson Road, Stornoway,
Isle of Lewis HS1 2LR
TMacNeil@churchofscotland.org.uk
01851 700820
01851 704238

Stornoway: St Columba (F GD H)
William J. Heenan BA MTh — 2012

St Columba's Manse, Lewis Street, Stornoway, Isle of Lewis HS1 2JF
WHeenan@churchofscotland.org.uk
01851 701546
01851 705933
07837 770589

Uig See Lochs-in-Bernera

B. In other appointments
Shadakshari, T.K. BTh BD MTh — 1998 2006

Head of Spiritual Care, Western Isles
Health Board

23D Benside, Newmarket, Stornoway, Isle of Lewis HS2 0DZ
tk.shadakshari@nhs.scot

Home   01851 701727
Office   01851 704704
            07403 697138

C. Retaining

Amed, Paul LTh DPS	1992	2015	(Barvas)	6 Scotland Street, Stornoway, Isle of Lewis HS1 2Q paul.amed@outlook.com	01851 706450
Jamieson, Esther M.M. (Mrs) BD	1984	2002	(Glasgow: Penilee St Andrew)	1 Redburn, Bayview, Stornoway, Isle of Lewis HS1 2UU iandejamieson@btinternet.com	01851 704789
Johnstone, Ben MA BD DMin	1973	2013	(Strath and Sleat)	Loch Alainn, 5 Breaclete, Great Bernera, Isle of Lewis HS2 9LT benonbernera@gmail.com	01851 612445
Maclean, Donald A. DCS	1988	1990	(Deacon)	8 Upper Barvas, Isle of Lewis HS2 0QX	01851 840454
Macleod, William	1957	2006	(Uig)	54 Lower Barvas, Isle of Lewis HS2 0QY	01851 840217

LEWIS Communion Sundays

Barvas	3rd Mar, Sep	Knock	3rd Apr, 1st Nov	Stornoway: Martin's Memorial	3rd Feb, last Aug
Carloway	1st Mar, last Sep	Lochs-Crossbost	4th Mar, Sep		1st Dec, Easter
Cross Ness	2nd Mar, Oct	Lochs-in-Bernera	1st Apr, 2nd Sep	Stornoway: St Columba	3rd Feb, last Aug
Kinloch	3rd Mar, 2nd Jun, 2nd Sep	Stornoway: High	3rd Feb, last Aug	Uig	3rd Jun, 4th Oct

(45) ORKNEY (F W)

Meets at Kirkwall on the first Wednesday of November 2022. On 1 January 2023 it will unite with the Presbyteries of Aberdeen and Shetland, Buchan, Gordon, Kincardine and Deeside and Moray to form the Presbytery of the North East and the Northern Isles. That new Presbytery will meet on-line on 10 January 2023 and thereafter as decided.

Clerk: MRS FREYA HENDERSON BEd Sweenalay, Rendall, Orkney KW17 2EX **01856 761598**
orkney@churchofscotland.org.uk
Depute Clerk: MS MARGARET A.B. SUTHERLAND LLB BA 13 Cursiter Crescent, Kirkwall, Orkney KW15 1XN **01856 873747**
mabs2@tiscali.co.uk

Birsay, Harray and Sandwick (F W)
Vacant
Interim Moderator: Linda J. Broadley The Manse, North Biggings Road, Dounby, Orkney KW17 2HZ 01856 771599
lindabroadley@btinternet.com 01856 771599

East Mainland (W)

Christopher Wallace BD DipMin	1988	2022	**eastmainlandchurch@gmail.com** The Manse, Holm, Orkney KW17 2SB Christopher.Wallace@churchofscotland.org.uk	01856 781797

Eday
Vacant
Session Clerk: Johan Robertson   essonquoy@btinternet.com   01857 622251

Evie and Rendall (F) linked with Firth (F H) linked with Rousay
Vacant   **Firth: 01856 761117**
Session Clerk, Evie and Rendall: Eileen Fraser   eileenocot@hotmail.co.uk   01856 761409
Session Clerk, Firth: Janis Dickey   rbdickey@hotmail.com   01856 761396
Interim Moderator: Linda J. Broadley   lindabroadley@btinternet.com   01856 771599

Firth See Evie and Rendall

Flotta (W) linked with Orphir and Stenness (H W)
Vacant
Martin W.M. Prentice BVMS DipCS   2013   2015   Stenness Manse, Stenness, Stromness, Orkney KW16 3HH   01856 851139
(Ordained Local Minister)   Cott of Howe, Cairston, Stromness, Orkney KW16 3JU   07795 817213
Session Clerk, Flotta: Isobel Smith   MPrentice@churchofscotland.org.uk   01856 701219
Session Clerk, Hoy and Walls: 01856 701363
Anderson Sutherland

Hoy and Walls (F)
Vacant
Interim Moderator: Marjory A. MacLean   MMacLean@churchofscotland.org.uk   01856 831648

Kirkwall: East (F H W) linked with Shapinsay (F W)
Julia M. Meason MTh MA MTh   2013   East Church Manse, Thoms Street, Kirkwall, Orkney KW15 1PF   01856 874789
JMeason@churchofscotland.org.uk

Kirkwall: St Magnus Cathedral (F H T W)
G. Fraser H. Macnaughton MA BD DipCPC   1982   2002   Cathedral Manse, Berstane Road, Kirkwall, Orkney KW15 1NA   01856 873312
FMacnaughton@churchofscotland.org.uk
June Freeth BA MA (Ordained Local Minister)   2015   Cumlaquoy, Orkney KW17 2ND   01856 721449
JFreeth@churchofscotland.org.uk

North Ronaldsay
Guardianship of the Presbytery
Interim Moderator: Kenneth Meason   kennymeason@yahoo.co.uk   01856 874789

Orphir and Stenness See Flotta

Tel/Fax

Papa Westray (W) linked with Westray (W)
Iain D. MacDonald BD DipChEd — 1993
The Manse, Hilldavale, Westray, Orkney KW17 2DW
IMacDonald@churchofscotland.org.uk
01857 677357
07710 443780

Rousay See Evie and Rendall

Sanday
Vacant
Interim Moderator: June Freeth
JFreeth@churchofscotland.org.uk
01856 721449

Shapinsay See Kirkwall: East

South Ronaldsay and Burray (F)
Marjory A. MacLean LLB BD PhD — 1991 2020
St Margaret's Manse, Church Road, St Margaret's Hope, Orkney KW17 2SR
MMacLean@churchofscotland.org.uk
01856 831648

Stromness (F H)
Vacant
Interim Moderator: June Freeth
5 Manse Lane, Stromness, Orkney KW16 3AP
JFreeth@churchofscotland.org.uk
01856 850203
01856 721449

Stronsay: Moncur Memorial (W)
David I.W. Locke MA MSc BD — 2000 2021
The Manse, Wardhill, Stronsay, Orkney KW17 2AG
DLocke@churchofscotland.org.uk
01857 616284

Westray See Papa Westray

C. Retaining

Butterfield, John A. BA BD MPhil DipTCP DipCC	1990	2022	(Stromness)	Bring Deeps, Buxa Road, Orphir, Orkney KW17 2RE	01856 811707
Graham, Jennifer D. (Mrs) BA MDiv PhD	2000	2011	(Eday with Stronsay: Moncur Memorial)	Lodge, Stronsay, Orkney KW17 2AN jdgraham67@gmail.com	01857 616487
Johnston, Wilma A. MTheol MTh	2006	2020	(East Mainland)	Notland, Denwick Road, Deerness KW17 2QL rev.wilmajohnston@gmail.com	01856 741318 07706 091968
Tait, Alexander	1967	1995	(Glasgow: St Enoch's Hogganfield)	Ingermas, Evie, Orkney KW17 2PH	01856 751477
Wishart, James BD	1986	2009	(Deer)	Upper Westshore, Burray, Orkney KW17 2TE jwishart06@btinternet.com	01856 731672

(47) ENGLAND (F)

Meets at London, in Crown Court Church, on the second Tuesday of February, and at St Columba's, Pont Street, on the second Tuesday of June and the second Saturday of October.

Clerk: REV. ALISTAIR CUMMING MSc CCS FInstLM FLPI | 50 Burgh Heath Road, Epsom KT17 4LX england@churchofscotland.org.uk | **07534 943986**

Corby: St Andrew's (F H W)
Vacant
Interim Moderator: Paul Middleton (Prof.) | The Manse, 43 Hempland Close, Corby, Northants NN18 8LR p.middleton@chester.ac.uk | 01244 378766

Corby: St Ninian's (F H W)
Vacant
Interim Moderator: William McLaren | The Manse, 46 Glyndebourne Gardens, Corby, Northants NN18 0PZ WMcLaren@churchofscotland.org.uk | **01536 265245** / 01536 669478 / 020 7584 2321

Guernsey: St Andrew's in the Grange (F H W)
Justin W. Taylor BTh MTh MTh | 2018 2022 | The Manse, Le Villocq, Castel, Guernsey GY5 7SB JTaylor@churchofscotland.org.uk | 01481 257345

Jersey: St Columba's (F H T W)
Vacant
Interim Moderator: Cameron H. Langlands | 18 Claremont Avenue, St Saviour, Jersey JE2 7SF Cameron.Langlands@slam.nhs.uk | 01534 730659 / 07971 169791

London: Crown Court (F H T W)
Scott M. Rennie MA BD STM FRSA | 1999 2022 | 53 Sidmouth Street, London WC1H 8JX SRennie@churchofscotland.org.uk | **020 7836 5643** / 020 7278 5022

London: St Columba's (F H T W) linked with Newcastle: St Andrew's (H T W)   office@stcolumbas.org.uk | **St Columba's: 020 7584 2321**
C. Angus MacLeod MA BD | 1996 2012 | 29 Hollywood Road, Chelsea, London SW10 9HT Angus.MacLeod@churchofscotland.org.uk | Office 020 7584 2321

William McLaren MA BD (Associate Minister) | 1990 2021 | St Columba's, Pont Street, London SW1X 0BD WMcLaren@churchofscotland.org.uk | Office 020 7584 2321

Newcastle: St Andrew's See London: St Columba's

B. In other appointments

Name			Appointment	Address	Contact
Binks, Mike	2007	2015	Auxiliary Minister – Churches Together in Corby	Hollybank, 10 Kingsbrook, Corby NN18 9HY MBinks@churchofscotland.org.uk	07590 507917
Cumming, Alistair MSc CCS FInstLM FLPI	2010	2013	Presbytery Clerk: Auxiliary Minister	50 Burgh Heath Road, Epsom KT17 4LX ACumming@churchofscotland.org.uk	07534 943986 07534 943986 02870 353869
Francis, James MBE BD PhD	2002	2009	Army Chaplain	37 Millburn Road, Coleraine BT52 1QT JFrancis@churchofscotland.org.uk	
Langlands, Cameron H. BD MTh ThM PhD MInstLM	1995	2012	Head of Spiritual and Pastoral Care, South London and Maudsley NHS Foundation Trust	Maudsley Hospital, Denmark Road, London SE5 8AZ Cameron.Langlands@slam.nhs.uk	020 3228 2815 07971 169791
Lovett, Mairi F. BSc BA DipPS MTh	2005	2013	Hospital Chaplain	Royal Brompton Hospital, Sydney Street, London SW3 6NP m.lovett@rbht.nhs.uk	020 7351 8060
MacKay, Stewart A. BA	2009	2020	Chaplain: Army	2 LANCS, Elizabeth Barracks, Pirbright, Woking GU24 0DT	
MacKenzie, Hector M.	2008		Chaplain: Army	5 Regiment Royal Artillery, Marne Barracks, Catterick Garrison DL10 7NP Hector.Mackenzie657@mod.gov.uk	
Mather, James BA DipArch MA MBA	2010		Auxiliary Minister: University Chaplain	24 Ellison Road, Barnes, London SW13 0AD JMather@churchofscotland.org.uk	Home 020 8876 6540 Work 020 7361 1670 Mbl 07836 715655
McLay, Neil BA BD MTh	2006	2012	Army Chaplain	2 (Training) Regiment Army Air Corps, Middle Wallop, Stockbridge SO20 8DY	
McMahon, John K.S. MA BD	1998	2012	Head of Spiritual and Pastoral Care, West London NHS Trust	Broadmoor Hospital, Crowthorne, Berkshire RG45 7EG john.mcmahonrev@westlondon.nhs.uk	01344 754098
Middleton, Paul (Prof) BMus BD ThM PhD FRSA FHEA	2000	2018	New Testament and Early Christianity, University of Chester	10 Raymond Street, Chester CH1 4EL p.middleton@chester.ac.uk	01244 378766
Thom, David J. BD DipMin	1999	2015	Army Chaplain	Army Foundation College, Uniacke Barracks, Penny Pot Lane, Killinghall, Harrogate HG3 2SE revdjt@gmail.com	
Walker, R. Forbes BSc BD ThM	1987	2013	School Chaplain, Emmanuel School, London	15 Selhurst New Court, Selhurst New Road, London SE25 5PT revrfw@gmail.com	
Ward, Michael J. BSc BD PhD MA PGCE	1983	2009	Training and Development Officer: Presbyterian Church of Wales	Apt 6, Bryn Hedd, Conwy Road, Penmaen-mawr, Gwynedd LL34 6BS revmw@btopenworld.com	07765 599816
Wright, Allan BVMS MRCVS	2021		Ordained Local Minister: Pioneer Minister to Veterinary Community in NE England	27 Prospect Terrace, Burnopfield, Newcastle NE16 6EL AWright@churchofscotland.org.uk	07984 541587

C. Retaining

Name			Appointment	Address	Contact
Anderson, Andrew F. MA BD	1981	2011	(Edinburgh: Greenside)	58 Reliance Way, Oxford OX4 2FG andrew.relianceway@gmail.com	01865 778397
Cairns, W. Alexander BD	1978	2006	(Corby: St Andrew's)	Kirkton House, Kirkton of Craig, Montrose DD10 9TB sandy.cairns@btinternet.com	07808 588045

Cameron, R. Neil   1976 2005   (Chaplain: Army)   neilandminacameron@yahoo.co.uk
Lunn, Dorothy I.M.   2002 2016   (Auxiliary Minister)   14 Bellerby Drive, Ouston, Co.Durham DH2 1TW   0191 492 0647
                                                                                            dorothylunn@hotmail.com

Macfarlane, Peter T. BA LTh   1970 1994   (Chaplain: Army)   4 rue de Rives, 37160 Abilly, France
Mills, Peter W. CB BD DD CPD   1984 2018   (East Neuk Trinity with St Monans)   16 Pearce Drive, Lawley, Telford TF3 5JQ
Ogg, M. Fiona (Mrs) BA BD   2012 2021   (Acharacle with Ardnamurchan)   6a Stamford Road, Essendine, Stamford PE9 4LQ
                                                                                            Fiona.Ogg@churchofscotland.org.uk
Wallace, Donald S.   1950 1990   (Chaplain: Royal Caledonian Schools)   7 Delfield Close, Watford, Herts WD1 3BL   01923 223289

ENGLAND – Church Addresses

Corby: St Andrew's   Occupation Road   **Jersey:**   Midvale Road, St Helier   **Newcastle:**   Sandyford Road
Corby: St Ninian's   Beanfield Avenue   **London:** Crown Court   Crown Court WC2
Guernsey: The Grange, St Peter Port   **London:** St Columba's   Pont Street SW1

(48) PRESBYTERY OF INTERNATIONAL CHARGES (F W)

Meets over the weekend of the second Sunday of March and October, hosted by congregations in mainland Europe.

Clerk: REV. DEREK G. LAWSON LLB BD   16 Rue de la Madeleine, 22210 La Chèze, France   **0033 6 09 57 66 71**
                                               international@churchofscotland.org.uk
                                               clerk@internationalpresbytery.net
                                               www.internationalpresbytery.net

Amsterdam: English Reformed Church (F T W)   info@erc.amsterdam
Vacant   Jan Willem Brouwersstraat 9, NL-1071 LH Amsterdam,   0031 20 672 2288
                                                    The Netherlands
Interim Moderator: Gillean P. MacLean   GMacLean@churchofscotland.org.uk   0041 21 323 98 28
                                                  Church address: Begijnhof 48, 1012WV Amsterdam

Bermuda: Christ Church, Warwick (F H W)   christchurch@logic.bm   **001 441 236 1882**
Alistair G. Bennett BSc BD   1978 2016   1 Steele's Drive, Paget PG03, Bermuda   001 441 236 0400
                                                  ABennett@churchofscotland.org.uk
                                                  Church address: Christ Church, Middle Road, Warwick, Warwick, Bermuda
                                                  Mailing address: PO Box WK 130, Warwick WK BX, Bermuda

Bochum: English-Speaking Christian Congregation (Associated congregation) (W)
Anja Nicole Stuckenberger
Ev. Stadtakademie Bochum, Westring 26a, 44787 Bochum
(Joint Pastors, not ministers of the CofS)
astuckenberger@ekvw.de
Emmanuel Mote-Ndasah
Church address: Pauluskircke, Grabenstrasse 9, 44787 Bochum
0049 234 962904 ext 661
0049 175 2518757

Brussels: St Andrew's (F H W)
Eric W. Foggitt MA BSc BD   1991   2020
secretary@churchofscotland.be
23 Square des Nations, B-1000 Brussels, Belgium
EFoggitt@churchofscotland.org.uk
Church address: Chaussée de Vieurgat 181, 1050 Brussels
0032 2 649 02 19
0032 2 672 40 56

Budapest: St Columba's (F W)
Aaron C. Stevens BA MDiv MACE   2004   2006
Locsei ut 14, 4e, 21a, 1147, Budapest, Hungary
AStevens@churchofscotland.org.uk
Szabina Sztojka *(Associate Minister,*   2021
sztojka.szabina@reformatus.hu
Reformed Church of Hungary)
Church address: Vörösmarty utca 51, 1064 Budapest
0036 30 567 6356
0036 70 615 5394

Colombo, Sri Lanka: St Andrew's Scots Kirk (F W)
Vacant
churchofficer@scotskirk.lk
73 Galle Road, Colpetty, Colombo 3, Sri Lanka
minister@standrewsscotskirk.org
Church address: 73 Galle Road, Colpetty, Colombo
Interim Moderator: Eric W. Foggitt
EFoggitt@churchofscotland.org.uk
0094 112 323 765
0094 112 386 774

0032 474 57 10 84

Geneva (F W)
Laurence H. Twaddle MA BD MTh   1977   2017
6 chemin Taverney, 1218 Geneva, Switzerland
LTwaddle@churchofscotland.org.uk
Church address: Auditoire de Calvin, 1 Place de la Taconnerie, Geneva
0041 22 788 08 31
0041 22 788 08 31

Gibraltar: St Andrew's (W)
Ewen D. MacLean BA BD DipBI   1995   2009
Flat 201 Sunrise, Royal Ocean Plaza, Ocean Village,
  Gibraltar GX11 1AA
Ewen.Maclean@churchofscotland.org.uk
Church address: Governor's Parade, Gibraltar
00350 200 77040

Lausanne: The Scots Kirk (F H W)
Gillean P. MacLean (Ms) BA BD   1994   2019
26 Avenue de Rumine, CH-1005 Lausanne, Switzerland
PGDipCouns CertPS
GMacLean@churchofscotland.org.uk
Church address: 26 Avenue de Rumine, Lausanne
0041 21 323 98 28

Lisbon: St Andrew's (F W)
Guardianship of the Presbytery

lisbonstandrewschurch@gmail.com
Rua Coelho da Rocha, N°75 - 1°
Campa de Ourique, 1350-073 Lisbon, Portugal
cofslx@netcabo.pt
Church address: Rua da Arriaga, Lisbon
00351 213 951 165

Session Clerk: Nina O'Donnell
sessionclerklisbon@gmail.com
00351 21 483 8750

Malta: St Andrew's Scots Church (H W)
Beata (Betsi) Thane   MA BD   2020

2 Casa Cappella, Triq L-Infanterija, KKP 1270 Ħal-Kirkop, Malta
minister@saintandrewsmalta.com
Church address: 210 Old Bakery Street, Valletta, Malta
00356 993 53246

Paris: The Scots Kirk (F W)
Vacant
Interim Moderator: Lawrence H. Twaddle

10 Rue Thimonnier, F-75009 Paris, France
LTwaddle@churchofscotland.org.uk
Church address: 17 Rue Bayard, 75009 Paris
0033 1 48 78 47 94
0041 22 788 08 31

Rome: St Andrew's (F W)
Vacant

Interim Moderator: Aaron C. Stevens

scotskirkrome@gmail.com
Via XX Settembre 7, 00187 Rome, Italy
Church address: Via XX Settembre 7, 00187 Rome
AStevens@churchofscotland.org.uk

Tel   0039 06 482 7627
      0039 06 487 4370
Fax   0036 70 615 5394

Rotterdam: Scots International Church (F W)   1997   2020
Graham Austin   BD

info@scotsintchurch.com
Schiedamse Vest 121, 3012BH Rotterdam, The Netherlands
GAustin@churchofscotland.org.uk
Church address: Schiedamsesingel 2, Rotterdam, The Netherlands

0031 10 412 4779
0031 10 412 5709

0031 10 412 5709

Trinidad: Greyfriars St Ann's, Port of Spain (W) linked with Arouca and Sangre Grande
Vacant
Interim Moderator: Alistair G. Bennett

50 Frederick Street, Port of Spain, Trinidad
ABennett@churchofscotland.org.uk

001 868 623 6684
001 441 236 0400

B. In other appointments
Born, Irene M.E.   BA DipCS   2008   Ordained Local Minister-Worship and Prayer Promoter
Bergpolderstraat 53A, NL-3038 KB   Rotterdam, The Netherlands
ibsalem@xs4all.nl
0031 10 265 1703

Evans-Boiten, Joanne H.G.   BD   2004 2018   Retreat Centre Director
Colomba le Roc, 510 Chemin du Faurat, Belmontet, 46800 Montcuq en Quercy, France
Joanne.evansboiten@gmail.com
0033 5 65 22 13 11

McGeoch, Graham G.   MA BD MTh PhD   2009 2017   Theology Lecturer
Faculdade Unida de Vitoria, R.Eng. Fabio Ruschi, 161 Bento Ferreira, Vitoria ES 29050-670, Brazil
graham@fuv.edu.br

| Ross, Matthew Z. LLB BD MTh FSAScot | 1998 | 2018 | Programme Executive for Diakonia and Capacity Building, World Council of Churches | World Council of Churches, Route de Ferney 150, Case Postale 2100, CH-1211 Geneva 2, Switzerland Matthew.Ross@wcc-coe.org | work 0041 22 791 6322 mob 0041 79 155 8638 |

C. Retaining

Brown, James M. MA BD	1982	2022	(Bochum: English-Speaking Christian Congregation)	Verkehrsstrasse 37, 44809 Bochum, Germany JBrown@churchofscotland.org.uk	0049 234 133363
Herbold Ross, Kristina M.	2008	2018	(Work Place Chaplain)	kristinaherboldross@gmail.com	
Homewood, I. Maxwell MSc BD	1997	2003	(Edinburgh: Drylaw)	Ander Fließwiese 26, D-14052 Berlin, Germany maxhomewood@me.com	0049 151 2758 6921
Lawson, Derek G. LLB BD	1998	2020	(Rotterdam: Scots International Church)	16 Rue de la Madeleine, 22210 La Chèze, France DLawson@churchofscotland.org.uk	0036 09 57 66 71
Pitkeathly, Thomas C. MA CA BD	1984	2004	(Brussels: St Andrew's)	77 St Thomas Road, Lytham St. Anne's FY8 1JP tpitkeathly@yahoo.co.uk	01253 789634
Reamonn, Paraic BA BD	1982	2018	(Jerusalem: St Andrew's)	395B Route de Mandement, 1281 Ruissin, Switzerland PReamonn@churchofscotland.org.uk	0041 22 776 4834
Stone, Lance B. BD MTh PhD	1978	2021	(Amsterdam: English Reformed Church)	Flat C Branksome Court, 2 Sudbourne Road, London SW2 5AQ	07443 321184

(49) JERUSALEM

Clerk:	**JOANNA OAKLEY-LEVSTEIN BA**		**St Andrew's, Galilee, PO Box 104, Tiberias 14100, Israel j.oak.lev@gmail.com**	**00972 50 5842517**

Jerusalem and Tiberias: St Andrew's (F W)

D. Stewart Gillan BSc MDiv PhD	1985	2022	**jerusalem@churchofscotland.org.uk** St Andrew's Scots Memorial Church, 1 David Remez Street, PO Box 8619, Jerusalem 91086, Israel SGillan@churchofscotland.org.uk	00972 2 673 2401
Muriel B. Pearson (Ms) MA BD PGCE (Associate Minister)	2004	2021	**tiberias@churchofscotland.org.uk** St Andrew's, Galilee, 1 Gdud Barak Street, PO Box 104, Tiberias 14100, Israel MPearson@churchofscotland.org.uk	+447951 888860

SECTION 6

Additional Lists of Personnel

LIST A – ORDAINED LOCAL MINISTERS

Those in active service. Where only one date is given it is the year of ordination and appointment. Contact details are under the relevant Presbytery in Section 5.

NAME	ORD	APP	APPOINTMENT	PRESBYTERY
Anderson, Fiona DipHE	2020	2020	Strathaven: Trinity	17 Forth Valley and Clydesdale
Archer, Morven (Mrs)	2013	2020		37 Inverness
Bellis, Pamela A. BA DipTheol	2014	—	Presbytery Assistant Minister	7 South West
Bissett, James	2016		Contin linked with Fodderty and Strathpeffer	39 Ross
Bom, Irene M.E. BA DipCS	2008		Worship Resourcing	48 International Charges
Breingan, Mhairi M. BSc CertCS	2011	2019	Paisley: St George's	14 Clyde
Brodie, Catherine J. MA BA MPhil PGCE	2017		Dundee: Fintry	29 Dundee
Crouch, Simon A. MCIPD CertCS	2019		Cushnie and Tough; and Upper Donside	33 Gordon
Don, Andrew MBA	2006	—	Newton	3 Lothian
Duncanson, Mary B. (Ms) BTh	2013	2013	Cromdale and Advie with Dulnain Bridge with Grantown-on-Spey	36 Abernethy
Forsythe, Ruth (Mrs) DipRS MCS	2017	2017	Glasgow: Knightswood Anniesland Trinity	16 Glasgow
Freeth, June BA MA	2015	2018	Kirkwall: St Magnus Cathedral	45 Orkney
Fyfe, Lorna K. BD	2020	—		17 Forth Valley and Clydesdale
Galbraith, David	2021		Maryculter Trinity	32 Kincardine and Deeside
Gourlay, Heather	2021		Supporting rural ministry in Angus	30 Angus
Gray, Ian	2013		Montrose: Old and St Andrew's	30 Angus
Grieve, Leslie E.T. BSc BA	2014	2017	Glasgow: Colston Wellpark	16 Glasgow
Hacking, Philip R.	2021	2022	Head of Spiritual Care and Bereavement, NHS Lothian	17 Forth Valley and Clydesdale
Haggarty, Kay O.N. BEd	2021		Edinburgh: Gracemount with Edinburgh: Liberton	1 Edinburgh and West Lothian
Hardman Moore, Susan (Prof.) MA MAR PhD FRHistS	2013		New College, University of Edinburgh	1 Edinburgh and West Lothian
Harrison, Frederick CertCT	2013	—		3 Lothian
Henderson, Derek R. MA DipTCP DipCS	2017		Abercorn linked with Pardovan, Kingscavil and Winchburgh	1 Edinburgh and West Lothian
Hogg, James	2018	—		7 South West
Hunt, David MSc PhD CertHE	2020	—	Alloway	7 South West
Hunt, Roland BSc PhD CertEd	2016		Glasgow: Carmyle linked with Glasgow: Mount Vernon	16 Glasgow
Johnston, June E. BSc MEd BD	2013		Bilston linked with Roslin	3 Lothian
Kirkland, Nikki J. BSc	2021	2020	Edinburgh: St Nicholas' Sighthill	1 Edinburgh and West Lothian
Lennox-Trewren, Norman D. CertCS	2018		Mearns Coastal	32 Kincardine and Deeside

Name	Ordained	Appointment	Presbytery
Macdonald, Ishabel	2011	Benbecula linked with Carinish	43 Uist
MacDonald, Monica J. (Mrs)	2014	Slamannan	17 Forth Valley and Clydesdale
MacKellar, Janet K. BSc ProfCertMgmt FCMI	2019	Kilmun, Strone and Ardentinny: The Shore Kirk	19 Argyll
MacPherson, Alexander J. MA BSc FRSA	2021	Cowal Kirk	19 Argyll
Mateos, Margaret B.	2018	Dunfermline: St Leonard's	24 Fife
Maxwell, David	2014	—	16 Glasgow
McKenzie, Janet R. (Mrs) BA DipHS CertCS	2016	Edinburgh: Tron Kirk (Gilmerton and Moredun)	1 Edinburgh and West Lothian
McLeod, Tom	2014	Craigie Symington linked with Prestwick: South	7 South West
Michie, Margaret (Mrs)	2013	Loch Leven Parish Grouping	28 Perth
Millar, Ian J. BA	2020	Craigrownie linked with Garelochhead linked with Rosneath: St Modan's	14 Clyde
Mitchell, Valerie A. MA FSA	2019	Presbytery-wide	33 Gordon
Morrison, Fiona S. BA	2019	—	37 Inverness
Morrison, John A. BSc BA PGCE	2013	Dallas linked with Forres: St Leonard's linked with Rafford	37 Inverness
Munro, Alastair RN BSc	2022	Dunblane: Cathedral	23 Stirling
Munro, Irene BA	2019	Presbytery Chaplain to vulnerable groups in residential care	39 Ross
Murphy, Jim	2014	—	17 Forth Valley and Clydesdale
Nicol, Robert D. MA	2013	Fortingall, Glenlyon, Kenmore and Lawers	27 Dunkeld and Meigle
Palmer, Sonia RGN	2017	Elgin: St Giles' and St Columba's South	35 Moray
Porteous, Brian W. BSc DipRM DipCS CertCounsS	2018	Kirkcaldy: Templehall and Torbain United	24 Fife
Prentice, Martin W.M. BVMS DipCS	2013	Flotta linked with Orphir and Stenness	45 Orkney
Quilter, Alison I. DipCS	2018	Polbeth Harwood linked with West Kirk of Calder	1 Edinburgh and West Lothian
Rattenbury, Carol BA	2017	Rosskeen	39 Ross
Sarle, Andrew BSc BD	2013	Falkirk: Bainsford	17 Forth Valley and Clydesdale
Somevi, Joseph K. BSc MSc PhD MRICS MRTPI MIEMA CertCRS	2015	Aberdeen: St Nicholas Kincorth, South of; and Aberdeen: Torry St Fittick's	31 Aberdeen and Shetland
Stanley, Lesley MA PhD FBTS	2021	Balfron with Fintry	23 Stirling
Steele, Grace M.F. MA BTh	2014	Presbytery-wide	27 Dunkeld and Meigle
Stevenson, Beverley	2020	—	17 Forth Valley and Clydesdale
Stevenson, Stuart CertCE	2011	Latheron	14 Clyde
Stewart, Heather (Mrs)	2017	—	41 Caithness
Stewart, William	2016	Presbytery-wide	34 Buchan
Stobo, Mary J. (Mrs) BA	2013	Community Healthcare Chaplain	40 Sutherland
Stott, Anne M.	2019	Presbytery Pioneer Worker, Bertha Park	28 Perth
Strachan, Pamela D. (Lady) MA (Cantab)	2015	—	4 Melrose and Peebles
Strachan, Willie D. DipYCW MBA CertCS	2013	Presbytery-wide	29 Dundee
Sturrock, Roger D. (Prof.) BD MD FCRP	2014	Glasgow: Kelvinside Hillhead and Glasgow: Wellington	16 Glasgow
Thomson, Mary Ellen (Mrs)	2014	Presbytery Chaplain to Care Homes	36 Abernethy

	ORD	RET		
Thorburn, Susan (Mrs) MTh	2014	2019	Mission Development Worker, Presbytery of Fife	28 Perth
Thorne, Joan I. BA TQFE CertCS	2019		Dyce	31 Aberdeen and Shetland
Tweedie, Fiona J. BSc PhD	2011	2014	Statistician, Church Offices	1 Edinburgh and West Lothian
Wallace, Mhairi (Mrs)	2013	2017	Kirkmichael, Tinwald and Torthorwald	7 South West
Watson, Michael D. CertCS	2013	2019	Traprain	3 Lothian
Watt, Kim CertThS	2015		Presbytery-wide	7 South West
Welsh, Rita M. BA PhD	2017		Edinburgh: Holy Trinity	1 Edinburgh and West Lothian
Whillis, David (Dr) DipHE	2020		Presbytery-wide minister to over 60s community	37 Inverness
White, Anne W. BA CQSW DipHE	2018		Falkirk: Grahamston United	17 Forth Valley and Clydesdale
Wright, Allan BVMS MRCVS	2021		Pioneer Minister to Veterinary Community in NE England	47 England

ORDAINED LOCAL MINISTERS (Retaining or Inactive)

Those who are retired and registered under the Registration of Ministries Act (Act 2, 2017, as amended) as 'R' (Retaining) or 'I' (Inactive). A few may be still registered as 'O' (eligible for an appointment) but are not in appointments. Only those 'Inactive' who have given consent under the GDPR to publication of their details are included. Contact details are under the relevant Presbytery in Section 5.

NAME	ORD	RET	PRESBYTERY
Allardice, Michael MA MPhil DipTheol FHEA	2014	2020	24 Fife
Anderson, David M. MSc FCOptom	1984	2017	38 Lochaber
Brown, Kathryn I. (Mrs)	2014	2019	17 Forth Valley and Clydesdale
Crossan, William	2014	2019	1 Edinburgh and West Lothian
Dee, Oonagh	2016	2019	7 South West
Dempster, Eric T. MBA	2013	2021	7 South West
Duncan, Esme (Miss)	2013	2017	41 Caithness
Edwards, Dougal BTh	2015	2017	30 Angus
Finnie, Bill H. BA DipSW CertCRS	2012	2022	16 Glasgow
Fulcher, Christine P. BEd CertCS	2013	2022	19 Argyll
Geddes, Elizabeth (Mrs)	2016	2021	14 Clyde
Kiehlmann, Peter BA (Dr)	2013	2018	47 England (not a member of Presbytery) PKiehlmann@churchofscotland.org.uk
Mack, Lynne (Mrs)	2015	2019	23 Stirling
Mathers, Alexena (Sandra)	2013	2018	17 Forth Valley and Clydesdale
McAllister, Anne C. (Mrs) BSc DipEd CCS	2013	2015	7 South West
Muirhead, Morag Y. (Mrs)	2014	2022	38 Lochaber
Nutter, Margaret A.E. BA BD MFPh	2014	2021	14 Clyde
Rennie, Lyall	2013	2019	41 Caithness
Robertson, Ishbel A.R. MA BD	2018	2018	14 Clyde

LIST B – AUXILIARY MINISTERS

Those in active service. Contact details are under the relevant Presbytery in Section 5.

NAME	ORD	APP	APPOINTMENT	PRESBYTERY
Binks, Mike	2007	2015	Churches Together in Corby	47 England
Buck, Maxine SRN ONC CertMgtS	2007	2015	Presbytery-wide	17 Forth Valley and Clydesdale
Campbell, Gordon A. MA BD CDipAF DipHSM CMgr MCMI MIHM AssocCIPD AFRIN ARSGS FRGS FSAScot	2001	2004	An Honorary Chaplain, University of Dundee	29 Dundee
Cumming, Alistair MSc CCS FInstLM FLPI	2010	2013	Presbytery Clerk, England	47 England
Gardner, Hilary M. (Miss)	2010	2018	Lairg linked with Rogart	40 Sutherland
Kinnear, Marion (Mrs) BD	2009	2021	Southern Lochaber Group	38 Lochaber
Macdonald, Michael J.	2004	2014	Alness	39 Ross
Mack, Elizabeth A. (Miss) DipPE	1994	2018	Lochend and New Abbey	7 South West
Mather, James BA DipArch MA MBA	2010		University Chaplain	47 England
Riddell, Thomas S. BSc CEng FIChemE	1993	1994	Linlithgow: St Michael's	1 Edinburgh and West Lothian
Shearer, Anne F. BA DipEd CertCS	2010	2018	Alva	23 Stirling
Wandrum, David C.	1993	2017	Carriden	17 Forth Valley and Clydesdale
Wilkie, Robert F. CertCS	2011	2012	Perth: Craigie and Moncrieffe	28 Perth

AUXILIARY MINISTERS (Retaining or Inactive)

Those who are registered under the Registration of Ministries Act (Act 2, 2017, as amended) as 'R' (Retaining) or 'I' (Inactive). A few may be still registered as 'O' (eligible for an appointment) but are not in appointments. Only those 'Inactive' who have given consent under the GDPR to publication of their details are included. Contact details are under the relevant Presbytery in Section 5.

NAME	ORD	RET	PRESBYTERY
Attenburrow, A. Anne BSc MB ChB	2006	2018	35 Moray
Birch, James PgDip FRSA FIOC	2001	2007	16 Glasgow
Brown, Elizabeth (Mrs) JP RGN	1996	2007	28 Perth
Cameron, Ann J. (Mrs) CertCS DCE TEFL	2005	2019	14 Clyde
Cloggie, June (Mrs)	1997	2006	23 Stirling

NAME	ORD	APP	
Craggs, Sheila A. (Mrs)	2001	2016	33 Gordon
Griffiths, Ruth I. (Mrs)	2004	2020	19 Argyll
Harrison, Cameron BSc MEd	2006	2010	24 Fife
Howie, Marion L.K. (Mrs) MA ARCS	1992	2015	7 South West
Jackson, Nancy M. CerThRS CertChS	2009	2015	7 South West
Kay, Elizabeth (Miss) DipYCS	1993	2007	29 Dundee
Kemp, Tina MA	2005	2021	14 Clyde
Landale, William S.	2005	2016	5 Duns
Lunn, Dorothy I. M.	2002	2016	47 England
MacDonald, Kenneth D. BA MA	2001	2006	16 Glasgow
MacFadyen, Anne M. (Mrs) BSc BD FSAScot	1995	2003	16 Glasgow
Mailer, Colin M.	1996	2005	17 Forth Valley and Clydesdale (not member of Presbytery) 25 Saltcoats Drive, Grangemouth FK3 9JP colinmailer@blueyonder.co.uk 01324 712401
Manson, Eileen (Mrs) DipCE	1994	2021	14 Clyde
McAlpine, John BSc	1988	2004	17 Forth Valley and Clydesdale (not member of Presbytery) Braeside, 201 Bonkle Road, Newmains, Wishaw ML2 9AA jonedmcalpine@aol.com 01698 384610
Moore, Douglas T.	2003	2019	7 South West
Morrison, Donald John	2001	2019	43 Uist
Paterson, Andrew E. JP	1994	2020	24 Fife
Paterson, Maureen (Mrs) BSc	1992	2010	24 Fife
Phillippo, Michael MTh BSc BVetMed MRCVS	2003	2011	31 Aberdeen and Shetland
Pot, Joost BSc	1992	2004	48 International Charges (not member of Presbytery) joostpot@gmail.com
Robson, Brenda PhD	2005	2019	1 Edinburgh and West Lothian (not a member of Presbytery) 22 Ratho Park Road, Ratho, Newbridge EH28 8NY BRobson@churchofscotland.org.uk 0131 281 9511
Shaw, Catherine A.M. MA	1998	2005	7 South West
Walker, Linda A.W. BA CertCS	2008	2022	37 Inverness
Zambonini, James LIADip	1997	2015	17 Forth Valley and Clydesdale

LIST C – THE DIACONATE

Those in active service. Contact details are under the relevant Presbytery in Section 5.

Prior to the General Assembly of 2002, Deacons were commissioned. In 2002 existing Deacons were ordained, as have been those subsequently.

NAME	ORD	APP	APPOINTMENT	PRESBYTERY
Beck, Isobel BD DCS	2014	2016	Kilwinning: Abbey	12 Ardrossan
Blair, Fiona (Miss) DCS	1994	2015	Beith	12 Ardrossan

NAME	COM/ORD	RET		PRESBYTERY
Brydson, Angela (Mrs) DCS	2015	2021	Community Outreach Worker, Southern Ministry Cluster	17 Forth Valley and Clydesdale
Cathcart, John Paul (Mr) DCS	2000	2017	Glasgow: Castlemilk	16 Glasgow
Corrie, Margaret (Miss) DCS	1989	2013	Armadale	1 Edinburgh and West Lothian
Crocker, Liz (Mrs) DipComEd DCS	1985	2015	Edinburgh: Tron Kirk (Gilmerton and Moredun)	1 Edinburgh and West Lothian
Cuthbertson, Valerie (Miss) DipTMus DCS	2003		Cumbernauld: Old	16 Glasgow
Evans, Mark (Mr) BSc MSc DCS	1988	2006	Head of Spiritual Care and Bereavement Lead, NHS Fife	1 Edinburgh and West Lothian
Gargrave, Mary S. (Mrs) DCS	1989	2002	Glasgow: Carnwadric	16 Glasgow
Hamilton, James (Mr) DCS	1997	2000	Glasgow: Maryhill	16 Glasgow
Hamilton, Karen M. (Mrs) DCS	1995	2014	Glasgow: Cambuslang	16 Glasgow
Herbert, Claire BD DCS	2019		Chaplain, Lodging House Mission, Glasgow	16 Glasgow
Love, Joanna R. (Ms) BSc DCS	1992	2009	Iona Community: Wild Goose Resource Group	16 Glasgow
McIntosh, Kay (Mrs) DCS	1990	2018	Edinburgh: Mayfield Salisbury	1 Edinburgh and West Lothian
McPheat, Elspeth (Miss) DCS	1985	2001	CrossReach: Manager, St Margaret's House, Polmont	1 Edinburgh and West Lothian
Pennykid, Gordon J. BD DCS	2015	2018	Chaplain, HM Prison Edinburgh	1 Edinburgh and West Lothian
Robertson, Pauline (Mrs) BA CertTheol BD DCS	2003	2016	Port Chaplain, Sailors' Society: Leith and Forth Estuary	1 Edinburgh and West Lothian
Scott, Pamela (Mrs) BD DCS	2017		Lochgelly and Benarty: St Serf's	24 Fife
Thomson, Jacqueline (Mrs) MTh DCS	2004	2008	Buckhaven and Wemyss	24 Fife
Wallace, Catherine (Mrs) PgDipC DCS	1987	2021	Clinical Manager, The Harbour Counselling Service, Perth	28 Perth
Wright, Lynda (Miss) BEd DCS	1979	2016	Community Chaplaincy Listening Co-ordinator, NHS Fife	24 Fife

THE DIACONATE (Registered as Retaining or Inactive)

Those who are retired and registered under the Registration of Ministries Act (Act 2, 2017, as amended) as 'Retaining' or 'Inactive.' A few may still be registered as 'O' (eligible for an appointment') but are not in appointments. Only those 'Inactive' Deacons who have given consent under the GDPR to publication of their details are included. Contact details are under the relevant Presbytery in Section 5.

NAME	COM/ORD	RET	PRESBYTERY
Allan, Jean (Mrs) DCS	1989	2011	29 Dundee
Beaton, Margaret S. (Miss) DCS	1989	2015	16 Glasgow
Bell, Sandra L.N. (Mrs) DCS	2001		39 Ross (not a member of Presbytery) 4 Munro Terrace, Rosemarkie, Fortrose IV10 8UR

Name			Presbytery
Buchanan, Marion (Mrs) MA DCS	1983	2019	3 Lothian (not a member of Presbytery) 40 Links View, Port Seton, Prestonpans EH32 0EZ 01875 814632
Crawford, Morag (Miss) MSc DCS	1977	2021	1 Edinburgh and West Lothian
Dunnett, Linda (Mrs) BA DCS	1976	2016	23 Stirling
Getliffe, Dot L.J. (Mrs) BA BD DipEd DCS	2006	2021	37 Inverness
Gilroy, Lorraine (Mrs) DCS	1988	1994	17 Forth Valley and Clydesdale
Gordon, Margaret (Mrs) DCS	1998	2012	1 Edinburgh and West Lothian
Gray, Christine M. (Mrs) DCS	1969	2003	16 Glasgow (not a member of Presbytery) 11 Woodside Avenue, Thornliebank, Glasgow G46 7HR 0141 571 1008
Gray, Greta (Miss) DCS	1992	2014	14 Clyde
Hughes, Helen (Miss) DCS	1977	2008	16 Glasgow
Johnston, Mary (Miss) DCS	1988	2003	14 Clyde (not a member of Presbytery) 19 Lounsdale Drive, Paisley PA2 9ED 0141 849 1615
King, Margaret MA DCS	2002	2012	35 Moray
Lundie, Ann V. (Miss) DCS	1972	2007	31 Aberdeen and Shetland
Lyall, Ann (Miss) DCS	1980	2022	16 Glasgow
MacDonald, Anne (Miss) BA DCS	1980	2022	16 Glasgow
Mackay, Kenneth D. DCS	1996	2020	27 Dunkeld and Meigle (not a member of Presbytery) 15 Bank Street, Blairgowrie PH10 6DE 01250 369029 07891 203403
MacKinnon, Ronald M. (Mr) DCS	1996	2012	7 South West
Maclean, Donald A. (Mr) DCS	1988	1990	44 Lewis
McCully, M. Isobel (Miss) DCS	1974	1999	14 Clyde (not a member of Presbytery) 10 Broadstone Avenue, Port Glasgow PA14 5BB 01475 742240 mi.mccully@btinternet.com
McLaren, Glenda M. (Ms) DCS	1990	2020	1 Edinburgh and West Lothian
McLellan, Margaret DCS	1986	2018	16 Glasgow
McNaughton, Janette (Miss) DCS	1982	2007	16 Glasgow (not a member of Presbytery) 4 Dunellan Avenue, Moodiesburn, Glasgow G69 0GB 01236 870180
Merrilees, Ann (Miss) DCS	1994	2006	1 Edinburgh and West Lothian (not a member of Presbytery) 7/1 Slaeside, Balerno EH14 7HL 0131 449 3325 amerrilees@gmail.com
Miller, Elsie M. (Miss) DCS	1974	2001	16 Glasgow
Mitchell, Joyce (Mrs) DCS	1994	2010	37 Inverness
Mulligan, Anne MA DCS	1974	2013	1 Edinburgh and West Lothian
Munro, Patricia M. BSc DCS	1986	2016	28 Perth
Nicholson, David (Mr) DCS	1994	2020	16 Glasgow
Nicol, Joyce (Mrs) BA DCS	1974	2006	14 Clyde (not a member of Presbytery) 93 Brisbane Street, Greenock PA16 8NY joycenicol@hotmail.co.uk 01475 723235 07957 642709
Ogilvie, Colin (Mr) BA DCS	1998	2015	17 Forth Valley and Clydesdale
Philip, Elizabeth A. C. (Mrs) MA BA PGCSE DCS	2007	2018	28 Perth
Porter, Jean T. (Mrs) BD DCS	2006	2022	23 Stirling
Rennie, Agnes M. (Miss) DCS	1974	2012	1 Edinburgh and West Lothian
Rose, Lewis (Mr) DCS	1993	2010	29 Dundee
Steele, Marilynn J. (Mrs) BD DCS	1999	2012	3 Lothian

Steven, Gordon R. BD DCS	1997	3 Lothian
Teague, Yvonne (Mrs) DCS	1965	1 Edinburgh and West Lothian
Urquhart, Barbara (Mrs) DCS	1986	11 Irvine and Kilmarnock
Wallace, Sheila D. (Mrs) BA BD DCS	2009	27 Dunkeld and Meigle
Wilson, Muriel (Miss) MA BD DCS	1997	7 South West
Wright, Lynda (Miss) BEd DCS	1979	24 Fife

LIST D – MINISTERS NOT IN PRESBYTERIES REGISTERED AS EMPLOYED OR RETAINING

Part 1.: ministers, registered under the Registration of Ministries Act (Act 2, 2017, as amended), who are **in appointments** but not members of a Presbytery.

Part 2.: ministers registered as 'Retaining' and authorised to perform the functions of ministry outwith an appointment covered by Category O (a charge) or Category E (an employed appointment), but not members of a Presbytery.

1. NAME	ORD	APP	APPOINTMENT	ADDRESS	TEL	PRES
Aiken, Ewan R. BA BD	1992	2014	CEO, Edinburgh Cyrenians	159 Restalrig Avenue, Edinburgh EH7 6PI	0131 467 1660	1
Davidson, Mark R. MA BD STM PhD PhD RN	2005	2011	Chaplain: Royal Navy	The Manse, Main Street, Kippen FK8 3DN	01786 871249	14
Drummond, Norman W. (Prof.) CBE MA BD DUniv FRSE	1976	1997	President, Columba 1400	c/o Columba 1400 Ltd., Staffin, Isle of Skye IV51 9JY	01478 611400	42
Hutchison, David S. BSc BD ThM	1991	2015	Chaplain: University of Aberdeen	40 The Lane, Alwoodley, Leeds LS17 7BS d.hutchison@abdn.ac.uk		31
Provan, Iain W. (Prof.) MA BA PhD	1991	1997	Biblical Studies	Regent College, 5800 University Boulevard, Vancouver BC V6T 2E4, Canada	001 604 224 3245	1
Scouler, Michael D. MBE BSc BD	1988	2018	Head of Spiritual Care	NHS Borders, Chaplaincy Centre, Borders General Hospital, Melrose TD6 9BS michael.scouler@borders.scot.nhs.uk	01896 826565	6
Shackleton, Scott J.S. QCVS BA BD PhD	1993	2021	Head of Faith Action Programme	121 George Street, Edinburgh EH2 4YN SShackleton@churchofscotland.org.uk	0131 225 5722	16
Smith, Hilary W. BD DipMin MTh PhD	1999	2016	Tutor in Theology, Vanuatu Spiritual Care Development Minister	Vaughan Park Anglican Retreat Centre, New Zealand oxfordsmith28@yahoo.co.nz	0064 21 0283 5435	35
Storrar, William F. (Prof.) MA BD PhD	1984	2005	Director, Center of Theological Inquiry	50 Stockton Street, Princeton, NJ 08540, USA		1
Strachan, David G. BD DPS FRSA	1978	1988	Producer, Religious Television	24 Kennay Place, Aberdeen AB15 8SG dgstrachan@btinternet.com	01224 324032	31

2. NAME	ORD	DEM	CHARGE/APP	ADDRESS	TEL	PRES
Anderson, David MA BD	1975	1999	(Fordyce)	Rowan Cottage, Aberlour Gardens, Aberlour AB38 9LD maurvid@hotmail.com	01340 871906	35
Anderson, Susan M. (Mrs) BD GRSM ARMCM	1997	2014	(Kilmarnock: St John's Onthank)	32 Murrayfield, Bishopbriggs, Glasgow G64 3DS susanbbriggs32@gmail.com	0141 772 6338	16
Auld, A. Graeme (Prof.) MA BD PhD DLitt FSAScot FRSE	1973	2008	(Principal, New College, University of Edinburgh)	Nether Swanshiel, Hobkirk, Bonchester Bridge, Hawick TD9 8JU a.g.auld@ed.ac.uk	01450 860636	6
Bardgett, Frank D. MA BD PhD	1987	2001	(Department of National Mission)	Tigh an Iasgair, Street of Kincardine, Boat of Garten PH24 3BY iasgair1@icloud.com	01479 831751	36
Black, James S.	1976	1978	(Associate, Paisley: St Ninian's Ferguslie)	7 Breck Terrace, Penicuik EH26 0RJ jsb.black@btopenworld.com	01968 677559	3
Blount, Graham K. LLB BD PhD	1976	2017	(Presbytery Clerk: Glasgow)	28 Alcaig Road, Mosspark, Glasgow G52 1NH Graham.Blount@churchofscotland.org.uk	0141 419 0746	16
Booth, Frederick M. LTh	1970	2005	(Helensburgh: St Columba)	Achnashie Coach House, Clynder, Helensburgh G84 0QD boothef@btinternet.com	01436 831858	14
Bradley, Andrew W. BD	1975	2007	(Paisley: Lylesland)	Flat 1/1, 38 Cairnhill View, Bearsden, Glasgow G61 1RP andrewwbradley@hotmail.com	0141 931 5344	16
Brown, Kathryn I. (Mrs)	2014	2019	(Ordained Local Minister)	1 Callendar Park Walk, Callendar Grange, Falkirk FK1 1TA kaybrown1cpw@talktalk.net	01324 617352	17
Brown, Robert F. MA BD ThM	1971	2008	(Aberdeen: Queen's Cross)	55 Hilton Drive, Aberdeen AB24 4NJ Bjacob546@aol.com	01224 491451	31
Brown, T. John MA BD	1995	2006	(Tullibody: St Serf's)	1 Callendar Park Walk, Callendar Grange, Falkirk FK1 1TA johnbrown1cpw@talktalk.net	01324 617352	17
Buchan, William BD DipTheol	1987	2001	(Kilwinning: Abbey)	9 Leafield Road, Biggar ML12 6AY billbuchan3@btinternet.com	01899 229253	17
Cairns, John B. KCVO LTh LLB LLD DD	1974	2009	(Aberlady with Gullane)	Bell House, Roxburghe Park, Dunbar EH42 1LR johncairns@mail.com	01368 862501	3
Christie, John C. BSc BD CBiol MRSB	1990	2012	(Interim Minister)	10 Cumberland Avenue, Helensburgh G84 8QG JChristie@churchofscotland.org.uk	01436 674078 07711 336392	14
Collard, John K. MA BD	1986	2019	(Interim Minister)	1 Nelson Terrace, East Kilbride G74 2EY JCollard@churchofscotland.org.uk	01355 520093	17
Cowell, Susan G. (Miss) BA BD	1986	1998	(Budapest: St Columba's)	3 Gavel Lane, Regency Gardens, Lanark ML11 9FB	01555 665509	17
Currie, David E.P. BSc BD	1983	2011	(Mission and Discipleship Council)	42 Onslow Gardens, Muswell Hill, London N10 3JX davidepcurrie@gmail.com	01355 248510	17

Name			Role	Address	Phone	No.
Cutler, James S.H. BD CEng MIStructE	1986	2011	(Black Mount with Culter with Libberton and Quothquan)	Grainstore, 11 Cuthill Towers Farm, Milnathort, Kinross KY13 9SE revjimc@outlook.com		17
Dawson, Michael S. BTech BD	1979	2005	(Associate: Edinburgh: Holy Trinity)	9 The Broich, Alva FK12 5NR mikpen.dawson@btinternet.com	01259 769309	23
Donaghy, Leslie G. BD DipMin PGDipPsych PhD FSAScot AVCM	1990	2004	(Dumbarton: St Andrew's)	53 Oak Avenue, East Kilbride G75 9ED les@donaghy.ie	07809 484812	17
Donaldson, George M. MA BD	1984	2015	(Caldercruix and Longriggend)	4 Toul Gardens, Motherwell ML1 2FE g.donaldson505@btinternet.com	01698 239477	17
Douglas, Colin R. MA BD STM	1969	2007	(Livingston Ecumenical)	34 West Pilton Gardens, Edinburgh EH4 4EQ colin.r.douglas@gmail.com	0131 551 3808	1
Drake, Wendy F. (Mrs) BD	1978	2007	(Cockpen and Carrington with Lasswade and Rosewell)	21 William Black Place, South Queensferry EH30 9QR revwdrake@hotmail.co.uk	0131 331 1520	1
Duff, Valerie J. (Miss) DMin	1993	2021	(Glasgow: Shawlands Trinity)	Flat 25, 2 Melrose Avenue, Rutherglen, Glasgow G73 3BU		16
Espie, Howard	2011	2014	(Mission Facilitator/Enabler, Edinburgh: Barclay Viewforth)	1 Sprucebank Avenue, Langbank, Port Glasgow PA14 6YX howardespie.me.com	01475 540391	1
Findlay, Henry J.W. MA BD	1965	2005	(Wishaw: St Mark's)	2 Alba Gardens, Carluke ML8 5US henryfindlay@btinternet.com	01555 759995	17
Gardner, Bruce K. MA BD PhD	1988	2011	(Aberdeen: Bridge of Don Oldmachar)	21 Hopetoun Crescent, Bucksburn, Aberdeen AB21 9QY drbrucekgardner@aol.com	07891 186724	31
Gauld, Beverly G.D.D. MA BD	1972	2009	(Carnwath)	7 Rowan View, Lanark ML11 9FQ	01555 665765	17
Gillies, Janet E. BD	1998	2014	(Tranent)	33 Castle Road, Stirling FK9 5JD jan.gillies@yahoo.com	01786 446222	23
Gordon, Elinor J. (Miss) BD	1988	2015	(Cumbernauld: Kildrum)	6 Balgibbon Drive, Callander FK17 8EU elinorgordon@btinternet.com	01877 331049	23
Grieg, Charles H.M. MA BD	1976	2016	(Dunrossness and St Ninian's incl. Fair Isle with Sandwick, Cunningsburgh and Quarff)	6 Hayhoull Place, Bigton, Shetland ZE2 9GA chm.greig@btinternet.com	01950 422468	31
Groves, Ian B. BD CPS	1989	2016	(Inverurie: West)	28 Parkhill Circle, Dyce, Aberdeen AB21 7FN ian@thegroves.me.uk	01224 774380	31
Hamilton, Helen D. (Miss) BD	1991	2002	(Glasgow: St James' (Pollok))	The Cottage, West Tilbouries, Maryculter, Aberdeen AB12 5GD helenhamilton125@gmail.com	01224 739632	32
Harper, Anne J.M. (Miss) BD STM MTh CertSocPsych	1979	2010	(Chaplain, Glasgow Royal Infirmary)	122 Greenock Road, Bishopton PA7 5AS	01505 862466	16
Haslett, Howard J. BA BD	1972	2010	(Traprain)	26 The Maltings, Haddington EH41 4EF howard.haslett@btinternet.com	01620 481208	3
Hobson, Diane L. (Mrs) BA BD	2002	2017	(Aberdeen: St Mark's)	173B Blatchcombe Road, Paignton, Devon TQ3 2JP diane.hobson@me.com	07850 962007	31

Name			(Charge/Position)	Address	Tel	No.
Hutchison, Alison M. (Mrs) BD DipMin	1988	2013	(Chaplain, Aberdeen General Hopsitals)	Ashfield, Drumoak, Banchory AB31 5AG ahutch@hotmail.co.uk	01330 811309	32
Jessamine, Alistair L. MA BD	1979	2011	(Dunfermline: Abbey)	11 Gallowhill Farm Cottages, Strathaven ML10 6BZ	01357 520934	17
Job, Anne J. BSc BD	1993	2010	(Kirkcaldy: Viewforth with Thornton)	5 Carse View, Airth, Falkirk FK2 8NY aj@ajjob.co.uk	01324 83094	17
Lusk, Alastair S. BD DipPS	1974	2010	(East Kilbride: Moncrieff)	9 MacFie Place, Stewartfield, East Kilbride G74 4TY		17
MacDonald, George BTh	1996	2021	(Bonnybridge: St Helen's)	60 Kennedy Way, Airth, Falkirk FK2 8GG gmd1946@gmail.com	01324 832782	17
MacGregor, Margaret S. (Miss) MA BD DipEd	1985	1994	(Calcutta)	16 Learmonth Court, Edinburgh EH4 1PB	0131 332 1089	1
MacLaine, Marilyn (Mrs) LTh	1995	2009	(Inchinnan)	37 Bankton Brae, Livingston EH54 9LA marilynmaclaine@btinternet.com	01506 400619	1
MacLean, Elspeth J. (Mrs) BVMS BD	2011	2021	(Forth: St Paul's)	17 Mameulah Crescent, Newmachar AB21 0WG revmum55@gmail.com		33
McCracken, Gordon A. BD CertMin	1988	2021	(Presbytery Clerk: Hamilton)	1 Kenilworth Road, Lanark ML11 7BL GMcCracken@churchofscotland.org.uk	07918 600720	17
McCulloch, John BA BA(Theol) PhD	2018	2021	(Jerusalem and Tiberias: St Andrew's)	JMcCulloch@churchofscotland.org.uk		49
McHaffie, Robin D. BD	1979	2016	(Cheviot Churches)	Shepherd's Cottage, Castle Heaton, Cornhill-on-Tweed TD12 4XQ robinmchaffie@btinternet.com	01890 885946	5
McKay, Johnston R. MA BA PhD	1969	2002	(Editor, BBC Scotland, Religious Programmes)	40 Sinton Park, Dunbar EH42 1ZP johnston.mckay@btinternet.com	07938 438391	3
McKean, Alan T. BD CertMin	1982	2018	(Avoch with Fortrose and Rosemarkie)	15 Park Road, Kirn, Dunoon PA23 8JL	01369 700016	39
McLean, Gordon LTh CertMS	1972	1992	(Edinburgh: Currie)	Beinn Dhorain, Kinnettas Square, Strathpeffer IV14 9BD gmaclean@hotmail.co.uk	01997 421380	39
McWilliam, Thomas M. MA BD	1964	2003	(Contin)	Flat 3, 13 Culduthel Road, Inverness IV2 4AG tommcw@tommcwl.plus.com	01463 718981	39
Morrice, Alastair M. MA BD	1968	2008	(International Church of Bishkek, Kyrgyzstan)	5 Brechin Road, Kirriemuir DD8 4BX ambishkek@swissmail.org	01575 574102	30
Morrison, Mary B. (Mrs) MA BD DipEd	1978	2000	(Edinburgh: Stenhouse St Aidan's)	174 Craigcrook Road, Edinburgh EH4 3PP	0131 336 4706	1
Muckart, Graeme W.M. MTh MSc FSAScot	1983	2009	(Kincardine, Croick and Edderton)	Torr Gorm, Davochfin, Dornoch IV25 3RW gw2m.kildale@gmail.com	01862 810428 07737 424565 07762 966393	40
Munro, Flora J. BD DMin	1993	2015	(Portlethen)	87 Gairn Terrace, Aberdeen AB10 6AY floramunro@aol.com		31
Murray, George M. LTh	1995	2011	(Glasgow: St Margaret's Tollcross Park)	6 Mayfield, Lesmahagow ML11 0FH george.murray7@gmail.com	01555 895216	16
Newell, Alison M. (Mrs) BD 1986	1986	2021	(Associate Chaplain, University of Edinburgh)	1A Inverleith Terrace, Edinburgh EH3 5NS alinewell@aol.com	0131 556 3505	1

Name			Position	Address / Email	Tel	No.
Nicholson, Thomas S. BD DPS	1982	2020	(Gordon: St Michael's with Greenlaw with Legerwood with Westruther)	Sandy Hill, St Margaret's Hope, Orkney KW17 2RN TNicholson@churchofscotland.org.uk		45
Niven, William W. LTh	1982	1995	(Alness)	4 Obsdale Park, Alness IV17 0TP	01349 884053	39
Parker, Carol Anne (Mrs) BEd BD	2009	2017	(Alloa: Ludgate)	The Cottages, Dornoch Firth Caravan Park, Meikle Ferry South, Tain IV19 1JX ca.parker76@icloud.com	01862 892292	39
Patterson, Philip W. BMus BD	1999	2020	(Army Chaplain)	33/5 Carnbee Avenue, Edinburgh EH16 6GA PPatterson@churchofscotland.org.uk	0131 664 0673	28
Penman, Iain D. BD DipMS	1977	2008	(Edinburgh: Kaimes Lockhart Memorial)	iainpenmanklm@aol.com	07931 993427	1
Pieterse, Ben BA BTh LTh	1968	2014	(Auchterderran Kinglassie)	15 Bakeoven Close, Seaforth Sound, Simon's Town 7975, South Africa benhp1@gmail.com		24
Pitkeathly, David G. LLB DipLP BD	1996	2021	(The Border Kirk)	11 Butlers Road, Horsham, Sussex RH13 6AJ david.pitkeathly@btinternet.com	07546 064607	47
Reid, A. Gordon BSc BD	1982	2008	(Dunfermline: Gillespie Memorial)	7 Arkleston Crescent, Paisley PA3 4TG reid501@fsmail.com	0141 842 1542 07773 300989	14
Robertson, Blair MA BD ThM	1990	2016	(Head of Chaplaincy and Spiritual Care, Greater Glasgow and Clyde Health Board)	West End Guest House, 282 High Street, Elgin IV30 1AG blair.robertson@tiscali.co.uk	07952 558766	35
Roderick, Maggie R. BA BD FRSA FTSI	2010	2018	(Menstrie)	34 Craiglea, Stirling FK9 5EE MRoderick@churchofscotland.org.uk	01786 478113	23
Saunders, Keith BD MSc CertPS	1983	2015	(Chaplain, Glasgow Western Infirmary)	1/2, 10 Rutherford Drive, Lenzie G66 3US revchap53@hotmail.com	0141 558 4338	16
Shanks, Norman J. MA BD DD	1983	2007	(Glasgow: Govan Old)	1 Marchmont Terrace, Glasgow G12 9LT rufuski@btinternet.com	0141 339 4421	16
Smith, Ronald W. BA BEd BD	1979	2011	(Falkirk: St James')	1F1, 2 Middlefield, Edinburgh EH7 4PF	0131 553 1174	1
Smith, William A. LTh	1972	1978	(Blairdaff with Monymusk)	82 Ashgrove Road West, Aberdeen AB16 5EE bill2us@aol.com	07900 896954 01224 681866	31
Speirs, Archibald BD	1995	2021	(Inverkip with Skelmorlie and Wemyss Bay)	27 Arnochrie Road, Paisley PA2 0LB archiespeirs1@aol.com	01505 815327	14
Spiers, John M. LTh MTh	1972	2004	(Giffnock: Orchardhill)	58 Woodlands Road, Thornliebank, Glasgow G46 7JQ j.spiers@icloud.com	0141 638 0632	16
Stevens, Linda (Mrs) BSc BD PGDipCouns	2006	2022	(West Angus Area Team Minister)	17 North Latch Road, Brechin DD9 6LE		30
Stewart, Charles E. BSc BD MTh PhD	1976	2010	(Chaplain, Royal Hospital School, Holbrook)	105 Sinclair Street, Helensburgh G84 9HY c.e.stewart@btinternet.com	01436 678113	14
Stewart, Fraser M.C. BSc BD	1980	2017	(Kilmuir and Logie Easter)	44 Great Glen Place, Inverness IV3 8FA fraserstewart1955@hotmail.com	01463 832589	37
Stewart, Margaret L. (Mrs) BSc MB ChB BD	1985	1988	(Deputy Leader, Iona Community)	28 Inch Crescent, Bathgate EH48 1EU famstewart@ormail.co.uk	01506 653428	1
Strachan, Ian M. MA BD	1959	1994	(Ashkirk with Selkirk)	'Cardenwell', Glen Drive, Dyce, Aberdeen AB21 7EN	01224 772028	31

NAME	ORD	DEM	CHARGE/APP	ADDRESS	TEL	PRES
Tallach, John M. MA MLitt DipPhil	1970	2010	(Cromarty)	29 Firthview Drive, Inverness IV3 8NS johntallach@talktalk.net	01463 418721	39
Thomson, Alexander BSc BD MPhil PhD	1973	2012	(Rutherglen: Old)	4 Munro Street, Dornoch IV25 3RA alexander.thomson6@btinternet.com	01862 811650	40
Thomson, Donald M. BD	1975	2013	(Tullibody: St Serf's)	50 Sighthill Road, Edinburgh EH11 4NY donniethomson@tiscali.co.uk		1
Thrower, Charles D. BSc	1965	2002	(Carnbee with Pittenweem)	Grange House, Wester Grangemuir, Pittenweem, Anstruther KY10 2RB charlesandsteph@btinternet.com	01333 312631	24
Torrance, Iain R. (Prof.) KCVO Kt DD FRSE	1982	2012	(President: Princeton Theological Seminary)	25 The Causeway, Duddingston Village, Edinburgh EH15 3QA irt@ptsem.edu	0131 661 3092	
Turnbull, Julian S. BSc BD MSc CEng MBCS	1980	1986	(Dumfries: Lochside with Terregles)	39 Suthren Yett, Prestonpans EH32 9GL jules@turnbull25.plus.com	01875 818305	3
Webster, John G. BSc	1964	1998	(Glasgow: St John's Renfield)	Plane Tree, King's Cross, Brodick, Isle of Arran KA27 8RG	01770 700747	7
Webster, Peter BD DipPS	1977	2014	(Edinburgh: Portobello St James')	6 Newton Park, Dunoon PA23 7ST peterwebster101@hotmail.com		19
Whyte, Ron C. BD CPS	1990	2013	(Alvie and Insh with Rothiemurchus and Aviemore)	13 Hillside Avenue, Kingussie PH21 1PA ron4xst@btinternet.com	01540 661101 07979 026973	36
Williamson, Magnus J.C.	1982	1999	(Fetlar with Yell)	Creekhaven, Houl Road, Scalloway, Shetland ZE1 0XA	01595 880023	31
Wilson, Andrew G.N. MA BD DMin	1977	2012	(Aberdeen: Rubislaw)	Auchintarph, Coull, Tarland, Aboyne AB34 4TT agn.wilson@gmail.com	01339 880918	32
Wyllie, Hugh R. MA DD FCIBS	1962	2000	(Hamilton: Old)	18 Chantinghall Road, Hamilton ML3 8NP hrwyllie@gmail.com	01698 420002	17
Young, Alexander W. BD ThM DipMin	1988	2017	(Kelson: Old and Sprouston)	9 Towerburn, Denhom TD9 8TB sandy.young45@yahoo.com	07489 241344	6

LIST E – MINISTERS NOT IN PRESBYTERIES (REGISTERED AS INACTIVE)

Ministers who are not members of a Presbytery but are registered as 'Inactive' under the Registration of Ministries Act (Act 2, 2017, as amended). Only those who have given consent under the GDPR to publication of their details are included.

NAME	ORD	DEM	CHARGE/APP	ADDRESS	TEL	PRES
Alexander, Douglas N. MA BD	1961	1999	(Bishopton)	West Morningside, Main Road, Langbank, Port Glasgow PA4 6XP	01475 540249	14
Barclay, Neil W. BSc BEd BD	1986	2006	(Falkirk: Grahamston United)	4 Gibsongray Street, Falkirk FK2 7LN neil.barclay@virginmedia.com	01324 874681	17

Name			(Position)	Address	Tel	No.
Beckett, David M. BA BD	1964	2002	(Edinburgh: Greyfriars, Tolbooth and Highland Kirk)	31/1 Sciennes Road, Edinburgh EH9 1NT / davidbeckett3@aol.com	0131 667 2672	1
Beautyman, Paul H. MA BD PGCCE	1993	2019	(Youth Adviser, Presbytery of Argyll)	59 Alexander Street, Dunoon PA23 7BB / paulbeautyman67@gmail.com	07572 813695	19
Bjarnason, Sven S. CandTheol CPS	1973	2011	(Tomintoul, Glenlivet and Inveraven)	14 Edward Street, Dunfermline KY12 0JW / sven@bjarnason.org.uk	01383 724625	24
Black, David W. BSc BD	1968	2008	(Strathbrock)	66 Bridge Street, Newbridge EH28 8SH / dw.black666@yahoo.co.uk	0131 333 2609	1
Black, Janette M.K. (Mrs) BD	1993	2006	(Assistant: Paisley: Oakshaw Trinity)	5 Craigiehall Avenue, Erskine PA8 7DB	0141 812 0794	14
Blakey, Ronald S. MA BD MTh	1962	2000	(Assembly Council)	24 Kimmerghame Place, Edinburgh EH4 2GE / kathleen.blakey@gmail.com	0131 343 6352	1
Brook, Stanley A. BD MTh CPS	1977	2016	(Newport-on-Tay)	4 Scotstoun Green, South Queensferry EH30 9YA / stan_brook@btinternet.com	0131 331 4237	1
Brown, Ronald H.	1974	1998	(Musselburgh: Northesk)	6 Monktonhall Farm Cottages, Musselburgh EH21 6RZ	0131 653 2531	3
Campbell, A. Iain MA DipEd	1961	1997	(Busby)	430 Clarkston Road, Glasgow G44 3QF / iaingillian@talktalk.net	0141 637 7460	16
Campbell, J. Ewen R. MA BD	1967	2005	(Auchterderran St Fothad's with Kinglassie)	20 St Margaret's Road, North Berwick EH39 4PJ	01620 890835	24
Chalmers, George A. MA BD MLitt	1962	2002	(Catrine with Sorn)	3 Cricket Place, Brightons, Falkirk FK2 0HZ	01324 712030	17
Cherry, Alastair J. BD BA FPLD	1982	2009	(Glasgow: Penilee St Andrew)	8 Coruisk Drive, Clarkston, Glasgow G76 7NG / ajcherry133@gmail.com	07483 221141	16
Chisholm, Archibald F. MA	1957	1997	(Braes of Rannoch with Foss and Rannoch)	32 Seabank Road, Nairn IV12 4EU / arch32@btinternet.com	01667 452001	37
Collins, Mitchell BD CPS	1996	2005	(Creich, Flisk and Kilmany with Monimail)	6 Netherby Park, Glenrothes KY6 3PL / collinsmit@aol.com	01592 742915	24
Cowie, James M. BD CCE	1977	2016	(Paris: The Scots Kirk)	24 Cowdrait, Burnmouth, Eyemouth TD14 5SW / jimcowie@europe.com	01890 781394	5
Cullen, William T. BA LTh	1984	1996	(Kilmarnock: St John's Onthank)	6 Laurel Wynd, Cambuslang, Glasgow G72 7BA	0141 641 4337	16
Cunningham, J.S.A. MA BD BLitt PhD	1992	2000	(Glasgow: Barlanark Greyfriars)	Kirkland, 5 Inveresk Place, Coatbridge ML5 2DA	01236 421541	16
Davidson, Ian M.P. MBE MA BD	1954	1994	(Stirling: Allan Park South with Church of the Holy Rude)	13/8 Craigend Park, Edinburgh EH16 5XX / ian.m.p.davidson@btinternet.com	0131 664 0074	1
Dick, J. Ronald BD	1973	2012	(Hospital Chaplain)	1 Viewfield Terrace, Leet Street, Coldstream TD12 4BL / ron.dick180@yahoo.co.uk	01890 882206	4
Dickson, Graham T. MA BD	1985	2005	(Edinburgh: St Stephen's Comely Bank)	43 Hope Park Gardens, Bathgate EH48 2QT / gtd194@googlemail.com	01506 237597	1
Donald, Robert M. BA LTh	1969	2005	(Kilmodan and Colintraive)	20 Avon Crescent, Broughty Ferry, Dundee DD5 3TX / robandmoiradonald@yahoo.co.uk		
Donaldson, Colin V.	1982	1998	(Ormiston with Pencaitland)	3A Playfair Terrace, St Andrews KY16 9HX / colinmarion80@gmail.com	01334 472889	24
Dunsmore, Barry W. MA BD	1982	2018	(Aberdeen: St Machar's Cathedral)	33 Young Road, Victoria Park, Dunblane FK15 0FT / barrydunsmore@gmail.com	01786 643287	23

Name			Position	Address	Tel	No.
Ferguson, Ronald MA BD ThM DLitt	1972	2001	(Kirkwall: St Magnus Cathedral)	Vinbreck, Orphir, Orkney KW17 2RE ronbluebrazil@aol.com	01856 811353	45
Finlay, Quintin BA BD	1975	1996	(North Bute)	Ivy Cottage, Greenlees Farm, Kelso TD5 8BT	07901 981171	6
Fleming, Alexander F. MA BD	1966	1995	(Strathblane)	11 Bankwood Drive, Kilsyth, Glaasgow G65 0GZ alex@koror99.com	01236 820915	16
Forbes, John W.A. BD	1973	1999	(Edzell Lethnot with Fern, Careston and Menmuir with Glenesk)	Little Ennochie Steading, Finzean, Banchory AB31 4LX jr6666@icloud.com	01330 850785	32
Fraser, Ian C. BA BD	1982	2008	(Glasgow: St Luke's and St Andrew's)	62 Kingston Avenue, Neilston, Glasgow G78 3JG ianandlindafraser@gmail.com	0141 563 6794	14
Galloway, Kathy J. (Mrs) BD DD DipPS	1977	2020	(Co-Leader, Iona Community)	20 Hamilton Park Avenue, Glasgow G12 8UU kathygalloway200@btinternet.com	0141 357 4079	16
Gillon, D. Ritchie M. BD DipMin	1994	2017	(Paisley: St Luke's)	12 Fellhill Street, Ayr KA7 3JF revgillon@hotmail.com	01292 270018	7
Gilmour, William M. MA BD	1969	2008	(Lecropt)	14 Pine Court, Doune FK16 6JE	01786 842928	23
Grainger, Harvey L. LTh	1975	2004	(Kingswells)	13 St Ronan's Crescent, Peterculter, Aberdeen AB14 0RL harveygrainger@btinternet.com	01224 739824	31
Grant, David I.M. MA BD	1969	2003	(Dalry: Trinity)	8 Mossbank Drive, Glasgow G33 1LS	0141 770 7186	16
Green, Alex H. MA BD	1986	2010	(Strathblane)	44 Laburnum Drive, Milton of Campsie, Glasgow G66 8HY lesvert@btinternet.com	01360 313001	16
Grier, James BD	1991	2005	(Coatbridge: Middle)	14 Love Drive, Bellshill ML4 1BY	01698 742545	17
Haddow, Angus H. BSc	1963	1999	(Methlick)	25 Lerwick Road, Aberdeen AB16 6RF marjory.haddow@gmail.com	01224 969521	31
Hamilton, David S.M. MA BD STM	1958	1996	(Lecturer, Practical Theology, University of Glasgow)	Linfield, Milton of Lawton, Arbroath DD11 4RU dandmhamilton@gmail.com	01241 238369	30
Harris, John W.F. MA	1967	2012	(Bearsden: Cross)	68 Mitre Road, Glasgow G14 9LL jwfh@sky.com	0141 321 1061	14
Harris, Samuel McC. OStJ BA BD	1974	2010	(Rothesay: Trinity)	56 Rowland Street, Skipton, North Yorkshire BD23 2DU mhar10@hotmail.com	01756 794505	7
Harvey, W. John BA BD DD	1965	2002	(Interim Minister, Edinburgh: Corstorphine Craigsbank)	501A Shields Road, Glasgow G41 2RF jonmol@phonecoop.coop	0141 429 3774 07709 651335	16
Hastie, George I. MA BD	1971	2009	(Mearns Coastal)	23 Borrowfield Crescent, Montrose DD10 9BR	01674 672290	30
Kerr, Hugh F. MA BD	1968	2006	(Aberdeen: Ruthrieston South)	33 Strathmore Court, 20 Abbey Drive, Glasgow G14 9JX		16
Kingston, David V.F. BD DipPTh	1993	2015	(Chaplain: Army)	2 Cleuch Avenue, North Middleton, Gorebridge EH23 4RP	01875 822026	3
Lamont, Stewart J. BSc BD	1972	2015	(Arbirlot with Carmyllie)	Mas des Pins, 23 Rue du 19 mars 1962, 11500 Quillan, France lamonts@lamonts.eu	0033 9 86 56 16 78	1
Lawrie, Robert M. BD MSc DipMin LLCM(TD) MCMI FCMI	1994	1998	(Fyvie with Rothienorman)	West Benview, Main Road, Langbank PA14 6XP revrmlawrie@gmail.com	01475 540240 07789 824479	14
Ledgard, J. Christopher BA CertTh	1969	1998	(Upper Donside)	Streonshalh, 8 David Hume View, Chirnside, Duns TD11 3SX	01890 817124	5

Name			(Position)	Address	Phone	
Liddiard, F.G. Bernard MA	1957	1971	(Brechin: Gardner Memorial and East)	34 Trinity Fields Crescent, Brechin DD9 6YF bernardliddiard@btinternet.com	01356 622966	30
Lindsay, W. Douglas BD CPS	1978	2004	(Eaglesham)	3 Drummond Place, Calderwood, East Kilbride, Glasgow G74 3AD	01355 234169	16
Lithgow, Anne R. (Mrs) MA BD	1992	2009	(Dunglass)	13 Cameron Park, Edinburgh EH16 5JY anne.lithgow@btinternet.com		1
Logan, Thomas M. LTh	1971	1995	(Clydebank: Abbotsford)	3 Duncan Court, Kilmarnock KA3 7TF thomasmlogan8@gmail.com	01563 524398	7
Macdonald, William J. BD CPS	1976	2002	(Board of National Mission: New Charge Development)	21 Muirfield Court, 20 Muirend Road, Glasgow G44 3QP williejohnmac@gmail.com	0141 384 3014	16
MacLeod, Roderick MBE MA BD PhD(Edin) PhD(open)	1966	2011	(Cumlodden, Lochfyneside and Lochgair)	Creag-nam-Barnach, Furnace, Inveraray PA32 8XU mail@revroddy.co.uk	01499 500629	19
Main, Alan (Prof.) TD MA BD STM PhD DD	1963	2001	(Practical Theology, University of Aberdeen)	Kirkfield, Barthol Chapel, Inverurie AB51 8TD a.main993@btinternet.com	01651 806773	31
McDonald, John A. MA BD	1978	1997	(Cumbernauld: Condorrat)	1 John Murray Court, Motherwell ML1 2QW	01324 871947	17
McDowall, Ronald J. BD	1980	2001	(Falkirk: Laurieston with Redding and Westquarter)	'Kailas', Windsor Road, Falkirk FK1 5EJ		17
McGillivray, A. Gordon MA BD STM	1951	1993	(Presbytery Clerk, Edinburgh)	36 Larchfield Neuk, Balerno EH14 7NL	0131 449 3901	1
McIntosh, Hamish N.M. MA	1949	1987	(Fintry)	Room 20, Pearson House, Erskine Home, Nursery Avenue, Bishopton PA7 5PU		23
McIntyre, Allan G. BD	1985	2017	(Greenock: St Ninian's)	9a Templehill, Troon KA10 6BQ agmcintyre@lineone.net	07876 445626	7
McIntyre, J. Ainslie MA BD	1963	1984	(University of Glasgow)	60 Bonnaughton Road, Bearsden, Glasgow G61 4DB jamcintyre@hotmail.com	0141 942 5143	14
McKenzie, Mary O. CPS	1976	1996	(Edinburgh: Richmond Craigmillar)	4 Dunellan Avenue, Moodiesburn, Glasgow G69 0GB maemck@btinternet.com	01236 870180	16
McKenzie, Raymond D. DipTh BD	1978	2012	(Hamilton: Burnbank with Hamilton: South)	25 Austine Drive, Hamilton ML3 7YE		17
McLachlan, Fergus C. BD	1982	1988	(Dunbarney with Forgandenny)	46 Queen Square, Glasgow G41 2AZ whitegoldfm@gmail.com	07544 721032	16
Millar, John L. MA BD	1981	1990	(Fort William: Duncansburgh with Kilmonivaig)	Flat 0/1, 12 Chesterfield Gardens, Glasgow G12 0BF johnmillar123@btinternet.com	0141 339 4090	38
Millar, Peter W. MA BD ThM PhD	1971	1998	(Warden, Iona Abbey)	6/5 Ettrickdale, Edinburgh EH3 5JN ionacottage@hotmail.com	0131 557 0517	1
Minto, Joan E. (Mrs) MA BD	1993	1997	(Wemyss)	1 Lochaber Cottages, Forres IV36 2RL joanminto.123@gmail.com	07800 669074	37
Morrison, Iain C. BA BD	1990	2003	(Linlithgow: St Ninian's Craigmailen)	Whaligoe, 53 Eastcroft Drive, Polmont, Falkirk FK2 0SU iain@kirkweb.org	01324 713249	17
Munro, Sheila BD DipPsych	1995	2021	(RAF Chaplain)	2 Moorcroft Drive, Airdrie ML6 8ES	07468 339330	37
Munton, James G. BA	1969	2002	(Coatbridge: Old Monkland)	32 Forth Park, Bridge of Allan, Stirling FK9 5NT	01236 754848	17
Murray, Douglas R. MA BD	1965	2004	(Lausanne: The Scots Kirk)	d-smurray@supanet.com	01786 831081	23

Name	Year	Year	(Position/Parish)	Address	Telephone	No.
Newlands, George M. (Prof.) MA BD PhD DLitt FRSA FRSE	1970	2008	(Professor of Divinity, University of Glasgow)	49 Highsett, Cambridge CB2 1NZ gnewlsnds@icloud.com	01223 569984 07786 930941	47
Owen, Catherine W. MTh	1984	1987	(Wishaw: Chalmers)	10 Waverley Park, Kirkintilloch, Glasgow G77 2BP katy.owen@talktalk.net	0141 776 0407	16
Petrie, Ian D. MA BD	1970	2008	(Dundee: St Andrew's)	27/111 West Savile Terrace, Edinburgh EH9 3DR idp-77@hotmail.com	0131 237 2857	1
Plate, Maria A.G. (Miss) BA LTh CQSW DSW	1983	2000	(South Ronaldsay and Burray)	Flat 29, 77 Barnton Park View, Edinburgh EH4 6EL riaplate@gmail.com	0131 339 8539	1
Poole, Ann McColl (Mrs) DipEd ACE LTh	1983	2003	(Dyke with Edinkillie)	Kirkside Cottage, Dyke, Forres IV36 2TF		35
Prentice, George BA BTh	1964	1997	(Paisley: Martyrs')	46 Victoria Gardens, Corsebar Road, Paisley PA2 9AQ g.prentice04@talktalk.net	0141 842 1585	14
Price, Peter O. CBE QHC BA FPhS	1957	1996	(Blantyre: Old)	22 Old Bothwell Road, Bothwell, Glasgow G71 8AW peteroprice@sky.com	01698 854032	17
Ramsay, Alan MA	1967	2007	(Fort William: MacIntosh Memorial)	12 Riverside Grove, Lochyside, Fort William PH33 7RD	01397 702054	38
Ramsay, Robert J. LLB NP BD	1986	2018	(Invergowrie)	50 Nethergray Road, Dundee DD2 5GT s3rjr@tiscali.co.uk	01382 562481	29
Reid, Albert B. BSc BD	1966	2001	(Ardler, Kettins and Meigle)	1 Mary Countess Way, Glamis, Forfar DD8 1RF abreid019@gmail.com	01307 840999	30
Reid, Janette G. BD CertMin	1991	2009	(Glasgow: St Andrew's East)	c/o Presbytery Office, 260 Bath Street, Glasgow G2 4JP tomandpatrich@gmail.com	07956 308687	16
Richardson, Thomas C. LTh ThB	1971	2004	(Cults: West)	19 Kinkell Road, Aberdeen AB15 8HR		31
Robertson, John M. BSc BD	1975	1992	(Campsie)	8 North Green Drive, Airth, Falkirk FK2 8RA	01324 832244	17
Rogerson, Stuart D. BSc BD	1980	2001	(Strathaven: West)	17 Westfield Park, Strathaven ML10 6XH srogerson@cnetwork.co.uk	01357 523321	17
Ross, Evan J. LTh	1986	1998	(Cowdenbeath: West with Mossgreen and Crossgates)	5 Arneil Place, Brightons, Falkirk FK2 0NJ	01324 719936	17
Scott, James F.	1957	1997	(Dyce)	5 Gullipen View, Callander FK17 8HN	01877 330565	23
Shannon, W.G. MA BD	1955	1998	(Pitlochry)	19 Knockard Road, Pitlochry PH16 5HJ	01796 473533	27
Sloan, Robert BD	1997	2014	(Fauldhouse: St Andrew's)	3 Gean Grove, Blairgowrie PH10 6TL	01250 875286	27
Smith, Richard BD	1976	2002	(Denny: Old)	Easter Wayside, 46 Kennedy Way, Airth, Falkirk FK2 8GB richards@uklinex.net	01324 831386	17
Spence, Sheila M. (Mrs) MA BD	1979	2010	(Kirk o' Shotts)	12 Machan Avenue, Larkhall ML9 2HE	01698 310370	17
Spowart, Mary G. (Mrs) BD	1978	1991	(Papa Westray with Westray)	Aldersyde, St Abbs Road, Coldingham, Eyemouth TD14 5NR	01890 771697	5
Steven, Harold A.M. OStJ LTh FSAScot	1970	2001	(Baldernock)	9 Cairnhill Road, Bearsden, Glasgow G61 1AT harold.allison.steven@gmail.com	0141 942 1598	14
Stewart, James C. MA BD STM FSAScot	1960	2000	(Aberdeen: Kirk of St Nicholas)	Ashley House Residential Home, 4 King's Gate, Aberdeen AB15 4EJ	01224 648878	31

Name			Location	Address	Phone	No.
Stirling, G. Alan S. MA	1960	1999	(Leochel Cushnie and Lynturk with Tough)	97 Lochlann Road, Culloden, Inverness IV2 7HJ	01463 798313	37
Taylor, Jane C. BD DipMin	1990	2013	(Insch-Leslie-Premnay-Oyne)	Timbers, Argyll Road, Kilcreggan G84 0JW jane.c.taylor@btinternet.com	01436 842336	14
Torrance, David W. MA BD	1955	1991	(Earlston)	38 Forth Street, North Berwick EH39 4JQ torrance103@btinternet.com	01620 895109	3
Watson, Valerie G.C. MA BD STM	1987	2018	(North and West Islay)	11 Roxburgh Street, Greenock PA5 4PU vgcwatson@btinternet.com	01475 787116	14
Watts, Anthony E. BD	1999	2013	(Glenmuick (Ballater))	7 Cumiskie Crescent, Forres IV36 2QB tonyewatts@yahoo.co.uk	01309 672418	37
Waugh, John L. LTh	1973	2002	(Ardclach with Auldearn and Dalmore)	58 Wyvis Drive, Nairn IV12 4TP jswaugh31@gmail.com	01667 456397	37
Webster, Brian G. BD BSc CEng MIEE	1988	2011	(Cambusbarron: The Bruce Memorial)	3/1 Cloch Court, 57 Albert Road, Gourock PA19 1NJ revwebby@aol.com		14
Whyte, Iain A. BA BD STM PhD	1968	2005	(Community Mental Health Chaplain)	14 Carlingnose Point, North Queensferry, Inverkeithing KY11 1ER iainisabelwhyte@gmail.com	01383 410732	24
Wilson, James H. LTh	1970	1996	(Cleland)	21 Austine Drive, Hamilton ML3 7YE wilsonjh@blueyonder.co.uk	01698 457042	17
Wilson, John M. (Ian) MA	1964	1995	(Adviser, Religious Education)	27 Bellfield Street, Edinburgh EH15 2BR ianandshirley@talktalk.net	0131 669 5257	1
Wilson, Thomas F. BD	1984	1996	(Aberdeen: North of St Andrew)	55 Allison Close, Cove, Aberdeen AB12 3WG	01224 873501	31
Wood, James L.K.	1967	1995	(Aberdeen: Ruthrieston West)	1 Glen Drive, Dyce, Aberdeen AB21 7EN james@jamesinez.plus.com	01224 722543	31

LIST F – HEALTH AND SOCIAL CARE CHAPLAINS

LOTHIAN

Head of Spiritual Care and Bereavement
Rev. Philp R. Hacking: philip.hacking@nhslothian.scot.nhs.uk; 0131 242 1991
Spiritual Care Office: The Royal Infirmary of Edinburgh, 51 Little France Crescent, Edinburgh EH16 4SA
Full details of chaplains and contacts in all hospitals: www.nhslothian.scot > Our Services > Spiritual Care > The Team

Chaplaincy team includes from the Church of Scotland:
Rev. Joanne G. Foster, Royal Infirmary of Edinburgh; joanne.foster2@nhslothian.scot.nhs.uk; 0131 242 1990
Rev. F. Lynne MacMurchie, Royal Edinburgh Hospital, Community Mental Health, Astley Ainslie Hospital; lynne.macmurchie@nhslothian.scot.nhs.uk; 0131 537 6775

Outwith NHS
Rev. Erica M. Wishart, St Columba's Hospice, 15 Boswall Road, Edinburgh EH5 3RW; EWishart@churchofscotland.org.uk; 0131 551 1381

BORDERS

Head of Spiritual Care
Rev. Michael D. Scouler; michael.scouler@borders.scot.nhs.uk; 01896 826565
Spiritual Care Department: Chaplaincy Centre, Borders General Hospital, Melrose TD6 9BS; 01896 826564
Further information: www.nhsborders.scot.nhs.uk > Patients and Visitors > Our services > Chaplaincy Centre

DUMFRIES AND GALLOWAY

Spiritual Care Lead
Rev. Nathan Mesnikoff, Dumfries and Galloway Royal Infirmary; 01387 246246 Ext 31544
DGRI Sanctuary Office, Cargenbridge, Dumfries DG2 8RX dg.spiritual-care@nhs.scot
Further information: https://dghscp.co.uk/spiritual-care-support

AYRSHIRE AND ARRAN

Spiritual Care
Point of contact for all chaplains: Susan Robertson, 01583 825988
University Hospital Crosshouse Chaplain: Karen Crosbie
University Hospital Ayr Chaplain: Elaine Hough
Ailsa Hospital: Suzanne Algeo
Further information: www.nhsaaa.net > Services A-Z > Chaplaincy service

LANARKSHIRE

Head of Spiritual Care and Wellbeing
Paul Graham, paul.graham@lanarkshire.scot.nhs.uk; 07717 815581
Spiritual Care and Wellbeing Office: Law House, Airdrie Road, Carluke ML8 5EP; spiritualcare@lanarkshire.scot.nhs.uk; 01698 754251
Further information: www.nhslanarkshire.org.uk > Our services A-Z > Spiritual care

GREATER GLASGOW AND CLYDE

Spiritual Care Service Manager: Dawn Allan;dawn.allan3@ggc.scot.nhs.uk
Chaplains Office, Inverclyde Royal Hospital, Larkfield Road, Greenock PA16 0XN; 07814 313249
Spiritual Care Administrator: chaplains@ggc.scot.nhs.uk
Further information: www.nhsggc.org.uk > Services Directory > Spiritual Care

Healthcare chaplains from Church of Scotland:
Rev. Paul G.R. Grant, Glasgow Royal Infirmary: 0141 201 6300
Rev. Jeanette L. Peel, Chaplains Office, Inverclyde Royal Hospital; 07903 681003; 01475 504759

FORTH VALLEY

Head of Spiritual Care: Tim Bennison
Spiritual Care Centre: Forth Valley Royal Hospital, Larbert FK5 4WR; 01324 566071
Further information: www.nhsforthvalley.com > Services A–Z > Spiritual Care Centre

Chaplaincy team includes from Church of Scotland:
Rev. Helen F. Christie, Forth Valley Hospitals

FIFE

Head of Spiritual Care and Bereavement Lead
Mr Mark Evans DCS, Department of Spiritual Care, Queen Margaret Hospital, Whitefield Road, Dunfermline KY12 0SU;
mark.evans59@nhs.scot; 01383 623623 ext 24136
Victoria Hospital, Kirkcaldy and NHS Fife Community Hospitals: Chaplain's Office: 01592 648158 or 01592 729675
Queen Margaret Hospital, Dunfermline: Chaplains Office: 01383 674136
Mental Health and Community Chaplain, Adamson and Stratheden Hospitals: 07976 918909
Further information: www.nhsfife.org > Spiritual Care

Chaplaincy team includes from the Church of Scotland:
Rev. Gordon I. Strang, Victoria Hospital, Kirkcaldy; 01592 648158
Rev. Eileen A. Miller, Queen Margaret Hospital, Dunfermline; 01383 674136

TAYSIDE

Head of Spiritual Care: Rev. Alan Gibbon
The Wellbeing Centre, Royal Victoria Hospital, Dundee DD2 1SP; lynne.downie@nhs.scot; 01382 423110
Further information: www.nhstayside.scot.nhs.uk > Our Services A–Z > Spiritual Care and Wellbeing

Chaplaincy team includes from the Church of Scotland:
Rev. Ian J.M. McDonald, Palliative Care Chaplain, Roxburghe House, Dundee; ian.mcdonald2@nhs.scot; 01382 423110

Outwith NHS
Rev. Ali R. Pandian, CHAS, Rachel House Children's Hospice, Avenue Road, Kinross KY13 8FX; APandian@churchofscotland.org.uk; 01577 865777

GRAMPIAN

Lead Chaplain
Gillian Douglas, Chaplains' Office, Aberdeen Royal Infirmary, Foresterhill, Aberdeen AB25 2ZN; gram.chaplaincy@nhs.scot; 01224 553166
Further information: www.nhsgrampian.co.uk > Home > Our services > A–Z > Spiritual Care

HIGHLAND

Lead Chaplain (Interim)
Janet Davidson, Raigmore Hospital, Old Perth Road, Inverness IV2 3UJ; janet.davidson@nhs.scot; 01463 704463
Further information: www.nhshighland.scot.nhs.uk/Services/Pages/Chaplaincy-Raigmore.aspx

Chaplaincy team includes from the Church of Scotland:
Rev. Michael A. Robertson, Raigmore Hospital; mike.robertson@nhs.scot; 01463 704463

WESTERN ISLES HEALTH BOARD

Lead Chaplain
Rev. T. K. Shadakshari, 23D Benside, Newmarket, Stornoway, Isle of Lewis HS2 0DZ; tk.shadakshari@nhs.scot;
(Office) 01851 704704; (Home) 01851 701727; (Mbl) 07403 697138

ORKNEY

Spiritual Care Team
ork.chaplaincy@nhs.scot; 01856 888184
Further information: www.ohb.scot.nhs.uk/service/chaplaincy-and-spiritual-care

SHETLAND

Spiritual Care Lead
Rev Canon Neil Brice, neil.brice@nhs.scot; 01595 743662; 07771 380989
Further information: www.shb.scot.nhs.uk/hospital/spiritualcare.asp

NHS SCOTLAND

Interim Head of Programme, Health & Social Care Chaplaincy & Spiritual Care, NHS Education for Scotland
Audrey Taylor, Principal Educator, NHS Education for Scotland; 07984 772697; @audreynesahp

Spiritual Care Specialist Research Lead
Rev. Iain J.M.Telfer, iain.telfer@nhs.scot; 01224 805120; 07554 222232
NHS Education for Scotland, Forest Grove House, Foresterhill Road, Aberdeen AB25 2ZP

Church of Scotland Chaplains in NHS ENGLAND
Rev. Dr Cameron H. Langlands, Head of Spiritual and Pastoral Care, South London and Maudsley NHS Foundation Trust, Maudsley Hospital, Denmark Road, London SE3 8AZ; Cameron.Langlands@slam.nhs.uk; 020 3228 2815; 07971 169791
Rev. Mairi F. Lovett, Chaplain, Royal Brompton Hospital, Sydney Sydney Street, London SW3 6NP; m.lovett@rbht.nhs.uk; 020 7351 8060
Rev. John K.S. McMahon, Head of Spiritual and Pastoral Care, West London NHS Trust, Broadmoor Hospital, Crowthorne, Berkshire RG45 7EG; john.mcmahonrev@westlondon.nhs.uk; 01344 754098

LIST G – CHAPLAINS TO HM FORCES

The three columns give dates of ordination and commissioning, and branch where the chaplain is serving: Royal Navy, Army, Royal Air Force, Royal Naval Reserve, Army Reserve, Royal Air Force Reserve, or where the person is an Officiating Chaplain to the Military.

NAME	ORD	COM	BCH	ADDRESS
Anderson, David P. BSc BD	2002	2007	A	DACG 4 Infantry Brigade and HQ North East, Bourlon Barracks, Pluymer Road, Catterick Garrison DL9 3AD
Ashley-Emery, Stephen BD DPS	2006	2019	RN	Portsmouth Flotilla, The Chaplaincy, Rodney Block, HMS Nelson, Queen Street, Portsmouth PO1 3HH Stephen.Ashley-Emery100@mod.gov.uk 02392 723000
Begg, Richard J. MA BD	2008	2016	A	1 Prince of Wales Royal Regiment, Royal Artillery Barracks, Repository Road, Woolwich, London SE18 4BH
Berry, Geoff T. BSc BD	2009	2012	A	3 SCOTS, Fort George, Ardersier, Inverness IV2 7TE
Blakey, Stephen A. BSc BD	1977	1977	OCM	Staff Chaplain, HQ Scotland, Forthside, Stirling FK7 7RR
Cobain, Alan R. BD	2000	2017	A	Infantry Training Centre, Vimy Barracks, Catterick Garrison DL9 3PS
Dalton, Mark F. BD DipMin RN	2002	2002	RN	The Chaplaincy, HMS Neptune, HM Naval Base Clyde, Faslane, Helensburgh G84 8HL mark.dalton242@mod.gov.uk
Davidson, Mark R. MA BD STM PhD PhD RN	2005	2011	RN	HMS Prince of Wales BFPO 364 Mark.Davidson122@d1o2o101.MND.R.MIL.UK
Duncan, John C. MBE BD MPhil	1987	2001	OCM	Waterloo Lines, Leuchars Station, St Andrews KY1 0JX
Frail, Nicola R. BLE MBA MDiv	2000	2012	A	HQ 1 Army Infantry Brigade, Delhi Barracks, Tidworth SP9 7DX
Francis, James MBE BD PhD	2002	2009	A	HQ Regional Command, Montgomery House, Queen's Avenue, Aldershot GU11 2JN
Gardner, Neil N. OStJ MA BD	1991	1991	OCM	Edinburgh Universities Officers' Training Corps, 301 Colinton Road, Edinburgh EH13 0LA
Jeffrey, Kenneth S. BA BD PhD DMin	2002	2021	AR	7 SCOTS, Queens Barracks, 131 Dunkeld Road, Perth PH1 5BT
Kellock, Chris N. MA BD	1998	2012	A	Defence Academy, Shrivenham, Swindon SN6 8LA
Lancaster, Craig MA BD	2004	2011	RAF	St Aidan's Church, RAF Lossiemouth, Moray IV31 6DS craig.lancaster102@mod.gov.uk
MacKay, Stewart A. BA	2009	2009	A	2 LANCS, Elizabeth Barracks, Pirbright, Woking GU24 0DT
MacKenzie, Hector M.	2008	2008	A	5 Regiment Royal Artillery, Marne Barracks, Catterick Garrison DL10 7NP
Macpherson, Duncan J. BSc BD	1993	2002	A	MAB, Ministry of Defence A Block, Regents Park Barracks, Albany Street, London NW1 4AZ
Mair, Michael J. BD	2014	2019	AR	32 (Scottish) Signal Regiment, 21 Jardine Street, Glasgow G20 6JU
McLay, Neil BD MTh	2006	2012	A	2 (Training) Regiment Army Air Corps, Middle Wallop, Stockbridge SO20 8DY
Rankin, Lisa-Jane BD CPS	2003		OCM	2 Bn Royal Regiment of Scotland, Glencorse Barracks, Penicuik EH26 0QH
Rowe, Christopher J. BA BD	2008	2008	AR	5 Military Intelligence Battalion, Edinburgh Castle, Edinburgh EH1 2NG
Selemani, Ecilo LTh MTh	1993		OCM	51 Military Brigade and HQ Scotland, Forthside, Stirling FK7 7RR
Thom, David J. BD DipMin DipPS DipLM	1999	2015	A	Army Foundation College, Uniacke Barracks, Penny Pot Lane, Killinghall, Harrogate HG3 2SE
van Sittert, Paul BA BD	1997	2011	A	32 Engineer Regiment, Marne Barracks, Catterick Garrison DL10 7NP
Young, David T. BA BD MTh	2007	2022	RAF	St Aidan's Church, RAF Lossiemouth, Moray IV31 6DS david.young137@mod.gov.uk

ACF: Army Cadet Force

Blackwood, Keith T. BD DipMin	2 Bn The Highlanders, ACF, Cadet Training Centre, Rocksley Drive, Boddam, Peterhead AB42 3BA	01334 857136
Dicks, Shuna M. BSc BD	2 Bn The Highlanders, ACF, Cadet Training Centre, Rocksley Drive, Boddam, Peterhead AB42 3BA	07891 501859
Mackenzie, Cameron BD	Lothian and Borders Bn, ACF, Drumshoreland House, Broxburn EH52 5PF	
McCulloch, Alen J.R. MA BD	1 Highlanders Bn, ACF, Gordonville Road, Inverness IV2 4SU	
Selemani, Eciio LTh MTh	Glasgow and Lanarkshire Bn, ACF, Gilbertfield Road, Cambuslang, Glasgow G72 8YP	
Stewart, Fraser M.C. BSc BD	1 Highlanders Bn, ACF, Gordonville Road, Inverness IV2 4SU	
Wilson, Fiona A. BD	West Lowland Battalion, ACF, Fusilier House, Seaforth Road, Ayr KA8 9HX	

ATC: Air Training Corps

Regional Chaplain, Scotland & N. Ireland		
Alistair K. Ridland MStJ MA BD DipDS MRAeS MInstLM RAFAC	chaplain.sni@rafac.mod.gov.uk	

North Scotland Wing

Wing Chaplain & 2405 Sqn	Russel Smith BD	russamtwo@yahoo.co.uk	01349 861011
107 (Aberdeen) Sqn	James L.K. Wood	james@jamesinez.plus.com	01224 722543
379 (County of Ross) Sqn	Michael J. Macdonald	Michael.Macdonald@churchofscotland.org.uk	01349 884268
423DF (Speyside) Sqn	Robert I.M. Anderson BD FInstLM	bobjimanderson@gmail.com	01343 835401
446 (Forres) Sqn	Donald K. Prentice BSc BD MSc MLitt	DPrentice@churchofscotland.org.uk	01309 672380
1298 (Huntly) Sqn	Kay F. Gauld BD STM PhD	KGauld@churchofscotland.org.uk	01464 820404
1796 (Thurso) Sqn	David J.B. Macartney BA	DMacartney@churchofscotland.org.uk	01847 811734
2367 (Banchory) Sqn	Frank Ribbons MA BD DipEd	FRibbons@churchofscotland.org.uk	01339 887267

Central Scotland Wing

Wing Chaplain & 2450 (Dudhope) Sqn	C. Graham D. Taylor BSc BD FIAB	AT Corps, MOD Leuchars KY16 0JX	01383 822316
775 (Burntisland) Sqn	Alan Sharp BSc BD	Unity Hall, Links Place, Burntisland KY3 9DY	07806 776560
859 (Dalgety) Sqn	Christine M. Sime BSc BD	CSime@churchofscotland.org.uk	01887 820242
1370 (Leven) Sqn	Jacqueline Thomson MTh DCS	Jacqueline.Thomson@churchofscotland.org.uk	01674 672447
1743 (Crieff) Sqn	Robert D. Nicol MA	RNicol@churchofscotland.org.uk	01333 320850
2288 (Montrose) Sqn	Ian A. McLean BSc BD DMin	IMcLean@churchofscotland.org.uk	
2435 (St Andrews) Sqn	Gavin R. Boswell BTheol	GBoswell@churchofscotland.org.uk	

South East Scotland Wing

Wing Chaplain	Regional Chaplain at present		
132 (North Berwick) Sqn	Neil J. Dougall BD DipMin DMin	NDougall@churchofscotland.org.uk	01620 892132
867 (Denny) Sqn	F. Derek Gunn BD	RevDerekGunn@hotmail.com	01324 624938
870 (Dreghorn) Sqn, Edinburgh	Peter Nelson BSc BD	PNelson@churchofscotland.org.uk	07500 057889
1716 (Roxburgh) Sqn	Sheila W. Moir MTheol	SMoir@churchofscotland.org.uk	01835 822255
2535 (Livingston) Sqn	Nelu I. Balaj BD MA ThD	NBalaj@churchofscotland.org.uk	01506 411888

West Scotland Wing

Wing Chaplain & 2166 (Hamilton) Sqn	I. Ross Blackman BSc MBA BD CertTh	RBlackman@churchofscotland.org.uk	01698 640185
327 (Kilmarnock) Sqn	Kristina I. Hine BS MDiv	KHine@churchofscotland.org.uk	01563 257172
498 (Wishaw) Sqn	Ian Douglas (Mr) (Reader)	IDouglas@churchofscotland.org.uk	07742 022423
1001 (Monklands) Sqn	Robert A Hamilton BA BD	RHamilton@churchofscotland.org.uk	01236 763022

SC: Sea Cadets

Campbell, Gordon MA BD	Sea Cadets Dundee, East Camperdown Street, Dundee DD1 3LG	
Fletcher, Suzanne G. BA MDiv MA DMin	Sea Cadets Dunbar, ACF Building, Castle Park Barracks, 33 North Road, Dunbar EH42 1EU	
MacKay, Colin (Mr)	Sea Cadets Wick, The Scout Hall, Kirkhill, Wick KW1 4PN	
May, John S. (Iain) BSc MBA BD	Sea Cadets Leith, Prince of Wales Dock, Leith, Edinburgh EH6 7DX	
Robertson, Pauline DCS BA CertTheol	Sea Cadets Musselburgh, 9-11 South Street, Musselburgh EH21 6AT	
Templeton, James L. BSc BD	Sea Cadets Methil, Harbour View, Methil KY8 3RF	
Wallace, Douglas W. MA BD	Sea Cadets East Kilbride, Army Reserve Centre, Whitemoss, East Kilbride G74 2HP	

LIST H – READERS

This list comprises active Readers only.

1. EDINBURGH AND WEST LOTHIAN

Devoy, Fiona (Mrs)	196 The Murrays Brae, Edinburgh EH17 8UH	fiona.devoy@yahoo.co.uk	01506 654950
Elliot, Sarah (Miss)	105 Seafield Rows, Seafield, Bathgate EH47 7AW	sarah.elliott6@btopenworld.com	0131 558 8210
Farrow, Edmund	14 Brunswick Terrace, Edinburgh EH7 5PG	edmundfarrow@blueyonder.co.uk	01506 842069
Galloway, Brenda (Dr)	16 Baron's Hill Court, Linlithgow EH49 7SP	dr.b.galloway82@gmail.com	0131 664 2366
Jackson, Kate (Ms)	3 Kedslie Road, Edinburgh EH16 6NT	katejackson1252@gmail.com	07901 501819
			0131 660 3007
Kerrigan, Herbert A. (Prof.) MA LLB QC	Airdene, 20 Edinburgh Road, Dalkeith EH22 1JY	kerrigan@kerriganqc.com	07725 953772
McFadzean, John	121 South Street, Armadale, Bathgate EH48 3JT	jmcfadzean2@gmail.com	01501 730260
Middleton, Alex	19 Cramond Place, Dalgety Bay KY11 9LS	alex.middleton@btinternet.com	01383 820800
Orr, Elizabeth (Mrs)	64a Marjoribanks Street, Bathgate EH48 1AL	liz-orr@hotmail.co.uk	01596 653116
Paxton, James	5 Main Street, Longridge, Bathgate EH47 8AE	jimpaxton1950@gmail.com	01501 772192
Pearce, Martin J.	4 Corbiehill Avenue, Edinburgh EH4 5DR	martin.j.pearce@blueyonder.co.uk	0131 336 4864
			07801 717222
Tew, Helen (Mrs)	5/5 Moat Drive, Edinburgh EH14 1NU	helentew9@gmail.com	07986 170802
Wilkie, David	55 Goschen Place, Broxburn EH52 5JH	david-fmu_09@tiscali.co.uk	01506 238644

3. LOTHIAN

Hogg, David MA	82 Eskhill, Penicuik EH26 8DQ	hogg-d2@sky.com	01968 676350
			07821 693946
Johnston, Alan C.	36 Foster Road, Penicuik EH26 0FL	alanacj2@gmail.com	01968 664860
			07901 501819
Millan, Mary (Mrs)	33 Polton Vale, Loanhead EH20 9DF	marymillan@gmail.com	0131 440 1624
			07814 466104
Waugh, Jacqueline (Mrs)	15 Garleton Drive, Haddington EH41 3BL	jacqueline.waugh@yahoo.com	01620 825007

Name	Address	Email	Phone
Yeoman, Edward T.N. FSAScot	75 Newhailes Crescent, Musselburgh EH21 6EF	edwardyeoman6@aol.com	0131 653 2291 / 07896 517666

4. MELROSE AND PEEBLES

Name	Address	Email	Phone
Selkirk, Frances (Mrs)	21 Park Crescent, Newtown St Boswells, Melrose TD6 0QR	f.selkirk@hillview2selkirk.plus.com	01835 823669

5. DUNS

Landale, Alison (Mrs)	Green Hope Guest House, Ellemford, Duns TD11 3SG	alison@greenhope.co.uk	01361 890242

6. JEDBURGH

Findlay, Elizabeth (Mrs)	7e Rose Lane, Kelso TD5 7AP	findlay290@gmail.com	01573 226641
Knox, Dagmar (Mrs)	3 Stichill Road, Ednam, Kelso TD5 7QQ	dagmar.knox.riding@btinternet.com	01573 224883

7. SOUTH WEST

Anderson, James BVMS PhD DVM FRCPath FIBiol MRCVS	67 Henrietta Street, Girvan KA26 9AN	jc.anderson2@talktalk.net	01465 710059
Barclay, Elizabeth (Mrs)	2 Jacks Road, Saltcoats KA21 5NT	mfiz98@dsl.pipex.com	07952 512720 / 01294 471855
Brookens, Aileen J. (Mrs)	Willow Cottage, Glenashdale, Whiting Bay, Isle of Arran KA27 8QW	aileenbrokens@gmail.com	01770 700535
Brown, S. Jeffrey BA	Skara Brae, Holm Park, 8 Ballplay Road, Moffat DG10 9JU	sjbrown@btinternet.com	01683 220475
Bruce, Andrew J.	57 Dockers Gardens, Ardrossan KA22 8GB	andrew_bruce2@sky.com	01294 605113
Cash, Marlane (Mrs)	5 Maxwell Drive, Newton Stewart DG8 6EL	marlaneg690@btinternet.com	01671 401375
Clarke, Elizabeth (Mrs)	Swallowbrae, Torbeg, Isle of Arran KA27 8HE	lizahclarke@gmail.com	01770 860219 / 07780 574367
Cooper, Fraser	5 Balgray Way, Irvine KA11 1RP	frasercooper1560@gmail.com	01294 211235
Corson, Gwen (Mrs)	7 Sunnybrae, Borgue, Kirkcudbright DG46 4SJ	gwendolyn@hotmail.com	01557 870328
Crosbie, Shona (Mrs)	4 Campbell Street, Darvel KA17 0DA	fawltytowersdarvel@yahoo.co.uk	01560 322229
Currie, Archie BD	55 Central Avenue, Kilbirnie KA25 6JP	Archie.Currie@churchofscotland.org.uk	01505 681474 / 07881 452115
Dodds, Alan	Trinco, Battlehill, Annan DG12 6SN	alanandjen46@talktalk.net	01461 201235
Gillespie, Janice (Miss)	12 Jeffrey Street, Kilmarnock KA1 4EB	janice.gillespie@tiscali.co.uk	01563 540009
Graham, Barbara (Miss) MA MLitt MPhil CertChSt	42 Annanhill Avenue, Kilmarnock KA1 2LQ	barbara.graham74@btinternet.com	01563 522108
Hamilton, Margaret A. (Mrs)	59 South Hamilton Street, Kilmarnock KA1 2DT	mahamilton1@outlook.com	01563 534431
Hunter, Jean C.Q. (Mrs) BD	Leucheram, Corrie, Isle of Arran KA27 8JB	j.hunter744@btinternet.com	01770 810218
Jackson, Susan (Mrs)	48 Springbells Road, Annan DG12 6LQ	peter-jackson24@sky.com	07498 714675
Jamieson, Ian A.	2 Whinfield Avenue, Prestwick KA9 2BH	ian4189.jamieson@gmail.com	01242 476898
Jamieson, John H. (Dr) BSc DEP DEdPsy AFBPsS CPsychol	22 Moorfield Avenue, Kilmarnock KA1 1TS	johnhjamieson@tiscali.co.uk	01563 534065
MacLean, Donald	1 Four Acres Drive, Kilmaurs, Kilmarnock KA3 2ND	donannmac@yahoo.co.uk	01563 538475

Name	Address	Email	Phone
MacLeod, Sharon (Mrs)	Creag Dhubh, Golf Course Road, Whiting Bay, Isle of Arran KA27 8QT	macleodsharon@hotmail.com	01770 700353
Matheson, David	44 Auchenkeld Avenue, Heathhall, Dumfries DG1 3QY	davidb.matheson44@btinternet.com	01387 252042
McCool, Robert	17 McGregor Avenue, Stevenston KA20 4BA		01294 466548
McGeever, Gerard (on sabbatical until 2023)	23 Kinloch Avenue, Stewarton, Kilmarnock KA3 3HQ	mcgeege1@gmail.com	01560 484331
McQuistan, Robert	Old Schoolhouse, Carsluith, Newton Stewart DG8 7DT	mcquistan@mcquistan.plus.com	01671 820327
Mills, Catherine (Mrs)	59 Crossdene Road, Crosshouse, Kilmarnock KA2 0IU	cfmills5lib@hotmail.com	01563 535305
Monk, Geoffrey	Hilbre Cottage, Laurieston, Castle Douglas DG7 2PW		01644 450679
Morrison, James	27 Monkton Road, Prestwick KA9 1AP	jamessmorrisonprestwick@gmail.com	01292 479313 / 07773 287852
Morton, Andrew A. BSc	19 Sherwood Park, Lockerbie DG11 2DX	andrew_morton@mac.com	01576 203164
Murphy, Ian	56 Lamont Crescent, Netherthird, Cumnock KA18 3DU	ianm_cumnock@yahoo.co.uk	01290 423675
Murray, Brian	19 Snowdon Terrace, Seamill KA23 9HN	brian.murray100@btinternet.com	01294 822272
Ogston, Jean (Mrs)	14 North Park Avenue, Girvan KA26 9DH	jeanogston@gmail.com	01465 713081
Robertson, William	1 Archers Avenue, Irvine KA11 2GB	willie.robert@yahoo.co.uk	01294 203577
Ronald, Glenn	188 Prestwick Road, Ayr KA8 8NP	glennronald@btinternet.com	01292 286861
Ross, Magnus M.B. BA MEd	39 Beachway, Largs KA30 8QH	m.b.ross@btinternet.com	01475 689572
Stewart, Christine (Mrs)	52 Kilnford Drive, Dundonald KA2 9ET	christistewart@btinternet.com	01563 850486
Whitelaw, David	9 Kirkhill, Kilwinning KA13 6NB	whitelawfam@talktalk.net	01294 551695

14. CLYDE

Name	Address	Email	Phone
Banks, Russell	18 Aboyne Drive, Paisley PA2 7SJ	margaret.banks2@ntlworld.com	0141 884 6925
Bird, Mary Jane (Miss)	Greenhill Farm, Barochan Road, Houston PA6 7HS	mjbird55@gmail.com	
Boag, Jennifer (Miss)	11 Madeira Street, Greenock PA16 7UJ	jenniferboag@hotmail.com	01475 720125
Davey, Charles L.	16 Divert Road, Gourock PA19 1DT	charlesdavey16@hotmail.co.uk	01475 631544
Hood, Eleanor (Mrs)	12 Clochoderick Avenue, Kilbarchan, Johnstone PA10 2AY	eleanor.hood.kilbarchan@ntlworld.com	01505 704208
MacDonald, Christine (Ms)	33 Collier Street, Johnstone PA5 8AG	christine.macdonald10@ntlworld.com	01505 355779
Marshall, Leon M.	Glenisla, Gryffe Road, Kilmacolm PA13 4BA	lm@stevenson-kyles.co.uk	01505 872417
Maxwell, Margaret A. (Sandra) (Mrs) BD	2 Grants Avenue, Paisley PA2 6AZ	sandra@maxwellmail.co.uk	0141 884 3710
McEwan, Alex	1/1 The Riggs, Milngavie G62 8LX	aleximcewan@gmail.com	0141 384 0274
McFarlan, Elizabeth (Miss)	20 Fauldswood Crescent, Paisley PA2 9PA	elizabeth.mcfarlan@ntlworld.com	01505 358411
McHugh, Jack	Earlshaugh, Earl Close, Bridge of Weir PA11 3HA	jackmchugh1@btinternet.com	01505 612789
Morgan, Richard	Annandale, School Road, Rhu, Helensburgh G84 8RS	themorgans@hotmail.co.uk	01436 821269
Rankin, Kenneth	20 Bruntsfield Gardens, Glasgow G53 7QJ	krankin@hotmail.co.uk	0141 880 7474

Name	Address	Email	Phone
Spooner, John R. BSc PGC(Mgt)	Onslow, Uplawmoor Road, Neilston, Glasgow G78 3LB	jrspooner@btopenworld.com	0141 881 5182 07481 008033
Theaker, Philip D. (Dr)	17 Kilmory Gardens, Skelmorlie PA17 5EX	ptheaker48@gmail.com	07904 919776

16. GLASGOW

Name	Address	Email	Phone
Allan, Phillip	34 Muirhead Way, Bishopbriggs, Glasgow G64 1YG	hampdenhorror@gmail.com	07954 497930
Fullarton, Andrew	Flat 2/2, 2263 Paisley Road West, Glasgow G52 3QA	drewf225@gmail.com	0141 883 9518
Horner, David J.	20 Ledi Road, Glasgow G43 2AJ	djhorner@btinternet.com	0141 637 7369
Kelly, George	25 Westerton, Lennoxtown G66 7LR	geojkelly@btinternet.com	0141 360 311739
Kilpatrick, Joan (Mrs)	39 Brent Road, Regent's Park, Glasgow G46 8JG	je-kilpatrick@sky.com	0141 621 1809
McFarlane, Robert	25 Avenel Road, Glasgow G13 2PB	robertmcfrln@yahoo.co.uk	0141 954 5540
Mcnally, Gordon	10 Melville Gardens, Bishopbriggs, Glasgow G64 3DF	gmcinally@sky.com	0141 563 2685
Millar, Kathleen (Mrs)	18 Greenwood Grove West, Stewarton Road, Glasgow G77 6ZF		07793 203045
Morrison, Graham	1/1, 40 Gardner Street, Glasgow G11 5DF		0141 579 4772
Morrison, Katie (Miss)	3b Lennox Court, 16 Stockiemuir Avenue, Bearsden G61 3JL	katiemorrison2003@hotmail.co.uk	0141 942 3024 07852 373840
Nicolson, John C.	2 Lindsaybeg Court, Chryston, Glasgow G69 9DD	john.c.nicolson@btinternet.com	0141 779 2447
Robertson, Lynne M. (Mrs) MA MEd	2 Greenhill, Bishopbriggs, Glasgow G64 1LE	emrobertsonmed@btinternet.com	0141 772 1323 07720 053981
Smith, Ann	52 Robslee Road, Thornliebank, Glasgow G46 7BX	maystead@hotmail.co.uk	0141 621 0638
Stead, May (Mrs)	9A Carrick Drive, Mount Vernon, Glasgow G32 0RW		07917 785109
Struthers, Ivar	7 McVean Place, Longcroft, Bonnybridge FK4 1QZ	ivar.struthers@btinternet.com	01324 841145
Tindall, Maragret (Mrs)	23 Ashcroft Avenue, Lennoxtown, Glasgow G65 7EN	margarettindall@aol.com	01360 310911

17. FORTH VALLEY AND CLYDESDALE

Name	Address	Email	Phone
Allan, Angus J.	Blackburn Mill, Chapelton, Strathaven ML10 6RR	angus.allan@hotmail.com	01357 300916
Beattie, Richard	4 Bent Road, Hamilton ML3 6QB	richardbeattie1958@hotmail.com	01698 420806
Codona, Joy (Mrs)	Dykehead Farm, 300 Dykehead Road, Airdrie ML6 7SR	jcodona772@btinternet.com	01236 767063 07810 770609
Douglas, Ian	24 Abbotsford Crescent, Strathaven ML10 6EQ	IDouglas@churchofscotland.org.uk	07742 022423
Duncan, Lorna M. (Mrs) BA	28 Solway Drive, Head of Muir, Denny FK6 5NS	ell.dee@blueyonder.co.uk	01698 813020
Grant, Alan	25 Moss-side Avenue, Carluke ML8 5UG	amgrant25@aol.com	01355 771419
Hastings, William Paul	186 Glen More, East Kilbride, Glasgow G74 2AN	wphastings@hotmail.co.uk	01355 521228
Henderson, William D.	48 Watson Street, High Blantyre G72 9SJ	bill_henderson@icloud.com	07954 167158
Hislop, Eric	1 Castlegait, Strathaven ML10 6FF	eric.hislop@tiscali.co.uk	01698 829938
Jardine, Lynette	1 Hume Drive, Uddingston, Glasgow G71 4DW	lpjardine@blueyonder.co.uk	01357 520003
Love, William	30 Barmore Avenue, Carluke ML8 4PE	janbill30@tiscali.co.uk	01698 812404
McCleary, Isaac	719 Coatbridge Road, Bargeddie, Glasgow G69 7PH	isaacmccleary@gmail.com	01555 751243 07908 547040

Name	Address	Email	Phone
McMillan, Isabelle (Mrs)	17 Castle Avenue, Airth, Falkirk FK2 8GA		07896 433314
Preston, Steven J.	24 Glen Prosen, East Kilbride, Glasgow G74 3TA	steven.preston1@btinternet.com	01355 237359 / 07752 120536
Scoular, Iain W.	15 Bonnyside Road, Bonnybridge FK4 2AD	scoulariain@gmail.com	01324 812395 / 07717 131596
Stevenson, Thomas	34 Castle Wynd, Quarter, Hamilton ML3 7XD	weetamgtr@gmail.com	01698 282263 / 07860 477344
Stewart, Arthur MA	51 Bonnymuir Crescent, Bonnybridge FK4 1GD	arthur.stewart1@btinternet.com	01324 812667
Struthers, Ivar B.	7 McVean Place, Bonnybridge FK4 1QZ	ivar.struthers@btinternet.com	01324 841145 / 07921 778208
White, Ian T.	4 Gilchrist Walk, Lesmahagow ML11 0FQ	iantwhite@aol.com	01555 890704

19. ARGYLL

Name	Address	Email	Phone
Allan, Douglas	1 Camplen Court, Rothesay, Isle of Bute PA20 0NL	douglasallan984@btinternet.com	
Binner, Aileen (Mrs)	Ailand, North Connel, Oban PA37 1QX England	binners@ailand.plus.com	01631 710264
Garrett, William		we.garrett@btinternet.com	
Logue, David	3 Braeface, Tayvallich, Lochgilphead PA31 89N	david@loguenet.co.uk	01546 870647
Malcolm, James	Courtyard Cottage, Barrmor View, Kilmartin PA31 8UN	jgmalcolm@btinternet.com	01546 510540
McHugh, Douglas	Tigh Na Criche, Cairndow, Argyll PA27 8BY	dmchugh6@gmail.com	01369 860147
McLellan, James A.	West Drimvore, Lochgilphead PA31 8SU	james.mclellan8@btinternet.com	01546 606403
Mills, Peter A.	Northon, Ganavan, Oban PA34 5TU	peter@peteramills.com	
Morrison, John L.	Tigh na Barnashaig, Tayvallich, Lochgilphead PA31 8PN	jolomo@thejolomostudio.com	01546 870637
Ramsay, Matthew M.	Portnastorm, Carradale, Campbeltown PA28 6SB	kintyre@fishermensmission.org.uk	01583 431381
Scouller, Alastair	15 Allanwater Apartments, Bridge of Allan, Stirling FK9 4DZ	scouller@globalnet.co.uk	01786 832496
Sinclair, Margaret (Ms)	2 Quarry Place, Furnace, Inveraray PA32 8XW	margaret_sinclair@btinternet.com	01499 500633
Stather, Angela (Ms)	1 Dunlossit Cottages, Port Askaig, Isle of Islay PA46 7RB	angstat@btinternet.com	01496 840726
Thornhill, Christopher R.	4 Ardfern Cottages, Ardfern, Lochgilphead PA31 8QN	c.thornhill@btinternet.com	01852 300011
Waddell, Martin	Fasgadh, Clachan Seil, Oban PA34 4TJ	waddell715@btinternet.com	01852 300395
Zielinski, Jenefer C. (Mrs)	7 Wallace Court, Ferguslie Street, Sandbank Dunoon PA23 8QA	jenefferzielinski@gmail.com	01369 706136

23. STIRLING

Name	Address	Email	Phone
Grier, Hunter	17 Station Road, Bannockburn, Stirling FK7 8LG	anneandhunter@gmail.com	01786 815192
McPherson, Alistair M.	Springpark, Doune Road, Dunblane FK15 9AR		01786 826850

24. FIFE

Name	Address	Email	Phone
Biernat, Ian	2 Formonthills Road, Glenrothes KY6 3EF	ian.biernat@btinternet.com	01592 741487
Brown, Gordon	Nowell, Fossoway, Kinross KY13 0UW	brown.nowell@hotmail.com.uk	01577 840248

Elder, Morag Anne (Ms)   5 Provost Road, Tayport DD6 9JE   benuardin@btinternet.com   01382 552218
Grant, Allan   6 Normandy Place, Rosyth KY11 2HJ   allan75@talktalk.net   01383 428760
               07449 278378
Mitchell, Ian G. QC   17 Carlingnose Point, North Queensferry, Inverkeithing KY11 1ER   igmitchell@easynet.co.uk   01383 416240

Monk, Alan   36 North Road, Saline KY12 9UQ   salinemonks@gmail.com   01383 851283
Muirhead, Sandy   7 Westpark Gate, Saline KY12 9US   sandy_muirhead@hotmail.com   01383 850077
Peacock, Graham   6 Balgove Avenue, Gauldry, Newport-on-Tay DD6 8SQ   grahampeacock6@btinternet.com   01382 330124

Smith, Elspeth (Mrs)   Glentarkie Cottage, Glentarkie, Strathmiglo, Cupar KY14 7RU   elspeth.smith@btinternet.com   01337 860824

27. DUNKELD AND MEIGLE
Howat, David P.   Lilybank Cottage, Newton Street, Blairgowrie PH10 6HZ   david@thehowats.net   01250 874715

Patterson, Rosemary (Mrs)   Rowantree, Golf Course Road, Blairgowrie PH10 6LJ   pattersonrose.c@gmail.com   01250 876607

Weidner, Karl J. BD CertTh   4 Drumkelbo Road, Meigle PH12 8AD   kweidner@btinternet.com   07523 091786

28. PERTH
Archibald, Michael   Wychwood, Culdeesland Road, Methven, Perth, PH1 3QE   michael.archibald@gmail.com   01783 840995

Benneworth, Michael   7 Hamilton Place, Perth PH1 1BB   mbenneworth@hotmail.com   01738 628093
Davidson, Andrew   95 Needless Road, Perth PH2 0LD   a.r.davidson.91@cantab.net   01738 620839
Stewart, Anne   Ballcraine, Murthly Road, Stanley, Perth PH1 4PN   anne.stewart13@btinternet.com   01738 828637
Yellowlees, Deirdre (Mrs)   Ringmill House, Gannochy Farm, Perth PH2 7JH   d.yellowlees@btinternet.com   01738 633773
               07920 805399

29. DUNDEE
Xenphontos-Hellen, Tim   23 Ancrum Drive, Dundee DD2 2JG   tim.xsf@btinternet.com   01382 630355
               (Work) 01382 567756

30. ANGUS
Beedie, Alexander W. (William)   68 Bloomfield Road, Arbroath DD11 3LQ   a.wbeedie38@gmail.com   01241 875001

Gray, Linda (Mrs)   8 Inchgarth Street, Forfar DD8 3LY   lindamgray@sky.com   01307 464039
Walker, Eric   12 Orchard Brae, Kirriemuir DD8 4JY   eric.line15@btinternet.com   01575 572082
Walker, Pat (Mrs)   12 Orchard Brae, Kirriemuir DD8 4JY   pat.line15@btinternet.com   01575 572082

31. ABERDEEN AND SHETLAND
Cooper, Gordon   1 Kirkbrae View, Cults, Aberdeen AB15 9RU   ga_cooper@hotmail.co.uk   01224 964165
Gray, Peter (Prof.)   165 Countesswells Road, Aberdeen AB15 7RA   pmdgray@bcs.org.uk   01224 318172
Greig, Martin   85 Macaulay Drive, Aberdeen AB15 8FL   mgreig@aberdeencity.gov.uk   07920 806332

32. KINCARDINE AND DEESIDE

Bell, Robert BSc FIStructE MICE	27 Mearns Drive, Stonehaven AB39 2DZ	r.bell282@btinternet.com	01569 767173 / 07733 014826
Broere, Teresa (Mrs)	3 Balnastraid Cottages, Dinnet, Aboyne AB34 5NE	broere@sbcco.com	01339 880058
Coles, Stephen	43 Mearns Walk, Laurencekirk AB30 1FA	steve@sbcco.com	01561 378400
McCafferty, W. John	Lynwood, Cammachmore, Stonehaven AB39 3NR	wjmccafferty@yahoo.co.uk	01569 730281
Middleton, Robin B. (Capt.)	7 St Ternan's Road, Newtonhill, Stonehaven AB39 3PF	robbiemiddleton7@hotmail.com	07768 925122 / 01569 730852
Simpson, Elizabeth (Mrs)	Connemara, 33 Golf Road, Ballater AB35 5RS	connemara33@yahoo.com	01339 755597

33. GORDON

Bichard, Susanna (Mrs)	Beechlee, Haddo Lane, Tarves, Ellon AB41 7JZ	smbichard@aol.com	01651 851345
Doak, Alan B.	17 Chievres Place, Ellon AB41 9WH	alanbdoak@aol.com	01358 721819
Findlay, Patricia (Mrs)	Douglas View, Tullynessle, Alford AB33 8QR	p.a.findlay@btopenworld.com	01975 562379

34. BUCHAN

Barker, Tim	South Silverford Croft, Longmanhill, Banff AB45 3SB	tbarker05@aol.com	01261 851839
Brown, Lillian (Mrs)	45 Main Street, Aberchirder, Huntly AB54 7ST	mabroon64@gmail.com	01466 780330
Forsyth, Alicia (Mrs)	Rothie Inn Farm, Forgue Road, Rothienorman, Inverurie AB51 8YH	aliciaforsyth56@gmail.com	01651 821359
Givan, James	Zimra, Longmanhill, Banff AB45 3RP	jim.givan@btinternet.com	01261 833318 / 07753 458664
Grant, Margaret (Mrs)	22 Elphin Street, New Aberlour, Fraserburgh AB43 6LH	mgrant3120@gmail.com	01346 561341
Hine, Kath (Ms)	2 Burnside Cottage, Rothiemay, Huntly AB54 7JX	kath.hine@gmail.com	01542 870680
MacLeod, Ali (Ms)	11 Pitfour Crescent, Fetterangus, Peterhead AB42 4EL	aliow1@hotmail.com	01771 622992 / 07821 670705
Macnee, Anthea (Mrs)	Wardend Cottage, Alvah, Banff AB45 3TR	macneeiain4@googlemail.com	01261 815647
Mair, Dorothy L. T. (Miss)	Flat F, 15 The Quay, Newburgh, Ellon AB41 6DA	dorothymair2@aol.com	01358 788832 / 07505 051305
McDonald, Rhoda (Miss)	16 St Andrew's Drive, Fraserburgh AB43 2PX	techmc@callnetuk.com	01346 514052
McFie, David	The Manse, Fordyce Terrace, New Deer, Turriff AB53 6TD	waverley710@gmx.co.uk	01771 644631
Pirie, Maggie (Mrs)	Uppermill Cottage, Auchterless, Turriff AB53 8AU	maggie.pirie@btinternet.com	01888 511059
Simpson, Andrew C.	10 Wood Street, Banff AB45 1JX	andy.louise1@btinternet.com	01261 812538
Sneddon, Richard	100 West Road, Peterhead AB42 2AQ	richard.sneddon@btinternet.com	

35. MORAY

Cumming, Grant	Dunedin, 2 Reidhaven Street, Elgin IV30 1QG	cumminggrant@gmail.com	01343 540023
Forbes, Jean (Mrs)	Greenmoss, Drybridge, Buckie AB56 5JB	dancingfeet@tinyworld.co.uk	01542 831646 / 07974 760337

Name	Address	Email	Telephone
Harrison, Christine BA	16 Allt-Na-Coire, Tomnavoulin, Ballindalloch AB37 9JE	chrstnhrrsn42@googlemail.com	01897 590630 / 07930 048565
36. ABERNETHY			
Bardgett, Alison (Mrs)	Tigh an Iasgair, Street of Kincardine, Boat of Garten PH24 3BY	iasgair10@icloud.com	01479 831751
Black, Barbara J. (Mrs)	Carn Eilrig, Nethy Bridge PH25 3EE	bjcarneilrig54@gmail.com	01479 821641
37. INVERNESS			
Appleby, Jonathan	91 Cradlehall Park, Inverness IV2 5DB	jon.wyvis@gmail.com	01463 791470
Cazaly, Leonard	9 Moray Park Gardens, Culloden, Inverness IV2 7FY	len_cazaly@btinternet.com	01463 794469
Cook, Arnett D.	66 Millerton Avenue, Inverness IV3 8RY	arnett.cook@btinternet.com	01463 224795
Dennis, Barry	5 Loch Ness View, Dores, Inverness IV2 6TW	barrydennis@live.co.uk	01463 751393
King, Fiona	23 Torr Gardens, Dores, Inverness IV2 6TS	kingdores@btinternet.com	01463 751293
MacInnes, Ailsa (Mrs)	Kilmartin, 17 Southside Road, Inverness IV2 3BG	ailsa.macinnes@btopenworld.com	01463 230321 / 07704 485055
Robertson, Hendry	Park House, 51 Glenurquhart Road, Inverness IV3 5PB	hendryrobertson046@btinternet.com	01463 231858 / 07929 766102
Roberston, Stewart J.H.	6 Raasay Road, Inverness IV2 3LR	sjhro@tiscali.co.uk	01463 417937
Roden, Vivian (Mrs)	15 Old Mill Road, Tomatin, Inverness IV13 7YW	vroden@btinternet.com	01808 511355 / 07887 704915
38. LOCHABER			
Gill, Ella (Mrs)	5 Camus Inas, Acharacle PH36 4JQ	ellagill768@gmail.com	01967 431834
Skene, William	Tiree, Gairlochy, Spean Bridge PH34 4EQ	bill.skene@lochaber.presbytery.org.uk	01397 712594
39. ROSS			
Finlayson, Michael R.	Amberlea, Glenskiach, Evanton, Dingwall IV16 9UU	finlayson935@btinternet.com	01349 830598
Greer, Kathleen (Mrs) MEd	17 Duthac Wynd, Tain IV19 1LP	greer2@talktalk.net	01862 892065
Jackson, Simon	Broomton Farm, Balintore IV20 1XN	simonjackson@procam.co.uk	01862 832831
Jamieson, Patricia A. (Mrs)	9 Craig Avenue, Tain IV19 1JP	happjam179@yahoo.co.uk	01862 893154
McAlpine, James	5 Cromlet Park, Invergordon IV18 0RN	jmca2@tiscali.co.uk	01349 852801
40. SUTHERLAND			
Baxter, A. Rosie (Dr)	Daylesford, Invershin, Lairg IV27 4ET	drrosiereid@yahoo.co.uk	01549 421326 / 07748 761694
Roberts, Irene (Miss)	Flat 4, Harbour Buildings, Main Street, Portmahomack, Tain IV20 1YG	ireneroberts43@hotmail.com	01862 871166 / 07854 436854
41. CAITHNESS			
MacDonald, Morag (Dr)	Orkney View, Portskerra, Melvich KW14 7YL	liliasmacdonald@btinternet.com	01641 531281
O'Neill, Leslie	Holytree Cottage, Parkside, Lybster KW3 6AS	leslie_oneill@hotmail.co.uk	01593 721738
O'Neill, Maureen (Mrs)	Holytree Cottage, Parkside, Lybster KW3 6AS	oneill.maureen@yahoo.com	01593 721738

42. LOCHCARRON-SKYE

Name	Address	Email	Phone
Lamont, John H. BD	6 Tigh na Filine, Aultbea, Achnasheen IV22 2JE	jhlamont@btinternet.com	07714 720753
MacRae, Donald E.	Nethania, 52 Strath, Gairloch IV21 2DB	dmgair@aol.com	01445 712235

43. UIST

MacNab, Ann (Mrs)	Druim Skilivat, Scolpaig, Lochmaddy, Isle of North Uist HS6 5DH	annabhan@hotmail.com	01876 510701

44. LEWIS

Macleod, Donald	14 Balmerino Drive, Stornoway, Isle of Lewis HS1 2TD	donaldmacleod25@btinternet.com	01851 704516
Macmillan, Iain	34 Scotland Street, Stornoway, Isle of Lewis HS1 2JR	iainmacmillan.alba34@gmail.com	01851 704826 / 07943 420817

45. ORKNEY

Dicken, Marion (Mrs)	12 MacDonald Park, St Margaret's Hope, Orkney KW17 2AL	mj44@hotmail.co.uk	01856 831687
Gillespie, Jean (Mrs)	16 St Colm's Quadrant, Eday, Orkney KW16 3PH	jrw2810@btinternet.com	01856 701406 / 01856 873271
Howard, Chris	Pegal, Glaitness Road, Kirkwall KW17 1BA	2201csb@gmail.com	07510 320607
Jones, Josephine (Mrs) BA CertEd LRAM	Moorside, Firth, Orkney KW17 2JZ	yetminstermusic@googlemail.com	01856 761899
Pomfret, Valerie (Mrs)	3 Clumly Avenue, Kirkwall, Orkney KW15 1YU	vpomfret@btinternet.com	
Robertson, Johan (Mrs)	Essonquoy, Eday, Orkney KW17 2AB	essonquoy@btinternet.com	01857 622251

47. ENGLAND

Menzies, Rena (Mrs)	40 Elizabeth Avenue, St Brelade's, Jersey JE3 8GR	menzfamily@jerseymail.co.uk	01534 741095
Milligan, Elaine (Mrs)	16 Surrey Close, Corby, Northants NN17 2TG	elainemilligan@ntlworld.com	01536 205259

48. INTERNATIONAL CHARGES

Campbell, Cindy (Mrs)	9 Cavello Heights, Sandys MA 05, Bermuda	cindyfcampbell@gmail.com	001 441 234 3797
Goodman, Alice (Mrs)	Route de Sallaz 23, Rivaz 1071, Switzerland	alice.goodman@epfl.ch	0041 21 946 1727

49. JERUSALEM

Name	Address	Email	Phone
Oakley-Levstein, Joanna (Mrs) BA	Mevo Hamma, 12934, Israel	j.oak.lev@gmail.com	00972 50584 2517

LIST I – MINISTRIES DEVELOPMENT STAFF

Ministries Development Staff support local congregations, parish groupings and presbyteries in a wide variety of ways, bringing expertise or experience to pastoral work, development, and outreach in congregation and community. Some may be ministers and deacons undertaking specialist roles: they are listed also in Section 5 (Presbyteries), with deacons further in List C of the present section.

1. EDINBURGH AND WEST LOTHIAN

Brown, Kenneth (Rev) BD	Livingston United – Church and Community Development Worker	Kenneth.Brown@churchofscotland.org.uk
Corrie, Margaret (Miss) DCS	Armadale – Parish Assistant	MCorrie@churchofscotland.org.uk
Crocker, Liz DipComEd DCS	Edinburgh: Tron Kirk (Gilmerton and Moredun) – Parish Assistant	ECrocker@churchofscotland.org.uk
de Jager, Lourens (Rev) PgDip MDiv BTh	Edinburgh: Portobello and Joppa – Associate Minister	LDeJager@churchofscotland.org.uk
Fejszes, Violetta (Dr)	Edinburgh: Old Kirk and Muirhouse – Parish Development Worker	VFejszes@churchofscotland.org.uk
Hirani, Hina	Edinburgh: Old Kirk and Muirhouse – Project Development Worker	HHirani@churchofscotland.org.uk
Hudson, Henry	Edinburgh: Gorgie Dalry Stenhouse – Community Outreach Worker	Henry.Hudson@churchofscotland.org.uk
Laoshe, Fadeke	Edinburgh: St Margaret's – Children, Youth and Family Worker	FLaoshe@churchofscotland.org.uk
Lawrie, Lesley	Livingston: Old – Community Outreach Worker	LLawrie@churchofscotland.org.uk
Lewis, Christein	Edinburgh: Old Kirk and Muirhouse – Young Person Development Worker	CLewis@churchofscotland.org.uk
MacPherson, Gigha K.	Edinburgh: St David's Broomhouse – Children and Family Worker	GMacPherson@churchofscotland.org.uk
McMullin, Michael BA	Edinburgh: Craigmillar Park; Priestfield; Reid Memorial – Community Project Worker	MMcMullin@churchofscotland.org.uk
Midwinter, Alan	Edinburgh: St David's Broomhouse – Pastoral Assistant	AMidwinter@churchofscotland.org.uk
Moodie, David	Edinburgh: Granton – Parish Assistant	DMoodie@churchofscotland.org.uk
Orr, Lorraine	Linlithgow: St Michael's – Pioneer and Community Outreach Worker	LOrr@churchofscotland.org.uk
Richardson, Ian (Dr)	Edinburgh: Holy Trinity – Discipleship Team Leader	IRichardson@churchofscotland.org.uk
Robertson, Douglas S. BEng BA MTh	Edinburgh: Gracemount – Church Leader and Project Worker	Douglas.Robertson@churchofscotland.org.uk
Stark, Jennifer MA MATheol	Edinburgh: Richmond Craigmillar – Community Project Worker	JStark@churchofscotland.org.uk

3. LOTHIAN

Billes, Shirley	Tranent – Youth and Families Worker	SBilles@churchofscotland.org.uk
McKenzie, Susan	Newton – Mission and Discipleship Outreach Worker	SMcKenzie@churchofscotland.org.uk
Pryde, Erika	Newton – Mission and Discipleship Outreach Worker	EPryde@churchofscotland.org.uk

4. MELROSE AND PEEBLES

5. DUNS

6. JEDBURGH

7. SOUTH WEST

Algeo, Paul	North Ayr Parish Grouping – Family/Development Worker	PAlgeo@churchofscotland.org.uk

Anderson, Peter	Stewarton 20s–40s Initiative – Mission Pioneer	PAnderson@churchofscotland.org.uk
Beck, Isobel BD DCS	Kilwinning Abbey – Deacon	IBeck@churchofscotland.org.uk
Blair, Fiona DCS	Beith – Parish Assistant	FBlair@churchofscotland.org.uk
Devlin, Brian	Stevenston: Ardeer linked with Livingstone – Community Mission Worker	BDevlin@churchofscotland.org.uk
Forsyth, Stuart	Irvine Virtual Church Initiative – Mission Pioneer	SForsyth@churchofscotland.org.uk
Hendry, Jill	Kilmarnock South Area – Growing Together with God – Mission Pioneer	JHendry@churchofscotland.org.uk
Hislop, Donna	Canonbie, Langholm & Border grouping - Children's, Youth and Family Worker	DHislop@churchofscotland.org.uk
Jenkinson, Barbara (Dr)	Dalmellington linked with Patna Waterside – Parish Assistant	BJenkinson@churchofscotland.org.uk
McKay, Angus BA	Cumbrae linked with Largs St John's – Parish Assistant	AMcKay@churchofscotland.org.uk
McTernan, Margaret (Rev) LLB MSW CertCP CertSWM	Presbytery Mission Pioneer Team Leader	MMcTernan@churchofscotland.org.uk
Muir, Alison	Irvine Towerlands Church Plant Initiative – Mission Pioneer	Alison.Muir@churchofscotland.org.uk
Templeton, Katrona	Irvine Open Door (Disability Inclusion) Initiative – Mission Pioneer	KTempleton@churchofscotland.org.uk
Thomson, Robert	Irvine Sports Development Initiative – Mission Pioneer	RThomson@churchofscotland.org.uk
Wardrop, Elaine	Kilmarnock: St Marnock's: Mission Development Worker	EWardrop@churchofscotland.org.uk

14. CLYDE

Burke, Maureen	Dumbarton churches – Pastoral Assistant	MBurke@churchofscotland.org.uk
Dungavell, Marie Claire	Dumbarton: Riverside linked with West – Development Worker	MCDungavell@churchofscotland.org.uk
Graham, Gillian	Clydebank: Waterfront linked with Dalmuir: Barclay – Children, Young People and Family Worker	GGraham@churchofscotland.org.uk
Wilson, Lorraine	Clydebank: Waterfront linked with Dalmuir: Barclay – Pastoral Assistant	LWilson@churchofscotland.org.uk

16. GLASGOW

Black, Karen	Glasgow: Garthamlock and Craigend – Family and Community Worker	KBlack@churchofscotland.org.uk
Boland, Susan (Mrs) DipHE(Theol)	Cumbernauld: Abronhill and Cumbernauld: Kildrum – Family Development Worker	SBoland@churchofscotland.org.uk
Burgess, June	Glasgow: Ruchazie – Mission Resources Worker	JBurgess@churchofscotland.org.uk
Cameron, Lisa	Glasgow: Carntyne – Children and Families Worker	LCameron@churchofscotland.org.uk
Carroll, Helen	Glasgow: Springburn – Church and Community Development Worker	HCarroll@churchofscotland.org.uk
Cathcart, John Paul DCS	Glasgow: Castlemilk – Deacon	John.Cathcart@churchofscotland.org.uk
Cuthbertson, Valerie S. (Miss) DCS	Cumbernauld: Old – Deacon	VCuthbertson@churchofscotland.org.uk
Gargrave, Mary S. (Mrs) DCS	Glasgow: Carnwadric – Deacon	Mary.Gargrave@churchofscotland.org.uk
Goodwin, Jamie	Glasgow: Govan and Linthouse – Arts and Worship Development Worker	JGoodwin@churchofscotland.org.uk
Graham, Susan	Glasgow: Sherbrooke Mosspark – Church and Community Outreach Worker	SGraham@churchofscotland.org.uk
Hamilton, James DCS	Glasgow: Maryhill – Deacon	James.Hamilton@churchofscotland.org.uk
Hamilton, Karen (Mrs) DCS	Cambuslang – Deacon	KHamilton@churchofscotland.org.uk
Herbert, Claire BD DCS	Lodging House Mission, Glasgow – Chaplain	CHerbert@churchofscotland.org.uk
Howie, Lamont	Glasgow: Drumchapel St Mark's – Community Outreach Worker	LHowie@churchofscotland.org.uk
Hyndman, Graham	Church House, Bridgeton – Youth Worker	GHyndman@churchofscotland.org.uk
Johnstone, Susan	Glasgow: Castlemilk – Community Development Worker	SJohnstone@churchofscotland.org.uk

Macdonald-Haak, Aileen D.	Glasgow: Carntyne – Development Worker, Older People	AMacdonald-Haak@churchofscotland.org.uk
Marshall, Kirsteen	Glasgow: St Christopher's Priesthill and Nitshill – Parish Assistant	KMarshall@churchofscotland.org.uk
McDougall, Hilary N. (Rev) MA PGCE BD	Presbytery – Depute Clerk and Congregational Facilitator	HMcDougall@churchofscotland.org.uk
McElhinny, Amy	Glasgow: Queen's Park Govanhill – Community Outreach Worker	AMcElhinny@churchofscotland.org.uk
McIlreavy, Gillian M.	Glasgow: Govan and Linthouse – Communications Worker	GMcIlreavy@churchofscotland.org.uk
McMahon, Deborah	Glasgow: Easterhouse – Children's and Development Worker Team Leader	DKeenan@churchofscotland.org.uk
McWilliam, David	Glasgow: Ruchazie – Project Support Worker	DMcWilliam@churchofscotland.org.uk
Milligan, Catriona	Glasgow: Gorbals – Community Development Worker	CMilligan@churchofscotland.org.uk
Morrison, Iain J.	Glasgow: Colston Milton – Community Arts Worker	IMorrison@churchofscotland.org.uk
Mubengo, Eddison	Rutherglen: West and Wardlawhill – Mission and Discipleship Worker	EMubengo@churchofscotland.org.uk
Peat, Derek A. (Rev) BA BD MTh	Presbytery – Strategy Officer	DPeat@churchofscotland.org.uk
Robertson, Douglas J.	Glasgow: Shettleston New – Discipleship Facilitator	DJRobertson@churchofscotland.org.uk
Thomas, Jay MA BA	Glasgow: St James' (Pollok) – Youth and Children's Worker	JThomas@churchofscotland.org.uk
Usher, Eileen	Glasgow: Cranhill, Ruchazie, Garthamlock and Craigend Parish Grouping – Family Worker	EUsher@churchofscotland.org.uk
Willis, Mags	Glasgow: Easterhouse – Youth Development Worker	MWillis@churchofscotland.org.uk
Wilson, Marie	Netherlee and Stamperland – Pastoral Assistant	Marie.Wilson@churchofscotland.org.uk
Young, Neil J.	Glasgow: St Paul's – Youth Team Leader	NYoung@churchofscotland.org.uk

17. FORTH VALLEY AND CLYDESDALE

Brydson, Angela (Mrs)	Southern Ministry Cluster – Community Outreach Worker	ABrydson@churchofscotland.org.uk
Robertson, Julie	Strathaven: Trinity – Children and Youth Development Worker	JRobertson@churchofscotland.org.uk

19. ARGYLL

Binner, Aileen	Presbytery – Hub Ministries Co-ordinator, South Argyll	ABinner@churchofscotland.org.uk
D'Silva, Emily	Kilmore and Oban – Parish Assistant	EDSilva@churchofscotland.org.uk
Hay, Alison	Presbytery – Ministries Co-ordinator, North and East Argyll	AHay@churchofscotland.org.uk
Whyte, Susan	Presbytery – Youth Worker – Team Leader	SWhyte@churchofscotland.org.uk
Wilson, John K. (Kenny)	Presbytery – Youth and Children's Worker	KWilson@churchofscotland.org.uk

23. STIRLING

Allen, Valerie L. (Rev) BMus MDiv DMin	Presbytery – Chaplain	VL2allen@btinternet.com

24. FIFE

Christie, Aileen	Lochgelly and Benarty: St Serf's – Outreach Worker	Aileen.Christie@churchofscotland.org.uk
Davie, Sandra	Glenrothes: St Margaret's – Children Youth and Family Worker	SDavie@churchofscotland.org.uk
Hutchison, John BA	Rothes Trinity Parish Grouping – Families Worker and Parish Assistant	JHutchison@churchofscotland.org.uk
Jones, Lauren	Kirkcaldy: Templehall and Torbain United – Community Outreach Worker	LJones@churchofscotland.org.uk
Kerr, Fiona	Methil: Wellesley – Parish Assistant	FKerr@churchofscotland.org.uk
Pringle, Iona M. BD	Kennoway, Windygates and Balgonie: St Kenneth's – Parish Assistant	IPringle@churchofscotland.org.uk
Scott, Pamela (Mrs) DCS	Lochgelly and Benarty: St Paul's – Parish Assistant	PScott@churchofscotland.org.uk
Thomson, Jacqueline (Mrs) MTh DCS	Buckhaven and Wemyss – Deacon	Jacqueline.Thomson@churchofscotland.org.uk

Thorburn, Susan (Rev) MTh — Eden Tay Cluster – Mission Development Worker — SThorburn@churchofscotland.org.uk
Ure, Irene — Glenrothes Area Partnership Development Co-ordinator — IUre@churchofscotland.org.uk

27. DUNKELD AND MEIGLE

28. PERTH
Slowman, Neil BA — Perth: Letham St Mark's – Community Development Worker — NSlowman@churchofscotland.org.uk
Smith, Jane — Perth: Riverside – Community Development Worker — JSmith@churchofscotland.org.uk
Stott, Anne M. (Rev) — Presbytery Pioneer Worker – Bertha Park — AStott@churchofscotland.org.uk

29. DUNDEE
Berry, Gavin R. — Dundee: Camperdown/Dundee: Lochee – Parish Assistant — GBerry@churchofscotland.org.uk
Clark, Ross — Dundee: Fintry – Discipleship, Mission and Development Worker — Ross.Clark@churchofscotland.org.uk
McKenzie, Matthew — Dundee: Lochee / Dundee: Camperdown – Youth and Families Worker — MMcKenzie@churchofscotland.org.uk
Reynolds, Scott E. BSc BA — Monifieth – Parish Assistant — SReynolds@churchofscotland.org.uk
Stirling, Diane BSc DipCPC BTh — Dundee: Craigiebank linked with Douglas and Mid Craigie – Parish Assistant — DStirling@churchofscotland.org.uk

30. ANGUS
Barakat, Shona — Montrose Area – Youth and Children's Worker — SBarakat@churchofscotland.org.uk

31. ABERDEEN AND SHETLAND
Amalanand, John C. — Aberdeen: South Holburn – Parish Assistant — JAmalanand@churchofscotland.org.uk
Angus, Natalie — Dyce – Youth and Family Worker — NAngus@churchofscotland.org.uk
Brankin, Cheryl L. (Mrs) BA — Presbytery – Depute Clerk — aberdeenshetland@churchofscotland.org.uk
Griffiths Weir, K. Ellen — Shetland – Youth and Children's Worker — EWeir@churchofscotland.org.uk
Joseph, Sundari C. (Dr) — Presbytery – Communications Officer — SJoseph@churchofscotland.org.uk
Mitchell, William — Aberdeen: St George's Tillydrone – Parish Assistant — WMitchell@churchofscotland.org.uk
Richardson, Frances — Shetland – Administrator and Treasurer — FRichardson@churchofscotland.org.uk
Simms, Michele MA — Shetland – Parish Development Worker — MSimms@churchofscotland.org.uk
Taylor, Valerie AssocCIPD PGDip — Aberdeen: Torry St Fittick's – Ministry Assistant — VTaylor@churchofscotland.org.uk
van Geete, Claire MSc — Aberdeen: North – Children and Families Development Worker — CVanGeete@churchofscotland.org.uk

32. KINCARDINE AND DEESIDE

33. GORDON
Adam, Pamela BD — Ellon – Parish Assistant — PAdam@churchofscotland.org.uk
Bruce, Nicola P.S. BA MTh — Ellon – Parish Assistant, Mission Development — NBruce@churchofscotland.org.uk
Cross, Peter — Ellon – Parish Assistant — PCross@churchofscotland.org.uk
Daramola, Ibidun (Rev) BA MA PhD — Skene – Associate Minister — IDaramola@churchofscotland.org.uk

Mikelson, Heather (Rev) — Presbytery - Mission Development Worker — HMikelson@churchofscotland.org.uk
Stigant, Victoria J. — Presbytery - Youth Work Facilitator — VStigant@churchofscotland.org.uk

34. BUCHAN
Dick, Janet — Presbytery – Mission and Discipleship Development Worker — Janet.Dick@churchofscotland.org.uk

35. MORAY
Baker, Paula (Mrs) — Birnie and Pluscarden linked with Elgin: High – Parish Assistant — PBaker@churchofscotland.org.uk

36. ABERNETHY
Black, Barbara — Tomintoul, Glenlivet and Inveraven – Parish Assistant — BBlack@churchofscotland.org.uk
Bowker, Thomas — Presbytery – Fresh Expressions Worker (South) — TBowker@churchofscotland.org.uk

37. INVERNESS

38. LOCHABER
MacLeod, Rory N. (Rev) BA BD — Fort William Kilmallie linked with Kilmonivaig – Team Minister — RNMacLeod@churchofscotland.org.uk

39. ROSS

40. SUTHERLAND

41. CAITHNESS
Petersen, Robert — Wick: Pulteneytown and Thrumster – Mission Development Worker — RPetersen@churchofscotland.org.uk
Rennie, Lyall (Rev) — Pentland – Parish Assistant — LRennie@churchofscotland.org.uk

42. LOCHCARRON-SKYE
Sikorski, Anne — Presbytery – Mission and Ministry Development Worker — ASikorski@churchofscotland.org.uk

43. UIST

44. LEWIS

45. ORKNEY

47. ENGLAND

McLaren, William (Rev) MA BD   London: St Columba's with Newcastle: St Andrew's – Associate Minister   WMcLaren@churchofscotland.org.uk

48. INTERNATIONAL CHARGES

LIST J – OVERSEAS LOCATIONS

AFRICA

MALAWI	**Church of Central Africa Presbyterian Synod of Livingstonia**		
	Dr Linus Malu (2018)	Legal Officer, Church and Society Department, Church and Society Department, PO Box 112, Mzuzu, Malawi mabuikemalu@yahoo.com	office +265 265 1 311 133 mobile +265 994 652 345 www.ccapsolinia.org
	Mr Gary Brough (2019)	Organisational Development Director, CCAP General Assembly Office, PO Box 112, Mzuzu, Malawi	mobile +265 883 626 500

MALAWI: CCAP Livingstonia, Nkhoma and Blantyre: MOZAMBIQUE: **Evangelical Church of Christ**; SOUTH SUDAN: **Presbyterian Church of South Sudan and Sudan**

	Rev Dr Kenneth R Ross (2019)	Theological Educator: Africa, based at Zomba Theological College, PO Box 130, Zomba KRoss@churchofscotland.org.uk	+265 1 524 419
ZAMBIA	**United Church of Zambia**		
	Mr Keith and Mrs Ida Waddell (2016)	Special Needs Support and Health Support, UCZ, Mwandi Mission, Box 60693, Livingstone, Zambia keithida2014@gmail.com	mobile (Keith) +260 977 143 692 mobile (Ida) +260 964 761 039 http://uczsynod.org
ZAMBIA	**United Church of Zambia**		
	Mrs Gina Oliver (2021)	Health Secretary, UCZ Synod, Nationalist Road at Burma Road, PO Box 50122, 15101 Ridgeway, Lusaka, Zambia jayamuleya@gmail.com	office 00260 964 761 039 mobile +260 765 194 738 http://uczsynod.org

ASIA

LAOS	Mr Tony and Mrs Catherine Paton (2009) (Mission Associates, staff of CMS)	Church Mission Society, Church of the Holy Spirit, Vientiane Lao People's Democratic Republic	www.the-chs.org.

EUROPE

ROME	Ms Fiona Kendall (2018) (Ecumenical appointment: Methodist Church UK; Global Ministries USA)	Mediterranean Hope, Federation of Protestant Churches in Italy, Via Firenze 38, 00138 Roma, Italy FKendall@churchofscotland.org.uk	00 39 (0)6 4825 120 www.mediterraneanhope.com

MIDDLE EAST
ISRAEL & PALESTINE
JERUSALEM   Rev Dr D. Stewart Gillan (2022)   St Andrew's Jerusalem, PO Box 8619, Jerusalem 91086, Israel   +972 2 673 2401
SGillan@churchofscotland.org.uk   www.standrewsjerusalem.org/
TIBERIAS   Rev Muriel C. Pearson (2021)   St Andrew's Galilee, PO Box 104, Tiberias 14100, Israel   https://standrewsgalilee.com/
MPearson@churchofscotland.org.uk   +447951 888860

The Faith Impact Forum also operates:

St Andrew's Scots Guesthouse, Jerusalem
Originally 'Hospice' and opened in 1930 beside St Andrew's Church in central Jerusalem.   23 bedrooms, meeting rooms, Fairtrade handcrafts sales.
General Manager: Mrs Lilian Lepejian, PO Box 8619, 1 David Remez Street, Jerusalem 910986, Israel.   www.scotsguesthouse.com   info@scotsguesthouse.com
+972 2 673 2401

The Scots Hotel, Tiberias
Hotel, Wellness Resort and Spa, established in 2004 in the historic compound of the Scottish Hospital.   69 bedrooms, restaurant, wine bar, swimming pool, spa,
historical visitors centre. General Manager: Mr Shaul Hadas, 1 Gdud Barak Street, Tiberias, Israel.   www.scotshotels.com   info@scotshotels.co.il
+972 4 671 0710

Tabeetha School, Jaffa
An English speaking school founded in 1863, where girls and boys of different languages, faiths and cultures are educated together through an English curriculum leading
to IGCSE, GCSE and A level qualifications accepted by universities in Israel and elsewhere. Executive Director: Mrs Mona Ashkar PO Box 8170, 21 Jeffet Street, Jaffa
61081, Israel.   www.tabeethaschool.org   +972 3 682 1581

See also the Presbyteries of International Charges and Jerusalem (Section 5: 48 and 49)

LIST K – PRISON CHAPLAINS

SCOTTISH PRISON SERVICE CHAPLAINCY ADVISER (Church of Scotland)
Rev. Dr Sheena Orr   SPS HQ, Calton House, 5 Redheughs Rigg, Edinburgh EH12 9HW   0131 330 3575; 07922 649160
sheena.orr@prisons.gov.scot

ADDIEWELL   HM Prison Addiewell, Station Road, Addiewell, West Calder EH55 8QA   01506 874500
Rev. Chris Galbraith   chris.galbraith@sodexogov.co.uk
Rev. Kay Gilchrist   KGilchrist@churchofscotland.org.uk

CASTLE HUNTLY   HM Prison Castle Huntly, Longforgan, Dundee DD2 5HL   01382 319388
Rev. Anne E. Stewart   anne.stewart2@prisons.gov.scot

CORNTON VALE   HM Prison and Young Offender Institution, Cornton Vale, Cornton Road, Stirling FK9 5NU   01786 835365
Rev. Dr Sheena Orr   sheena.orr@prisons.gov.scot
Mrs Deirdre Yellowlees   deirdre.yellowlees@prisons.gov.scot

DUMFRIES
Rev. Neil Campbell
HM Prison Dumfries, Terregles Street, Dumfries DG2 9AX
neil.campbell2@prisons.gov.scot
01387 294214

EDINBURGH
Mr Gordon Pennykid DCS
Rev. Keith Graham
Rev. David Swan
Rev. Bob Akroyd (Free Church)
HM Prison Edinburgh, 33 Stenhouse Road, Edinburgh EH11 3LN
gordon.pennykid@prisons.gov.scot
KEGraham@churchofscotland.org.uk
david.swan@prisons.gov.scot
robert.akroyd@prisons.gov.scot
0131 444 3115

GLASGOW: BARLINNIE
Rev. Jill Clancy
Rev. Paul Innes (Assemblies of God)
Rev. Jonathan Keefe
Rev. John Murfin (Elim)
HM Prison Barlinnie, 81 Lee Avenue, Riddrie, Glasgow G33 2QX
jill.clancy@prisons.gov.scot; JClancy@churchofscotland.org.uk
paul.innes@prisons.gov.scot
jonathan.keefe@prisons.gov.scot
john.murfin@prisons.gov.scot
0141 770 2059

GLENOCHIL
Rev. Graham Bell (Baptist)
HMPrison Glenochil, King o' Muir Road, Tullibody FK10 3AD
graham.bell@prisons.gov.scot
01259 767211

GRAMPIAN
Rev. Alison Harvey (Episcopal)
Mrs Julie Innes (Assemblies of God)
HM Prison and Young Offender Institution, South Road, Peterhead AB42 2YY
alison.harvey@prisons.gov.scot
julie.innes@prisons.gov.scot
01779 485744

GREENOCK
Contact Chaplaincy Adviser
HM Prison Greenock, Old Inverkip Road, Greenock PA16 9AH
01475 787801

INVERNESS
Rev. Dr Hugh Watt
Rev. John Beadle (Methodist)
HM Prison Inverness, Duffy Drive, Inverness IV2 3HN
hugh.watt@prisons.gov.scot
john.beadle@methodist.org.uk
01463 229020

KILMARNOCK
Rev. John Murfin (Elim)
HM Prison Kilmarnock, Mauchline Road, Kilmarnock KA1 5AA
john.murfin@prisons.gov.scot
01563 548928

LOW MOSS
Rev. Martin Forrest
Rev. Paul Innes (Assemblies of God)
Rev. John Craib (Baptist)
HM Prison Low Moss, 190 Crosshill Road, Bishopbriggs, Glasgow G64 2QB
martin.forrest@prisons.gov.scot
paul.innes@prisons.gov.scot
john.craib@prisons.gov.scot
0141 762 9727

PERTH
Rev. Margaret Shuttleworth
Mrs Deirdre Yellowlees
Chaplaincy Centre, HM Prison Perth, 3 Edinburgh Road, Perth PH2 7JH
margaret.shuttleworth@prisons.gov.scot
deirdre.yellowlees@prisons.gov.scot
01738 458216

POLMONT
Rev. Hillary Nyika (Baptist)
Chaplaincy Centre, HM Young Offender Institution Polmont, Brightons, Falkirk FK2 0AB
hillary.nyika@prisons.gov.scot
01324 722241

SHOTTS
Rev. John Caldwell (Apostolic Church UK)   HM Prison Shotts, Canthill Road, Shotts ML7 4LE   01501 824071
Rev. Murdo MacLean   john.caldwell@prisons.gov.scot
    murdo.maclean@prisons.gov.scot

LIST L – UNIVERSITY CHAPLAINS

ABERDEEN
Rev. Marylee Anderson MA BD   m.anderson@abdn.ac.uk   01224 272137
Rev. David S. Hutchison BSc BD ThM   d.hutchison@abdn.ac.uk   01224 272137

ABERTAY, DUNDEE
Vacant

CAMBRIDGE
Rev. Nigel Uden (U.R.C. and C. of S.)   nigel.uden@downingplaceurc.org   01223 314586

DUNDEE
Rev. Fiona C. Douglas MBE MA BD PhD   f.c.douglas@dundee.ac.uk   01382 384156
Rev. Gordon A. Campbell MA BD (Honorary)   g.a.campbell@dundee.ac.uk   01382 384045

EDINBURGH
Rev. Harriet A. Harris MBE BA DPhil   chaplain@ed.ac.uk   0131 650 2595; 07896 244792
Rev. Geoffrey Baines (Associate Chaplain)   g.baines@ed.ac.uk   0131 650 9502; 07940 348121
Rev. Dr Urzula Glienecke (Associate Chaplain)   urzula.glienecke@ed.ac.uk

EDINBURGH NAPIER (Honorary Chaplains)
Rev. Karen K. Campbell BD MTh DMin   chaplaincy@napier.ac.uk
Rev. Michael J. Mair BD   KKCampbell@churchofscotland.org.uk   0131 447 4359
    MMair@churchofscotland.org.uk   0131 334 1730

GLASGOW
Rev. Carolyn Kelly PhD   chaplain@glasgow.ac.uk   0141 330 4160
Rev. Roger D. Sturrock BD MD FCRP (Honorary)   churchofscotland@glasgow.ac.uk   0141 339 0454
Rev. Elizabeth J. Blythe MDiv (Honorary Assistant)   churchofscotland-2@glasgow.ac.uk   07885 536984

GLASGOW CALEDONIAN
Rev. Alastair S. Duncan MA BD   ADuncan@churchofscotland.org.uk   07968 852083

HERIOT-WATT, EDINBURGH
Rev. Jane M. Howitt MA BD   J.M.Howitt@hw.ac.uk   0131 451 4508

OXFORD
Rev. Helen Garton (U.R.C. and C. of S.)   minister@saintcolumbas.org   01865 606910

ROBERT GORDON, ABERDEEN
Rev. Canon Isaac. M. Poobalan BD MTh DMin — chaplaincy@rgu.ac.uk — 01224 640119

ST ANDREWS
Rev. Donald G. MacEwan MA BD PhD — dgm21@st-andrews.ac.uk — 01334 462865
Rev. Samantha J. Ferguson MTheol (Assistant) — sjf6@st-andrews.ac.uk — 01334 461766
Rev. Jane L. Barron BA DipEd BD — jlb31@st-andrews.ac.uk

STIRLING
Rev. Lesley Stanley MA PhD FBTS — lesley.stanley@stir.ac.uk — 01786 467164

STRATHCLYDE, GLASGOW
Rev. Meg Masson — meg.masson@strath.ac.uk — 0141 548 2212

LIST M – WORK PLACE CHAPLAINS

Work Place Chaplaincy Scotland — **info@wpcscotland.co.uk**
National Director: Rev. Andrew Gregg — Andrew.Gregg@wpcscotland.co.uk — 07834 748129

For a list of Work Place Chaplaincy key contacts see: www.wpcscotland.co.uk > Contact Us

Outwith WPCS:
Chaplain to the UK Oil and Gas Industry — Rev. Gordon T. Craig — gordon.craig@ukoilandgaschaplaincy.com — 01224 882600
www.ukoilandgaschaplaincy.com

LIST N – REPRESENTATIVES ON COUNCIL EDUCATION COMMITTEES

Council	Representative	Email	Phone
Aberdeen City	Ms Hilda Smith	smithh09@hotmail.com	01224 311309
Aberdeenshire	Rev. Carl J. Irvine	CIrvine@churchofscotland.org.uk	01467 629163
Angus	Vacant		
Argyll and Bute	Rev. Alexander J. MacPherson	SMacPherson@churchofscotland.org.uk	01369 707969
City of Edinburgh	Mrs Fiona E. Beveridge	fbeveridge1@gmail.com	0131 661 8831
Clackmannanshire	Rev. Sang Y. Cha	SCha@churchofscotland.org.uk	01259 213872
Comhairle nan Eilean Siar	Rev. Hugh M. Stewart	berneralwuig@btinternet.com	01851 672388
Dumfries and Galloway	Mr Robert McQuistan	mcquistan@mcquistan.plus.com	01671 820327

Presbytery	Name	Email		Phone
Dundee City	Ms Margaret McVean	margaret.mcvean@btinternet.com		01382 860894
East Ayrshire	Rev. Dr Allan S. VInt	AVint@churchofscotland.org.uk		01290 518528
East Dunbartonshire	Mrs Barbara Jarvie	jarviebj@gmail.com		01360 319729
East Lothian	Mr Ray Lesso	ray.lesso@gmail.com		07884 448224
East Renfrewshire	Mrs Fiona M. Gilchrist	fionagilchrist0@gmail.com		0141 391 9551
Falkirk	Mrs Agnes Mullen	mullenagnescc@gmail.com		07447 393343
Fife	Mr Brian W. Blanchflower	brian.blanchflower@btinternet.com		01383 874258; 07759 944452
Glasgow City	Mr James Hamilton DCS	James.Hamilton@churchofscotland.org.uk		0141 558 3195; 07584 137314
Highland	Mr William Skene	bill.skene@lochaber.presbytery.org.uk		01397 712594
Inverclyde	Rev. David W.G. Burt	dwgburt@btinternet.com		07971 431185
Midlothian	Mrs Elizabeth Morton	elizabethmorton180@gmail.com		0131 663 8916
Moray	Ms. Sheila A. Brumby	sheilabrumby50@btinternet.com		01340 831588
North Ayrshire	Mr Andrew J. Bruce	andrew_bruce2@sky.com		07484 150461
North Lanarkshire	Vacant			
Orkney Islands	Rev. G. Fraser H. Macnaughton	FMacnaughton@churchofscotland.org.uk		01856 873312
Perth and Kinross	Mrs Margaret B. Conroy	margaretbconroy@hotmail.com		07817 627725
Renfrewshire	Miss Mary Jane Bird	mjbird55@gmail.com		
Scottish Borders	Rev. Dr Adam J.J. Hood	AHood@churchofscotland.org.uk		01289 332787
Shetland Islands	Ms. K. Ellen Griffiths Weir	EWeir@churchofscotland.org.uk		
South Ayrshire	Rev. David R. Gemmell	DGemmell@churchofscotland.org.uk		01292 864140
South Lanarkshire	Ms Gillian D. Coulter	gillcoulter55@yahoo.com		01899 810339
Stirling	Mr Colin O'Brien	cobrien20@btinternet.com		01360 660616
West Dunbartonshire	Vacant			
West Lothian	Mrs Lynne McEwen	lynnemcewen@hotmail.co.uk		07933 352935

LIST O – MINISTERS ORDAINED FOR SIXTY YEARS AND UPWARDS

Year	Date	Name	Charge
1948	6 October	George Davidson Wilkie OBE BL	(Kirkcaldy: Viewforth)
1949	14 February	Hamish Norman Mackenzie McIntosh MA	(Fintry)
1950	28 December	Donald Stewart Wallace	(Chaplain: Royal Caledonian Schools)
1951	6 November	Alexander Gordon McGillivray MA BD STM	(Edinburgh: Presbytery Clerk)
1953	21 October	Donald Maciver Ross MA	(Industrial Mission Organiser)
1953	6 December	Mark Wilson	(Church of North India)
1954	17 January	Arthur William Alexander Main MA BD	(Kirkintilloch: St David's Memorial)
1954	6 June	Ian Murray Pollock Davidson MBE MA BD	(Stirling: Allan Park South with Stirling; Church of the Holy Rude)
1955	10 August	Michael Muir Dickie BSc	(Ayr: Castlehill)
1955	14 November	David Wishart Torrance MA BD	(Earlston)

Year	Date	Name	
1956	14 December	William Gault Shannon MA BD	(Pitlochry)
1957	5 June	John Murdo Smith	(Lochmaddy)
	11 January	William Macleod	(Uig)
	8 April	Thomas Stewart McGregor MBE MA BD	(Chaplain: Edinburgh Royal Infirmary)
	23 June	James Finlay Scott	(Dyce)
	15 July	Alexander Brown Cairns MA	(Turin)
	3 November	George Gordon Cameron MA BD STM	(Edinburgh: Juniper Green)
	7 November	Robert Milne Tuton MA	(Glasgow: Shettleston Old)
	24 November	Archibald Freeland Chisholm MA	(Braes of Rannoch with Foss and Rannoch)
	24 November	Francis George Bernard Liddiard MA	(Brechin: Gardner Memorial and East)
		Peter Owen Price CBE QHC BA FPhS	(Blantyre: Old)
1958	20 April	Eric John Alexander MA BD	(Glasgow: St George's Tron)
	11 June	William Moncur McKenzie DA	(Dumfries: Troqueer)
	13 July	Donald William Fraser MA	(Monifieth)
	23 October	David Sage Millen Hamilton MA BD STM	(Lecturer, Practical Theology, University of Glasgow)
	14 December	Francis Campbell Tollick BSc DipEd	(Port Glasgow: St Martin's)
	23 December	John McLeod MA	(Resolis and Urquhart)
1959	10 March	Sydney Edwin Peebles Beveridge BA	(Brydekirk with Hoddom)
	16 March	Robert James Stewart MA BD STM	(Orwell with Portmoak)
	12 April	Ian Morrison Strachan MA BD	(Ashkirk with Selkirk)
	31 May	John Russell MA	(Tillicoultry)
	21 June	Angus Wilson Morrison MA BD	(Kildalton and Oa)
	5 July	James Lindsay Wilkie MA BD	(Executive Secretary, Board of World Mission)
	28 October	Andrew Stark Taylor BTh FPhS	(Greenock: The Union)
1960	6 January	Alasdair James Morton MA BD DipEd FEIS	(Bowden with Newtown)
	13 January	Ralph Colley Philip Smith MA STM	(Director, Audio-Visual Productions)
	June	Alexander John Geddes MA BD	(Stewarton: St Columba's)
	5 July	Derek Haley BD DPS	(Chaplain: Gartnavel Royal Hospital, Glasgow)
	15 July	Iain McDougall Roy MA BD	(Stevenston: Livingstone)
	13 September	James Charles Stewart MA BD STM	(Aberdeen: Kirk of St Nicholas)
	14 September	George Alan Simpson Stirling MA	(Leochel Cushnie and Lynturk with Tough)
	21 September	James Alexander Simpson BSc BD STM DD	(Interim Minister, Brechin Cathedral)
	17 November	Alistair Andrew Benvie Davidson MA BD	(Grange with Rothiemay)
1961	8 April	Douglas Niven Alexander MA DipEd	(Bishopton)
	26 April	Archibald Iain Campbell MA BD	(Busby)
	26 April	John Pattison Cubie MA BD	(Caldwell)
	21 May	James Harkness KVCO CB OBE QHC MA DD	(Chaplain General, Army)
	17 June	Donald Rutherford Gaddes	(Kelso: North and Ednam)
	June	Sidney Hall Coleman BA BD MTh	(Glasgow: Merrylea)
	24 October	James Barbour Lawson MA BD	(South Uist)
	17 November	Alexander Cunningham MA BD	(Glasgow: Presbytery Clerk)
		Robin Graeme Brown BA BD	(Birsay with Rousay)

1962

11 January	John Mackenzie Kellet MA	(Edinburgh: Leith South)
4 March	Ian Andrew Moir MA BD	(Adviser for Urban Priority Areas)
6 April	Alastair Fleming McCormick	(Creich with Rosehall)
12 June	David Ferguson Huie MA BD	(Rome: St Andrew's)
24 June	David Reid MSc LTh FSA Scot	(Largoward with St Monans)
26 August	Ronald Stanton Blakey MA BD MTh	(Assembly Council)
25 September	John Diamond Rennie MA	(Broughton, Glenholm and Kilbucho with Skirling with Stobo and Drumelzier with Tweedsmuir)
10 October	John Spencer MA BD	(Dumfries: Lincluden with Holywood)
11 November	Donald Murray Stephen TD MA BD ThM	(Edinburgh: Marchmont St Giles')
14 December	George Angus Chalmers MA BD MLitt	(Catrine with Sorn)
December	Hugh Rutherford Wyllie MA DD FCIBS	(Hamilton: Old)

LIST P – DECEASED MINISTERS AND DEACONS

The following ministers and deacons have died since the list in the previous volume of the Year Book was compiled.

NAME	ORD	RET	CHARGE
2021			
Annand, James Mitchell MA BD	1955	1995	(Lockerbie: Dryfesdale)
Baird, William Welsh Halliday	1972	1979	(Patna with Waterside and Lethanhill)
Cameron, John William Morrison MA BD	1957	1996	(Edinburgh: Liberton)
Clark, Thomas Legerwood BD	1985	2008	(Orphir with Stenness)
Cowie, George Strachan BSc BD	1991		Clerk, Presbytery of Glasgow
McLaughlin, Catherine H.	2014	2018	(Ordained Local Minister, Glasgow: Kelvinbridge)
Moyes, Sheila Alice DCS	1957	1991	(General Secretary, Scottish Council of YWCA)
Muir, Margaret Alison MA LLB BD	1989	2012	(Glencaple with Lowther)
Nicoll, Ewen Sinclair MA BD	1973	1998	(Arrochar with Luss)
Palit, Stephen MA	1961	1983	(Dundonnell)
Ritchie, Garden William Murray	1961	1995	(Ardersier with Petty)
Sharp, James	2005		Ordained Local Minister: Clerk, Presbytery of International Charges
Warner, Kenneth DipArch DipTP BD	1981	2008	(Halkirk and Westerdale)
Whiteford, John Deas MA BD CQSW DipSW	1988	2016	(Glasgow: Newlands South)
Wright, Eric John	1975	1983	(Associate, Glasgow: St George's Tron)
2022			
Allan, William Grainger	1964	1978	(Kirkcudbright: St Cuthbert's)
Cameron, John Urquhart BA BSc PhD BD ThD	1974	2008	(Dundee: Broughty Ferry St Stephen's and West)
Chisholm, Henry Norwell	1955	1973	(Overseas Council: Freeport, Grand Bahama)

Name			Location
Drysdale, James Henry Dunn Craig LTh	2006	1987	(Blackbraes and Shieldhill)
Duncan, Robert Farrell MTheol PGCE	2001	1986	(Lochgelly: St Andrew's)
Edmonds, Donald Kinloch MA BD STM DMin	1974	1969	(Hillhousewood St Christopher's)
Elston, Peter Kenneth	1999	1963	(Dalgety)
Ferguson, David James	2001	1966	(Bellie with Speymouth)
Fleming, Hamish Kirkpatrick MA	2001	1966	(Banchory Ternan: East)
Forsyth, James LTh	2000	1970	(Fearn Abbey with Nigg: Chapelhill)
Gordon, Laurie Young	1995	1960	(Aberdeen: John Knox)
Gordon, Peter Mitchell MA BD	1995	1958	(Airdrie: West)
Hamilton, William Douglas BD	2009	1975	(Greenock: Westburn)
Heggie, Thomas Pryde BSc BD	1985	1976	(Nairn: Old)
Houston, Graham Richard BSc BD MTh PhD	2010	1978	(Cairngryffe with Symington)
Lang, Isabel Patricia BSc	2003	1996	(Dunoon: The High Kirk)
MacCormick, Moira Grace LTh BA	2003	1986	(Buchlyvie with Gartmore)
Macfarlane, Thomas Gracie BSc ARTC BD PhD	1992	1956	(Glasgow: South Shawlands)
MacLeod, Malcolm (Calum) BA BD	2018	1979	(Rutherglen: Old)
McAlister, Donald John Barker MA BD PhD	1989	1951	(North Berwick: Blackadder)
McGregor, Duncan James MIFM	1996	1982	(Channelkirk with Lauder: Old)
McIndoe, John Hedley MA BD STM DD	2000	1960	(London: St Columba's with Newcastle: St Andrew's)
Mead, Jeffrey Maurice BD	2021	1978	(Kirkinner with Mochrum with Sorbie)
Milton, Eric Gordon	1994	1963	(Blairdaff with Chapel of Garioch)
Pattison, Kenneth John MA BD STM	2004	1967	(Kilmuir and Logie Easter)
Reid, Alan Anderson Stuart MA BD STM DipEd	1995	1962	(Bridge of Allan: Chalmers)
Rettie, James Alexander BTh	1999	1981	(Melness and Tongue)
Sawyer, John Frederick Adam BD PhD	2002	1964	(Professor, Religious Studies, Lancaster University)
Seaman, Ronald Stanley MA	2007	1967	(Dornock)
Shackleton, William MA	1996	1960	(Greenock: Wellpark West)
Stoddart, Alexander Grainger LTh	2001	1975	(Meldrum and Bourtie)
Sutherland, Denis Ian MA BD	1995	1963	(Glasgow: Hutchesontown)
Tait, Agnes (Mrs) DCS	2014	1995	(Deacon, East Kilbride: Greenhills and East Kilbride: Moncrieff)
Taylor, Alan Thomas BD	2005	1980	(Kilninian and Kilmore with Salen and Ulva with Tobermory with Torosay and Kinlochsplevie)
Thom, Helen BA DipEd MA DCS	1988	1959	(Tynecastle School, Edinburgh)
Trimble, Robert DCS	1998	1988	(Deacon, Kirkcaldy: Templehall)
Walker, Ian BD MEd DipMS	2007	1973	(Rutherglen: Wardlawhill)
Whiteford, Alexander LTh	2013	1996	(Ardersier with Petty)
Whyte, Isabel Helen BD DipCE	2005	1993	(Chaplain, Queen Margaret Hospital, Dunfermline)

SECTION 7

Legal Names and Scottish Charity Numbers: Presbyteries and Congregations

Those presbyteries, all congregations in Scotland, and those congregations furth of Scotland which are registered with OSCR, the Office of the Scottish Charity Regulator

For a complete list of legal names see:
www.churchofscotland.org.uk > Resources > Yearbook > Section 7

Further information
All documents, as defined in the Charities References in Documents (Scotland) Regulations 2007, must specify the Charity Number, Legal Name of the congregation, any other name by which the congregation is commonly known and the fact that it is a Charity. For more information, please refer to the Law Department circular on the Regulations on the Church of Scotland website.

www.churchofscotland.org.uk > Resources > Law Department Circulars > Charity Law

SECTION 8

Church Buildings: Ordnance Survey National Grid References

Please go to: www.churchofscotland.org.uk > Resources > Yearbook > Section 8

SECTION 9

Parish and Congregational Changes

The parish structure of the Church of Scotland is constantly being reshaped as the result of unions, linkages and the dissolutions.

Section 9A, 'Parishes and Congregations: names no longer in use', records one of the inevitable consequences of these changes, the disappearance of the names of many former parishes and congregations. There are, however, occasions when for legal and other reasons it is important to be able to identify the present-day successors of those parishes and congregations whose names are no longer in use and which can therefore no longer be easily traced. A list of all such parishes and congregations, with full explanatory notes, may be found at:

www.churchofscotland.org.uk/Resources/Yearbook > Section 9A

Section 9B, 'Recent Readjustment and other Congregational Changes', below, lists all instances of union, linkage and dissolution, since the compilation of the 2021–22 Year Book.

3. Lothian	**Glencorse** dissolved
	Penicuik: St Mungo's and **Penicuik: South and Howgate** united as **Penicuik: Trinity**
16. Glasgow	**Glasgow: Knightswood St Margaret's** and **Glasgow: Temple Anniesland** united as **Glasgow: Knightswood Anniesland Trinity**
	Kirkintilloch: Hillhead and **Kirkintilloch: St Columba's** united as **Kirkintilloch: St Columba's Hillhead**
	Twechar dissolved
24. Fife	**St Andrews: Hope Park and Martyrs** and **Strathkinness** united as **St Andrews: St Mark's**
30. Angus	**Brechin: Cathedral** dissolved
	Brechin: Gardner Memorial renamed **Brechin**

31. Aberdeen and Shetland	**Aberdeen: St George's Tillydrone** and **Aberdeen: St Machar's Cathedral** united as **Aberdeen: St Machar's Cathedral**
	Bucksburn Stoneywood and **Newhills** united as **Brimmond**
35. Moray	**Alves and Burghead** linked with **Kinloss and Findhorn, Dallas** linked with **Forres: St Leonard's** linked with **Rafford, Dyke and Edinkillie**, and **Forres: St Laurence** transferred to Presbytery of Inverness
37. Inverness	**Alves and Burghead** linked with **Kinloss and Findhorn, Dallas** linked with **Forres: St Leonard's** linked with **Rafford, Dyke and Edinkillie**, and **Forres: St Laurence** transferred from Presbytery of Moray
45. Orkney	**Flotta** linked with **Orphir and Stenness**: linkage with **Hoy and Walls** severed
48. International Charges	**Costa del Sol: Fuengirola** dissolved

Presbytery of Edinburgh and **Presbytery of West Lothian** united as **Presbytery of Edinburgh and West Lothian**

Presbytery of Annandale and Eskdale, Presbytery of Dumfries and Kirkcudbright, Presbytery of Wigtown and Stranraer, Presbytery of Ayr, Presbytery of Irvine and Kilmarnock and **Presbytery of Ardrossan** united as **Presbytery of the South West**

Presbytery of Lanark, Presbytery of Hamilton and **Presbytery of Falkirk** united as **Presbytery of Forth Valley and Clydesdale**

Historical Note
The presbyteries created in 1581 (or shortly thereafter) included the Presbyteries of Edinburgh and of Linlithgow. Following the 1929 union, Linlithgow was split into the Presbyteries of Bathgate, and of Linlithgow and Falkirk. At the 1964 General Assembly Bathgate was renamed Livingston and Bathgate. In 1976 Livingston and Bathgate was renamed West Lothian, and Linlithgow and Falkirk was renamed Falkirk, with transference of some charges between the two.

The 1581 presbyteries included the Presbyteries of Dumfries, Wigtown, Kirkcudbright, Ayr, and Irvine. In 1622 the Presbytery of Stranraer was formed from part of Wigtown. By 1638, three more presbyteries were formed from parts of Dumfries: Lochmaben, Middlebie (renamed Annan in 1743) and Penpont, then in 1743 Langholm was formed from part of Middlebie. Following the 1929 union, Dumfries and Penpont were united as the Presbytery of Dumfries, and Lochmaben and Annan were united as the Presbytery of Annandale; Langholm was subsumed within a new Presbytery of Hawick; and Irvine was split into the Presbyteries of Irvine and Kilmarnock and of Ardrossan. At the 1963 General Assembly, Stranraer and Wigtown were united as the Presbytery of Wigtown and Stranraer. In 1976, the two presbyteries of Dumfries and Kirkcudbright were united as the Presbytery of Dumfries and Kirkcudbright. In 1978 Annandale was renamed Annandale and Eskdale.

The 1581 presbyteries included the Presbyteries of Hamilton and of Lanark. In 1643 a Presbytery of Biggar was formed from parts of the Presbyteries of Peebles and Lanark. Following the 1929 union, Biggar and Lanark were united as the Presbytery of Lanark. For the Presbytery of Falkirk, see above.

SECTION 10

Congregational Statistics 2021

Comparative Statistics: 1981–2021

	2021	*2011*	*2001*	*1991*	*1981*
Communicants	283,600	432,348	590,824	770,217	938,930
Elders	23,575	34,436	43,499	46,899	47,900

NOTES ON CONGREGATIONAL STATISTICS

Com   Number of communicants at 31 December 2021.

Eld   Number of elders at 31 December 2021.

G   Membership of the Guild including Young Woman's Groups and others as recorded on the 2021 annual return submitted to the Guild Office.

In21   Ordinary General Income for 2021. Ordinary General Income consists of members' offerings, contributions from congregational organisations, regular fund-raising events, income from investments, deposits and so on. This figure does not include extraordinary or special income, or income from special collections and fund-raising for other charities.

M&M   Final amount allocated to congregations to contribute for Ministries and Mission after allowing for Presbytery-approved amendments up to 31 December 2021, but before deducting stipend endowments and normal allowances given for locum purposes in a vacancy or guardianship.

–18   This figure shows 'the number of children and young people aged 17 years and under who are involved in the life of the congregation'.

The statistics for the congregations now in the united Presbyteries of Edinburgh and West Lothian, of the South West, and of Forth Valley and Clydesdale are shown under the new presbyteries.

Some congregations were united or dissolved after 31 December 2021. Their statistics are shown as the entities they were at that date, but their names are shown in italics – details of the readjustment are given in Section 9B.

Figures may also not be available for congregations which failed to submit the appropriate schedule. Where the figure for the number of elders is missing, then in nearly every case the number of communicants relates to the previous year.

Congregation	Com	Eld	G	In21	M&M	–18
1. Edinburgh and West Lothian						
Abercorn	64	8	-	14,281	9,916	-
Pardovan, Kingscavil and Winchburgh	217	27	-	40,803	33,430	-
Armadale	431	36	19	-	41,916	46
Avonbridge	40	-	-	-	6,746	-
Torphichen	108	15	-	-	16,138	-
Bathgate: Boghall	184	20	23	97,265	50,759	30
Bathgate: High	405	35	17	86,448	51,925	30
Bathgate: St John's	307	14	18	-	33,494	42
Blackburn and Seafield	207	39	-	106,408	36,463	74
Blackridge	54	9	-	24,739	11,520	-
Harthill: St Andrew's	154	7	21	-	30,704	5
Breich Valley	99	10	11	30,871	20,969	6
Broxburn	302	20	-	-	42,579	7
Edinburgh: Balerno	485	46	22	-	73,112	-
Edinburgh: Barclay Viewforth	264	28	-	205,895	106,899	49
Edinburgh: Blackhall St Columba's	592	50	-	192,326	100,796	4
Edinburgh: Bristo Memorial Craigmillar	32	-	-	38,469	21,209	-
Edinburgh: Broughton St Mary's	156	23	-	59,568	49,059	13
Edinburgh: Canongate	322	31	-	-	79,016	-
Edinburgh: Carrick Knowe	306	42	35	-	36,287	250
Edinburgh: Colinton	751	40	-	-	104,562	15
Edinburgh: Corstorphine Craigsbank	346	24	-	100,304	57,222	33
Edinburgh: Corstorphine Old	350	25	40	84,887	61,704	25
Edinburgh: Corstorphine St Anne's	343	46	55	101,790	61,540	45
Edinburgh: Corstorphine St Ninian's	530	72	32	171,950	88,600	25
Edinburgh: Craiglockhart	328	38	21	-	75,752	25
Edinburgh: Craigmillar Park	137	8	25	-	33,454	1
Edinburgh: Reid Memorial	177	9	-	111,142	58,267	-
Edinburgh: Cramond	842	79	-	233,885	163,792	23
Edinburgh: Currie	411	27	35	-	77,723	24
Edinburgh: Dalmeny	96	5	-	50,585	20,343	15
Edinburgh: Queensferry	492	50	44	-	64,505	45
Edinburgh: Davidson's Mains	389	58	-	-	109,921	45
Edinburgh: Drylaw	73	10	-	45,295	12,832	7
Edinburgh: Duddingston	362	37	-	-	66,702	150
Edinburgh: Fairmilehead	473	46	27	166,048	78,903	14
Edinburgh: Gorgie Dalry Stenhouse	165	15	-	-	66,997	22
Edinburgh: Gracemount	20	4	-	25,314	9,499	13
Edinburgh: Liberton	644	55	49	245,756	109,995	45
Edinburgh: Granton	138	19	-	-	25,255	15
Edinburgh: Greenbank	636	72	31	-	122,876	270
Edinburgh: Greenside	86	20	-	-	30,128	2
Edinburgh: Greyfriars Kirk	293	32	-	-	85,921	10
Edinburgh: High (St Giles')	445	34	-	-	158,643	-
Edinburgh: Holy Trinity	206	31	-	151,445	77,631	60
Edinburgh: Inverleith St Serf's	283	28	26	101,948	61,481	-
Edinburgh: Juniper Green	266	25	-	119,215	54,916	30
Edinburgh: Kirkliston	205	29	43	89,891	54,716	37

Congregation	Com	Eld	G	In21	M&M	–18
Edinburgh: Leith North	123	18	-	61,876	39,192	4
Edinburgh: Leith St Andrew's	136	18	-	76,050	42,571	-
Edinburgh: Leith South	238	41	-	83,014	67,351	111
Edinburgh: Liberton Northfield	122	12	-	54,145	24,692	62
Edinburgh: Marchmont St Giles'	197	26	10	112,256	73,083	76
Edinburgh: Mayfield Salisbury	424	51	-	256,691	124,492	45
Edinburgh: Meadowbank	23	3	-	35,012	26,601	1
Edinburgh: Morningside	365	56	-	-	104,195	35
Edinburgh: Morningside United	101	9	-	55,475	909	9
Edinburgh: Murrayfield	426	21	-	-	80,440	39
Edinburgh: Newhaven	135	13	-	88,876	42,532	124
Edinburgh: Old Kirk and Muirhouse	86	17	-	27,266	21,420	125
Edinburgh: Palmerston Place	338	34	-	-	93,915	-
Edinburgh: Pilrig St Paul's	184	12	15	78,689	31,936	-
Edinburgh: Polwarth	134	20	-	89,563	50,434	5
Edinburgh: Portobello and Joppa	727	69	69	-	128,812	163
Edinburgh: Priestfield	99	14	-	75,592	47,290	26
Edinburgh: Ratho	171	10	-	-	31,863	13
Edinburgh: Richmond Craigmillar	78	7	-	-	12,887	14
Edinburgh: St Andrew's and St George's West	274	41	-	200,681	141,342	8
Edinburgh: St Andrew's Clermiston	138	7	-	-	31,350	2
Edinburgh: St Catherine's Argyle	81	6	-	-	33,078	24
Edinburgh: St Cuthbert's	239	23	-	-	72,918	-
Edinburgh: St David's Broomhouse	112	15	-	28,200	17,953	15
Edinburgh: St John's Colinton Mains	178	19	-	56,767	33,555	32
Edinburgh: St Margaret's	175	26	22	56,828	35,718	3
Edinburgh: St Martin's	78	11	-	-	12,649	8
Edinburgh: St Michael's	287	24	31	72,429	41,629	10
Edinburgh: St Nicholas' Sighthill	301	16	-	-	21,943	16
Edinburgh: St Stephen's Comely Bank	113	11	-	-	55,197	20
Edinburgh: Slateford Longstone	164	9	25	40,310	20,478	15
Edinburgh: Stockbridge	181	11	-	-	51,941	-
Edinburgh: Tron Kirk (Gilmerton and Moredun)	79	9	-	46,376	15,439	15
Edinburgh: Wardie	449	43	48	165,421	77,095	78
Edinburgh: Willowbrae	89	13	-	48,504	31,079	-
Fauldhouse: St Andrew's	164	8	-	-	24,179	6
Kirknewton and East Calder	279	34	31	-	52,095	45
Kirk of Calder	431	31	-	71,278	45,341	4
Linlithgow: St Michael's	1,220	95	45	-	145,000	108
Linlithgow: St Ninian's Craigmailen	336	32	45	-	36,821	33
Livingston: Old	270	29	15	-	51,255	65
Livingston: United	229	31	-	62,858	40,215	715
Polbeth Harwood	141	10	-	-	14,572	3
West Kirk of Calder	209	16	-	-	40,902	38
Strathbrock	244	19	18	-	52,499	-
Uphall: South	155	21	-	41,263	31,310	12
Whitburn: Brucefield	156	18	22	-	50,451	-
Whitburn: South	308	27	-	61,409	41,902	69

Congregation	Com	Eld	G	In21	M&M	–18
3. Lothian						
Aberlady	160	15	-	-	22,717	-
Gullane	296	22	-	-	37,179	14
Belhaven	475	25	42	-	48,129	42
Spott	101	5	-	13,566	10,688	-
Bilston	71	3	14	-	6,310	-
Roslin	176	7	-	16,870	14,569	-
Bonnyrigg	507	49	28	-	60,455	18
Cockenzie and Port Seton: Chalmers Memorial	148	26	21	67,922	45,555	60
Cockenzie and Port Seton: Old	186	17	18	-	26,293	10
Cockpen and Carrington	132	20	33	-	21,420	4
Lasswade and Rosewell	217	17	-	35,250	20,950	25
Dalkeith: St John's and King's Park	463	30	28	-	57,871	70
Dalkeith: St Nicholas Buccleuch	300	15	-	45,316	26,182	-
Dirleton	158	12	-	-	36,092	5
North Berwick: Abbey	225	28	32	-	46,512	182
Dunbar	308	13	20	92,147	63,594	11
Dunglass	254	9	-	-	18,154	15
Garvald and Morham	31	5	-	-	6,598	4
Haddington: West	190	13	-	-	29,299	2
Gladsmuir	141	13	-	-	14,759	4
Longniddry	274	39	22	76,930	39,864	4
Gorebridge	136	10	-	123,118	62,999	60
Haddington: St Mary's	446	40	-	-	59,039	15
Humbie	63	9	-	23,408	14,817	19
Yester, Bolton and Saltoun	252	26	-	54,185	28,683	36
Loanhead	264	27	27	-	32,196	32
Musselburgh: Northesk	265	13	26	51,209	31,593	27
Musselburgh: St Andrew's High	228	20	14	58,392	35,008	-
Musselburgh: St Clement's and St Ninian's	55	5	-	11,992	12,633	-
Musselburgh: St Michael's Inveresk	330	34	-	73,823	46,659	6
Newbattle	271	23	-	56,106	31,217	43
Newton	76	1	-	16,154	11,137	1
North Berwick: St Andrew Blackadder	539	24	25	172,553	90,972	70
Ormiston	120	7	27	-	23,066	5
Pencaitland	126	3	-	-	19,370	1
Penicuik: North	345	28	-	54,403	38,952	30
Penicuik: St Mungo's	160	17	15	67,872	37,708	-
Penicuik: South and Howgate	55	7	-	-	28,974	-
Prestonpans: Prestongrange	214	14	14	58,340	32,643	6
Tranent	190	14	30	54,864	33,433	6
Traprain	644	35	27	88,314	80,115	23
Tyne Valley	253	24	-	63,166	49,015	-
4. Melrose and Peebles						
Ashkirk	29	3	-	7,770	6,461	-
Ettrick and Yarrow	138	10	-	22,174	26,163	-
Selkirk	300	21	-	64,952	34,830	37
Bowden and Melrose	608	40	22	100,252	66,445	25
Broughton, Glenholm and Kilbucho	114	7	18	13,688	10,201	-

Congregation	Com	Eld	G	In21	M&M	–18
Carlops	46	11	-	-	13,917	5
Kirkurd and Newlands	66	11	8	10,884	13,760	1
Skirling	56	6	-	10,623	5,030	1
Tweedsmuir	34	3	-	-	3,957	-
West Linton: St Andrew's	151	15	-	-	20,688	-
Caddonfoot	140	12	-	16,279	10,092	1
Stow: St Mary of Wedale and Heriot	125	10	-	-	16,985	-
Channelkirk and Lauder	348	13	15	-	33,117	3
Dryburgh District Churches	302	26	14	33,103	33,173	4
Earlston	315	17	8	32,922	27,690	27
Eddleston	96	6	-	-	9,087	-
Peebles: Old	354	20	-	-	55,841	-
Stobo and Drumelzier	75	7	-	-	13,532	1
Galashiels	624	37	31	-	85,549	39
Innerleithen, Traquair and Walkerburn	266	23	25	-	33,258	2
Lyne and Manor	85	7	-	18,534	17,224	-
Peebles: St Andrew's Leckie	446	28	-	162,504	62,671	45

5. Duns

Congregation	Com	Eld	G	In21	M&M	–18
Ayton and District Churches	259	17	12	18,796	25,933	1
Berwick-upon-Tweed: St Andrew's Wallace Green and Lowick	265	16	-	-	31,088	3
Chirnside	69	5	-	13,109	10,681	16
Hutton and Fishwick and Paxton	56	4	-	11,280	9,562	5
Coldingham and St Abbs	48	12	-	29,484	23,497	17
Eyemouth	86	20	16	39,483	20,394	7
Coldstream and District Parishes	352	26	-	45,402	36,751	-
Eccles and Leitholm	124	12	12	-	15,255	-
Duns and District Parishes	534	26	33	74,411	58,198	40
Fogo	70	10	-	-	5,635	5
Gordon: St Michael's	54	6	-	6,470	7,237	5
Greenlaw	68	3	11	-	11,037	-
Legerwood	51	7	-	-	5,195	6

6. Jedburgh

Congregation	Com	Eld	G	In21	M&M	–18
Ale and Teviot United	361	21	15	-	28,639	10
Cavers and Kirkton	89	7	-	10,794	11,161	-
Hawick: Trinity	436	32	38	36,372	23,908	40
Cheviot Churches	271	18	33	-	37,396	-
Hawick: Burnfoot	61	10	-	14,086	13,545	1
Hawick: St Mary's and Old	306	16	12	36,189	25,733	5
Hawick: Teviot and Roberton	176	13	12	51,005	28,954	7
Hawick: Wilton	234	18	-	-	26,863	64
Teviothead	51	3	-	-	3,494	-
Hobkirk and Southdean	121	16	10	-	14,676	5
Ruberslaw	205	14	11	27,325	20,782	6
Jedburgh: Old and Trinity	515	10	18	59,116	35,459	-
Kelso Country Churches	172	14	5	-	24,265	-
Kelso: North and Ednam	858	63	-	-	66,874	8
Kelso: Old and Sprouston	401	22	-	-	28,767	2
Oxnam	116	12	-	-	7,223	8

Congregation	Com	Eld	G	In21	M&M	–18
7. South West						
Alloway	865	79	-	-	113,552	100
Annan: Old	306	32	41	50,219	32,103	-
Dornock	97	8	-	-	6,413	1
Annan: St Andrew's	403	31	42	56,158	32,598	30
Brydekirk	43	4	-	-	5,736	-
Annbank	217	18	14	-	11,513	-
Tarbolton	255	22	22	-	27,661	38
Applegarth, Sibbaldbie and Johnstone	102	6	10	3,346	8,706	-
Lochmaben	181	15	24	55,066	35,839	-
Ardrossan: Park	342	26	26	-	41,305	74
Ardrossan and Saltcoats: Kirkgate	170	29	24	65,190	46,464	4
Arnsheen Barrhill and Colmonell: St Colmon	95	9	-	20,933	15,979	5
Ballantrae	212	14	8	35,509	27,303	5
Auchinleck	280	13	28	-	21,361	3
Catrine	82	8	-	13,302	12,110	-
Ayr: Auld Kirk of Ayr	366	46	-	-	42,549	-
Ayr: Castlehill	476	31	38	94,965	47,110	60
Ayr: Newton Wallacetown	170	32	35	-	60,428	9
Ayr: St Andrew's	186	18	-	-	30,151	50
Ayr: St Columba	888	92	48	-	135,826	8
Ayr: St James'	280	22	-	-	34,199	101
Ayr: St Leonard's	329	39	-	-	56,495	-
Dalrymple	116	11	-	-	14,589	-
Ayr: St Quivox	99	18	-	40,617	26,591	-
Balmaclellan, Kells and Dalry	109	11	12	26,649	22,168	-
Carsphairn	71	6	-	8,803	5,435	-
Barr	30	2	-	-	2,821	-
Dailly	98	7	-	-	8,761	-
Girvan: South	216	20	17	-	18,103	-
Beith	585	51	19	88,024	55,806	20
Bengairn Parishes	147	14	-	23,362	23,808	-
Castle Douglas	306	21	17	-	30,728	2
Border Kirk	253	36	-	-	33,329	-
Brodick	111	15	-	-	26,781	-
Corrie	24	4	-	15,088	11,028	-
Lochranza and Pirnmill	56	10	-	-	14,396	-
Shiskine	52	9	17	-	16,980	-
Caerlaverock	97	7	-	7,910	7,624	-
Dumfries: St Mary's-Greyfriars'	276	26	26	-	35,267	-
Caldwell	196	-	-	-	33,984	-
Dunlop	334	31	14	70,704	44,297	75
Canonbie United	76	8	-	26,439	19,725	7
Liddesdale	91	8	-	27,545	18,783	-
Closeburn	157	12	-	21,809	16,524	3
Kirkmahoe	142	11	-	-	17,153	-
Colvend, Southwick and Kirkbean	149	10	-	-	46,564	-
Corsock and Kirkpatrick Durham	45	9	-	-	13,818	1
Crossmichael, Parton and Balmaghie	159	8	9	-	17,900	-
Coylton	293	17	-	29,397	20,685	-

Congregation	Com	Eld	G	In21	M&M	–18
Drongan: The Schaw Kirk	143	14	12	-	21,004	-
Craigie and Symington	249	21	16	-	30,801	-
Prestwick: South	214	33	20	82,267	46,745	95
Crosshill	104	9	20	10,456	8,959	-
Maybole	218	22	11	56,150	33,381	1
Crosshouse	205	28	15	45,204	33,427	8
Cumbrae	173	15	28	43,704	35,434	1
Largs: St John's	582	26	-	90,634	65,428	-
Cummertrees, Mouswald and Ruthwell	162	14	-	-	22,091	-
Dalbeattie and Kirkgunzeon	319	19	-	-	29,981	-
Urr	147	8	-	-	11,578	-
Dalmellington	108	12	-	8,179	12,596	15
Patna: Waterside	118	6	-	-	13,028	-
Dalry: St Margaret's	444	47	-	-	76,422	20
Dalry: Trinity	132	15	-	-	46,655	8
Dalton and Hightae	163	6	-	-	12,276	-
St Mungo	42	9	-	-	8,571	-
Darvel	254	20	27	-	26,106	4
Dreghorn and Springside	365	-	26	72,939	49,936	-
Dumfries: Maxwelltown West	296	30	23	76,663	44,835	8
Dumfries: Northwest	229	7	-	-	17,882	-
Dumfries: St George's	426	46	19	111,433	56,388	13
Dumfries: St Michael's and South	576	39	21	-	51,993	-
Dumfries: Troqueer	223	15	16	116,345	45,953	41
Dundonald	397	29	32	-	38,433	43
Dunscore	161	16	-	-	17,128	13
Glencairn and Moniaive	127	5	-	22,056	18,934	-
Durisdeer	120	5	-	-	13,008	8
Penpont, Keir and Tynron	139	10	-	-	16,174	4
Thornhill	110	7	-	-	15,964	-
Ervie Kirkcolm	158	9	-	14,565	13,333	8
Leswalt	251	16	-	21,304	14,391	4
Fairlie	161	15	15	54,081	39,665	-
Largs: St Columba's	284	10	-	74,220	42,947	38
Fenwick	271	20	23	-	30,684	-
Fisherton	109	13	-	-	9,718	5
Kirkoswald	171	16	8	31,043	19,186	12
Galston	494	-	50	73,274	53,954	-
Gatehouse and Borgue	218	16	-	-	31,837	15
Tarff and Twynholm	122	11	22	18,250	17,473	1
Girvan: North	486	36	-	-	39,307	7
Glasserton and Isle of Whithorn	79	4	-	-	11,034	-
Whithorn: St Ninian's Priory	288	7	16	33,791	21,453	22
Gretna: Old, Gretna: St Andrew's, Half Morton and Kirkpatrick Fleming	265	15	-	21,573	30,414	1
Hoddom, Kirtle-Eaglesfield and Middlebie	171	17	-	-	19,091	2
Hurlford	244	17	18	-	31,903	1
Inch	164	11	6	11,273	12,465	30
Luce Valley	196	14	16	43,336	27,965	7
Irongray, Lochrutton and Terregles	150	21	-	29,604	20,028	-

Congregation	Com	Eld	G	In21	M&M	–18
Irvine: Fullarton	353	-	40	126,882	60,540	-
Irvine: Girdle Toll	127	10	16	-	19,100	2
Irvine: St Andrew's	223	-	23	-	22,424	-
Irvine: Mure Relief	378	33	18	59,806	47,793	65
Irvine: Old	296	20	-	58,158	36,317	1
Kilbirnie: Auld Kirk	252	22	-	-	29,487	-
Kilbirnie: St Columba's	440	32	-	49,256	33,316	-
Kilmarnock: Kay Park	406	57	13	123,575	72,137	10
Kilmarnock: New Laigh Kirk	713	68	37	214,985	119,945	90
Kilmarnock: St John's Onthank	145	14	-	22,166	22,175	-
Kilmarnock: St Kentigern's	254	22	-	47,380	27,693	2
Kilmarnock: St Marnock's	1,001	50	53	203,863	147,015	10
Kilmaurs: St Maur's Glencairn	262	-	20	-	31,815	-
Kilmory	25	4	-	-	8,006	-
Lamlash	68	11	26	27,354	21,490	4
Kilwinning: Abbey	454	50	23	104,177	62,117	14
Kilwinning: Mansefield Trinity	164	11	17	-	29,103	8
Kirkconnel	188	9	-	-	17,687	-
Sanquhar: St Bride's	315	15	11	-	22,403	-
Kirkcowan	93	10	-	-	18,029	-
Wigtown	131	10	9	33,007	17,984	30
Kirkcudbright	421	23	-	71,334	47,054	3
Kirkinner	98	5	6	2,867	11,233	-
Mochrum	207	9	16	-	13,399	4
Sorbie	84	8	-	-	12,701	-
Kirkmabreck	105	12	12	15,303	12,135	-
Monigaff	222	7	-	-	10,879	4
Kirkmaiden	145	9	-	11,772	16,452	10
Kirkmichael	182	14	18	28,043	12,552	2
Straiton: St Cuthbert's	147	11	18	-	11,551	5
Kirkmichael, Tinwald and Torthorwald	338	32	12	-	27,280	-
Kirkpatrick Juxta	90	5	-	7,324	6,644	-
Moffat: St Andrew's	286	31	20	-	37,023	34
Wamphray	51	4	-	-	5,031	10
Langholm, Eskdalemuir, Ewes and Westerkirk	420	22	10	-	37,741	15
Largs: Clark Memorial	544	66	-	122,145	71,058	20
Lochend and New Abbey	177	17	10	40,208	21,676	-
Lockerbie: Dryfesdale, Hutton and Corrie	388	33	28	43,904	35,971	-
Lugar	147	10	17	18,358	12,408	-
Old Cumnock: Old	301	18	22	-	33,128	10
Mauchline	322	14	30	-	41,231	3
Sorn	121	11	11	16,022	10,855	1
Monkton and Prestwick: North	215	24	18	75,579	49,329	1
Muirkirk	142	13	-	-	10,644	-
Old Cumnock: Trinity	268	18	24	38,882	24,303	15
New Cumnock	411	25	11	-	35,489	35
Newmilns: Loudoun	144	-	-	-	20,500	-
Ochiltree	206	19	12	-	18,358	8
Stair	197	17	21	-	27,157	-
Penninghame	350	18	17	88,274	56,859	27

Congregation	Com	Eld	G	In21	M&M	–18
Portpatrick	195	9	11	-	16,353	-
Stoneykirk	216	14	11	-	21,464	1
Prestwick: Kingcase	491	65	20	82,719	60,861	25
Prestwick: St Nicholas'	443	51	28	-	67,998	12
Saltcoats: North	205	18	11	40,421	23,645	7
Saltcoats: St Cuthbert's	202	30	12	69,535	46,336	12
Stevenston: Ardeer	90	13	-	-	21,104	11
Stevenston: Livingstone	170	16	12	42,579	26,210	13
Stevenston: High	186	15	23	75,023	46,504	24
Stewarton: John Knox	237	28	24	-	51,764	40
Stewarton: St Columba's	400	-	43	94,424	51,964	-
Stranraer	825	35	22	-	94,297	30
Troon: Old	695	47	-	128,037	74,111	100
Troon: Portland	400	44	-	-	67,591	7
Troon: St Meddan's	549	61	29	-	72,294	99
Tundergarth	28	4	-	-	4,999	-
West Kilbride	342	39	-	121,006	68,077	92
Whiting Bay and Kildonan	62	9	-	29,365	20,265	3

14. Clyde

Congregation	Com	Eld	G	In21	M&M	–18
Arrochar	53	15	-	-	12,000	-
Luss	79	13	8	33,645	28,103	2
Baldernock	158	13	-	-	19,060	1
Milngavie: St Paul's	617	88	87	186,945	101,265	27
Barrhead: Bourock	387	31	32	-	48,276	75
Barrhead: St Andrew's	316	35	20	-	73,542	233
Bearsden: Baljaffray	353	7	38	-	47,089	110
Bearsden: Cross	497	64	21	-	89,392	37
Bearsden: Killermont	498	53	33	-	83,468	120
Bearsden: New Kilpatrick	1,081	98	53	291,541	154,945	47
Bearsden: Westerton Fairlie Memorial	281	29	36	-	56,400	4
Bishopton	583	51	-	-	58,620	30
Bonhill	334	37	-	-	36,744	-
Renton: Trinity	130	12	-	-	17,150	8
Bridge of Weir: Freeland	358	37	-	133,995	73,043	80
Bridge of Weir: St Machar's Ranfurly	274	22	26	85,207	51,215	28
Cardross	333	40	26	-	47,349	30
Clydebank: Faifley	165	11	26	49,496	23,161	19
Clydebank: Kilbowie St Andrew's	205	22	15	48,061	24,368	91
Clydebank: Radnor Park	89	13	-	30,414	20,273	-
Clydebank: Waterfront	127	22	-	-	26,839	19
Dalmuir: Barclay	140	20	-	39,374	24,126	9
Craigrownie	129	14	-	29,683	21,220	-
Garelochhead	118	12	-	-	26,526	4
Rosneath: St Modan's	76	10	18	22,522	14,904	5
Dumbarton: Riverside	420	58	31	-	59,127	170
Dumbarton: St Andrew's	90	16	-	21,465	15,848	-
Dumbarton: West Kirk	129	20	-	-	30,284	85
Duntocher: Trinity	160	16	48	-	25,842	-
Elderslie Kirk	377	33	22	-	55,023	60

Congregation	Com	Eld	G	In21	M&M	–18
Erskine	280	25	49	-	54,737	120
Gourock: Old Gourock and Ashton	523	54	17	120,810	65,243	367
Greenock: St Ninian's	197	13	-	-	15,820	18
Gourock: St John's	355	45	-	-	69,519	140
Greenock: East End	45	6	-	14,203	5,375	12
Greenock: Mount Kirk	285	29	-	-	34,654	135
Greenock: Lyle Kirk	653	45	12	-	79,247	77
Greenock: St Margaret's	144	27	-	-	21,707	3
Greenock: Wellpark Mid Kirk	419	42	-	-	54,826	65
Greenock: Westburn	466	55	20	-	65,723	26
Helensburgh	731	52	22	223,298	105,803	15
Rhu and Shandon	149	15	7	-	36,927	-
Houston and Killellan	644	61	51	-	81,974	250
Howwood	98	14	20	37,890	26,275	5
Johnstone: St Paul's	294	52	-	-	43,228	85
Inchinnan	215	29	27	-	34,145	11
Inverkip	278	23	17	-	41,495	2
Skelmorlie and Wemyss Bay	202	32	-	65,722	42,179	5
Johnstone: High	173	28	15	82,204	50,127	46
Johnstone: St Andrew's Trinity	168	20	-	-	19,841	44
Kilbarchan	373	48	25	100,561	67,285	10
Kilmacolm: Old	324	37	-	-	68,177	20
Kilmacolm: St Columba	117	17	-	-	50,095	7
Kilmaronock Gartocharn	165	10	-	-	15,280	3
Lomond	320	33	18	95,709	59,060	-
Langbank	105	11	-	-	24,278	-
Linwood	136	14	25	-	25,321	1
Milngavie: Cairns	282	29	-	152,109	86,950	12
Milngavie: St Luke's	318	12	-	64,769	40,485	4
Neilston	363	24	9	102,076	62,633	130
Old Kilpatrick Bowling	186	9	-	-	36,360	49
Paisley: Abbey	393	34	-	-	94,026	45
Paisley: North	368	38	-	53,983	58,664	6
Paisley: Oakshaw Trinity	391	62	-	-	59,581	91
Paisley: St George's	352	52	25	121,022	77,451	92
Paisley: St Mark's Oldhall	364	49	47	121,330	59,156	60
Paisley: Sherwood Greenlaw	290	51	-	116,156	67,804	42
Paisley: South	347	46	-	111,445	73,365	24
Paisley: West	285	45	-	53,237	43,151	54
Port Glasgow: Hamilton Bardrainney	195	17	13	31,095	25,060	40
Port Glasgow: New	424	53	16	-	46,458	233
Renfrew: North	515	63	28	-	65,824	140
Renfrew: Trinity	254	16	13	-	55,009	12

16. Glasgow

Congregation	Com	Eld	G	In21	M&M	–18
Bishopbriggs: Kenmure	211	20	19	65,413	57,552	35
Bishopbriggs: Springfield Cambridge	554	-	65	134,154	78,281	-
Broom	397	43	-	139,685	71,672	15
Burnside Blairbeth	394	32	70	-	121,772	30
Busby	177	25	18	86,393	38,786	10

Congregation	Com	Eld	G	In21	M&M	–18
Cadder	537	62	43	-	81,931	73
Cambuslang	516	-	30	-	77,436	-
Cambuslang: Flemington Hallside	293	-	32	-	35,728	-
Campsie	128	18	19	49,230	31,150	11
Chryston	275	-	12	-	74,304	-
Cumbernauld: Abronhill	150	12	24	-	36,374	-
Cumbernauld: Condorrat	259	28	29	-	44,017	72
Cumbernauld: Kildrum	224	20	-	38,315	33,346	2
Cumbernauld: St Mungo's	145	-	-	-	19,643	-
Cumbernauld: Old	261	39	-	62,962	40,021	38
Eaglesham	449	-	32	-	75,225	-
Fernhill and Cathkin	204	21	10	-	27,060	55
Gartcosh	66	10	-	-	11,326	68
Glenboig	93	7	-	12,376	8,194	-
Giffnock: Orchardhill	268	38	-	-	83,070	21
Giffnock: South	525	48	31	-	91,988	15
Giffnock: The Park	227	-	-	52,215	36,702	-
Greenbank	669	61	59	194,673	114,607	250
Kilsyth: Anderson	218	-	39	-	38,328	-
Kilsyth: Burns and Old	340	27	30	-	43,871	19
Kirkintilloch: Hillhead	65	-	-	-	12,744	-
Kirkintilloch: St Columba's	188	25	34	-	52,716	10
Kirkintilloch: St David's Memorial Park	469	-	20	-	44,813	-
Kirkintilloch: St Mary's	612	-	-	147,694	64,314	-
Lenzie: Old	384	42	-	129,447	70,727	46
Lenzie: Union	518	-	48	210,827	95,940	-
Maxwell Mearns Castle	236	24	-	-	84,196	46
Mearns	518	37	-	-	103,366	30
Milton of Campsie	291	-	32	77,224	43,798	-
Moodiesburn	113	8	-	67,137	30,895	23
Netherlee and Stamperland	779	64	54	-	135,987	-
Newton Mearns	328	35	27	-	62,598	-
Rutherglen: Old	187	22	-	71,451	33,678	6
Rutherglen: Stonelaw	272	23	-	-	72,411	-
Rutherglen: West and Wardlawhill	422	-	-	75,711	40,997	-
Stepps	188	12	-	58,346	29,866	5
Thornliebank	108	11	19	56,753	24,577	3
Torrance	178	-	-	98,800	53,852	-
Twechar	63	10	-	-	8,576	1
Williamwood	351	42	24	103,012	56,381	455
Glasgow: Baillieston Mure Memorial	291	27	36	-	44,912	102
Glasgow: Baillieston St Andrew's	239	19	17	-	36,336	14
Glasgow: Balshagray Victoria Park	107	23	-	-	50,863	2
Glasgow: Barlanark Greyfriars	49	12	10	-	12,566	128
Glasgow: Blawarthill	150	19	20	-	9,914	42
Glasgow: Bridgeton St Francis in the East	60	12	11	32,752	18,136	18
Glasgow: Broomhill Hyndland	431	-	19	156,540	97,616	-
Glasgow: Calton Parkhead	74	-	-	15,513	7,460	-
Glasgow: Cardonald	242	35	-	95,428	56,667	55
Glasgow: Carmunnock	156	20	-	32,180	26,634	-

Congregation	Com	Eld	G	In21	M&M	–18
Glasgow: Carmyle	64	4	-	17,178	10,216	47
Glasgow: Kenmuir Mount Vernon	109	11	-	87,171	32,082	50
Glasgow: Carntyne	214	17	-	52,213	40,222	100
Glasgow: Carnwadric	67	8	-	-	17,671	6
Glasgow: Castlemilk	108	19	21	-	15,064	12
Glasgow: Cathcart Old	233	-	18	-	45,395	-
Glasgow: Cathcart Trinity	272	40	28	-	91,607	22
Glasgow: Cathedral (High or St Mungo's)	390	-	-	96,877	67,753	-
Glasgow: Causeway (Tollcross)	152	-	16	-	27,751	-
Glasgow: Clincarthill	179	-	31	87,575	45,684	-
Glasgow: Colston Milton	48	6	-	-	7,454	7
Glasgow: Colston Wellpark	74	9	-	24,441	16,974	1
Glasgow: Cranhill	32	-	-	-	6,200	-
Glasgow: Croftfoot	224	35	26	-	43,576	81
Glasgow: Dennistoun New	151	27	-	-	44,451	6
Glasgow: Drumchapel St Andrew's	145	38	-	-	23,648	45
Glasgow: Drumchapel St Mark's	74	-	-	-	2,894	-
Glasgow: Easterhouse	54	-	-	-	10,344	-
Glasgow: Eastwood	147	39	18	113,459	53,906	11
Glasgow: Gairbraid	119	-	-	-	14,441	-
Glasgow: Gallowgate	29	-	-	-	14,985	-
Glasgow: Garthamlock and Craigend	53	-	-	-	3,605	-
Glasgow: Gorbals	93	11	-	28,316	16,741	11
Glasgow: Govan and Linthouse	136	23	30	-	51,616	58
Glasgow: Hillington Park	255	-	21	77,033	33,270	-
Glasgow: Ibrox	103	24	-	93,332	25,163	32
Glasgow: John Ross Memorial (for Deaf People)	51	-	-	-	-	-
Glasgow: Jordanhill	336	-	34	189,741	85,197	-
Glasgow: Kelvinbridge	46	-	-	25,995	28,413	-
Glasgow: Kelvinside Hillhead	139	18	-	-	36,724	-
Glasgow: King's Park	463	-	-	131,214	72,685	-
Glasgow: Kinning Park	120	-	-	-	17,662	-
Glasgow: Knightswood St Margaret's	123	16	-	-	23,891	4
Glasgow: Langside	200	-	-	88,539	52,685	-
Glasgow: Maryhill	144	12	3	58,050	17,247	76
Glasgow: Merrylea	224	-	-	-	38,998	-
Glasgow: Newlands South	358	36	-	116,697	72,032	15
Glasgow: Partick South	81	9	-	44,751	32,545	15
Glasgow: Partick Trinity	119	-	-	-	45,144	-
Glasgow: Pollokshaws	79	18	-	-	22,315	8
Glasgow: Pollokshields	109	18	-	-	36,844	10
Glasgow: Possilpark	85	-	-	-	15,463	-
Glasgow: Queen's Park Govanhill	110	26	-	106,191	58,749	9
Glasgow: Robroyston	53	-	-	-	4,917	-
Glasgow: Ruchazie	26	6	-	-	1,628	15
Glasgow: Ruchill Kelvinside	64	-	-	-	27,749	-
Glasgow: St Andrew and St Nicholas	263	25	17	-	40,326	195
Glasgow: St Andrew's East	46	10	18	-	16,216	-
Glasgow: St Andrew's West	140	15	14	-	50,491	-
Glasgow: St Christopher's Priesthill and Nitshill	173	8	-	-	17,350	10

Congregation	Com	Eld	G	In21	M&M	–18
Glasgow: St Columba	123	-	-	-	12,880	-
Glasgow: St David's Knightswood	143	14	26	-	43,235	17
Glasgow: St Enoch's Hogganfield	94	11	16	-	16,786	2
Glasgow: St George's Tron	65	-	-	-	2,466	-
Glasgow: St James' (Pollok)	97	20	28	36,567	22,697	45
Glasgow: St John's Renfield	273	-	-	140,763	78,005	-
Glasgow: St Paul's	27	7	-	25,067	4,062	275
Glasgow: St Rollox	73	-	-	41,769	23,588	-
Glasgow: Sandyford Henderson Memorial	168	15	-	161,971	82,399	8
Glasgow: Sandyhills	205	22	43	66,818	36,911	-
Glasgow: Scotstoun	67	-	-	-	30,811	-
Glasgow: Shawlands Trinity	201	23	-	75,218	49,796	98
Glasgow: Sherbrooke Mosspark	287	40	20	-	88,484	19
Glasgow: Shettleston New	190	-	23	-	41,632	-
Glasgow: Springburn	178	22	17	-	32,888	60
Glasgow: Temple Anniesland	201	19	-	-	51,361	55
Glasgow: Toryglen	54	-	-	13,110	9,816	-
Glasgow: Trinity Possil and Henry Drummond	44	-	-	63,223	33,357	-
Glasgow: Tron St Mary's	82	-	-	-	21,596	-
Glasgow: Wallacewell	35	3	-	-	1,350	8
Glasgow: Wellington	94	-	-	123,981	58,345	-
Glasgow: Whiteinch	74	-	-	-	29,239	-
Glasgow: Yoker	91	-	-	-	8,951	-

17. Forth Valley and Clydesdale

Airdrie: Cairnlea	459	45	20	-	73,490	81
Calderbank	110	10	12	-	14,145	-
Airdrie: Clarkston	287	30	15	61,609	40,768	130
Airdrie: High	245	30	-	-	34,112	100
Caldercruix and Longriggend	133	8	-	56,933	29,754	3
Airdrie: Jackson	297	42	14	107,998	48,989	150
Airdrie: New Monkland	247	26	26	61,575	38,853	83
Greengairs	101	9	-	-	12,170	1
Airdrie: New Wellwynd	621	83	-	167,095	90,718	127
Airdrie: St Columba's	198	14	-	-	10,668	-
Airth	118	7	18	-	23,043	35
Bellshill: Central	133	30	24	-	30,540	14
Bellshill: West	389	30	-	-	35,549	6
Biggar	271	20	24	106,037	57,693	25
Black Mount	64	4	14	-	11,226	4
Blackbraes and Shieldhill	135	19	16	-	16,730	-
Muiravonside	147	13	-	-	23,524	-
Blantyre: Livingstone Memorial	164	16	-	63,615	25,152	62
Blantyre: St Andrew's	152	18	-	48,553	25,797	6
Blantyre: Old	222	15	-	46,395	41,868	7
Bo'ness: Old	272	23	8	-	32,713	4
Bo'ness: St Andrew's	313	12	-	44,039	28,049	25
Bonnybridge: St Helen's	165	16	-	-	29,941	-
Bothkennar and Carronshore	152	16	-	48,078	20,141	7
Bothwell	433	42	37	-	67,187	21

Congregation	Com	Eld	G	In21	M&M	–18
Brightons	521	26	37	-	76,292	190
Cairngryffe	130	12	8	21,068	18,443	7
Libberton and Quothquan	74	9	-	-	10,114	-
Symington	124	13	-	27,188	17,315	-
Carluke: Kirkton	526	42	25	101,590	72,049	445
Carluke: St Andrew's	153	11	13	43,495	27,061	3
Carluke: St John's	486	41	23	-	49,166	14
Carnwath	86	9	13	-	11,045	-
Carstairs	150	11	19	43,235	25,507	2
Carriden	316	33	18	37,068	34,660	-
Chapelhall	171	22	29	40,130	22,742	17
Kirk o' Shotts	146	9	-	-	15,196	14
Cleland	129	6	-	13,583	14,004	-
Wishaw: St Mark's	231	22	29	58,551	36,996	146
Coalburn and Lesmahagow	399	23	21	161,582	75,062	1
Coatbridge: Blairhill Dundyvan	214	22	16	41,951	35,027	67
Coatbridge: Middle	221	33	27	-	23,623	123
Coatbridge: Calder	237	13	-	30,783	28,039	-
Coatbridge: Old Monkland	84	12	-	45,596	26,353	-
Coatbridge: New St Andrew's	476	41	26	97,182	62,499	143
Coatbridge: Townhead	107	18	-	18,513	17,909	28
Crossford	124	4	-	-	17,924	-
Kirkfieldbank	72	6	-	-	10,799	2
Dalserf	160	21	20	-	39,502	4
Denny: Old	261	36	18	45,105	33,278	35
Haggs	204	26	-	30,689	20,253	20
Denny: Westpark	344	28	19	78,473	57,478	36
Douglas Valley	249	20	31	-	33,342	-
Dunipace	157	19	-	58,093	32,560	75
East Kilbride: Claremont	358	37	-	-	72,757	15
East Kilbride: Greenhills	128	10	9	-	17,003	4
East Kilbride: Moncrieff	498	40	35	166,644	62,166	160
East Kilbride: Mossneuk	250	8	-	33,275	16,328	41
East Kilbride: Old	572	48	22	-	69,980	24
East Kilbride: South	126	20	-	62,659	39,555	149
East Kilbride: Stewartfield	25	5	-	8,978	7,664	-
East Kilbride: West	236	19	-	-	27,746	2
East Kilbride: Westwood	276	22	-	-	38,402	5
Falkirk: Bainsford	98	11	-	-	16,892	75
Falkirk: Camelon	147	14	-	-	36,953	4
Falkirk: Grahamston United	374	50	14	-	9,514	-
Falkirk: Laurieston	149	19	17	32,641	19,271	-
Redding and Westquarter	107	12	-	25,116	13,785	-
Falkirk: St Andrew's West	361	22	-	59,742	44,055	19
Falkirk: Trinity	408	30	14	156,013	90,006	35
Forth: St Paul's	288	19	28	-	30,594	138
Grangemouth: Abbotsgrange	274	40	-	-	33,162	111
Grangemouth: Kirk of the Holy Rood	252	25	-	-	29,584	3
Grangemouth: Zetland	462	50	51	83,253	60,913	33
Hamilton: Cadzow	326	42	28	99,072	63,195	40

Congregation	Com	Eld	G	In21	M&M	–18
Hamilton: Gilmour and Whitehill	96	18	-	52,444	24,881	-
Hamilton: West	161	29	-	-	34,917	25
Hamilton: Hillhouse	330	27	-	-	49,157	100
Hamilton: Old	420	57	-	-	91,282	50
Hamilton: St John's	435	42	30	-	72,572	180
Hamilton: South	123	16	19	50,643	28,105	6
Quarter	88	11	-	24,911	13,174	-
Hamilton: Trinity	238	18	-	49,951	27,746	4
Holytown	126	21	13	-	25,340	31
New Stevenston: Wrangholm Kirk	66	8	-	-	19,184	2
Kirkmuirhill	138	7	30	104,709	48,413	-
Lanark: Greyfriars	437	44	24	-	47,726	65
Lanark: St Nicholas'	428	36	18	120,930	63,301	61
Larbert: East	542	50	34	-	76,582	40
Larbert: Old	229	18	-	85,659	41,590	50
Larbert: West	306	26	24	67,951	38,055	1
Larkhall: New	314	55	31	-	72,765	80
Larkhall: Trinity	141	16	17	47,564	20,830	-
Law	156	11	29	-	24,472	49
Motherwell: Crosshill	221	34	47	61,876	44,072	-
Motherwell: St Margaret's	344	14	-	-	21,252	7
Motherwell: Dalziel St Andrew's	400	53	47	149,610	73,649	75
Motherwell: North	119	21	25	-	34,890	-
Wishaw: Craigneuk and Belhaven	107	20	-	40,200	24,868	9
Motherwell: St Mary's	590	88	43	-	83,201	432
Motherwell: South	381	50	48	-	49,364	145
Newarthill and Carfin	167	20	-	-	39,725	62
Newmains: Bonkle	98	15	-	31,892	19,473	5
Newmains: Coltness Memorial	160	18	19	-	32,782	-
Overtown	251	31	9	66,364	29,463	70
Polmont: Old	291	21	-	91,019	53,326	17
Shotts: Calderhead Erskine	359	30	22	-	48,062	-
Slamannan	88	6	-	-	15,616	25
Stenhouse and Carron	282	19	-	-	34,295	-
Stonehouse: St Ninian's	338	49	37	-	3,343	97
Strathaven: Avendale Old and Drumclog	425	52	35	123,775	70,336	1
Strathaven: Trinity	812	117	37	165,477	92,570	122
Uddingston: Burnhead	245	21	7	-	28,904	17
Uddingston: Old	343	38	21	-	80,951	20
Uddingston: Viewpark	352	58	8	-	61,462	18
Upper Clyde	169	7	12	-	16,934	5
Wishaw: Cambusnethan North	371	36	-	-	41,816	35
Wishaw: Cambusnethan Old and Morningside	330	27	-	42,935	39,765	60
Wishaw: Old	165	20	-	-	19,722	30
Wishaw: South Wishaw	246	24	22	-	46,686	13

19. Argyll

Appin	79	12	15	-	14,029	1
Lismore	34	7	-	-	8,581	2
Ardchattan	75	10	-	-	16,826	6

Congregation	Com	Eld	G	In21	M&M	–18
Coll	17	3	-	6,224	2,257	-
Connel	97	15	3	-	18,892	6
Ardrishaig	111	16	17	26,214	18,867	-
South Knapdale	29	4	-	-	8,507	2
Barra	30	3	-	-	8,504	-
South Uist	41	7	-	19,537	9,478	4
Bute, United Church of	383	32	19	-	40,198	-
Campbeltown: Highland	307	24	-	35,710	20,830	-
Saddell and Carradale	139	15	7	-	18,117	-
Southend	204	14	14	-	15,363	3
Campbeltown: Lorne and Lowland	636	34	-	-	49,027	14
Colonsay and Oronsay	9	2	-	10,889	6,629	1
Cowal Kirk	664	77	51	-	104,527	17
Craignish	39	3	-	-	4,762	-
Gigha and Cara	25	6	-	7,644	5,143	-
Kilcalmonell	30	10	-	-	5,908	5
Killean and Kilchenzie	109	8	-	-	13,415	1
Glassary, Kilmartin and Ford	80	8	-	-	12,098	-
North Knapdale	29	6	-	-	19,502	-
Glenorchy and Innishael	38	6	-	-	6,650	-
Strathfillan	24	6	-	2,316	5,967	-
Iona	11	4	-	-	10,099	-
Kilfinichen and Kilvickeon and the Ross of Mull	24	3	-	6,173	3,649	-
Jura	20	6	-	4,702	4,651	-
North and West Islay	93	24	7	-	28,586	-
South Islay	111	17	-	45,750	32,198	2
Kilbrandon and Kilchattan	98	17	-	18,972	16,039	-
Kilninver and Kilmelford	50	6	-	-	6,813	8
Kilchrenan and Dalavich	31	7	-	14,284	11,141	5
Muckairn	98	14	-	20,928	13,889	-
Kilfinan	29	5	-	6,868	4,524	-
Kilmodan and Colintraive	57	5	-	-	12,682	-
Kyles	75	13	-	32,125	22,033	-
Kilmore and Oban	388	42	21	68,977	47,087	6
Kilmun, Strone and Ardentnny: The Shore Kirk	135	14	14	-	25,063	1
Lochgilphead	97	12	19	29,327	23,294	-
Lochgoilhead and Kilmorich	59	10	-	29,497	19,959	3
Strachur and Strachlachlan	93	11	10	14,439	16,419	-
North Mull	134	19	-	-	35,019	11
Rothesay: Trinity	285	33	13	-	31,953	1
Skipness	16	2	-	7,744	6,236	-
Tarbert, Loch Fyne and Kilberry	85	10	17	51,432	17,443	-
Tiree	53	6	-	-	9,260	3
West Lochfyneside: Cumlodden, Inveraray and Lochgair	103	16	12	-	28,111	2

23. Stirling

Congregation	Com	Eld	G	In21	M&M	–18
Aberfoyle	61	5	12	12,081	8,571	-
Port of Menteith	51	9	-	20,435	8,904	-
Alloa: Ludgate	266	17	10	67,345	36,604	15
Alloa: St Mungo's	293	34	18	59,706	35,863	13

Congregation	Com	Eld	G	In21	M&M	–18
Alva	397	52	-	83,038	46,143	115
Balfron	105	12	-	-	20,033	-
Fintry	92	8	-	-	15,327	-
Balquhidder	54	4	-	-	11,835	3
Killin and Ardeonaig	73	8	3	-	14,078	7
Bannockburn: Allan	232	29	-	44,667	27,145	10
Cowie and Plean	143	-	-	-	5,590	-
Bannockburn: Ladywell	326	13	-	-	16,104	11
Bridge of Allan	614	39	40	-	65,415	65
Buchanan	88	7	-	-	15,817	-
Drymen	201	21	-	55,754	39,460	12
Buchlyvie	143	10	-	22,666	16,049	10
Gartmore	56	8	-	-	13,882	6
Callander	462	18	24	72,980	60,645	20
Cambusbarron: The Bruce Memorial	250	21	-	72,770	41,854	30
Clackmannan	307	21	29	65,463	46,893	34
Dollar	205	20	52	82,860	51,940	20
Glendevon	26	-	-	-	2,164	-
Muckhart	70	6	-	-	14,327	8
Dunblane: Cathedral	718	66	27	212,224	108,553	184
Dunblane: St Blane's	268	24	30	80,851	54,147	9
Lecropt	126	13	-	44,252	19,617	1
Fallin	224	7	-	-	16,517	15
Gargunnock	103	9	-	-	17,339	5
Kilmadock	70	8	-	12,764	16,566	-
Kincardine-in-Menteith	66	3	-	-	10,981	4
Killearn	311	-	46	83,548	50,491	-
Kippen	161	14	10	32,724	21,737	-
Norrieston	78	8	10	19,554	16,166	1
Logie	440	28	25	80,452	47,826	10
Menstrie	295	19	25	47,865	37,878	-
Sauchie and Coalsnaughton	365	16	12	42,222	31,115	7
Stirling: Church of The Holy Rude	117	14	-	-	21,149	-
Stirling: Viewfield Erskine	202	16	9	-	18,828	5
Stirling: North	324	25	20	86,425	29,807	16
Stirling: Park	447	43	-	-	68,851	30
Stirling: St Mark's	146	7	-	38,965	14,507	15
Stirling: St Ninian's Old	544	57	-	-	52,637	55
Strathblane	145	16	38	68,183	38,140	11
Tillicoultry	484	54	27	83,034	46,032	48
Tullibody: St Serf's	274	17	25	-	31,243	6

24. Fife

Congregation	Com	Eld	G	In21	M&M	–18
Aberdour: St Fillan's	317	14	-	57,201	42,690	5
Anstruther and Cellardyke: St Ayle	336	35	31	54,952	50,083	4
Crail	274	19	44	44,333	28,622	3
Auchterderran Kinglassie	267	21	20	-	32,582	6
Auchtertool	63	11	-	-	5,763	3
Kirkcaldy: Linktown	194	25	26	51,155	32,528	3
Balmerino	101	10	-	-	14,456	-

Congregation	Com	Eld	G	In21	M&M	–18
Wormit	146	12	28	-	20,580	-
Beath and Cowdenbeath: North	199	14	-	48,042	30,890	-
Boarhills and Dunino	118	8	-	19,707	19,553	-
St Andrews: Holy Trinity	238	24	30	-	53,940	-
Buckhaven and Wemyss	184	18	11	-	27,504	-
Burntisland	236	27	12	-	38,265	4
Cairneyhill	81	17	-	20,574	15,055	-
Limekilns	214	29	-	-	41,523	1
Cameron	88	10	-	21,455	13,342	-
St Andrews: St Leonard's	381	-	20	128,025	68,392	-
Carnbee	80	7	-	-	9,148	-
Pittenweem	204	11	12	-	11,474	-
Carnock and Oakley	132	17	19	-	29,061	2
Ceres, Kemback and Springfield	287	18	13	-	63,704	7
Cowdenbeath: Trinity	238	25	11	57,523	40,576	11
Creich, Flisk and Kilmany	71	10	-	20,041	14,270	-
Culross and Torryburn	50	10	-	39,484	27,611	-
Cupar: Old and St Michael of Tarvit	447	29	22	121,690	71,544	-
Monimail	68	11	-	-	13,774	-
Cupar: St John's and Dairsie United	555	40	19	-	61,996	14
Dalgety	431	34	25	111,463	68,319	50
Dunfermline: Abbey	467	42	-	121,182	74,263	27
Dunfermline: East	92	7	-	133,391	15,747	70
Dunfermline: Gillespie Memorial	100	14	11	-	20,390	15
Dunfermline: North	131	-	-	21,314	15,267	-
Dunfermline: St Andrew's Erskine	153	18	14	49,966	28,207	-
Dunfermline: St Leonard's	259	22	28	-	41,394	39
Dunfermline: St Margaret's	180	25	-	65,164	39,247	23
Dunfermline: St Ninian's	128	21	20	50,431	29,797	35
Dunfermline: Townhill and Kingseat	148	19	-	51,708	34,881	-
Dysart: St Clair	361	22	11	-	28,090	-
East Neuk Trinity	260	19	30	66,183	49,597	4
St Monans	190	9	23	-	35,407	4
Edenshead	269	19	11	-	28,900	-
Falkland	98	9	-	-	21,614	-
Freuchie	109	16	23	24,110	16,061	7
Glenrothes: Christ's Kirk	154	14	17	37,238	18,802	2
Glenrothes: St Columba's	305	39	-	61,601	32,013	33
Glenrothes: St Margaret's	223	25	22	52,867	31,213	58
Glenrothes: St Ninian's	181	24	11	64,004	40,536	7
Howe of Fife	255	14	-	-	33,576	7
Inverkeithing	166	16	-	-	37,153	15
North Queensferry	42	5	-	-	9,629	-
Kelty	207	17	17	50,862	40,528	2
Kennoway, Windygates and Balgonie: St Kenneth's	361	31	45	84,722	56,007	2
Kilrenny	85	10	-	23,036	19,472	-
Kinghorn	196	20	-	-	41,975	8
Kingsbarns	62	-	-	-	11,445	-
Kirkcaldy: Abbotshall	389	28	-	84,994	39,648	15
Kirkcaldy: Bennochy	349	27	17	-	46,095	6

Congregation	Com	Eld	G	In21	M&M	–18
Kirkcaldy: Pathhead	280	21	28	-	38,623	60
Kirkcaldy: St Bryce Kirk	289	24	18	79,466	48,593	11
Kirkcaldy: Templehall and Torbain United	271	23	18	65,515	40,887	75
Largo	259	23	18	75,138	43,893	5
Largoward	44	8	-	8,836	4,860	12
Leslie: Trinity	112	11	-	12,624	10,206	-
Leuchars: St Athernase	233	21	16	-	24,110	6
Leven	382	-	30	-	54,378	-
Lindores	250	29	-	38,090	27,663	45
Lochgelly and Benarty: St Serf's	178	32	-	53,805	36,887	25
Markinch and Thornton	394	26	-	-	51,661	10
Methil: Wellesley	252	25	10	-	29,074	94
Methilhill and Denbeath	162	16	22	29,168	17,675	7
Newport-on-Tay	317	37	-	81,207	41,965	22
Rosyth	189	18	-	-	19,644	4
St Andrews: Hope Park and Martyrs'	424	36	16	-	85,100	-
Strathkinness	72	2	-	-	11,889	-
Saline and Blairingone	129	18	-	29,185	25,413	-
Tulliallan and Kincardine	188	24	38	46,297	30,092	64
Tayport	196	9	-	-	26,161	-

27. Dunkeld and Meigle

Aberfeldy	147	12	-	104,562	25,253	74
Dull and Weem	119	12	11	-	20,551	-
Grantully, Logierait and Strathtay	126	9	6	-	24,332	4
Alyth	581	23	-	55,966	45,197	4
Ardler, Kettins and Meigle	343	17	22	-	26,537	-
Bendochy	67	7	-	-	15,151	-
Coupar Angus: Abbey	238	18	-	-	21,721	-
Blair Atholl and Struan	92	10	-	-	18,867	-
Braes of Rannoch	18	4	-	-	5,663	-
Foss and Rannoch	72	8	-	-	8,297	-
Blairgowrie	630	43	28	115,861	64,860	29
Caputh and Clunie	117	13	-	14,671	17,434	-
Kinclaven	125	10	15	19,505	12,835	-
Dunkeld	299	24	-	105,337	61,378	25
Fortingall, Glenlyon, Kenmore and Lawers	92	14	12	-	23,295	-
Kirkmichael, Straloch and Glenshee	62	4	-	-	11,370	-
Rattray	236	15	-	27,559	19,802	-
Pitlochry	282	26	17	64,313	45,616	-
Tenandry	33	7	-	24,118	13,714	-

28. Perth

Aberdalgie and Forteviot	165	11	-	20,707	14,374	-
Aberuthven and Dunning	177	9	-	35,266	29,987	10
Abernethy and Dron and Arngask	247	21	-	29,296	31,557	6
Almondbank Tibbermore	166	13	18	-	27,658	4
Methven and Logiealmond	128	17	-	-	14,887	-
Ardoch	142	11	27	-	23,298	15
Blackford	83	-	-	26,604	13,159	-

Congregation	Com	Eld	G	In21	M&M	–18
Auchterarder	501	33	35	-	78,894	53
Auchtergaven and Moneydie	443	-	20	-	28,680	-
Redgorton and Stanley	285	11	27	19,837	23,569	70
Cargill Burrelton	77	14	17	29,631	18,336	25
Collace	97	6	-	12,806	8,857	-
Cleish	111	9	14	26,436	22,823	-
Fossoway: St Serf's and Devonside	182	12	-	47,429	29,682	-
Comrie	323	26	19	-	54,415	-
Dundurn	51	8	-	15,256	10,378	-
Crieff	512	-	12	68,924	48,257	-
Dunbarney and Forgandenny	484	26	21	92,841	49,624	20
Errol	234	15	-	-	29,763	13
Kilspindie and Rait	63	-	-	4,651	9,018	-
Kinross	591	31	30	149,118	67,758	50
Mid Strathearn	289	24	14	46,184	43,123	12
Muthill	207	16	9	41,099	27,660	14
Trinity Gask and Kinkell	37	-	-	-	5,189	-
Orwell and Portmoak	348	32	23	62,788	45,507	12
Perth: Craigie and Moncrieffe	459	22	10	-	51,654	76
Perth: Kinnoull	337	37	17	-	39,174	70
Perth: Letham St Mark's	394	7	-	112,182	63,935	10
Perth: North	719	40	34	-	113,367	10
Perth: Riverside	62	6	-	47,951	25,090	41
Perth: St John's Kirk of Perth	335	29	-	-	50,986	-
Perth: St Leonard's-in-the-Fields	361	29	-	-	44,799	1
Perth: St Matthew's	332	31	17	94,540	59,655	170
St Madoes and Kinfauns	259	28	-	75,623	37,600	113
Scone and St Martins	737	35	26	98,014	63,444	40

29. Dundee

Congregation	Com	Eld	G	In21	M&M	–18
Abernyte	83	10	-	16,913	12,224	3
Inchture and Kinnaird	131	22	-	35,659	22,481	10
Longforgan	150	11	7	-	29,472	-
Auchterhouse	116	11	18	27,847	14,160	2
Monikie and Newbigging and Murroes and Tealing	404	19	13	33,135	27,250	-
Dundee: Balgay	222	17	-	-	31,577	-
Dundee: Barnhill St Margaret's	605	39	56	-	83,257	29
Dundee: Broughty Ferry New Kirk	530	38	24	-	56,655	37
Dundee: Broughty Ferry St James'	125	9	22	-	17,311	6
Dundee: Broughty Ferry St Luke's and Queen Street	241	27	10	-	31,808	12
Dundee: Broughty Ferry St Stephen's and West	260	22	-	48,481	27,386	-
Dundee: Dundee (St Mary's)	468	41	-	69,914	41,400	-
Dundee: Camperdown	64	8	-	17,872	14,775	-
Dundee: Chalmers Ardler	139	17	-	-	44,453	7
Dundee: Coldside	154	16	-	-	28,000	2
Dundee: Craigiebank	101	8	-	-	13,721	-
Dundee: Douglas and Mid Craigie	86	9	-	-	11,573	-
Dundee: Downfield Mains	224	12	21	98,104	48,706	130
Dundee: Fintry	84	5	-	-	26,125	36
Dundee: Lochee	350	18	30	-	33,190	325

Congregation	Com	Eld	G	In21	M&M	–18
Dundee: Logie and St John's Cross	187	15	18	-	37,472	8
Dundee: Meadowside St Paul's	258	22	15	-	25,366	3
Dundee: St Andrew's	352	35	19	92,162	56,117	7
Dundee: Menzieshill	222	13	-	-	17,922	23
Dundee: St David's High Kirk	137	14	19	-	25,344	14
Dundee: Steeple	136	19	-	-	77,305	2
Dundee: Stobswell	309	28	-	-	33,278	-
Dundee: Strathmartine	205	24	18	-	28,852	-
Dundee: Trinity	344	26	-	-	29,255	32
Dundee: West	233	23	18	-	31,670	-
Dundee: Whitfield	33	4	-	-	8,024	-
Fowlis and Liff	129	11	-	-	24,739	-
Lundie and Muirhead	242	22	-	36,141	23,590	-
Invergowrie	223	43	18	52,321	33,156	9
Monifieth	501	48	34	-	56,377	-

30. Angus

Congregation	Com	Eld	G	In21	M&M	–18
Aberlemno	177	11	-	27,074	15,702	14
Guthrie and Rescobie	198	8	-	-	15,065	-
Arbirlot	122	8	-	-	14,520	-
Carmyllie	87	12	-	-	15,716	-
Arbroath: Old and Abbey	355	24	-	80,269	38,413	5
Arbroath: St Andrew's	473	39	36	138,920	77,262	40
Arbroath: St Vigeans	420	38	12	-	37,323	6
Arbroath: West Kirk	737	71	34	92,982	67,238	49
Barry	162	6	18	26,394	13,760	4
Carnoustie	246	19	18	72,825	40,870	7
Brechin: Cathedral	387	-	-	-	37,080	-
Brechin	375	21	-	46,897	32,426	-
Farnell	115	12	-	-	9,934	10
Carnoustie: Panbride	576	29	-	73,211	41,977	24
Colliston	155	5	6	-	11,623	-
Friockheim Kinnell	111	7	15	14,437	12,967	-
Inverkeilor and Lunan	103	7	-	16,700	13,594	2
Dun and Hillside	324	32	32	-	30,455	-
Dunnichen, Letham and Kirkden	206	13	11	28,879	19,960	-
Eassie, Nevay and Newtyle	180	13	17	-	17,270	15
Edzell Lethnot Glenesk	310	21	16	35,950	26,159	9
Fern Careston Menmuir	91	8	-	-	12,783	4
Forfar: East and Old	415	38	26	-	62,960	36
Forfar: Lowson Memorial	549	42	23	102,509	68,367	8
Forfar: St Margaret's	393	27	16	63,008	45,644	60
Glamis, Inverarity and Kinettles	320	25	-	40,712	38,130	10
Montrose: Old and St Andrew's	508	38	14	-	45,462	48
Montrose: South and Ferryden	249	17	-	58,676	32,238	6
Oathlaw Tannadice	97	7	-	17,339	16,144	-
The Glens and Kirriemuir United	1,019	70	34	-	66,746	12
The Isla Parishes	127	12	11	-	23,981	2

Congregation	Com	Eld	G	In21	M&M	–18
31. Aberdeen and Shetland						
Aberdeen: Bridge of Don Oldmachar	153	10	-	-	24,998	19
Aberdeen: Craigiebuckler	668	58	21	-	65,319	-
Aberdeen: Ferryhill	272	34	-	79,639	47,970	-
Aberdeen: High Hilton	340	26	18	35,635	30,575	50
Aberdeen: Holburn West	271	32	15	87,123	57,786	9
Aberdeen: Mannofield	744	63	29	-	81,061	-
Aberdeen: Midstocket	381	36	38	-	61,568	25
Aberdeen: North	337	33	22	-	63,845	4
Aberdeen: Queen's Cross	360	40	-	-	73,554	8
Aberdeen: Rubislaw	359	55	36	117,536	79,226	13
Aberdeen: Ruthrieston West	187	23	10	62,495	42,808	4
Aberdeen: St Columba's Bridge of Don	211	12	-	-	48,221	100
Aberdeen: St George's Tillydrone	71	7	-	-	8,099	4
Aberdeen: St John's Church for Deaf People	82	3	-	-	-	-
Aberdeen: St Machar's Cathedral	361	30	-	138,113	82,232	8
Aberdeen: St Mark's	338	43	32	94,714	76,837	8
Aberdeen: St Mary's	248	34	-	57,011	39,362	45
Aberdeen: St Nicholas Kincorth, South of	274	26	-	-	36,966	68
Aberdeen: St Stephen's	130	18	15	-	38,633	21
Aberdeen: South Holburn	359	32	28	70,987	57,387	2
Aberdeen: Stockethill	83	6	-	32,197	11,053	7
Aberdeen: Torry St Fittick's	249	14	18	-	33,006	128
Aberdeen: Woodside	118	27	17	-	32,011	3
Bucksburn Stoneywood	355	11	-	-	17,707	-
Cults	597	56	32	157,117	96,700	37
Dyce	781	44	34	-	59,932	188
Kingswells	265	18	12	-	24,706	-
Newhills	305	19	17	-	62,477	52
Peterculter	463	42	-	98,451	58,002	58
Shetland	770	84	97	-	97,700	81
32. Kincardine and Deeside						
Aberluthnott	57	8	-	-	10,172	-
Laurencekirk	203	6	-	-	14,315	1
Aboyne-Dinnet	244	9	11	40,544	24,960	12
Cromar	176	13	-	22,753	19,577	2
Arbuthnott, Bervie and Kinneff	251	-	-	67,049	36,855	-
Banchory-Ternan: East	449	25	11	67,850	47,562	8
Banchory-Ternan: West	551	15	12	-	61,295	30
Birse and Feughside	191	14	-	29,783	24,748	6
Braemar and Crathie	165	-	-	-	36,012	-
Drumoak-Durris	352	8	-	50,718	35,678	-
Glenmuick (Ballater)	214	14	-	-	24,954	1
Maryculter Trinity	124	13	12	-	28,584	25
Mearns Coastal	197	10	-	22,411	23,219	-
Mid Deeside	458	34	17	-	38,433	14
Newtonhill	204	9	14	-	19,652	48
Portlethen	242	12	-	45,879	36,686	6
Stonehaven: Carronside	708	19	-	-	45,715	4

Congregation	Com	Eld	G	In21	M&M	–18
Stonehaven: Fetteresso	495	-	39	-	87,893	-
West Mearns	395	14	13	-	37,723	5

33. Gordon

Barthol Chapel	63	6	8	-	6,698	1
Tarves	231	13	31	-	24,800	24
Belhelvie	293	29	15	-	50,253	25
Blairdaff and Chapel of Garioch	277	17	-	-	22,633	2
Cluny	154	8	-	21,490	16,565	-
Monymusk	87	4	-	16,743	11,668	35
Culsalmond and Rayne	152	5	-	-	9,871	4
Daviot	133	7	-	7,357	9,497	3
Cushnie and Tough	216	9	-	13,534	15,584	1
Echt and Midmar	242	11	-	31,556	19,364	7
Ellon	1,242	66	-	183,691	97,789	19
Fintray Kinellar Keithhall	125	8	-	18,972	23,272	-
Foveran	180	6	-	-	26,019	5
Howe Trinity	403	15	24	-	42,187	20
Huntly Cairnie Glass	551	6	9	-	32,841	-
Insch-Leslie-Premnay-Oyne	299	24	13	-	31,278	58
Inverurie: St Andrew's	835	22	-	-	58,289	-
Inverurie: West	516	41	22	-	45,940	6
Kemnay	403	30	-	65,695	47,132	32
Kintore	603	30	-	-	53,455	40
Meldrum and Bourtie	332	18	27	60,074	42,102	2
Methlick	293	24	14	-	39,475	50
New Machar	332	16	-	45,799	38,362	15
Noth	177	5	-	21,999	17,849	-
Skene	1,012	61	41	147,006	79,464	136
Strathbogie Drumblade	361	25	19	-	33,315	16
Udny and Pitmedden	219	19	12	44,798	37,681	30
Upper Donside	307	16	-	-	25,059	25

34. Buchan

Aberdour	92	7	9	-	8,149	-
Pitsligo	74	7	-	-	8,696	-
Auchaber United	87	9	-	-	11,808	-
Auchterless	159	12	-	27,003	14,613	1
Banff	336	19	-	-	46,256	-
King Edward	121	9	-	19,639	14,311	22
Crimond	129	12	-	18,530	14,409	-
Lonmay	88	8	9	-	11,172	-
Cruden	294	18	16	38,021	22,697	1
Deer	502	13	17	-	33,468	-
Fraserburgh: Old	394	41	41	-	60,716	20
Fraserburgh: South	231	16	-	-	23,253	-
Inverallochy and Rathen: East	65	6	-	-	9,812	11
Fraserburgh: West	376	40	-	48,660	34,512	97
Rathen: West	67	8	-	8,450	6,702	-
Fyvie	155	12	10	-	22,887	-

Congregation	Com	Eld	G	In21	M&M	–18
Rothienorman	92	6	-	15,076	9,101	15
Longside	346	22	-	58,224	40,566	32
Macduff	513	27	20	-	49,178	105
Marnoch	317	17	12	33,534	21,764	8
Maud and Savoch	164	12	-	23,422	16,954	8
New Deer: St Kane's	232	12	15	42,568	23,747	8
Monquhitter and New Byth	241	17	8	17,796	17,096	-
Turriff: St Andrew's	410	23	11	-	21,996	42
New Pitsligo	229	5	-	-	12,648	15
Strichen and Tyrie	321	17	13	-	28,588	6
Ordiquhill and Cornhill	126	10	8	7,978	6,909	13
Whitehills	247	5	18	16,736	20,604	-
Peterhead: New	443	22	28	-	42,270	9
Peterhead: St Andrew's	344	16	15	29,427	24,880	5
Portsoy	244	10	21	-	23,452	-
St Fergus	88	4	9	-	7,098	-
Sandhaven	63	6	-	-	2,700	32
Turriff: St Ninian's and Forglen	483	19	15	73,337	37,391	6

35. Moray

Congregation	Com	Eld	G	In21	M&M	–18
Aberlour	191	7	26	33,981	21,826	-
Bellie and Speymouth	305	17	18	-	38,147	90
Birnie and Pluscarden	170	17	7	37,989	27,248	25
Elgin: High	203	28	-	64,708	34,343	26
Buckie: North	273	24	32	-	27,275	14
Rathven	53	11	14	-	10,593	-
Buckie: South and West	188	-	-	-	25,054	-
Enzie	45	3	-	-	6,621	-
Cullen and Deskford	239	13	11	33,862	36,281	-
Duffus, Spynie and Hopeman	191	27	-	43,784	31,240	20
Elgin: St Giles' and St Columba's South	454	-	37	99,384	65,732	-
Findochty	34	8	10	-	11,635	20
Portknockie	48	8	13	-	12,244	38
Keith: North, Newmill, Boharm and Rothiemay	404	38	16	33,435	59,170	2
Keith: St Rufus, Botriphnie and Grange	787	-	24	-	41,566	-
Knockando, Elchies and Archiestown	198	11	5	-	22,828	18
Rothes	249	12	21	-	22,649	18
Lossiemouth: St Gerardine's High	179	-	13	-	28,866	-
Lossiemouth: St James'	178	-	20	40,913	25,377	-
Mortlach and Cabrach	271	-	12	-	21,248	-
St Andrew's-Lhanbryd and Urquhart	280	39	24	59,890	39,012	4

36. Abernethy

Congregation	Com	Eld	G	In21	M&M	–18
Abernethy	125	12	-	-	31,335	12
Boat of Garten, Carrbridge and Kincardine	155	16	27	39,584	22,102	17
Alvie and Insh	51	3	-	-	17,340	10
Rothiemurchus and Aviemore	57	7	-	15,548	10,624	4
Cromdale and Advie	52	3	-	13,656	13,767	-
Dulnain Bridge	29	5	-	2,880	7,220	-
Grantown-on-Spey	154	14	-	47,522	25,634	10

Congregation	Com	Eld	G	In21	M&M	–18
Kingussie	59	13	-	-	16,501	10
Laggan and Newtonmore	89	15	-	46,611	30,060	12
Tomintoul, Glenlivet and Inveraven	114	8	-	-	16,178	-

37. Inverness

Alves and Burghead	96	14	23	-	20,788	10
Kinloss and Findhorn	59	18	-	18,619	20,015	-
Ardersier	35	6	-	20,997	12,081	-
Petty	30	-	11	-	9,883	-
Cawdor	138	-	-	18,750	17,500	-
Croy and Dalcross	34	7	15	-	12,481	2
Culloden: The Barn	200	17	-	81,521	46,198	44
Dallas	41	4	-	-	9,845	-
Forres: St Leonard's	125	-	22	-	27,637	-
Rafford	41	-	-	13,663	9,151	-
Daviot and Dunlichity	43	5	-	-	9,657	2
Moy, Dalarossie and Tomatin	29	5	10	-	6,674	5
Dores and Boleskine	50	5	-	5,872	12,321	-
Dyke and Edinkillie	144	10	8	-	24,909	9
Forres: St Laurence	299	-	16	60,582	38,924	-
Inverness: Crown	451	50	26	89,021	59,109	25
Inverness: Dalneigh and Bona	130	10	11	-	27,499	64
Inverness: East	184	16	-	-	62,250	14
Inverness: Hilton	207	8	-	84,240	39,026	35
Inverness: Inshes	213	14	-	175,557	92,695	45
Inverness: Kinmylies	63	8	-	47,482	21,986	45
Inverness: Ness Bank	480	-	23	-	79,720	-
Inverness: Old High St Stephen's	306	32	-	106,448	59,899	-
Inverness: St Columba's	61	-	-	61,283	17,500	-
Inverness: Trinity	155	19	10	51,271	36,412	-
Kilmorack and Erchless	78	9	-	-	30,040	4
Kiltarlity and Kirkhill	101	13	-	-	26,005	23
Nairn: Old	304	35	16	-	64,081	14
Nairn: St Ninian's and Auldearn and Dalmore	195	14	27	-	36,006	-
Urquhart and Glenmoriston	83	5	-	45,380	31,357	5

38. Lochaber

Acharacle	28	4	-	-	13,004	12
Ardnamurchan	13	4	-	10,162	5,416	12
Ardgour and Kingairloch	38	4	11	-	7,624	5
Morvern	28	4	7	-	5,926	-
Strontian	24	3	-	-	3,558	3
Duror	33	6	13	12,400	8,381	-
Glencoe: St Munda's	32	4	-	-	9,205	-
Fort Augustus	54	8	-	-	11,215	2
Glengarry	27	5	12	-	6,764	2
Fort William Kilmallie	351	31	25	68,585	61,952	9
Kilmonivaig	46	13	10	-	17,416	3
Kinlochleven	40	7	11	23,866	12,815	-
Nether Lochaber	32	6	-	16,178	10,454	-
North West Lochaber	71	10	-	29,116	17,789	8

Congregation	Com	Eld	G	In21	M&M	–18
39. Ross						
Alness	62	8	-	-	15,551	12
Avoch	16	2	-	9,367	7,962	1
Fortrose and Rosemarkie	68	5	-	32,685	17,625	6
Contin	33	9	-	-	11,061	2
Fodderty and Strathpeffer	90	17	-	21,245	16,358	6
Cromarty	35	6	-	-	6,950	-
Resolis and Urquhart	77	8	-	-	23,735	-
Dingwall: Castle Street	117	12	-	-	23,877	15
Dingwall: St Clement's	141	20	13	-	36,273	-
Fearn Abbey and Nigg	38	-	-	-	10,559	-
Tarbat	26	4	-	-	6,730	4
Ferintosh	134	17	16	-	25,649	10
Invergordon	85	8	-	-	31,009	-
Killearnan	71	14	-	-	25,048	-
Knockbain	22	6	-	-	10,058	-
Kilmuir and Logie Easter	56	7	14	-	19,127	-
Kiltearn	52	6	-	-	18,248	-
Lochbroom and Ullapool	32	5	-	21,047	17,222	10
Rosskeen	98	11	12	-	24,328	25
Tain	78	8	19	-	25,179	7
Urray and Kilchrist	71	14	-	54,012	27,936	11
40. Sutherland						
Altnaharra and Farr	20	-	-	-	6,691	-
Melness and Tongue	18	2	-	-	12,552	-
Assynt and Stoer	12	2	-	30,995	7,121	15
Clyne	34	9	-	-	18,447	-
Kildonan and Loth Helmsdale	28	6	-	9,645	9,709	4
Creich	12	4	-	-	8,406	1
Kincardine Croick and Edderton	14	5	-	11,207	12,293	-
Rosehall	17	2	-	-	6,103	4
Dornoch Cathedral	252	25	33	-	65,636	20
Durness and Kinlochbervie	26	3	-	-	10,404	30
Eddrachillis	6	2	-	-	9,428	-
Golspie	28	5	5	16,042	17,374	-
Lairg	16	3	8	14,859	13,604	-
Rogart	11	-	-	-	8,211	-
41. Caithness						
Halkirk Westerdale	72	6	8	-	8,066	-
Watten	11	1	-	-	4,676	-
Latheron	46	8	7	-	14,145	15
North Coast	29	8	17	-	13,420	8
Pentland	93	10	22	-	22,800	15
Thurso: St Peter's and St Andrew's	116	16	-	-	31,335	17
Thurso: West	133	21	16	50,752	28,064	4
Wick: Pulteneytown and Thrumster	174	10	23	41,873	30,438	2
Wick: St Fergus	130	20	-	27,198	23,581	-

Congregation	Com	Eld	G	In21	M&M	–18
42. Lochcarron-Skye						
Applecross, Lochcarron and Torridon	47	5	6	-	19,457	-
Bracadale and Duirinish	31	4	6	-	18,177	-
Gairloch and Dundonnell	68	4	-	61,902	40,632	7
Glenelg Kintail and Lochalsh	56	9	11	34,912	24,582	-
Kilmuir and Stenscholl	41	-	-	33,337	18,110	-
Portree	83	14	-	60,812	36,351	5
Snizort	28	-	-	44,321	19,681	-
Strath and Sleat	104	6	-	85,770	57,573	-
43. Uist						
Benbecula	59	10	15	40,634	21,528	2
Carinish	64	7	14	-	27,872	-
Berneray and Lochmaddy	25	2	7	-	10,076	-
Kilmuir and Paible	25	4	-	-	18,328	6
Manish-Scarista	20	4	-	-	19,300	7
Tarbert	69	7	-	-	33,648	18
44. Lewis						
Barvas	70	8	-	-	37,937	18
Carloway	44	4	-	25,477	14,947	5
Cross Ness	58	4	-	38,838	23,566	11
Kinloch	30	4	-	-	22,370	17
Knock	21	1	-	-	16,916	10
Lochs-Crossbost	8	3	-	-	10,231	7
Lochs-in-Bernera	28	-	-	-	9,217	-
Uig	13	3	-	-	12,110	15
Stornoway: High	82	7	-	-	34,297	25
Stornoway: Martin's Memorial	329	12	-	191,192	85,034	60
Stornoway: St Columba	124	7	30	-	54,042	148
45. Orkney						
Birsay, Harray and Sandwick	258	29	22	-	23,210	6
East Mainland	217	15	5	14,834	17,987	-
Eday	2	1	-	-	1,571	-
Evie and Rendall	63	4	-	-	14,915	32
Firth	63	4	-	20,121	10,844	11
Rousay	10	2	-	4,556	4,624	-
Flotta	20	8	-	-	2,907	-
Orphir and Stenness	115	12	-	-	14,761	-
Hoy and Walls	32	6	-	3,285	4,497	2
Kirkwall: East	275	16	19	-	35,984	9
Shapinsay	33	6	-	7,983	5,689	5
Kirkwall: St Magnus Cathedral	437	26	20	-	41,798	-
North Ronaldsay	6	3	-	-	1,003	-
Papa Westray	7	4	-	11,804	4,339	3
Westray	75	18	21	-	17,679	45
Sanday	42	7	5	-	6,529	-
South Ronaldsay and Burray	102	4	11	22,604	9,923	-
Stromness	265	29	13	-	24,304	2
Stronsay: Moncur Memorial	46	6	-	9,314	7,579	1

Congregation	Com	Eld	G	In21	M&M	–18
47. England						
Corby: St Andrew's	191	-	-	-	19,477	-
Corby: St Ninian's	137	11	-	50,697	20,602	1
Guernsey: St Andrew's in the Grange	172	21	-	69,281	41,893	5
Jersey: St Columba's	105	13	-	69,478	33,709	5
London: Crown Court	191	31	3	-	55,515	18
London: St Columba's	759	54	-	-	219,378	20
Newcastle: St Andrew's	102	14	-	-	8,903	17
48. International Charges						
Amsterdam: English Reformed Church	347	12	-	-	-	15
Bermuda: Christ Church Warwick	469	39	-	-	-	42
Brussels: St Andrew's	265	19	-	-	-	20
Budapest: St Columba's	27	-	-	-	-	-
Colombo, Sri Lanka: St Andrew's Scots Kirk	103	-	-	-	-	-
Costa del Sol: Fuengirola	14	3	-	-	-	-
Geneva	211	14	-	-	-	10
Gibraltar: St Andrew's	23	6	-	-	-	2
Lausanne: The Scots Kirk	120	12	-	-	-	13
Lisbon: St Andrew's	50	6	-	-	-	2
Malta: St Andrew's Scots Church	36	4	-	-	-	2
Paris: The Scots Kirk	88	8	-	-	-	11
Rome: St Andrew's	81	-	-	-	-	-
Rotterdam: Scots International Church	183	11	-	-	-	48
Trinidad: Greyfriars St Ann's, Port of Spain with Arouca and Sangre Grande	227	15	-	-	-	-

INDEX OF MINISTERS

Ministers who are members of a Presbytery are designated 'A' if holding a parochial appointment in that Presbytery, 'B' if in other appointments or 'C' if 'Retaining'. 'A-1, A-2' etc. indicate the numerical order of congregations in the Presbyteries of Edinburgh and West Lothian, South West, Clyde, Glasgow, Forth Valley and Clydesdale, and Fife.

Also included are ministers listed in Section 6:

(1) Ministers who have resigned their seat in Presbytery but registered as Retaining or Employed (List 6-D1: in an appointment; List 6-D2: not in appointments);

(2) Ministers who have resigned their seat in Presbytery but registered as Inactive (List 6-E);

(3) Ministers serving overseas (List 6-J) – see also Presbyteries 48 and 49;

(4) Ordained Local Ministers and Auxiliary Ministers, who are listed both in Presbyteries and in List 6-A and List 6-B respectively;

(5) Ministers ordained for sixty years and upwards (List 6-O); and

(6) Ministers who have died since the compilation of the last Year Book (List 6-P).

For a list of the Diaconate, see List 6-C.

Abeledo, B.J.A.	Dunkeld/Meigle 27A	Annand, J.M.	List 6-P
Ableitner, J.M.	Glasgow 16A-16	Archer, M.	Inverness 37B
Acklam, C.R.	Argyll 19C	Archer, N.D.C.	Inverness 37C
Adams, D.G.	Fife 24C	Arif, R. Forth V./Clydesdale 17A-43	
Adams, J.M.	Moray 35A	Armitage, W.L.	
Adamson, R.A.	South West 7C	Edinburgh/W. Lothian 1C	
Afrin, N.A.	Glasgow 16A-113	Armstrong, G.B.	Clyde 14A-60
Aitchison, J.W.		Armstrong, W.R.	Clyde 14C
	Edinburgh/W. Lothian 1C	Arnott, A.D.K.	Melrose/Peebles 4C
Aitken, E.R.	List 6-D1	Ashley-Emery, S.	
Aitken, F.R.	South West 7C	Edinburgh/W. Lothian 1B	
Aitken, I.M.	Aberdeen/Shetland 31A	Astles, G.D.	Lothian 3A
Aitken, J.D.		Atkins, Y.E.S.	Lothian 3C
	Edinburgh/W. Lothian 1A-23	Atkinson, G.T.	Abernethy 36A
Albon, D.A.	South West 7A-47	Attenburrow, A.A.	Moray 35C
Alexander, D.N.	List 6-E	Auld, A.G.	List 6-D2
Alexander, E.J.	Glasgow 16C	Austin, G.	Int. Charges 48A
Alexander, H.J.R.			
	Edinburgh/W. Lothian 1C	Bain, B.	Moray 35C
Alexander, I.W.		Baird, K.S. Edinburgh/W. Lothian 1C	
	Edinburgh/W. Lothian 1B	Baird, W.W.H.	List 6-P
Allan, R.S.T.		Baker, C.M.	South West 7C
	Forth V./Clydesdale 17A-61	Balaj, N.I.	
Allan, W.G.	List 6-P	Edinburgh/W. Lothian 1A-88	
Allardice, M.	Fife 24C	Ballentine, A.M.	Perth 28C
Allen, V.L.	Stirling 23B	Barber, P.I. Edinburgh/W. Lothian 1C	
Allison, A.	Lothian 3C	Barclay, I.C. Edinburgh/W. Lothian 1B	
Allison, R.N.	Lothian 3A	Barclay, N.W.	List 6-E
Alston, C.M.	Fife 24A-41	Barclay, S.G.	Glasgow 16B
Amed, P.	Lewis 44C	Bardgett, F.D.	List 6-D2
Anderson, A.F.	England 47C	Barge, N.L.	Argyll 19C
Anderson, D.	List 6-D2	Barr, D.L.C.	Kincardine/Deeside 32A
Anderson, D.M.	Lochaber 38C	Barr, G.R.	Fife 24C
Anderson, D.P.	Argyll 19B	Barr, T.L.	Perth 28C
Anderson, D.U.		Barrett, L.M.	Dundee 29C
	Edinburgh/W. Lothian 1C	Barrie, A.A.	Caithness 41A
Anderson, F.		Barrie, A.P. Forth V./Clydesdale 17C	
	Forth V./Clydesdale 17A-109	Barrie, D.	Stirling 23A
Anderson, R.A.	South West 7C	Barron, J.L.	Fife 24A-14
Anderson, R.J.M.	Moray 35C	Bartholomew, D.S.	South West 7C
Anderson, S.M.	List 6-D2	Baxendale, G.M.	
Andrews, J.E.	Inverness 37C	Forth V./Clydesdale 17C	
Baxter, R.	Glasgow 16A-123		
Beattie, C.J.	Glasgow 16A-20		
Beattie, W.R.	Ross 39A		
Beautyman, P.H.	List 6-E		
Becker, A.E.	South West 7C		
Beckett, D.M.	List 6-E		
Beebee, G.W.	Fife 24A-11		
Begg, R. J.	Stirling 23B		
Bell, G.K.	Ross 39C		
Bell, I.W.	Clyde 14C		
Bell, J.L.	Glasgow 16B		
Bell, M.	Clyde 14C		
Bellis, P.A.	South West 7B		
Bender, A. C.	Moray 35A		
Bennett, A.G.	Int. Charges 48A		
Beresford, H. J.	South West 7A-95		
Berry, G.T.	Lothian 3B		
Beveridge, S.E.P.	South West 7C		
Bezuidenhout, L.C.	Moray 35C		
Bezuidenhout, W.J.	Argyll 19A		
Bicket, M.S. Edinburgh/W. Lothian 1C			
Billes, R.H.			
Edinburgh/W. Lothian 1A-19			
Binks, M.	England 47B		
Birch, J.	Glasgow 16C		
Bircham, M.F.	Perth 28A		
Birnie, C.	Fife 24A-29		
Birse, G.S.	South West 7C		
Birss, A.D.	Kincardine/Deeside 32C		
Bissett, J.	Ross 39B		
Bjarnason, S.S.	List 6-E		
Black, A.R.	South West 7C		
Black, D.R.	Glasgow 16A-94		
Black, D.W.	List 6-E		
Black, G.W.G.	Fife 24A-20		
Black, I.W.	Glasgow 16C		
Black, J.M.K.	List 6-E		
Black, J.S.	List 6-D2		
Black, S.	Glasgow 16A-44		
Black, W.B.	Glasgow 16C		
Blackman, I.R.			
Forth V./Clydesdale 17A-71			

Huie, D.F.	List 6-O	Kennon, S.	Perth 28A	Logan, A.T.	Edinburgh/W. Lothian 1C
Hume, D.	South West 7A-1	Kenny, E.S.S.	Fife 24C	Logan, T.M.	List 6-E
Humphrey, J.W.	Angus 30C	Kent, R.M.	Forth V./Clydesdale 17C	London, D.K.	Lothian 3A
Hunt, M.J.	Angus 30A	Kenton, M.B.		Lough, A.J.	Edinburgh/W. Lothian 1C
Hunt, R.	Glasgow 16A-54		Edinburgh/W. Lothian 1A-89	Louw, D.	Inverness 37A
Hunt, T.G.	Inverness 37C	Kerr, A.	Edinburgh/W. Lothian 1C	Love, S.	Glasgow 16A-62
Hunter, A.G.	Glasgow 16C	Kerr, A.D.C.	Dundee 29A	Lovett, M.F.	England 47B
Hunter, W.F.	Fife 24A-40	Kerr, B.	Forth V./Clydesdale 17A-80	Lowey, M.	Kincardine/Deeside 32A
Hutcheson, N.M.	South West 7C	Kerr, H.F.	List 6-E	Ludik, C.B.	Moray 35A
Hutchison, A.M.	List 6-D2	Kesting, S.M.	Fife 24C	Lunan, D.W.	Glasgow 16C
Hutchison, D.S.	List 6-D1	Keyes, J.A.	Glasgow 16A-11	Lunn, D.I.M.	England 47C
		Kiehlmann, P.	List 6-A	Lusk, A.S.	List 6-D2
Inglis, A.	Edinburgh/W. Lothian 1C	Kimmitt, A.I.M.	Moray 35A	Lyall, M.G.	
Irvin, S.D	Glasgow 16A-42	Kimmitt, A.W.D.	Fife 24A-37		Forth V./Clydesdale 17A-113
Irvine, C.J.	Gordon 33A	Kingston, D.V.F.	List 6-E	Lyon, M.M.	Lothian 3A
Irving, D.R.	South West 7C	Kinnear, M.	Lochaber 38B	Lyons, E.D.	South West 7A-133
Irving, W.D.	Edinburgh/W. Lothian 1C	Kinnear, M.A.	Lochaber 38A		
Izett, W.A.F.	Stirling 23C	Kinsey, L.	Aberdeen/Shetland 31A	Macalister, E.E.	Gordon 33C
		Kirk, S.M.	Buchan 34A	Macartney, D.J.B.	Caithness 41A
Jack, A.M.	Stirling 23B	Kirkland, N.J.		Macaskill, D.M.	Lewis 44A
Jack, J.A.P.			Edinburgh/W. Lothian 1A-75	Macaulay, G.D.	Lothian 3C
	Edinburgh/W. Lothian 1A-31	Kirkland, S.R.M.	Glasgow 16A-31	MacCormick, M.G.	List 6-P
Jackson, N.M.	South West 7C	Kirkwood, G.	Glasgow 16A-81	Macdonald, A.	Clyde 14C
Jackson, W.	South West 7C	Kirkwood, J.A.	Dundee 29A	Macdonald, C.D.	Glasgow 16A-21
Jaffrey, A.	Buchan 34A	Kisitu, T.M.		Macdonald, F.A.J.	Melrose/Peebles 4C
Jamieson, A.J.	Glasgow 16A-69		Edinburgh/W. Lothian 1A-75	MacDonald, G.	List 6-D2
Jamieson, E.M.M.	Lewis 44C	Knox, A.	Clyde 14A-40	Macdonald, I.	Uist 43A
Jamieson, G.D.		Knox, J.W.	Dunkeld/Meigle 27C	MacDonald, I.A.	
	Edinburgh/W. Lothian 1C	Kuzma, A.P.	Inverness 37A		Edinburgh/W. Lothian 1A-40
Jamieson, H.E.		Kyle, C.A.E.	South West 7C	MacDonald, I.D.	Orkney 45A
	Forth V./Clydesdale 17A-27			MacDonald, I.M.M.	Uist 43A
Janse van Vuren, H.I.		Lacy, D.W.	South West 7C	MacDonald, J.W.	Perth 28C
	Edinburgh/W. Lothian 1A-92	Lafontaine, L.M.		MacDonald, K.D.	Glasgow 16C
Jefferson, M.S.	Melrose/Peebles 4A		Edinburgh/W. Lothian 1A-16	Macdonald, M.	
Jeffrey, K.S.	Aberdeen/Shetland 31B	Laidlaw, V.W.N.	Fife 24C		Forth V./Clydesdale 17C
Jenkins, G.F.C.	Fife 24C	Laing, D.A.	Stirling 23A	Macdonald, M.C.	
Jessamine, A.L.	List 6-D2	Laing, D.J.H.	Dundee 29C		Forth V./Clydesdale 17A-14
Job, A.J.	List 6-D2	Lamarti, S.H.	South West 7C	Macdonald, M.J.	Ross 39A
Johnson, C.I.W.	Glasgow 16C	Lamb, A.D.	Kincardine/Deeside 32C	MacDonald, N.	
Johnston, C.D.	Jedburgh 6A	Lamont, S.J.	List 6-E		Forth V./Clydesdale 17A-105
Johnston, J.E.	Lothian 3A	Lancaster, C.	Moray 35B	Macdonald, N.M.	
Johnston, J.P.N.	Aberdeen/Shetland 31A	Landale, W.S.	Duns 5C		Forth V./Clydesdale 17A-114
Johnston, M.G.	Glasgow 16B	Landman, A.	South West 7A-37	MacDonald, R.I.T.	South West 7A-22
Johnston, M.H.	Glasgow 16A-85	Lane, M.R.	Fife 24C	Macdonald, S.	Ross 39A
Johnston, R.	Glasgow 16A-25	Lang, I.P.	List 6-P	Macdonald, W.J.	List 6-E
Johnston, R.W.M.	Glasgow 16C	Langlands, C.H.	England 47B	MacDougall, L.I.	
Johnston, T.N.	Fife 24C	Lawrie, D.R.	Fife 24A-3		Forth V./Clydesdale 17A-100
Johnston, W.A.	Orkney 45C	Lawrie, R.M.	List 6-E	MacDougall, M.I.	Perth 28A
Johnstone, B.	Lewis 44C	Lawson, D.G.	Int. Charges 48C	Macdougall, M.M.	Melrose/Peebles 4C
Johnstone, H.M.J.	Glasgow 16C	Lawson, J.B.	Perth 28C	MacEwan, D.G.	Fife 24B
Johnstone, M.E.	Glasgow 16A-60	Lawson, K.C.		MacEwan, J.A.I.	Abernethy 36C
Jones, A.M.	Lochaber 38A		Edinburgh/W. Lothian 1C	MacFadyen, A.M.	Glasgow 16C
Jones, A.M.	Lothian 3C	Ledgard, J.C.	List 6-E	Macfarlane, J.	Argyll 19C
Jones, J.O.	Argyll 19A	Lees, A.P.	Clyde 14C	Macfarlane, P.T.	England 47C
Jones, R.	Forth V./Clydesdale 17C	Legge, R.	Moray 35C	Macfarlane, T.G.	List 6-P
Jones, W.G.	South West 7A-103	Leitch, D.G.	Fife 24C	Macgregor, A.	Buchan 34C
		Leitch, M.	Clyde 14C	Macgregor, J.	Perth 28C
Kavanagh, J.A.	Glasgow 16A-32	Lennox, L.I.	South West 7C	MacGregor, J.	Glasgow 16A-6
Kay, D.	Clyde 14C	Lennox-Trewren, N.D.		MacGregor, M.S.	List 6-D2
Kay, E.	Dundee 29C		Kincardine/Deeside 32A	MacGregor, N.I.M.	Inverness 37C
Keating, G.K.	South West 7C	Levison, C.L.	Melrose/Peebles 4C	Machado, K.	Glasgow 16A-102
Keefe, J.A.	Glasgow 16A-97	Liddiard, F.G.B.	List 6-E	MacInnes, D.M.	Glasgow 16A-72
Keil, A.H.	Edinburgh/W. Lothian 1C	Lillie, F.L.	Dundee 29C	Macintyre, T.	South West 7C
Kellett, J.M.	Melrose/Peebles 4C	Lincoln, J.	Ross 39C	MacIver, N.	Uist 43C
Kellock, C.N.	Lothian 3B	Lind, G.K.	South West 7C	Mack, E.A.	South West 7A-114
Kelly, C	Glasgow 16B	Lind, M.J.	Argyll 19C	Mack, K.L.	Lothian 3A
Kelly, E.R.	Glasgow 16B	Lindsay, W.D.	List 6-E	Mack, L.	Stirling 23C
Kelly, T.C.	Perth 28C	Lines, C.M.D.	Fife 24A-13	Mackay, G.C.	Glasgow 16A-50
Kelly, W.W.	South West 7C	Linford, V.J.	Melrose/Peebles 4A	Mackay, K.J.	Edinburgh/W. Lothian 1C
Kemp, T.	Clyde 14C	Lithgow, A.R.	List 6-E	Mackay, L.E.	
Kennedy, G.		Lochrie, J.S.	South West 7C		Forth V./Clydesdale 17A-81
	Edinburgh/W. Lothian 1A-24	Locke, D.I.W.	Orkney 45A	Mackay, M.H.	South West 7C

INDEX OF PARISHES AND PLACES

Numbers on the right of the column refer to the Presbytery in which the district lies. Names in brackets are given for ease of identification. They may refer to the name of the parish, which may be different from that of the district, or they distinguish places with the same name, or they indicate the first named place within a union.

INDEX OF SUBJECTS

344   Index of SUBJECTS